D1176025

Readings in the Sociology of Language

Readings in the Sociology of Language

Edited by

JOSHUA A. FISHMAN

Yeshiva University

MOUTON PUBLISHERS · THE HAGUE · PARIS · NEW YORK

First Printing: 1968
Second Printing: 1970
Third Printing: 1972
Fourth Printing: 1977

ISBN: 90-279-1528-8

Printed in The Netherlands

Dedicated to the memory of
Uriel Weinreich,
who was always both
teacher and friend.

Contents

Introduction

Joshua A. Fishman

THE SOCIOLOGY OF LANGUAGE

Professional linguists have long been aware that languages differ from each other in many patterned respects. Similarly, professional sociologists have long been aware that societies differ from each other in many patterned respects. However, for several reasons, there has thus far been too little realization in either camp that language and society reveal various kinds and degrees of patterned co-variation. The sociology of language represents one of several recent approaches to the study of the patterned co-variation of language and society.

Under 'language' one may be concerned with different *codes* (e.g., English, Chinese, Swahili), *regional varieties* within a single code (e.g., the English of Boston, New York, Philadelphia or Norfolk), *social class varieties* of a particular regional variant (e.g., the English of lower- middle- and upper-class Bostonians), *stylistic varieties* related to levels of formality (e.g., public address vs. casual conversational usage), etc. Each of these varieties may be studied either from the point of view of actual verbal communication or from the point of view of idealized language norms. Furthermore, each of these language varieties may be examined at the level of *sound patterns*, at the level of *vocabulary*, at the level of *grammatical* features, at the level of *meaning*, etc. Under "society" one may be concerned with dyadic encounters, small group interaction, large group functioning, the articulation of social classes and sectors, contacts and contrasts between entire nations, etc. Furthermore, each of these social groupings may be examined with respect to heterogeneity of composition, permeability of group barriers, status-role patterns, context of interaction, norm restrictiveness and stability, etc.

Obviously languages and societies are both highly varied (vis-à-vis others) as well as highly diversified (internally). However, these variations and diversities reveal many patterns or regularities rather than purely random or idiosyncratic manifestations. The sociology of language inquires into the co-variation of diversity and of pattern in these two fields. Since *languages* normally function in a social matrix and since *societies* depend heavily on language as a medium (if not as a symbol) of interaction it is certainly appropriate to expect that their observable manifestations, language behavior and social behavior, will be appreciably related in many lawful ways. Some of the very designations of language variants carry social implications (e.g., formality levels, regional variants, social class variants, etc.). Some of the very designations of social groupings carry distinct communicative implications (dyadic encounters, small group interactions, international contacts, etc.). Thus it may be that language and society not only reveal *lawful co-variation* but that each may provide *additional insight into the other*. To the extent that this is true the sociology of language is not only a "possible field of inquiry" (there are infinitely many such fields) but a "fruitful field of inquiry" (these may be far fewer) as well.

The term "sociolinguistics" is often used interchangeably with "the sociology of language". The latter usage seems to me to be preferable for the purposes of this volume and for some general purposes that may be briefly mentioned here. The primary purpose for which these *Readings* have been brought together is to interest students of social behavior in the language determinants, concomitants or consequences of that behavior. Although particular studies in this field of inquiry may more appropriately view either language behavior *or* social behavior as the independent or the dependent variable for their immediate purposes it is my fundamental bias to view society as being broader than language and, therefore, as providing the context in which all language behavior must ultimately be viewed. It seems to me that the concept "sociology of language" more fully implies this bias than does the term "sociolinguistics", which implies quite the opposite bias. However, I have certainly made no effort to rule out of these *Readings* studies whose methodological and conceptual apparatus indicate that "sociolinguistics" rather than "sociology of language" is closer to their authors' point of departure or ultimate goal. Quite the contrary. There is nothing that the sociology of language needs at the *present* time as much as it needs work and workers with sensitivity and sympathy for the contributions of "the other field". As a newly developing interdisciplinary field the sociology of language may well be approached, at the present time, either via topics, concepts and methods primarily derived from linguistics, or via topics, concepts and methods derived from the sciences of social behavior. Indeed, it is inevitable that "borrowed" topics, concepts and methods will predominate until students of the sociology of language clarify a sufficient number of topics, concepts and methods that are more uniquely appropriate and more fully integrated in terms of their own needs and interests. Thus, the expression "sociology of language" is more an indication of future-oriented perspectives than of currently feasible or desirable differentiation and delimitation.

There are many reasons for the mutual isolation of sociology and linguistics that go beyond those usually applicable to distantly related fields with separate academic recognition and separate scholarly traditions. Linguistics, particularly American linguistics during at least the first half of this century, has been primarly a "formal discipline", almost along the lines of abstract mathematics. It has concentrated on the analysis of language structure. Thus, language "per se", in the form of a corpus of sounds and smaller or larger units of meaning, has been examined for its patterns, as if it were something that existed above and beyond its users and its uses. Psychologizing and sociologizing have not only been *ignored* (as leading in "exolinguistic" directions) but have been *attacked* in former years by the most distinguished American linguists as dangerous and misleading pursuits. In contrast to the mainstream of American linguistics, linguists with strong sociocultural interests have represented a smaller parallel tradition, usually under the rubric of "anthropological linguistics". Unfortunately, this co-tradition long considered language and culture as monolithic (though relatable) wholes.

Any objective evaluation of linguistics would have to admit that its early strictures resulted in much rigorous and fruitful work within a narrow sphere of interests. The obvious successes of linguistics within this narrow sphere probably underlie the greater security feelings evident in recent years with respect to stepping outside the usual topics of this discipline. In addition, these successes have led to a greater awareness of the unnecessary and unwise limitations imposed by procrustean frameworks relative to the *current* frontiers and unsolved problems of the discipline. Thus it is that various schools of "mentalistic linguistics" have recently become major sources of stimulation in modern linguistic science. Hopefully, "sociolinguistics" may prove to be similarly stimulating when it reaches greater consensus as to its goal and procedures.

If the development of linguistics has been such as to produce a particular insensitivity to the relationship between language behavior and social behavior the same has been true for sociology, particularly for American sociology. American sociology has also sought rigor and respectability via formalism. It has gravitated away from its early interests in the ethnology of social progress and social problems to a predominant concern with large-scale social structure and quantitative analysis, neither of which are likely to draw upon language behavior as a source of primary data. A concern with language has been contraindicated on yet another score; namely, language is often considered to be omnipresent and therefore of no significance in differentiating social behavior. The latter view is undoubtedly related to the monoglot and urbanized nature of the societies best known to the founding fathers of American and European sociology. In addition, American sociology has long been primarily non-comparative and American sociologists themselves, overwhelmingly monolingual. As a result of all of the above limitations in outlook, most macrotopics in the sociology of language (i.e., those topics that represent the traditional core of this field, e.g., multilingualism and ethno-national solidarity, long term trends in language maintenance and language shift, language standardization and language planning, etc.) strike many American sociologists as dealing with matters both foreign and marginal to "society" as they know it. It is only in quite recent years that interest in the developing nations, in small group dynamics, in social change as a community or neighborhood process, and in the network concomitants of unity and diversity at the national level have made many sociologists more receptive to the pursuit of several traditionally "sociolinguistic" topics and to the development of new ones.

Many of the above observations imply that the two parent-disciplines involved in the sociology of language would each stand to gain if their joint offspring developed into a robust interdisciplinary field of specialization. Sociology might gain a number of very reliable (linguistic) indicators of social class and social interaction. In addition, sociology might gain new insight into processes of group formation and dissolution, into social change, social integration and social cleavage. Above all, sociology would come to realize that this "taken for granted" variable, language, shows great and yet patterned diversity in its own characteristics and in the characteristics of its uses and users. Linguists, on the other hand, stand to gain even more, for there is a very real sense in which the sociology of language might be said to be crucial for the solution of many of the "hard core" problems of modern structural linguistics. If the sociology of language were to provide a fuller realization that what has hitherto been viewed as merely "free variation" around an ideal norm of language structure or usage is itself socially patterned in terms of users and uses, this would be a major contribution to linguistics per se. In addition, more and more linguists might come to realize that the categories represented by "natural" human groups (whether these be generational, religious, ethnic, educational, occupational, etc.) merely represent a reflection of "folk sociology". The sociologist's categories and strata are frequently no more than handy ways of getting at recognizably different rates of various social behaviors: friendship patterns, attitudes, competitive or cooperative processes, socialization patterns, leisure activities, political behaviors, interactions across group boundaries, etc. An awareness of *these behaviors* (other than of the categories through which they are easily located) probably represents the basic potential contribution of the sociology of language to the science of linguistics.

It is certainly true that sociologists spend a great deal of time defining social categories and refining the ways of operationally recognizing them. It is also true that linguists spend a great deal of time on exhaustive presentations and analyses of the phonology and morphology of languages. However, in both cases these pursuits are really means or way-stations in a programmatic progression. The community of sociologists recognizes, however dimly, that it must go on from categories and rates to relationships and processes. Thus, it may be highly disturbing to sociologists to discover that some linguists not only have a superficial interest in the *nature* of social categories but that they are also content to stop their "social inquiries" at the categorical level. Similarly, linguists are rightly concerned when sociologists who become interested in language merely recognize such linguistic categories as "pure language" and "mixed language" (or language and dialect) without due concern for the complexity of the linguistic designata involved. Thus, the sociology of language may well become the avenue whereby the sociologist interested in behavior through language will lose his naive "linguistic enlightenment" at the same time that the linguist aware of the social context of language will lose his naive "social outlook". Ultimately this field will prepare its own interdisciplinary specialists (not unlike the anthropological linguists and the social psychologists of today) who will be fully at home in both parent disciplines at the same time that they seek to explore and to organize the co-varying diversities within the sociology of language proper. Until that time arrives most work in the sociology of language will tend to fall short of the ideal, either on the linguistic or on the sociological side. The *Readings* here presented to the student should therefore be considered as representing an *approximation* to a field which is in the process of conceptual and methodological development. They do not represent ideal solutions to the recognized problems of this field. All of them, I hope, represent interesting attempts to cope with these problems. Most of them, I believe, are representative of what is currently considered to be "work of good quality" (although frequently of a preliminary or introductory nature) in this field. Nevertheless, I hope and expect that many of them will be replaced by much better studies within a relatively few years.

A final difference (between the parent disciplines of a sociology of language) deserves to be mentioned here, for it pertains directly to the selection of items for inclusion in these *Readings*. Linguistic field work and linguistic publications frequently reveal a tradition (akin to that of folkloristic and ethnographic studies) of exhaustive enumeration devoid of major theoretical guidelines. Indeed, linguists point with pride at their ability to derive benefit from old grammars based upon intensive work with a single informant, even when the theoretical portions of such publications no longer deserve any attention whatsoever. Sociologists are not only rarely able to understand the technical analyses lavished upon such exhaustive inventories, but, more importantly, they are rarely likely to consider them *worth* analyzing, regardless of whether they deal with the morphophonemics of southern apple pickers, the epithets of northern delinquents, or the language of kings. Sociological research is normally approached from a more theoretical point of view, such that certain concerns at a level "higher than description" guide data collection and data analysis. The data themselves, while ideally gathered in painstaking detail, are usually analyzed and presented statistically (both in descriptive and in inferential terms) rather than enumeratively. Since the methodology of social research has improved markedly in recent years, it is not infrequent for sociologists to be more pleased with their old theories than with their old data.

All in all, most linguistic presentations are likely to prompt the sociologist to ask, "How can you be sure of your findings?" By this query he indicates that he is looking for a demonstration (such as those with which he is familiar) that in *appropriately selected individuals or groups* among whom certain behavioral patterns are shown to occur (or not to occur, or to occur more or less frequently than in other groups) there is a marked *tendency* for certain linguistic regularities (in terms of the *basic structure* rather than the *manifest content* of communication) also to be present. He expects many exceptions to this co-occurrence tendency but also expects to account for these exceptions (subsequently) via factors temporarily assigned to "error variance". The linguist is equally likely to ask, "How can you be sure of your findings?" when faced with sociological presentations. He is looking for a complete inventory of language data (rather than for categorical summaries of data) and for a demonstration of complete lawfulness in relationships (rather than "tendencies" strong enough to come through tests of significance or repeated samples). In view of the audience for which the present volume is intended, and in view of this field of inquiry as I would like to see it, I have tended to prefer the sociologist's to the linguist's definition of data and of demonstration. Nevertheless, once again, I have included several papers that clearly represent quite a different approach to these matters.

At this early point in the development of the sociology of language, it seemed premature to impose a highly detailed conceptual framework on a book of *Readings*. Not only have I been concerned that this selection be useful to a wide variety of differently organized courses in departments of sociology, anthropology, speech, communication and linguistics, but I have also been eager to include provocative papers and topics even where I have not been entirely sure whether a more tightly organized or conceptually integrated approach to the sociology of language would find them to be substantively admissible. Thus, while denying admission to most studies in psycholinguistics and in mass communication, I have not tried to be similarly exclusivistic with respect to studies of an anthropological, historical, social-psychological or political science nature. Finally, while relying mainly on a number of established topic areas as the basis for grouping studies into sections I have also ventured a few broad groupings that are less widely recognized. These approaches to selecting *Readings* and to grouping them results from some *compromises* between my personal topical biases and my personal conceptual hunches as to the most likely lines of development in the sociology of language during the next few years. As a result of these two quite different approaches to the selection and organization of readings, many of the items included lend themselves to inclusion in more than one section of this volume.

To begin with (in Section I) I have tried to present a number of papers that may provide the student with greater perspective on the sociology of language as only one of several disciplines viewing language in a behavioral context. It is my hope that this section will do more than provide the student with many crucial terms and concepts. Hopefully, it will also indicate that as much as the sociology of language represents a broader view (than either of its parent disciplines thus far holds with respect to language and social behavior) it too must be seen in broader scientific and intellectual perspective.

The following section (Section II) represents an attempt to enter the sociology of language from its more microscopic pole. Here we encounter studies of small group processes, beginning with dyadic encounters and progressing to much longer interactions between somewhat larger face-to-face groups. Unfortunately this area within the sociology of language is still rather meagerly developed. My prediction is that it will receive much more attention during the next few years, to the end that interlocutor, setting, topic and other integrative variables will loom large in our efforts to organize the entire field of the sociology of language.

Section III presents studies that are concerned with larger categories of mankind (social stratification) and with the within-group and between-group organization (social structure) of these categories. Here I have examined the literature on economic, religious, racial, and other traditioned groups functioning within a common national or cultural framework.

In Section IV the size of the social groupings under consideration is once more enlarged, this time to the full socio-cultural level. However, in addition, the studies presented were selected from the point of view of *reflecting* cultural values and socio-cultural change.

Section V is one of two devoted to multilingualism. Multilingualism has long been a topic recognized by sociologists, linguists, anthropologists, and others as shedding light on many aspects of language learning, language use and behaviors toward language, all of these being topics that are theoretically crucial and yet extremely difficult to analyze in monolingual settings. This fact may justify the inclusion of two sections on multilingualism. However, whereas Section V concentrates on the social, cultural, political and other concomitants of relatively widespread and enduring multilingualism, Section VI is concerned with the circumstances and processes that result in stable or unstable multilingualism.

The final section, Section VII may strike some readers as representing an "applied concern". Actually, language planning is often guided by quite theoretical considerations and, oftener yet, its procedures and outcomes may be productive of new theoretical insights into language-society relationships.

I expect that this particular sectional organization may seem less useful within a few years, particularly as the sociology of language begins to crystallize around integrative concepts and methodologies.

A few guiding principles or self-imposed limitations were adhered to in preparing this selection of readings.

1. No selections from the "classics" of linguistics or of sociology;
2. No selections authored by editor;
3. No more than a single selection by any given author (except in cases of co-authorships);
4. No selections from other *Readers* familiar to students of the sociology of language (unless items appeared nowhere else);
5. Minimization of technical linguistic material beyond the grasp of most social scientists;

6. No substantive comments or corrections by editor;
7. Articles in commonly known European languages to be given in the original language of publication;
8. Preference for recent and integrative presentations.

These principles reflect personal biases concerning the desired relationship between *Readings* and other texts that should be brought to the attention of students, as well as biases concerning the ethics of preparing *Readers*. I do not necessarily recommend these biases to others since they may reflect nothing more than one individual's approach to working with students and colleagues.

I am indebted to many individuals for their help in the preparation of this volume. Several friends and colleagues suggested readings for possible inclusion and helped me revise earlier outlines. Foremost among these are Susan Ervin, John J. Gumperz, Dell Hymes, William Labov, and, particularly, Leonard Savitz. My indebtedness to the authors and publishers who permitted me to reprint their works is obvious. Finally, to the staff and Fellows of the Center for Advanced Study in the Behavioral Sciences, with whose help this volume was originally conceived during the 1963-64 academic year, and to my fellow participants in the SSRC-NSF Sociolinguistic Seminar held at Indiana University during the Summer of 1964, with whose help many additional readings were located and this preface was written, go my boundless thanks for truly colleagueal interest and assistance.

JOSHUA A. FISHMAN
Professor of Psychology and Sociology,
Yeshiva University

New York, N.Y.
August, 1964

Editor's note: In the nearly four years since the papers included in this volume were selected and the foregoing introductory remarks written the sociology of language has undergone a remarkable growth and a very encouraging degree of acceptance within the ranks of both sociology and linguistics. As a result, some of the formulations advanced four years ago no longer seem to be as appropriate today as they were at that time, while others, on the other hand, have been confirmed or appear to be even more strongly supported now than they were then. This selection of papers should still be found to be stimulating and useful, to instructors and students alike, even though a large number of outstanding new papers dealing with the sociology of language have recently been published. In a rapidly maturing field such as this, collections of reading may need to be revised frequently although, at the same time, a smaller group of papers will doubtlessly come to be regarded as "classics" of a kind. Many papers of this latter type are doubtlessly included in this volume.

Section I

PERSPECTIVE ON THE SOCIOLOGY OF LANGUAGE

Thomas A. Sebeok

COMMUNICATION IN ANIMALS AND IN MEN; THREE REVIEWS

Communication among social bees. By Martin Lindauer *(Harvard Books in Biology*, No. 2) (Cambridge, Mass., Harvard University Press, 1961), ix + 143 pp.
Porpoises and sonar. By Winthrop N. Kellogg (Chicago, University of Chicago Press, 1961), xiv + 177 pp.
Man and dolphin. By John C. Lilly (Garden City, N. Y., Doubleday and Company Inc., 1961), 312 pp., 20 plates.

Generations of linguists, as well as other scientific observers of language, have followed with fascination the exquisitely fashioned series of studies of bee colonies and, in particular, the detailed accounts of the dances which foraging honey bees perform on their return to the hive and which serve to inform their nest mates of the presence of food, its direction, distance, and quality, reported by K. von Frisch. Based on the pioneer efforts of Rösch during the 1920's,[1] the researches of von Frisch and of his fellow-investigators will surely abide as one of the most impressive achievements of contemporary science. To be fully savored – for their thoroughness, rigor, and elegance and, indeed, for sheer exhilaration – one should follow his verba ipsissima, perhaps most readily available in a collection of three lectures delivered in the course of a tour of the United States early in 1949.[2]

[1] G. A. Rösch, "Untersuchungen über die Arbeitsteilung im Bienenstaat", *Z. vergleich. Physiol.*, 2 (1925), 571-631; 12 (1930), 1-71.

[2] K. von Frisch, *Bees: Their vision, chemical senses, and language* (Ithaca, N. Y., 1950); cf. the review by J. Lotz, *Word*, 7, 66-7, emphasizing the importance of this book for semiotics in general and for linguistics in particular. See also von

From the point of vantage of human communication, the story of the dancing bees has sometimes been treated as a kind of scientific parable, a primitive behavior pattern from which various Aesopian lessons may be drawn. Thus one of the most eminent psychologists of language, Bühler, citing an early monograph by von Frisch,[3] argued – metaphorically anticipating a cybernetic model – that no animal community can exist without a steering mechanism guiding the social relations of the community members, and that this entails an interchange of signs as much as an interchange of matter: "Und diese Steuerungsmittel die wir exact beobachten können, sind das vormenschliche Analogon zur Sprache." A systematic interchange of matter among the members of an animal community is, in fact, inconceivable to Bühler without an accompanying interchange of signs, which leads him to conclude, "soweit muss eine biologisch wohlfundierte Sprachtheorie ausholen und dan noch eine letzte Horizonterweiterung vornehmen." [4]

Viewing language from an anthropological perspective, Kroeber repeatedly turned his attention to comparisons and contrasts with communication systems in other species,[5] notably the bee. His particular concern was to illuminate the distinction between signs and symbols as to both their mechanism and their function. "I have discussed the facts with several linguists", he wrote, but we "seemed to take the attitude that the bees' informations must be mere signs or signals", and "scarcely tried to analyze away the symbolic nature of these informations". He therefore undertook to examine the matter more closely. While, in so doing, he shed light on several facets of language, he failed to resolve to his own satisfaction his initial query, whether the communicative techniques used by the bees are "genuinely or pseudosymbolic" – possibly because the nature of the opposition between his key concepts, "sign" and "symbol", is itself by no means unclouded.[6]

At least four linguists have pondered *Apis mellifera* as a source of

---

Frisch, *The dancing bees* (London, 1954), a translation of the 5th edition of his *Aus dem Leben der Bienen* (Berlin, 1953).

[3] "Über die 'Sprache' der Bienen", *Zool. Jahrb.* (Abt. allg. Zool. und Physiol.), 40 (1923), 1-186.

[4] K. Bühler, *Sprachtheorie* (Jena, 1934), vi-vii. Among other psychologists of language who have commented on the implications of von Frisch's findings, see, for example, F. Kainz, *Psychologie der Sprache*, 2 (Stuttgart, 1943), 174-7; R. Brown, *Words and things* (Glencoe, Ill., 1958), 157-70; and L. S. Vygotsky, *Thought and language* (New York, London, 1962), 41.

[5] Cf. the obituary by D. Hymes, *Lg.*, 37 (1961), 1-28, especially the references on p. 14.

[6] A. L. Kroeber, "Sign and symbol in bee communications", *Proc. Nat. Acad. Sci.*, 38 (1952), 753-7.

insights about *Homo sapiens*. Laziczius, in an attempt to elucidate the three constitutive factors of verbal communication which were so fashionable in his day – the emotive, the conative, and the referential – described the last as the "most human" of all: the bee, he explained, can be the source of a message and its destination, but the message does not denote, i.e. has no cognitive function. If one were to transmute such messages into human speech, they would be interjections: from the addresser's standpoint they generate tension. and from the addressee's they are imperatives spurring to circumscribed action.[7] It must be remembered that these remarks of Laziczius were, like Bühler's, based on von Frisch's early work; but while the formal properties of this communication system had been accurately observed and meticulously described even then, it took two more decades to crack the code. Lotz has pointed out how instructive it may be "to those linguists who exclude the study of meaning from linguistics proper" to follow the unfolding of this story: "After his first hypothesis was refuted, that of a two-word code, with the round dance standing for pollen and the wiggling dance for the nectar, the dance was interpreted as a symptom of general excitement, without further meaning. In 1946, however, von Frisch himself was able to prove that the dance represented a method of conveying very explicit information."[8]

Lotz was also the first linguist to make a structural analysis of bee communication, with a view to providing a basis for systematic comparison with the structure of language. The results were compressed into a diagram, Fig. 1.[9]

The features which distinguish language from the fabric of bee communication were concisely enumerated by Lotz and, repeating him, reassayed by Benveniste.[10] In a broader framework, they were later examined by Hockett on at least four occasions.[11] During the very decade in which these various glottocentric interpretations were being sharpened and called to the attention of linguists, however, much was happening in biology. Zoology and psychology have converged and a

[7] Gy. Laziczius, *Általános nyelvészet* [General linguistics] (Budapest, 1942), 135.

[8] J. Lotz, "Symbols make man", in Lynn White Jr. (ed.), *Frontiers of knowledge in the study of man* (New York, 1956), 228.

[9] Reproduced, with the author's permission, from Fig. 4 of J. Lotz, "Speech and language", *JASA*, 22 (1950), 715.

[10] E. Benveniste, "Animal communication and human language: The language of the bees", *Diogenes*, 1 (1952), 1-7.

[11] C. F. Hockett, *A course in modern linguistics* (New York, 1958), Ch. 64; "Animal 'languages' and human language", in J. N. Spuhler (ed.), *The evolution of man's capacity for culture* (Detroit, 1959), 32-9; "The origin of speech", *Sci. Am.*, 203 (1960), 88-96; and "Logical considerations in the study of animal communication", in W. E. Lanyon and W. N. Tavolga (eds.), *Animal sounds and communication* (Washington, D. C., 1960), 392-430.

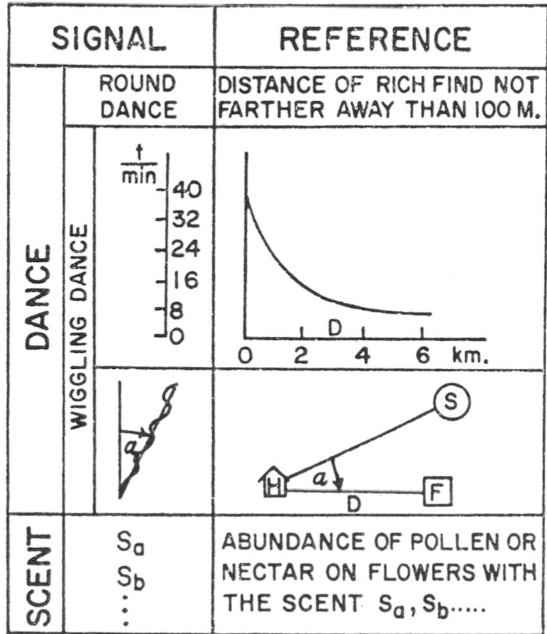

Figure 1. The structure of bee communication [1950].

H is the hive; *F* is the field; *S* is the sun; *D* is the distance between the hive and the find; *α* is the deviation of the wiggling from the vertical line, the angle between the direction toward the sun and toward the find from the hive; *t/min* is turns per minute; S_a, S_b are various scents.

special discipline called ethology has matured which comprehends, in the narrow sense, the comparative anatomy of gesture of animal species or, more broadly, the scientific study of animal behavior.[12] Important advances were being anounced in the phylogenetic analysis of more or less complex signalling movements, directed towards members of the same species or those of other species sharing the actor's

[12] For background, see R. A. Hinde, "Some recent trends in ethology", in S. Koch (ed.), *Psychology: A study of a science 2, General systematic formulations, learning, and special processes* (New York, 1959), 561-610. For surveys of the recent literature, W. H. Thorpe, "Comparative psychology", *Ann. rev. psych.*, 12 (1960), 27-50; M. Lindauer, "Ethology", *ibid.*, 13 (1961), 35-70; and D. G. M. Wood-Gush, "Comparative psychology and ethology", *ibid.*, 14 (1963), 175-200. The most comprehensive account is the book of F. Kainz, *Die 'Sprache' der Tiere* (Stuttgart, 1961), a separate review of which will appear in an early issue of *Am. anthrop.* P. Marler, "The logical analysis of animal communication", *J. theoret. biol.*, 1 (1961), 295-317, is an attempt by a zoologist to approach animal communication systems as a whole, using models developed by C. W. Morris and C. Cherry.

environment; and the unifying concept of "ritualization" was introduced[13] and critically explored.[14] As for the bee, it was gradually revealed that all the essential characteristics of the actor's performance in the communication dance are found to be present in other insects, but that their combined potentialities for social regulation have remained unrealized elsewhere. The widely accepted belief that the bee's field of semantic reference is rigidly restricted to information about the location of food and its quality was then shattered by Lindauer's discovery that an almost identical code is used in indicating possible sites for a future hive.[15]

Literally following in his teacher's footsteps, Lindauer toured North America ten years after von Frisch. In the spring of 1959 he delivered the Prather Lectures in Biology at Harvard University, and his delightful *Communication among social bees* is based on them. The book brings together pertinent facts uncovered since von Frisch was in our midst, and focuses upon four specific problem areas: Are there simple, elementary (i.e. phylogenetically older) forms of communication in *Apis mellifera* which might turn out to be components of the dance? Does the dance occur in related species and genera and, if so, in what forms and with what significance? Does the dance reveal previously unsuspected ranges of meaning? And finally, what is the physiology of the sensory mechanisms through which information is transferred?

The opening sentence of Lindauer's text reads: "In the last analysis, all animals are social beings." The chief implication of this assertion is that all organic alliances presuppose a measure of communication: Protozoa interchange signals;[16] an aggregate of cells becomes an organism by virtue of the fact that the component cells can influence one another. Metazoa assemble in various kinds of alliances. Minimally, they must come together to form a temporary tandem for mating, thus enabling their species to continue. When the sexual partners remain together until the offspring appear, we may speak of a family community, that is, a group whose members STAY together but become differentiated – a type of process realized in most dramatic fashion by insect colonies. On the other hand, members of a species not necessarily stemming from one mother may COME together and

[13] N. Tinbergen, " 'Derived' activities; their causation, biological significance, origin and emancipation during evolution", *Quart. rev. bio.*, 27 (1952), 1-32.

[14] A. D. Blest, "The concept of 'ritualisation' ", in W. H. Thorpe and O. L. Zangwill (eds.), *Current problems in animal behaviour* (Cambridge, England, 1961), Ch. IV.

[15] M. Lindauer, "Schwarmbienen auf Wohnungssuche", *Z. vergleich. Physiol.*, 37 (1955), 263-324.

[16] This is discussed e.g. by J. B. S. Haldane, "La signalisation animale", *L'année biol.*, 58 (1954), 89-98.

become integrated into "interest communities", joined together, for instance, for mutual protection – like a school of dolphins.[17] In all such unions – whether transient or persistent, closed or open, divergent or convergent, simple or complex – creatures of the same species must locate and identify each other; moreover, they must give information as to what niche they occupy in territory as well as status in the social hierarchy, and as to their momentary mood.[18]

It has been pointed out that a linguist approaching a totally unknown language acts as a cryptanalyst: he receives messages not destined for him and not knowing their code.[19] The student of animal communication also resembles a cryptanalyst, but he is faced with some problems which need not occupy the observer of speech: thus, initially, he cannot even be sure through what physical channel or channels the presumed messages are being transmitted. Since "any form of energy propagation can be explored for communication purposes",[20] and many forms are in fact at the disposal of animals, one of his first tasks is to specify the sense or constellation of senses employed in the message-processing situations which he is observing. When describing speech phenomena, many linguists, at the crossroads of conflicting approaches, continue to employ a mixed nomenclature, drawing for their technical vocabulary now on articulatory, now on acoustic, and sometimes on perceptual phonetics; the resulting montage may show seams, but the total picture makes sense. The zoologist, attempting to identify communication in a given group of animals, may likewise define the event by the manner in which the signal is encoded, passed on, or decoded; however, the classification chosen leads one into quite different realms of discourse, which appear far from being blended into a harmonious synthesis. Sometimes the action of an effector organ is featured, for instance in the description of the signalling system of fireflies, of which the chemistry has been worked out in considerable detail.[21] At other times, properties of the intervening medium are emphasized, for instance in studies of the sonic (and ultrasonic) emissions of the bottlenose dolphin, where excellent spectrographic representations of signals-plus-noise have not yet been supple-

[17] Cf. A. Alpers, *Dolphins: The myth and the mammal* (Cambridge, Mass., 1961), 85-6, 102-3.

[18] These phenomena are discussed in regard to the dragonfly, and generally, in A. Portmann, *Animals as social beings* (New York, 1961).

[19] R. Jakobson and M. Halle, *Fundamentals of language* (The Hague, 1956), 17-9.

[20] R. M. Fano, *Transmission of information* (New York, London, 1961), 9.

[21] J. B. Buck, "Studies on the firefly: II. The signal system and colour vision in *Photinus pyralis*", *Physiol. zool.*, 10 (1937), 412-9; W. D. McElroy and H. H. Seliger, "Biological luminescence", *Sci. Am.*, 207 (1962), 76-89.

mented by a definitive description of the underlying mechanism to explain the results, let alone of the "meanings" of the recorded exchanges.[22] More often than not, the spotlight falls upon the action of a receptor organ, as the dog's sense of smell.[23] A signal encoded by one means, say chemical, may be variously interpreted, say by the olfactory sense of the gustatory sense. On the other hand, signals of quite varied origin – produced, say by discoloration of the body's cover or by a gross movement (such as the change in the position of a horse's ear) – may all be decoded through the visual channel. A classification at the receptor stage seems to yield, on the whole, a much simpler and more heuristically useful framework, as illustrated, for example, by Marler's comprehensive survey.[24]

"The most primitive communication undoubtedly takes place by *chemical* means", Lindauer tells us (2), yet the chemical senses play an important role in the life of most animals, with the probable exception of birds. Lindauer considers chemical communication "primitive" because the possibilities for modulation are highly restricted. It is true that the stag, for example, can broadcast two different scent signals: one, by marking the trail, to keep the herd together; the other, by delimiting the boundaries of his territory, to warn off rival males. But to accomplish the emission of two kinds of information he must use two anatomically separated organs, the hoof glands and the eye glands. As almost anyone who has run over a polecat on a highway knows, a shocking message (ethanethiol) is abruptly produced but cannot be so rapidly turned off. In this very lack of flexibility, however, lies the one distinct advantage of chemical signals: by these means, an individual is capable of communicating with another in the future and, what is even more remarkable, an individual is also capable, by virtue of delayed feedback, of communicating with himself in the future.[25] A spectacular illustration of the persistence in time of chemical

[22] J. C. Lilly and A. M. Miller, "Sounds emitted by the bottlenose dolphin", *Science*, 133 (1961), 1689-93; "Vocal exchanges between dolphins", *ibid.*, 134 (1961), 1873-6. See also J. J. Dreher, "Linguistic considerations of porpoise sounds", *JASA*, 33 (1961), 1799-1800. Context-specific sounds produced by the dolphin have recently been described and illustrated by M. C. Caldwell, R. M. Haugen, and D. K. Caldwell in their brief report on "High-energy sound associated with fright in the dolphin", *Science*, 138 (1962), 907-8; and by J. C. Lilly, in his "Distress call of the bottlenose dolphin; Stimuli and evoked behavioral responses", *ibid.*, 139 (1963), 116-8.

[23] S. Neuhaus, "Die Unterscheidungsfähigkeit des Hundes für Duftgemische", *Z. verg. Physiol.*, 39 (1956), 25-43.

[24] P. Marler, "Developments in the study of animal communication", in P. R. Bell (ed.), *Darwin's biological work: Some aspects reconsidered* (Cambridge, 1959), 150-206, 329-34.

[25] Cf. J. B. S. Haldane, "Animal communication and the origin of human lan-

signs is the retention by a salmon of odor impressions from youth to maturity (i.e. over three to five years), enabling its return from the sea to its precise parent stream.[26] Canine predators, among other mammals (bears, bisons, etc.), put urine very much to the same uses that we put another chemical, ink – a substance which, Uldall once justly complained, "has not received the same attention on the part of linguists that they have so lavishly bestowed on the substance of air".[27] Yet the graphic manifestation of language, script, no less than speech, has its functional analog elsewhere in the animal kingdom, and in particular throughout the mammalian orders.

The transmission of food – and, along with the nourishment, information vital to the colony – constitutes another elementary form of communication among bees. The social significance of the food exchange (trophallaxis) is threefold. First, the quality of the fare imparts information to the foragers about the extent of the competition to which their territory is subject (only the best food sources release the alerting dance). Second, the water demand for temperature regulation is reported and finely attuned by this means, the extent of the need being accurately gauged by the delivery time. Third, since the food contains minute portions of a substance picked up by licking the queen's body, all bees in a hive are kept constantly aware of her presence or absence and react to her removal, in a matter of hours, by preparations to replace her.

Having briefly disposed of food as a symbol conductor, Lindauer devotes all of the remaining four of his five chapters to communication by dancing. The olfactory sense, the sense of taste, the eye, the gravitational sense organs, and the time sense are all discussed, but he pays no attention in this book, even in passing, to the much disputed question whether honey bees can perceive sound waves and, if so, whether information is transmitted by this means from one bee to another. For a consideration of the acoustic behavior of bees, one must turn to other sources, for instance Haskell's handbook.[28] Suggestions that foraging bees use sound in communicating distance of a food source to other

---

guage", *Sci. progress*, 43 (1955), 390. E. O. Wilson's "Chemical communication among animals", *Recent progress*, 19 (1963), 673-716, and his less technical introduction, "Pheromones", *Sci. Am.*, 208 (1963), 100-14, constitute the best reviews and theoretical analyses of communication among animals by means of the transfer of chemical substances.

[26] A. D. Hasler, "Homing orientation in migrating fishes", *Ergebnisse d. Biol.*, 23 (1960), 94-115.

[27] H. J. Uldall, "Speech and writing", *Acta ling.*, 4 (1944), 11-6.

[28] P. R. Haskell, *Insect sounds* (Chicago, 1961). Lindauer did prove, however, that humming in the stingless bee, *Meliponini*, has "something to do" with the collector's alerting other hive bees (76).

workers in the hive deserve particularly careful evaluation in the light of Lindauer's own stricture that "unsolved questions still remain concerning the sensory performances for *distance* indication" (111), and evidence which is now available showing that sound, at least in the range of 600 to 2,000 cps., is in fact used by bees for information exchange.[29]

Assuming the uses of the round dance, the global near-deixis, and of the tail-wagging dance, the calibrated far-deixis,[30] in the search for food to be widely known, Lindauer describes them, at the outset of his second chapter, only in summary fashion. In this context, one misses a report of the highly interesting experiment which was carried out by W. Steche years before the current excitement about the feasibility of interspecies communication, namely, between man and dolphin; he in fact demonstrated man's ability to communicate as a honey bee does. Steche equipped a working hive with a faintly perfumed artificial bee whose oscillations on the comb surface he could control remotely by electronic links; manipulating his wooden bee with levers, he succeeded in programming the live bees that crowded around the imitation insect to head in a prescribed direction to seek and find nectar.[31]

29 A. M. Wenner, "Communication with queen honey bees by substrate sound", *Science*, 138 (1962), 446-7. The nature of the bee's sound receptor is unknown, but to elicit a series of "quacks", the vibrations had to be transmitted directly through the hive material, i.e. when the generator's sound was sent through the air, the bee did not respond. – A few months after I had finished this review, I had an opportunity to visit the laboratory of H. Esch, at the University of Munich, and to observe a series of new discoveries about bee communication. Very briefly, these appear to be as follows. The tail-wagging dance carries no information unless accompanied by a whirring sound, i.e. it is a redundant gesture commonly known as an intention movement. The duration of the sound informs the worker bees about the distance of the nectar supply; thus a whir of 0.4 seconds indicates 200 meters, of 8 seconds 10,000 meters and so forth. The higher the quality of the food-find, the more vehement the dancer's whir – whereby quality and distance are additionally coupled in an economic relationship. The sound is not a monologue, for the scout's drumming is followed by short, chirping beeps emitted by the watching workers, seemingly meaning: "message understood". When the scout senses the bees she stops dancing, thus enabling a worker to approach her and smell the odor of the nectar she has found. If she fails to stop, she is stung to death. Popular reports of dramatic experiments have appeared in *Time* (May 31, 1963), and the German magazine *Der Spiegel* (June 19, 1963). Cf. H. Esch, "Über die Schallerzeugung beim Werbetanz der Honigbiene", *Z. vergleich. Physiol.*, 45 (1961), 1-11; and his later semipopular restatement, "Auch Lautäusserungen gehören zur 'Sprache' der Bienen", *Die Umschau in Wissenschaft und Technik*, 10 (1962), 293-6.

30 Cf. H. Frei, "Systèmes de déictiques", *Acta ling.*, 4 (1944), 111-29.

31 "How to talk to a bee", *Time*, 9 Feb. 1959, p. 34. Possible agricultural uses of communication with bees through the vibratory code are discussed in L. and M. Milne, *The senses of animals and men* (New York, 1962), 35-6.

Unlike a bird's nest, which is simply an incubator turned into a cradle, a bee-hive serves not only as a nursery but also as the colony's meeting place, social center – in a word, home. It is therefore hardly surprising that the search for a dwelling of high quality looms as a problem for a bee community next only to the search for food. Yet it became known only within the past decade that the dances of the bees play a decisive role in conveying information about shelter; in the rest of Chapter 2, Lindauer spells out the ways in which this is accomplished. He traces how the scout bees announce the location of suitable nesting places by means of the dance in the cluster; how, before moving, the swarm "agrees" upon one of the nesting places offered; how this "agreement" comes about; how the quality of a nesting place is evaluated; and which bees function as house hunters. The pragmatic import of the tail-wagging dance, we learn, depends not upon variation in the formal expression but rather upon the attendant physical context of the same gesture pattern. Hockett has already pointed this out,[32] but his observation needs one qualification: although the form of the dance is identical, there are significant differences in duration. The message, being a call of concern to the entire swarm, often lasts more than five minutes and may continue for an hour. Lindauer relates the history of one suspenseful "debate" which lasted for five days, and the exceptional case of one aerial tug of war which ended, after a fortnight's dancing, without an agreement. The biological function of duration, under normal circumstances, is obvious: the longer the dance, the more bees can visit the chosen site and thereupon act as guides for the swarm. In the lifetime of a worker, a house-hunt is a very rare, perhaps unique, event, whereas there are many opportunities to communicate about sources of crops to be exploited for food.

"Is a structural dialectology possible?", we may ask with Weinreich,[33] extending his question to the domain of animal communication. A survey of recent developments in the experimental study of bird songs, at least, leaves no room for doubt that the answer will be affirmative: "It is well known that in many cases the song of the species can be sufficiently constant and distinct to serve as a specific recognition mark, but yet can vary within these limits sufficiently to indicate subspecific, racial and local populations."[34] From a wealth of data, one might cite the chaffinch, where the effects of geographic boundaries have been shown to result in "true" dialectic formation (i.e. in local variations which are not based on genetic discontinuities). The dialect areas may range in size from an isolated glen in Scotland

32 "Logical considerations ...", *op. cit.*, 410.
33 *Word*, 10 (1954), 388-400.
34 W. H. Thorpe, *Bird-song* (Cambridge, 1961), 99.

to a mosaic of very small pieces, delimited by a road or a railroad, as described by H. Sick, in the Stuttgart region;[35] and may exhibit differences both in inventory and in distribution. Synchronic dialectology, Weinreich defines, "compares systems that are partially different and analyzes the 'synchronic consequences' of these differences within the similarities". This was the procedure followed in a series of engrossing experiments with wild crows. Crows in this country are known to exhibit distinctive alarm notes inducing other crows to disperse, distress calls when caught, and assembly calls emitted when they sight a bird of prey or a cat. These calls were tape-recorded and, when played to wild crows in an American woodland, elicited much the same reactions. When, however, these tape recordings were tested on crows in France, either there was no response or the French crows assembled where the Americans would have fled. Captive Pennsylvania crows respond "abnormally" to the calls of Maine crows and vice versa; but crows free to migrate between the two regions construct a diasystem which enables them to understand both local dialects.[36]

Since the appearance of the book under review, the topic of the third chapter has received special attention from von Frisch himself.[37] Both treatments deal with what we might designate, still using Weinreich's terminology, diachromic dialectology, namely the phenomenon of divergence: "it studies the growth of partial differences at the expense of similarities and possibly reconstructs earlier stages of greater similarity". Observations carried out on six races – Italian, Austrian, German, Punic, Caucasian, and Egyptian – within the species *Apis mellifera* soon showed communicative variations in respect both to the area indicated, respectively by a round and a tail-wagging dance, and to the dancing rhythm. Thus if the distance between the hive and the food source is 100 meters, the number of complete revolutions of the figure-eight-shaped dance per 15 seconds for each race was calculated, respectively, as 7.95, 8.4, 9, 9.05, 9.8 and 9.25. Given such minute geographic variations, one cannot help wondering whether bees would misunderstand each other if different races were placed together to make a mixed colony. Being members of the same species, an Austrian bee (*A. mellifera carnica*) and an Italian bee (*A. mellifera ligustica*) can interbreed; if put together in a colony, they work together in harmony; and the dance of one will arouse the other – yet they experience confusion whenever they attempt to com-

[35] "Über die Dialektbildung beim 'Regenruf' des Buchfinken", *J. orn.*, 87 (1939), 568-92.

[36] H. Frings et al., "Reactions of American and French species of *Corvus* and *Larus* to recorded communication signals tested reciprocally", *Ecology*, 39 (1958), 126-31; H. and M. Frings, "The language of crows", *Sci. Am.*, 201 (1959), 119-31.

[37] "Dialects in the language of bees", *Sci. Am.*, 207 (1962), 79-87.

municate: "If, for example, an Austrian bee receives information from an Italian bee about a food place 100 meters from the nest, she will fly 120 meters, because she interprets the 'Italian dialect' in her Austrian way. And conversely, the Italian bee will fly only 80 meters when given information for 100 meters by an Austrian bee" (61). The experiment reported by Lindauer is reminiscent of the "test the informant" method designed to measure the degree to which members of one speech community can understand the utterances of members of another,[38] but a linguist is bound to envy the precision with which his aparian colleague is able to record and represent the extent of variation.

It is comforting to have access to informants, but in passing from dialectology to comparative linguistics their lack or the absence of their written residue are hardly decisive handicaps. It has now been shown that phylogenetic research is equally feasible, among the bee's taxonomic relatives, in respect to the dance complex – a sophisticated behavior pattern which also leaves no paleontological record, as fossils of, say, termite nests, by way of petrified proof. In trying to track the dancing instinct backwards in time, one must start with descriptive statements of existing structures of communication in species of *Apis* other than *mellifera*. To accomplish this, Lindauer journeyed to the original home of our honey bee, the Indo-Malayan region, which is the habitat of all other known species of this genus: *A. indica*, the giant *A. dorsata*, and the dwarf *A. florea*. In brief what he found was this. All four species use essentially the same method of communication – by round dances and tail-wagging dances – as far as food provision and search for housing sites are concerned. With respect to the indication of distance (which is expressed in the rhythm of the tail-wagging dance), only minor differences appeared, although these were more pronounced than those among the strains within the species. With respect to the indication of direction, however, Lindauer did make one crucial discovery, namely, that the dwarf bee is incapable of transposing light to gravity. That is to say, members of this species can dance only on a horizontal surface. Von Frisch characterizes theirs as "a clearly more primitive social organization and a corresponding less highly developed language" (83).

To regress still further on the evolutionary scale, Lindauer and his associates turned to the bees most closely related to the *Apini*, the stingless bees of the subfamily *Meliponini*. All eleven species so far investigated were found to "have a means of communication that enables them to alert other bees and to guide them to a specific goal"

[38] C. F. Voegelin and Z. S. Harris, "Methods for determining intelligibility among dialects of natural languages", *Proc. APS*, 95 (1951), 322-9.

(72), but their technique differs in many points from that of their relatives. The essential difference lies in the fact that *Meliponini* newcomers are not directed to their goal by information imparted exclusively in the hive (direction and distance information are not even incorporated in their alerting system), but are also guided by trail marks and pilot bees beyond the hive. Although their solution may seem less elegant to us, it is just as successful as the honey bee's and, in at least one respect, superior: Communication fails when honey bees are required to report a feeding place much above or below the hive,[39] but not so in the stingless bees.

As the linguist cautiously probes from costructs such as linguistic families toward wider historical reconstructions which some call, "by an unfortunate biological metaphor", phyla and macro-phyla,[40] so the ethologist searches out traits common to all social insects and, beyond, to solitary species. As far as the social insects are concerned, one must single out what is undoubtedly the most complex chemical communication system yet described: E. O. Wilson's brilliant work with fire ants (*Solenopsis saevissima*).[41] In the course of his investigations, Wilson measured the information transmitted in the odor trails of the fire ants and then compared the results with the information content of the honeybee's waggle dance. It turned out that the two message-types transmit similar quantities of information, to wit, 3 to 5 bits for direction and 2 for distance. In other words, each species, with radically different systems, manages to employ, accurately, an 8- to 32-point compass and 4-interval scale, as may be summarized in Fig. 2.[42] A combination of alerting and indicating of direction are traits shared among the ants and the stingless bees. As a concluding reference in this context should be recorded the curious dancing behavior of the fly

[39] K. von Frisch, H. Heran, and M. Lindauer, "Gibt es in der 'Sprache' der Bienen eine Weisung nach oben und unten?", *Z. vergleich. Physiol.*, 35 (1953), 219-45.

[40] H. Hoijer, in a comment to C. F. Voegelin, "The dispersal factor in migrations and immigrations of American Indians", in R. H. Thompson (ed.), *Migrations in New World culture history* (Tucson, Arizona, 1958), 47-62. It may be interesting to recall, in passing, that Darwin himself, on the other hand, used "languages" as a key metaphor: "a breed, like a dialect of a language"; "It may be worth while to illustrate this view of classification, by taking the case of languages"; "Rudimentary organs may be compared with the letters in a word"; etc. Cf. S. E. Hyman, *The tangled bank* (New York, 1962), 33; and, more generally, A. Schleicher, *Die Darwin'sche Theorie und die Sprachwissenschaft* (Weimar, 1873).

[41] "Chemical communication among workers of the fire ant", *Animal behaviour*, 10 (1962), 134-64.

[42] Reproduced, with the author's permission, and that of the editors of *Animal behaviour*, from Fig. 5, *loc. cit.*, 154.

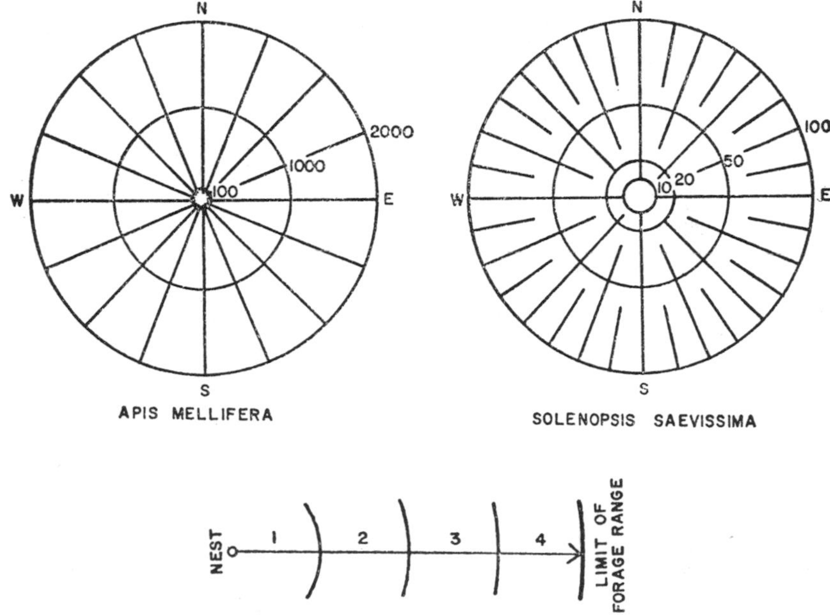

Figure 2. Diagrammatic representations of the amounts of information transmitted in the honeybee (race *carnica*) waggle dance and the fire ant odor traii.

Upper left: The "bee compass", indicating that the worker honeybee receives up to 4 bits of information with respect to distance, or the equivalent of acquiring information necessary to allow it to pinpoint a target within one of 16 equiprobable angular sectors. The compass lines are represented arbitrarily as bisecting the sectors. The amount of direction information remains independent of distance, given here in meters.

Upper right: The "fire and compass", showing approximately how direction information increases with distance, given here in millimeters. In both compasses only parts of the potential distance ranges are shown.

Lower: "Distance scale" of both bee and fire ant communication. Approximately 2 bits are transmitted, providing sufficient information for the worker to pinpoint at target within one of four equal concentric divisions between the nest and the maximum distance over which a single message can normally apply.

Phormia regina. A series of extremely interesting observations by V. G. Dethier [43] gives a plausible hint that here physiology has located one of the essential roots of the elaborate bee dance.

[43] "Communication by insects: Physiology of dancing", *Science*, 125 (1957), 331-6.

Sensory aspects in the determination of distance and of directional information are treated in Lindauer's fourth chapter, while in the last he takes up certain special problems concerning solar orientation (including reports about the behavior of bees raised by artificial illumination, and the solar compass in competition with terrestrial landmarks).

Before leaving the bees for the dolphins, I should like to make two digressive observations, the first of them stimulated by J. H. Greenberg. In reviewing Hockett's chapter on "Man's place in nature", and, in particular, in connection with Hockett's treatment of bee communication, Greenberg, "as a human", insists that he "would like to win out over the bees by more than a technical knock-out".[44] He appears to mean that there is a single structural trait which distinguishes their system of communication from ours: "All human languages including written and other representations which permit one-to-one conversion on the sentence level are universal metalanguages and only human language has this property." If exchanged cues and propositions about codification and relationship between the communicators is "metacommunication",[45] then clear instances of such higher-order social interchanges can be found among many animals. The metacommunicative messages used by rhesus monkeys, enabling them to distinguish between play and nonplay, have received particularly careful attention,[46] and a form of instinctive behavior in the honeybee has been recorded which surely falls into this category. When a worker leaves the hive for field duties, she carries a sample of her particular colony odor (which, as a result of the actual flow of wax, pollen, and nectar, presents a certain uniformity throughout the hive) locked in a special scent sac. Upon her return she opens her scent gland as though displaying a pass badge to the guard bees. The odor of a strange worker causes bellicose behavior, but bees with the matching home odor are admitted.[47] When individual b_1, of the colony C, sends a signal s_x to individuals b_n of C, this event can be represented by a simple formula:

$$b_1 \rightarrow s_x \rightarrow b_n$$

In the situation described by Köhler, however, the signal consists of a

44 *Am. anthrop.*, 63 (1961), 1140-5, esp. the last paragraph on p. 1144.

45 Cf. J. Ruesch and G. Bateson, *Communication* (New York, 1951), 209. See now also Hockett, "The problem of universals in language", in Greenberg (ed.), *Universals of language* (Cambridge, Mass., 1963), 10, where he deals with this property under the label "reflexiveness".

46 S. A. Altmann, "Social behavior of anthropoid primates: Analysis of recent concepts", in E. L. Bliss (ed.), *Roots of behavior* (New York, 1962), 277-85.

47 F. Köhler, "Wache und Volksduft im Bienenstaat", *Z. f. Bienenforsch.*, 3 (1953), 57-63.

special fragrance, C_f, which functions to insure that further communication, advantageous to that particular C, can thereupon be initiated; the wrong stimulus may lead to an attack, followed by a scuffle, ending with the kill of the adversary. This signal is, therefore, metacommunicative, s_m :

$$b_1 \rightarrow s_m \rightarrow b_n \dashrightarrow b_1 \rightarrow s_x \rightarrow b_n$$

My second observation relates to a hypothesis recently developed in some detail elsewhere:[48] that whereas subhuman species characteristically exchange messages that are coded in analog fashion, in speech some information is coded thus and other information is coded digitally. As far as the bees are concerned, it is clear that their behavior resembles that of an analog computer (as has already been noted by both a zoologist and another linguist[49]), that is, a control machine of the more-or-less type, and not at all of a digital computer, of a yes-or-no type.

Lindauer's book, supplemented by reports of other findings published elsewhere, makes it possible now to adjust and expand somewhat the column on bee dancing in Hockett's latest table (1960) of 13 design features. In that version, he had marked five slots positively: (2) broadcast, (4) interchangeability, (7) semanticity, (10) displacement, and (11) productivity. A "yes" should also be entered in row (5) for total feedback – since any dancer will cease to emit messages in the absence of an "audience"; and in row (8) for arbitrariness – since the gesture can, after all, be decomposed into elements used to transmit specific portions of information. In addition, one should remember that the field of semantic reference comprehends both food source and nesting site. In feature (1), Hockett combined the transmitter, the channel, and the receiver into one single category, "vocal-auditory"; but it would be much better to keep the three stages strictly apart: the auditory component in the total ribbon of bee communication, for example, invites separate inquiry. Further important features include a transcoding potential,[50] that is, an ability to convert directional vectors from a visual field (positive phototaxis) to a gravitational field (negative geotaxis); and finally, the capacity for a restricted form of metacommunication.

Aristotle was the first natural historian who alluded to the dancing

[48] T. A. Sebeok, "Coding in the evolution of signalling behavior", *Beh. sci.*, 7 (1962), 430-42.

[49] Haldane (1954), 97; Hockett (1959), 35.

[50] C. F. H. Kalmus, "Analogies of language to life", *Lg. and speech*, 5 (1962), 15-25; and Sebeok, *loc. cit.*, fn. 4.

bees: "on reaching the hive they throw off their load (*aposeíontai* "they shake themselves"), and each bee on his return is accompanied by three or four companions." Aristotle was also the first marine biologist who accurately classed the dolphin with the mammals, adding: "The dolphin, when taken out of the water, gives a squeak and moans in the air. ... For this creature has a voice (and can therefore utter vocal or vowel sounds), for it is furnished with a lung and a windpipe; but its tongue is not loose, nor has it lips, so as to give utterance to an articulate sound (or a sound of vowel and consonant in combination)." [51]

From 330 B.C. until yesterday man's understanding of the bottlenose dolphin, *Tursiops truncatus* – actually, a toothed whale of small size – grew very slowly indeed, as chronicled by Alpers.[52] Then, in 1961, three book-length studies were published in the United States: one by Kellogg and another by Lilly, in addition to Alpers' skillful blend of fact and legend (not to mention L. Szilard's clever satirical piece on the voice of the dolphins [53]). The reports of Kellogg and of Lilly could thus be viewed as climaxing centuries of accumulated observations. On the other hand, they could also, and perhaps more aptly, be regarded as major if tentative opening moves in a new scientific game: marine biocoustics. The existence of animal communication by sound (underwater creatures communicate by other means too, of course: electric fish distort their own high-voltage fields; one member of the squid family squirts a radiant cloud to hide behind) in the "silent world" of the ocean depths came to the serious attention of the scientific community only within the last quarter of a century. "Roars, knocks, honks, squeals, 'popping of corks' – old sounds from new places" are now under intense investigation in their natural environment by means of a hydrophone system; [54] and the literature of the field has already reached staggering proportions.[55]

[51] *Hist. anim.*, 624 and 536, by D. W. Thompson.

[52] *Op. cit.* (fn. 17), 241-4.

[53] *The voice of the dolphins and other stories* (New York, 1961).

[54] H. N. Tavolga and J. C. Steinberg, "Marine animal sounds", *Science*, 134 (1961), 288.

[55] J. M. Moulton, "References dealing with animal acoustics particularly of marine forms, Second compilation", 1962, and "Addendum to second compilation", April, 1962 (mimeographed), contain over 1500 references. For a more general introduction to bioacoustics, cf. G. Tembrock, *Tierstimmen* (Wittenberg Lutherstadt, 1959), including 23 pages of further references. Although acoustical studies of captive cetaceans have concentrated for the most part on the bottlenose dolphin, the sonic activities of the pilot whale, the spotted porpoise, the harbor porpoise, the Atlantic saddleback dolphin, the white-sided porpoise, and, lately, the white whale have also been recorded. The pertinent literature is cited in the introductory paragraphs of M. P. Fish and W. H. Mowbray, "Production of underwater sound by the white whale or beluga, *Delphinapetrus leucas* (Pallas)", *Sears Foundation: J. of marine res.*, 20 (1962), 149-62.

The whistles, squeals, chirps, clicks, rasps, and other noises of marine mammals have suggested three areas of inquiry: orientation by echolocation, intraspecies communication, and interspecies communication. Kellogg's research program is devoted largely to the way in which porpoises navigate, and his book presents impressive evidence showing the workings of their sonar system – how they avoid obstacles while swimming at night or in turbid water, and how they locate fish for food. The author is a psychologist noted for his flair in conducting imaginative experiments with large-brained mammals: thirty years ago, he and Mrs. Kellogg adopted a seven-month-old chimpanzee into their home, and compared her with their baby son.[56] In the present instance, his work carries on a tradition embodied in D. R. Griffin's masterpiece on acoustic orientation in bats, in certain nocturnal birds, and among blind men.[57] In pleasant contrast with Lilly's perfervid prose, Kellogg's exposition is lean; where the former relies heavily on rhetoric, the latter marshals data dispassionately in their logical array.

Kellogg's first chapter positions the bottlenose dolphin, *Tursiops truncatus*, in common usage also called a porpoise, in the taxonomic order of *Cetacea*, among the toothed whales or *Odontoceti*, and concludes with the description of a dramatic incident, foreshadowing the particularized substance of the rest of his book, in the course of which, by a lucky concatenation of circumstances, he succesfully recorded the underwater noises made by a school of some twenty wild dolphins in their natural state. ("Never before that time – and never since – have we been fortunate enough to capture such an auditory event on magnetic recording tape" (10). That is to say, virtually all observations, by all researchers in this field, relate to captive and often solitary animals.)

The second chapter deals primarily with the dolphin's order of intelligence, meaning its ability to learn from experience. According to Kellogg, an accurate assessment "is not yet possible because of the dearth of experimental research on the subject" (25); although Lilly predicts, from an elaborate argument based chiefly on anatomical considerations, that *Tursiops* will prove to be as intelligent as man (Appendix Two, 225-94). The dolphin appears to differ from other mammals in one striking respect, namely, the extent to which its vocalization can be modified. In seeming contradiction to the assertions of B. F. Skinner, that "Well-defined emotional and other innate

[56] W. N. Kellogg and L. A. Kellogg, *The ape and the child* (New York, 1963).

[57] *Listening in the dark* (New Haven, 1958). Pp. 260-77 of Griffin's book deal with echolocation in the ocean, and constitute a résumé of findings up to the date of its publication. Echo ranging in the sea lion has just been discovered, as reported by T. C. Poulter in "Sonar signals of the sea lion", *Science*, 139 (1963), 753-5.

responses comprise reflex systems which are difficult, if not impossible, to modify by operant reinforcement", and that "Vocal behavior below the human level is especially refractory",[58] dolphins can readily be trained to vocalize for a reward. Lilly goes much further and claims to have unique evidence for some degree of mimicking of human laughter, human or electronically produced whistles, "Bronx cheers" and similar noises, and ("These are the most subjective of all judgments of the sounds emitted by dolphins") words (201-2). However this may be, the zoologist R. J. Andrew has reviewed the implications of these and other discussions of the acquisition of high intelligence and the ability of vocal mimicking in the broad perspective of human evolution, and has come to certain pertinent conclusions: that the intelligence of a dolphin is of an order somewhere between that of a dog and that of a chimpanzee; that, in view of our vast ignorance of the causes of the evolution of the capability for sound mimicry in birds or man, "it would be foolish to assume that the cetaceans cannot mimic", but that such behavior is bound to be adaptive – involving, as we might say, a set of messages serving to establish, prolong, or discontinue contact, to check whether the network is in operating condition, or, to use B. Malinowski's terse phrase, phatic communion.[59] One residual fact, with interesting if disturbing implications for the evolution of speech, is the evident ease with which dolphins can be trained to vocalize in order to obtain rewarding stimulation, and how markedly this contrasts with findings in primates[60] for which visual messages are, by and large, much more important.[61] As Andrews

58 *Verbal behavior* (New York, 1957), 463. That vocal behavior can be brought under stimulus control in birds has been demonstrated by J. H. Grosslight, P. C. Harrison, and C. M. Weiser, in two studies reported in their "Reinforcement control of vocal responses in the mynah bird (*Gracula religiosa*)", *The psych. record*, 12 (1962), 193-201. S. M. Sapon has "succeeded in conditioning vocal responses in a normally silent animal – the white laboratory rat ... These sounds function as operants by which a hungry or thirsty animal may acquire food and/or water" (personal communication, 10 Dec. 1962).

59 R. J. Andrew, "Evolution of intelligence and vocal mimicking", *Science*, 137 (1962), 585-9. Cf. Sebeok, *loc. cit.* L. Eiseley, in rhapsodic reaction to Lilly's work, "The long loneliness – man and the porpoise: Two solitary destinies", *The American scholar*, 30 (1960-61), 57-64, advances the notion that the dolphin's echo-ranging "instrument" is a finger surrogate, and he depicts (63) "another kind of lonely, almost disembodied intelligence floating in the wavering green fairyland of the sea – an intelligence possibly near or comparable to our own but without hands to build, to transmit knowledge by writing, or to alter by one hairsbreadth the planet's surface".

60 E.g. C. Hayes, *The ape in our house* (New York, 1951).

61 Among baboons, "most communication between troop members is gestural and without vocal accompaniment", as reported by S. L. Washburn and I. DeVore, "Social behavior of baboons and early men", in S. L. Washburn, ed. *Social Life*

states the point: "if a primate is trying to solve a problem it does not vocalize (unless it is giving up and going into a tantrum). If it is made to vocalize, then its attention is no longer on the problem, or on the reward that awaits its solution; that it will learn to use vocalization to obtain a reward is therefore most unlikely." The dolphin, however, with its wide repertoire of sounds, vocalizes frequently and under various circumstances.

In his third chapter, Kellogg surveys the kinds of sounds encountered in the ocean: of crabs and shrimp, of fishes. He explains the significance of such noises and stresses their importance for man at peace (fishing) and at war. He shows how the propagation of sound in water differs from that in air. In the next chapter, he introduces the reader to the principle of so(und) n(avigation) a(nd) r(anging), and inquires whether water noises emitted by whales are suitable for use as echo-ranging signals. In the case of the dolphin, there is an obvious similarity with man's electronic sonar, but there are two major differences: the frequency of emission of the dolphin's pinging sound varies over a wide range, whereas that of human sonar is usually constant; and the intensity of the animal noises may also be markedly altered within a single burst of ranging signals (52). The nature of the signal itself forms the topic of the fifth chapter. The echoes which bounce back from objects that are in the animal's way, supplying information about distance and direction, can be seen and photographed

---

of early man (New York, 1961), 101-2. Gorillas are said by G. B. Schaller, *The mountain gorilla* (Chicago, 1963), 272, to "coordinate the behavior within the group primarily by employing certain postures and gestures ... It is probable that facial expressions emphasize and elaborate information communicated by other means ... Vocalizations notify the others of a specific emotional state of the performer, alerting them to watch for gestures which communicate further information." Howler monkeys, on the other hand, living in dense tropical forests, frequently rely on vocalizations in situations in which a semiterrestrial primate would use a visual signal (S. A. Altmann, personal communication, 3 Dec. 1962). For a systematic study of primate displays, see R. J. Andrew, "The origin and evolution of the calls and facial expressions of the primates", *Behaviour*, 20 (1963), 1-109. We may tentatively explain the predominance of the acoustic channel in the human (and in the dolphin) – in contradistinction to the situation among the apes – in terms of an economic shift from a vegetarian to an omnivorous existence (i.e. requiring hunting); R. Ascher and C. F. Hockett suppose that "the communicative behavior of the great apes may be somewhat more subtle and complex than has yet been realized" in order "to account for the apparently less highly developed vocal-auditory signalling of the great apes", in their unpublished paper, "The human revolution" (1963). A popularized report of recent field studies among chimpanzees offers some hints concerning their "tremendous variety of calls", but also stresses their gestures and contact movements; see J. Goodall, "My life among wild chimpanzees", *Nat. geog.*, 124 (1963), 272-308, esp. the section "Calls and gestures serve as language", 289-91.

on the screen of a cathode-ray oscilloscope, and the auditory pattern can be brought within the more limited perceptual range of the human ear and brain by reducing the play-back speed of the recording tape.

The question of just how the dolphin produces sound signals remains unresolved (70): the cetaceans have no vocal cords. The dolphin's whistling, incidentally, can be seen – in the shape of a stream of bubbles emerging from its blowhole – as well as heard, but whether or not this message is redundant cannot be answered pending further data on its visual acuity in water. The receptor organs are much better known: accordingly, Kellogg details the dolphin's acoustic analyzer in his sixth chapter.

The perception of submerged targets was studied, under controlled conditions, at the Marine Laboratories of Florida State University, as set forth in the seventh chapter. The dolphin's auditory scanning is shown to consist of the emission of a continuous series of sound signals for echolocation plus binaural localization. How the stream of information produced by auditory scanning is instantly classified and associated with previously stored impulses in the animal's brain is, again, beyond present knowledge; we can but speculate about its similarity to the mechanical counterpart of such a receptor system: a sonar apparatus with one transmitter and two independent receivers, hooked up to an electronic computer capable of decoding and processing the input – all stored within a single compact unit (104-5). In addition, the dolphin's acoustic analyzer "performs a kind of frequency analysis for every echo which is received" (123); that is, the animal can easily perceive distinctions between separate objects of the same area but of different material. The eighth and ninth chapters demonstrate the predominance, if not exclusive involvement, of the auditory sense, after elimination of the visual, olfactory (the dolphin has none), gustatory, tactual, and thermal; the experiment designed to prove that the dolphin does not simply "follow its taste buds" (135-42) is particularly ingenious and conclusively confirms that the acoustic modality is the sole sensory avenue employed by the dolphin to discriminate a blocked passageway from an open one. Attempts to jam the echo-ranging process by broadcasting back to the dolphins tape recordings of their own sonar signals from an earlier session have failed: evidently they are able to distinguish between genuine and recorded signals (149). In his concluding chapter, Kellogg emphasizes "that porpoise sonar is quite a different matter from carrying on a conversation" (157), because in speech the direct sound intensity is much greater than the echoes, whereas in sonar the echoes carry the relevant information and the task is to isolate one particular kind of echo from others which may be stronger or of different composition. The returning signal "denotes" – that is, implies the ability to interpret, evaluate, and identify – features of the environment, including distance, direction, speed, size, shape, and perhaps the texture of the object delineated by the echo.

By a curious trick of a typographer's art, beginning with his book's half title, repeated on the title page and thereafter in the running head of each even-numbered page, Lilly's anthropomorphic imagination is given physical force: "Man" is printed in roman type, "*and Dolphin*" contrastively in italics. His work is imbued with what Ruskin called the "pathetic fallacy", the rhetorical device which humanizes animals or which, applied downward, projects man into the non-human world. The author himself is well aware of this (104 ff.) but his metaphoric intuition proves stronger than his scientific discipline (303 ff.), and we find that, with due assistance from the mass media – *Life* magazine, the Jack Paar show – Lilly's dolphins have moved into the swim of contemporary American mythology. Like Blake's Tiger, Lilly's Dolphin is at once something less and something more than man, a visionary creature, symbol as well as thing. With this figure in a double narrative, on the level of science and on the level of myth, he has written a strange, irritating, anecdotal, and provoking book. His obsessive concern is with the interaction of the two species named in the title; his first sentence sets the tone: "Within the next decade or two the human species will establish communication with another species: non-human, alien, possibly extraterrestrial, more probably marine; but definitely highly intelligent, perhaps even intellectual" (11). This leitmotiv recurs from the first chapter, "The possibilities of interspecies communication", through the twelfth, "Implications". If the passages were shaped to shock, épater, as it were, le bourgeois, they will leave sober workers in the behavioral and life sciences unmoved: not because of the freshness of the confrontation but because of the triviality of the data so far. Moreover, Lilly's "method of describing results has a high degree of subjectivity to it. It can be inexact, and even completely mistaken" (196), and the matter of mimicry thus stands, inconclusively, where Andrew left it. The following tragicomic episode, which ends chapter 11, "The voices of the dolphin" (203), is cited in full to convey something of the flavor of this book. Lilly is working with a dolphin named Lizzie:

> Someone suggested that I would be late for dinner if I didn't leave and said, 'It's six o'clock!' very loudly. The tape recorded this on the air channel; in a few seconds on the underwater channel Lizzie, near the hydrophone, putt-putted, Baby [another dolphin] answered with a short fast series of whistles, and Lizzie very loudy came out with a 'humanoid' sentence, the meaning of which (if any) has puzzled several of us since. It may have been a poor copy of 'It's six o'clock.' But I was caught first by another 'meaning.' It sounded

to me like 'This is a trick!' with a peculiar hissing accent. Other people have since heard the tape and come to the same conclusion.

This was the last recording from Lizzie; we found her dead next morning. Our grief was painful and our mourning long. It was a great disappointment to lose her just as she started to make sounds of this sort.

The term *zoosemiotics* – constructed in an exchange between Rulon Wells and me – is proposed for the discipline, within which the science of signs intersects with ethology, devoted to the scientific study of signaling behavior in and across animal species. A survey of the vast and widely ramified literature of ethology, supplemented by repeated spot checks of ongoing research projects, reveals that the study of signaling behavior in animals has, by and large, been taxonomically parochial: even Darwin's great pioneer work, on *The expression of the emotions in man and animals* (London, 1872), dealt, in the main, with the domestic cat and dog. A great variety of animals has since been more or less minutely scrutinized, both in the natural environment (after J. S. Huxley and K. Lorenz) and in captivity (after H. Lissman and N. Tinbergen), but usually in one particular species (or, sometimes, in closely related forms, say, of the genus *Apis*) rather than guided by overarching theoretical considerations relevant to problems of communication in general, including especially speech. The task for the immediate future will be to treat, comprehensively and exhaustively, the achievements of zoosemiotics from Darwin through J. von Uexküll to the present day; to arrange and display the data in a format relevant to the study of language, that is, by matching logical concepts derived from sociobiology with those developed in linguistics; and, using each species, so to say, as a miniature paradigm which throws light upon language observed as a peculiar combination of distinctive features, of which all or almost all components, considered alone, have their separate evolutionary roots,[62] to consolidate and build upon what has been established about the protocultural foundations of human adaptation.

Whitney's conception of language as a social institution, unfolded in necessary antithesis to Schleicher's simple-minded Darwinism, is now itself in need of revision as we recollect L. Bloomfield's aphorism:[63] "Language creates and exemplifies a twofold value of some human actions." Language has, as he put it, both a biophysical and a biosocial aspect. Speech is, of course, a biological phenomenon in several related senses. Since all systems in science have a biological component, the lin-

[62] Cf. O. Koehler, "Thinking without words", *XIV International Congress of Zoology* (Copenhagen, 1956), 75-88.
[63] *Linguistic aspects of science* (Chicago, 1939), 8.

guistic system observed includes the linguist-observer.[64] Speech, furthermore, is carried on by human beings, a species of animal; it is not only a part of animal behavior but undoubtedly the principal means of biological adaptation for man, an evolutionary specialization that arose from prehuman behavioral adaptation of which we seek to trace the paths as one objective of zoosemiotics.

In 1936 Jakobson asked, in Copenhagen:[65] "Est-il besoin aujourd'hui de rappeler que la linguistique appartient aux sciences sociales et non à l'histoire naturelle? N'est-ce pas un truisme évident?" Twenty-five years later, he himself gave the answer as, in Helsinki, he called attention to the "direct homology between the logic of molecular and phonemic codes",[66] implying a vision of new and startling dimensions: the convergence of the science of genetics with the science of linguistics. A fundamental unity of viewpoint has been provided by the discovery that the problem of heredity lies, in effect, in the decipherment of a script, that genes are sections of the molecular chains of DNA which contain messages coded in particular sequences of nucleotide bases,[67] in a manner persuasively reminiscent of the way in which bundles of binary features are linked into sequences of phonemes. Genetics and linguistics thus emerge as autonomous yet sister disciplines in the larger field of communication sciences, to which, on the molar level, zoosemiotics also contributes.

From *Language*, 39 (1963), 448-466. Reprinted with permission.

[64] Cf. G. G. Simpson, "Biology and the nature of science", *Science*, 139 (1963), 81-8.

[65] *Selected writings*, 1 (The Hague, 1962), 234.

[66] "Concluding remarks", in A. Sovijärvi and A. Aalto (edd.), *Proceedings of the Fourth International Congress of Phonetic Sciences* (The Hague, 1962), xxviii.

[67] T. Dobzhansky, *Mankind evolving* (New Haven-London, 1962), 39.

Floyd G. Lounsbury

LINGUISTICS AND PSYCHOLOGY

THE FIELD OF LINGUISTICS

The linguistics of today has developed in a rather remarkable isolation from the psychological disciplines. Influences from psychology have been indirect, coming through the general intellectual climate of the recent decades – to which behaviorist psychology has contributed its share – rather than by direct contact. It is not our task here to account for this, but rather to sketch some areas of central concern in linguistics which may be considered as potential areas for psychological exploration. First we should note some of the commonly accepted limitations on the scope of the discipline.

Linguistics is concerned with the structure of the verbal response. Only within relatively narrow limits is it concerned with the stimulus conditions under which a verbal response is produced or with the nature of the stimulus-response connection and its establishment in the individual. It is primarily descriptive and formulative, rather than interpretive. In this, it is akin to certain behaviorist schools of experimental psychology. In the former respect, however, its goals are rather different from those of psychology.

It is concerned with verbal responses only up to a certain level of complexity. Levels of complexity or structural integration in the verbal response are of at least two sorts: phonological and grammatical. The former include the distinctive phonetic feature, the phoneme, the syllable, one or more orders of stress groups, one or more kinds of pause groups, and several internationally defined groups. The latter include the distinctive morphemic feature, the morpheme, and several intermediate levels of morphological and syntactic structures, on up to the sentence in its various types. Languages differ from one another considerably in the way in which units in one of the hierarchies tie in with units in the other hierarchy, but they agree at least to the extent of a fair correlation – not quite perfect – between certain maximum units of the one kind and certain maximum units of the other kind. These are the sentence types of a language. Linguistics deals with all of the levels of either types, up to and including the sentence. Except when a linguist ventures into logic, discourse analysis, content analysis, or literary criticism, his field of investigation does not extend to verbal responses of a larger magnitude or of a higher order of internal complexity than these.

The research problems which linguists undertake are generally not of the sort that psychologists undertake when they study verbal behavior. This is not to deny psychological relevance to the former or linguistic relevance to the latter, however. Many of the problems of linguistics do relate to questions that are properly a concern of psychology or of one or another of its subdisciplines. And psychological studies of verbal behavior throw light on particular points in linguistic theory.

The linguist's special concern is with the "structure of language in its grammatical, phonological, and – somewhat less frequently – semantic aspects. Many of the problems of special concern to psychologists are of secondary concern to the linguist. Some of these are the acquisition of language, concept formation, the instrumental use of language, the study of individual differences in various specific verbal skills, the measurement of these, their relation to problem solving, second-language learning, etc., the relation of verbal patterns to various types of nonverbal behavior and to personality, the study of the statistical properties of language, or word associations, response latencies, symbolism, phenomena of interference, speech pathology, etc., and even perception. They are all relevant to linguistics ultimately, but are subordinated to the study of structure in language. The linguist wants to see them not as isolated items or as illustrations of psychological principles, but rather as they can be related to the total theory of language structure. We proceed to sketch a few of the aspects of this. The selection and presentation are from the standpoint of linguistics and the interests of its practioners rather than from the point of view and the interests of psychologists. We do not attempt a review of the psychological literature on language. That is the function of another paper in this series (65). Rather, we attempt a brief synoptic view ot topics which are in the foreground in current literature on structural linguistics.

THE STRUCTURES OF AN UTTERANCE, OF A LANGUAGE, AND OF LANGUAGE

Utterances can be said to have "structures", languages to have "structural patterns", and language (in general) to have certain "structural characteristics" or "general properties". There are differences between these. For short, one often uses the term "structure" indiscriminately – not only of utterances, but also of a language, and of language. Its special sense in each of these contexts must be understood. The structure (i.e., structural pattern) of a language is a phenomenon of a different order of abstraction and of greater generality and comprehensiveness than the structure of an utterance. The structural characteristics or general properties of language are, in turn, of a still different order. In this case, one refers to the properties which are common to the stuctural patterns of all languages, that is, of language in general, or of the phenomenon of language.

For linguists the starting point in analysis is the utterance – or rather a corpus of these from a single speaker or several speakers from one speech community. From the study of these – and with continued recourse to native speakers so that the corpus can be amplified as becomes necessary – one arrives at a formulation of the structural pattern of language. The study involves various kinds of data processing, analysis, abstracting, hypothesis formulation and testing, and carrying out experiments. The approach is both "clinical" and "experimental". It is directed toward the construction of a theory of the forms of the language in question, such as will account for the data at hand at any one time and will also have predictive power so as to stand the test of any further accumulation of data from the same language.

From the comparative and contrastive study of the structural patterns of many languages and, most importantly, from the progress which is made toward an analytic method of equal applicability to all languages, there are the beginnings of an understanding also of the "structure" of language, that is, a theory of the general nature of the organization of language behavior.

It is this third kind of structure – whatever can be said about the properties of languages in general – that would seem to be of the greatest relevance to psychology. Only this can be said to characterize the behavior of man as a species. Generalizations of a lower order, which are the principal product of linguistic researches, characterize the linguistic behavior of men in particular societies – Englishmen, Americans, Germans, Chinese, Iroquois, or some subgroup within these or other societies. These are of interest to linguists and to culture historians. They may, however, be of interest to psychologists also, in so far as one or another of the structural patterns of these particular languages can be shown to *exemplify* a structural characteristic of language in general. That is to say, they may be of some interest as illustrations of general principles.

Unfortunately for present purposes, the general science of language is still in its infancy. Despite notable successes in the construction of theories of particular languages, the general theory of language structure and of language universals is still in the stage of tentative formulation, and its relation (or reduction) to psychological laws is still largely speculative. A few of the more obvious general characteristics of language structure are sketched below, together with comment – where such is possible – on their psychological relevance. We beg indulgence for the excursion into grammar. If it does not seem to relate immediately to psychological problems, we should not on this account pass it by. At least it points up some aspects of the rather amazing complexity of the behavior that goes into the production of sentences. Surely this is in some sense a problem for psychology, especially as psychology may be concerned with the hierarchical organization of behavioral sequences. If at certain points we seem to be describing not so much the nature of language as what linguists do with it or to it, it should be confessed that this is true. We are concerned with the models that linguists construct in order to account, in as simple and comprehensive a manner as possible, for the regularities they observe in specimens of linguistic behavior.

THE PROPOSITION

The propositional sentence is a universal in human language. This is not to say that all utterances are statements of propositions; it does mean that there is no human society whose speech patterns do not permit of both *a primary reference* and *an ascription* (of something to it, or of it to something) within a single speech act.[1] This is a uniquely human attribute. The proposition is absent, to the best of our knowledge, from the possible communicative vocal acts of all other species. The specific form or set of alternative forms which the proposition assumes in different languages shows considerable variation. This variation, however, does not controvert the universality of the proposition itself.

Inherent in this statement of a simple and obvious fact are some

[1] Phrasing this in terms of a reference and an ascripiton is, of course, a semantic description. The correlated units of linguistic form can be given nonsemantic formal definitions for particular languages, but not for languages in general.

rather large questions for comparative psychology and neurology. A young child's first statement of a proposition – his first subject-predicate equation or complete sentence, e.g., "Baby, crying!" (an actual case) – is preceded by the development of a very extensive naming vocabulary based on recognition of both static and dynamic qualities of things in his environment, with the vocabulary in part already morphologically differentiated. In turn, all of this rests upon the unfolding – prior to and concurrently with the growth in vocabulary – of a phonological system which is not yet that of adult speech, but which already has a fair degree of internal differentiation and a structure of its own. None of these – the phonological capacity, the naming capacity, or the constructional capacity – seems to have a true analog in the vocal behavior of other animal species. The quasi analogs which do exist appear to differ drastically both in degree and in quality.[2]

BRANCHING AND LAYERING

In speaking of the structure of an utterance (proposition or otherwise), one understands that it is a unit of some sort which is made up of parts. There are fair reasons for assuming that if more than two parts are present in the make-up of a unit, more than one level must be involved in its construction.

Linguistic structures can be described as "branching" and as "layered". The import of these terms may perhaps best be seen by way of an example. Consider the latter portion of the first sentence of this section: *one understands that it is a unit of some sort which is made*

[2] On crucial differences between human and infrahuman communication see Hockett (28, 569-586; 29) and White (78, 79). On the notion of evolution in language see Greenberg (21). It should be noted that neither linguistics nor cultural anthropology has much to offer that is relevant to the question of the origin of language (cf. Sturtevant, 73, 40-50). On the semiotic base present in gesture and its interpretation in animal behavior, see G. H. Mead (60). For an insightful speculation concerning the nature of the transition from the prelinguistic species of Homo to Homo sapiens, see Krantz (36), on pithecanthropine brain size, the relation of its probable growth curve to the maturation cycle, and its linguistic and cultural consequences. It should be noted that no transitional stage in the origin and evolution of languages has survived for observation by modern man. Note also that, contrary to popular notions, as well as to earlier scholarly interpretations (45, 46, 72; contrast 35, 38), the languages of even the most primitive peoples cannot be characterized as "primitive" languages by any valid or consistently applied criterion. All languages – so far as their phonological base, their formal syntactic apparatus, their lexical derivational potential, and their adaptability to communicative needs are concerned – appear to be quite on a par with one another. This statement applies to their formal resources, not to their semantic content. Primitive levels of lexical development of particular semantic areas are well known.

up of parts. The first few layers of its structure divide (i.e., branch) as follows:

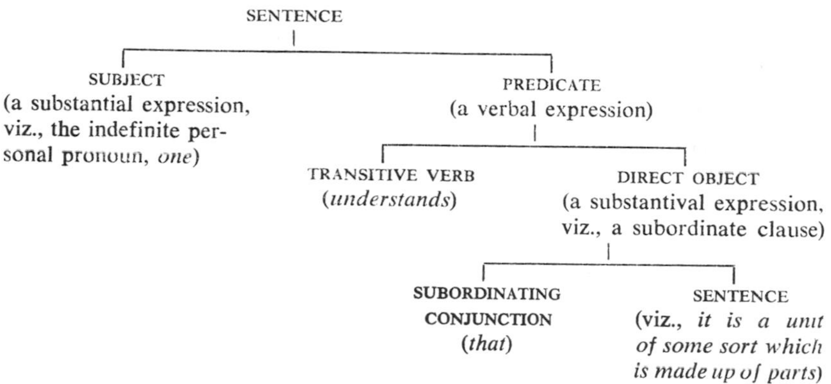

The reader may be disappointed to note that this is nothing more than the traditional parsing which he learned in grammar school. He might have expected something more novel and revealing from linguistics. There is, in fact, considerably more to it than meets the eye. A few of these matters are taken up briefly in following sections. It is, moreover, a representation of but one aspect of the structure of the sentence, other aspects of which would require different representations. The choice of an English example is undramatic because of our familiarity with this type of structure. A sentence from an exotic language could have been used to show structures of quite different sorts.

The remaining layers may be left for the reader to take apart. The first of these, the resolution of the inner sentence into a subject and a predicate, is the same as that for the outer sentence, of course. Beyond that, different structures appear.

RECURSION

In the above diagram of a branching and layering structure, we began with a sentence (*One understands that*...) and ended with a sentence (*It is a unit of some sort which*...). Though different in specific content and different in structure on the second and further lower layers, they are identical in structure on the first lower layer and are members of the same form class (tokens of the same type), viz., SENTENCE, i.e., the SUBJECT-PREDICATE construction of English.

This points up a characteristic and important feature of language structure in general, namely, its recursive potential. It is a special case

– a peculiar and pervasive one – in the general derivational potential of a language. It is an aspect of the capacity for using constructions of a particular type as constituents in other constructions, which may be of a different type or (immediately or ultimately) of the same type as the original. This latter possibility – especially as it involves encapsulating sentences within sentences – makes for theoretically indefinite expandability, limited in practice only by certain external considerations of another order.[3] The mechanics of such encapsulation differs greatly from language to language – some exotic varieties of it strike us as quite bizarre – but the basic functions performed and the general consequences for the adaptability of the language tool are essentially the same.

The inner sentence can be subjected to its own analysis of branches and layers, as was the first, or outer, sentence.

ALTERNATIVES

At the third layer of the inner sentence, we find that the predicate does not resolve into TRANSITIVE VERB + DIRECT OBJECT as in the outer sentence, but into COPULA + PREDICATE NOUN. These are but two of the substitutable alternative types which may serve as predicates in English sentences. Other common ones are intransitive verb (a "nonwanting" verb, which is therefore potentially complete in itself as a predicate) and COPULA + PREDICATE ADJECTIVE.

"Alternatives" are different in their internal structure and identity, but are the same in their external structural relations. They are members of the same form class (tokens of the same type) at the next higher layer of structure.

Other examples of alternatives which concern the form class of substantival expressions are noted in the next section.

IMMEDIATE CONSTITUENTS

As is apparent from the preceding sections, an utterance, a complex verbal response, cannot be regarded merely as a unidimensional concatenation of unit response-segments, in spite of its apparently linear array in time; it must be seen as a many-layered edifice, a construction of parts, each of which is in turn a construction of parts, and so on from the highest to the lowest in the order of layers.

[3] On recursion in syntax and its import for an adequate model of language structure, see Chomsky (7, 9, 10).

Most constructions are seen as two-part constructions. Longer chains which may – in the context of certain problems – be viewed as many-part constructions are resolvable on further analysis into successive layers of two-part constructions.

The parts of a construction are its "constituents". Every linguistic unit except the highest and the lowest dealt with is seen simultaneously 1. as a construction made up of smaller constituents, 2. as a constituent in a particular larger construction, and 3. as a member of a form class defined by its "distribution", or range of possible constructional contexts. It must be characterized in each of these capacities and may be named accordingly. Thus, the expression *that it is a unit*... in our diagram sentence is a subordinate clause when described as a construction. When described as a constituent in the construction in which it finds itself in this sentence, it is a direct object of a transitive verb. When described as a member of a form class, it is a substantival expression (along with nouns, noun phrases, pronouns, etc.). All of these roles need to be specified in its grammatical characterization.

The members of a form class may represent several different kinds of constructions. Thus, as noted, there are many varieties of substantival expressions, as these are considered from the vantage point of the next lower layer. Also, any member of a form class may enter into a number of different kinds of constructions and accordingly be different kinds of constituents. Thus, a substantival expression may be the subject of a predicate, the direct object of a transitive verb, the object of a preposition, a predicate-noun expression, an appositional complement to a noun, etc. To be a member of the form class substantival expressions is, by definition (for English), to be capable of serving in any of these constituent roles; for a form class, as noted, is defined in terms of its distribution.

Linguistic analysis proceeds by the method of "immediate constituents", i.e., by division of a larger unit into two immediate constituents. The brief illustration given above of the branching and layering in structure proceeded in this fashion. The parsing above no doubt appeared simple. In fact, however, the determination of the hierarchy of immediate-constituent divisions in longer forms always presents serious problems. In the illustrative sentence which was used above, there are at least two other places that might seriously be considered as choices for the first immediate-constituent division. These would yield not a SUBJECT-PREDICATE CONSTRUCTION at the top layer of analysis, but would give constructions of other sorts requiring different characterizations. In the end, a systematic pursuit of a different set of policies in immediate-constituent division would, in fact, produce a different grammar of the same language. Among the alternative procedures which may be considered, there is one which is based strongly on phonological considerations – especially those of juncture – as applied to the spoken forms of sentences in their textual environments.

In general, the guiding consideration in making such choices is one which involves 1. maximum substitutability of parts on both sides of the division, 2. maximum productivity of the end formulation, and 3. maximum simplicity in the statement of the total structural pattern. These are not independent criteria, but are related ultimately to the same thing.

In working toward a solution that satisfies these desiderata, there are some who are willing to believe that they are discovering the structural pattern which inheres in the language, while others consider that they are merely constructing a model of the simplest and most highly predictive form that can generate the forms of utterances in the given language. The latter view would seem to be the safer. It leaves open the question of *the* structure of the language, and it carries no suggestion or commitment as to the psychological validity of the formulation. It leaves the field open for alternative analyses and it can entertain, without prejudice to itself, the posing of psychological questions which may be asked in connection with language structure in its varied facets and alternative interpretations.

At the present time, a point of view which holds that linguistics offers not so much a discovery as an evaluative procedure is gaining ascendancy. It permits one to choose from among different grammars or models of a language that which is the "best" according to a stated set of criteria.

Languages differ greatly in their roster and hierarchy of specific constructional patterns. An illustration from another language, especially from a non-Indo-European language, might have shown some of the novelty that was lacking in the English example excerpted from this paper.[4]

HISTORY AND ACTUALITY

Of two constructions made according to the same pattern, one may be an *ad hoc* construction of the moment and the other may be a repetition or reuse of one coined long ago, often heard, and much employed as a whole unit, e.g., as an idiom, a cliché, or a high frequency phrase of some sort. It is apparent that as behavioral events they are quite different and that in some sense their psychological statuses in the

[4] On immediate constituents see Wells (77), Gleason (15, chap. 10), Hockett (28, chap. 17).

structure of the actual speaking behavior may be quite different. This may be reflected in a number of ways other than that of their grammatical structure, which is presumed constant. They may be characterized by different internal entropy profiles. They may have different text frequencies. They may have different latency patterns, these being reflected in observably different timing patterns and in differences in the introduction of hesitation pauses. Yet in terms of their grammatical structure, they may be the same.

The point to be made is that the structural pattern of a language – its grammar – serves as a guide for the manufacture of one's speaking stock in trade. Some of this is old, familiar, and quite automatic at any given time – some of it is new as of the moment and may even be hesitatingly put together. Old and new alike exhibit the same structural patterns except for the relatively rare cases where there is a legacy of old forms which where coined in a no longer productive pattern. The old, in fact, furnish the models for generating the new. In a psychological account taking of linguistic behavior, more than the grammatical structure of utterances needs to be reckoned with. In particular, indexes of latency must be attended to. Usage as well as system requires study.[5]

TRANSFORMATIONS

We turn again to the excerpted sentence which was used for purposes of illustration. In *Branching and Layering*, its analysis was carried to the point of recursion to another sentence. In *Alternatives*, the next two layers in the structure of this inner sentence were indicated. A further step would lead to the next lower layer, which divides into a NOUN PHRASE (*a unit of some sort*) and an ADJECTIVAL EXPRESSION consisting of a relative clause (*which is made up of parts*). The next step leads to the analysis of the relative clause.

Here again, alternative analyses present themselves. All clauses, relative included, share the SUBJECT-PREDICATE construction. An immediate-constituent analysis of the relative clause might then follow this division, identifying the relative pronoun as the subject and the remainder as the predicate. In the evaluative procedure which must follow any decision and which weighs the merits of the decision (in terms of final simplicity and potential account-taking capacity) against

[5] On hesitation pauses and their relation to the transitional-probability structure of a language (as opposed to the grammatical structure), see Lounsbury (57), and Maclay and Osgood (59). Also of interest in this connection are Goldman-Eisler (16, 17).

other possible decisions, two weaknesses are inherent in taking the SUBJECT-PREDICATE division as the first in the analysis of the relative clause. One is that the relative pronoun is in certain respects fundamentally different from all other members of the class of substantival expressions which may serve as subjects or objects or predicate nouns. The other and more serious weakness is that this decision fails to identify or take account of an important and fundamental relationship between any relative clause and a corresponding independent clause of the sentence form – as, for example, the analysis of the subordinate clause above showed its relation to a corresponding independent sentence.

In such cases, one identifies the construction as a "transformation" of some other construction (i.e., of one of the so-called "kernel" constructions), states the relationship between the two, and then proceeds to analyze the constituency of the latter. In the present case, that of the relative clause in our illustration, this amounts to a different decision as to where to place the first immediate-constituent division. It involves the suppression of one of the canons of immediate-constituent analysis, viz., a rule not to divide within a word prior to dividing between words, the justification of which may perhaps be called into question. It is as though in the present case we were to regard the relative pronoun *which* as consisting of, or representing, a relative morpheme (*wh-*) and a pronominal morpheme (identifiable with the morpheme of *it*), and then make an immediate-constituent analysis of RELATIVE SUBORDINATOR (*wh-*) + SENTENCE (*it is made up of parts*) instead of an immediate SUBJECT + PREDICATE analysis.

The concept of transformation is needed to account for aspects of structure (of which the present example represents only one type among many) which would escape an accounting by immediate-constituent analysis of phrase and clause structure except by a *tour de force* such as indicated above. In particular, transformation analysis uncovers a great many *masked recursions* that would otherwise remain undetected. Since the degrees and manners of masking of recursive structures vary greatly from language to language, one result of transformational analysis, which undercuts this masking, is to lead linguistics a step closer to a general model for the syntax of language. It also raises the question of the status of the word as a linguistic unit. Clearly, in the analysis of one aspect of language structure, the word can be violated. Yet it is surely a unit in another aspect of structure. We are dealing with linguistic units of some sort in each case.[6]

[6] On transformations see Harris (24), Chomsky (9, 10), Lees (41, 42), Householder (33), and Gleason (15, chap. 13). The notion of transformation is a recent innovation in structural linguistics, though unformalized analogs to it are old in

CONDITIONED VARIANTS

A frequent phenomenon in the structure of languages is that the context in which a unit appears imposes certain constraints upon the form which the unit may assume. A unit may thus appear differently in different contexts. This kind of contextual determination may be found at all levels:

1. In phonology, in the determination of allophones of phonemes (e.g., whether a *t* in English is an aspirated stop, an unaspirated stop, an unreleased stop with simultaneous glottal closure, a lightly articulated voiced or voiceless flap, a simple glottal stop, etc.);
2. In morphophonemics, in the determination of allomorphs of morphemes;
3. In syntax, in the determination of alternant forms (allotagmas) which particular constructions (tagmemes) must assume in particular larger constructional contexts;
4. In morphology, in the determination of the particular form of an inflectable word – the "allolog", we might say – which it must have in a particular syntactic context.

All of these result in a redundancy between a form and its context, each implying something of the other.

The last case just mentioned, which concerns inflected forms of words, is the weakest as an example of the phenomenon of contextual determination, but it is one of the most interesting. We return once more to our earlier sample sentence for illustrations. In the outer sentence, in the context of the subject *one*, the verb of the predicate must take the form *understands*, not *understand*. Similarly, in the inner sentence, in the context of the subject *it*, the copula of the predicate must be *is*, not *are*.

Inflection in some languages is carried into several dimensions of variation, resulting in multidimensional paradigms running into hundreds or even thousands of forms. Dimensions may be such familiar ones as those of person, number, mode, aspect, tense, voice, etc., or they may involve quite novel criteria (criteria of context, with or without definite correlates in reference). A single form from such a paradigm may be characterized in each of several dimensions. – For example, it may be second person, singular, preterite, subjunctive. The person and number specifications may be required by the particular subject with which the verbal predicate is in construction; the modal specification may be required by a part of the outer context in which

---

traditional school grammars – such as, for example, the rules for "converting" an active sentence into a passive sentence, those for converting indicative into interrogative sentences, etc.

this subject-predicate construction (as an inner sentence) finds itself; while the tense specification may perhaps be restricted by still another part of the context.

In the case just described, each of the inflectional features of the word is a *conditioned* feature of that word, and the resulting form of the word may be described as a *conditioned variant*, or allolog of the word. There is a resulting condition of redundancy; given the context of the word, the particular form of the word – with its special features – may be predicted. And conversely, the special features of the word are an index to the nature of its context, permitting prediction of the latter (within limits) or at least narrowing down its possibilities. Given this situation, the features by which inflected forms differ may be said to be "conditioned", "determined", or "nondistinctive" features.

This type of case, however, represents something of an ideal case. The sentences in which this state of affairs obtains may be termed "model sentences". Actual discourses, however, may occasionally or even frequently contain sentences which deviate from the model by the omission of parts of the model context which are fully predictable from the particular variant of the word. Thus, for example, in Portuguese one may sometimes hear simply *sei* in place of *eu sei* (*I know*), or *sabes* in place of *tu sabes* (*you know*). In such instances, where the presumed conditioning part of the model context is absent, the inflectional feature can no longer be described as contextually determined or as nondistinctive.

This is the state of affairs with much of the morphological inflection of words. In many sentences a particular inflected form can be regarded as a conditioned variant in the proper sense of the term. Yet in other sentences it may be the only source for a feature of the message. It may thus alternate between the status of a conditioned variant and the status of a syntactic construction internal to the word. Inflectional categories are only rarely devoid of referential (denotational) content. In optimum cases, they may be semantically defined – e.g., second person, plural. In some of the more frequent cases, however, the referential content is irregular, shifting from instance to instance, often null, and without common feature (cf. the gender distinctions in German, French, etc.). The semantic definitions, even where these are possible, give no clue to the linguistic status of the inflectional categories. Their linguistic definitions are contextual ones, in terms of their distributions or their "privileges of occurrence". (The latter is not quite the same as the former. A definition in terms of privileges of occurrence is essentially a definition in terms of a form's distribution in what were called "model sentences" above.)

It is rather surprising to see how different languages can be from one another in this particular respect. This kind of interconditioning between syntactic environments and inflectional morphology of words can be virtually nil in some languages (e.g., Chinese) but can be carried to staggering lengths in others. This can be disconcerting to the linguist or psychologist who inclines to a view of the basic sameness of all languages in their fundamental structural characteristics. What is true of the interconditioning between syntactic environments and the inflectional morphology of words is also true of the relations between environment and the forms of morphemes. Some languages have hardly any morphophonemic irregularities (e.g., the Cuzco dialect of Quechua), while others have incredible amounts of it (e.g., the Iroquoian languages). It does not seem that there is as much difference between languages in respect to the corresponding phenomenon on the phonemic level. All languages have a good deal of it. Some may seem to have more of it than others, but this is a function of our ethnocentricity. A case in point is described in the next section.

STIMULUS EQUIVALENCE

Linguistics has developed a considerable apparatus for handling problems of what might be regarded as stimulus equivalence in language structure. This phenomenon in language and the apparatus to deal with it in linguistics seems most often to have attracted the attention of psychologists. It relates (in a very general way) to the problems of constancy, conditioned similarity, and criterial attributes which have interested perception psychologists, learning theorists, and those who study concept formation.

Linguists themselves never cease to be amazed at the identifications and groupings into equivalence classes which they discover in the structures of the languages they work with. They find them in phonological equivalences, in grammatical equivalences, and in lexical equivalences. Many of them are indeed novel and unusual, given the conditioning of one's own different language background. It is on these that the so-called "Whorf hypothesis", or the "linguistic-relativity hypothesis", is based. We consider here an example from phonology. Examples from lexicon are found in the next section.

The writer has done intensive field work on a language – Cayuga, one of the languages of the Iroquoian family – which exhibits conditioned alternations and resulting stimulus equivalences of types such as those in the following pairs of disyllabic and monosyllabic sequences: *gahə̃n* and *k'hãə̃n*; *diho* and *t'hyo*; *gũha* and *k'hwa*; *driho* and *t'hryo* (or *čhryo*). The paired types are quite unlike in over-all acoustic properties, and they are perceived as very unlike by listeners (like ourselves) who have a different perceptual preconditioning to speech sounds from that which native speakers of this language have. When the differences between the alternants in these pairs were pointed out by the writer to his language informants, however, they declared that they never were aware that there was any difference between them.

Cayuga speech also has a liberal sprinkling of "whispered" syllables. (They are syllables – *ka*, *tro*, *nyũ*, *wi*, for example, which are pronounced entirely without voice. Phonetically this is not quite the same as whispering, for a whisper has another added articulatory feature.) These voiceless syllables alternate in a regular way with voiced syllables which are followed by *h*. Speakers who have been questioned about this and informed of the point at issue have replied that they had never noticed before that these syllables were whispered, or that there was any difference between them and the voiced types (followed by *h*) with which they alternate.

Besides these, Cayuga has many metathesized pairs in similar alternation, where the metatheses affect the relative order of vowels and the glottal stop (as it does with vowels and *h* in the first examples cited). These alternations too escape detection by the very ones who produce them.

The Cayuga words pronounced *onũhsagáhɛ̃n* (*window*) and *deyonh*^{ŭ}*sák'h'ãĩn* (*two windows*) produce drastically different auditory impressions on a phonetician or on an English-speaking listener or one who speaks almost anything but Cayuga. But to the Cayuga they sound the same, except that the second word begins with *de-* (a prefix associated here with reference to *two* things). So it is also with *gˀoník'hwaˀ* (*her mind*) and *godiˀnigũ̆haˀ* (*their minds*). The second word has a syllable *-di-* which makes it a plural form. Here again the acoustic impression to the outsider is drastically different as between the two words, but not at all so to the native speaker, who notices only the presence or absence of the syllable *-di-*. Similarly in *ɛ̃hat'hryóˀdaat* (*he will work*) and *ɛ̃hɛ̃nadríhoˀdaat* (*they will work*), the difference in the pronominal prefixes *-ha-* (*he*) versus *-hɛ̃na-* (*they*) is noticed, but the remaining differences are not.

The Cayuga listener is obviously not responding to the same features of the acoustic stimulus that an outsider would pick up. We would probably not be far wrong if we concluded that in the native speaker there is a learned *nonperception* (a conditioned indifference) to some of these features. If, instead of objectively reporting the total acoustic stimulus as we have done above in our phonetic transcriptions, we should obliterate the distinctions: 1. between voiced and voiceless sounds both in consonants and in vowels; 2. between the two possible orders of a vowel and a laryngeal, e.g. between *aʾ* and *ʾa* and between *ah* and *ha*, etc.; 3. between syllabic and monosyllabic vocalic segments; 4. between stressed and unstressed vowels; and 5. if we drop the special mark of nasalization, the tilde, on the two nasalized vowels, we would probably come closer to representing what the native speaker hears. We should then write the above examples as *onuhsakahɛn* and *teyonuhsakahɛ̇n* (instead of the phonetically more accurate *onũhsagáhɛ̃n* and *deyonh*$^{\tilde{u}}$*sákhʻãĩn*), *koʾnikuhaʾ* and *kotiʾnikuhaʾ* instead of *gʾoníkʻhwaʾ* and *godiʾnig*$^{\tilde{u}}$*ha*), and *ɛhatrīhoʾtaat* and *ɛ̇hɛ̀natrihoʾtaat* (instead of *ɛ̃hatʻhryóʾdaat* and *ɛ̃hɛ̃nadríhóʾdaat*). Now the paired members begin to look as much alike in transcription as they seem to sound alike to the Cayugas. What we have accomplished is to suppress from our transcription the representation of features of the acoustic stimulus (voicing, syllabicity, laryngeal order, and position of the accent) which do not serve as cues for differential responses on the part of the native subjects and to retain a representation only of those features which do serve as cues – the distinctive features of this language.[7]

This process is called "phonemicizing" the transcription.[8] For an outsider, one must give rules for converting the phonemic representation back into phonetics. Otherwise it would be impossible for him to read the transcription to make it sound like the original language. For the native speaker, however, the rules are built into his habits already. The basis of the Cayuga rules – as the reader may already have observed from the examples – is syllable count, the distinction between even and odd-numbered syllables. The details of the rules are too complex to be given here. An almost identical system was found by Sapir in Southern Paiute. It is described in his monograph on that language (68) as well as in the famous paper "The Psychological Reality of Phonemes" (67). The two cases are of independent historical develop-

[7] The above is a slight oversimplification of the facts. Fuller details are presented in another paper (58). It is possibly also an overinterpretation of the facts because it can be argued that perception is of a total whole, a gestalt, and that within this no feature can be said to be devoid of stimulus value, whatever its redundancy and predictability from context. It should be remarked in this connection that linguists generally make a point of avoiding psychological interpretations of the structural facts of a language – a rule of caution which the present writer has allowed himself to neglect for the moment.

[8] A transcription which suppresses all but the cue-bearing phonetic features (the *independent variables* of a phonological system) is known as a "phonemic" transcription. This contrasts with a "phonetic" transcription, which registers all features that a given phonetician is able to discriminate and report, without regard to their structural status or cue-bearing function in the particular language at hand.

ment. Cayuga and Southern Paiute are neither phylogenetically related nor influenced by geographic proximity.[9]

The method of phonemics is not one of psychological experimentation; rather, it involves the search for circumstantial evidence as to the distinctiveness or nondistinctiveness of phonetic features in naturally occurring speech data. The only "psychological" test which the linguist performs is to ascertain whether two phonetically different forms are the same or different as linguistic stimuli to natives. The specific purpose of the same-or-different test is to determine whether a particular feature of phonetic difference is a result of *free variation* or of *contrast*. Beyond this, one studies the distributions of phonetic types (the inventory of phonetic environments in which they occur). In particular, one seeks to determine whether two phonetic types which are similar in some features but different in others are in *complementary distribution* or in *contrast*. If a rule can be formulated whereby the occurrence of one or another of two such phonetic types is shown always to be a function of the phonetic context, then they can be regarded as conditioned variants of one unit. The "phoneme" is generally regarded as a class of phone types which have a phonetic feature in common and whose differences are either in complementary distribution or in free variation in respect to their environments. Alternatively, it can be regarded as the phonetic feature (or bundle of features) shared by all the members of such a class, i.e., the defining features of the class, or necessary and sufficient conditions for membership in the class. Given the specification of a phoneme and of the environment in which it occurs in any instance, the selection of the allophone – i.e., the particular member of the class of conditioned variants – follows automatically.

It is generally assumed that the allophones of a phoneme are in some sense equivalent stimuli. They are defined so that they share the same distinctive features (features that function as cues for differential responses in the given language) and differ from one another only by nondistinctive features (those which do not function as cues). Granting the assumption, one may see in this phenomenon in phonology – as some psychologists have seen it – an anaolg to the phenomenon of constancy, which has been studied by perception psychologists

[9] Sapir's paper (67) is one of the classic pioneer papers in the then (1933) new theory of phonemics. It contains interesting data on the interpretive responses of a native speaker to one of the phonological problems of Southern Paiute, and it gives a partial phonemicization of the phonetic data. Sapir's phonemicization – or "phonologic orthography" as he called it in this paper – does not go far enough, however. It misses the solution of both the geminate stops and the voiceless syllables. Lounsbury (58) suggests a reinterpretation based on the structural analogies with Cayuga.

largely in connection with visual-concept formation. The notion may perhaps be extended also to analogs in lexicon, such as those described in the next section.

Examples just as pertinent as the Cayuga ones could be found in English. It is difficult to make the point with English examples, however, for the phonetic differences which would have to be described in distinguishing the allophones of English phonemes would seem like phonetic hair-splitting to an English-speaking reader. But one society's hair's breadth can be another's chasm. Every linguist has struggled in a strange language over distinctions so subtle (from his point of view) that he has wondered how the speakers of that language can ever pick up the cues. These same distinctions, however, seem gross and obvious to the native speakers. On the other hand, some differences that seem gross and obvious to us (such as those mentioned for Cayuga) may escape detection by others, including the very ones who produce them. There seems to be no absolute metric that can be applied to acoustic space when, in language behavior, it is subject to so much learned perceptual distortion.[10]

THE CLASSIFICATORY FUNCTION OF LINGUISTIC FORMS

Linguistic forms act as classifiers of their referents, for it is through the use of the forms that distinctions are drawn and ambiguities allowed in the construction of messages which report on (or otherwise relate to) things, situations, and events. We will use the term "first-line distinctions" to designate distinctions of reference which are made, in usage, by the naming vocabulary of a language; and the term "first-line ambiguities" to refer to the ambiguities of reference which are present in that same usage. Sharper distinctions than those given by the naming vocabulary can, of course, be drawn by the addition of modifying constructional devices, and some of the first-line ambiguities may be thereby eliminated. Every language has qualifying and limiting constructions by means of which reference may be sharpened, when necessary, beyond the degree provided by the conventional usage of its naming vocabulary.

[10] In regard to the learned perceptual distortion of phonetic space, Liberman et al. (50) have designed experiments to test whether the observed sharper stimulus discriminations in the region of phoneme boundaries are an effect of learning, and, if so, whether this represents "acquired distinctiveness" near phoneme boundaries or "acquired similarity" within the ranges of variation of phonemes. The results support the assumption that the discrimination peak at phoneme boundaries is a result of learning, and they point in the direction of acquired distinctiveness.

The first-line distinctions and ambiguities are of considerable interest in their own right, however. These are the referential distinctions which are most economically made and the hardest to avoid (those most accessible in the "code"), and the ambiguities in reference which are the likeliest to be present and the most cumbersome to remove. Anthropologists, linguists, and psychologists have entertained numerous interesting hypotheses concerning these. The referential classifications made through lexicon often vary strikingly from language to language and are seen to exhibit different classificatory principles in different languages. It is posited that the principles of referential classification embodied in lexical usage in a given speech community bear some relation to their relative utility in communication in that community and to the frequency with which the distinctions implied by them are of crucial significance. This, in turn, it is posited, may be a function of the ways in which a people's social interactions and their activities in relation to their natural and man-made environments are organized.

Some of the best cases in support of this hypothesis come from special vocabularies such as those of kinship systems, numeration, ethnobotanical, ethnozoological and ethnometeorological terminologies, etc. Other convincing examples can be found in the vocabularies and/or inflectional apparatus related to the forms of respect and familiarity, authority and deference, social distance and solidarity, etc. Some of those who have speculated on these matters see language as organizing a very large part of one's perceptual habits, and would see even the grammar of a language as related to an underlying "world view" or perceptual orientation which may characterize the culture of a particular speech community. Clearly this is a fertile field for hypothesis formulation.[11] As an example of the classificatory function in lexical usage, we shall cite a few instances from kinship terminologies.

Lexical units in kinship terminologies can differ, as between different societies, in two aspects of their meanings: the "personnel-designating" aspect and the "role-symbolizing" aspect.[12] Thus the meanings of the "father" terms of various kinship systems may differ in regard to who may be named "father" (or the equivalent) and what it means to be a "father" in that society. In our society, as the term is applied to real relatives (i.e., excluding the metaphoric extensions to nonrelatives), the reference term is applied by an individual to but one person: the one whom we understand as one's father (though as a term of address it may be extended to a stepfather and to a father-in-law as well). In a great many societies (those having what anthropologists call Iroquois-

[11] In fact, it has been a favorite field for quite untrammeled speculations (cf. Whorf, 80, especially pp. 57, 134, 160, 207, 233; Lee, 39, 40; and Hoijer, 31).

[12] This distinction is drawn from Schneider and Roberts (71).

type kinship systems), the "father" term is applied not only to one's father, but to one's father's brothers and male cousins as well. In still other societies (those having Crow-type kinship systems), the "father" term applies to one's father, father's brothers, father's sister's sons, father's sister's daughter's sons, and sometimes to the father's mother's brothers as well. Aside from the question of who may be classed under the same kinship label as the father, there is also the question of what the label implies in the way of expected behavior. In one society, the relevant term may mean an authoritarian figure who is the head of the family; in another, the analogous term may mean something quite different.[13] The personnel-designating aspects of the meanings of kinship terms are analyzed by isolating the dimensions of referential features which are distinctive in the given system and by defining each labeled kin class in terms of the distinctive features of that class, i.e., in terms of those which state the necessary and sufficient conditions for membership. The role-symbolizing aspects may be analyzed from associated behavioral data in somewhat analogous ways.

The effects of different classificatory principles applied to the same set of elements can be seen in the following examples. Consider the following pairs of kin types:

1. Brother, sister
2. Father's brother's son, father's brother's daughter
3. Mother's sister's son, mother's sister's daughter
4. Father's sister's son, father's sister's daughter
5. Mother's brother's son, mother's brother's daughter.

In our kinship usage, the types of 1 are classed as brother and sister, while those of 2, 3, 4, and 5 are classed as cousins. In the Iroquois-type usages, the 1, 2 and 3 types are all brothers and sisters, while only those of 4 and 5 are cousins. In Crow-type usages the types of 1, 2, and 3 are again brothers and sisters, while those of 4 are classed as father and aunt, and those of 5 are son and daughter to a man, but nephew and niece to a woman. In Omaha-type usages, the types of 1, 2, and 3 are brothers and sisters, while those of 4 are nephew and niece to a man, but son and daughter to a woman, and those of 5 are uncle and mother. (There are no cousin classes in Crow- or Omaha-type usages.)

These different classifications result from the recognition of different dimensions of distinctive features. In our system, the primary dimension is degree of collaterality, with generation as a secondary dimension of limited applicability. (Our cousin class, which consists of second and

[13] Cf. Schneider and Gough (70, especially Schneider, 1-29; Fathauer, 247-249; Basehart, 291; Gough, 363-366).

higher-degree collaterals, extends into ascending and descending generations.) In systems of the Iroquois type, the primary dimensions are those of generation and bifurcation (the distinction between "parallel" and "cross" kin types). In those of the Crow type, the primary dimensions are a skewed generation measure (in whose computation females rank a social generation higher than their male siblings in certain contexts) and bifurcation. In those of the Omaha type, they are a differently skewed generation measure (the mirror image of Crow generation, in whose computation the roles of the sexes are reversed) and bifurcation.[14] It should be noted that the particular generation measure, whether straight or skewed, must be applied first in the Iroquois, Crow, and Omaha systems, inasmuch as the reckoning of bifurcation (whether a kin type is to be regarded as parallel or as cross) is dependent on the prior specification of generation in all systems.

The different principles of classification are not arbitrary quirks of particular languages, but linguistic reflections of important legal and social realities in particular societies. The first-line distinctions drawn by a kinship lexicon are simply the most useful ones for the given society. The fact that certain types of systems recur independently among peoples in distant parts of the world reflects the phenomenon of convergence in basic aspects of social structure, i.e., of similar adaptive responses to similar conditioning factors.

THE RELATIONS OF A LINGUISTIC FORM

The primary relations of a linguistic form have been variously categorized. C. W. Morris's familiar partitioning of these (63, 64), which puts them as "pragmatic", "semantic", and "syntactic" at a first level of categorization, was intended to apply to the relations of linguistic forms as well as to those of other and more general kinds of signs. We shall speak only of its application to linguistic forms, but we shall preserve Morris's terminology in referring to the latter as "signs".

1. Of the three varieties of relations, the "pragmatic" is the least well defined. It was meant to embrace the "expressive" aspects of the linguistic act, relating a linguistic sign to its users. "User" appears here to include both the producer for whom the linguistic sign is consciously or unconsciously an instrument, and whose disposition it expresses, and

[14] The above is not a sufficient description of the modes of generation reckoning in these systems. Actually there are four different varieties of so-called "Crow-type" generation reckoning, and a mirror-image set of four varieties of "Omaha-type". The formal analysis of these systems, their typology, and hypotheses concerning their social determinants are presented in papers by the present writer (55, 56).

any additional audience upon whom the sign acts as a stimulus, and whose interpretant response it also expresses (63, p. 7). Of the three relations specified by Morris, "pragmatics" is the one of most traditional interest to psychologists. The full gamut of psychological writings concerned with language, ranging from Freud to Skinner to Osgood, bears witness to this. It is, incidentally, the one of least traditional interest to linguists.

2. The "semantic" relation in this scheme of things is that between linguistic signs and "the objects to which [they] are applicable" (63, p. 6). "Object" here is an overly concrete term for what is intended, viz., objects, qualities, conditions, etc., whether actually existent or only describable or imaginable. Semantics in the present scheme, then, has to do with "reference", in the widest sense of this term. It is not a traditional interest in either psychology or linguistics, though linguists have not avoided dealing with it in at least an offhand, practical sort of way, and anthropologically oriented linguists (or linguistically oriented anthropologists) have made it a subject of theoretical, as well as practical, concern. It has of course, long been a subject of theoretical concern in philosophy. (In the anthropological approach to reference, since this is based on usage representing a society-wide pragmatism of sorts and reflecting a so-called "linguistic relativity", the line of division between pragmatics and semantics becomes somewhat blurred.)

Semantic analysis is facilitated by recognizing different *modes of reference* in the relationship between a linguistic sign and its object, viz., the relation between a sign and its *object as a thing*, and the relation between a sign and its *object as an exemplar of a kind or member of a class*. The former relation has been called "denotation" and the latter "designation" (63, p. 5).

Although some writers have used "kind of object" and "class of objects" as essentially equivalent terms (*ibid.*), it is important in descriptive semantics to make a further distinction between them. A semantic *class* may be defined merely by the sign which is its label, i.e., as the set of objects to which a given linguistic sign is applied. This tells us nothing about the *kind*, however; i.e., it does not tell us what distinctive qualities the members of the class have in common, other than their name. But any naturally formed class of things, arrived at pragmatically by stimulus generalization, is assumed to have some distinctive quality or combination of qualities in common, which furnished the basis for the generalization manifested in the common labeling response. A natural class of this type contrasts with unnatural classes, or pseudoclasses, which have no distinctive inherent qualities in common at all except their name (e.g., the class of girls named Mary as opposed to the class of those named Helen) or a feature of their name (e.g., the class of things named by masculine nouns in German as opposed to the class of things named by feminine nouns in German). Such classes are not based on stimulus generalization, but on random individual acts of name bestowal from out of a limited stock (as in the first example) or upon a traditional but arbitrary classification whose presumed former natural basis, if any, is a matter of prehistory (as in the latter example). It is the task of descriptive semantic analysis to isolate and abstract from the members of a label-defined class of objects what are their common distinctive inherent features that also make them as "kind", if indeed they are. We may restrict the use of the term "designation" to the relation of a sign to the class of its objects and adduce a later term of Morris, "signification", for the relation of a sign to the distinctive features of the class of its objects, i.e., to the attributes which specify the kind of object to which it is applicable (64, pp. 17, 20, 354).

While theoretical semantics, as already noted, is one of the traditional interests of philosophy, its applied aspect – the descriptive or "structural" semantic analysis of the lexicons of natural languages – is at present a concern of linguistically oriented anthropologists and psychologists. Areas of lexicon investigated by them include such lexical sets or semantic "fields" as the vocabularies of spatial and temporal orientation (27), color terminologies (5, 11, 37, 43, 44), pronominal categories (4, 12, 74), native botanical ("ethnobotanical") taxonomies (12), primitive taxonomies of disease (14), and above all, systems of kinship terms (18, 20, 52, 55, 56, 75, 76). The usual procedure in such undertakings is to move from (*a*) the compilation of raw lexicographic data on particular denotations, to (*b*) the assembling of the denotata of each single linguistic form as a semantic class of objects, or designatum, to (*c*) the discovery – when possible – of the classificatory dimensions imposed upon the field by native linguistic usage, and (*d*) the specification of the distinctive features defining each of the constituent semantic classes as a kind, to (*e*) an ordering of the semantic units of the various hierarchical levels within the total structure of the system.

Success in the third and fourth of these steps, viz., in the discovery of the significant variables of stimulus features and the specification of the defining features of each semantic class, is not always assured – especially when working with exotic systems such as anthropologists most often work with; for one can never know in advance what cues the people of a given society may be responding to in their linguistic classificatory behavior (cf. *The Classificatory Function of Linguistic Forms*). Analytic successes, however, as they accumulate in solving problems of this kind, may lead – and in some lexical domains have led – to a fairly comprehensive theory of the psychological and sociological possibilities for variation in linguistic classificatory behavior. As such a theory develops – as it has already in the field of kinship organization – it becomes increasingly easier to arrive at the solutions to newly discovered, or old but as yet unsolved, individual systems. Moreover, the determinants of the classificatory structures are often revealed, and this aspect of structure in language can be seen as related to other social and cultural phenomena.

3. The "syntactic" relation, the third of the varieties recognized in Morris's outline, is "the formal relation of *signs to one another* ... in abstraction from the relations of signs to objects or to interpreters" (63, pp. 6, 13). It is the aspect of language which is the principal concern of linguistics. It is the one of least traditional interest in psychology, although in recent times with the advent of information theory there has been an interest on the part of some psychologists in the probabilistic aspects of this relation (61, chap. 4; 62; 66; esp. §§ 2.3, 5.1-5). Since then, however, it has been adequately demonstrated that no stochastic model can generate the syntactic structures of a language (7, 9, 10).

The "formal relations which signs have to one another" are generally viewed as belonging to two elementary varieties: (*a*) those of a constituent to its partner-constituent within a construction, and (*b*) those of a constituent to an alternative constituent which may take its place in a similar construction with the same partner. The types of relations in this basic dichotomy have been variously categorized as "syntagmatic" and "associative", "*in praesentia*" and "*in absentia*", "contiguity" and "similarity", "combination" and "selection", "distribution" and "commutation", etc. (34, part II; 69, part II, chap. 5; 54).

R. Jakobson has noted that aphasic disturbances may affect one or the other or both of these facets of linguistic structure. He has referred to the resulting disturbances as the "contiguity disorder" and the "similarity disorder", respectively (34, part II).

Responses to word-association tests show the same two associative relations between the words: the sequential contiguity variety and the substitutional similarity variety. The familiar special cases of antonyms and synonyms as associative responses may be due to either contiguity, or similarity relations: contiguity, because both antonyms and synonyms are frequently linked in conventional phrases (*black and white, great and small, summer and winter*); and similarity, because of both syntactic and semantic similarity. (*Syntactic similarity:* membership in the same substitution class and substitutability in many of the same syntactic frames. *Semantic similarity:* sharing of all defining features but one – all but the last in the hierarchy of defining referential features in the case of antonyms, and all but one of context in the case of synonyms.)

Selection of the antonym is a fairly frequent form of tongue slip with some persons.

The same relations are involved also in the well-known and long-classified figures of speech, metaphor and simile on the one hand, and metonymy and synecdoche on the other. The nineteenth-century American philosopher C. S. Peirce recognized them in a typology of signs, in the dichotomy of "icon" and "index", the former owing its special character as a sign to the similarity principle, and the latter to the contiguity principle. Sir James G. Frazer recognized the same principles operating in a special form of sign behavior, primitive magic, and in his *Golden Bough* made these the criteria for defining the two main subdivisions of sympathetic magic: "homeopathic", based on the similarity principle, and "contagious", based on the contiguity principle. These same notions of similarity and contiguity relations were fundamental to nineteenth-century association psychology, and they survive into twentieth-century learning theory in a refined form as two of the basic variables in stimulus conditioning.[15]

These relations, manifest in the sequential arrangement of forms and in the replaceability of forms, are the fundamental syntactic relations within any layer of structure in language. Passing from layer to layer, there are the relations of constituent to construction, of form to transform, etc., which characterize the derivational structures of sentences and the derivational patterns of a language. Something of the nature of these relations was suggested in earlier sections. Their specification constitutes the major part of the descriptive syntax of a language.

Morris, in his sketch of the "syntactic" branch of the theory of signs, focused on the "logical syntax" of Carnap as an example of the kind of investigations that were to be included under the heading of "syntactics". He noted how this "deliberately neglects what has here been called the semantical and the pragmatical dimensions of semiosis to concentrate upon the logico-grammatical structure of language, i.e., upon the syntactical dimension of semiosis" (63, p. 14). The nature of the analysis envisioned for descriptive syntactics is indicated in his précis of logical syntax:

> In this type of consideration a "language" becomes any set of things related in accordance with two classes of rules: *formation rules*, which determine permissible independent combinations of members of the set (such combinations being called sentences), and *transformation rules*, which determine the sentences which can be obtained from other sentences. These may be brought together under the term "*syntactical rule*." Syntactics is, then, the consideration of signs and sign combinations in so far as they are subject to syntactical

[15] These two paragraphs are adapted from a previous publication of the writer (54).

rules. It is not interested in the individual properties of the sign vehicles or in any of their relations except syntactical ones, i.e., relations determined by syntactical rules (63, p. 14).

"Logical syntax", however, is at best a very special case in the syntactics of languages, being "the pure syntactic of *the language of science*" (64, p. 279). This last restriction imposes drastic limits on the kinds of sentences and the kinds of discourses to which it is applicable and even to the "language" to which it is applicable; since the language is not necessarily any one of those employed in scientific discourses (e.g., English, German, etc.), but a sort of international and artificial one consisting of a relatively small set of logical relations expressible (though in different ways) in all of these and abstracted from these; and whose selection from the total set of syntactic relations possible in a natural language introduces certain considerations of both a semantic and a pragmatic sort.

As for the syntactics of natural languages, Morris noted correctly that grammar, as usually developed in linguistics (which should be the syntactic description of natural languages), "is both semantical and syntactical in nature" (64, p. 280). The inclusion of semantic specifications has become something of an issue. The post-Bloomfieldian dogma in American linguistics has long upheld the desideratum of exclusion of semantic considerations from linguistics. Though certain theorists have attempted to formulate the analysis of phonology in such a way that it might – in theory, though only clumsily in practice – be carried out without recourse to questions of meaning differentiation (1, 8, 9, 23, 26), it has generally been considered impossible, or at least unfeasible, to eliminate it from grammar. (We have included it above when constructions were identified not only by the form classes and the order of the constituents which comprise them, but also by the functions of the constituents in the given constructions.) Thus, grammar has remained functional, and the identification of grammatical constructions has included specification of the semantic relations between constituents. Recently, however, a new school of linguists in this country has undertaken a completely semantics-free theory of grammar, fulfilling Morris's prophecy for "syntactics' in its linguistic application, as well as the post-Bloomfieldian dream of getting rid of meaning altogether. (In another sense also this new linguistics would seem to be a fulfillment of Morris's forecast, for it is the first to incorporate an explicit theory of sentence transformations.)

There is, of course, no compelling reason why studies of language *must* be compartmentalized in precisely this way. As intimated earlier, we are reporting not so much on what language *is* (for it cannot be said with certainty that any one view of this is adequate) as on what linguists do to it. And this is what they are doing to it now.

LINGUISTICS AND THE PSYCHOLOGY OF LANGUAGE

It would perhaps be desirable to conclude this paper with some suggestions of a programmatic sort for the development of the psychology of language – suggestions which might represent the linguists' points of view toward this subject. Actually, few linguists have given much thought to the subject (at least not in print). And the writer hardly feels competent to formulate linguistic problems as psychological questions, in spite of the fact that he feels that many of the issues that divide linguists of different schools are at bottom questions for the psychology of language.[16] The best that he can do at present is to give a sketch – as has been done in the preceding sections of this paper – of the things that linguists see in language and let the psychologists themselves decide whether any of these look as though they might hold something worth exploring by their methods. The writer is of the opinion that all aspects of linguistic behavior – from the molecular components of articulation and perception to the highest levels of behavioral organization that are involved in speaking and in the comprehension of speech – are appropriate topics and provide important problems for psychological inquiry into language. The foregoing sketch is far from an adequate map of this territory. If, however, it should reveal a few features of the terrain that are not yet common knowledge among psychologists, it will have served its purpose.

REFERENCES

1. Bloch, B., "A set of postulates for phonemic analysis", *Language*, 24 (1948), 3-46.
2. Bloomfield, L., *Language* (New York, Holt, 1933).
3. Brown, R. W., "Language and categories", in J. S. Bruner, et al., *A study of thinking* (New York, Wiley, 1956), 247-312.
4. Brown, R. W., & Gilman, A., "The pronouns of power and solidarity", in T. A. Sebeok (ed.), *Style in language* (New York, Wiley, 1960).
5. Brown, A. W., & Lenneberg, E. H., "A study in language and cognition", *J. abnorm. Psychol.*, 49 (1954), 454-462.
6. Chomsky, N., Review of B. F. Skinner, *Verbal behavior*, in *Language*, 35 (1959), 26-58.
7. Chomsky, N., Review of C. F. Hockett, *A manual of phonology*, in *Int. J. Amer. Ling.*, 23 (1957), 223-234.

[16] For a discussion of some of the basic issues upon which linguists disagree, and the psychological questions underlying these issues, see an account in the *Biennial Review of Anthropology*, 1961 (53, pp. 279-299).

8. Chomsky, N., "Semantic considerations in grammar", *Inst. Lang. Ling. Monogr.*, No. 8 (1955), 141-150.
9. Chomsky, N., *Syntactic structures* (The Hague, Mouton & Co., 1957).
10. Chomsky, N., "Three models for the description of language", *IRE Trans. Inf. Theor.*, 1956, IT-2 (3), 113-124.
11. Conklin, H. C., "Hanunoo color categories", *S.W. J. Anthrop.*, 11 (1955), 339-344.
12. Conklin, H. C., "Lexicographical treatment of folk taxonomies", *Int. J. Amer. Ling.*, 28 (1962), 119-141.
13. Cooper, F. S., et al., "Some input-output relations observed in experiments on the perception of speech", in *Second International Congress on Cybernetics* (Namur, Belgium, Association International de Cybernétique, 1958), 930-941.
14. Frake, C. O., "The diagnosis of disease among the Subanun of Mindanao", *Amer. Anthrop.*, 63 (1961), 113-132.
15. Gleason, H. A., Jr., *An introduction to descriptive linguistics*, 2nd ed., revised (New York, Holt, 1961).
16. Goldman-Eisler, F., "A comparative study of two hesitation phenomena", *Lang. Speech*, 4 (1961), 18-26.
17. Goldman-Eisler, F., "The predictability of words in context and the length of pauses in speech", *Lang. Speech*, 1 (1958), 226-232.
18. Goodenough, W. H., "Componential analysis and the study of meaning", *Language*, 32 (1956), 195-216.
19. Goodenough, W. H., "Cultural anthropology and linguistics", *Inst. Lang. Ling. Monogr.*, No. 9 (1957), 167-173.
20. Goodenough, W. H., "Property, kin, and community on Truk", *Yale Univer. Publ. Anthrop.*, No. 46 (1951).
21. Greenberg, J. H., "Language and evolution", in B. J. Meggers (ed.), *Evolution and anthropology: a centennial appraisal* (Washington, Anthropological Society of Washington, 1959).
22. Greenberg, J. H., "Order of affixing: a study in general linguistics", in J. H. Greenberg (ed.), *Essays in linguistics* (= *Viking Fund Publ. in Anthrop.*, No. 24) (New York, Wenner-Gren Foundation, 1957), 86-94.
23. Halle, M., "The strategy of phonemics", *Word*, 10 (1954), 197-209.
24. Harris, Z. S., "Co-occurrence and transformation in linguistic structure", *Language*, 33 (1957), 283-340.
25. Harris, Z. S., "Distributional structure", *Word*, 10 (1954), 146-162.
26. Harris, Z. S., *Methods in structural linguistics* (Chicago, Univer. Chicago Press, 1951).
27. Haugen, E., "The semantics of Icelandic orientation", *Word*, 13 (1957), 447-459.
28. Hockett, C. F., *A course in modern linguistics* (New York, Macmillan, 1958).
29. Hockett, C. F., "Animal 'languages' and human language", in J. N. Spuhler (ed.), *The evolution of man's capacity for culture* (Detroit, Mich., Wayne Univer. Press, 1959), 32-39.
30. Hockett, C. F., "Biophysics, linguistics, and the unity of science", *Amer. Scientist*, 36 (1948), 558-572.
31. Hoijer, H., "Cultural implications of some Navaho linguistic categories", *Language*, 27 (1951), 111-120.
32. Hoijer, H. (ed.), *Language in culture* (= *Amer. Anthrop. Assn. Memoir*, No. 79) (Chicago, Univer. Chicago Press, 1954).

33. Householder, F. W., "On linguistic primes", *Word*, 15 (1959), 231-239.
34. Jakobson, R., & Halle, M., *Fundamentals of language* (The Hague, Mouton & Co., 1956).
35. Koppers, W., "Lévy-Bruhl und das Ende des 'prälogischen Denkens' der Primitiven", *Sonderabdr. d. 18. int. Sozialkongresses*, Bd. IV (Rome, 1950).
36. Krantz, G. S., "Pithecanthropine brain size and its cultural consequences", *Man*, 61 (1961), 85-87.
37. Landar, H. J., Ervin, S. M., & Horowitz, A. E., "Navaho color categories", *Language*, 36 (1960), 368-382.
38. Laycock, D. C., "Language and society: twenty years after", *Lingua*, 9 (1960), 16-29.
39. Lee, D. D., "Conceptual implications of an Indian language", *Phil. Sci.*, 5 (1938), 89-102.
40. Lee, D. D., "Linguistic reflection of Wintu thought", *Int. J. Amer. Ling.*, 10 (1944), 181-187.
41. Lees, R. B., Review of N. Chomsky, *Syntactic structures*, in *Language*, 33 (1957), 375-408.
42. Lees, R. B., "The grammar of English nominalizations", *Ind. Univer. Res. Cent. Anthrop., Folkl., Ling. Publ.*, No. 12 (1960).
43. Lenneberg, E. H., "Color naming, color recognition, color discrimination: a reappraisal", *Percept. mot. Skills*, 12 (1961), 375-382.
44. Lenneberg, E. H., & Roberts, J. M., "The language of experience: a study in methodology", *Ind. Univer. Publ. Anthrop. Ling.*, Mem. 13 (1956).
45. Lévy-Bruhl, L., *La mentalité primitive* (Paris, 1922).
46. Lévy-Bruhl, L., *Les fonctions mentales dans les sociétés inférieures*, 3rd ed. (Paris, 1918).
47. Liberman, A. M., et al., "Minimal rules for synthesizing speech", *J. Acoust. Soc. Amer.*, 31 (1959), 1490-1499.
48. Liberman, A. M., et al., "Some results of research on speech perception", *J. Acoust. Soc. Amer.*, 29 (1957), 117-123.
49. Liberman, A. M., et al., "The discrimination of relative onset-time of components of certain speech and nonspeech patterns", *J. exp. Psychol.*, 61 (1961), 379-388.
50. Liberman, A. M., et al., "The discrimination of speech sounds within and across phoneme boundaries", *J. exp. Psychol.*, 54 (1957), 358-368.
51. Liberman, A. M., Delattre, P. C., & Cooper, F. S., "Some cues for the distinction between voiced and voiceless stops in initial position", *Lang. Speech*, 1 (1958), 153-167.
52. Lounsbury, F. G., "A semantic analysis of the Pawnee kinship usage", *Language*, 32 (1956), 158-194.
53. Lounsbury, F. G., "Language", in B. J. Siegel (ed.), *Bien. Rev. Anthrop.*, 1961, 279-322.
54. Lounsbury, F. G., "Similarity and contiguity relations in language and in culture", *Inst. Lang. Ling. Monogr.*, No. 12 (1959), 123-128.
55. Lounsbury, F. G., "The formal analysis of Crow and Omaha-type kinship terminologies", in W. H. Goodenough (ed.), *Explorations in cultural anthropology* (New York, McGraw-Hill, 1964).
56. Lounsbury, F. G., "The structural analysis of kinship semantics", *Proceedings Ninth International Congress of Linguists* (The Hague, Mouton & Co., 1964).
57. Lounsbury, F. G., "Transitional probability, linguistic structure, and systems of habit-family hierarchies", in C. E. Osgood and T. A. Sebeok (eds.), *Psycho-*

linguistics: a survey of theory and research problems (= *Ind. Univer. Publ. Anthrop. Ling.*, 10) (1954), 93-101.
58. Lounsbury, F. G., "Voiceless vowels, their phonological status and conditioning factors in Cayuga, Comanche, and Southern Paiute". Unpublished ms.
59. Maclay, H., and C. E. Osgood, "Hesitation phenomena in spontaneous English speech", *Word*, 15 (1959), 19-44.
60. Mead, G. H. (C. W. Morris, ed.), *Mind, self and society* (Chicago, Univer. Chicago Press, 1934).
61. Miller, G. A., *Language and communication* (New York, McGraw-Hill, 1951).
62. Miller, G. A., "Speech and language", in S. S. Stevens (ed.), *Handbook of experimental psychology* (New York, Wiley, 1951). 789-810.
63. Morris, C. W., *Foundations of the theory of signs. Int. encycl. of unified science.* Vol. 1, No. 2 (Chicago, Univer. Chicago Press, 1938).
64. Morris, C. W., *Signs, language and behavior* (Englewood Cliffs, N.J., Prentice-Hall, 1946).
65. Osgood, C. E., see p. 244, vol. 6 of *Psychology: A Study of a Science*, ed. by Sigmund Koch (New York, McGraw-Hill, 1963).
66. Osgood, C. E., & Sebeok, T. A. (eds.), *Psycholinguistics: a survey of theory and research problems* (= *Ind. Univer. Publ. Anthrop. Ling.*, Mem. 10) (1954).
67. Sapir, E., "La réalité psychologique des phonèmes", *J. de Psychol. normale et pathologique*, 30 (1933), 247-265. Also in D. G. Mandelbaum (ed.), *Selected writings of Edward Sapir* (Berkeley, Calif., Univer. Calif. Press, 1949), 46-60.
68. Sapir, E., "Southern Paiute, a Shoshonean language", *Proc. Amer. Acad. Arts Sci.*, 65, No. 1 (1930).
69. Saussure, F. de (C. Bally and A. Sechehaye, eds.), *Cours de linguistique générale* (Paris, Payot, 1916). Also W. Baskin (trans.), *Course in general linguistics* (New York, Philosophical Library, 1959).
70. Schneider, D. M., & Gough, K. (eds.), *Matrilineal kinship* (Berkeley, Calif., Univer. Calif. Press, 1961).
71. Schneider, D. M., & Roberts, J. M., "Zuni kin terms", *Lab. Anthrop. Note Book*, No. 3 (1956), 1-23.
72. Sommerfelt, A., *La langue et la société: caractères sociaux d'une langue de type archaïque* (Oslo, H. Aschehoug & Co. [W. Nygaard], 1938).
73. Sturtevant, E. H., *An introduction to linguistic science* (New Haven, Conn., Yale Univer. Press, 1947).
74. Thomas, D., "Three analyses of the Ilocano pronoun system", *Word*, 11 (1955), 204-208.
75. Wallace, A. F. C., & Atkins, J., "The meaning of kinship terms", *Amer. Anthrop.*, 62 (1960), 58-80.
76. Wallace, A. F. C., "Culture and cognition", *Science*, 135 (1962), 351-357.
77. Wells, R. S., "Immediate constituents", *Language*, 23 (1947), 81-117.
78. White, L. A., "On the use of tools by primates", *J. Comp. Psychol.*, 34 (1942), 369-374. Reprinted in L. A. White, *The science of culture* (New York, Farrar, Straus, 1949), 40-48.
79. White, L. A., "The symbol: the origin and basis of human behavior", *Philos. Sci.*, 7 (1940), 451-463. Reprinted in L. A. White, *The science of culture* (New York, Farrar, Straus, 1949), 22-39.
80. Whorf, B. L. (J. B. Carroll, ed.), *Language, thought, and reality: selected writings of Benjamin Lee Whorf* (New York, Wiley, 1956).

From *Psychology: A Study of A Science*, ed. by Sigmund Koch (New York, McGraw-Hill, 1963), vol. 6, 552-582. Reprinted with permission.

Susan M. Ervin and Wick R. Miller

LANGUAGE DEVELOPMENT

During the last thirty-five years, much of the work of American psychologists, influenced to some extent by the functional studies of Piaget, has been directed toward quantitative and normative aspects of child language. This work has been summarized by McCarthy (69). Additional foreign research has been summarized by Kainz (52) and El'konin (26).[1] We will focus our attention on current trends, in particular on work that has been guided by modern structural linguistics.[2]

The most important contribution that modern linguistics has brought to child language studies is its conception of what a language is. A language is a system that can be described internally in terms of two primary parts or levels – the phonological (sound system) and the grammatical. A complete description of a language would include an account of all possible phonological sequences and also a set of rules by which we can predict all the possible sentences in that language.

We can study the child's developing language system from two viewpoints; first, the child's own system – a description of his own sound

1 We gratefully acknowledge the contributions of A. G. Bratoff in finding, translating, and interpreting Soviet research reports. Thanks are due also to Volney Strefflre for many bibliographical suggestions. – The preparation of this chapter has been facilitated by a grant from the Department of Health, Education, and Welfare to the Institute of Human Development, University of California, Berkeley. Facilities have also been provided by the Center for Human Learning under support of the National Science Foundation.

2 A brief account of linguistically oriented studies is given by Carroll (17). Brown and Berko (8) summarize psycholinguistic methods used in child language studies and, in addition, discuss some of the more important linguistic concepts that are basic to this approach.

system and the set of rules he uses to form sentences – and, second, progress in the mastery of the linguistic system of the model or adult language. Since the advent of linguistically oriented research, more attention necessarily has come to be given to the analysis of individual cases. Among adults of the same language community, differences in the linguistic system are slight. Among young children, who are developing an internal linguistic system, differences are much greater. Cross-individual comparisons of linguistic elements are not appropriate if there is a possibility that the elements may occupy a different structural position in the system. It is necessary, first, to develop techniques and to discover units through the study of individual systems before comparisons between individuals, or group studies, are possible. For this reason, many of the studies herein reported are analyses of the rules of individual systems.

Since these analyses are producing the most significant changes in current views of language among psychologists, this chapter will give attention primarily to the analysis of the internal system of sound and syntax. Considerations of space have led to the omission of systematic treatment of the semantic and functional aspects of language acquisition which a complete discussion would require.

PHONOLOGY

Prelinguistic Stage

All human languages have certain distinctive properties: (*a*) they are learned; (*b*) they include conventional, arbitrary signs for meanings or for referents which may be displaced in time or space; (*c*) they include conventional units and rules for the combination of those units. It is evident that the vocalizing infant does not have a language. Though he may respond to adult language, we cannot begin to analyze the structure of his own language until he has at least two systematically contrasted meaningful words, a point usually reached by the end of the first year (69).

Spectrographic studies of sound during the first few months of infancy indicate that vocal behavior is very unstable. The speech organs are employed in breathing, eating, crying, or gurgling. The cortex is immature and the speech-like sounds which do occur show extreme fluctuations and defy analysis by the ordinary phonetic classifications applicable to speech under more stable cortical control (68, 60).

The most striking change in the months immediately following is the acquisition of increasing control over volume, pitch, and articulatory position and type, a control manifested by continuity or repetition of these features. The best recent study of this phase of development is by Tischler (92). In a study of seventeen children in contrasted social situations, he noted that there was a gradual increase in the frequency of vocalization. It reached its peak at eight or ten months of age, then declined. Between the eighth and the twelfth month, almost all conceivable sounds occur, including some not in the adult language.

An important theory regarding changes during the prelinguistic stage has been offered by Mowrer (73). He suggested that there is secondary reinforcement in hearing one's self speak as the rewarding parent speaks. This suggestion would account for both increasing quantity of sound and increasing approximation to adult sounds. There are a few data to test this theory. The prelinguistic sounds of deaf and hearing children are indistinguishable in the first three months, but there is a gradual decrease in the range of sounds uttered by the deaf after the age of six months (60), with each child specializing idiosyncratically. Thus, the hearing of a variety of speech sounds may increase the range of sounds used by the child, but we do not know if the hearing of a particular range of sounds influences the particular range used by the child. A study of children from two different language communities would shed some light on this problem.

Unfortunately, most studies which have been done at this stage and which have used adequate samples (43, 44, 45, 46) have two serious defects for our purpose. One is that they have seldom recorded the complete range of infant sounds, providing no record of rounded front vowels (as in French "tu", German "böse"), glottal trills, implosives, or clicks. The other is that they have not separated sounds uttered during babbling or cooing and those constituting variants in systematic language. Linguists have noted marked differences in vocal behavior even when babbling and language occurred at the same age.

Passive Control

It is usually assumed that passive control of phonological features antedates active control, that a child can hear a phonetic contrast, such as that between "s" and "sh", before he can produce it. The reader may have had the common experience of having his imitation of the child's speech rejected; Brown and Berko (8) give an example: "That's your fis?" "No, my fis." "That's your fish." "Yes, my fis." Hearing a contrast may be a necessary but not sufficient condition for producing it.

Little is known about the order of learning to hear differences in various aspects of intonation, stress, and quality in voices. The only study on this subject is reported by Shvarchkin (25), in which he taught children between 11 and 22 months Russian words differing only in one phoneme at a time. He presented his results as a series of phonemic features that distinguish groups or classes of phonemes. The phonemic features are learned in a given order.[3] By the end of the second year the children could distinguish all the phonemes of Russian. While techniques which could be expected to yield comparable results to those of this important study have been applied in this country, the results have not been presented according to sounds or features (83, 91). Information on the actual phonetic cues used by the child could be obtained by using artificially constructed vocalic stimuli. Such studies have been conducted by psychoacousticians on adults, but not on children.

The System of Contrasts

Just before the transition to the use of meaningful words, there is sometimes a period of complete silence or decreased babbling, but often babbling continues into the linguistic stage.

The use of meaningful words marks the onset of an active phonological system replacing unsystematic phonetic preference. Now for the first time we are dealing with true language, and we may examine the systematic structure of the sound contrasts employed by the child to distinguish meaningful words. A few examples from Joan, described by Velten (93), will serve as an illustration. At 22 months, Joan had *bat* (bad), *dat* (cut), *bap* (lamb), and *dap* (cup). In these words, [b-] and [d-] can be seen to contrast, in that they signal differences of meanings in otherwise identical words. These four words also illustrate a phenomenon that applied to all of Joan's vocabulary at this time. Four stops were found, [b], [p], [d], and [t]. The voiced stops, [b] and [d], occurred only in initial position, never final, whereas the voiceless stops [p] and [t], occurred only in final position, never initial. The stops [b] and [p] did not contrast in the same position and therefore were *allophones* of the *phoneme* /p/,[4] and, similarly, [d] and [t] were allophones of /t/.

Jakobson has developed a very influential hypothesis about the de-

[3] Vowel distinctions are learned first. The order of acquisition for the remaining features is: (*a*) vowels *vs.* consonants; (*b*) sonorants *vs.* articulated obstruants; (*c*) plain *vs.* palatalized consonants; (*d*) nasals *vs.* liquids; (*e*) sonorants *vs.* unarticulated obstruants; (*f*) labials *vs.* linguals (i.e., nonlabials); (*g*) stops *vs.* fricatives; (*h*) front *vs.* back linguals; (*i*) voiceless *vs.* voiced consonants; (*j*) blade *vs.* groove sibilants; (*k*) liquids *vs.* /y/.

[4] The symbols [. . .] are customarily used for phonetic writing, and /. . ./ for phonemic writing. The choice of the symbols /p/ and /t/ rather than /b/ and /d/ is arbitrary in representing Joan's phonemes. The concept of phonemic analysis is also applicable to adult speech. A fuller discussion is given by Brown (7, pp. 27-50) and Hockett (40, chaps. ii-xiii).

velopment of child language (49). His approach is summarized and applied by Velten (93) and Leopold (62). The hypothesis is that the development of the sound system can be described in terms of successive contrasts between features that are maximally different and which permeate the whole system. Thus, the first distinction is between a vowel and a consonant, since vowels and consonants are more different than any other part of the system. Next, the child might learn to contrast a stop with a nonstop, e.g., /p/ and /m/, or /p/ and /f/. Theoretically, the child could double his stock of consonants with each pair of contrasting features. When Joan, discussed in the preceding paragraph, learned to contrast /p/ and /b/, she also learned to contrast /t/ and /d/. In short, she learned the contrasting voiced-voiceless feature and applied it to all her stop phonemes. Thus, this theory presents an economical process of learning since the number of contrasting features is much smaller than the number of phonemes. Radical changes in the system come at once rather than through the gradual approximation of the adult phonemes one by one.

Are contrasts of features acquired suddenly as Jakobson hypothesizes? Evidence on phonology stems largely from diary reports about single children (1, 12, 20, 36, 62, 63, 93). These reports tend to support the notion of acquisition of features.

Jakobson also suggested an order in the acquisition of contrasting features. He suggested that the order reflects the prevalence of the contrasting features among the languages of the world. It is possible that the more common contrasts are both acoustically or visually distinct and easier to articulate. Evidence has been presented for acoustic confusion of /t/ and /k/ by adults (71). The contrast of /p/ *vs.* /t/ or /k/ is also acoustically confused, but, in normal situations, a visual cue is provided. There is probably a relation between the visual cue and the fact that children usually develop a contrast between labial (e.g., /p/) and nonlabial (e.g., /t/, /k/) consonants well before they develop a contrast between dental (e.g., /t/) and velar (e.g., /k/) consonants.

Among adults, auditory confusions are more common among phonemes similar in manner of articulation (e.g., /p/ and /t/) than phonemes similar in place of articulation (e.g., /p/ and /b/) (71). Children, however, frequently make substitutions that differ in manner of articulation. Stops replace the corresponding fricative (e.g., "thing" may become *ting*), and semivowels or vowels replace liquids (e.g., "rabbit" may become *wabbit*; "bottle" may become *batto*) (63, 91). Degree of difficulty in articulation is probably the crucial factor. Thus, stops (e.g., /p/, /t/) are usually acquired earlier than fricatives (e.g., /f/, /th/), probably because a more delicate adjustment of the tongue is necessary for the fricatives. Caution must be exercised in ascribing articulatory difficulty, because no simple measure of articulatory difficulty exists, and judgments are usually made *post hoc* from acquisition problems.

There is adequate evidence from diary reports to warrant an examination of the generalizations which have the widest support. These generalizations, which follow, appear to be the most tenable current hypotheses, but they must be viewed with extreme caution, in view of the small sample and restricted range of languages. (*a*) The vowel-consonant contrast is one of the earliest, if not the earliest, contrast for all the children. (*b*) A stop-continuant contrast is quite early for all children. The continuant is either a fricative (e.g., /f/) or a nasal (e.g., /m/). When two consonants differing in place of articulation but identical in manner of articulation exist, the contrast is labial *vs.* dental (e.g., /p/ *vs.* /t/, /m/ *vs.* /n/). (*d*) Contrasts in place of articulation precede voicing contrasts. (*e*) Affricates (ch, j) and liquids (l, r) do not appear in the early systems. (*f*) In the vowels, a contrast between low and high (e.g., /a/ and /i/) precedes front *vs.* back (e.g., /i/ and /u/). (*g*) Consonant clusters such as /st/ and /tr/ are generally late. In regard to contrasts at different positions within the word, certain tendencies are observed. Children normally acquire initial consonants before final or medial consonants, and consonantal contrasts often apply to initial position before other positions. On the basis of evidence from research on convergent *vs.* divergent habits, this order is what we would expect. Templin's report (91) of articulation problems in children three years and older supports these positional generalizations as well as the generalizations in order of appearance of contrasts.

In addition to acoustic, visual, and articulation factors, the size of the vocabulary may play a part in the development of contrasts. Velten, in the only thorough study of the problem (93), has provided some measures of the maximum possible number of vocabulary items in his daughter's speech. He reported that, at 22 months, she actually used 86 per cent of the words possible, given her word pattern (consonant-vowel or consonant-vowel-consonant) and her available stock of phonemes. Naturally, this meant she had a great many homonyms. She could expand the possibilities either by using disyllabic words or by expanding the phonemic contrasts employed. The correlation of increasing vocabulary and increasing complexity of the system is obvious, but we do not know what induces change. The few descriptions available suggest wide differences between children in the extent to which they maximize vocabulary potential in a given system. There may be certain points where homonyms are so dysfunctional that the system changes.

Rules of Substitution

In addition to describing the sound system of the child as a self-contained system, one can describe the relation between the adult's and child's system by rules of susbtitution.[5] If the child has a smaller stock of phonemes than the adult, it is obvious that the child must make certain substitutions; one phoneme must serve for two or more adult phonemes. Ordinarily, these rules reveal remarkable consistency (2, 63, 93).

It is an oversimplification to state that one phoneme in the child's system substitutes for several in the adult's system. The reverse is also frequent. Articulatory assimilation is one of several factors that can produce this result (1, 20, 63). One can hear similar assimilations in adult speakers – e.g., nightin-gale *vs.* nighting-gale. Templin's results suggest that medial unvoiced consonants tend to be voiced – especially /-t-/, also often voiced by adults – and that final voiced consonants tend to be unvoiced (91).

Complex substitution rules are often the result of anticipation. Morris Swadesh[6] observed such a pattern with his son. Final and medial consonants of the adult's words were dropped by the child. The initial consonant was replaced by a nasal if a noninitial nasal was found in the adult's word; a labial was replaced by the labial nasal /m/, and a nonlabial was replaced by /n/: *blanket* /me/, *green* /ni/, *candy* /ne/. Complicated substitutions of this type are not at all uncommon, but they are ordinarily not recognized by the parent.

Adult allophones are frequently allocated to different phonemes by the child (1, 63, 93). Thus, the adult's prevocalic /r/ is often represented in the child's system as /w/, but in other positions it often becomes a vowel or is lost. In adult speech, /r/ is formed with rounded lips before vowels, unrounded lips elsewhere; lip-reading research suggests that /r/ and /w/ are visually very similar before vowels (104).

Not infrequently an allophonic feature of the adult's language is reinterpreted by the child and becomes phonemic – i.e., it becomes contrastive – because the factors that condition the adult's allophonic feature are not represented in the child's phonological system (93). The relation between the adult's and child's phonological system and pattern of allophones can become extremely complex. Chao (20) presented evidence which suggests that the complex patterns found for one child were in part due to different physiological capabilities of the child and the adult – specifically, the difference in relative size of the tongue and mouth cavity.

[5] Similar techniques of language comparison are employed in the study of bilingualism and second language learning (99).

[6] Personal communication.

The child's phonological system is not a static system. Today's substitution rules are not tomorrow's rules. And, yesterday's rules are still to be found with some words today. The results are archaisms, found in almost every child's vocabulary. We have observed a child who learned to distinguish /t/ from /k/. She continued, unless corrected, to use an earlier word /ta/ for *car*. Velten (93) and Leopold (63) observed this phenomenon and, also, hypercorrections at times of change. We have noticed that new and old forms are sometimes stylistic variants; for example, the earlier form may be used in "baby-talk" or in talking to parents, the new form with outsiders. Archaisms are probably more common among children who have a relatively larger vocabulary and more primitive phonological system. In such a case, a newly acquired contrast must apply to a larger number of vocabulary items. Some vocabulary items are missed, and archaisms result.

The reverse of archaisms is also found, but less often. Chao (20) reports a case of a Mandarin-speaking child who applied a newly learned contrast to one frequently occurring word but not to other words for which the new contrast would have been appropriate.

By the fourth year, the child's phonological system closely approximates the model, and the remaining deviations are usually corrected by the time the child enters school. Occasionally, earlier substitution patterns persist, and the child is usually described as having speech problems. Applegate (2) describes the rules of substitution for such a child.

Grammar

Children display no evidence of systematic grammar when they first begin to use words at about the age of ten months, yet most observers agree that by four years the fundamentals are mastered. The acquisition of grammar is one of the most complicated intellectual achievements of children. How does the child learn the grammatical structure of the language? Before attempting to answer this question, we must understand something of the nature of grammar and specify some of the grammatical devices used by languages. Try to construct a sentence from a string of English words: *house, hat, ski, John, man, drop*. Out of these we can construct among others the sentence *the man dropped his skis and hat at John's house*. The most obvious addition is order. Secondly, we have added markers in the form of function words (*and, the, his, at*) and suffixes (*-ed, -s, -'s*). Together, markers and order are employed for any of several functions. They identify classes (*the* identifies a noun), they specify relations (*and* relates *skis* to *hat*; *'s* relates *John* to *house*; order indicates the subject-object relationship), or they signal meanings (plurality, possession, and tense are signalled by markers). A third device is *prosody*, or characteristic intonation and stress patterns.

The unit for grammatical analysis is the *morpheme*, the smallest element in speech to which meaning can be assigned. A word may be composed of one or more morphemes; *cats* consists of two morphemes, *cat* and the plural suffix. Morphemes, like phonemes, may take various forms. The plural morpheme appears as /-s/, /-z/, /-əz/, /-ən/, or a vowel change in *cats, dogs, bridges, oxen,* and *men*. All of these various forms of the plural morpheme are called *allomorphs*.

Morphemes are divided into classes, and sentences are composed of certain ordered sequences of classes. Morpheme classes are comparable to traditional parts of speech but are identified in terms of substitutions in linguistic contexts rather than in terms of meaning. Thus, the morphemes that fit in the sentence, "The ________ was good", constitute a class. Morpheme classes can be divided into two groups, lexical and function classes. Lexical classes are few in number but have many members. In English these include nouns, verbs, adjectives, and certain adverbs. Function classes constitute a larger number of small, closed classes. In English these include conjunctions, prepositions, auxiliaries, and suffixes such as the plural and past tense morphemes.

More detailed treatment of morphemic and grammatical analysis can be found elsewhere (8, 31, 40). In the remainder of this chapter the term "word" will be used in place of "morpheme", except where the distinction between them is necessary.

Passive Grammatical Control

The child's first word normally appears before the first birthday, but a year may pass before the child forms his first two-word sentence. During this period the child cannot be said to have an active grammatical system, or grammatical rules for forming sentences, because the words are not combined into sentences. All his utterances are one-word sentences. At this stage, however, the very young child may have a passive grammatical system, rules for decoding or understanding many adult patterns, but the appropriate experimental techniques have not yet been applied to study children so young. A few studies with older children have been made that bear on the problem of passive grammatical patterns.

In Russian, as in English, the subject and predicate constitute the largest units of the sentence; these in turn can be subdivided into smaller units. Karpova (53) has reported an ingenious study on sentence analysis by Soviet preschool children. They were trained with pictures, then with isolated words, to list, count, and then report which was first, second, and so on. Then sentences were presented. The majority of children five to seven tended to hear two parts, a subject and a predicate. When they heard more, they more often segregated concrete nouns; less often verbs and adjectives; and least often, function words.

Porter (78) observed that in identifying verbs in written sentences, children seven to thirteen and adults relied primarily on structure, relatively little on meaning. He asked them to find a word like "jumped" in "the cow jumped the fence". He used both meaningful and nonsense sentences, varying the cues available – meaning, markers, and order. Prosodic cues were not available since the sentences were written. Children tended to select on the basis of position, adults more often on the basis of markers. Thus, in the nonsense sentence, "docib hegof gufed rupan tesor", children more often thought "hegof" was the verb, and adults chose "gufed".

The two forementioned studies were concerned with the identification of units belonging to lexical classes. The understanding of markers or function words can be studied both from a syntactic and semantic standpoint. Sokhin (87) studied the understanding of a Russian locative preposition by children 23 to 41 months of age. He asked the children, for example, to "put the ring on the block" or to "put the block on the block". The youngest children seemed to depend so heavily on situational probabilities that they could not understand these instructions. Eighteen of the children, between 26 and 36 months of age, who understood the difference between "on" and "under", still were unable to put the block on the block; and when told to put the ring on the block did the reverse half the time. Thus, they could discriminate the semantic contrast between different prepositions but could not distinguish the syntactic difference between the object of the verb and the object of the preposition, and the semantic contrast thereby signalled. Fourteen children 26-41 months of age were relatively successful in this task.

Derivational suffixes were studied by Bogoyavlenski (26). He contrasted four Russian derivational suffixes, a diminutive, an augmentative, and two suffixes (*-nik, -shchik*) that formed agentive nouns from nouns and verbs. The agentive suffixes are like the English suffix *-er* in *farmer* and *worker*. It was found that the children had much more difficulty in understanding words using the agentive suffixes, evidently because there is a more radical semantic change involved.

The Unmarked Grammatical System

Our knowledge is relatively well developed regarding children's sound systems and includes elegant and detailed descriptions of particular children's sytems, which can be a prelude to generalizations when more children have been studied. The same is not truc of children's grammatical systems. For this reason, the treatment in this section must rely largely on a few studies of individual cases now in progress.

Observers have agreed that when true sentences appear, sentences composed of two or more words, they seem to be abbreviated or "telegraphic" versions of adult sentences (10, 57). *That's the ball* becomes *that ball; where's the ball* becomes *where ball.* Function words are almost completely lacking at this stage. Recent studies of individual children show that even in these early sentences there are systematic regularities of order (5, 10, 11, 72). How seriously are we to take these regularities? There are grave difficulties in defining children's classes and establishing grammatical rules on internal evidence alone, without analogy to the adult system. A linguist studying an adult language can test his generalizations by composing sentences and asking a speaker to correct him. This is not possible with the young children who view adult imitations of their speech as amusing (11). Furthermore, adult informants correct inconsistencies and slips, but children's "errors" (that is – inconsistencies) are indistinguishable from shifts in the structure. There is, of course, a point in time when children begin to correct their own inconsistencies, thereby revealing the existence of a norm, which may be the same or different from the adult norm.

In spite of these difficulties, certain regularities of sequences are apparent and have been found independently by different investigators. Braine found them as early as 18 months of age in the first two-word sentences (5). It is possible that the regularities in the early sentences merely reflect memorization of sequential probabilities in adult speech. Only novel sentences can show this is not the case. All studies by these investigators have revealed sentences which are systematic by the induced rules of the child's grammar, but "strange" in adult English. Miller and Ervin reported *all-gone puzzle*; and Braine, *all-gone sticky, other fix,* and *the up*. Braine points out that the strangeness of an utterance is no criterion of its grammaticality at this age.

We assume that the development of grammar arises from the economy of coding words into classes. It would tax the capacities of any mind immensely to remember the millions of utterances heard; if the words are coded into grammatical classes, it is not necessary to store specific utterances as such. If class probabilities or rules rather than specific sequences are remembered, new sequences can be generated.

There must be an important relation between the frequency of sequences and learning of classes. We suggest that one way grammatical classes are created is through a sequence consisting of a very frequent item and a highly variable item. The frequent item corresponds to what

Jenkins and Palermo (50) term an *operator*. In an inflected language, the operator may be an inflectional prefix or suffix even if it is invariant in the child's speech. In English, a function word or another high-frequency word is used as the defining frame; e.g., words such as *that, where, it, off, on, want, see, all-gone*. In a language in which only equiprobable lexical items existed, classes would be very hard to learn. Jenkins and Palermo have suggested that operators are necessary for the development of word classes. There is no proof that this is the case, but the evidence so far available supports this contention.

The child's first two-word sentences are frequently something like *that truck, that baby*, and *where dolly, where truck*. If the child has used *that* and *where* as operators for identifying a class, he can generate a new sentence – *where baby*. An operator occurs in a fixed position; i.e., in either first or second position. The remainder of the vocabulary forms a single, undifferentiated class and can occur with any operator (5). Very soon, the remainder is divided into classes; certain operators occur exclusively or almost exclusively with certain words. The classes tend to reflect class distinctions of the model language, e.g., some children use *it* as an operator only after words that are transitive verbs in the model language.

The evidence from three studies conducted by Miller and Ervin (72), Brown and Fraser (10) and Braine (5) reveals a high degree of similarity in the existence of such sequences of high-frequency and low-frequency items. Braine observed that children had periods of concentrated use of certain operators with particularly high frequency, using the favorite with a variety of other words, as new vocabulary was acquired.

A second feature in the evolution of classes may be the common semantic properties of referents. Thus, nouns often refer to things and verbs to actions. Brown has observed that children's classes are more semantically consistent than adults'. He has also demonstrated that preschool children select a picture of action when asked to find "sibbing", a picture of a container or simple object when asked to find "a sib", and a picture of confetti-like material when asked to find "some sib". The word "sib" is, of course, nonsense to the children, but they can select the most probable semantic properties of "sib" by the marker which identifies the word class: "–ing" (verb), "a–" (count noun), and "some–" (mass noun) (6).

If grammatical rules simply stated allowable sequences of words, it would be necessary to have one set of rules for two-word sentences, a different set of rules for three-word sentences, and so on. In sentences of more than two words, certain words are nested so that it is necessary to deal with only two units at a time. Thus in the sentence *many birds fly*, the first two words are nested and occupy the same structural position as the first word in the sentence *birds fly*. One rule will account for the subject-predicate sequence in both sentences, and another rule will account for the two-word sequence that composes the subject of the first sentence. The principle of nesting (or immediate constituent analysis, as it is termed in linguistics) is described in detail by Hockett (40, chap. xvii). Preliminary evidence suggests that nesting is learned early, but the child sometimes develops his own system before learning the system of the adult language (5, 72). It is difficult to assess the evidence, however, because nested constructions are usually delineated by markers which are largely lacking in the early grammatical systems.

The Marked Grammatical System

Word classes in the early grammatical system are identified primarily in terms of order. As the child starts using more and more function words and suffixes, the classes are also identified by markers. Nouns are words that occur after *the* and before the plural suffix; verbs are words that can occur after *can* and before *-ing*. At this time it is convenient to describe the child's grammatical system as a simplified version of the model, along with additional grammatical rules to account for features that have no counterpart in the model.

Rapid progress is commonly observed when the child enters this phase of development. Velten (93) reported in his daughter's speech from 27 to 30 months a swift development of prepositions, demonstratives, auxiliaries, articles, conjunctions, possessive and personal pronouns, the past-tense suffix, the plural suffix, and the possessive suffix. At first, the use of markers is usually optional and often inconsistent, and only gradually does the child's usage approach that of the adult's, with increasing subdivision of classes (16).

Most observers have noted that before a contrast occurs consistently, one of the alternate forms is preferred. Gvozdev has added that, in the case of the Russian child, there is free variation observable just prior to mastery (36). Comparisons of different studies are difficult because the criteria of mastery are different. The fact that a given child says *toys* and *eyes* does not necessarily indicate that he has mastered the plural suffix. We must know if the use was spontaneous or imitated, if the singular *toy* and *eye* are used, if there is a contrast in meaning between the singular and plural forms, and if the formation is productive, i.e., if the plural suffix can be added to new nouns. Berko (4) developed a technique which involved asking children to make new formations using nonsense words. The child was told: "This is a wug. Now there are two of them. There are two ______." The appropriate response is, of course, "wugs". Using this technique, Berko found that four- to seven-year-old children knew the rules for forming the plural and possessive for nouns and the past tense and third person singular for verbs. Their greatest difficulties were partly phonological in nature; e.g., they had difficulty in adding the plural suffix "-s" to items that ended in a sibilant, such as "tass", perhaps because such forms were interpreted as already including a plural suffix. Miller and Ervin (72) used this technique with younger children in studying the acquisition of the plural. The tests were repeated at monthly intervals, and both meaningful and nonsense items were used. They found that the plural was usually learned before the child was three years old, but there were large individual differences. Learning of the plural for meaningful words almost always preceded that of the plural for nonsense words that had a similar phonological shape, but the interval between the two was surprisingly short.

Mastery of familiar forms precedes their generalization. The patterns are then extended to irregular forms, so that along with the regular pairs like *dog-dogs* or *walk-walked,* regularized pairs are found: *man-mans, foot-foots*, (or *feet-feets*), *go-goed, break-breaked.* Guillaume (35) also was struck with his children's tendency to regularize verbs; *battre* became *batter, rire* became *rier*. Even very common verbs such as *prendre* and *tenir* were affected. He reported the only statistics suggesting why such regularization occurs; he found that though the French verbs employing a regular pattern were used only 36.2 per cent of the time, they constituted 76 per cent of the different verbs used.

Syntactic contrasts are often added to the less obvious required markers when the contrast is semantically important. In *I talked to him yesterday*, time is marked by both *-ed* and *yesterday*; in *two books*, plurality is marked by both *two* and *-s*. The child will sometimes use the more specific syntactic indicator (*yesterday* and *two*) in place of the less specific suffix (*-ed* and *-s*). A child is probably more apt to use a syntactic device if his phonological system does not allow him to use the suffix. Miller and Ervin (72) reported one case in which the child lacked final sibilants and used *one-two* in place of the standard plural: *one-two shoe* meant more than one shoe. Such a child, though she would fail a standardized test of the plural, would fail for phonological, not grammatical, reasons. Grammatically, she did have a plural signal. We do not know if such syntactic indicators are commonly acquired before suffix contrasts for phonological or other reasons. Gvozdev has reported that in the observations he has made in Russia these indicators are acquired at the same time (36).

There has been little systematic study of the order of acquisition of contrasts indicated by markers for English-speaking children. Russian linguists have done some work along these lines. Gvozdev (36) contends that the order of evolution depends on meaning. Russian gender contrasts appear relatively late because of their lack of strong semantic support, and the conditional mood, which is grammatically quite simple, occurs a year after the past-tense contrast for reasons of semantic difficulty.

An important aspect of language has been raised by Chomsky's transformational analysis (21). Transformations are complex derivations from a simple or kernel sentence. Compare the following sets of sentences, each of which contains a kernel sentence and a question, a negative, an emphatic, an elliptical, and a progressive transformation of the kernel:

HE GOES.	HE WENT.	HE'LL GO.
Does he go?	Did he go?	Will he go?
He doesn't go.	He didn't go.	He won't go.
He *does* go.	He *did* go.	He *will* go.
He does.	He did.	He will.
He's going.	He was going.	He will be going.

A number of rules can be formulated which apply to more than one transformation. In the first four transformations, the auxiliary *do* is added if there is no auxiliary. A past tense or third-person-singular suffix is shifted from the main verb to the auxiliary. Additional, nontransformational rules must be applied to account for contractions and irregular forms; e.g., *go* plus *-ed* becomes *went*. The great advantage of a transformational account is that a small number of rules compared to a larger number of possible sentences results in an economy of description and a potential economy in learning as well. The transformation theory remains controversial in linguistics; in the field of language acquisition it is an ingenious hypothesis, which deserves testing.

Whether transformations are imitated or productive requires testing with novel sentences. Then one can discover if the sentences represent simply independent, unrelated patterns without effect upon each other. We should expect that, if transformations are acquired as operations, they should appear suddenly and influence much of the language at once, just as morphological regularities do. Miller and Ervin (72) present evidence from one child supporting this expectation.

Grammatical Development After Four Years Of Age

There have been very few structural analyses of language in older children. What material is available (4, 16, 38) suggests that by the age of four most children have learned the fundamental structural features of their language and many of the details. There is then a long period of consolidation, a period of overlearning so that grammatical habits become automatic. Some irregular patterns are learned. Other irregular patterns, already learned, still must become firmly established. A six-year-old often uses forms such as *buyed* and *bought*, or *brang* and *brought* interchangeably. When he corrects himself, changes *buyed* to *bought*, he indicates that he knows the adult norm but has not yet developed a firmly established habit. Less frequent patterns, such as the use of *too* with positive sentences and *either* with negative sentences, are yet to be learned. The child must still acquire certain grammatical patterns that are associated with difficult semantic patterns, such as passive transformations and causal patterns with *why* and *because*.

We have pointed out that sentences can be produced by memorizing sequences. The evolution into classes based on substitution in the same contexts is gradual. The process continues over many years and affects many verbal habits, even when children's sentences seem to conform to adult grammar. Thus, during the primary school years, there is a marked increase in the tendency to give free associations that are grammatically similar to the stimulus word. This tendency is earliest and strongest with nouns and adjectives and weakest with function words (9, 27). Experimentally, it has been found that such associations derive from occurrence in identical linguistic contexts (27, 70), that is, in the same conditions that we have suggested lead to the learning of grammatical classes. In pursuing the link between grammar and association, Brown and Berko (9) found that when children were asked to use nonsense words after they had heard them in sentences, they had difficulty. They were most successful with count nouns and adjectives. Their progress in mastery of classes showed the same sequential development found in mastery of word associations.

For diagnostic purposes, it would be useful to have standardized tests for various aspects of grammatical development. While there have been many separate studies of individual features (69), no standardization norms are available. The most common quantitative measures employed to assess development in standardization studies, such as Templin's (91), have been sentence length – as judged by adult words – and frequency of structural features, such as phrases and subordination. Brown and Fraser (10) compared sentence length in two-year-olds with certain other factors, such as presence of specific auxiliary verbs, and found a high correlation. When age is allowed to vary, all of these features tend to be correlated, since all change with age. One important precaution should be observed in finding appropriate measures of grammatical development. Adult usage differs in the various subcultures of any community. A good developmental measure for general use should include only those features common to all adult speech in the presence of children.

Language Differences

Comparison of acquisition of different languages may provide some clues to the bases of the particular sequences observed. For example, it has been commonly observed in English that the child who does not yet make a contrast in plurality simply uses no marker at all. The plural suffix in adult speech has a double function; it is both a semantic signal and a noun marker. Usually children say *dog* for both adult *dog* and *dogs*. Why this choice? Frequency and ease of articulation may dictate which of the alternative forms is preferred. As for frequency, *toys, eyes, shoes* may occur so often in the plural that this form is preferred by the child. On the other hand, the development of final consonant contrasts and consonant clusters is usually late, so that the singular of words with consonant finals may be preferred. Languages which use prefixes rather than suffixes might show a different pattern, but no evidence is available.

Most contrasts in English consist of a marker *vs.* no marker. By preferring the unmarked form, the child not only fails to signal a semantic contrast but also lacks a class marker. In some languages, on the other hand, the noun must occur with an inflectional suffix. Before they have inflectional contrasts, children have preferences in the form they use. Thus, these forms would be available as class markers to distinguish nouns from verbs when the child begins to form sentences, even before he uses them contrastively.

To what extent do different language structures condition different learning patterns? This is a question that has not yet received study. Kluckhohn suggested that Navaho children, who must learn an extremely complicated language, are more retarded in their language development than English-speaking children (19). Leopold (62) has stated that syntax (grammatical rules that apply to arrangements between words) comes before morphology (grammatical rules that apply to arrangements of morphemes within words) in the child's grammatical development. Leopold did his work with an English- and German-speaking child, and these are languages in which syntax plays a more important role than morphology. Burling (12) describes the development of a child learning Garo, a language in which morphology plays a more important role. He found that morphology and syntax appeared simultaneously and were of equal importance for the child.

Derivational suffixes (as distinct from inflectional suffixes) such as *-ly* in *wiggily, -y* in *fussy, -er* in *gunner*, play a less important role in

English than in some other languages, such as Russian. Berko (4) found that American children, ages four to seven, avoided such suffixes, preferring compounds or syntactic constructions. When they were asked, for example, what they would call a very tiny "wug", most children responded with phrases like *baby wug, teeny wug,* or *little wug.* A large number of adults responded with *wuglet, wuggie, wuggette,* or *wugling.* Russian children studied by Bogoyavlenski (26) readily formed derivatives using suffixes such as the diminutive.

LANGUAGE SOCIALIZATION

Cultures differ markedly in their practices in and attitudes toward language teaching. Baby talk furnishes an example. At one extreme is Comanche with a uniform and formalized baby talk (19). Baby talk has also been reported for Arabic, Gilyak, and Nootka cultures (3, 29, 82). At the other extreme are the Hidatsa, who claim to use no baby talk at all. They state, "We don't like baby talk. ... When they talk, we want them to talk just like us, right from the start" (96). The Mohave claim newborn children can understand speech (24). It is not known whether these differences are related to any differences in the rate of language acquisition. But we can expect that language instruction will be more casual among the Mohave, for example, than among the Hidatsa.

Baby languages in various societies cast some light on adult views of children's language systems. Baby vocabularies frequently bear a systematic relation to adult vocabularies and have three common features: employment of articulatory simplifications, tending to the use of stops and nasals and the elimination of consonant clusters;[7] use of reduplications, such as *byebye* and *mama*; and the use of special suffixes which may be peculiar to baby talk or may also be used as endearments or diminutives, such as the English suffix *-y* in *doggy, horsey, Billy, sweety.* Grammatical simplification is probably also a feature of the baby talk used in speaking to children, though this feature has not often been thus described.

Steward (90) compared two cultures that differ radically in their tolerance of the peculiarities of child language. He found stuttering more common in the society that made more rigid demands on the young

[7] Whether the articulatory changes are actually simplifications is arguable, since the criteria of simplicity are unclear. Pharyngeal fricatives are common in Arabic baby words (29), and glottalized consonants are found in Acoma baby words (authors' notes). Both of these sounds are difficult for second-language learners. It may be significant that a number of words in the formalized baby vocabulary of both languages are not systematically related to adult words.

speaker. This study is novel in its analysis of a variety of socialization practices related to language learning.

Societies may differ greatly in the amount and type of verbal stimulation given children. Irwin (46) has shown that speech development may be affected by reading to children. Children of multiple births are known to be retarded in language development (69), implying the importance of siblings in the kind of language the child learns. Hockett (39) has suggested that older children are the most important environmental force in shaping the younger child's speech habits. If this is the case, we can expect to find differences across cultures that correlate with differences in the amount and kind of contact found among children.

The development of good miniature tape-recorders makes possible the study of the evolving relation between speech forms and social functions, a study neglected even in the analysis of adult language (42, 88). There have been occasional comparisons of children's speech in different social conditions (37, 41, 97). The study of the nonlinguistic factors that condition the choice of differing linguistic forms offers another point of departure. A nice example is provided by Fischer (30) who studied the stylistic alternation of the participal suffix *-ing vs. -in* among children in a New England town. He found the alternation was related to personality (the "good boy" said *-ing*), to situational formality, and to the type of word used (*swimmin, chewin, hittin*, vs. *correcting, reading, visiting*). There was a slight tendency for girls to use *-ing* more than boys. Social class, in this relatively unstratified group, was not a significant factor.

Studies of the functional development of language are dependent on adequate descriptions of the behavior under study, the linguistic system of the child. As knowledge of the significant properties of children's language increases, it seems probable that more attention will be focused on the evolving differentiated usage of children, which results in the complex functional argots of adults, and on the features of the environment, which alter the rate of change in various aspects of the system.

LANGUAGE AND COGNITION

There has been a great interest in the past decade in the effects of language or label learning on nonverbal behavior. Soviet research, with a slightly different focus, has been concerned with the relation between the "first and second signal systems". Since the early 1950's, there has been a resurgence of research in this field in the Soviet Union. English summaries are found in Luria (66) and the collection edited by Ivanov-

Smolenskii (48). Because Soviet research is less familiar to us, we will give it somewhat disproportionate attention.

In this country, many of the studies have been done on adults, since the questions have been framed in terms of general behavior theory rather than developmental changes. There appear to be three explanatory frameworks employed in American studies:

(*a*) *Acquired distinctiveness.* Verbal training during the acquisition of labels alters the similarity of stimulus material, even on a single stimulus dimension, affecting discriminability.

(*b*) *Verbal mediation.* Though discriminability might be unaffected, verbal responses permit chaining, bringing to bear any prior reactions learned to the verbal responses themselves. Delay or stimulus complexity increases the effect.

(*c*) *Dimensional salience.* Verbal training may lead to selective attention to certain dimensions of the environment, as revealed in tasks requiring sorting of complex materials.

Acquired Distinctiveness

It has not been shown that psychophysical discrimination is altered by the acquisition of labels. In a study of speakers from different language communities, with different categories for color names, Lenneberg found that the capacity to discriminate hues was the same, even though the labels were differently distributed on the hue continuum (59). The only form of discrimination known to be affected by language is that of speech sounds themselves. Liberman showed the ability of adults to hear differences between sounds which are discreet in articulation but on the same acoustic continuum is clearly improved at phoneme boundaries (65). An example is the contrast between *do* and *to*, differing only in one feature on the acoustic continuum. The studies have shown that there is improved discrimination at phoneme boundaries, but no acquired similarity, or decrease in discrimination, within the phoneme. Why is there such a difference between the effects of acquiring labels for colors and sounds? One explanation may be that we make hue discrimination daily, without the use of color names, in our transactions with the physical world – judging contours, distances, and so on. We
tory frameworks employed in American studies:

Verbal Mediation

Many investigations which have been called studies of acquired distinctiveness actually seem to involve the occurrence of verbal mediation. In fact, the speech-sound studies, such as Liberman's, may involve comparison not of two heard speech sounds but of two utterances reinterpreted by the listener in terms of his own phonemic system – i.e., response mediation. Verbal mediation involves a response by the subject, and we may group the studies into two categories – those which are concerned with the distinctiveness of the response-produced cues, and those which are concerned with their chaining.

Spiker and his associates are among those who have studied the first of these two problems with children as subjects (89). An example is a study by Hayne Reese (80), in which children were taught in two stages. First they learned labels for colored lights; then they learned a motor response to the lights. Reese contrasted four different pairs of labels, differing in the distinctiveness of the labels. The most similar was *wug-wog* with phonetically similar vowels, then *zim-zam* with less similar vowels, and the most different were *lev-mib* and *wug-zam*. Reese found that there were differences in both the time it took to learn the labels and the time it took to learn the motor responses for the different groups. The more distinct the labels, the more quickly they were learned, and the more easily the motor response was learned. Evidently the ease in learning the motor response did not reflect merely the distinctiveness of the labels, but rather the mastery of the labeling response which took longer with the similar labels. Whether an alternative type of distinctive response which was nonverbal might have been equally effective is not known. A theoretical discussion of related studies has been presented by Goss (33).

Studies on delayed response suggest that verbal mediation is important in a variety of ways. Brown and Lenneberg (7) showed that if there was a delay after a color chip was shown, subjects tended to recognize the color, to choose it from among many, not so much in terms of its hue as in terms of its label. Thus, if a pale lavender blue was called "blue" by a subject, he tended to identify it later as bluer than it actually had been. This study has not been repeated with children, but the phenomenon is very striking and predictable in adults.

Spiker has pretrained children with labels for stimuli in a delayed-reaction experiment and thereby improved their performance (89). He designed the labels to fit the performance categories. The children remembered the correct response later because they had verbal labels which corresponded.

Oléron (76) has noted that deaf children were inferior to hearing children in their ability to solve double alternation problems of the type "left twice – right twice". He later found that the children did not know how to count and assumed that counting might help solve such problems. A study by Carrier with deaf children also suggests the importance of verbal mediation (15). He noted that hearing children judged black or dark objects to be heavier than similar light or white objects.

Before adolescence, deaf children did not make such judgments. He had to teach these children the terms "heavy" and "light" for concepts they already had. Clearly the deaf children were unlikely to know the double meaning of "light".

Michèle Vincent (95) has found differences between deaf and hearing children, less than eight years of age, in sorting tasks. Verbal mediation was assumed to be the critical factor. Two blocks, alike with respect to one dimension, were displayed, and the children were asked to choose the third. Wrong choices were corrected. The deaf were more than a year retarded. In a similar study meaningful categories, such as animals, were employed (94). Deaf children of eight behaved like hearing children of six years. When the hearing children were asked to justify their choices, subsequent performance improved. Presumably, this procedure increased the probability of verbal mediation. Studies comparing deaf and hearing children have the hazard that many features of experience are likely to differ and that some organic defects besides deafness may be present.

It has been common to compare children before and after they can verbalize a contrast and to assume that verbalization reflects the availability of verbal mediation. Of course, where the verbal skill has not been taught by the experimenter, the verbalization and the performance may both reflect a third factor. The Kendlers' recent work with reversal shifts seems to solve this difficulty (55, 56). Subjects are trained to criterion on a task requiring response to one of two available cues – such as size or color – and then a new rule is made. The new rule may simply be a reversal – if white was correct, now black is correct – or it may involve a shift to the other cue. Children between five and seven years found the two equally difficult, but, if young children were taught to mention the relevant cue, reversal was easier. For the older children, who presumably verbalized spontaneously anyway, the teaching had no effect, except that teaching them to mention the irrelevant cue impaired performance.

These studies assume the occurrence of a covert or implicit response. One way to test the occurrence of such covert responses is to condition a reaction to them. Volkova found that a response conditioned to the word "right" occurred if the children were given arithmetic problems that were correctly solved and that a response conditioned to the word "ten" occurred when the stimulus was "five plus five" (79).

Dimensional Salience

The sorting studies of Vincent, mentioned above, suggest the presence of verbal mediation, but it is possible that sorting or grouping tasks might be affected simply by the relative salience of different dimensions. Such salience varies with experience, and dimensions commonly codified by vocabulary or grammar would tend to be noticed more often. Casagrande (18), in a study connected with the Southwestern Project in Comparative Psycholinguistics, compared Navaho- and English-dominant Navaho children who lived on the Navaho reservation. The Navaho language includes a set of verbs referring to handling of objects, with a different verb for long rigid objects, mushy objects, flat flexible objects, and so forth. The classification of objects into these categories is similar to the classification of objects into the gender categories of European languages, except that the Navaho categories display marked semantic consistency. Since verbs of handling are prominent in the vocabulary of children, Casagrande believed the children might attend to the pertinent properties of objects earlier if they spoke primarily Navaho. He asked them to choose from two others a block to match a model, allowing matching on either of two dimensions. Between the ages of three and eight, there were marked differences, the Navaho-dominant children choosing the block similar in form, the English-dominant that similar in color.

This study has been concerned with the impact of the learning of language on nonverbal processes. While positive results have been found, in many studies the total effect is relatively slight and only barely statistically significant. It is possible to exaggerate the importance of verbal processes in simple tasks involving objects and motor responses. In studies involving aiming, mechanical puzzles, or various kinds of visuo-motor co-ordination such as that reported by Ervin (28), verbal training can interfere with performance. It may distract by supplying an additional task or by drawing disproportionate attention to part of the relevant stimulus complex. In the experiment by Ervin, a verbally trained group was generally inferior but was better one difficult item where the usual strategies discovered by visuo-motor experience were inappropriate. In the Casagrande study, a control group of Massachusetts city nursery-school children chose the form match as often as the Navaho-dominant Indian children. Perhaps their training with form-boards and other nursery toys had led them to focus on form as more relevant than color. This kind of experience may have had the same effects as the training supplied by speaking Navaho. And even verbal mediation does not, perhaps, have to be verbal. The complex problem-solving of primates on multiple-sign problems, and the level of play involving planning which can be sustained by deaf children before they receive speech training, suggests that alternative representational processes are available.

Soviet Research

A central interest of Soviet research has been in the changing relation between verbal and nonverbal processes as children's mastery of language increases and on the evolution of the self-directive role of language. While there is overlap, for example, with American studies of verbal mediation, the experimental questions have been quite different. The focus has been much more developmental, and the labels studied have been labels acquired in natural language learning. Age is usually the variable of chief interest.

At the earliest ages, children do not distinguish vocal from other auditory stimuli. This was found to be the case at seven to eight months of age, but three months later conditioning to words occurs four times faster than to other sound stimuli (26). There is considerable evidence from American research that children at first respond to the sound properties of words and only later to meaning. The classic experiment of Riess ([illegible]) found that, even at the age of eight, children generalized most to homophones, or words that sound like the training word, and that it was only in adolescence that synonyms became predominant. Also, it is known that children give rhyming or alliterative responses on word-association tests much more often than adults, with a sharp decline in the early school years (27).

There have been many studies of stimulus generalization between words and referents. Korbatov (58), using a bell or the word "ring" and various visual and auditory stimuli, tested generalization at various ages and degrees of training. The youngest and least-trained most often responded to all the stimuli. Then there was a stage of reacting only to the bell and "ring" and not to other stimuli, and finally of reacting to the identical stimulus. When the training stimulus was the bell, the reactions tended to be more primitive in these terms than when the training stimulus was the word. Thus, at the lowest level of training, 70 per cent of the 4- to 6-year-olds and 10 per cent of the 15- to 16-year-olds showed diffuse stimulus generalization after training with the bell. At the same age, 40 per cent of the youngest and none of the oldest gave such reactions when trained to the word. Specific training with a particular stimulus has effects similar to an increase in age. Studies of the generalization of inhibition of responses have given somewhat similar results, but the interpretation of the results is complicated by the tendency of young children to be very reactive, and thus show little generalization of inhibition (84).

In a study on mediated generalization, Narodnitskaia (74) conditioned a response to a green light and nonresponse to a blue light. It was found that the discrimination generalized not only to *green* and *blue* but to *leaf, grass, sky* and *sea*. Some of the children actually said the word *green* when given these secondary verbal stimuli rather than giving a motor response. Since the effect was strongly related to age, the experimenter tried to induce mediation by giving word-association training to the 5-year-old children but failed to increase the amount of mediated generalization.

Another type of mediation training was attempted by Gerasimchuk (32). Children sorted and discussed drawings, for instance, of red chicks and yellow buckets. Then they were conditioned discriminatively to a red and a yellow light. Among the 11- to 12-year-olds, there were 13 out of 20 children who reacted to the word *chick*, for example, although with a long latency.

All of these studies display experimentally the increasingly differentiated linkage of word and referent as the child grows older. A somewhat different frame of reference has been used by the psychologists influenced by Vigotsky and Luria. Luria was an associate of Vigotsky in the early thirties at the time of Vigotsky's vigorous and original work on the functions of language in the adaptive behavior of the child (97, 98). The recent resurgence of interest in this approach has resulted in the publication of a series of studies, many summarized by Luria in English (66). In the most ambitious of these projects, Luria and Yudovich (67) separated two speech-retarded twins and gave intensive verbal training to one. They describe vividly the great changes in behavior which accompanied training, particularly changes in the complexity and integration of play.

A series of single experimental studies was concerned with the evolution of self-control in the child through the use, first, of overt and, then, of covert verbal responses. These studies are reported by Luria (66). If a child under sixteen months was engaged in on-going activity, or saw a salient stimulus, he was unresponsive to instructions. A child, told several times to put rings on a peg, would begin to do it; but, once the task was under way, instructions to stop merely increased his activity.

A child trained to press a bulb whenever a light went on would press it continuously, once he began. He would stop if the light went out or a bell rang; but, in the absence of these stimuli, children under age three would turn to continuous pressure. After age three, a self-produced cue would work, consisting either of a second movement after pressure, and *now* or *boo* said when the light appeared. Thus, language helped to demarcate the short time duration when pressure was to be made. When they were silent, children under age four, trained to use the verbal cue, continued pressing too long.

If a child under age four was told to say *press twice*, Tikhomirov (66) has shown that he pressed continuously. But if he said *one-two* or *boo-boo* he responded by pressing only twice. Here we see an overt form of the verbal control that Oléron (76) found deaf children lacked in double alternation problems.

A similar difficulty developed in efforts to train children to differentiate between a red and a blue light. At age three and a half a child could only discriminate with accompanying verbal instructions; otherwise he generalized his response to both. If the children were taught to say *now* or *press* to the red and *don't* to the blue, an even higher percentage pressed for the blue stimulus than before. Silence for the blue light was the only effective support for discrimination. After the age of four, such supports were not necessary. In general, Luria concludes that after four and a half years words cease merely to generate impulsive responses and become differentiated signals. This point is supported by the evidence of increasing importance of semantic rather than phonetic properties of words.

Although Vigotsky warned against identifying thought with subvocal speech (9, pp. 44-45), these studies imply that verbal control of behavior developmentally undergoes two changes: it comes to be semantically distinctive rather than merely a trigger; and it progresses from the utterances of another to overt utterances by the subject to covert responses. The American studies, conducted largely at ages after this development is well under way, have shown the role of language in certain operations involving visible and tangible stimuli. As yet, little is known about the effects of language on cognition of a more complex type, such as the problems in natural science and mathematics investigated by Piaget. Nor has evidence been sought on an even more difficult implication, namely, the suggestion of G. H. Mead that the learning of language is crucial to the ability to categorize one's self and one's acts and hence crucial to social and moral behavior.

BIBLIOGRAPHY

1. Albright, R. W., and Albright, Joy Buck, "Application of Descriptive Linguistics to Child Language", *J. Speech Research*, 1 (1958), 257-61.
2. Applegate, Joseph R., "Phonological Rules of a Subdialect of English", *Word*, 17 (1961), 186-93.
3. Austerlitz, Robert, "Gilyak Nursery Words", *Word*, 12 (1956), 260-79.
4. Berko, Jean, "The Child's Learning of English Morphology", *Word*, 14 (1958), 150-77.
5. Braine, Martin D. S., "The Ontogeny of English Phrase Structure: The First Phase", *Language*, 39 (1963), 1-13.
6. Brown, Roger W., "Linguistic Determinism and the Part of Speech", *J. Abnorm. Soc. Psychol.*, 55 (1957), 1-5.
7. Brown, Roger W., *Words and Things* (Glencoe, Illinois, Free Press, 1958).

8. Brown, R. W., and Berko, Jean, "Psycholinguistic Research Methods", in *Handbook of Research Methods in Child Development*, edited by P. H. Mussen (New York, [illegible] Wiley & Sons, 1960), [illegible].
9. Brown, R. W., and Berko, Jean, "Word Association and the Acquisition of Grammar", *Child Develpm.*, 31 (1960), 1-14.
10. Brown, Roger, and Fraser, Colin, "The Acquisition of Syntax", in *The Acquisition of Language*, edited by Ursula Bellugi and Roger Brown, *Child Development Monographs*, 29 (1964), 43-79.
11. Brown, Roger, Fraser, Colin, and Bellugi, Ursula, "Explorations in Grammar Evaluation [illegible] for Grammars Written for the Speech of Children", in *The Acquisition of Language*, edited by Ursula Bellugi and Roger Brown, *Child Development Monographs*, 29 (1964), 79-92.
[illegible] "Language Development of [illegible] and English-speaking Children", [illegible]
[illegible] "Effect of [illegible] Preschool Children", *J. [illegible]*, 40 (194[illegible]), [illegible]
[illegible] "The Role of Mediating Verbal Responses [illegible]", *J. Genet. Psychol.*, [illegible]
[illegible]
[illegible] "Determinants [illegible]", *Child Develpm.*, [illegible]
[illegible]
Ervin, Susan M., "Changes with Age in the Verbal Determinants of Word Association", *Amer. J. Psychol.*, 74 (1961), 361-72.
Ervin, Susan M., "Transfer Effects of Learning a Verbal Generalization", *Child Develpm.*, 32 (1961), 153-64.

29. Ferguson, Charles A., "Arabic Baby Talk", in *For Roman Jakobson: Essays on the Occasion of his Sixtieth Birthday*, compiled by Morris Halle et al. (The Hague: Mouton & Co., 1956), 12[illegible].
30. Fischer, John L., "Social Influences on the Choice of a Linguistic Variant", *Word* 14 (1958), [illegible].
31. Fries, Charles Carpenter, *The Structure of English* (New York: Harcourt, Brace & Co., 1952).
32. [illegible], W. H., "(Gantt), Data on Initial Conditioned Connection in the General Course of a Child", in *Works of the* [illegible] (Moscow: Academy of Medical Sciences USSR, 1952) [illegible].

[illegible]

Vol. II) (Moscow, Academy of Sciences, U.S.S.R., 1956) (Washington, National Science Foundation, 1960).
49. Jakobson, Roman, and Halle, Morris, *Fundamentals of Language* (The Hague, Mouton & Co., 1956).
50. Jenkins, J. J., and Palermo, D. S., "Mediation Processes and the Acquisition of Linguistic Structure", in *First-Language Acquisition*, edited by Ursula Bellugi and R. Brown. *Child Development Monographs*, 29 (1964), 141-169.
51. Kahane, Henry, Kahane, Renée, and Saporta, Sol, "Development of Verbal Categories in Child Language", *Int. J. Amer. Linguistics* (= *Publications of the Indiana University Research Center in Anthropology, Folklore, and Linguistics*, 9) (1958).
52. Kainz, Friedrich, *Psychologie der Sprache*, Vol. II (Stuttgart, Ferdinand Enke, 1960), 1-161.
53. Karpova, S. N., "Osoznanie slovesnogo sostava rechi rebyonka doshkolnogo vozrasta" [Awareness of the Word Content of Speech of a Preschool Child], *Vop. Psikhol.*, 1 (1955), 43-55.
54. Kaverina, E. K., *O razvitii rechi detei pervykh dvukh let zhizni* [On the Development of Child Language in the First Two Years of Life] (Moscow, Medgiz, 1950).
55. Kendler, H. H., and Kendler, T. S., "The Effect of Verbalization on Reversal Shifts in Children", *Science*, 134 (1961), 1619-20.
56. Kendler, T. S., Kendler, H. H., and Wells, D., "Reversal and Nonreversal Shifts in Nursery School Children", *J. Comp. Physiol. Psychol.*, 53 (1960), 83-87.
57. Konish, Teruo, "On the Development of Language in Infants", *Jap. J. Child Psychiat.*, 1 (1960), 62-74.
58. Korbatov, B. M., "Study of the Dynamic Transmission of a Conditioned Connection from One Cortical Signalling System into the Other", in *Works of the Inst. Higher Nerv. Activity* (= *Pathophysiological Series*, Vol. II), edited by Ivanov-Smolenskii (Moscow, Academy of Science, U.S.S.R., 1956), 92-107 (Washington, National Science Foundation, 1960).
59. Lenneberg, E. H., "Color Naming, Color Recognition, Color Discrimination: A Reappraisal", *Percept. Mot. Skills*, 12 (1961), 375-82.
60. Lenneberg, E. H., "Speech as a Motor Skill with Special Reference to Nonaphasic Disorders", in *First-Language Acquisition*, edited by Ursula Bellugi and R. Brown. In preparation for submission to *Child Development Monographs*.
61. Leopold, Werner F., *Bibliography of Child Language* (Evanston, Illinois, Northwestern University Press, 1952).
62. Leopold, Werner F., "Patterning in Children's Language Learning", *Language Learning*, 5 (1953-54), 1-14.
63. Leopold, Werner F., *Speech Development of a Bilingual Child: A Linguist's Record*, 4 vols. (= *Northwestern University Studies in the Humanities*) (Evanston, Illinois, Northwestern University, 1939-49).
64. Lewis, M. M., *Infant Speech* (New York, Humanities Press, 1951).
65. Liberman, A. M., Harris, Katherine S., Kinney, Jo Ann, and Lane, H., "The Discrimination of Relative Onset-Time of the Components of Certain Speech and Nonspeech Patterns", *J. Exp. Psychol.*, 61 (1961), 379-88.
66. Luria, A. R., *The Role of Speech in the Regulation of Normal and Abnormal Behavior* (New York, Liveright Pub. Corp., 1961).
67. Luria, A. R., and Yudovich, F. Ia., *Speech and the Development of Mental Processes in the Child* (London, Staples Press, 1959).

68. Lynip, A. W., "The Use of Magnetic Devices in the Collection and Analyses of the Preverbal Utterances of an Infant", *Genet. Psychol. Monogr.*, 44 1951), 221-62.

69. McCarthy, Dorothea A., "Language Development in Children", in *Manual of Child Psychology*, edited by Leonard Carmichael (New York, John Wiley & Sons, 1954), 492-630.

70. McNeill, David, "The Development of Paradigmatic Word-Associations under Experimental Conditions". Unpublished Doctor's dissertation, University of California at Berkeley (1962).

71. Miller, G. A., and Nicely, Patricia, "An Analysis of Perceptual Confusions among Some English Consonants", *J. Acoustical Soc. Amer.*, 27 (1955), 338-52.

72. Miller, Wick, and Ervin, Susan, "The Development of Grammar in Child Language", in *First-Language Acquisition*, edited by Ursula Bellugi and R. Brown. *Child Development Monographs*, 29 (1964), 9-34.

73. Mowrer, O. H., *Learning Theory and the Symbolic Processes* (New York, John Wiley & Sons, 1960).

74. Naroditskaia, G. D., "A Study of the Question of the Phenomenon of the So-called Secondary Excitation in the Cerebral Cortex of Children", in *Works of the Inst. Higher Nerv. Activity* (= *Pathophysiological Series*, Vol. II), edited by Ivanov-Smolenskii (Moscow, Academy of Science, U.S.S.R., 1956), 131-39 (Washington, National Science Foundation, 1960).

75. Naroditskaia, G. D., "Complex Dynamic Structure in Children of Different Ages", in *The Central Nervous System and Behavior* (Princeton, Josiah Macy Foundation and National Science Foundation, 1960), 670-77.

76. Oléron, P., "Une Contribution à la Psychopathologie Différentielle: Les Caractéristiques Psychologiques Determinées par la Surdi-mutité", *Biotopologie*, 15 (1954), 1-12.

77. Pike, Evelyn G., "Controlled Infant Intonation", *Language Learning*, 2 (1949), 21-24.

78. Porter, Douglas, "Preliminary Analysis of the Grammatical Concept 'Verb' ". Unpublished paper, Harvard Graduate School of Education (1955).

79. Razran, G., "Soviet Psychology and Psychophysiology", *Behavioral Science*, 4 (1959), 35-48.

80. Reese, H. W., "Transfer to a Discrimination Task as a Function of Amount of Stimulus Pretraining and Similarity of Stimulus Names". Unpublished Doctor's dissertation, State University of Iowa (1958).

81. Reiss, B. F., "Genetic Changes in Semantic Conditioning", *J. Exp. Psychol.*, 36 (1946), 143-52.

82. Sapir, Edward, "Nootka Baby Words", *Int. J. Amer. Linguistics*, 5 (1929), 118-19.

83. Schiefelbusch, R. L., and Lindsey, Mary Jeanne, "A New Test of Sound Discrimination", *J. Speech and Hearing Disorders*, 23 (1958), 153-59.

84. Seredina, M. I., "Selective Irradiation of Extinguishing Inhibition at Different Age Levels", in *Works of the Inst. Higher Nerv. Activity, op. cit.*, 108-21.

85. Shepard, Winifred, and Schaeffer, Maurice, "The Effect of Concept Knowledge on Discrimination Learning", *Child Develpm.*, 27 (1956), 173-78.

86. Smith, Stanley L., and Goss, Albert E., "The Role of the Acquired Distinctiveness of Cues in the Acquisition of a Motor Skill in Children", *J. Genet. Psychol.*, 87 (1955), 11-24.

87. Sokhin, F. A., "O formirovanii iaazykovykh obobshcenii v protsesse reche-

vogo razvitiia" [On the Formation of Language Generalizations in the Process of Speech Development], *Vop. Psikhol.*, 5 (1959) 112-23.
88. Soskin, W. F., and John, Vera, "The Study of Spontaneous Talk", in *Streams of Behavior*, edited by Roger Barker (New York, Appleton-Century-Crofts, 1963), 228-282.
89. Spiker, C. C., "Verbal Factors in the Discrimination Learning of Children", in *Basic Cognitive Processes in Children*, edited by John C. Wright and Jerome Kagan, *Monograph of the Society for Research in Child Development*, 28, No. 2 (1963), 53-69.
90. Stewart, J. L., "The Problem of Stuttering in Certain North American Indian Societies", *J. Speech Hearing Disorders, Monogr. Suppl.* 6 (1960), [illegible]
91. Templin, Mildred C., *Certain Language Skills in Children: Their Development and Interrelationships* (= *Inst. Child Welfare Monogr. Ser.*, No. 26) (Minneapolis, University of Minnesota Press, 1957).
92. [illegible], Hans, "Schreien, Lallen und Erstes Sprechen in der Entwicklung des Säuglings", *Z. Psychol.*, [illegible]
93. Velten, H. V., "The Growth of Phonemic and Lexical Patterns in Infant Language", *Language*, 19 (1943), 281-92.
94. Vincent, Maurice, "Les Classifications d'Objets et leur Formulation verbale chez l'Enfant", *Enfance*, [illegible]
95. Vincent, Michèle, "Sur le Rôle du Langage [illegible]", *Enfance*, [illegible], 443-61.
96. [illegible]
97. Vygotsky, L. S., *Thought and Language* [illegible]
98. Vygotsky, L. S., "Thought and Speech", *Psychiatry*, [illegible]
99. Weinreich, Uriel, *Languages in Contact* [illegible] Circle of New York, 1953).
100. Weir, M. W., and Stevenson, H. W., "The Effect of Verbalization in Children's Learning as a Function of Chronological Age", *Child Developm.*, [illegible]
101. [illegible] *Development*, Vol. XV, No. 51 [illegible]
102. Whorf, Benjamin Lee, [illegible] Cambridge, Mass., Technology Press, 1956).
103. [illegible] "Syllabic and Phonetic Structure of [illegible]
104. [illegible] "Phoneme Perception in [illegible]

[illegible] National Society for [illegible] (Chicago, NSSE, 1963) [illegible] Reprinted with permission.

Dell H. Hymes

THE ETHNOGRAPHY OF SPEAKING*

INTRODUCTION

The role of speech in human behavior has always been honored in anthropological principle, if sometimes slighted in practice. The importance of its study has been declaimed (as by Malinowski [1935]), surveyed with insightful detail (as in Sapir [1933]), and accepted as a principle of field work (see citations in Hymes 1959).

That the study of speech might be crucial to a science of man has been a recurrent anthropological theme. Boas (1911) found in the linguistic realm [illegible] phenomena particularly [illegible] [illegible] phenomena. [illegible] Some anthropologists have seen language and hence linguistics as basic to a science of man because it provides a link between the biological and socio-cultural levels. Some have seen in modern linguistic methodology a model or harbinger of a general methodology for studying the structure of human behavior.

American anthropology has played an important part in the progress of linguistics in this country, through the careers of Boas, Sapir, Bloomfield, and their students, and through the opportunities offered by American Indian languages. It has contributed to the development of

* I should like to dedicate this paper to Roman Jakobson. He has generously given his time to discuss it with me, and his criticisms have led to many improvements. If at some points I have had to follow my own bent, just because of that I want to state clearly my debt to the stimulation of his ideas, and my belief that his work is a model to anthropology of a broad integrating approach to language.

particular techniques and concepts, and has used linguistics as a tool for other lines of research. In both respects, anthropology's involvement with linguistics has come to be shared now by psychology. Having assimilated modern advances in linguistics, many psychologists have contributed studies of considerable relevance and value in recent years. One need cite only the work of Charles Osgood, George Miller, and Roger Brown. Hybridization between linguistic concepts, and the technologies of the computers and experimental psychology, is producing perhaps the most rapidly growing sector in the study of speech, one with which anthropology must keep informed liaison.

Indeed, diffusion of the tools of modern linguistics may be a hallmark of the second half of this century. In the course of such diffusion, presumably three things will hold true: 1. the discipline of linguistics will continue to contribute studies of the history, structure, and use of languages; 2. in other disciplines, linguistic concepts and practices will be qualified, reinterpreted, subsumed, and perhaps sometimes re-diffused in changed form into linguistics; 3. linguistics will remain the discipline responsible for coordinating knowledge about verbal behavior from the viewpoint of language itself.

In any event, the joint share of linguistics and psychology in the burgeoning study of verbal behavior seems vigorous and assured. Has anthropology a share apart from some of its practitioners becoming linguists and psychologists, and apart from its traditional role as an intellectual holding company under the ægis of culture? Is the role of prime collaborator of linguistics among the sciences now to pass to psychology? Sheer weight of numbers may determine. It would be of no importance were it not for the value to linguistics and anthropology of a strengthening, not a relaxing, of mutual concern.

In one regard, there is no danger of lapse. Modern linguistics is diffusing widely in anthropology itself among younger scholars, producing work of competence that ranges from historical and descriptive studies to problems of semantic and social variation. Most such work is on well-defined linguistic problems; its theoretical basis is established, its methodology well grounded, and its results important, especially for areas in which languages rapidly dwindle in number. There is no need to detail the contribution which such work makes to anthropological studies, nor to argue its permanent value to linguistics proper. If anything, the traditional bonds between linguistics and anthropology in the United States are more firmly rooted now than a decade ago.

What may lapse is an opportunity to develop *new* bonds, through contributions to the study of verbal behavior that collaboration between anthropology and linguistics can perhaps alone provide. This is more than a matter of putting linguistics to work in the study of other scientific problems, such as cognitive behavior or expressive behavior. The role of speech in both is important, and has engaged anthropological attention: the cognitive problem in association with the name of Whorf, the expressive problem more recently under the heading of "paralinguistics". But to pursue these problems, and to try to give them firm anthropological footing, is to broach the study of a new problem area, one of which little account is taken.

There are indeed several underdeveloped intellectual areas involving speech to which anthropology can contribute. All are alike in that they need fresh theoretical thought, methodological invention, and empirical work, and have roots in anthropology's vocation as a comparative discipline. Among these areas are the revitalization of dialectology (perhaps under the heading of "sociolinguistics"); the place of language in an evolutionary theory of culture; the semantic typology of languages; and the truly comparative study of verbal art.[1] Fortunately, all those mentioned have begun to attract attention. For the anthropological study of behavior there is another area of importance, one that seems general, central, and neglected. It can be called the *ethnography of speaking*.

In one sense this area fills the gap between what is usually described in grammars, and what is usually described in ethnographies. Both use speech as evidence of other patterns; neither brings it into focus in terms of its own patterns. In another sense, this is a question of what a child internalizes about speaking, beyond rules of grammar and a dictionary, while becoming a full-fledged member of its speech community. Or, it is a question of what a foreigner must learn about a group's verbal behavior in order to participate appropriately and effectively in its activities. The ethnography of speaking is concerned with the situations and uses, the patterns and functions, of speaking as an activity in its own right.

What the content of this area may be in detail, what a description of it as a system might be like – these things are hard to state, although I shall attempt it in this paper. Field studies devoted to the topic hardly exist, nor has there been much attention to what the theory and method of such studies would be. Occasional information can be gleaned, enough to show that the patterns and functions of speaking can be very different from one group to another – how speech enters into socialization and education, for example, may differ strikingly. But the evidence is not enough to itemize all variables, or to show a system. Hence the

[1] Towards the first of these, see Gumperz (1961); towards the other three, see respectively, Hymes (1961c, 1961a, and 1960a [for the typology at the close of the latter]). Such developments will require rapprochement with established philological disciplines, which control much of the essential data.

orientation of what follows must be toward the field work that is necessary.

Why undertake such field work? [illegible] because the phenomena are there, ready to be brought into order, so that systematic description can contribute to a comparative study of the cross-cultural variations in a major mode of human behavior (a "comparative speech-ography" beside comparative religion, comparative law, and the like) and to its place in theory; for the contribution to other kinds of concern, such as studies of the formation of personality in early years.

I shall attempt to bring out the nature and problems of this area by [illegible] from the role of speech as a factor in cognitive [illegible] with the ethnographic [illegible] of the [illegible]

[illegible]

[illegible] and semantic [illegible]. If [illegible] behavior [illegible] (Hymes [illegible]), but we cannot adequately [illegible] the role of semantic habits [illegible] without knowledge of the semantic habits that are available to [illegible], and such knowledge can be gained only by [illegible] words, we need a semantic analysis that is a part of ethnography.

The need for such an ethnographic semantics has been pointed out [illegible], and it is the theme of Malinowski's *Coral Gardens and Their Magic*, Part II. How to implement an ethnographic semantics, however, how to devise its methodology, largely remains. Malinowski saw clearly the need to analyze meaning in contexts of use, but his method amounted in practice to massive narrative. An ethnographic semantics may be bulky, but it need not be on principle interminable, nor endlessly ad hoc. It should be more than a narrative reflection of reality. It should be a structural analysis, achieving the economies of the rules of a grammar in relation to a series of analyses of texts.

In the past generation Jakobson and his associates have done most to develop such a structural semantics. In recent years a fresh wave of American interest has appeared in significant papers by linguists such as Haugen (1957) and Joos (1958), and by ethnographers such as Conklin (1955, 1962), Goodenough (1956a, 1957), and Lounsbury (1956). Here as in other studies there are two general approaches, as Jakobson has so brilliantly set forth: on the one hand to trace an item with all the various contexts in which it can occur, characterizing it in terms of its ability to co-occur with other items; and on the other hand to take an item within a set which can occur in particular contexts, and characterize it in terms of its substitutability for other items of the set. The two approaches have various names, such as the syntagmatic and paradigmatic axes (see Jakobson and Halle 1956). The first approach is essentially that of a concordance; the second approach can be thought of as that of contrast within a frame, or better, contrast within a context-defined frame. Here I want to side with those who consider the latter as more fundamental of the two, since it validates the structural relevance of the items whose distribution is studied by the first approach, and adds information of its own; and assert that use of this fundamental "contrast within a frame" approach must lead linguistics into ethnography, and ethnography into analysis of patterns of speaking.

Here I can only outline the argument. The paradigmatic approach involves discovering a relevant frame or context, identifying the items which contrast within it, and determining the dimensions of contrast for the items within the set so defined. The approach has been successful for phonology and grammar, but only partly so for lexicon. Indeed, it is much disputed that a structural approach can be applied to the whole of a language, when the whole of vocabulary is considered. Yet it would be remarkable, and should be a source of embarrassment, if the paradigmatic principle fundamental to the core of language should fail us here. Recognizing this, linguists associated with the glossematic theory have proposed modes of analysis of "content-structure" and defended the possibility of extending them to all of lexicon on principle. These modes may prove fruitful, despite theoretical criticisms, although some seem to smack too much of the ad hoc and arbitrary at present. In any case, these approaches tend to stay within received bodies of linguistic data rather than to move outward into the exploration of speech behavior and use. Such exploration is essential, whether one is concerned with semantics delimited as dealing with designation and intension, or whether one is concerned also with what one might then term "pragmatic meaning", as the ethnography of speaking must be. (Cf. Firth's inclusion in his conception of "semantics" of this pragmatic dimension of meaning, which he places beyond lexicography in the province of "sociological linguistics" (1935, 27).)

The need for such exploration is easy to see. One source of the present impasse in structural analysis of content is precisely the limitations of the contexts available in the usual linguistic materials. The usual corpus provides sufficient contexts for phonological and grammatical analysis, but for semantic analysis of only a few limited sets of frequently recurring elements, such as case-endings and prepositions. That is one reason Wells writes, regarding the possibility of structural analysis of items such as the Latin stem *tabul-*, "the only reliable method now available depends upon treating it as a member of some C[ontent]-paradigm. This we do not see how to do" (Wells, 1957).

Scholars sometimes have been willing also to posit dimensions of contrast for a few other domains, apparently universal or "given", such as kinship terms, numerals, pronouns. But in fact even the seemingly most obvious domains cannot be taken for granted. It may sometimes be assumed that, although languages segment experience differently, what they segment is the same, as if it were a matter of different jigsaw puzzles fashioned from the same painting. But recent work shows that structural analysis of meaning must first demonstrate that a domain *is* a domain for speakers of the language in question. What the domain includes, what it excludes, what features define it and its elements, cannot be prescribed in advance, even for kinship (cf. Conant 1961) or color terms (Conklin 1955). (The principle is generally true for cultural phenomena; cf., on residence rules, Goodenough (1956b), and on the structure of the family, Adams (1960).)

The exploration of native contexts of use to validate domains is the basis of the success of Conklin and Frake, and it points the way for the structural analysis of all of speech. All utterances occur contrastively in contexts, but for much of lexicon and most larger units of speech, the contextual frames must be sought not in the usual linguistic corpus, but in behavioral situations. One must reciprocally establish the modes and settings of behavior relevant to speech, and the sets of verbal items that occur within them; dimensions of contrast and rules of use, whether purely semantic (designative) or concerned with other imports and functions, can then be found. (The sets would often not be perceived from a formal linguistic point of view, being formally diverse, e.g., a set of greetings may range from "Hi" to "It's a damned good thing you got here when you did, Jack".)

The approach of course requires the structural analysis of the community in relation to speech that would constitute an ethnography of speaking. This approach is an answer to the problem posed by Hjelmslev (1957, 283): "Une description structurale ne pourra s'effectuer qu'à condition de pouvoir réduire les classes ouvertes à des classes fermées."

For understanding and predicting behavior, contexts have a cognitive significance that can be summarized in this way. The use of a linguistic form identifies a range of meanings. A context can support a range of meanings. When a form is used in a context, it eliminates the meanings possible to that context other than those that form can signal; the context eliminates from consideration the meanings possible to the form other than those that context can support. The effective meaning depends upon the interaction of the two. (Recently stated by Joos (1958), this principle has also been formulated by Bühler (1934, 183) and Firth (1935, 32).)

Important also is the point that the cognitive role of speech is not all-or-nothing, but a matter of what, where, and when. Speech is cognitively more important in some activities than others, some times more than others, for some persons more than others, for some societies more than others. The amount and kind of influence may change as between the child and the adult, and there are the obvious problems of the relative importance of their languages for multilinguals.

Such concern with speech in contexts of behavior leads toward analysis of individual patterns in particular native situations. If, from a grammar, we can not read off the role that speech habits play in present-day behavior, neither can we do so from an experimental situation novel to the culture. Nor can the assessment be made from compartmentalized accounts of speech habits and of other habits, compared point-for-point in some millennial future. The analysis must be made on the ground. We must know what patterns are available in what contexts, and how, where, and when they come into play. The maxim that "meaning is use" has new force when we seriously study the role of semantic habits in behavior.

In sum, description of semantic habits depends upon contexts of use to define relevant frames, sets of items, and dimensions of contrast. Moreover, persons and groups may differ in the behavior that is mediated by speech. Thus analysis of the role of speech in cognitive behavior leads into analysis of the ethnographic context of speech.

The same holds true for the role of speech in expressive behavior. Of course there is a cognitive aspect to expressive behavior, insofar as it presupposes the sharing of a code, so that semantic habits do not exhaust the cognitive role of speech. Likewise, there is an expressive aspect to the cognitive style of an individual or group, and in general, all speech phenomena can be interpreted by a hearer as expressive of a speaker. But expressive studies tend to emphasize speech as an aspect of personality, and to throw into prominence features of speech, such as tone of voice and hesitation pauses, that lie outside lexicon and grammar — phenomena which have recently been systematized in a preliminary way under the heading of "paralinguistics". (For a general survey of both cognitive and expressive aspects of personality, linguistically viewed, see Hymes (1961b).) The principal study to result so far from the work in paralinguistics, that of Pittenger, Hockett and Danehy (1960) is based on the heuristic, if somewhat intuitive, use of the principle of contrast within a frame, applied to the unfolding of a psychiatric interview. Indeed, the main task confronting paralinguistics is to determine the import of the phenomena it has isolated by further study of their contrastive use in situations. In general, advances in analysis of the expressive role of speech also lead into analysis of the ethnographic context.[4]

Among other anthropological concerns which lead into such analysis, there is the aspect of culture change involving programs of fundamental education, concerned with literacy and multilingualism. In introducing new uses for indigenous forms of speech, and in extending foreign forms of speech into local contexts, the patterns and functions of speaking on both sides need to be analyzed, so as to anticipate points of congruence and conflict (cf. Weinreich 1953 and Hymes 1961c).

Now it is time to consider how the analysis of the ethnographic context of speech may be carried out. There are a number of lines of research whose goals overlap those of an ethnography of speaking, and whose results and methods must contribute. Since these lines of research have generally not raised or had the particular focus and scope that is of concern here, it is worthwhile, perhaps necessary, to take this opportu-

[4] Mahl (1959) has discussed an "instrumental model of language" in contrast to a "representational" one. He argues that "the instrumental model is the more generally valid one for purposes of inferring states and traits from language behavior" (p. 89), and that the instrumental model is more closely linked to behavior than the representational (cognitive, or lexicon-and-grammar focused) model. But a cognitive approach may be concerned with the effect of a speech derived symbolic map on problem-solving, planning, and the like, and hence can also be called "instrumental", since it also deals with speech as tool using behavior. In exploring the signalling of emotional states, Mahl deals with what will here be termed expressive function, and in pointing to the effect of this signalling on the behavior of others, he deals with what will here be termed directive function. His use of "instrumental" subsumes the two. I particularly value Mahl's analysis because he insists on "including the situational and/or the nonlexical contexts of messages" (p. 107) and in effect demands the equivalent of an ethnography of speaking in relation to the analysis of speech events for certain psychological purposes.

tunity to broach the descriptive problem and to outline a method of approach. My way of getting at it is of course without prejudice to ways that prove rewarding to others. Approaches to ethnographic analysis devised under linguistic influence, although they may diverge, are likely to show strong resemblance at many points.[4]

DESCRIPTIVE ANALYSIS OF SPEAKING

The descriptive focus is the speech economy of a community. The scope is all behavior relevant to a structural ("emic", in Pike's terminology) analysis of this. The approach is not to consider behavioral reality a pie and the speech economy a unique slice. It is a question of an organizing perspective on a social reality that is the same for differing analytical frameworks. I believe that structural analyses in this particular framework will be of value in its own right and will [illegible] from other perspectives.

By structural analysis is meant more than the placing of data in an articulated set of categories. Such placing is a necessary starting point, and also a desired outcome, when systems that have been individually analyzed are studied comparatively. But for the individual system, structural analysis means a selective and moral commitment to the individual discovery of units, criteria, and patterns that are valid in terms of the system itself. An illustration is the relation between phonetics as a starting point, the phonemic analysis of a given language, and the use of the results of that analysis in general linguistics, e.g., in phoneme typology; or, more loosely, [illegible] as a starting point, the ethnographic analysis of [illegible], and the [illegible] the results of that analysis in [illegible]. The fundamental precondition then for an ethnography of speaking [illegible] is the getting at individual "systems" [illegible] analogous to [illegible] and [illegible] part of a practical phonemics. The [illegible] is [illegible] *a priori*.

The point seems obvious, but experience shows it to be easily mistaken. Let me put it another way. What would be an appropriate so-

[4] E. T. Hall, *The Silent Language*, is especially worthwhile. Details apart, my only reservation is that the 10 primary message systems, the 3 levels of culture, the 3 components of messages, the 3 principal types of patterning, and the 100-category map of culture should be taken only [illegible]. In particular the 10 primary message systems seem [illegible] rather than rooted in biology, and the components (set, isolate, pattern) and pattern types (order, selection, congruence) seem a valid but partial extrapolation of a linguistic model. Several such extrapolations, particularly those of Hall and Trager, of Jakobson, of Pike (1954, 1955, 1960), and of Uldall, have each their contribution to perspective, but none has yet carried the day. The Hall and Trager framework of components (set, isolate, pattern) converges in a noteworthy way with the trimodal framework (manifestation, feature, distribution modes) of Pike.

provement, or correction, of what follows? Not an argument that there *really are* 3, or 8, or 76, factors or functions of speech – in general. That would be equivalent to arguing how many phonemes there *really are* – in general. The problem, of course, is how many phonemes, or factors and functions, there are in some one determinate system. What the range in number of factors and functions may be, what invariants of universal scope there may be – answers to these questions may perhaps be glimpsed now, but must wait for demonstration on the structural analyses of many systems. An appropriate improvement or correction, then, is one that contributes to that job, that makes of this paper a better practical phonetics and phonemics.

It can be asked: to what extent is analysis from the perspective of speaking itself valid structurally to a given case? Activity defined as speaking by one group may be defined as something else by another. But differences of this sort are themselves of interest. Some behavior will be organized and defined in terms of speaking in every group, and the import of this behavior may be missed if not investigated as such. Only a focus on speaking answers the structural question, and provides data for comparative study of the differential involvement of speaking in the structure of behavior in different groups. In one sense, a comparative ethnography of speaking is but one kind of comparative study of the utilization of cultural resources.

Note that the delimitation of the speech economy of a group is in relation to a population or community, however defined, and not in relation to the homogeneity or boundaries of a linguistic code. If several dialects or languages are in use, all are considered together as part of the speech activity of the group. This approach breaks at the outset with a one language–one culture image. Indeed, for much of the world the primary object of attention will not coincide with the units defined as individual languages. The patterning of a linguistic code will count as one among several analytical abstractions from verbal behavior. In cultural terms, it will count as one among several sets of speech habits. The specialization of particular languages or varieties to particular situations or functions, and the implications of each for personality, status, and thinking, will be a normal part of a description. Standard analysis of each code will of course be necessary, but the broader framework seems more "natural", indeed, more properly anthropological. The structure of this argument also applies if the focus of attention is not a population but an individual personality.[4]

[4] Aberle (1960) argues that language has been an inadequate model for culture-and-personality studies, having only two terms, the individual and the shared cultural pattern, whereas a third term, the cultural system in which persons participate but do not share, is necessary. In Aberle's terms, I am saying here that the

A necessary step is to place speaking within a hierarchy of inclusiveness: not all behavior is communicative, from the viewpoint of the participants; not all communication is linguistic; and linguistic means include more than speech. One can ask of an activity or situation: is there a communicative act (to oneself or another) or not? If there is, is the means linguistic or non-linguistic (gesture, body-movement) or both? In a given case, one of the alternatives may be necessary, or optional, or proscribed. The allocation of communication among behavior settings differs from group to group: what, for example, is the distribution of required silence in a society – as opposed to occasions in which silence, being optional, can serve as a message? (To say that everything is communication is to make the term a metaphor of no use. If necessary, the wording could be changed to: not all behavior is message-sending ... not all message-sending is linguistic ... etc.) The allocation of communicative means may also differ. For any group, some situations must be speech situations, some may be, some cannot be. Which situations require writing, derivative codes of singing, whistling, drumming, non-linguistic uses of the voice or instruments, or gesture? Are certain messages specialized to each means?

The distribution of acts and means of communication in the round of behavior is one level of description. Patterns of occurrence and frequency are one kind of comparison between groups. Much more complex is the analysis of the communicative event itself. (In discussing it, I shall refer to speech and speaking, but these terms are surrogates for all modes of communication, and a descriptive account should be generalized to comprise all.) Let me emphasize again that what I present is not a system to be imposed, but a series of questions to be asked. Hopefully, the questions will get at the ingredients, and from the ingredients to the structure of speaking in a group.

There seem to be three aspects of speech economy which it is useful to consider separately: *speech events*, as such; the *constituent factors* of speech events; and the *functions of speech.* With each aspect, it is a question of focus, and a full description of one is partly in terms of the rest.

Speech Events

For each aspect, three kinds of questions are useful. Taking first the speech events within a group, what are instances of speech events? What classes of speech events are recognized or can be inferred? What are the dimensions of contrast, the distinctive features, which differen-

two-term model is inadequate for linguistics studies as well. "Ethnography of speaking" involves a speech equivalent of "cultural system".

tute them? This will include reference to how factors are represented [illegible] functions served [illegible] what is their pattern of occurrence, their distribution [illegible] selected aspects?

[illegible] ethnographic [illegible] of speech events and [illegible] through words which name them. Some classes of speech events in our culture are well known: Sunday morning sermon, [illegible] address, pledge of allegiance. Other classes are suggested by colloquial expressions such as: heart-to-heart talk, salestalk, [illegible]

[illegible]

[illegible] what can serve [illegible]

[illegible] Speech Events

Each speech event can be said to be comprising several components, and the analysis of these is a major aspect of an ethnography of speaking. Seven types of component or factor can be discriminated. Every speech event involves 1. a Sender (Addresser); 2. a Receiver (Addressee); 3. a Message Form; 4. a Channel; 5. a Code; 6. a Topic; and 7. Setting (Scene, Situation).[4]

In what follows I am most immediately indebted to Roman Jakobson's pres-

The set of seven types of factor is an initial (etic) framework. For any group, the indigenous categories will vary in number and kind, and their instances and classes must be empirically identified. For example, Sender and Addresser, or Receiver and Addressee, need not be the same. Among the eastern Chinookan groups, a formal occasion is marked (defined) by the fact that the words of a chief or sponsor of a ceremony are repeated by a special functionary to the assembled people. In general the categories of these ... factors must be investigated in relation to the role system of the group studied. [illegible]

[illegible]

It has already been noted that the [illegible] gives [illegible] on the speech habits of a population. The range is from communities with different levels of a single dialect to communities in which most individuals command several different languages. The presence of argots, jargons, forms of speech disguise, and the like enters here. Terms such as "dialect", "variety", "vernacular", "level", [illegible] in

[illegible] of factors and functions [illegible] concluding remarks to the Conference on Style held at Indiana University, April 1958, sponsored by the Social Science Research Council. The published statement identifies six factors and corresponding functions (Jakobson 1960). Jakobson's rich discussion should be carefully read. I have also pervasive debts to Kenneth Burke, Kenneth L. Pike, [illegible] (1951) and Barker and Wright (1955).

discussion now (see Ferguson and Gumperz 1960, Hill 1958, Kenyon 1948). It is clear the status of a form of speech as a dialect, or language, or level, cannot be determined from linguistic features alone, nor can the categories be so defined. There is a sociocultural dimension (see Wolff 1959, on the non-coincidence of objective linguistic difference and communicative boundary), and the indigenous categories must be discovered, together with their defining attributes and the import of using one or another in a situation. Depending on attitude, the presence of a very few features can stamp a form of speech as a different style or dialect.[6]

The Topic factor points to study of the lexical hierarchy of the languages spoken by a group, including idioms and the content of any conventionalized utterances, for evidence and knowledge of what can be said. To a large extent this means simply that semantic study is necessary to any study of speaking. An ethnography of speaking does also call special attention to indigenous categories for topics. One needs to know the categories in terms of which people will answer the question, "What are they talking about?", and the attributes and patterns of occurrence for these categories. The old rhetorical category of *topoi* might go here as well.

The Setting factor is fundamental and difficult. It underlies much of the rest and yet its constituency is not easily determined. We accept as meaningful such terms as "context of situation" and "definition of the situation" but seldom ask ethnographically what the criteria for being a "situation" might be, what kinds of situations there are, how many, and the like. Native terms are one guide, as is the work of Barker and Wright (1955) to determine *behavior settings* and to segment the continuum of behavior.[7]

[6] The phenomena which Voegelin treats as "casual" vs. "non-casual" belong here. Voegelin (1960) sees the need for an empirical, general approach to all forms of speech in a community, discussing their variation in number and kind between communities, and the situational restrictions on their use. His discussion takes "casual" as a residual, unmarked category, whereas the need is to assume that all speech manifests some positively marked level or style, and to discover the identifying traits. He generalizes that neither formal training nor specialized interest contributes to proficiency in casual speech, and that judgments of proficiency are not made, but evaluations of proficiency among the Menominee (Bloomfield 1927) and the Crow (Lowie 1935) show that this implication of "causal" is misleading. Indeed, for some groups, most utterances might have to be classed in Voegelin's terms as "non-casual", for training in proper speaking is intensive and proficiency stressed (e.g., the Ngoni of Nyassaland and many groups in Ghana).

[7] Jakobson treats the last two factors (his Context and Referent) together as one factor. To stress my descriptive concern with factors, I eschew the theoretically laden term "Context" for a factor here, retaining "Setting" (cf. Barker and Wright 1955) with "Scene" (Burke 1945) and "Situation" (Firth 1935, following Mali-

Some of the import of these types of factors will be brought out with regard to the functions of speech. With regard to the factors themselves, let us note again that native lexical categories are an important lead, and that contrast within a frame is a basic technique for identifying both instances and classes, and for discovering their dimensions of contrast.

Given the relevant instances and classes for a group, the patterning of their distribution can be studied. One way is to focus on a single instance or class, hold it constant, and vary the other components. As a sort of concordance technique, this results in an inventory, a description of an element in terms of the combinability of other elements with it. As a general distributional technique, this can discover the relations which obtain among various elements: whether co-occurrence is obligatory, or optional, or structurally excluded. Sometimes the relation will hold for only two elements (as when a certain category of Receiver may be addressed only by a certain category of Sender), sometimes for several. The relation may characterize a class of speech events.

In this way we can discover the rules of appropriateness for a person or group. (And indications that such rules have been violated are of special help in discovering them.) From a linguistic (Code) point of view, such rules may account for variance in the speech material on which a description is based, explaining why some grammatically possible utterances do not occur (e.g., to illustrate each type of factor: because the informant is not an appropriate Sender, the linguist not an appropriate Receiver, a different choice of words or order is preferred, the sequence is sung and cannot be dictated apart from that mode of

---

nowski) as alternatives. As factors, I distinguish Setting and Topic because the same statement may have quite different import, as between, say, a rehearsal and a performance. In one sense, it is simply a question of what one has to inventory in describing the speech economy of a group. Settings and Topics seem to me to involve two obviously different lists, and lists on the same level as Addressers, Addressees, Channels, etc. Put otherwise, "Who said it? Who'd he say it to? What words did he use? Did he phone or write? Was it in English? What'd he talk about? Where'd he say it?" seem to me all questions of the same order. With functions I cannot avoid using "Context". I agree with Jakobson that referential function involves context (as an earlier section makes plain), but find this no difficulty if a function may be defined in relation to more than one factor. I also agree with Jakobson that all aspects of a speech event are aspects of context from one point of view, but I have argued that all aspects may be viewed in terms of *any* one factor; and the level at which all are aspects of context merges all, not just context and reference, while the level at which the others are distinct seems to me to distinguish context and reference as well, as I hope the illustrations, especially the literary ones, show. Certainly if reference is less than the total import of a sentence, then shifting the line "And seal the hushéd casket of my soul" from early in the sonnet "To Sleep" to its close (as manuscripts show Keats did), enhanced the effect of the line and its contribution to the poem, without changing its reference.

channel, the sequence indicates a speech variety or level which the informant avoids or must not use, the topic is tabued, the *situation* which would elicit the utterance has never occurred or been imagined, such a thing is said only in a context to which the linguist has no access). From an ethnographic point of view, the discovery of such rules of appropriateness is of practical importance for participant observation, and it is central to the conception of speaking as a system. *One way that patterns of speaking constitute a system is in virtue of restrictions on the co-occurrence of elements.*

Relevant data have been noted by ethnographers, especially as incident to lexical items of interest, such as kin terms. Linguists have taken account of such data when intrusive into the formal code, as when different morphemic shapes or different paradigms are used according to the sex of the speaker and hearer. (Haas 1944 is the best treatment.) The participants in speech may then be admitted as environments for use of the principle of complementary distribution, and the different forms treated as lexically or grammatically equivalent; but such data are likely to be regarded as a special case of grammar rather than as an opening into the broader system of speaking. Such facts have sometimes served as curiosities for theories of 'men's' and 'women's' 'languages'; but serious characterization of speech differences between men and women in a society hardly exists.

A descriptive analysis of patterns of speaking in terms of situational instances of the constitutive factors of speech events is worthwhile in its own right, [illegible] We may consider relations between elements, or consider [illegible]

The virtue of this focus is of course that it is what we often have to work with, namely, text of one sort or another. Inquiry of the sort is common in and out of science. But in our own society the success of such inquiry presupposes a knowledge of the relations – diagnostic, probabilistic – that obtain among the constitutive elements of speech events. We share in the patterns of speaking behind the text or message and can intuitively ask of ourselves what would be different if the

Sender were different?; if the Sender's motives were different?; and so on. In another society this contrast-within-a-frame technique must appeal to an explicit analysis of patterns of speaking.

Functions in Speech Events

The third aspect of speech events is that of function. Within anthropology the functions of speech (or language) have usually been discussed in terms of universal functions. While it is important to know the ways in which the functions of speaking are the same in every group and for every personality, our concern here is with the ways in which they differ. One way to approach this is to reverse the usual question, "what does a language contribute to the maintenance of personality, society, and culture?" and to ask instead, "what does a personality, society, or culture contribute to the maintenance of a language?" Especially if we ask the question in situations of culture change, we can see the various functional involvements of speech and of given languages.

Some elements of standard languages have defined for them functions and normative attitudes. These are not common to all languages, and serve to contrast their roles. To illustrate: among the Hopi-Tewa the language serves prestige, unifying, and separatist functions, and there is great language pride as well as language loyalty. Among the Eastern Cherokee the hierarchy of functions seems just the reverse; the retention of the language serves mainly a separatist function, and there is no attitude of positive loyalty or pride. Perhaps we think too much in terms of nineteenth-century European linguistic nationalism to notice that some languages do not enjoy the status of a valued emblem of group identity. The Fulnio of Brazil have preserved group identity over three centuries by giving up their territory to maintain their language and major ceremony; but the Guayqueríes of Venezuela have preserved group identity by maintaining a set of property relations. Of indigenous language and religion there has been no trace for generations. One suspects that the Guayqueríes' involvement with their language differed from that of the Fulnio.

When only a few speakers of a language are left in a community, the survival of the language becomes almost entirely dependent on its manifest and latent functions for the personalities concerned. Thus Swanton rescued an important and independent Siouan language, Ofo, partly because he happened to be in the unsuspected presence of the last speaker, and followed up a chance remark. But it was partly due to the personality of the woman, who could be an informant because she had spoken the language frequently to herself in the years since all other speakers had died.

These examples of the broad functional involvements of speech, and of languages, raise questions that can be answered only within general ethnography or social anthropology. While the same holds for an ethnography of speaking at other points, insofar as it is a special focus and not a separate subject-matter, it looms large here because the necessary conceptual framework exists almost entirely outside linguistics. There are still points and progress to be made, however, by concentrating on the linguistic discussions of the function of speech in terms of the constructive factors of the speech event.

Within the tradition of linguistics, functions of speech have commonly been an interpretation of factors of the speech event in terms of motive or purpose, obtaining a set of functions, one for each factor discriminated. Sometimes a particular feature, a linguistic category, or literary genre is associated with a function. For example, the 1st person pronoun, interjections, and the lyric poem have been associated with expressive function (focus on the Sender within the speech event); the 2nd person pronoun, imperatives, and rhetoric or dramatic poetry with the directive function; and the 3rd person pronoun, and epic poetry, with the referential function.[8]

Some conception of speech functions must figure in any theory of behavior, if it is to give any account of speaking. The same holds for an account of language in a theory of culture. Indeed, rival views on many issues involving speech can best be interpreted as involving differing assumptions about the importance or existence of various functions. For an ethnography of speaking, then, the question is not, should it have a conception of speech functions, but, what should that conception be?

There can be only a preliminary outline at present, and, as a guide for field work, its concern should be for scope and flexibility. It should not conceive the functions of speech too narrowly, as to number or domain, and it should not impose a fixed set of functions. While some general classes of function are undoubtedly universal, one should seek to establish the particulars of the given case, and should be prepared to discover that a function identifiable in one group is absent in another.

One can point to seven broad types of function, corresponding to the

[8] Snell (1952) attempts to subsume all linguistic features, including parts of speech and grammatical categories, under Bühler's classification of three types of linguistic function ("Auslösung", "Kundgabe", "Darstellung", equivalent to Snell's "Wirkungs-, Ausdrucks- und Darstellungsfunktion", and corresponding to directive, expressive, and referential function here). This might be valuable to the coding of personality expression in speech. But Snell's linguistic base is narrowly within Indo-European, the application is *a priori*, and three functions are not enough. His work has been reviewed as interesting, but not convincing (Winter 1953).

seven types of factor already enumerated. (Each type can be variously named, and the most appropriate name may vary with circumstances; alternatives are given in parentheses.) The seven are: 1. Expressive (Emotive); 2. Directive (Conative, Pragmatic, Rhetorical, Persuasive); 3. Poetic; 4. Contact; 5. Metalinguistic; 6. Referential; 7. Contextual (Situational).

In the simplest case, each of the types of function can be taken as focussing upon a corresponding type of factor, and one can single out questions and comments, and units as well, that primarily are associated with each.

"You say it with such feeling" points to expressive function, and a language may have units which are conventionally expressive, such as French [h] ("Je te H'aime") and English vowel length ("What a fiiiiiiiine boy"), used to convey strong feeling. (A feature can be conventionally an expressive device only where it is not referential, i.e., for phonic features, not functioning phonemically to differentiate lexical items.) 'Do as I say, not do as I do" points to directive function, and imperatives have been cited as primarily directive units. "What oft was thought, but ne'er so well expressed" points to poetic function, focussed on message form, as does "The sound must seem an echo to the sense". Feet, lines, and metrical units generally are primarily poetic in function. "If only I could talk it instead of having to write it" and "Can you hear me?" point to contact function; breath groups may be channel units, in the case of speaking, as are pages in the case of print. "Go look it up in the dictionary" points to metalinguistic function, to concern with the code underlying communication; words such as "word", and technical linguistic terms, which make talk about the code possible, serve primarily metalinguistic function. Quotation marks have metalinguistic function when they signal that a form is being cited or glossed, but channel function when enclosing quoted or imagined speech. "What are you going to talk about?", "What did he have to say?" focus on topic and point to referential function. Most lexical and grammatical units are primarily referential, and are analyzed by descriptive linguistics in terms of that function. "When will you tell him?", "As mentioned above", "You can't talk like that here!!", "If you're going to use that scene at all, you'll have to put it later in the play", are primarily contextual in function, as are a sign flashing "On the Air" and the statement of scene at the beginning of an act of a play ("(Elsinore. A platform before the castle)").

All features of the speech event, including all features of the linguistic code, may participate in all of the functions. This point must be made, because certain features are often treated exclusively in terms of a single function. But, as Kenneth Burke has pointed out, any utterance, for example, even an interjection, may secondarily serve as a title for contexts to which it is appropriate, and hence have a referential aspect. [illegible]

III.) Even narrowing the perspective to that of a single participant in the situation, more than one function is usually present in a given speech event. Jakobson's way of handling this is to consider that all types of functions are always compresent, and to see a given speech event as characterized by a particular hierarchy of functions. There are clear cases of the validity of this approach, as when expressive function (signalled perhaps by intonation) dominates referential function, and there are interesting cases of its manipulation, as when a teen-age daughter protests, "But all I said was...", editing out the intonation that had been perceived as insult. She is claiming the privileged status generally ascribed to the referential function in our culture. Our cultural view is the opposite of the fact, however, if the Dutch linguist de Groot (1949) is right in his "Law of the Two Strata", which asserts that whenever the referential and expressive import of a message conflict, the expressive import is overriding. Such conflict had been noted by Sapir (1931), and it underlies Bateson's concept of the "double bind" of many children who become schizophrenic. Conflict, however, raises doubt that all messages can be analyzed in terms of a hierarchy of functions such that one function is dominant. The defining characteristic of some speech events may be a balance, harmonious or conflicting, between more than one function. If so, the interpretation of a speech event is far from a matter of assigning it to one of seven types of function.

This brings us to a second problem, that of the relation of particular functions to the constituent factors of speech events. Although types of function have been presented in a preliminary way as correlates of types of factor, the relationships between the two are more complex. Indeed, it would be a great mistake to analyze an actual situation as if each type of factor simply determined a single type of function.

Here is where an ethnographic approach diverges perhaps from that sketched by Jakobson. Jakobson's work represents a decisive advance for anthropology and linguistics. It inspires concern with speech functions, which have had only sporadic attention in recent years; it breaks with the confinement of most schemes to two or three functions (referential : expressive : conative),[9] and it recognizes that all features of a message may participate in all functions. But regarding the relation of functions to factors, Jakobson states:

> Each of these six factors determines a different function of language. Although we distinguish six basic aspects of language, we could, however, hardly find verbal messages that would fulfill only one function. The diver-

[9] When earlier work distinguishes more than two or three functions, it usually is elaborating within one of these. Ogden and Richards list five functions in *The Meaning of Meaning*, but their focus is on the Sender's intention, and the elaboration falls within the expressive type.

sity lies not in monopoly of some one of these several functions, but in a different hierachical order of functions. The verbal structure of a message depends primarily on the predominant function. (Jakobson 1960, 353)

The divergence may be only verbal, however, since Jakobson has subsequently said that "determine" is not the right word, and that rather each type of function is focussed upon, centered upon a given factor. Such a view does not exclude participation of more than one. Certainly it is doubtful that particular functions of a concrete case can ever be defined in terms of factors singly. The definition seems always to involve two or more factors (or instances or classes within a type of factor).

Thus, the expressive function of features must be defined in relation to referential function. The function which Malinowski called "phatic communion" can be taken as a kind of alternating or reciprocal expressive function of speech, as when housewives exchange stories about their children or anthropologists about their field work. Now, having designated a factor of "CONTACT, a physical channel and psychological connection between the addresser and the addressee, enabling both of them to enter and stay in communication" (p. 353), Jakobson correlates with it "messages primarily serving to establish, to prolong, or to discontinue communication to check whether the channel works ('Hello, do you hear me?'), to attract the attention of the interlocutor or to confirm his continued attention" and places "phatic communion" here ("This set for CONTACT, or in Malinowski's terms PHATIC function" (p. 355).) The psychological connection between participants in communication seems to me significantly independent of the nature and state of the channel, and referrable primarily to them rather than to it. Messages to establish, prolong or discontinue communication may neither intend nor evoke a sense of communion; there may be a clear channel and no rapport. The resolution is probably to take the reference to "a physical channel" and "psychological connection" as indicating two main subtypes of contact function. (Thomas Sebeok has pointed out the importance of the factor of noise also in relation to analysis of channel and contact.) In any case, if phatic communion is a function of speech in the behavior of a group, it must be identified empirically and particulars given as to participants and situations. Even if universal, phatic communion differs greatly in its occasions and importance from group to group, and ethnographically cannot be read off as the equivalent of one factor.

More striking is the case of the factor of Message Form. This cannot be associated directly or univocally with Poetic function. The relation between a printed message and a Receiver (not Addressee) acting as proof-reader is a pure and obvious case of a function associated with message-form. And the more the proof-reader can divorce his response to the message-form from concern with any other aspect, especially reference, the better. Moreover, any sustained concern with the poetic aspect of message-form must take it in relation with other factors. Use of phonic substance is interpretable only in relation to reference: the phonemes in "The murmuring of innumerable bees" suggest bee-sound only in connection with the topic announced by the meaning of the words. (Pope's passage on "The sound must seem an echo to the sense" illustrates this.) Recent work on criteria for stylistic analysis has taken as fundamental that the stylistic value of a feature depends upon its perception in relation to a delimited verbal context (Riffaterre 1959). (Jakobson has subsequently explained that the label "poetic" should not be misleading; in his view "poetic" function need not concern poetry, but concerns any case of *Einstellung* on the message, so that the message becomes from a certain point of view self-sufficient. Poetry as such would thus be but a principal sub-type, proof-reading perhaps a minor one.)

In general, a message or feature has a particular function in behavior only for specified classes of participants in the speech event. An act of speech may have directive and no referential value for someone who knows nothing of the language involved. Many misunderstandings arise from situations in which the referential value of a message is understood, but not the expressive or directive import, because the Receiver does not share the Sender's conventional understandings, or code, for these. In short, speech functions must be defined in contexts of use.

The delimitation of speech functions brings out one of the ways in which speaking constitutes a system. If the speech economy of a group is stated in terms of the broad incidence of various factors, this constitutes a simple system; [illegible] To constitute a functional system, the speech economy would have to be not only analyzable into structure of parts, but also be such that the condition of some of these parts determines whether a certain property G will occur in the system; the parts are subject to variation such that if nothing compensates for the variation, G will no longer occur; if one (or some) of these parts vary within certain limits, the other of these parts will vary so as to compensate for the "initial variation" and G will be maintained; if one (or some) of these parts vary beyond certain limits, compensation will be impossible and G will no longer occur. When these conditions are met, the parts of the system can be called "functional" with respect to G. (Nagel 1953, 1956. I am indebted to Francesca Cancian at this point.)

It is easy to see how phonemes constitute a functional system, as when variation in one is compensated for by variation in another to maintain phonemic distinction. Such interpretation is well known in linguistics, and indeed, phonemic theory such as that of André Martinet (1955) should be better known as an example of a structural-functional theory of change. Interpretation of speaking in such terms is a challenge that has not generally been met. For any one speech function in the behavior of a group, the various factors (Sender, Receiver, etc.) can be taken as state-coordinates whose values vary within certain limits to maintain it. Communication can be taken as a cover-term for most of the specific functions, or as a very general function in its own right. If it is taken as a property being maintained, we can see that it in fact may depend upon the values of other functions. This might be in terms of a whole community, as in the analysis of the maintenance or loss of intelligibility between dialects. Let us consider single speech events. The members of a group have conceptions and expectations as to the distribution of speech functions among situations, and insofar as several functions are compresent, it is a matter of expectations as to relative hierarchy. These expectations may be anything from formal cultural norms to the projection of individual needs. If two persons meet, and perceive the situation in terms of conflicting hierarchies of speech function, communication will be broken off or the other person silently judged unfavorably, unless adjustment is made.

Let us take the relation of expressive and referential functions, broadly conceived. A group of wives may be chatting about personal experiences with children. If another woman insists on exact information, she is failing to perceive dominance of expressive or phatic function in the situation. Polite inquiry is appropriate, but not persistent challenge as to fact. Or a group of wives may be discussing children in behavioral science terms. If another woman interposes purely associative and biographical comments about her own children, she is failing to perceive the dominance of a referential function. Evidence is appropriate, but not anecdotes irrelevant to the views and theory being exchanged. In either case, the offender may be excluded from communication, or avoided under similar circumstances later. A good deal of interpersonal behavior can be examined in similar terms. In general, instances of the breaking off of communication, or uneasiness in it, are good evidence of the presence of a rule or expectation about speaking, including differences in functional hierarchy.

Three aspects of speech economy have been outlined now, the speech events, their constitutive factors, and various types of functions. Each is one perspective on the whole of verbal behavior, and full description of each must be partly in terms of the others. An approach in these terms should be useful whether one's interest is a comparative study of human behavior, or the behavior typical of a group, or the varying behavior of individuals within a group.

SPEECH IN SOCIALIZATION

I now want to survey the role of speaking in socialization. In one sense this role is one part of the kind of descriptive analysis that has been proposed. In another sense, it is a question of the induction of new recruits into the ongoing adult system. Whichever perspective is chosen, and we often shift back and forth in ordinary thinking, it is worthwhile to single out speech in socialization because, from a comparative viewpoint, it has been entirely neglected; there is far too little attention to it in the study of individual groups; and it presumably underlies much of the variation in individual adult behavior.

Studies of the child's acquisition of speech have concentrated on mastery of the code for referential function. Far too few such studies have been informed by modern linguistics as to the structural nature of what it is the child learns, but the number is increasing. Adequate studies of the child's acquisition of the other functions of speech have been more or less unknown to American linguistics and anthropology, but recently the work of Russian psychologists on the directive function has gained recognition (Luria 1959; Luria and Yurovich 1959). The Russian scholars consider the child's acquisition of speech ("the secondary signalling system") in interaction with adults as fundamental to the child's development of control over its own behavior and of its picture of the world. Their experimental work has shown that the development of capacity to understand an utterance (referential function) does not have as automatic consequence the capacity to respond adequately, to have behavior directed by it. The capacity for the directive functioning of speech develops independently and by stages in the first years of life. Thus before the age of 1½ years a child responds to a verbal request for a toy fish by getting and handing the object, but is not able to do so if another toy (say a cat) is closer, and between it and the fish. It will orient toward the object named, but maintain the directive function of the word only until the external situation (the toy cat) conflicts, then grasp and offer the intervening toy. At 3 to 3½ years, if a child is to perform a certain task of pressing a ball, it will not achieve the necessary control over its responses if simply given preliminary verbal instructions, but if it gives itself the appropriate verbal commands, it will succeed. At this age, however, the success is only for positive commands. If the child gives itself the command "Don't press", it not only fails to stop pressing, but presses even harder. Only at the age of 4 to 4½ years does the verbal command "Don't press" actually acquire inhibitory effect, according to these studies.

Thus the directive function of speech depends partly upon maturation, and is partly independent of the dependence upon maturation of control of referential function. As for another salient function, the expressive, observations indicate that it begins to be acquired quite early. Expressive use of intonation and other features may precede referential control. In short, the three most prominent types of function (referential, expressive, directive) appear to develop in childhood in partial independence of each other and in varying relation to the process of maturation.

It also appears that mastery of these functions varies in education and adult life. The basic patterns of the referential function, of grammar and lexicon, are shared as prerequisites to the maintenance of communication at all. There are of course differences at some levels of control of resources for reference. And there seems to be a quite looser rein as to the other functions and greater individual variability. Individuals differ greatly, for example, in control of intonation patterns in our society; some never learn the right intonation for announcing a joke, and some, having learned a certain intonation as students, as part of a pattern of quick repartee, carry it in later life into situations in which it acts to cut off every conversational sequence. And if we extend our horizon from the usual scope of linguistic descriptions to the full repertoire of conventional linguistic habits, to the recurrent linguistic routines and situational idioms of daily verbal behavior, variation in individual mastery is even more apparent. The consequences range from socal discomfort to exclusion from or failure in significant areas of activity, because ignorant or maladroit; or, on the other hand, recruitment for and success in certain areas, because adept. There may be a consequence for the possibility of psychotherapy. Such differences may characterize whole subcultures that in basic patterns share the same language.[10]

Concern with differences in individual verbal behavior leads to concern with differences in the role of speech in socialization, and through that, to differences which obtain between groups, whether subcultures or whole societies. Russian psychologists emphasize that the vital functions of speech are acquired in interaction with adults, but seem not to consider the consequences for their experimental norms of different

[10] Cf. the work now being done by Basil Bernstein (1958, 1959, 1960a, 1960b, 1961). He contrasts two modes of speech, *formal* and *public*, associated with the English middle-class and lower-class, respectively. Bernstein finds that the two modes arise because two social strata place different emphases on language potential, that once this emphasis is placed, the resulting modes of speech progressively orient speakers to different types of relationships to objects and persons, and that this is reflected in differences of verbal intelligence test scores, of verbal elaboration of subjective intent, and otherwise.

cultural patterns of interaction. This lack they share with most writers, who, if they point out the socialization importance of language, do so in a generic way.[11]

The role of speech in socialization, the context of its acquisition, may vary in every aspect of the patterning of speech events, factors, and functions. Some kinds of variation can be highlighted in a notes-and-queries way with respect to the speech materials and resources available, the processes often stressed in study of personality formation, social structure and organization, and cultural values and beliefs.

What are the cognitive and expressive resources of the linguistic codes of the community? What portion of these are available to children, to what extent and in what sequence? Among the Nupe there are few terms for sexual matters and most knowledge about them is acquired by observation and experience. If there is more than one linguistic code, which is learned first, if either is? (Among the Chontal of Oaxaca, children learn a "second language", Spanish, first, in the home, and Chontal and some other aspects of native culture only in adolescence.) Is there a specialized baby-talk? If so, what is its content (referential, expressive, directive)? Are there verbal games, perhaps metalinguistic in that they draw attention to features of the code as such? (Since much significance has been attached to the child's acquisition of personal pronouns, and means of self-reference, these should be singled out.) What are the *linguistic routines* which the child is taught or can acquire?

A linguistic routine is a recurrent sequence of verbal behavior, whether conventional or idosyncratic. Its pattern may be obvious and concrete, as in single sequences such as the numerals 1 to 10, the days of the week, the ABC's, or as in antiphonal sequences such as in many children's games, as well as adult games and ceremonies. Or the pattern may not be obvious because it is not concrete, but consists of some regular sequence of emotion or topic. Instruction may be couched as "Then he says . . . and then you say . . .", but often it is not a matter of the exact words. (In magic and instruction from supernatural helpers, of course often it is.) Or it may be a formal pattern such as a limerick. Feedback may be involved, and the patterning of the routine resemble a branching tree diagram. (A good "line" or salesman's pitch has alternative ways of reaching the same goal.) A vast portion of verbal behavior in fact consists of recurrent patterns, of linguistic routines. Description

[11] George Herbert Mead is one example. Another is A. Irving Hallowell, whose inventory article on "Culture, Personality, and Society" states: "A necessary condition for socialization in man is the learning and use of a language. But different languages are functionally equivalent in this respect, and one language is comparable with another because human speech has certain common denominators" (Hallowell 1953, p. 612).

has tended to be limited to those with a manifest structure, and has not often probed for those with an implicit pattern. Analysis of routines includes identification of idomatic units, not only greeting formulas and the like, but the full range of utterances which acquire conventional significance, for an individual, group, or whole culture. Description is usually limited to idioms of phrase length which, because their reference is not predictable from their parts, must be independently listed in a dictionary as lexical units (e.g., "kick the bucket"). Even for clear referential categories such as those of place and personal names, a carefully considered description of the status and formation of idioms is rare (see Hoijer 1948, 182-3 for a fine example), and conventionalization in terms of other functions is important in behavior and personality formation. There are utterances conventionalized in metalinguistic and contextual function, but especially interesting here are those with directive or expressive function. A child's play in imitation of adult roles, as a girl with her dolls, may reveal many of the conventionalized sequences of her family – sequences which have recurred in situations until in some sense they "name", "stand for" the situation and carry a significance, expressive or directive, not predictable from their constituent parts. A mother may find herself using expressions to her child that her own mother had used to her, and with horror, having sworn as a child never to do so.

The number and range of such idioms varies between individuals, families, groups. These and linguistic routines play a great part in the verbal aspect of what Lantis (1960) points to as "vernacular culture", the handling of day-to-day situations, and they are essential in verbal art, in the oral performance of myths, sung epics, many speeches and lectures. The text of these is not identical from one performance to the next, but the general sequence is more or less constant, and most of the verbal content is drawn from a standard repertoire. They fill the slots of a speech, as words fill the slots of a sentence. (Their presence can sometimes be detected when a performer finds himself not communicating. Sequences which he has drawn on as ready coin may prove to have no conventional value for a new audience, which struggles for an interpretation of something intended merely as formulas or labels.) The acquisition of conventional sequences, both idioms and routines, is a continuous process in life, and herein resides some of the theoretical interest, for to a great extent these sequences exist in the cambium between idiosyncrasy and culture. They exhibit persisting effort toward the patterning and predictability of behavior. Some sequences become idiomatic for a person or group because of a memorable novelty (see Hockett 1958, 304ff.), but more because sensed as appropriate or as needed. Most do not achieve generality or persistence, but some would lose value if they did, being intended or enjoyed as distinctive, or private to a few.

Turning to the formation of personality, how does speaking figure in the economy of punishment and reward, as alternative to physical acts (spanking, hugging) and to deprivation or giving of things such as candy? At what stage in psycho-sexual development is pressure about speech applied, if any is? How intensive is it? Autobiographical materials from Ghanian students reveal great childhood anxiety about speech. When is socialization pressure about weaning, toilet-training, self-feeding and the like applied in relation to the child's verbal development? In some groups it is after the demands can be verbally explained, in some not. What is the incidence of stuttering and other speech defects, if any? There is evidence that this depends upon socialization pressures, being absent in some groups, and perhaps among the Pilagá characteristic of girls rather than, as among us, of boys. If there is bilingualism, do speech defects appear in both or but one language? How much does speech figure in the transmission of skills and roles? Among some groups, such as the Kaska (Canada), it figures very little. Does a baby talk facilitate or retard acquisition of adult speech patterns? Is speaking a source of pleasure, of oral, perhaps erotic gratification? That some languages are extremely rich in vocabulary showing sound symbolism, some quite poor, suggests differential enjoyment of the phonic substance of language.

From the viewpoint of the social system of the group, how does speaking enter into definition of the roles acquired or observed by children? In what way does this determine or reflect how speaking is acquired? How relatively significant is speaking in aggressive roles, such as that of warrior? of shaman or priest? (Perhaps the role of speaking in interaction with parents will correspond to the role of speaking in interaction with enemies or the supernatural.) How do residence rules, marriage rules, and the like affect the composition of the household in which the child learns to speak? In affecting the number and relative ages of children, these things affect the rate of mastery of adult patterns; there is evidence that singletons master speech more rapidly, children near the same age less rapidly, twins most slowly. Twins and children near the same age may develop and rely on their own verbal code vis-à-vis each other. If there is multilingualism, are the roles and settings of the languages kept distinct? If so, the child probably will acquire the languages without confusion, but if not, there may be personality difficulties. Are there situations and roles in which it is necessary to translate between two languages? If not, the child may very well master each without acquiring ability to do so. Such external factors have much to do with the effect of multilingualism on personality, including cognitive structure. In what settings are children required to speak, forbidden, permitted? What proportion of total behavior settings for the group permit the presence and speaking of children? A Russian visitor to France was astonished when the children of his host kept silent at the table; Russian children would have been reprimanded for *not* joining in the conversation with a guest.

The values and beliefs of the group of course pervade all this. What are the beliefs regarding children as participants in speech? Some believe neonates capable of understanding speech. The Ottawa believed the cries of infants to be meaningful, and had specialists in their interpretation. The Tlingit believed the talk of women to be the source of conflict among men, and an amulet was placed in a baby girl's mouth to make her taciturn. Are skill and interest in speech demanded, rewarded, ignored, or perhaps repressed? The Ngoni of Nyasaland value skill in speech, believing it part of what constitutes a true Ngoni, and so take pains to instill it in children and maintain it in adults. The remarkable polyglot abilities of Ghanian students in Europe perhaps reflect similar values in their own cultures. What values are held and transmitted with regard to the language or languages spoken? We have noted presence and absence of pride as between the Hopi-Tewa and Eastern Cherokee. The problem of bilingualism among immigrant children in the United States has been noted as one of the sense of inferiority associated with the non-English language. Concern for excellence of speech seems universal, but the degree and manifestation vary. Some groups tolerate sloppy pronunciation, some do not. If baby talk is present, is it believed easier for children? In sounds and forms it may in fact be as hard as the adult equivalents, and have the latent function of delaying the child's acquisition of these. What evidential status is accorded the statements of children? What degree and kind of intellectual awareness of speaking is present? What folk conceptions of a metalinguistic sort, as reflected in words for linguistic features or the abstraction of these for use in games and speech surrogates? Neighboring dialects may differ, as when one group of Mazatec abstract the tones of their language for a whistled code, while the Soyaltepec Mazatec do not. Bloomfield (1927) has ascribed the erroneous and sometimes injurious folk conceptions about language in our own culture to mistaken generalization from learning of writing, a later and conscious matter, relative to the largely unconscious learning of speech. Values and beliefs regarding speaking, or a language, may be interwoven with major institutions, and much elaborated, or peripheral and sketchy.

CONCLUSION

Speech cannot be omitted from a theory of human behavior, or a special theory for the behavior of a particular group. But whether we focus on the cognitive or expressive or directive role of verbal behavior, or on the role of speech in socialization, we find a paucity of descriptive analysis of "ethological" studies of speaking in context. There are to be sure many studies that are in one way or another linguistic. But either speaking is taken for granted, or used as means to other ends, or only special kinds of speaking (or writing) are valued and considered. Of speaking as an activity among other activities, of the analysis of its patterns and functions in their own right, there is little. There are bits of data and anecdotes, and a variety of conceptual schemes which impinge, but there are no well focussed field studies or systematic theories. The angle of vision has not been such as to bring speaking into focus.

Herein lies the responsibility for the degree of sterility that has dogged a good deal of anthropological discussion of language and culture. The relation between language and culture seems a problem, it crops up whenever a thoughtful anthropologist tries to construct an integrated view of culture or behavior, yet discussion usually trails off irresolutely. We may set language and culture side by side, and try to assess similarities and differences; or we may try to see if something, a method or a model, that has worked for language will work for culture; or we may look to a future of point-for-point comparisons, once all partial cultural systems have been neatly analyzed; or we may redefine or subdivide the problem. We do not want to usher language out of culture; a suggestion to that effect some years ago was quickly suppressed. But having kept language within culture, many seem not very sure what to do about it (except perhaps to recall that some of our brightest friends are linguists, and a credit to the profession).

I do not want to seem to reject efforts such as those characterized above: In particular, there is much to be gained from a determination of the properties of language which are generically cultural and those which are not. The search for formal analogues between linguistics and other systems can be revealing, and some extensions of linguistic-like methodology to other areas of culture seem quite important. Indeed, I would see linguistics in this case as an avenue for the introduction into anthropology of qualitative mathematics. But successes along these lines will not put an end to the language-and-culture problem. It will remain uneasily with us because of the terms in which it is posed, terms which preclude an ultimate solution, if we think of such a solution as being a general theory of culture or of behavior that will integrate the phenomena we consider linguistic with the rest. The difficulty is that we have tried to relate language, described largely as a formal isolate, to culture, described largely without reference to speaking. We have tried to relate one selective abstraction to another, forgetting that much that is pertinent to the place of speech in behavior and culture has not been taken up into either analytic frame. The angle of vision has been in effect a bifurcated one, considering speech primarily as evidence either of formal linguistic code or of the rest of culture.

Why has this been so? Neglect of speaking seems tolerable, I think, because of several working assumptions. Speech as such has been assumed to be without system; its functions have been assumed to be universally the same; the object of linguistic description has been assumed to be more or less homogeneous; and there has been an implicit equation of one language = one culture.

To put these working assumptions in qualified form: a. the relation of language to speech has been conceived as that of figure to ground. Structure and pattern have been treated in effect as pretty much the exclusive property of language (*la langue : la parole*). For speech as a physical phenomenon, there is a truth to this view. The qualitatively discrete units of the linguistic code stand over against continuous variation in the stream of speech. For speech as a social phenomenon, the case is different. Speaking, like language, is patterned, functions as a system, is describable by rules.[12]

b. The functions of speech have been of concern only with regard to properties judged (correctly or not) to be universal. Or, if differences have been of concern, these have been differences in the content of the code, along Whorfian lines, not differences in speaking itself. Speaking as a variable in the study of socialization has been largely ignored. (Speaking is not even mentioned in the section on "Oral Behavior" of the article, "Socialization", in the *Handbook of Social Psychology* (Child 1954).)

c. Descriptive method has been concerned with a single language or dialect, isolable as such and largely homogeneous. There has been much concern for neatness and elegance of result, and often a readiness to narrow the object of attention so as to achieve this. The object may be defined as one or a few idiolects, the habit of one or a few individuals (and in their roles as speakers, not as receivers); awkward data have often been excluded, if they could be identified as loanwords or a difference of style. The homogeneously conceived object has been a stand-

[12] Because the distinction *la langue : la parole* usually implies that only the former has structure, Pike has rejected it (1960, 52). I follow him in assuming that *la parole* has structure also, but believe that the distinction can be usefully retained. Within Pike's system, it can perhaps be treated as a difference in focus.

point from which to view speech phenomena in general. Looking out from it, many speech phenomena appear as variation in or of it, due perhaps to personality, social level, or situation. Recently the support for a broader conception of the object of linguistic attention has increased, through concern with bilingual description, a unified structure of several dialects, the relations between standard and colloquial varieties of languages, and the like. But most such work remains tied to the conception of a single language as primary and the locus of structure. Gleason has shown concern for "generalizations about linguistic variation as a characteristic feature of language. Here is the basis for a second type of linguistic science" (1955, 285ff.). But this second type of linguistic science is seen as thoroughly statistical, in contrast to the qualitative nature of descriptive linguistics. The possibility for a second type of linguistic science that is structural is not conceived.

d. Multilingualism of course has never been denied, but the use of linguistic units in ethnological classification, a prevailing cultural rather than societal focus, an individuating outlook, all have favored thinking of one language = one culture.

The sources of these working assumptions cannot be traced here, except to suggest that they are an understandable part of the ideology of linguistics and anthropology during their development in the past two generations. One need has been to refute fallacies about primitive languages, to establish the quality of all languages *sub specie scientia*, and this has been in accord with the relativistic message of cultural anthropology. To pursue differences in function among languages might seem to give aid and comfort to the ethnocentric. Another need has been to secure the autonomy of the formal linguistic code as an object of study, apart from race, culture, history, psychology, and to develop the appropriate methods for such study. The complexity and fascination of this task turns attention away from speech, and concentrates it on the regularities of the code. Not all variables can be handled at once. Part of the anthropological background has been noted in d. above. We should add that where the one language = one culture equation has been conceptually dissolved, it has been in terms of historical independence, rather than in terms of complex social *inter*dependence between, say, several languages in a single culture.

Now it is desirable to change these assumptions, and to take as a working framework: 1. the speech of a group constitutes a system; 2. speech and language vary cross-culturally in function; 3. the speech activity of a community is the primary object of attention. A descriptive grammar deals with this speech activity in one frame of reference, an ethnography of speaking in another. So (what amounts to a corollary, 3b), the latter must in fact include the former. The number of linguistic codes comprised in the ethnography of speaking of a group must be determined empirically.

Nothing said here should be taken to belittle linguistics and philology in their current practice. Malinowski, who advocated an ethnography of speech similar in spirit, if different in form, claimed a debt to the standard linguistic disciplines, yet treated them as grey dust against the fresh green of the field. For any work involving speech, however, these disciplines are indispensable (and Malinowski's efforts failed partly for lack of modern linguistics). Anthropology needs them and should foster them. What I am advocating is that anthropology recognize interests and needs of its own, and cultivate them; making use of linguistics, it should formulate its own ethnographic questions about speech and seek to answer them.[13]

We may be entering a period in which the pioneering studies of speech will be distributed among many disciplines. The new impetus in psychology is a case in point. A special opportunity, and responsibility, of anthropology is for comparative study of the patterning and functions of speech. This is a fundamental empirical problem for a science of behavior, one for which I propose the name "ethnography of speaking".

REFERENCES CITED

Aberle, David F.

1960 "The influence of linguistics on early culture and personality theory", in *Essays in the Science of Culture in Honor of Leslie A. White.* Gertrude E. Dole and Robert L. Carneiro, eds. (New York, Crowell), 1-29.

Adams, Richard N.

1960 "An inquiry into the nature of the family", in *Essays in the Science of Culture in Honor of Leslie A. White.* Gertrude E. Dole and Robert L. Carneiro, eds. (New York, Crowell), 30-49.

[13] Jakobson suggests the well known term "sociology of language" and insists that these concerns cannot be eliminated from linguistics. Linguistics and sociology should indeed develop this area, but so should anthropology, and for comparative perspective its contribution is essential. I am writing here chiefly to persuade that contribution. Moreover, I look for much of that contribution to come from those younger anthropologists who are reviving ethnography as a proud intellectual discipline, and for whom "ethnography", "ethnoscience", "ethnotheory" are significant and prestigeful terms. Hence the "ethnography" of my slogan. As for the "speaking", it reflects a theoretical bias that I hope shortly to be able to develop in more detail, relating it to a variety of other ideas, including some of Talcott Parsons', I am especially sorry not to say more about Firth's work here. Only when the paper was long overdue at the printer did I discover that Firth had clearly posed the general problem of factors and functions of speech more than a generation ago (1935). In large part I have only come upon a concern already there in his writings, unfortunately unread, although I differ from his conceptualization at several points. (Cf. Firth 1935, 1950, and Bursill-Hall 1960.)

Barker, Roger G., and Louise Shedd
1961 "Behavior units for the comparative study of cultures", in *Studying Personality Cross-culturally*. Bert Kaplan, ed. (Evanston, Row, Peterson), 457-476.

Barker, Roger G., and Herbert F. Wright
1955 *Midwest and its children, the psychological ecology of an American town* (Evanston, Row, Peterson).

Bernstein, Basil
1958 "Some sociological determinants of perception. An inquiry into subcultural differences", *The British Journal of Sociology*, 9 (2), 159-174.
1959 "A public language: some sociological implications of a linguistic form", *The British Journal of Sociology*, 10 (4), 311-326.
1960a "Language and social class (research note)", *The British Journal of Sociology*, 11 (3), 271-276.
1960b "Sozio-Kulturelle Determinanten des Lernens. Mit besonderer Berücksichtigung der Rolle der Sprache", *Kölner Zeitschrift für Soziologie und Sozialpsychologie*, Sonderheft 4, 52-79.
1961 "Aspects of language and learning in the genesis of the social process", *Journal of Child Psychology and Psychiatry*, 1, 313-324.

Bloomfield, Leonard
1927 "Literate and illiterate speech", *American Speech*, 2, 432-439.

Boas, Franz
1911 "Introduction", in *Handbook of American Indian Languages*. F. Boas, ed. (= *Bureau of American Ethnology, Bulletin* 40, pt. 1), 1-83.

Bühler, Karl
1934 *Sprachtheorie* (Jena).

Burke, Kenneth
1945 *A grammar of motives* (New York, Prentice-Hall).
1951 *A rhetoric of motives* (New York, Prentice-Hall).
1953 "Freedom and authority in the realm of the poetic imagination", in *Freedom and Authority in Our Time*. Lyman Bryson, Louis Finkelstein, R. M. MacIver, Richard McKeon, eds. Conference on Science, Philosophy and Religion (New York, Harper), 365-375.
1955 "Linguistic approach to problems of education", in *Modern Philosophies and Education* (= *Fifty-fourth yearbook of the National Society for the Study of Education*, Part I) (Chicago), 259-303.
1957 *The philosophy of literary form. Studies in symbolic action*. Revised edition, abridged by the author (New York, Vintage Books K-51).
1958 "The poetic motive", *The Hudson Review*, 11, 54-63.

Bursill-Hall, G. L.
1960 "Levels analysis: J. R. Firth's theories of linguistic analysis I", *The Journal of the Canadian Linguistic Association*, 6 (2), 124-135.

Child, Irvin L.
1954 "Socialization", in *Handbook of Social Psychology*. Gardner Lindzey, ed. (Cambridge, Addison-Wesley), 2, 655-692.

Conant, Francis P.
1961 "Jarawa kin systems of reference and address: a componential comparison", *Anthropological Linguistics*, 3 (2), 19-33.

Conklin, Harold C.
1955 "Hanunóo color categories", *Southwestern Journal of Anthropology*, 11 (4), 339-344.

1959 "Linguistic play in its cultural setting", *Language*, 35 (4), 631-636.
1962 "Lexicographical treatment of folk taxonomies. Workpaper for Conference on Lexicography, Indiana University, Nov. 11-12, 1960", in *Problems in Lexicography*, Fred W. Householder and Sol Saporta, eds. (= *Supplement to International Journal of American Linguistics*, vol. 28, no. 2 – *Indiana University Research Center in Anthropology, Folklore and Linguistics, Publication 21*) (Bloomington).

De Groot, A.
1949 "Structural linguistics and syntactic laws", *Words*, 5, 1-12.

Elmendorf, William W., and Wayne Suttles
1960 "Pattern and change in Halkomelem Salish dialects", *Anthropological Linguistics*, 2 (7), 1-32.

Ferguson, Charles, and John J. Gumperz, eds.
1960 *Linguistic diversity in South Asia: studies in regional, social, and functional variation* (= *Indiana University Research Center in Anthropology, Folklore, and Linguistics, Publication 13*) (Bloomington).

Firth, J. R.
1935 "The technique of semantics", *Transactions of the Philological Society* (London). Reprinted in his *Papers in Linguistics 1934-1951* (London, Oxford University Press, 1957), 7-33.
1950 "Personality and language in society", *Sociological Review*, 42 (II), 8-14. Ledbury, England. Reprinted in his *Papers in Linguistics 1934-1951* (London, Oxford University Press, 1957), 177-189.

Frake, Charles O.
1961 "The diagnosis of disease among the Subanun of Mindanao", *American Anthropologist*, 63 (1), 113-132.

Gleason, H. A., Jr.
1955 *An introduction to descriptive linguistics* (New York, Holt).

Goodenough, Ward H.
1956a "Componential analysis and the study of meaning", *Language*, 32 (1), 195-216.
1956b "Residence rules", *Southwestern Journal of Anthropology*, 12, 22-37.
1957 "Cultural anthropology and linguistics", in *Report of the Seventh Annual Round Table Meeting on Linguistics and Language Study*. Paul L. Garvin, ed. (= *Georgetown University Monograph Series on Language and Linguistics*, No. 9) (Washington D. C.), 167-173.

Gumperz, John J.
1961 "Speech variation and the study of Indian civilization", *American Anthropologist*, 63 (5), 976-988.

Haas, Mary R.
1944 "Men's and women's speech in Koasati", *Language*, 20, 142-149.
1951 "Interlingual word taboos", *American Anthropologist*, 53, 338-344.

Hall, Edward T.
1959 *The silent language* (New York, Doubleday).

Hallowell, A. Irving
1953 "Culture, personality, and society", in *Anthropology Today, an Encyclopedic Inventory*. Prepared under the chairmanship of A. L. Kroeber (Chicago, University of Chicago Press), 597-620.

Haugen, Einar
1957 "The semantics of Icelandic orientation", *Word*, 13 (3), 447-459.

Hill, Trevor
1958 "Institutional linguistics", *Orbis*, 7, 441-455 (Louvain).

Hjelmslev, Louis
1957 "Dans quelle mesure les significations des mots peuvent-elles être considérées comme formant une structure?", *Reports for the Eighth International Congress of Linguists*, 2, 268-286 (Oslo).

Hockett, Charles F.
1958 *A course in modern linguistics* (New York, Macmillan).

Hoijer, Harry
1948 "The structure of the noun in the Apachean languages", *Actes du XXVIIIe Congrès International des Américanistes (Paris 1947)* (Paris, Société des Américanistes), 173-184.

Hymes, Dell H.
1959 "Field work in linguistics and anthropology" (Annotated bibliography), *Studies in Linguistics*, 14, 82-91.
1960a "Ob-Ugric metrics", *Anthropos*, 55, 574-576.
1960b "Phonological aspects of style: some English sonnets", in *Style in Language*. T. A. Sebeok, ed. (Cambridge, The Technology Press, and New York, Wiley), 109-131.
1961a "On typology of cognitive styles in language (with examples from Chinookan)", *Anthropological Linguistics*, 3 (1), 22-54.
1961b "Linguistic aspects of cross-cultural personality study", in *Studying Personality Cross-culturally*. Bert Kaplan, ed. (Evanston, Row, Peterson), 313-359.
1961c "Functions of speech: an evolutionary approach", in *Anthropology and Education*. Fred Gruber, ed. (Philadelphia, University of Pennsylvania Press).
1961d Abstract of Vachek (1959), *International Journal of American Linguistics*, 27, 166-167.

Jacobs, Melville
1945 *Kalapuya texts* (= *University of Washington Publications in Anthropology*, 11) (Seattle).

Jakobson, Roman
1960 "Concluding statement: linguistics and poetics", in *Style in Language*. T. A. Sebeok, ed. (Cambridge, The Technology Press, and New York, Wiley), 350-373.

Jakobson, Roman, and Morris Halle
1956 *Fundamentals of language* (The Hague, Mouton).

Joos, Martin
1958 "Semology: a linguistic theory of meaning", *Studies in Linguistics*, 13 (3), 53-70.

Kenyon, John S.
1948 "Cultural levels and functional varieties of English", *College English*, 10, 31-36. Reprinted in *Readings in Applied English Linguistics*. H. B. Allen, ed. (New York, Appleton-Century-Crofts), 215-222.

Lantis, Margaret
1960 "Vernacular culture", *American Anthropologist*, 62, 202-216.

Lévi-Strauss, Claude
1958 *Anthropologie structurale* (Paris, Librairie Plon).

Lounsbury, Floyd G.
1956 "A semantic analysis of the Pawnee kinship usage", *Language*, 32 (1), 158-194.

Lowie, Robert H.
1935 *The Crow Indians* (New York, Rinehart).

Luria, A. R.
1959 "The directive function of speech I, II", *Word*, 15, 341-352, 453-464.

Luria, A. R., and F. Ia. Yurovich
1959 *Speech and the development of mental processes in the child.* J. Simon, translator (London, Staples Press).
Mahl, G. F.
1959 "Exploring emotional states by content analysis", in *Trends in Content Analysis.* I. Pool, ed. (Urbana, University of Illinois Press), 83-130.
Malinowski, Bronislaw
1935 *Coral gardens and their magic*, II: *The language of magic and gardening* (London).
Martinet, André
1955 *Economie des changements phonétiques* (= *Bibliotheca Romanica, series prima, Manualia et Commentationes*, X) (Berne, Editions A. Francke).
Nagel, Ernst
1953 "Teleological explanation and teleological systems", in *Vision and action.* Sidney Ratner, ed. (New Brunswick, Rutgers University Press).
1956 "A formalization of functionalism", in his *Logic without metaphysics, and other essays in the philosophy of science* (Glencoe, Free Press).
Newman, Stanley S.
1940 "Linguistic aspects of Yokuts style", in *Yokuts and Western Mono Myths.* Ann Gayton and S. S. Newman (eds.) (= *University of California Publications, Anthropological Records*, 5), 4-8.
Ogden, C. K., and I. A. Richards
1923 *The meaning of meaning* (London).
Pike, Kenneth L.
1954, 1955, 1960 *Language in relation to a unified theory of the structure of human behavior*, I, II, III. Preliminary edition (Glendale, Summer Institute of Linguistics).
Pittenger, Robert, Charles F. Hockett, and J. S. Danehy
1960 *The first five minutes* (Ithaca, Paul Martineau).
Riffaterre, Michael
1959 "Criteria for style analysis", *Word*, 15, 154-174.
Robins, R. H.
1959 "Linguistics and anthropology", *Man*, 59, 175-178.
Sapir, Edward
1931 "Communication", *Encyclopedia of the Social Sciences*, 4, 78-81.
1933 "Language", *Encyclopedia of the Social Sciences*, 9, 155-169.
Sinclair, Angus
1951 *The conditions of knowing* (London, Routledge and Kegan Paul).
Slama-Cazacu, Tatiana
1961 *Langage et contexte* (The Hague, Mouton).
Smith, M. G.
1957 "The social functions and meaning of Hausa praise singing", *Africa*, 27, 26-44.
Snell, Bruno
1952 *Der Aufbau der Sprache* (Hamburg, Claassen Verlag).
Uldall, Hans
1957 *Outline of glossematics*, I (= *Traveaux du Cercle Linguistique de Copenhague*, X) (Nordisk Sprog Kulturførlag).
Vachek, Josef
1959 "The London group of linguists", *Sborník Prací Filosofické Fakulty Brěnské University*, Ročnik 8 (Rada Jazykovidná, A7), 106-113.

Voegelin, C. F.
1960 "Casual and noncasual utterances within unified structure", in *Style in Language*. T. A. Sebeok, ed. (Cambridge, The Technology Press, and New York, Wiley, 57-68).

Weinreich, Uriel
1953 *Languages in contact* (Linguistic Circle of New York).

Wells, Rulon
1957 "Is a structural treatment of meaning possible?", *Reports for the Eighth International Congress of Linguists*, 1, 197-209 (Oslo).

Winter, Werner
1953 Review of Bruno Snell, *Der Aufbau der Sprache*, in *Language*, 29, 193-195.

Wolff, Hans
1959 "Intelligibility and inter-ethnic attitudes", *Anthropological Linguistics*, 1 (3), 34-41.

From *Anthropology and Human Behavior*, T. Gladwin and Wm. C. Sturtevant, eds. (Washington, D. C., Anthropol. Society of Washington, 1962), 13-53. Reprinted by permission and with minor revision (addition of the final paragraph missing in the original publication).

M. A. K. Halliday

THE USERS AND USES OF LANGUAGE

In Chapters 2 and 3 we discussed some theories and methods that have been developed in linguistics and phonetics for the description of how language works. As said in Chapter 1, decsription is not the only approach to the study of language. There are other branches of linguistics: one may for example treat language historically, showing how it persists and modifies through time. In application to language teaching, it is descriptive linguistics that is the most important. Even for this purpose, however, description is not the only type of linguistic study which is relevant.

In this section we are concerned with the branch of linguistics which deals, to put it in the most general terms, with the relation between a language and the people who use it. This includes the study of language communities, singly and in contact, of varieties of language and of attitudes to language. The various special subjects involved here are grouped together under the name of 'institutional linguistics'.

There is no clear line dividing institutional from descriptive linguistics; the two, though distinct enough as a whole, merge into one another. The study of context leads on to the analysis of situation types and of the uses of language. The descriptive distinction into spoken and written language naturally involves us in a consideration of the different varieties of language they represent. In institutional linguistics we are looking at the same data, language events, but from a different standpoint. The attention is now on the users of language, and the uses they make of it.

There are many ways of finding patterns among people. Some patterns are obvious: everyone is either male or female, with a fairly clear line between the two. Some, equally obvious, are less clearly demarcated: people are either children or adults, but we may not be sure of the assignment of a particular individual. Humorously, we may recognize all sorts of *ad hoc* patterns, like W. S. Gilbert's classification of babies into 'little liberals' and 'little conservatives'. The human sciences all introduce their own patterning: people are introverts or extroverts; negriform, mongoliform, caucasiform or australiform; employed, self-employed, non-employed or un-employed. No clear boundaries here, though the categories, statistically defined and, sometimes, arbitrarily delimited, are useful enough. Other patterns, such as national citizenship, are thrust upon us, often with conflicting criteria: each state tends to have its own definition of its citizens.

In linguistics, people are grouped according to the language or languages they use. This dimension of patterning is sometimes applied outside linguistics: a nation, in one view, is defined by language as well as by other factors. On the other hand, the category of 'nation' defined politically has sometimes been used in linguistics to give an institutional definition of 'a language': in this view 'a language' is a continuum of dialects spoken within the borders of one state. On such a criterion, British English and American English are two languages, though mutually intelligible; Chinese is one language, though Pekingese and Cantonese are not mutually intelligible; and Flemish, Dutch, German, Austrian German and Swiss German are five languages, though the pairing of mutually intelligible and mutually unintelligible dialects does not by any means follow the various national boundaries.

This is not the only way of defining 'a language'; there are as many definitions as there are possible criteria. Even within institutional linguistics various criteria are involved, each yielding a definition that is useful for some specific purpose. The concept of 'a language' is too important to be taken for granted; nor is it made any less powerful by the existence of multiple criteria for defining it. But we have to be careful to specify the nature of this category when we use it.

In institutional linguistics it is useful to start with the notion of a LANGUAGE COMMUNITY, and then to ask certain questions about it. The language community is a group of people who regard themselves as using the same language. In this sense there is a language community 'the Chinese', since they consider themselves as speaking 'Chinese', and not Pekingese, Cantonese and so on. There is no language community 'the Scandinavians'; Norwegians speak Norwegian, Danes Danish and Swedes Swedish, and these are not regarded as dialects of the 'Scandinavian language', even though they are by and large all mutually intelligible. The British, Americans, Canadians, Australians and others call their language 'English'; they form a single language community.

This method of recognizing a language community has the advantage that it reflects the speakers' attitude toward their language, and thus the way they use it. All speakers of English, for example, agree more or less on the way it should be written. At the same time, like all institutional linguistic categories and most of the basic categories of the human sciences, it is not clearcut, because people do not fall into clearcut patterns. There is a minor tendency for Americans to regard themselves as using a different language from the British, and this is again reflected in minor variations in orthography. But it is a mistake to exaggerate this distinction, or to conclude therefrom that there is no unified English-speaking language community.

Some of the questions that can be asked about a language community and its language are these. First, what happens when it impinges on other language communities? Second, what varieties of its language are there? Under the second question come these subdivisions: varieties according to users (that is, varieties in the sense that each speaker uses one variety and uses it all the time) and varieties according to use (that is, in the sense that each speaker has a range of varieties and chooses between them at different times). The variety according to users is a DIALECT; the variety according to use is a REGISTER. Third, what attitudes do the speakers display towards their language and any or all of its varieties?

2

Situations in which one language community impinges on another have been called 'language contact' situations. Such situations are characterized by varying degrees of bilingualism. Bilingualism is recognized wherever a native speaker of one language makes use of a second language, however partially or imperfectly. It is thus a cline, ranging in terms of the individual speaker, from the completely monolingual person at one end, who never uses anything but his own native language or 'L1', through bilingual speakers who make use in varying degree of a second language or 'L2', to the endpoint where a speaker has complete mastery of two languages and makes use of both in all uses to which he puts either. Such a speaker is an 'ambilingual'.

True ambilingual speakers are rare. Most people whom we think of as bilingual restrict at least one of their languages to certain uses: and in any given use, one or the other language tends to predominate. There are probably millions of L2 English speakers throughout the world with a high degree of bilingualism, but who could neither make love or do the washing up in English nor discuss medicine or space travel in their L1. Even those who have learnt two languages from birth rarely perform all language activities in both; more often than not a certain amount of specialization takes place.

This distinction between an L1 and an L2, a native and a non-native or learnt language, is of course not clearcut. Moreover it cuts across the degree of bilingualism. Some bilingual speakers, including some who are ambilingual, can be said to have two (occasionally more) native languages. There is no exact criterion for this; but one could say arbitrarily that any language learnt by the child before the age of instruction, from parents, from others, such as a nurse, looking after it, or from other children, is an L1. It is clear, however, that only a small proportion of those who learn two or more languages in this way become ambilingual speakers; and conversely, not all ambilinguals have two L1s.

A point that has often been observed about native bilingual, including ambilingual, speakers is that they are unable to translate between their L1s. This does not mean of course that they cannot learn to translate between them. But translation has to be learnt by them as a distinct operation; it does not follow automatically from the possession of two sets of native language habits. This has been linked with the fact that those with two L1s are usually not true ambilinguals: that they have usually specialized their two or more native languages into different uses. But this cannot be the only reason, since even those who approach or attain true ambilingualism are still usually unable to translate without instruction. It appears that it is a characteristic of an L1, defined in the way suggested above, to operate as a distinct set of self-sufficient patterns in those situations in which language activity is involved. However ambilingual the speaker is, in the sense that there is no recognizable class of situation in which he could not use either of his languages, there is always some difference between the actual situations in which he uses the one and those in which he uses the other, namely that each of the two is associated with a different group of participants.

This raises the question: how unique is or are the native language or languages in the life of the speaker? No sure answer can yet be given to this question. It is clear that for the great majority of bilingual speakers the L2 never replaces the L1 as a way of living; nor is it intended to do so. We may want to attain a high degree of competence in one or more foreign languages, but we usually do not expect thereby to disturb the part played in our lives by the native one. On the other hand those who move permanently to a new language community may, if they move as individuals and not as whole families, abandon at least the active use of their native language and replace it throughout by an L2.

This in itself is not enough to guarantee a particular degree of attainment in the L2. Some speakers are more easily content: they may, for example, not try to adopt the phonetic patterns of the L2 beyond the point where they become comprehensible to its native speakers. Others may simply fail to achieve the standard of performance that they themselves regard as desirable. In this way they cut down the role played by language in their lives. On the other hand there is clearly no upper limit to attainment in an L2. The L2 speaker may live a normal, full life in his adopted language community, absorb its literature and even use the language for his own creative writing, as Conrad and Nabokov have done so successfully with English. Whether the learnt language will ever be so 'infinitely docile', in Nabokov's words, as the native language, it is hard to say. Certainly the user of an L2 may learn to exploit its resources as widely as do its native speakers; and though he is more conscious of these resources than the majority of native speakers, in this he merely resembles that minority who have learnt to be conscious of how their native language works: principally the creative writers, literary analysts and linguists. But while one can set no limit to the possible degree of mastery of an L2, it remains true that such a level of attainment is rarely aimed at and still more rarely achieved.

The individual speaker, in contact with a new language community, may react by developing any degree and kind of bilingualism within this very wide range. Over language communities as a whole, in contact-situations, certain patterns tend to emerge. Sometimes the solution adopted, at least in the long term, is not one of bilingualism. What happens in these instances is either that one language community abandons its own language and adopts that of the other – here there will be a transitional period of bilingualism, but it may be very short; or that a mixed language develops which incorporates some features of both.

Such mixed languages have usually had either English or French as one of their components; less frequently Dutch or Potruguese. Those that remain restricted to certain uses, as many have done, without ever attaining the full resources of a language, are called PIDGINS. Some mixtures, however, have developed into full languages; these are known as CREOLES. In some areas, for example in language communities in Sierra Leone, Haiti, Mauritius and Melanesia, creoles are acquired by children as their L1. Here they have full status as community languages, and there is not necessarily any bilingualism at all. The fact that in most of these areas children are expected to acquire a second language as L2 at school reflects the social status of the mixed languages, but is entirely without prejudice to their linguistic status as full community languages.

In other instances the long term solution has been one of as it were institutionalized bilingualism. This frequently takes the form of a LINGUA FRANCA. One language comes to be adobted as the medium of some activity or activities which the different language communities perform in common. It may be a common language for commerce, learning, administration, religion or any or all of a variety of purposes: the use determines which members of each language community are the ones who learn it.

Latin was such a lingua franca for a long period in the history of Europe; in certain countries it retains this status to the present day, though to a much restricted extent, as the lingua franca of religion. Among other languages which have been linguae francae at certain times, over certain areas and for certain uses, are Arabic, Malay, Hausa, Classical and Mandarin (Pekingese) Chinese, Swahili, Sanskrit, French, Russian and English. Since the lingua franca normally operates for certain specific purposes, it is often a more or less clearly definable part of the language that is learnt as L2. There may even develop a special variety for use as a lingua franca, as with Hindustani and 'bazaar Malay'. These are distinct in practice from the mixed pidgins and creoles, in that each has clearly remained a variety of its original language; but it is difficult to draw an exact theoretical distinction.

Languages such as English and Russian, which are widely learnt as second languages in the world today, are a type of lingua franca. They are a special case only in the sense that they are being learnt by unprecedentedly large numbers of people and for a very wide range of purposes, some of which are new. In any serious study of the problems and methods of teaching English as a second language it is important to find out what these purposes are, and how they differ in different areas and according to the needs of different individuals. Possibly the major aim that is common to all areas where English is taught as L2 is that of its use in the study of science and technology. But there are numerous other aims, educational, administrative, legal, commercial and so on, variously weighted and pursued in different countries.

The task of becoming a bilingual with English as L2 is not the same in all these different circumstances; and it is unfair to those who are struggling with the language, whether struggling to learn it or to teach it, to pretend that it is. English is 'a language' in the sense that it is not Russian or Hindi; any two events in English are events in 'the same' language. But if we want to teach what we call 'a language', whether English or any other, as a second or indeed also as a first language, we must look a little more closely at the nature of the varieties within it.

3

In one dimension, which variety of a language you use is determined by who you are. Each speaker has learnt, as his L1, a particular variety of the language of his language community, and this variety may differ at any or all levels from other varieties of the same language learnt by other speakers as their L1. Such a variety, identified along this dimension, is called a 'dialect'.

In general, 'who you are' for this purpose means 'where you come from'. In most language communities in the world it is the region of origin which determines which dialectal variety of the language a speaker uses. In China, you speak Cantonese if you come from Canton, Pekingese if you come from Peking and Yunnanese if you come from Yunnan.

Regional dialects are usually grouped by the community into major dialect areas; there may, of course, be considerable differentiation within each area. The dialects spoken in Canton, Toishan, Chungshan and Seiyap, all in Kwangtung province, are clearly distinct from one another; but they are all grouped under the general name of 'Cantonese'.

Within Cantonese, the local varieties form a continuum: each will resemble its neighbours on either side more closely than it resembles those further away. Among major dialect areas, there is usually also a continuum. There may be a more or less clear dialect boundary, where the occurrence of a bundle of ISOGLOSSES (lines separating a region displaying one grammatical, lexical, phonological or phonetic feature from a region having a different feature at the same place in the language) shows that there are a number of features in which the dialects on either side differ from each other: but the continuum is not entirely broken. Thus there is a fairly clear distinction between Cantonese and Mandarin in the area where the two meet in Kwangsi, and there is indeed a strip of country where the two coexist, many villages having some families speaking Cantonese and some speaking Mandarin. Nevertheless the variety of Cantonese spoken in this dialect border region is closer to Mandarin than are other varieties of Cantonese, and the Mandarin is closer to Cantonese than are other varieties of Mandarin.

This situation represents a kind of median between two extremes: an unbroken continuum on the one hand, as between Mandarin and the 'Wu' or lower Yangtsze dialect region, and a sharp break on the other, as between Cantonese and Hakka in Kwangtung. In this case the reason for the break is that the Hakka speakers arrived by migration from the north roughly a thousand years after the original settlement of Kwangtung by the ancestors of the modern Cantonese speakers.

This general dialect pattern turns up in one form or another all over the world. An instance of wide dialectal variety in modern Europe is provided by German. Here we have to recognize three, and possibly four, different language communities. The Flemings, in Belgium, speak Flemish, though this is now officially regarded as a variety of Dutch; the Dutch speak Dutch; Germanic speakers in Switzerland regard themselves, in general, as speaking a distinct 'Swiss-German'. The Germans and the Austrians, and the Swiss in certain circumstances, regard themselves as speaking German. But over the whole of this area there is one unbroken dialect continuum, with very few instances of a clear dialect boundary; ranging from the High German of Switzerland, Austria and Bavaria to the Low German of Northwest Germany, Holland and Belgium.

The normal condition of language is to change, and at times and in places where there is little mobility between dialect communities there is nothing to cause the various dialects of a language to change in the same direction. Under these conditions dialects tend to diverge from each other at all levels, perhaps most of all in phonology and phonetics. It may happen that mutual intelligibility is lost; that the language community is as it were broken up into dialect regions such that there are many pairs of regions whose speakers cannot understand one another. This happened in China. There are six major dialects in modern China: Mandarin, Cantonese, Wu, North Min, South Min and Hakka; each of which is mutually unintelligible with all the others.

This situation tends to be resolved by the emergence of one dialect as a lingua franca. In China, the spoken lingua franca has traditionally been the Pekingese form of the Mandarin dialect. But under the empire very few people from outside the Mandarin-speaking area ever learnt Mandarin unless they were government officials. Mandarin was the language of administration and some literature; but classical Chinese remained the lingua franca for most written purposes, being supplemented as an educational medium, since it could no longer function as a spoken language, by the regional dialects. In nationalist China some progress was made towards introducing Mandarin as a 'second language' in schools, and the process has continued in communist China, where with the expansion of educational facilities Mandarin is now regularly taught at some stage in the school career. It is in fact becoming a 'standard' or 'national' language.

A similar process took place in Germany. 'Standard German' of course is 'standard' only for the language community that considers itself as speaking German (not, however limited to Germany itself). The concept of a standard is defined in relation to the language community: to a Dutchman 'standard' could only mean standard Dutch, not standard German.

In Germany, and similarly in China, there is no suggestion that the dialect chosen as the 'standard' language is any better than any other dialect. A modern state needs a lingua franca for its citizens, and there are historical reasons leading to the choice of one dialect rather than another. It may have been the one first written down, or the language of the capital; or it may, as in Germany, include a somewhat artificial mixture of features from different dialects. Nor is there any suggestion that those who learn the standard language should speak it exactly alike. The aim is intelligibility for all purposes of communication, and if a Cantonese speaks Mandarin, as most do, with a Cantonese accent, provided this does not affect his intelligibility nobody will try to stop him or suggest that his performance is inferior or that he himself is a less worthy person.

In the history of the English language, dialects followed the familiar pattern. In the fifteenth century England was a continuum of regional dialects with, almost certainly, some mutual unintelligibility. With the rise of urbanism and the modern state, a standard language emerged; this was basically the London form of the South-east Midland dialect, but with some features from neighbouring areas, especially from the South-central Midlands. The orthography, which in Middle English had varied region by region, became more and more standardized according to the conventions associated with this dialect. As in other countries, for ease of communication, the notion of a 'correct' orthography grew up: by the late seventeenth century educated people were expected to spell alike, although in earlier times individuality had been tolerated in spelling just as it had been (and still was) in pronunciation.

The emergence of a standard language gives rise to the phenomenon of 'accent', which is quite distinct from 'dialect'. When we learn a foreign language, we normally transfer patterns from our native language on to the language we are learning. These may be patterns at any level. Those of form, however, and most of those of phonology and orthography, tend to be progressively eliminated. This is because they may seriously impair intelligibility; they are less directly interrelated, thus reinforcing each other less; and they are easier to correct once observed, because they are not patterns of muscular activity. With phonetic patterns, on the other hand, there is greater intelligibility tolerance, more reinforcement and much greater difficulty in correction even when they are observed. Transference of phonetic habits, in other words, is easier to tolerate and harder to avoid than transference at other levels. So we usually speak with a 'foreign accent', even when our grammar and lexis are in general conformity with the native patterns of the learnt language.

So also when a speaker learns a second dialect. He generally speaks it with 'an accent': that is, with phonetic features of his native dialect. The learning of a standard language is simply the learning of a second dialect, the dialect that happens to have been 'standardized'. Most speakers, learning the standard language of their community, continue to speak with the phonetics of their native dialect, and there is usually no loss in intelligibility.

It is quite normal for members of a language community which has a standard language to continue to use both the native and the learnt (standard) dialect in different situations throughout their lives. This happens regularly in China and even Germany. But while in a rural community, where there is less movement of people, the native dialect is appropriate to most situations, in an urban community the relative demands on native and standard dialect are reversed. The population is probably made up of speakers of various different dialects, so that the standard language becomes a lingua franca amongst them; in addition there is greater mobility within and between towns.

As a consequence, many speakers drop their native dialect altogether, having very few situations in which to use it, and replace it with the standard language. In so doing, they transfer to the standard language the phonetics of the native dialect, speaking it with a regional 'accent'. In time, this form of the standard language with regional accent comes to be regarded itself as a dialect. Today, for example, people use the term 'Yorkshire dialect' equally to refer both to the speech of Leeds, which is standard English with generalized West Riding phonetics, and to the speech of Upper Wharfedale, which is an 'original' West Riding dialect. Since urban speech forms expand outwards at the expense of rural ones, the longer established dialects of England are disappearing and being replaced by the standard spoken with the various regional accents.

This process is liable to happen anywhere where there is a high degree of industrialization and consequent growth of cities. What is peculiar to England, however, is the extent to which, concurrently with this process, a new dimension of dialect differentiation has come into operation. In most countries, even those highly industrialized like Germany, the way a person speaks is determined by the place he comes from: he speaks either the regional dialect or the standard language with regional accent. In England, however, and to a lesser extent in France, Scotland, Australia and the United States, a person's speech is determined not only by the region he comes from but also by the class he comes from, or the class he is trying to move into. Our dialects and accents are no longer simply regional: they are regional and social, or 'socio-regional'. Nowhere else in the world is this feature found in the extreme form it has reached in England. It is a feature of English life which constantly amazes the Germans and others into whose national mythology the facts, or some version of them, have penetrated.

The dialect structure of England today can be represented by a pyramid. The vertical plane represents class, the horizontal one region. At the base, there is wide regional differentiation, widest among the agricultural workers and the lower-paid industrial workers. As one moves along the socio-economic scale, dialectal variety according to region diminishes. Finally at the apex there is no regional differentiation at all, except perhaps for the delicate shades which separate Cambridge and Oxford from each other and from the rest.

This regionally neutral variety of English, often known as 'RP', standing for 'received (that is, generally accepted) pronunciation', carries prestige and may be acquired at any stage in life. It tends to be taught by example rather than by instruction. Certain institutions, notably the preparatory and public schools, create, as part of their function, conditions in which it can be learnt. The speaker of this form of English has, as is well known, many social and economic advantages. There are, for example, many posts for which he will automatically be preferred over a candidate who does not speak it. If there are any posts for which the opposite is true, as is sometimes claimed, these are posts which are not likely to arouse serious competition.

When a speaker states what language he regards himself as speaking, he is defining a language community. By implication a language community may be delimited regionally, although national frontiers may enter into the definition of the region. When he states what dialect he speaks, he is defining a dialect community. Here again the delimitation that is implied is normally regional; but there are some countries, notably England, in which it is socio-regional. If the community has a standard language, there may be not only dialects but also accents: in other words 'new dialects', varieties of the standard language with regional or socio-regional phonetic patterns. The line dividing dialect and accent is often not clearcut, and the speaker may well conflate the two. All his observations, but especially those on dialect and accent, may be coloured by value-judgements; but the discussion of these we leave to the final section of this chapter.

4

A dialect is a variety of a language distinguished according to the user: different groups of people within the language community speak different dialects. It is possible also to recognize varieties of a language along another dimension, distinguished according to use. Language varies as its function varies; it differs in different situations. The name given to a variety of a language distinguished according to use is 'register'.

The category of 'register' is needed when we want to account for what people do with their language. When we observe language activity in the various contexts in which it takes place, we find differences in the type of language selected as appropriate to different types of situation. There is no need to labour the point that a sports commentary, a church service and a school lesson are linguistically quite distinct. One sentence from any of these and many more such situation types would enable us to identify it correctly. We know, for example, where 'an early announcement is expected' comes from and 'apologies for absence were received'; these are not simply free variants of 'we ought to hear soon' and 'was sorry he couldn't make it.'

It is not the event or state of affairs being talked about that determines the choice, but the convention that a certain kind of language is appropriate to a certain use. We should be surprised, for example, if it was announced on the carton of our toothpaste that the product was 'just right for cleaning false teeth' instead of 'ideal for cleansing artificial dentures'. We can often guess the source of a piece of English from familiarity with its use: 'mix well' probably comes from a recipe, although the action of mixing is by no means limited to cookery – and 'mixes well' is more likely to be found in a testimonial.

The choice of items from the wrong register, and the mixing of items from different registers, are among the most frequent mistakes made by non-native speakers of a language. If an L2 English speaker uses, in conversation, a dependent clause with modal 'should', such as 'should you like another pint of beer, ...', where a native speaker would use a dependent clause with 'if', he is selecting from the wrong register. Transference of this kind is not limited to foreigners; the native schoolboy may transfer in the opposite direction, writing in his Shakespeare essay 'it was all up with Lear, who couldn't take any more of it'.

Linguistic humor often depends on the inappropriate choice and the mixing of registers: P. G. Wodehouse exploits this device very effectively. Fifty years ago the late George Robey used to recite a version of 'The house that Jack built' which ended as follows: '... that disturbed the equanimity of the domesticated feline mammal that exterminated the noxious rodent that masticated the farinaceous produce deposited in the domiciliary edifice erected by Master John'.

Dialects tend to differ primarily, and always to some extent, in substance. Registers, on the other hand, differ primarily in form. Some registers, it is true, have distinctive features at other levels, such as the voice quality associated with the register of church services. But the crucial criteria of any given register are to be found in its grammar and its lexis. Probably lexical features are the most obvious. Some lexical items suffice almost by themselves to identify a certain register: 'cleanse' puts us in the language of advertising, 'probe' of newspapers, especially headlines, 'tablespoonful' of recipes or prescriptions, 'neckline' of fashion reporting or dressmaking instructions. The clearest signals of a particular register are scientific technical terms, except those that belong to more than one science, like 'morphology' in biology and linguistics.

Often it is not the lexical item alone but the collocation of two or more lexical items that is specific to one register. 'Kick' is presumably neutral, but 'free kick' is from the language of football. Compare the disc jockey's 'top twenty'; 'thinned right down' at the hairdresser's (but 'thinned out' in the garden); and the collocation of 'heart' and 'bid' by contrast with 'heart' and 'beat'.

Purely grammatical distinctions between the different registers are less striking, yet there can be considerable variation in grammar also. Extreme cases are newspaper headlines and church services; but many other registers, such as sports commentaries and popular songs, exhibit specific grammatical characteristics. Sometimes, for example, in the language of advertising, it is the combination of grammatical and lexical features that is distinctive. 'Pioneers in self-drive car hire' is an instance of a fairly restricted grammatical structure. The collocation of the last four lexical items is normal enough in other structures, as in 'why don't you hire a car and drive yourself?'; but their occurrence in this structure, and in collocation with an item like 'pioneer' or 'specialist', is readily identifiable as an advertising slogan.

Registers are not marginal or special varieties of language. Between them they cover the total range of our language activity. It is only by reference to the various situations and situation types in which language is used that we can understand its functioning and its effectiveness. Language is not realized in the abstract: it is realized as the activity of people in situations, as linguistic events which are manifested in a particular dialect and register.

No one suggests, of course, that the various registers characteristic of different types of situation have nothing in common. On the contrary, a great deal of grammatical and lexical material is common to many of the registers of a given language, and some perhaps to all. If this was not so we could not speak of 'a language' in this sense at all, just as we should not be able to speak of 'a language' in the sense of a dialect continuum if there was not a great deal in common among the different dialects.

But there tends to be more difference between events in different registers than between different events in one register. If we failed to note these differences of register, we should be ignoring an important aspect of the nature and functioning of language. Our descriptions of languages would be inaccurate and our attempts to teach them to foreigners made vastly more difficult.

It is by their formal properties that registers are defined. If two samples of language activity from what, on non-linguistic grounds, could be considered different situation-types show no differences in grammar or lexis, they are assigned to one and the same register: for the purpose of the description of the language there is only one situation-type here, not two. For this reason a large amount of linguistic analysis is required before registers can be identified and described. It is one thing to make a general description of English, accounting, to a given degree of delicacy, for all the features found in some or other variety of the language. Most native speakers will agree on what is and what is not possible, and the areas of disagreement are marginal. It is quite another thing to find out the special characteristics of a given register: to describe for example the language of consultations between doctor and patient in the surgery.

For such a purpose very large samples of textual material are needed. Moreover much of the language activity that needs to be studied takes place in situations where it is practically impossible to make tape recordings. It is not surprising, therefore, that up to now we know very little about the various registers of spoken English. Even studies of the written language have only recently begun to be made from this point of view. For this reason we are not yet in a position to talk accurately about registers; there is much work to be done before the concept is capable of detailed application.

While we still lack a detailed description of the registers of a language on the basis of their formal properties, it is nevertheless useful to refer to this type of language variety from the point of view of institutional linguistics. There is enough evidence for us to be able to recognize the major situation types to which formally distinct registers correspond; others can be predicted and defined from outside language. A number of different lines of demarcation have been suggested for this purpose. It seems most useful to introduce a classification along three dimensions, each representing an aspect of the situation in which language operates and the part played by language in them. Registers, in this view, may be distinguished according to field of discourse, mode of discourse and style of discourse.

'Field of discourse' refers to what is going on: to the area of operation of the language activity. Under this heading, registers are classified according to the nature of the whole event of which the language activity forms a part. In the type of situation in which the language activity accounts for practically the whole of the relevant activity, such as an essay, a discussion or an academic seminar, the field of discourse is the subject-matter. On this dimension of classification, we can recognize registers such as politics and personal relations, and technical registers like biology and mathematics.

There are on the other hand situations in which the language activity rarely plays more than a minor part: here the field of discourse refers to the whole event. In this sense there is, for example, a register of domestic chores: 'hoovering the carpets' may involve language activity which, though marginal, is contributory to the total event. At the same time the language activity in a situation may be unrelated to the other activities. It may even delay rather than advance them, if two people discuss politics while doing the washing up. Here the language activity does not form part of the washing up event, and the field of discourse is that of politics.

Registers classified according to field of discourse thus include both the technical and the non-technical shopping and games-playing as well as medicine and linguistics. Neither is confined to one type of situation. It may be that the more technical registers lend themselves especially to language activity of the discussion type, where there are few, if any, related non-language events; and the non-technical registers to functional or operational language activity, in which we can observe language in use as a means of achievement. But in the last resort there is no field of activity which cannot be discussed; and equally there is none in which language cannot play some part in getting things done. Perhaps our most purely operational language activity is 'phatic communion', the language of the establishment and maintenance of social relations. This includes utterances like 'How do you do!' and 'See you!', and is certainly non-technical, except perhaps in British English where it overlaps with the register of meteorology. But the language activity of the instructor in the dance studio, of the electrician and his assistant, of the patient consulting the doctor in the surgery, or of research scientists in the performance of a laboratory experiment, however technical it may be, is very clearly functioning as a means of operation and control.

This leads to 'mode of discourse', since this refers to the medium or mode of the language activity, and it is this that determines, or rather correlates with, the role played by the language activity in the situation. The primary distinction on this dimension is that into spoken and written language, the two having, by and large, different situational roles. In this connection, reading aloud is a special case of written rather than of spoken language.

The extent of formal differentiation between spoken and written language has varied very greatly among different language communities and at different periods. It reached its widest when, as in medieval Europe, the normal written medium of a community was a classical language which was unintelligible unless learnt by instruction. Latin, Classical Arabic, Sanskrit and Classical Chinese have all been used in this way. By comparison, spoken and written varieties of most modern languages are extremely close. The two varieties of French probably differ more than those of English; even popular fiction in French uses the simple past (preterite) tense in narrative. But spoken and written English are by no means formally identical. They differ both in grammar and in lexis, as anyone by recording and transcribing conversation can find out.

Within these primary modes, and cutting across them to a certain extent, we can recognize further registers such as the language of newspapers, of advertising, of conversation and of sports commentary. Like other dimensions of classification in linguistics, both descriptive and institutional, the classification of modes of discourse is variable in delicacy. We may first identify 'the language of literature' as a single register; but at the next step we would separate the various genres, such as prose fiction and light verse, as distinct registers within it. What is first recognized as the register of journalism is then subclassified into reportage, editorial comment, feature writing and so on.

Some modes of discourse are such that the language activity tends to be self-sufficient, in the sense that it accounts for most or all of the activity relevant to the situation. This is particularly true of the various forms of the written mode, but applies also to radio talks, academic discussions and sermons. In literature particularly the language activity is as it were self-sufficient. On the other hand, in the various spoken modes, and in some of the written, the utterances often integrate with other non-language activity into a single event. Clear instances of this are instructions and sets of commands. The grammatical and lexical distinction between the various modes of discourse can often be related to the variable situational role assigned to language by the medium.

Third and last of the dimensions of register classification is 'style of discourse', which refers to the relations among the participants. To the extent that these affect and determine features of the language, they suggest a primary distinction into colloquial and polite ('formal', which is sometimes used for the latter, is here avoided because of its technical sense in description). This dimension is unlikely ever to yield clearly defined, discrete registers. It is best treated as a cline, and various more delicate cuts have been suggested, with categories such as 'casual', 'intimate' and 'deferential'. But until we know more about how the formal properties of language vary with style, such categories are arbitrary and provisional.

The participant relations that determine the style of discourse range through varying degrees of permanence. Most temporary are those which are a feature of the immediate situation, as when the participants are at a party or have met on the train. At the opposite extreme are relations such as that between parents and children. Various socially defined relations, as between teacher and pupil or labour and management, lie somewhere intermediately. Some such registers may show more specific formal properties than others: it is probably easier to identify on linguistic evidence a situation in which one participant is serving the others in a shop than one involving lecturer and students in a university classroom.

Which participant relations are linguistically relevant, and how far these are distinctively reflected in the grammar and lexis, depends on the language concerned. Japanese, for example, tends to vary along this dimension very much more than English or Chinese. There is even some formal difference in Japanese between the speech of men and the speech of women, nor is this merely a difference in the probabilities of occurrence. In most languages, some lexical items tend to be used more by one sex than the other; but in Japanese there are grammatical features which are restricted to the speech of one sex only.

It is as the product of these three dimensions of classification that we can best define and identify register. The criteria are not absolute or independent; they are all variable in delicacy, and the more delicate the classification the more the three overlap. The formal properties of any given language event will be those associated with the intersection of the appropriate field, mode and style. A lecture on biology in a technical college, for example, will be in the scientific field, lecturing mode and polite style; more delicately, in the biological field, academic lecturing mode and teacher to student style.

The same lecturer, five minutes later in the staff common room, may switch to the field of cinema, conversational mode, in the style of a man among colleagues. As each situation is replaced by another, so the speaker readily shifts from one register to the next. The linguistic differences may be slight; but they may be considerable, if the *use* of language in the new situation differs sharply from that in the old. We cannot list the total range of uses. Institutional categories, unlike descriptive ones, do not resolve into closed systems of discrete terms. Every speaker has at his disposal a continuous scale of patterns and items, from which he selects for each situation type the appropriate stock of available harmonies in the appropriate key. He speaks, in other words, in many registers.

He does not, normally, speak in many dialects, since a dialect represents the total range of patterns used by his section of the language community. But he may, as a citizen of a nation, learn a second dialect for certain uses, and even a third and a fourth. In Britain, choice of dialect is bound up with choice of register in a way that is unique among the language communities of the world: it is a linguistic error to give a radio commentary on cricket in cockney or sing popular songs in the Queen's English. Many of the languages of older nations show some such mutual dependence between dialect and register.

In the newer nations, this is less apparent; instead there is often a tendency for the register to determine, not the choice of dialect, but the choice of language. Machine translation will in time make it possible for each community to use its own language for all purposes. Meanwhile, in many parts of the world, it is necessary to learn a second language in order to be equipped with a full range of registers; and foreign language teaching has become one of the world's major industries. By the time when it is no longer necessary for anyone to learn a foreign language in order to be a full citizen of his own community, it may well be recognized as desirable for everyone to do so in order to be a citizen of the world.

5

It is the individual who speaks and writes; and in his language activity dialect and register combine. In the dialect range, the finer the distinctions that are recognized, the smaller, in terms of number of speakers, the unit which we postulate as the dialect community becomes. Eventually we reach the individual. The individual is, so to speak, the smallest dialect unit: each speaker has his own IDIOLECT.

Even the homogeneity of the idiolect is a fiction, tenable only so long as we continue to treat language SYNCHRONICALLY, in abstraction from time. As soon as we consider DIACHRONIC varieties of language, taking in the dimension of persistence and change in time, we have to recognize that changes take place not only in the transmission of language from one generation to the next but also in the speech habits of the individual in the course of his life.

Literacy retards linguistic change. But even in a community with a high literacy rate we can usually observe some differences in speech between successive generations. The individual member of the dialect community may retain his own idiolect unchanged; or he may adopt some features of the dialect of the next generation, even consciously adjusting his language performance to incorporate the neologisms of the young. At the least these will enter into his receptive use of language. In this sense the smallest dialectal unit is not the individual but the individual at a certain period in his life. Here we are approaching the theoretical limit of delicacy on the dialect dimension.

In the register range, the countless situations in which language activity takes place can be grouped into situation types, to which correspond the various uses of language. A corpus of language text in a given use is marked off by its formal properties as a register. Registers, like dialects, can be more and more finely differentiated; here again we can approach a theoretical limit of delicacy, at least in imagination, by progressive sub-classification of features of field, mode and style.

Ultimately, register and dialect meet in the single speech event. Here we have reached the UTTERANCE, the smallest institutional unit of language activity. In arriving through dialect and register at the 'piece of activity', we have completed the circuit which led from this in the first place, via the description of substance and form, through context, to language in use. Viewed descriptively, the speech event was the occurrence of a formal item 'expounded' in substance. Viewed institutionally, it is an utterance in a situation, identifiable by dialect and register.

In the last resort, since each speaker and each situation is unique, each single utterance is also itself unique. But, as we saw at the beginning, the uniqueness of events is irrelevant to their scientific description, which can only begin when different events are seen to be partially alike. We become interested in one piece of language activity when we can show that it has something in common with another.

It is possible to group together a limited number of utterances according to what they have in common in dialect and register. One way of so delimiting a language variety is to retrace our steps a little up these two scales, to where we meet the individual as a participant in numerous situations. We can then define a set of language events as the language activity of one individual in one register. This intersection of idiolect and register provides an institutional definition of individual style.

Some registers are extremely restricted in purpose. They thus employ only a limited number of formal items and patterns, with the result that the language activity in these registers can accommodate little idiolectal or even dialectal variety. Such registers are known as RESTRICTED LANGUAGES. This is by no means a clearly defined category: some restricted languages are more restricted than others. Extreme examples are the 'International Language of the Air', the permitted set of wartime cable messages for those on active service, and the bidding code of contract bridge. Less restricted are the various registers of legal and official documents and regulations, weather forecasts, popular song lyrics, and verses on greeting cards. All these can still be regarded as restricted languages.

The individual may still sometimes be recognizable even under the impersonal uniformity of a restricted language. This is often due to PARALINGUISTIC features: these are features, such as voice quality and handwriting, which do not carry formal contrasts. (In languages in which voice quality does carry formal contrasts it is not paralinguistic but linguistic.) Such features, like the phonetic and phonological characteristics by which an individual is sometimes marked out, will appear in a restricted language just as in an unrestricted register. Occasionally we even come across individual formal patterns in a restricted language: there is the bridge player who expects her partner, but not her opponent, to interpret correctly her private structural distinction between 'one club' and ' a club'.

Except in restricted languages, it is normally assumed that individuals will differ in their language performance. In spoken registers the individual may stand out within his own dialect community through idiosyncratic phonetic habits. That he would of course stand out in a dialect community other than his own is trivial, since it is no more relevant to his linguistic individuality than the fact that an Englishman would stand out in France by speaking English. Even phonology gives some scope to individual variety: the present authors pronounce 'transparent plastic' in three phonologically different ways. Graphological practice is more uniform: we no longer tolerate individual spelling, though punctuation is allowed to vary somewhat.

Nevertheless, even in written registers the individual stands out. His language is distinctive at the level of form. A person's idiolect may be identified, through the lens of the various registers, by its grammatical and lexical characteristics. This is how we recognize the individual qualities of a particular writer. All linguistic form is either grammar or lexis, and in the first instance it is the grammatical and lexical features of the individual writer's language, together with a few features of punctuation, that constitute his 'style'.

Individual style, however, is linked to register. It is the writer's idiolect, especially the grammar and lexis of the idiolect, in a given register. Insofar as 'style' implies literary style, register here means literary, including poetic, genre and medium. Style is thus linguistic form in interrelation with literary form.

If we refer to 'the style of Pope' we presumably imply that there is something in common to the language of the *Essays*, the *Satires* and other works: that they constitute in some sense a single idiolect. In fact, 'style', like other, related concepts, must be recognized to be variable in delicacy: each genre, and each individual work, has its style. If it is assumed from the start that two texts are alike, the differences between them may be missed or distorted. It is a sound principle of descriptive linguistics to postulate heterogeneity until homogeneity is proved, and the study of literary texts is no exception. By treating the *Satires* and the *Essays* as different registers we can display the similarities as well as the dissimilarities between them.

Literature forms only a small part of written language, but it is the part in which we are most aware of the individual and most interested in the originality of the individual's language. At the same time it is of the essence of creative writing that it calls attention to its own form, in the sense that unlike other language activity, written or spoken, it is meaningful as activity in itself and not merely as part of a larger situation: again, of course, without a clear line of demarcation. This remains true whether or not the writer is consciously aiming at creating an individual variety. Thus the linguistic uniqueness of a work of literature is of much greater significance than the individuality of a variety of language in any other use.

The language activity of one user in one use: this concept will serve as the fundamental variety of a language. Such an individual variety is a product of both dialect and register, and both are involved in its study.

Dialectology is a long-established branch of linguistic studies. In Britain, which has lagged notably behind other European countries and the United States, large scale dialect survey work did not begin until after the Second World War; but the three national surveys now being conducted at the universities of Leeds, Edinburgh and Wales have amassed a large amount of material and the first results are now in course of publication.

Serious work on registers is even more recent in origin. Very large samples of texts have to be subjected to detailed formal analysis if we wish to show which grammatical and lexical features are common to all uses of the language and which are restricted to, or more frequent in, one or more particular register. Such samples are now being collected and studied at University College London, in the Survey of English Usage under the direction of Professor Randolph Quirk; and related work is in progress at the universities of Edinburgh and Leeds. The study of registers is crucial both to our understanding of how language works and in application to literary analysis, machine translation and native and foreign language teaching.

6

Languages in contact, dialects and registers are three of the major topics of institutional linguistics. The fourth and last to be considered is the observation of the attitudes of members of a language community towards their language and its varieties. Here we mention briefly some of the attitudes that are relevant to the present discussion, with commentary where necessary.

Most communities show some reverence for the magical powers of language. In some societies, however, this respect is mingled with, and may be eclipsed by, a newer set of attitudes much more disdainful of the language, or of a part of it. The value judgments that underlie these attitudes may be moral or aesthetic, or they may rest on a pragmatic appeal to efficiency. The degree of social sanction they carry varies according to the language community; but whether the judgments and attitudes are social or individual, the individual expounding them frequently claims objectivity for his opinions. A typical formulation is: 'Obviously it is better (or: 'Everybody agrees that it is better') to say, or write, this than that, because' either 'it's clearer' or 'it sounds better' or 'it's more correct'. Less common, and more sophisticated, are 'because the best people do it' and 'because I prefer it'.

The most far-reaching among such value judgments are those passed on whole languages. Those who argue that it is necessary for English to remain the language of government, law, education or technology in former colonies sometimes claim, in support of their view, that the national languages are not suitable for these purposes. This reason is even put forward by the native speaker of the languages concerned.

The arguments for and against the use of English in such situations are complex; but this particular factor is irrelevant, because it is not true. This misapprehension, that some languages are intrinsically better than others, cannot just be dismissed as ignorance or prejudice; it is a view held by people who are both intelligent and serious, and can bring forward evidence to support it. Nevertheless it is wholly false and can do a great deal of harm.

Essentially, any language is as good as any other language, in the sense that every language is equally well adapted to the uses to which the community puts it. There is no such thing as a 'primitive' language. About the origins of language, nothing is known; there is merely a tangle of conflicting speculation, none of it falling within linguistics. But there is evidence that speech in some form goes back at least a hundred thousand years, and quite certainly no society found in the world today, or known to us in history, represents anything but a stage long after language had become a fully developed form of social activity. If historians or anthropologists use 'primitive' as a technical term, to designate a certain stage of social development, then the term may be transferred to the language used by a community that is in that stage; but it is *not* a linguistic classification and tells us nothing whatever about the nature of the language concerned.

Among the languages in the world today, there is no recognizable dimension of *linguistic* progress. No language can be identified as representing a more highly developed state of language than any other. Worora, in Western Australia, is as well adapted to the needs of the community which developed it as English is to our own. Neither language could be transferred to the other society without some changes, because the needs and activities are different; in both cases new lexical items would have to be added. But only the lexis would be affected, and only a portion of that. There would be no need for any changes in the grammar. At most there might be a statistical tendency for certain grammatical changes to take place over a very long period; but no simple change would be predictable in any given instance, none would be bound to occur, and certainly none would be necessary to the continued efficiency of the language.

In other words, the changes that would be necessary in Worora, for it to operate as a full language in the modern world, would be those that were also necessary to English as it was before the modern period. Middle English, even Elizabethan English, was not adapted to the needs of a modern state either. One could no more describe an electronic computer in Middle English than in Worora. Different languages have different ways of expanding their lexis, determined by their own internal structure: Chinese, for example, coins scientific terminology in a very different way from Japanese, being a language of a very different type. But all languages are capable of incorporating the lexical additions they require.

Whether or not it is economically feasible for the language of a very small community to be used as a medium for all the purposes of the modern world is of course an entirely different question, which each community has the right to decide for itself. It is worth pointing out that in the next generation machine translation will probably become efficient enough, and cheap enough, to overcome the problem of translating all the material such a community would need to have translated from other languages. Whatever considerations may affect the choice of a language for science or administration in a newly independent nation, this at least can be made clear: all languages are equally capable of being developed for all purposes, and no language is any less qualified to be the vehicle of modern science and technology than were English and Russian some centuries ago.

A type of language that particularly attracts adverse value judgments is the mixed language. As long as this remains a pidgin, it can be nobody's L1 and has not the status of a language; it exists only in certain restricted varieties. But in those communities which have developed a mixed language as their L1, the new language has thereby gained full stature and become a completely effective medium of language activity.

In any case a creole is only an extreme result of a normal phenomenon in the development of language: linguistic borrowing. There is no reason why a language with such a history should be less effective than any other. They are languages in the defined sense of the word; some of them are already used as literary media, and they would be fully viable as media of education and science. At present they tend to be more discriminated against than languages with a more conventional history. But there is no justification for discriminating against any language whatever. In most parts of the world today, including Britain, there has to be some measure of linguistic policy and planning; decisions may have to be taken, for example, to establish certain languages as the national languages of a new nation. What matters is that the real issues and problems should not be allowed to become clouded by false notions that one language may be objectively inferior to another.

Many speakers from communities whose language is in some or other respect denied full status, while they would not maintain that their own L1 was in any way inferior, and might vigorously reject such a suggestion, nevertheless in their language activity, as speakers, accept and thereby help to perpetuate its diminished status. In countries where English, or some other L2, is the mark of education and social standing, conversation in the government office or college staff common room normally takes place in English. Alternatively, if the L1 is allowed into these surroundings, no sentence in it is complete without at least one item from English.

This is sometimes explained on the grounds that the speakers do not share a common L1, as indeed they may not. It often is in countries which face a really difficult national language problem that a foreign language flourishes as a lingua franca. As is well known, many speakers from minority communities, whose language is not a strong candidate for national status, so firmly oppose the claims of any other language from within the country that they prefer to assign this status to a foreign language, which at least has the merit of being neutral. Probably this is at best a temporary solution; moreover there is reason to suggest that shelving the problem makes it more difficult to solve in the future.

But the lacing of L1 utterances with L2 items is not confined to multilingual societies. It is likely to happen wherever a foreign language is a mark of social distinction and the sole medium of language activity in certain registers. English probably occupies this position more than any other language. There are of course no grounds on which the linguist, who observes and describes this phenomenon, could object to it as a use of language: it works. But he may also reasonably point out that the use of English in situations for which the L1 is adequately developed, and of English items in L1 utterances where L1 items are available, tends to inhibit the progress of the L1 towards regaining its full status in the community.

7

Within our own language community, value judgments on English as a whole are relatively rare. Occasionally one hears it compared unfavourably with French, by those who subscribe to the myth, sedulously kept alive by the French themselves, that French is a 'more logical' language. What are extremely common, however, are value judgments on varieties of English: sometimes referring to registers but principally to dialects. The English language community, especially the British section of it, is almost certainly unique in the extent to which its members pass judgment on varieties of their language. One of the few other communities that at all resembles us in this respect is the French. The English attitudes are of course bound up with the socio-regional character of our dialects; as such, they are class attitudes rather than individual attitudes. Nearly all the widely accepted value judgments can be traced to this origin, though some reflect it more directly than others.

It is at the new urban dialects, the varieties of the standard language with regional accent, that the most severe criticisms are levelled. The original dialects, now confined to the rural areas, have become quaint. They are tolerated; sometimes they may be praised, as 'soft', 'pleasant', or even 'musical'. And, somewhat inconsistently, though it is the rural dialects which provide the only instances of pairs of mutually unintelligible varieties remaining in England, it is often on grounds of incomprehensibility that criticism is directed at the urban dialects.

Perhaps the most frequent complaint is that formulated in various terms implying some sort of linguistic decay. The urban dialects are said to be 'slovenly', 'careless' or 'degenerate'. Similar terms were used about English and French in the nineteenth century, by those who regarded all recent linguistic change as a process of degeneration and decay. It is implied, and sometimes stated explicitly, that in the urban dialects there has been some loss of the communicative power of language.

This is simply nonsense. All the dialects, including all forms of standard English, are subject to change, both through the normal tendency of language to change and as a result of external factors such as movement of populations. Rate of change in language varies considerably, between different languages, between dialects, and at different times and places; even at different levels within the same variety of a language. English has altered rather strikingly over the last thousand years; the dialect now functioning as standard English is one of those that has changed the most, though it is difficult to measure comparative rates of change very accurately.

To the way of thinking that these attitudes represent, probably the slovenliest people in the world would be the French and the north Chinese: Parisian and Pekingese are the result of a high rate of change over long periods. There is no difference between the type of change undergone by these two languages and that which has affected the dialectal varieties of English, including the dialect that has become standardized and its modern regional derivatives.

There is actually no such thing as a slovenly dialect or accent. That the dialect of Sheffield or Birmingham has evolved in a different direction from one's own is hardly a matter for reproach, and anyone who labels it 'debased' is committing two errors. First, he is assuming that one type of standard English preserves an earlier variety of the language from which others have deviated; this is not true. Second, he is claiming that there is merit in this imagined conservation; if there was, such merit might appropriately be claimed by the Italians, the Cantonese and the Germans in reproach to their slovenly neighbours the French, the Pekingese and the English.

Traditionally, this charge of debasement rested on straightforward moral grounds: it was wrong and irresponsible to let the language fall into decay. More recently the same imputed shortcoming has come to be criticized from another point of view, that of the loss of efficiency. Since the fault is imaginary, the grounds on which it is censured might seem unimportant. But one comment at least is called for. Many people, including for a time some linguists, have been taken in by the spurious rigour of some pseudo-scientific 'measurements' of the 'efficiency' of language. There is no evidence whatever that one language, or one variety of a language, can be more efficient than another. Nor is there, either in our intuitive judgment or yet in mathematics or linguistics, any means of measuring whatever such efficiency might be. Information theory, which has a place in the quantitative description of a language, implies nothing about the relative efficiency of languages or the effectiveness of language activity.

A second accusation has been brought against the urban dialects that is somewhat different from that of slovenliness, in either its moral or its utilitarian form. This is an aesthetic criticism. The dialects are labelled 'harsh', 'grating', 'guttural', – this probably refers to the higher frequency, in some varieties, of glottal closure unaccompanied by oral stops – or simply 'ugly'.

Here the person judging is on safer ground, if he means that he personally does not like the sound of certain varieties of English: no one can dispute that. The formulation may be a general one, but there is a broad human tendency to generalize one's prejudices, and we probably all know people who would not distinguish between 'I dislike the sound of Cardiff English' and 'Cardiff English is ugly'.

It is true that there is often a wide range of agreement in these aesthetic judgments. What is not realized, however, is that they are usually learnt. An Indian brought up in the Indian musical tradition will not agree with European judgments on European music, and a European who does not know the Chinese language and Chinese cultural values does not appreciate – that is, agree with Chinese judgments of – the sounds of Chinese poetry. Whether or not the adult ever does produce an unconditioned aesthetic response, in general what we like is as much a result of what we have learnt to like socially as of what we have grown to like individually. In language, we know already that people from different language communities respond quite differently to the aesthetic qualities of the dialects of a given language: a Persian or a Japanese not knowing English would be as likely to prefer Birmingham to RP as the other way round. The chief factor in one's evaluation of varieties of a language is social conditioning: there is no universal scale of aesthetic judgment. Those who dislike the Birmingham accent often do so because they know that their children will stand a better chance in life if they do not acquire it.

It is thus the socio-regional pattern of English dialect distribution that gives rise to both the aesthetic and the moral or pragmatic value judgments on the urban and rural dialects, insofar as these judgments are held in common by a large section of our language community. In many countries such judgments either are not passed at all or, if they are, are regarded both by those who pass them and by those who listen to them as subjective expressions of personal taste. Foreign students in Britain listen in polite wonder while their teatime hosts in Leeds or Manchester explain how important it is that they should not copy the speech of their landladies: 'everybody agrees', they are told, that this is an ugly, distorted form of English.

Not everybody does agree, in fact: such views seem to be most general among speakers of mildly regional varieties of Standard English. But when these attitudes are shared by those who themselves speak the dialect, and no other, they become rather harmful. A speaker who is made ashamed of his own language habits suffers a basic injury as a human being: to make anyone, especially a child, feel so ashamed is as indefensible as to make him feel ashamed of the colour of his skin.

Various courses of instruction are available in spoken English, under headings such as 'Speech and Drama', 'Elocution' and 'Normal Voice and Speech'. In general three different kinds of instruction take place. The first is concerned with techniques of speaking on the stage and in public; this is a form of applied phonetics, and is often very successful. The second is concerned with personal attainments such as voice quality and clarity in speech, and is often linked to aspects of social behaviour under the general heading of 'developing the personality'; these aspects lie outside the scope of application of linguistics or phonetics.

In the third type of instruction, which is again applied phonetics, the individual is taught to use some accent of English other than the one he has acquired naturally. This may be for particular professional purposes, as in the schools where dance-band leaders and pop singers can acquire the pronunciation considered appropriate to their calling, and the courses in which actors, for the purpose of character parts, may learn reasonable imitations of regional accents or at least a conventional Mummerset. It may, on the other hand, be for general social purposes; classes are held where those who speak with a regional accent can learn a pronunciation which they have found carries greater social prestige and better prospects of employment. Here the teaching is catering for social attitudes to language; but they are still recognized as social attitudes.

In the extreme forms of such accent-teaching, however, the particular accent taught is extolled by those who teach it as 'more beautiful' and 'better' than any other. This accent is generally a variety of RP with a number of special vowel qualities and lip postures. Sometimes the speech of a particular individual is held up as a model for imitation; but more often an absolute aesthetic merit is claimed for the way of speaking that is taught. Some of the teachers have themselves been taught that there is a scale of values on which vowels may be judged, ranging from 'bad and ugly' to 'good and beautiful'. The teacher is thus attempting to alter the speech of her pupils for reasons which seem to her sensible and obvious, but which are inexplicable to most of the pupils. The view that some sounds are inherently higher or lower than others on an absolute scale of aesthetic values has no evidence to support it, though it is of interest to phoneticians to know how widely it is held.

Perhaps the most uncomfortable of all the conflicts of approach between linguists and phoneticians on the one hand and teachers of 'speech' (who may invoke the authority of these disciplines) on the other, are those centring on the subject commonly known as 'Normal Voice and Speech'. This subject is included within the curriculum for speech therapists, in which phonetics also plays a prominent part. 'Normal' here is used prescriptively; the assumption is that one particular accent of English is in some way 'normal', all others being 'abnormal', and that the 'normal' accent is RP. Such judgments, as we have seen, reflect no property of the accent itself, but merely the social standing of those who have acquired it.

If all the patients treated by speech therapists belonged to this group, the confusion would do no actual harm. But those with speech defects are a representative cross-section of the whole population, the majority of whom do not speak RP, so that the background provided by 'Normal Voice and Speech' is both culturally loaded and, for many, therapeutically irrelevant. Many phoneticians continue to provide courses for students of speech therapy because they hope to give an objective training which will counterbalance the prescriptive nature of 'Normal Voice and Speech'; but the harnessing of two such differently conceived subjects in a single course can only be likened to an attempt to combine astronomy with domestic science, or perhaps rather chemistry with alchemy.

8

The English tendency to linguistic intolerance is not confined to strictures on the sounds of language. Value judgments also flourish in grammar. In grammar, however, the features subjected to those judgments are on the whole not dialectal. Many dialectal grammatical patterns pass unnoticed in speech provided the speaker is using the phonetics of RP: even such a markedly regional clause structure as that exemplified by 'they've never been to see us haven't the Joneses' is tolerated in spoken English if the accent is an acceptable one. It would not on the other hand be tolerated in writing.

In grammar we have a set of arbitrary prescriptions and proscriptions relating to particular patterns and items. Some are applied to written English only, others to both spoken and written. Neither the prescribed nor the proscribed forms correspond to any particular regional varieties. As with the dialectal prescriptions, there are various ways of giving a bad name to the proscribed forms: they are called 'slipshod' and 'crude', sometimes simply 'wrong'. 'Incorrect', taken from a different register, is sometimes used as if it was an explanation of 'wrong'.

In this context 'slipshod' and 'crude' are meaningless, and a native speaker of English who happened not to know which of a pair of forms was approved and which censured would have no evidence whatsoever for deciding. As effective language activity, there is nothing to choose between 'do it as I do' and 'do it like I do', just as soup has the same food value however it is eaten (or whether it is 'eaten' or 'drunk'). 'Wrong' is a social judgment: what is meant is 'the best people use this form and not that form'. These are in effect social conventions about language, and their function is that of social conventions: meaningless in themselves, they exert cohesive force within one society, or one section of a society, by marking it off from another.

As we have seen, all languages have formally distinct varieties. What is unusual about the language situation in Britain is the extent to which rules are consciously formulated for what is regarded as appropriate grammatical behavior. Other communities have sometimes attempted to impose patterns of linguistic form, generally without much success; at the most, what is prescribed is the distinction between the spoken and the written language, some forms being rejected as inappropriate to the latter. Conventions in the spoken language are normally confined to lexical taboos: certain items are not to be used before children, strangers or members of the opposite sex. In Britain, rules are made for speech as well as for writing, and the speaker's grammar contributes, alongside his phonetics and phonology, to his identification on the social scale.

Since 'incorrect' linguistic behaviour whether dialectal or otherwise may be counted against one in many situations, the solution chosen by many speakers, in face of the prevalent attitudes, is to acquire a second idiolect. Indeed so strong is the feeling that there are correct and incorrect forms of linguistic behaviour that if one asks, as the present writers have asked many groups of university students, 'what is the purpose of the teaching of English in English schools?' a frequent answer is 'to teach the children to speak and write correct English'. The old observation that parents in the new dialect regions send their children to school so that they can be taught to 'talk proper' is by no means out of date. The subject of native language teaching is taken up in Chapter 8; suffice it to say here that if children have to learn new speech habits, it is the social attitude to their dialect, and no fault of the dialect itself, that is forcing them to do this: at least they need not be taught that their own speech is in some way inferior or taboo.

Some voices are raised against the prevailing attitudes, and some of the rules are occasionally called into question. Priestley once wrote, in *English Journey* (London, Heinemann in association with Gollancz, 1934, p. 290), "Standard English is like standard anything else – poor tasteless stuff." Hugh Sykes-Davies, in *Grammar Without Tears* (London, The Bodley Head, 1951, pp. 131-2), suggested reversing the polarity of prescription and proscription: "the use of the indirect cases of *who* should be avoided wherever possible by putting the preposition at the end of the sentence, and making *that* the relative, or omitting the pronoun altogether. It is better to say 'the man I found the hat of' than 'the man whose hat I found'". But here the speaker is still being told how to behave; there is still a right and a wrong in language.

Serious interest in dialectal varieties of the language is fostered by such bodies as the Yorkshire Dialect Society, which publishes both literary work in, and academic studies of, the Yorkshire dialects, urban as well as rural. Detailed surveys of the dialects of England, Wales and Scotland are, as has been mentioned, now well advanced. The Linguistic Survey of Scotland takes account of urban varieties of Scots; and although the English Dialect Survey has not yet turned its attention to the new dialects in England this is because the original, now rural, dialects are fast disappearing and must be recorded first. And teachers and university students seem to be becoming increasingly aware of the artificial and arbitrary nature of the conventional notions of 'good English' and 'bad English'.

Interwoven with the highly prescriptive attitudes towards the linguistic behaviour of individuals is a strong protective feeling for the language as a whole. Unlike the selective judgments, which are rare among language communities, the defensive 'leave our language alone' attitude is very commonly found. Perhaps the most striking instance of this in Britain is the fierce resistance to any suggestions for spelling reform. So strongly is the feeling against it that it seems unlikely at present that any orthographic revision of English will be undertaken for a long time.

Not all language communities are equally conservative in this respect. The Chinese, whose traditional orthography is even more difficult to master than ours, and is a serious barrier to the learning of the standard language, have recently embarked on what is probably the most far-reaching programme of script reform ever attempted in any language community. Intense interest was aroused from the start; and although this was by no means all favourable, some tens of thousands of suggestions, and over six hundred reformed scripts, were submitted to the committee which first drafted the new proposals.

It has been argued that if the English expect their language to operate as an international medium they should consider reforming the script in the interests of foreign learners. On the other hand any project for doing so would face enormous difficulties. The linguist, as a linguist, does not take sides in this issue, though as a private citizen he may; but he is qualified to act as a consultant, and to make suggestions as to how best to revise the orthography if it is once decided to do so. Apart from this, the role of linguistics at this stage is to help clear the air for rational discussion of the problem, as of all the other problems that are raised by the complex and deep-rooted attitudes of the members of a language community towards their language.

From: Halliday, M. A. K., McIntosh, Angus, and Strevens, Peter, *The Linguistic Sciences and Language Teaching* (London, Longmans, 1964). Reprinted with permission.

Section II
LANGUAGE IN SMALL-GROUP INTERACTION

— — — — — — — — — — — — — — — — — — — —

Henry L. Lennard and Arnold Bernstein

INTERDEPENDENCE OF THERAPIST AND PATIENT VERBAL BEHAVIOR

One kind of interdependence of behavior occurring in social systems which is of interest to sociologists is the trend toward similarity in performance or orientation. As Homans puts it, "The more frequently persons interact with one another, the more alike in some repects both their activities and their sentiments tend to become." [1] And as Newcomb says, "There is, in fact, no social phenomenon which can be more commonly observed than the tendency of freely communicating persons to resemble one another in orientation towards objects of common concern." [2]

We wanted to learn whether or not interacting individuals become more alike in the course of psychotherapy, and if so, with respect to which communicational variables.

Traditional theories of psychotherapy have always maintained the view that the patient, like Peer Gynt, should become more "himself" in the course of therapy, rather than be transformed into a facsimile of the therapist. Our findings (with respect to specific aspects of therapist and patient communication patterns) can be interpreted as bearing out Homans's hypothesis that interacting individuals tend to become more alike as time passes. But whether this means that the patient tends to become more like his therapist as treatment continues or is merely internalizing the communicational patterns he observes during treatment will depend upon how much of a therapist's behavior during treatment is a role he is playing and how much of it truly represents himself. To

[1] Homans, *The Human Group*, p. 120.
[2] Newcomb, "An Approach to the Study of Communicative Acts", *Psychological Review*, LX (1953), 393-404.

the extent that a therapist "is himself" (i.e., expresses his own values, preferences, etc.) during treatment, a patient may indeed grow to resemble him; but to the extent that the therapist is not "himself", the patient would merely incorporate those aspects of the therapist's behavior characteristic of the role assumed by him in the particular therapy.

Our results bear on this controversy only indirectly, since communication content was not analyzed directly in relation to specific values and orientation.[3] We did not code our material in terms of similarity in actual values expressed, but only as to whether or not the participants' communication was centered on the same subject or the same mode of communication. One can nevertheless hold that similarity in *what* and *how* one communicates does bear on the question of similarity in values.

The first step in investigating these questions was to examine the natural unit, the therapeutic session. Correlations between given types of therapist and patient verbal behavior were computed. Specifically, correlations were computed between percentage of therapist propositions and percentage of patient propositions which were of the same kind, that is, which were classified in the same category. This was done for three aspects of communication. We are using the term "similarity' to express the fact of an increasing correlation over time between patient and therapist with respect to the following three kinds of communicative sets: 1. primary system references, 2. evaluative communications, and 3. affective communications.

1. Primary system references, it will be remembered, deal with reciprocal therapist-patient role relations. They revolve around the obligations and activities of therapist and patient vis-à-vis each other. These references frequently consist of discussions of the purposes of therapy. Primary system references sometimes constitute more than half of all therapist communications during the initial hours of therapy but by the tenth hour of therapy may comprise less than 20 percent of all therapist communications. This is a critical area during the early period of therapy. The exchange of communications between therapist and patient regarding their respective roles is one avenue through which the patient "learns" the patient role and is enabled to function within it.

2. Evaluative propositions are those which give or ask for appraisals or statements of value. This category covers two of the Bales Interaction Progress categories. It was felt that evaluation of behavior was an especially recurrent feature of therapy and that, therefore, tendencies toward similarities in the trends of therapist and patient verbal behavior would have an opportunity to emerge and could be assessed.

3. Affective propositions are those which are directed toward or ex-

[3] A method for such an analysis was tentatively formulated, but it could not be applied because a sponsor for this aspect of the research could not be found.

press feelings or emotions. As we have seen, the eliciting of information about patient affect is widely regarded as a primary purpose of the therapeutic interaction. Whether an increase in the number of therapist communications about affect results in an increased patient affective yield is a question of theoretical as well as practical interest.

In order to examine the possibility of an increase over time in the percentage of patient or therapist propositions defined in the above dimensions, we computed Pearson's coefficient of correlation (r) for three groups of sessions: sessions one and two; sessions five and six; and two sessions from the third and fourth months of therapy. Table I presents the correlations for the above three dimensions at three times in therapy.

TABLE I

Increase in Similarity of the Therapist and Patient Behavior Over Time

	Correlations between percentage of therapist and patient propositions		
	Sessions 1 and 2	*Sessions 5 and 6*	*2 Sessions from 3rd and 4th months*
Primary System	.72	.66	.88
Evaluation	.36	.45	.58
Affect	.23	.43	.70

n = 48 sessions (8 therapist-patient pairs)

Table I shows that, for each dimension of communication, there is over time an increase in correlation, with an especially marked increase in the correlations for affective propositions.[4] These findings suggest that there is over time an increase in similarity of patient and therapist behavior with regard to these three areas.

One explanation for this increasing similarity of behavior is that it results from an increasing responsiveness of the patient and therapist toward each other's verbalizations. An increase in sensitivity would imply that if the patient discusses the process of therapy (primary system), the therapist is more likely to respond with propositions which are also about therapy. Similarly, if the therapist inquires of the patient as to how he felt about some event, the patient is more likely to respond with some proposition about his feelings. Our usage defines responsiveness simply as responding with the same subject or mode of communication.[5]

[4] This finding is altogether to be expected, in the light of one of the well-known goals of analytic therapy, i.e., the freeing of the patient to express his feelings.

[5] We do not mean to imply that responsiveness on the part of the therapist is always "therapeutic" in the sense of responding to the patient's "needs". We are aware that responsiveness may also constitute therapist fulfillment of patient demands.

How *degree* of responsiveness is measured is discussed later. We are here concerned with the process by which responsiveness is increased in therapy. This process can logically assume any of three different forms: 1. increasing responsiveness of the patient toward the therapist; 2. increasing responsiveness of the therapist toward the patient; or 3. increasing responsiveness of each toward the other.

Proceeding from one point of view it could be that the tendency toward symmetry observed in our data is due to 1. an increased sensitivity on the part of the patient to the therapist's communications. From this vantage point, it is the therapist who extends positive sanctions for appropriate behavior (as exhibited by relevant verbal responses) and imposes negative sanctions for inappropriate behavior. It is the therapist who "knows" what the patient's role is, and it is the patient who must "learn" it by responding appropriately. However, it might be argued that increasing similarity is due to 2. an ever-increasing sensitivity of the therapist to the patient, as the therapist learns more about the patient. In this view, the therapist does not dominate the relationship, but is skilled in "following" wherever the patient leads. And finally, following through on the sociological generalization summarized by the Homans and Newcomb statements at the outset of this chapter, one would suspect that 3. both participants in a system contribute to the emergence of symmetry.

Since we have determined the correlations between therapist and patient propositions in eight actual therapies, we are in a position to specify which if any of the above hypotheses apply. In order to do this, we constructed an Index of Patient Responsiveness and an Index of Therapist Responsiveness.

The indices of responsiveness are based on comparing the character of a response (by the patient or by the therapist) with the character of the immediately preceding statement. Each index of responsiveness is defined as the ratio between the frequency of similar responses and the frequency of dissimilar responses. A ration of 1.0 for the patient means that the patient responded in a similar manner *exactly as often* as he responded in a dissimilar manner. If the ratio were .5, it would mean that the patient responded in a similar manner only *one-half* as often as he responded in a dissimilar manner. Thus a ratio of 9.0 for the therapist means that the therapist responded in a similar manner 9 times as often as he responded in a dissimilar manner.[6]

[6] The Index of Patient Responsiveness is computed in three steps. The instructions which follow deal with the affective dimension, but they can be made applicable to any other dimension by replacing the term "affective" with the appropriate phrase.

1. Calculate the proportion of therapist affective statements that are followed

Thus, if the Index of Therapist Responsiveness is higher in later phases of therapy than during the initial phases, it indicates that the therapist is becoming more sensitive to the patient's statements. In order to examine change over time, we grouped the sessions into four time periods: sessions one and two, sessions three through five, sessions six through eight, and two sessions taken from the third and fourth months of therapy. Then the Index of Patient Responsiveness and the Index of therapist Responsiveness were computed for each time period for the three different dimensions of Primary System Responsiveness, Evaluation, and Affect. The means for all eight patient-therapist pairs are reported in Tables II, III, and IV.

TABLE II

Primary System Responsiveness Over Time

	Indices of primary system responsiveness				
	Sessions 1-2	*Sessions 3-5*	*Sessions 6-8*	*2 Sessions from 3rd and 4th months*	*All Sessions*
Patients	4.8	9.0	21.0	32.0	16.7
Therapists	5.9	9.4	8.1	11.5	8.7
			n = 9,314 statements		

by patient affective statements. This is the proportion of similar affective responses.

2. Calculate the proportion of therapist nonaffective statements which are followed by patient affective statements. This is the proportion of dissimilar responses.

3. Divide the proportion of similar responses by the proportion of dissimilar responses. This gives an Index of Patient Responsiveness to affect. This Index is really a ratio of the frequency with which the patient responds in a similar manner to the frequency with which he responds in a dissimilar manner.

In order to illustrate this procedure, a simple example is worked through these three steps:

1. Let us assume that for a certain group of sessions there are a total of 1000 therapist affective statements, 500 of which are followed by patient affective statements. This yields us a .50 similar response.

2. In this same group of hours, there are also 1000 therapist nonaffective statements, 250 of which are followed by patient affective statements. This gives us a .25 dissimilar response.

3. Dividing the proportion of similar responses (.50) by the proportion of dissimilar responses (.25) gives us a ratio of 2.0, which is the Index of Patient Responsiveness to Affect for the particular groups of hours. This index tells us that the patient responded in a similar manner twice as often as he responded in a dissimilar manner. If the ratio were 1.0, it would mean that the patient responded in a similar manner exactly as often as he responded in a dissimilar manner. If the ratio were .5, it would mean that the patient responded in a similar manner only one-half as often as he responded in a dissimilar manner.

The Index of Therapist Responsiveness is computed in the same way, except that the word "patient" is substituted for the word "therapist", and vice versa.

Table II shows that for Primary System Responsiveness both the Index of Patient Responsiveness and the Index of Therapist Responsiveness increase strikingly from the earlier to later hours. Thus, in this case, the increased similarity of behavior seems to be due to the increased sensitivity of *both* the patient and the therapist to each other. However, it should be noted that the patient sensitivity increases at a more rapid rate than the therapist, and that the patient has a higher overall average responsiveness.

TABLE III

Evaluative Responsiveness Over Time

	Indices of evaluative responsiveness				
	Sessions 1-2	*Sessions 3-5*	*Sessions 6-8*	*2 Sessions from 3rd and 4th months*	*All Sessions*
Patients	2.0	1.9	1.8	1.7	1.9
Therapists	1.4	1.2	1.3	1.2	1.3
	n = 9,314 statements				

Table III shows that for Evaluative Propositions there is *no* increase either in the Index of Patient Responsiveness or in the Index of Therapist Responsiveness. Thus, in the case of evaluation, none of the above three hypotheses seems to apply, and the observed increase in correlations must be due to some other process. It is possible that there is a "delayed response" which escapes detection at this microscopic level of analysis. In other words, when the therapist gives an evaluative statement, the patient's evaluative response may be delayed for several interactions due to lack of immediate comprehension or the necessity for some thought before responding appropriately, etc. If this is the case, such a delayed sensitivity would not manifest itself in these indices since they reflect only the immediately following response. However, we may note that the averages show the patient to be on the whole more responsive than the therapist.

Turning now to our final category, Affective Propositions, Table IV shows only a slight increase in the Index of Therapist Responsiveness

TABLE IV

Affective Responsiveness Over Time

	Indices of affective responsiveness				
	Sessions 1-2	*Sessions 3-5*	*Sessions 6-8*	*2 Sessions from 3rd and 4th months*	*All Sessions*
Patients	1.6	1.9	2.2	2.0	1.9
Therapists	1.7	1.9	1.9	1.9	1.9
	n = 9,314 statements				

and only a small increase in the Index of Patient Responsiveness. The increases in both therapist and patient affective responsiveness were so small that we might have overlooked a significant finding had we not examined each therapist separately. When we look at the indices computed separately for each therapist, we note two quite distinct patterns. The indices for therapist A and therapist B consistently increase over time, while the indices for therapist C and therapist D remain about the same or actually *decrease*. Thus it appears that the increased similarity of behavior of therapists A and B and their patients is due to increasing sensitivity of both patients and therapists, while this is not true of therapists C and D, since neither they nor their patients show any consistent increase. A variety of measurements have shown that therapists A and B are more "active" than the other two. Perhaps active therapists "teach" their patients to become more sensitive to verbalization about affect. What might not have been expected was that the active therapists *themselves* would become more sensitive, while the more passive therapists did not. The question now remains, why is there an increasing correlation over time for the passive therapists as well as for the active therapists (see Table I), even though no corresponding increase in responsiveness is measured by our index? Evidently, the increase in correlation must be due to a delayed rather than an immediate response.

Finally, one may ask why responsiveness differs both in magnitude and in rate of increase among these three dimensions. In comparing responsiveness to primary system references with responsiveness to evaluative and affective propositions, we note a markedly higher responsiveness in the former than in the latter two dimensions. Not only is responsiveness to primary system reference initially high, but it increases at a faster rate for both patients and therapists. For example, the Index of Patient Responsiveness to primary system references in the later sessions shows that patients gave similar responses 32 times as often as they gave dissimilar responses! This strikingly higher sensitivity may be related to the fact that primary system references are based on a specific substantive content, while the other two dimensions are based on characteristics of statements which are unrelated to the statements' specific content. In other words, a proposition coded as a primary system reference referred to concrete subject matter (therapy as a process).

On the other hand, a proposition which expressed opinion, wish, or preference was coded as Evaluative, regardless of subject matter under discussion. Similarly, a proposition which referred to any kind of feeling or emotion was coded as Affective, regardless of the subject matter under discussion. Thus, the patient and therapist when communicating along the substantive dimension (Primary System Reference) were prob-

TABLE V

Affective Responsiveness Over Time by Individual Therapist

	Indices of affective responsiveness			
	Sessions 1-2	*Sessions 3-5*	*Sessions 6-8*	*2 Sessions from 3rd and 4th months*
Therapist A	1.2	1.8	1.9	3.1
Patients [a]	1.6	1.7	2.7	2.1
Therapist B	1.5	1.9	1.9	2.4
Patients	1.5	2.2	2.7	3.4
Therapist C	1.9	1.9	2.4	1.1
Patients	1.8	1.8	1.7	.7
Therapist D	2.2	2.1	1.5	.8
Patients	1.7	2.1	1.9	1.7
	n = 80 sessions (9,314 statements)			

[a] The Index of Patient Responsiveness used here represents the average score for the two patients of each therapist.

ably more aware of whether they were responding in a similar or dissimilar manner, than when communicating along the more abstract dimensions (evaluation and affect). This difference in awareness of degree of similarity may account for the striking difference in sensitivity.

A further factor which might have contributed to this extraordinary increase in Primary System Responsiveness (as contrasted with the smaller increase in Affective Responsiveness) may lie in the relative changes that occur in the frequency distributions of Primary System and Affective communications from the earlier to the later sessions. Primary System communications decrease considerably from the earlier to the later sessions, while verbalization about affect increases. It may therefore be the case that the occurrence of a Primary System communication in the later sessions is an especially significant signal.

SUMMARY

In this chapter we first correlated patient and therapist treatment sessions with respect to three dimensions of communicative acts (i.e. primary system references, evaluative and affective references). For example, the correlation coefficient for primary system references gave us a picture of the extent to which sessions high in therapist primary system references were also high in patient primary system references. We found that for each dimension there was an increase in the correlation between patient and therapist by session over time. The increase in the correlation for affective communication was especially marked.

There is then a growing similarity of patient and therapist behavior over time with respect to these three areas. Hypotheses were then formulated to account for this increase in similarity. Since the increase in similarity might be due to a change brought about by one or both of the participants, the data was analyzed to determine to which participant, patient or therapist, it could be attributed.

A participant may contribute to growing similarity of behavior during the session by responding with a proposition similar in kind to the one introduced by the other participant. The results suggested that for primary system communication, both therapist and patient are responsible for increased similarity. With regard to evaluative propositions, it was the patient who was more responsive throughout. There is, however, no increase in the responsiveness of either patient or therapist over time. With regard to affective references, two of the therapists (the two more active ones) and their patients show an increase in sensitivity.

A trend toward similarity is one type of interdependence noted between therapist and patient communications. It was to the specification of such phenomena that we referred, when we mentioned as our purpose the identification of latent social processes not within the awareness of the participants in a therapeutic system.

From: *The Anatomy of Psychotherapy: System of Communication and Expectation*, by Henry L. Lennard et al. (New York, Columbia University Press, 1960), pp. 90-101. Reprinted with permission.

Lorna Marshall

SHARING, TALKING AND GIVING: RELIEF OF SOCIAL TENSIONS AMONG !KUNG BUSHMEN

This paper describes customs practiced by the !Kung Bushmen in the Nyae Nyae region of South West Africa, which help them to avoid situations that are likely to arouse ill will and hostility among individuals within the bands and between bands. Two customs which seem to be especially helpful and which I describe in detail are meat-sharing and gift-giving. I mention also the !Kung habits of talking, aspects of their good manners, their borrowing and lending, and their not stealing.[1]

The common human needs for co-operation and companionship are particularly apparent among the Nyae Nyae !Kung. Independent living, outside the band structure,[2] does not exist for individuals. Nuclear families do not live alone. The arduous hunting-gathering life would be impossible without the co-operation and companionship of a larger group. Moreover, in this society the ownership of the resources of food and water is organized through the headmen of bands, and individuals have rights to these resources by being members of a band connected to the headman by some near or remote kin or affinal bond. The !Kung are also extremely dependent emotionally on the sense of belonging and on companionship. Their need to avoid loneliness, I think, is actually visible in the way families cluster together in their werfs and in the way people sit, often touching someone else, shoulder against shoulder, ankle

[1] This description of the !Kung in the Nyae Nyae region is based on observations made during our several expeditions between 1951 and 1959. Changes in the conditions under which the !Kung live are to be expected, and how these changes will affect the practice of the customs here described we do not know.
[2] Lorna Marshall, "!Kung Bushman Band Organization", *Africa*, vol. xxx, no. 4 (Oct. 1960).

across ankle. Comfort and security for them lie in belonging to their group, free from hostility or rejection.

Their security and comfort must be achieved side by side with self-interest and much jealous watchfulness. Altruism, kindness, sympathy, or genuine generosity were not qualities which I observed often in their behaviour. However, these qualities were not entirely lacking, especially between parents and offspring, between siblings and between spouses. One mother carried her sick adult daughter on her back for three days in searing summer heat for us to give her medicine. *!*Naoka carried her lame son, Lame ≠Gao, for years. Gau clucked and fussed over his second wife, Khuan//a when she was sick. When *!*U had a baby, her sister, Di*!*ai, gathered veldkos for her for five days. On the other hand, people do not generally help each other. They laugh when the lame man, Kham, falls down and do not help him up. *!*U's jealous eyes were like those of a viper when we gave more attention to her husband, ≠ Toma, than to her because he was much more ill. And, in the extreme, there is the report from the 1958 expedition of an instance of callous indifference in one band and the probable abandonment of a dying old childless woman, an old aunt, when her sister, with whom she lived, had died.

Occasions when tempers have got out of control are remembered with awe. The deadly poisoned arrows are always at hand. Men have killed each other with them in quarrels – though rarely – and the *!*Kung fear fighting with a conscious and active fear. They speak about it often. Any expression of discord ("bad words") makes them uneasy. Their desire to avoid both hostility and rejection leads them to conform in high degree to the unspoken social law. If they do deviate they usually yield readily to expressed group opinion and reform their ways. I think that most *!*Kung cannot bear the sense of rejection which even mild disapproval makes them feel. They also conform strictly to certain specific useful customs which are like instruments for avoiding discord.

TALKING AND "TALKS"

I mention talking as an aid to peaceful social relations because it is so very much a part of the daily experience of the *!*Kung and, I believe, usefully serves three particular functions. It keeps up good open communication among the members of the band; through its constantly flowing expression it is a salutary outlet for emotions; and it serves as the principal sanction in social discipline. Songs are also used for social discipline. The *!*Kung say that a song composed specifically about someone's behaviour and sung to express disapproval, perhaps from the deepest shadow of the werf at night, is a very effective means of bringing people who deviate back into the pattern of approved behaviour. Nevertheless, during our observations, songs were not used as much as talking. If people disapprove of an individual's behaviour, they may criticize him or her directly, usually putting a question, "Why do you do that?" or they may gossip a bit or make oblique hints. In the more intense instances "a talk" may ensue.

The !Kung are the most loquacious people I know. Conversation in a !Kung werf is a constant sound like the sound of a brook, and as low and lapping, except for shrieks of laughter. People cluster together in little groups during the day, talking, perhaps making artifacts at the same time. At night families talk late by their fires, or visit at other family fires with their children between their knees or in their arms if the wind is cold.

There always seems to be plenty to talk about. People tell about events with much detail and repetition and discuss the comings and goings of their relatives and friends and make plans. Their greatest preoccupation and the subject they talk about most often, I think, is food. The men's imaginations turn to hunting. They converse musingly, as though enjoying a sort of day-dream together, about past hunts, telling over and over where game was found and who killed it. They wonder where the game is at present and say what fat bucks they hope to kill. They also plan their next hunts with practicality. Women (who, incidentally, do not talk as much as men) gave me the impression of talking more about who gave or did not give them food and their anxieties about not having food. They spoke to me about women who were remembered for being especially quick and able gatherers, but did not have pleasurable satisfaction in remembering their hot, monotonous, arduous days of digging and picking and trudging home with their heavy loads.

Another frequent subject of conversation is gift-giving. Men and women speak of the persons to whom they have given or propose to give gifts. They express satisfaction or dissatisfaction with what they have received. If someone has delayed unexpectedly long in making a return gift the people discuss this. One man was excused by his friends because his wife, they said, had got things into her hands and made him poor, so that he now had nothing suitable to give. Sometimes, on the other hand, people were blamed for being ungenerous ("far-hearted') or not very capable in managing their lives, and no one defended them for these defects or asked others to have patience with them.

As far as we know, only two general subjects are taboo in conversation. Men and women must not speak openly together of sexual matters except as they make jokes in the joking relationship. The !Kung avoid speaking the names of the gods aloud and do not converse about the gods for fear of attracting their attention and perhaps their displeasure. They told us their myths, but only when we asked them to. It is evidently not the habit of these Bushmen to recount the myths as they sit by their fires. They do not invent stories. They said they had no interest in hearing things that are not true and wonder why anybody has.

While a person speaks the listeners are in vibrant response, repeating the phrases and interposing a contrapuntal "eh". "Yesterday", "eh", "at Deboragu", "eh", "I saw old /Gaishay". "You saw Old /Gaishay", "eh, eh". "He said he had seen the great python under the bank." "EH!", "The PYTHON!" "He wants us", "eh, eh, eh", "to help him catch it". The "ehs" overlap and coïncide with the phrase and the people so often all talk at once that one wonders how anyone knows what the speaker has said.

Bursts of laughter accompany the conversations. Sometimes the !Kung laugh mildly with what I would call a sense of humour about people and events, often they shriek and howl as though laughter were an outlet for tension. They laugh at mishaps that happen to other people, like the lions eating up someone else's meat, and shriek over particularly telling and insulting sexual sallies in the joking relationship. Individual singing of lyrical songs, accompanied by the *//guashi*, or snatches of the medicine music, the playing of rhythmical games, the ceremonial dances themselves occupy the evenings, as well, but mostly the evening hours are spent in talk.

"A talk", as the !Kung call it, differs from a conversation or an arranged, purposeful discussion. It flares spontaneously, I believe from stress, when something is going on in which people are seriously concerned and in disagreement. I think that no formalities control it. Anyone who has something he wants to say joins in. People take sides and express opinions, accusing, denying, or defending persons involved. I witnessed one "talk" only, in 1952, which I mentioned before[3] and should mention again in this context. It occurred over a gift-giving episode at the time of !Nai's betrothal and involved persons in Bands 1 and 2 who were settled near together at the time. Khuan//a, the mother of /Gunda, !Nai's fiancé, had diverted a gift which people thought was making its way to Gao Medicine, the present husband of !Nai's mother. Instead of giving it to him at the time when an exchange of gifts was in order, she gave it to one of her relatives. !Nai's mother's sister, !U, sitting at her own scherm, began "the talk" by letting it be known what she thought of Khuan//a, in a voice loud enough to be heard in the two werfs, a startling contrast to the usual low flow of talk. Di!ai, !Nai's mother, sitting with her shoulder pressed against her sister's, joined in. People in the werfs went to sit at each other's scherms, forming little

[3] Lorna Marshall, "Marriage Among !Kung Bushmen", *Africa*, vol. xxix, no. 4 (Oct. 1959), pp. 352-3.

groups who agreed and supported each other. From where they sat, but not all at once and not in an excited babble, they made their remarks clearly, with quite long pauses between. Some expressed themselves in agreement with *!*U as she recounted Khuan//a's faults and deviations, past and present. Khuan//a's family and friends, who had moved to sit near her, denied the accusations from time to time, but did not talk as much or as loudly as *!*U. Khuan//a muttered or was silent. *!*U said she disapproved of her sister's daughter marrying the son of such a woman, but would reconsider her position if Khuan//a gave the expected gift to Gao Medicine. The talk lasted about twenty minutes. At that point Khuan//a got up and walked away and the "talk" subsided to *!*U's mutterings and others' low conversation. In a few days Khuan//a gave Gao Medicine a present, not the gift in question, but one which satisfied Gao, and, as they said, "they all started again in peace".

There is a third form of verbal expression which might be called a "shout" rather than a "talk", but as far as I know the *!*Kung have no special name for it. It is a verbal explosion. Fate receives the heat of the remarks in a 'shout".

We were present on two such occasions, one in 1952, the other in 1953. Both were in response to the burning of scherms. In both instances little children, whose mothers had taken their eyes off them though they were only a few feet away, had picked up burning sticks from the fire, had dropped them on the soft, dry bedding grass in the scherms and, at the first burst of flame, had sensibly run outside unscathed. On the first occasion, the two children, who were about three years old, were frightened and were soothed and comforted by their mothers and other relatives. They were not scolded. On the second occasion, Khuan//a, the two-year-old granddaughter of Old ≠ Toma and *!*Gam, had set fire to her grandparents' scherm. She was not apparently frightened at all and was found placidly chewing her grandfather's well-toasted sandal. She was not scolded either. What was especially interesting was the behaviour of the Bushmen. On both occasions they rushed to the burning scherms, shouting all at once, in extremely loud, excited voices, volcanic eruptions of words. The men made most of the noise, but the women were also talking excitedly. No one tried to do anything, nor could they, for the scherms burned like the fiery furnace. I asked the interpreters to stand close to one person at a time and try to hear what he said. People were telling where they had been when the fire started, why they had not got there sooner. They shouted that mothers should not take their eyes off their children, that the children might have been burned. They lamented the objects which had been destroyed – all in the greatest din I have ever heard humans produce out of themselves. It went on for about eight or ten minutes in bursts, then tapered off for another ten. While Old

≠ Toma's scherm was burning, he and his wife, *!* Gam, the great maker of beads, sat on one side weeping. After the shouting had subsided, a dozen or more people set about looking for Old ≠ Toma's knife blade and arrow points and picking up what beads they could find for *!* Gam in the cooling ashes. The two instances of "shouts" provided examples of the vehemence which vocal expression can have and vividly illustrated the *!* Kung way of venting emotion in words.

There is still another kind of talk, not conversation, which I consider to be an outlet for tension and anxiety. We happened to hear it only in relation to anxiety about food and do not know if other concerns sometimes find expression in this way. It occurs in varying degrees of intensity. It is a repeating of something over and over and over again. For instance, whether it is actually so or not, someone may be reiterating that he has no food or that no one has given him food. The remarks are made in the presence of other individuals, but the other individuals do not respond in the manner of a discussion or conversation. In an extreme instance we saw a woman visitor go into a kind of semi-trance and say over and over for perhaps half an hour or so in ≠ Toma's presence that he had not given her as much meat as was her due. It was not said like an accusation. It was said as though he were not there. I had the eerie feeling that I was present in someone else's dream. ≠ Toma did not argue or oppose her. He continued doing whatever he was doing and let her go on.

All these ways of talking, I believe, aid the *!* Kung in maintaining their peaceful social relations by keeping everyone in touch with what others are thinking and feeling, releasing tensions, and keeping pressures from building up until they burst out in aggressive acts.

From: *Africa*, 31 (1961), pp. 231-246. Only pp. 231-235 are presented here. Reprinted with permission.

Martin Joos

THE ISOLATION OF STYLES

This paper starts out from certain speech phenomena which have usually been named under two separate headings, and undertakes to unify them as far as possible by treating one of them as the independent variable or "cause", the other as the dependent variable or "effect" in popular terminology. The independent variable has been called "levels of usage" and the like; I call it "style". The dependent variable will be a large fraction of that variability which has been called "free variation" and "free alternation", including even "free" grammatical and lexical choices. The labeling as "independent" and "dependent" is from the viewpoint of the speaker; for the listener, of course, the resultant speech phenomena are stimuli from which he derives the "style" categories that governed the speaker. Switching from the speaker's to the listener's viewpoint then would seem to reverse the labels "independent" and "dependent", "cause" and "effect", between the two correlated categories. But for clarity in discussion it is expedient to adopt one of the two viewpoints as our standard; and the choice here is moreover clearly forced if we desire to prepare for further discussion from the "Transformation" standpoint which is becoming current today: then the speaker's viewpoint is the dominant one, and the listener's task is regarded as one of reconstruction, by trial and error, to match what the speaker presumably did straightforwardly.

The terms "free variation" and "free alternation" have been misunderstood by taking the word "free" in the sense that it has in the romantic theory of "free will". Actually, the word "free" is used in linguistics to mean merely "not yet accounted for". It is the technical label for whatever clearly does not need to be accounted for during the current operation in analysis; and to assume that it will never need to be accounted for in later operations would be a serious misunderstanding. A certain phenomenon might never be accounted for in your lifetime or mine, but the label "free" does not excuse us from trying. The descriptive linguist is committed to a deterministic philosophy; without determinism, he could never have gotten started, and having put his hand to the plow he can never turn back.

Naturally, the analyst can't explain everything at once and we are familiar with several things he does to relieve himself from doing so. In doing English phonology, he may observe an apical [s] here and a laminal [s] there; but he can easily convince himself that this has nothing to do with phonemics, so he relegates it to pre-linguistics and feels sure that it will never concern him later when he moves on into grammar and semantics. And the semantic agreement between /íygòw/ and /égòw/ (both *ego*) does not interfere with his establishing a phonemic difference; but this time he shifts the item along the line in the opposite direction, well aware that he may have to deal with it later on in "metalinguistics". Besides this line, along which he can shift items into the "past" or the "future" as he moves from pre-linguistics toward metalinguistics, sidewise directions have also been recognized recently, leading into such areas as the "vocalizations", associated systems which are not part of the "language" in the narrower sense but rather hitchhikers upon it. And all such things are "free" while we are working elsewhere.

I suppose that "style" in my sense of the term would belong to metalinguistics, and it might be wise to outline that area as thoroughly as possible before dealing with this category within it. Instead of doing that, I am going to try to make style define itself, by internal coherence among heterogeneous phenomena. Why "heterogeneous"? I will illustrate by starting out within phonology, taking the data at first entirely from my own speech.

One large group of my words, the *hut* group, always has the mid-central vowel-phoneme; but the quality varies, by "free variation", roughly from higher-mid to lower-mid. A second group, the *hot* group, always has the low-central phoneme, with qualities varying from much advanced to somewhat retracted from accurately central, but always without rounding. But then a third group, the *not* group (including *watch* and *probable* among others), has not only all the qualities of the *hot* group but also a much more retracted and noticeably rounded vowel; and this latter possibility is called "free alternation" as soon as we decide to assign the extra qualities to another phoneme, the low-back vowel-phoneme. In the *hut* and *hot* groups, with constant phoneme membership, we instead speak of "free variation".

Now consider the sentence *It's not hot*. The last two words may agree in vocalic quality, but only as long as this is within the range of variation of the *hot* group of words. The phenomena begin to be somewhat heterogeneous, though, when this *not* is in the low-back vowel-phoneme. True, the *hot* in such a sentence will then have a retracted quality (still unrounded, and less retracted than the *not* vowel then, thus still belonging to the low-central vowel-phoneme), and will not have an advanced variety of *hot* vowel: but this is heterogeneous to the extent that the retraction is phonemic in one word and not in the other.

Suppose we tried to describe this situation without departing farther from phonology than morphophonemics. We would then speak of a "long component" of rounding and retracting, affecting *hot* and *not* differently because they belong to different morphophonemic categories. But that would be only a tautology, not yet a correlation between two variables, because the component, considered as "cause", is homogeneous with the "effect". This is "pseudo-explanation".

Next we note that the lower-mid qualities in *hut* words occur in context with the low-back phoneme in *not* words; then the postulated long component would lower the *hut* vowel and retract the others, and this begins to be too heterogeneous to be a good tautology. But that is no loss, because it is on the road to being something that is worth more than a tautology.

We are forced to abandon the long component entirely, at least as a phonological component, when we notice that *Maybe not!* regularly has the *hot* phoneme, while *Perhaps not!* quite often has the low-back vowel-phoneme. (All these may be personal idiosyncrasies, but that isn't going to do any harm, I promise you.) Now it becomes almost compellingly attractive to postulate something else instead of a phonological long component. What I do is to say that in my "formal style" the vowel of *hut* is lower-mid and the *hot* and *not* words are retracted, the latter perhaps even phonemically, while my "casual style" has the opposite poles of these phonological differences; and *maybe* is my "casual" word while *perhaps* is a "formal" replacement thereof. And if an extrinsic explanation is wanted, we can say that these "styles" belong with what is called "set" in psychology, now that the rigors of pristine behaviorism have somewhat abated, so that it is even respectable to speak of "intentions". Still, that is psychology, not descriptive linguistics.

How could we define such "styles" entirely within the frame of reference of descriptive linguistics? Evidently, by showing that items identified by the usual descriptive criteria, as phonological items, grammatical items, lexical items, flock together in close context with each other to form groups of items which we should be willing to call stylistic groups or "styles". The number of styles must be finite, preferably rather small. The segregation of items into styles must be inexplicable by the criteria of phonology, by the criteria of grammar, by the criteria of semantics in the strict sense. Therefore the membership of each style-group of items must be linguistically heterogeneous; for if only phonological items, for example, were grouped together, that would only be more phonology, and similarly for the other types. The items forming the styles must not be all the linguistic items of the type in the language – the style-segregated items must not exhaust the speech-phenomena – otherwise this would be a segregation into distinct languages, or at least dialects, and that is not what we mean by "styles". The notion of "close context" had better not be defined in advance; obviously, the context must be larger than a grammatical construction, but small enough so that styles can shift within a conversation – that is one of the things we need the notion of "styles" for, namely so that we can say that a speaker has changed styles somewhere between two points in his discourse; and I suggest that the observation of many such events will define "close context" for us in due course, unless the whole theory collapses. That is to say, if we ever get a believable description of English styles, the several styles will be found to be correlated to an equal or greater number of sociologically definable occasions; presumably to a greater number of occasions, certainly not to a smaller number of occasions, for obvious reasons.

In the remainder of this paper, I am going to say more than I know for sure, of course, and less than I think I know. Tentatively, then, I recognized exactly five styles, which I have called 1. intimate, 2. casual, 3. consultative, 4. formal, and 5. frozen. It is routine to alternate, within a single discourse, between two styles which are neighbors on this scale; for example, a discourse which alternates between casual style and consultative style is a quite ordinary colloquial discourse, and familiar discourse alternates between casual and intimate styles. More artful speech, for example preaching, draws upon more than two basic styles, apparently, in extreme cases to such an extent as to make it unanalyzable for the present.

Having protected myself against counter-examples in this way, I proceed to list a few characteristic phenomena in various styles of American English. I start with consultative style, and from now on I am trying to mention only quite widespread phenomena instead of taking the items from my own speech. For a fairly pure sample of consultative style, see the conversation on typewriters in *The Structure of English*, by C. C. Fries, pp. 50-51. Nearly all the raw data in the Fries book are either consultative or casual – that is to say "colloquial" as mentioned above – and the consultative material predominates there. This is the most regular and most easily described of the English styles. It has got to be relatively regular, because it is the norm for conversations between strangers, where bafflement would be anti-social. If we undertake to describe all English systematically, we do well to describe consultative style first, then add modifications for the other styles. Therefore, consultative style has mostly negative markers – it is marked, so to say, by the absence of all those markers which are characteristic of the other styles individually. Still, a few positive markers of consultative style can be listed. By far the most conspicuous is the use, at fairly regular intervals, of brief insertions of speech by the person who is playing the role of "listener". These insertions nearly all belong to the list *yes, that's right, oh, I see, yeah, unhunh, o-oh, yes I know, well* (the last being used to reverse the roles between speaker and listener, so that it is not exactly an "insertion"). Other positive markers of consultative style are the all-purpose noun *thing*, the all-purpose preposition *on*, the measure-approximators *about* and *or so*, which protect fluency.

Every such marker not only has its "meaning" in the usual semantic sense, but also serves to define the style and thereby to define the social occasion the way the speaker wants that occasion to be, so that each marker has double function: it is part of the linguistic code, but it is also a label of the style – it is a code-label. The formal jokester may attempt to get a ludicrous picture out of *I'd like to see you on a typewriter*; the trained social animal simply takes *on* as the code-label for consultation.

The social occasion and its adequate style are dynamically correlated, of course: in one direction of this correlation, the speaker uses the style that suits the occasion; in the other direction, the speaker defines the occasion for the listener (and for himself) by his "choice" of style. This process is so important to man in society that the code-labels are among the most important items in speech. In this respect, the casual-style code-label *Come on!* is especially interesting because its meaning slides freely all along between the two poles of its double function, from "consider yourself among friends" as in *Come on, cheer up!* to "you're invited" as in *Come on, we're going to the pool.* I have not identified any other purely arbitrary code-label of casual style. But its systematic features are much easier to notice. These are especially (a) ellipsis and (b) slang. The ellipses of casual style are apparently ancient and historically stable. One is the absence of article at the beginning of a sentence: *Friend of mine saw it. Coffee's cold.* Another is the absence of subject at the beginning of a sentence: *Bought it yesterday. Makes no difference.* Then a conjugating auxiliary may also be absent: *Leaving? Seen John lately? Done it again!* A few resultant formulas have been promoted to consultative and even to formal style: *Thank you. Sorry!* Something like ellipsis is the use of minimum ("weak") stress where grammar would allow tertiary stress, with accompanying vowel-alternation, as in *c'n* /kin/ instead of *càn*

/kaæn/. In my consultative speech, the weak form is normal inside the clause, but the tertiary at its beginning; in my casual speech, the weak form is used in both places; in my formal speech, the tertiary both places:

Casual	*Consultative*	*Formal*
C'n I help you?	Can I help you?	Can/May I help you?
I c'n help you.	I c'n help you.	I can help you.

Parallel rules apply to most of the modals and conjugators; and because such words occur in such a large fraction of our clauses, even a fairly small sample of speech is easily classified as to style by these three accent-rules. In contrast to the stable ellipses, slang performs the same social-intergration functions by virtue of being ephemeral; there is no room here for discussing this in detail.

Many of us in our colloquial styles have a distinction in meaning between *That's not enough* "That is insufficient" and *That isn't enough* "That is not quite sufficient", and similarly in general: full *not* modifies the following text, but *n't* negates the whole predication. All such distinctions are wiped out by the formal ban on weak forms; thus both these sentences are replaced by formal *That is not enough.* A long chapter could be written on the numerous defects of formal style resulting from such neglect of elementary patterns. Another sample is that *He was wounded* is required to carry both the meanings of colloquial *He was wounded (when he arrived at the hospital)* and *He got wounded.* Further, formal speech discourages those insertions by which a consultative listener keeps the speaker informed of the effectiveness of his speech. Therefore, formal speech can not be automatic, as colloquial speech easily may be; formal discourse is always clumsy unless the speaker has been thoroughly trained and watches himself carefully. Accordingly, formal speech is little used for socially important purposes; it is pretty well restricted to the imparting of information, a rather antisocial act.

The leading code-label of formal American English seems to be the word *may*, otherwise little used, to replace both *might* and *can: That may cause trouble.* In some areas, *should* replaces *ought to.* And so on. Also, Latinisms are at home in formal style, for instance interrogative adverbial phrases at sentence-beginning: *From whom did you get it* "Who did you get it from?" A very common and often troublesome formalism is automatically to put an adverb before its infinitive instead of inside or after the infinitive. The list could easily be extended by copying from old-fashioned rhetoric books. But the schools can't always be held directly responsible for our formalisms. Half-educated people who have learned that formal style is syntactically more elaborate will always be capable of cultivating elaboration without school guidance: *for the puspose of* instead of *for*, and so on.

Intimate style and frozen style must remain without discussion here for lack of timc. The samples given from the three central styles ought to be enough to show what this is all about. But one negative specification might as well be added: these styles of course have only the most accidental sort of connection with what is commonly called "correctness".

From: *Monograph Series on Languages and Linguistics (Georgetown University)*, 12 (1959), pp. 107-113. Reprinted with permission.

Susan M. Ervin-Tripp

AN ANALYSIS OF THE INTERACTION OF LANGUAGE, TOPIC AND LISTENER

In this paper we shall examine some of the characteristics of sociolinguistic research, and illustrate with a detailed example.[1] The companion field of psycholinguistics (Osgood and Sebeok 1954; Saporta 1961) has concentrated heavily on individual psychology: perception, learning, individual differences, pathology. Social psychology has appeared primarily in attitude studies (Osgood *et al.* 1957: 189-216), not in psycholinguistic research concerning socialization and acculturation, or small group and institutional behavior. Thus, in the very fields which overlap most with sociology and sociolinguistics, psycholinguistic research is least developed.

Sociolinguists study verbal behavior in terms of the relations between the setting, the participants, the topic, the functions of the interaction, the form, and the values held by the participants about each of these (Hymes 1962: 25). Verbal behavior (talk and its equivalents) is the center of this definition, but of course a complete description of the system must include gestures or pictures when they are functional alternatives to linguistic signs. Verbal behavior is everywhere structured as a highly cohesive system, and therefore it is a convenient starting point. Others might want to deal with a larger set of communicative acts including, for instance, the dance, and exchange of tangible objects.

[1] The point of view and the sources in this article have both been enriched by discussions with Dell Hymes and John Gumperz. The study of Japanese bilinguals mentioned below was supported by the National Science Foundation. The author is especially grateful to Yaeko Nishijima Putzar and Naomi Litt Quenk for their work on this project.

SETTING

We shall use the term *setting* here in two senses, that of *locale*, or time and place, and that of *situation*, including the "standing behavior patterns" (Barker and Wright 1954: 45-46) occurring when people encounter one another. Thus situations include a family breakfast, a faculty meeting, a party, Thanksgiving dinner, a lecture, a date. Social situations may be restricted by cultural norms which specify the appropriate participants, the physical setting, the topics and functions of discourse, and the style. Obviously, situations vary as to which of these restrictions exist and the degree of permissible variation, so that a sermon may allow less style variation than a party. By altering any of these features, one might either create a reaction of social outrage, change the situation to a new one (date becomes job interview), or enter a situation lacking strong normative attributes, and allowing maximal variation.

One of the major problems for sociolinguists will be the discovery of independent and reliable methods for defining settings. The folk taxonomy of a given society (Conklin 1962: 120) might provide lexical categories for the definition of settings. However, the folk taxonomy may be too gross or too fine to indicate classifications of value to the social scientist. The high degree of regularity of elliptical constructions in waiter-to-cook request forms suggests that there is a setting class for which there is no common name in English. Thanksgiving and Christmas dinner behavior has common properties though we have no generally accepted superordinate terms for both events.

Joos (1962: 13) has given a classification of five major setting varieties in his own cultural system; these he defines by style types as intimate, casual, consultative, formal, and frozen. The fact that only the first two correspond to common usage suggests that the folk taxonomy may be inadequate for the level of generality Joos sought. It would be desirable to couch the discriminanda of settings in terms permitting cross-cultural comparisons. Joos' hypothesis (1962: 10) that all "national languages" have five styles is testable only if the division of types he described is not arbitrary.

PARTICIPANTS

For most sociolinguistic analyss the important features of participants will be sociological attributes. These include the participants' status in the society, in terms such as sex, age, and occupation; their roles relative to one another, such as an employer and his employee, a husband and his wife; and roles specific to the social situation, such as hostess-guest, teacher-pupil, and customer-salesgirl.

In any act of communication, there is a "sender" and a "receiver" (Hymes 1962: 25) who together may be called interlocutors. In addition, there may be present an audience which is not the primary addressee of the message. The role of sender, or speaker, is rarely distributed in equal time to all participants. There appear to be four factors which affect the amount of talking of each participant. One factor is the situation. In informal small-group conversation the roles of sender and receiver may alternate; in a sermon the sender role is available to only one participant; in choral responses in a ritual, or in a question period following a lecture, the role of sender is allocated at specific times. A second, related, determinant of the amount of talking is the role the participant has in the group and his social and physical centrality. He may be a therapy patient, chairman, teacher, or switchboard operator, so that his formal role requires communication with great frequency; he may informally play such a role, as in the case of a raconteur, or an expert on the topic at hand. There is a personal constant carried from group to group. The net effect of the second and third factors is that the sending frequency of participants in a group is almost always unequal, and has been shown to have regular mathematical properties in informal discussion groups (Stephan and Mishler 1952; Bales and Borgatta 1955). Because relative frequency of speaking is steeply graded, not evenly distributed, in a large group the least frequent speaker may get almost no chances to speak. The "receiver" role also is unequally distributed even in face-to-face groups, being allocated to the most central, the most powerful, those with highest status, the most frequent speakers, and under conditions where agreement is desired, the most deviant (Hare 1962: 289; Schachter 1951).

TOPIC

The manifest content or referent of speech is here called the topic. Topically equivalent sentences may be different in form so that topic is maintained through a paraphrase or translation. Compare these two sentences paraphrased from Watson and Potter (1962: 253):

"Every episode of conversation has a focus of attention."
"There is a single topic in each homogeneous unit of interaction."

In the terms of Watson and Potter's definitions, these sentences are topically equivalent. Also equivalent are the following: "Shut up!" "Please be quiet." "Tais-toi."

Topic includes both gross categories such as subject matter (economics, household affairs, gossip), and the propositional content of utterances. It is the topic which is the concern of cognitive structure studies such as those of kin systems, which differentiate "grandmother" and "mother" but not "mother" and "mommy".

Obviously some expressive speech (ouch!) and some routines (hi!) do not have a manifest topic. Such contentless speech could usually be replaced by gestures. In traditional treatments of language, topic is considered essential and typical because of its absence in most non-human and non-linguistic communication. It seems more appropriate to consider referential speech as simply one sub-category of speech. Topically dissimilar utterances or utterances with and without referential content can be functional equivalents. From a functional standpoint, the following could be equivalents in some situations:

"I'm sorry" = "Excuse me."
"Hi" = "How are you."

FUNCTIONS OF THE INTERACTION

Within a given setting, verbal discourse may vary in function. We use "function" to refer to the effect on the sender of his actions. Skinner (1957: 2) has pointed out that in its social uses language may be viewed as operant (rewarded or punished) behavior, which affects the speaker through the mediation of a hearer. The distinction between topic and function is similar to the one between manifest and latent content, as employed in content analysis. A difference is that since in many speech situations the addressee is known, and subsequent behavior of the sender is known, it is more often possible to delineate functions in ordinary speech than in the texts for which content analysis often is employed.

The following system was developed to account for the initiation of dyadic interactions. It is not intended to cover continuous discourse, but merely initiations. The criterion of classification was the hearer response which could terminate the interaction to the satisfaction of the initiator.

a. *Requests for goods, services, or information.*
The overt behavior of the hearer is manipulated, e.g. "What time is it?", "Please pass the potatoes", "Slow down!"

b. *Requests for social responses.*
The desired hearer reactions are often not explicit or even consciously known to the speaker. The subcategories often used are those derived from Murray's need system (1938: 315) which includes recognition, dominance, self-abasement, nurturance, affiliation. Behaviorally, overt hearer responses which might be elicited are applause, sympathetic words, laughter, a hug, or an angry retort, but often

hearer reactions are covert, e.g. "What a gorgeous dress you're wearing!", "A weird thing happened to me today", "You're a fool."

c. *Offering information or interpretation.*
Spontaneous instruction evidently based on the belief the hearer would be gratified to learn. Analogous to spontaneous offer of goods or services, e.g. "That's Orion", "Did you hear about the fire?"

d. *Expressive monologues.*
Expressions of joy, sorrow, anger, talking to oneself, muttering. The sender reacts to an external stimulus, a feeling, or a problem, without attending to the hearer's comments, which may be minimal or absent.

e. *Routines.*
Greetings, thanks, apologies, offers of service by waitresses and salespeople, where the alternatives are extremely restricted, and hence predictable.

f. *Avoidance conversations.*
Conversation is started only because the alternative activity is unpleasant or the sender is satiated; any hearer will do, and topics are highly variable. Water-cooler conversations in an office, coffee breaks during study sessions, bus-stop discourse.

A somewhat similar system was developed by Soskin and John (1963) to classify all the utterances in natural conversations. Their system, for instance, differentiates "signones" in which the speaker describes his own state or opinions, from "regnones" in which he tries to influence another's behavior. They point out that "signones" such as "I'm still thirsty" or "that tasted good" may in a benign and nurturant environment be used "as a consciously manipulative act". In purely functional terms, such "signones" are requests for goods, services, or information. Thus Soskin and John's classification seems in part to be formal. It is important to treat form separately from function just because there may be systematic discrepancies between manifest and latent function, as indicated in these examples. This point will be discussed further in the next section.

Because functions may not always be explicit, one way to discern latent functions is to examine the sender's reaction to various outcomes. The reason we know that "Got a match?" is sometimes a social demand rather than a demand for a match is that the speaker may go on chatting even if he fails to get a match. If he primarily wanted the match he would go elsewhere for one. Avoidance conversations are typically masked in the manifest content of other function classes. Small children at bed-time may make plausible requests; these could be unmasked if a functionally equivalent alternative response were given, for instance, if one brought crackers in response to a glass of water. Certain conversational functions perhaps must always be masked in a given society; others must be masked for certain receivers or in certain settings. Masking permits functional ambiguity. A woman's remark to her escort, "It's cold outside tonight", might either be an expressive monologue or a request for his coat. Presumably such ambiguity may lead to social embarrassment because of differences in interpretation by speaker and hearer.

FORMAL FEATURES OF COMMUNICATION

The form of communication may be viewed as having four aspects. The *channel* might be spoken language, writing, telegraphic signals, etc. As we have indicated, gestural signals on occasion may be systematic alternatives to speech and in such cases are part of the significant verbal exchange. The *code* or *variety* consists of a systematic set of linguistic signals which co-occur in defining settings. For spoken languages alternative codes may be vernaculars or superposed varieties. *Sociolinguistic variants* are those linguistic alternations linguists regard as free variants or optional variants within a code, that is, two different ways of saying the same thing. *Non-linguistic vocal signals* include the range of properties called paralinguistic (Trager 1958; Pittenger *et al.* 1960) which lack the arbitrary properties of linguistic signals.

Linguists have been concerned primarily with codes rather than with the other three classes of formal variation. A discussion of code distinctions especially pertinent to social variations can be found in Gumperz (1961, 1962). He distinguishes between the *vernacular*, the speech used within the home and with peers, and the *superposed variety* which is "the norm in one or more socially definable communication situations". Superposed varieties include many types, from occupational argots to koines used for trade and regional communication, such as Melanesian Pidgin and Swahili. A special type of vernacular-koine relation exemplified in Greece, German Switzerland, Arab countries, and China, has been called *diglossia* by Ferguson (1959). These all are illustrations of code variations.

A speaker in any language community who enters diverse social situations normally has a repertoire of speech alternatives which shift with situation. Yet linguists have generally focussed on relatively pure codes. They do this by trying to control the speech situation with the informant and to keep him from using borrowed forms without identifying them. They also may seek out monolinguals who have mastered only one vernacular, and whose speech constitutes therefore a recognizable norm (though not necessarily a highly valued norm in the larger community).

Language communities label some alternative varieties, especially those which either are different enough to interfere with intelligibility, or are identified with specific social groups. "Folk linguistics" of dialect perception and of classification into language and dialect taxonomies bears on the values attached to speaking in a certain way. As Weinreich has pointed out, "accent" perception is systematically biased (1953: 21).

It may sometimes be difficult to isolate the features of superposed varieties, because they normally co-exist in a single speaker and therefore may interpenetrate. One must seek defining situations demanding rigid adherence to a code (as in prayers) to isolate the features of the code. These may be hard to find in societies like our own with great tolerance for stylistic variability in a given situation. Where the formal difference in varieties is great, as in some diglossias, interpenetration may be more effectively inhibited. Obviously, where code-switching and interpenetration or borrowing are permissible, they become available to mark role and topic shifts within a setting (Gumperz 1964a).

Sociolinguistic variants have received very little attention. Examples are the systematic array of deletions available in answers and requests, as in "Coffee", vs. "Would you give me some coffee, please?"

Request sentences provide some excellent examples of formal variation with functional and topical equivalence. If we use Soskin and John's six categories (1963), we find that requests could take any form, as in the following examples:

"It's cold today." (structone)
"Lend me your coat." (regnone) (Also "would you mind lending...?")
"I'm cold." (signone)
"That looks like a warm coat you have." (metrone)
"Br-r-r." (expressive)
"I wonder if I brought a coat." (excogitative)

We could also classify these utterances by more conventional grammatical terms, as declarative, imperative, and interrogative.

It is clear that the selection of these alternatives is not "free" but is conditioned by both situational and personal factors. Student observations have shown that the imperative form is used most often to inferiors in occupational settings, and more often for easy than difficult or unusual services. The yes-no question is the most typical request form to superiors. Informants regarding cross-cultural differences have reported great variation in the "normal" request form to employees, in such cases of alternatives as:

"There's dust in the corner" vs. "Sweep the dust from the corner."
"It's haying time" vs. "Start the haying tomorrow."

Morphological as well as syntactic options may be available as sociolinguistic variants, as illustrated by Fischer's analysis (1958) of the alternation between the participial suffixes /in/ and /iŋ/. Obviously the choice of referential synonyms (Conklin 1962) is socially conditioned, as anyone reflecting on English synonyms for body functions will recognize. In fact, the number of referential synonyms may be indicative of the complexity of attitudes towards the referent. Brown and Ford (1961) have observed that the number of terms of address in America is usually directly related to intimacy, nicknames and endearments permitting marking of attitude variations.

The intercorrelation of these variables has been demonstrated in a variety of studies. The following are illustrative:

1. *Participant-function-form.* Basil Bernstein (1962) has discovered systematic differences between middle-class and working-class adolescent conversation groups in England. These may be summarized as greater emphasis on offering information and interpretation in middle-class groups and on requests for social responses in working-class groups. The effects on form of these function differences were great. The middle-class boys used fewer personal pronouns, a greater variety of adjectives, a greater variety of subordinate conjunctions, more complex syntax, and more pauses.

2. *Participant-form.* Charles Ferguson (1964), has pointed out that in many languages there is a style peculiar to the situation of an adult addressing an infant. The common formal features may include a change in lexicon, simplification of grammar, and formation of words by reduplications, simplifying of consonant clusters, and general labialization.

Brown and Gilman (1960) examined many aspects both contemporary and historical of the selection of "tu" and "vous" in French address, and the corresponding terms in Italian and German. They found that the selection was based primarily on the relation of sender and receiver, and that historically the selection had been based on relative power, whereas currently relative intimacy is more important. They found national differences, such as greater emphasis on kin-intimacy in Germany and on camaraderie in France and Italy. They also found that personality and ideology influenced individual differences in the sender's selection.

Joan Rubin (1962) found that the choice of Spanish or Guaraní for address in Paraguay was desirable in terms of the same set of dimensions – "solidarity" and "power" or status, and sometimes setting. She gives the example of the use of Spanish by men courting women, and the switch to Guaraní with marriage. Thus in a multilingual society a code shift can mark the same contrasts as a sociolinguistic variation in a single language.

Another kind of participant-form study is illustrated by Putnam and O'Hern's analysis (1955) of the relation between social status, judged by sociological indices, and linguistic features of speech in a Negro community in Washington, D. C. This study has many similarities in method to dialect geography, but adds a procedure of judge's blind ratings of status from tapes, to make a three-way comparison possible between objective status, perceived status, and specific features. Labov (1964), gives a sophisticated analysis of a status-form relation.

3. *Function-setting.* A comparison of interactions of a nine-year-old boy at camp and at home, by Gump, Schoggen and Redl (1963) showed systematic functional changes even in such a sub-category as interactions addressed to adults. The percentage of "sharing" (which was primarily verbal) was higher at camp, and the percentage of "submissive" and "appeal" behavior toward adults was higher at home. Sharing included asking opinion, playing with an adult, competing, telling a story. The child's shifts in behavior may have been effects of the variations in adult-initiated interaction.

Soskin and John (1963: 265) used a set of categories which were partially functional in analyzing tapes of a couple on vacation, and showed significant variations with setting. Explicitly directive utterances were most frequent by the wife in the cabin, and by the husband out rowing, where he gave her instructions. Informational utterances were most common for both at meal times.

4. *Topic-form.* In a study of New England children, John Fischer (1958) collected evidence of several factors related to the alternation of the participial suffix /iŋ/ vs. /in/. He found the selection to depend on sender ("typical" vs. "good" boy), and on topic of discourse. He heard "visiting", "correcting", and "reading" vs. "swimmin", "chewin", and "hittin". The topical distribution suggests that behind the alternation by topic lies an alternation by participants, with /iŋ/ being heard from adults, especially teachers, and /in/ being heard from peers.

John Gumperz (1946b), describes the effects of topic on the alternation in Norway between a rural dialect and standard North Norwegian. He found that the type of formal alternation depended on the social properties of the group of addressees.

5. *Setting-form.* Changes of form with setting have been frequently described. Some excellent examples of a shift between a spoken dialect and a superposed variety are provided by Ferguson (1959), for example the shift from classical to colloquial Arabic which accompanies a shift from formal lecturing to discussion in a classroom. Herman (1961) has given a number of examples of the influence of setting on code selection in Israel, pointing out that immigrants speak Hebrew more often in public than in private situations.

Sociolinguistic variations and paralinguistic features were noted by Andrea Kaciff and Camille Chamberlain who compared children's speech in a pre-school playground with their role-playing in a playhouse. The material was reported in an unpublished term paper. They found certain lexical changes, such as the use of role-names in address: "Go to sleep, baby, say goo-goo." They found that the children playing the role of the mother adopted a sing-song intonation especially when rebuking the play child. This intonation was not used by the children except in imitative play, and had been observed by another student in a study of adults' speech to other people's children.

In ordinary social life all of these interacting variables tend to vary together. The public setting of the Israeli immigrants included a different audience than the private setting; the address of adults to children is different in participants, topics, and form at once. In using naturalistic situations, we can discern the critical factors in determination of alternations only if we can find in nature comparisons in which other possibly relevant factors are held constant. An example is lecturing vs. class discussion in diglossia, where the topics and participants and functions may remain the same but only the situation changes, and with it the form. Where it is not possible to find such orderly experimental situations, an appropriate sequel to the ethnographic method is the social experiment. We shall describe one below.

A JAPANESE BILINGUAL EXPERIMENT

Bilingual speech is convenient to study because the formal changes are vividly apparent. There are many forms of social relation between two language communities. American immigrants, for example, range through a wide spectrum in the diversity of function-language distributions. At one extreme might be an old storekeeper in Chinatown. He rarely needs any knowledge of English except to ask limited-response questions of his customers, or to tell the cost of an item. On the whole, he is like a tourist with request forms and a vocabulary limited to the goods or services exchanged. If he employs English in restricted settings, he may succeed in communicating with a minimum of knowledge of English grammar or phonology.

At the opposite extreme are immigrants who have married Americans and raised families here. They typically vary widely in the functional distribution of their use of English, frequently employing English for as many uses as their native language at home before. The limitations in their use of English occur in certain aspects of the code. They may have gaps in their English vocabulary, reflecting differential exposure, for instance, to rural life in the two countries. They may have difficulties learning a new sound system after adolescence; it is clear that aptitude, personality, and perhaps willingness to lose one's identity as a foreigner vary. Japanese women, for example, often do not respect Nisei, and may not wish to be taken for Nisei. Yet it is common to find women who have extensive mastery of the vocabulary and grammar of English, and whose English dominance is so great that they may be unable to speak their native tongue without intrusions at all levels from English.

The first step in the experimental study of Japanese-American speech in terms of the topic-audience-language correlations was an ethnographic description of their covariance, based on informant interviews. Thousands of Japanese women marry Americans every year, and come to this country to live and to raise their American offspring. In the San Francisco area, they are generally isolated socially from the American Japanese who seem un-Japanese to them, from the immigrant Japanese, who are older and of rural backgrounds, and from the temporary officials and business personnel from Japan. Usually they do not live in areas with Japanese shops. As a result of their isolation, they use Japanese in three situations: visits to Japan; jobs (for some) in Japanese restaurants; and talks with bilingual friends. The women who took part in the study usually had friends who were also "war brides". These were their confidantes, their recourse when worried. With these friends, in Japanese, they reminisced about Japan, discussed news from home, gossiped; Japanese was the language of social interchange and expressive monologues.

By contrast, the functions of English covered a range varying for different women. For all, it was the language for talking of goods and services, for shopping. In a few marriages, the husband was a companion and confidant, teaching a large variety of English words, teaching about American activities and values, discussing many topics. Such women had learned the subtleties of social interchange in English. In other families, the absence of the husband at sea, or his silence, left the wife with little occasion to use English at home. One woman who spoke little English at the time of her marriage reported that the couple "spoke the language of the eyes". It is quite clear that there was not an equivalent distribution of functions for Japanese and English for most of the women interviewed.

The women spoke English primarily with their husbands, children, and neighbors. We would expect that when they spoke English the content would reflect the objects, experiences, and points of view encountered in this country. With their Japanese friends, language shifted with topic – American food, clothing, and husbands being discussed in English, and matters Japanese or personal concerns being discussed in

Japanese. Some reported never using English with Japanese friends except when the husbands were present, a situation presumably altering the topical distribution of conversations.

LANGUAGE AND CONTENT

Our first hypothesis is that as language shifts, content will shift. This hypothesis was tested earlier for French and American content (Ervin 1964; Lambert 1963). In this case, we have the explicit hypothesis that wherever monolingual American women and Japanese women tested in Japan differ in content, the bilingual women will tend to show an analogous content shift with language, even though the situations are otherwise identical. A Japanese interviewer saw each woman twice in the same setting, and tape recorded the sessions. At the first, only Japanese was used, and at the second, only English. Verbal materials employed were word associations, sentence completions, semantic differentials, problem stories, and Thematic Apperception Tests.

Here are some illustrative examples, the speaker being the same for the Japanese and English. Where the American and Japanese monolingual comparison groups gave a particular item uniquely or more frequently than the other language group, the word is marked with (A) or (J).

MOON: (Japanese) moon-viewing (J), zebra-grass (J), full moon (J), cloud (J)
(English) sky (A), rocket (A), cloud (J)

NEW YEARS DAY: (Japanese) pine decoration (J), rice-cake (J), feast (J), kimono (J), seven-spring-herbs (J), shuttlecock (J), tangerine (J), foot-warmer (J), friends (A)
(English) new clothes, party (A), holidays (A)

TEA: (Japanese) bowl (J), saucer (A), green (J), tea-cake (J), tea-ceremony (J)
(English) teapot, kettle, tea leaf (A), party (A), green tea (J), lemon (A), sugar (A), cookies (J)

Similar contrasts may be illustrated with sentence completions. The informants heard (and read) the first half of the sentence. The same woman's responses in both languages are cited below:

1. WHEN MY WISHES CONFLICT WITH MY FAMILY...
   (Japanese) It is a time of great unhappiness.
   (English) I do what I want.
2. I WILL PROBABLY BECOME ...

(Japanese) a housewife.
(English) a teacher.

3. REAL FRIENDS SHOULD . . .
(Japanese) help each other.
(English) be very frank.

On the last point, many women mentioned in attitude interviews that they particularly admired the frankness of American women.

It was found that when the sentences were weighted by their frequency in the American and Japanese monolingual comparison groups, the bilingual women's sentences were significantly less "Japanese" in content when the women spoke English. This change in content could not be simulated by women who did not change language but were instructed to give "typically Japanese" or "typically American" answers at the two sessions. Thus the change in the associations and the sentence completions is an effect of language, and not of self-instruction or set.

In the preceding experiment, everything was held constant except language, and the effects of a specified language on content were examined. It was expected that in the relatively abnormal situation of a Japanese woman forced to speak English to another Japanese woman, content typical of conversations between Americans would more often appear. This shift presumably would reflect English discourse with neighbors and husband and thematic material from the English mass media.

PARTICIPANT AND FORM

In a second experiment, the receiver was changed in each session, but the language was consistently English. The women were interviewed either by a Caucasian American or by a Japanese interviewer. Again, the women were in an abnormal situation when they were asked to speak English with another Japanese woman. The effects on the style of English were clear when the two situations were compared. With the Japanese listener, there was much more disruption of English syntax, more intrusion of Japanese words, and briefer speech.

A Japanese person provides an imperfect model of English, and as a listener is tolerant of and can understand Japanese intrusions. On the whole, the Japanese women are very tolerant of interpenetration of the two languages. We had found with French in the United States that those who had frequent discourse with other bilinguals had the highest incidence of borrowing of each language in the other (Ervin 1955). Thus we can say that bilinguals who speak only with other bilinguals may be on the road to merger of the two languages, unless there are strong pressures to insulate by topic or setting.

TOPIC AND FORM

In this experiment, it is possible to compare topics within each interview. In the word-associations, a stimulus word might be considered a topic. We know that some topics are more closely connected with life in the United States, others with Japan. For example, "love", "marriage", and "kitchen" have American associations for these women. On the other hand, "mushroom" and "fish" and "New Year's Day" are strongly associated with Japanese life. When we weighted the English responses according to their frequency in the monolingual norm groups in Japan and the United States, it appeared that the war brides were closer to American women when associating to "love", "marriage", and "kitchen" but closer to Japanese women for the other three topics. This was true even though, as we have seen, these "Japanese" topics elicited less characteristically Japanese content when the language used was English, not Japanese.

In one part of the interview, the informants were asked to explain or describe, in English, a set of 14 topics. The topics designed to be associated with English were the husband's work and leisure activities, American housekeeping, American cooking, and shopping for food and clothing here. Another set of topics was designed to be more frequent in Japanese: Japanese festivals, Japanese New Year's Day, Japanese cooking and housekeeping, Doll Festival, and street story-tellers. The last two topics in each set were accompanied with photographs of the event to be described.

From this procedure we found that it was not the receiver alone, nor the topic alone, which affected speech but a specific combination of the two. When the informants were instructed to speak English, they had difficulty only when they spoke of Japanese topics. The combination of a Japanese receiver and a Japanese topic almost always demands the use of Japanese in a normal situation. The effect of artificially violating this rule was that the women's speech was disrupted. They borrowed more Japanese words, had more disturbed syntax, were less fluent, and had more frequent hesitation pauses. Thus a simple change in the topic and listener had a marked effect on the formal features of speech even though the most obvious formal change, a switch of code, was not allowed.

In the analysis both of content and form changes, we had assumed that a bilingual is like two monolinguals with a single nervous system. The differences in two settings or audiences of a bilingual are viewed as extensions of the differences in monolinguals. But there are limits to this simplified explanation. One is a cognitive limit. There are reasons to believe that it is very hard to maintain in one nervous system two category systems with only slight differences between them. This is true whether it be a semantic system such as color terminology (Ervin 1961) or a phonemic system (Gumperz 1962). Thus there are pressures constantly towards a merger of the two systems of the bilingual. Also, the very fact that a larger repertoire of alternative behavior is available to the bilingual makes him a victim of the special signs of response-competition, such as hesitation pauses and less fluency.

The second limit to this explanation lies in the very functional specialization we mentioned before. No bilingual, however fluent in two languages, has exactly equivalent experiences in both language communities. One may have been learned at home, one at school. One may have been learned in childhood, the other in adolescence. Perhaps now one is used at work and one in the family. Even in multilingual communities such as those of India and Switzerland, some specialization exists. Robert Lowie, who grew up in a German-speaking family in the United States, reported a deliberate effort to keep an equivalent vocabulary (1945). He failed, for he could not control the difference in frequency or social context for the lexicon he required.

Thus, we cannot expect that a woman whose direct experience as a wife and mother was entirely in the United States would have, even when speaking Japanese, quite the same content as a woman in Japan. Her familiarity with these domains of life will be second-hand in some sense. In the same way, a woman who has never raised children in the United States will have most of the domain of meaning involving childhood much more fully developed in Japanese.

Finally, to the extent that the norms for Japanese and American monolingual behavior are current, they misrepresent the realities of contact, for these Japanese women know the Japan of five or ten years ago, not rapidly-changing contemporary Japan and its language.

METHODS IN SOCIOLINGUISTICS

If we examine the research which satisfies our definition of sociolinguistics, we find the methods used appear to be of four general types:

1. *Studies of the speech of social groups.* It has long been a practice among linguists and sociologists to study certain properties of the speech (usually the code) of pre-defined classes of speakers. We have, for example, studies reporting homosexual jargon (Cory 1952: 103-113) and thieves' jargon (Sutherland 1937). Dialect atlas studies have selected speakers by geographical criteria and mapped the distribution of selected code features such as special lexicon (e.g. spider vs. frying-pan) and pronunciation (e.g. /griysiy/ vs. /griyziy/). Traditionally none of these

studies takes the larger social community as a unit; speakers are selected out of context, and we may not know whether their speech varies with setting or receiver. We might expect, for instance, that "criminals" might use different speech to judges, parole officers, patrolmen, and cell-mates, and Sutherland reports that this is the case (1937).

2. *Ethnographic studies.* A form of study discussed in detail by Hymes (1962) would employ traditional methods of observation and interview to study when speech is used at all, and variations according to setting and participants. Naturalistic observations such as those of Barker and Wright (1954), Barker (1963), Watson and Potter (1962), Coser (1960) and Newman (1955) have ranged widely over the inter-correlational problems we have mentioned earlier. However, the draw-back of such studies is that normally there is so much variation at once that we can find descriptive information about distributions but little definitive knowledge of which of the co-varying features may be effective. In the paper of Gump, Schoggen, and Redl (1963), for instance, a child's behavior in two social settings was compared – but the settings involved different participants, different activities, and different physical surroundings. The authors point out that the child changed his forms of interaction, but it is not clear that this would have happened had his family been transported to a camp setting.

3. *Experimental studies.* Inevitably, experiments set up artificial situations. That is just their purpose, for they allow artificial constraints on normal co-variance, permitting us for example to control the social composition of juries (Strodtbeck *et al.* 1957), the size of the group (Bales and Borgatta 1955), or the power relation of participants (Cohen 1958) without varying any other significant features. Such studies would normally be based first on ethnographic research to explore the distribution of speech in the natural community so that extrapolation might be made to the artificial situation.

4. *Distribution of forms.* One can start with the analysis of formal alternatives and employ any of the above methods to study the determinants of the alternation. Fischer (1958), Brown and Gilman (1960), and Brown and Ford (1961) have done just this. This kind of study lends itself to a form of analysis we might call the description of equivalence patterns. For example, in some languages, the stylistic alternation which occurs when a man speaks to his superior rather than to a peer is similar to the alternation which occurs when a woman speaks to a man rather than to another woman. This is just a fragment of what is undoubtedly a wider set of corresponding alternations. If we looked at all societies in which such sets of correspondences occur, they might have common features, such as inferior ascribed status for women.

Another example is suggested by the distribution of the features of baby talk. The alternation which accompanies speech to adults vs. speech to infants has some similarities to the alternations between neutral vs. affectionate speech between intimates. Should this relation turn out to be universal, we might hunt for manipulable variables to test the psychological basis of the correspondence. If it is not universal, we need to know what systematic differences have individual analogues that can be studied (the baby-talk user vs. the non-baby-talk user).

These equivalence structures in verbal behavior are similar to the lexical classes which so interest cognitive theorists, for similarity in formal verbal behavior implies testable similarities in other types of behavior such as perception, memory, or emotional response.

This treatment of sociolinguistics has placed the face-to-face verbal encounter at the center of the definition. In contrast, a macroscopic approach to sociolinguistics might consider codes rather than finer formal contrasts, societal functions (such as education or law) rather than individual functions, institutionally classified settings (such as churches and mass media) rather than finer differentiations of setting in local communities, and values about language use as expressed in administrative actions and political behavior rather than merely in community norms and attitudes toward speakers of particular languages or dialects.

If one examines the generalizations in the studies we have cited, we find that frequently they are special instances of more general social or psychological propositions. Brown and Ford (1961), for instance, noted that changes in address forms are expected to be initiated by the higher status participant; probably all respect behavior is so. Herman (1961) explicitly couched his study of multilingual code-switching in a broader framework of a theory of choice behavior.

Yet language is distinct in certain respects. Unlike other formally coded social behavior it can have semantic content. The internal imitations of external speech constitute a kind of portable society, both the voice of conscience and a categorization system, promoting socialization even of private behavior. Most of the uniquely human forms of social behavior are dependent on shared language, so that the structure of language use in society may be related to societal functioning in unique ways. If this is the case, sociolinguistics will contribute a new dimension to the social sciences rather than provide further exemplifications of the otherwise known.

REFERENCES CITED

Bales, R. F., and Borgatta, E.F.
1955 "A study of group size: Size of group as a factor in the interaction profile", in *Small groups*, Paul Hare, E. F. Borgatta and R. F. Bales, eds. (New York, Knopf).
Barker, R. G.
1963 *The stream of behavior* (New York, Appleton-Century-Crofts).
Barker, R. G., and Wright, H. F.
1954 *Midwest and its children* (Evanston, Row, Peterson).
Bernstein, Basil
1962 "Social class, linguistic codes and grammatical elements", *Language and Speech*, 5, 221-240.
Brown, R. W., and Ford, M.
1961 "Address in American English", *Journal of Abnormal and Social Psychology*, 62, 375-385.
Brown, R. W., and Gilman, Albert
1960 "The pronouns of power and solidarity", in *Style in language*, T. A. Sebeok, ed. (New York, Wiley).
Cohen, Arthur R.
1958 "Upward communication in experimentally created hierarchies", *Human Relations*, 11, 41-53.
Conklin, Harold C.
1962 "Lexicographical treatment of folk taxonomies", *International Journal of American Linguists*, 28, 119-141.
Cory, D. W.
1952 *The homosexual in America* (New York, Greenberg).
Coser, Rose
1960 "Laughter among colleagues", *Psychiatry*, 23, 81-96.
Ervin, Susan M.
1955 "The verbal behavior of bilinguals: The effects of language of report on the Thematic Apperception Test content of adult French bilinguals". Ph.D. dissertation. University of Michigan. Microfilm Abstracts 55, 2228.
1961 "Semantic shift in bilingualism", *American Journal of Psychology*, 74, 233-241.
1964 "Language and T.A.T. content in bilinguals", *Journal of Abnormal and Social Psychology*, 68, 500-507.
Ferguson, C. A.
1959 "Diglossia", *Word*, 15, 325-340.
1964 "Baby-talk in six languages", *American Anthropologist*, 66, 6, part 2, 103-114.
Fischer, John L.
1958 "Social influences on the choice of a linguistic variant", *Word*, 14, 47-56.
Gump, Paul V., Schoggen, Phil, and Redl, Fritz
1963 "The behavior of the same child in different milieus", in *The Stream of Behavior*, R. G. Barker, ed. (New York, Appleton-Century-Crofts).
Gumperz, John J.
1958 "Dialect differences and social stratification in a North Indian village", *American Anthropologist*, 60, 668-682.
1961 "Speech variation and the study of Indian civilization", *American Anthropologist*, 63, 976-988.
1962 "Types of linguistic communities", *Anthropological Linguistics*, 4, 28-35.
1964a "Hindi-Punjabi code-switching in Delhi", in *Proceedings of the Ninth*

International Congress of Linguists, Cambridge, Mass., 1962, Horace G. Lunt, ed. (The Hague), 1115-1124.

1964b "Linguistic and social interaction in two communities", *American Anthropologist*, 66, 6, part 2, 137-153.

Hare, A. Paul

1964 "Linguistic and social interaction in two communities", *American Anthropologist*, 66, 6 part 2, 137-153.

1962 *Handbook of small group research* (Glencoe, Free Press).

Herman, Simon

1961 "Explorations in the social psychology of language choice", *Human Relations*, 14, 149-164.

Hymes, Dell

1962 "The ethnography of speaking", in *Anthropology and Human behavior*, T. Gladwin and W. Sturtevant, eds. (Washington D.C., Anthropological Society of Washington).

Joos, Martin

1962 *The five clocks* (= Supplement 22 to *International Journal of American Linguistics*, 28, Part V).

Labov, William

"Phonological correlates or social stratification", *American Anthropologist*, 66, 6, part 2, 164-176.

Lambert, Wallace E.

1963 "Psychological approaches to the study of language, Part II: On second-language learning and bilingualism", *The Modern Language Journal*, 47, 114-121.

Lowie, Robert

1945 "A case of bilingualism", *Word*, 1, 249-260.

Murray, Henry A.

1938 *Explorations in personality* (Cambridge, Harvard University Press).

Newman, Stanley

1955 "Vocabulary levels: Zuni sacred and slang usage", *Southwest Journal of Anthropology*, 11, 345-354.

Osgood, C. E., and Sebeok, T. A.

1954 *Psycholinguistics* (= Supplement to *International Journal of American Linguistics*, 20, Memoir 10).

Osgood, C. E., Suci, George J., and Tannenbaum, Percy H.

1957 *The measurement of meaning* (Urbana, University of Illinois Press).

Pittenger, Robert E., Hockett, C. F., and Danehy, John J.

1960 *The first five minutes* (Ithaca, Paul Martineau).

Putnam, G. N., and O'Hern, Ettna M.

1955 *The status significance of an isolated urban dialect* (= *Language Dissertations*, No. 53).

Rubin, Joan

1962 "Bilingualism in Paraguay", *Anthropological Linguistics*, 4, 52-8.

Saporta, Sol

1961 *Psycholinguistics* (New York, Holt, Rinehart, and Winston).

Schachter, Stanley

1951 "Deviation, rejection, and communication", *Journal of Abnormal and Social Psychology*, 46, 190-207.

Skinner, B. F.

1957 *Verbal behavior* (New York, Appleton-Century-Crofts).

Soskin, William F., and John, Vera

1963 "The study of spontaneous talk", in *The stream of behavior*, R. G. Barker, ed. (New York, Appleton-Century-Crofts).

Stephan, F. F., and Mishler, E. G.
1952 "The distribution of participation in small groups: An exponential approximation", *American Sociological Review*, 17, 598-608.

Strodtbeck, F. L., James, Rita M., and Hawkins, C.
1957 "Social status and jury deliberations", *American Sociological Review*, 22, 713-719.

Sutherland, E.
1937 *The professional thief* (Chicago, University of Chicago Press).

Trager, George
1958 "Paralanguage: a first approximation", *Studies in Linguistics*, 13, 1-12.

Watson, Jeanne, and Potter, Robert J.
1962 "An analytic unit for the study of interaction", *Human Relations*, 15, 245-263.

From *American Anthropologist*, 66 (1964), no. 6, part 2; pp. 86-102. Reprinted with permission.

Philip K. Bock

SOCIAL STRUCTURE AND LANGUAGE STRUCTURE *

The search for valid analogies between the structure of language and the structure of other aspects of culture is an important part of modern anthropological thought. Recent students of this problem seem to fall into two general groups: 1. those followers of Whorf who, in a variety of ways, are seeking *congruencies* between the language and the cultural values, perceptions, or practices of some particular society, and 2. those who, like Pike, are attempting to formulate unified theories of the structure of human behavior within which language appears as a special, though central, case (Pike 1954-1960).

The present paper is in the latter tradition. I shall suggest several analogies between language structure and social structure. These analogies have elsewhere led to the formulation of descriptive statements of the structural units of a community and the relationships among these units.[1]

Fundamental to this undertaking is the proposition that all linguistic forms (morphemes, morphological and syntactic structures, etc.) constitute a sub-class of the more general category *cultural forms*. Following Redfield's definition of culture as "conventional understandings, manifest in act and artifact" (1941, 132), I propose to define a cultural form as:

* The first portion of this paper was read at the annual meeting of the American Anthropological Association in San Francisco, November, 1963. I am indebted to Kenneth L. Pike, Dell H. Hymes, and the late Clyde Kluckhohn for assistance and encouragement.

[1] Bock (1962, 154-249). The ethnographic and ethnohistorical sections of my dissertation can be found in Bulletin No. 213 of the National Museum of Canada, Ottawa, Canada, 1966.

a set of inter-related, partially arbitrary expectations, understandings, beliefs or agreements, shared by the members of some social group, which can be shown to influence (or to have influenced) the behavior of some members of that group (Bock 1962, 15).

Linguistic forms are cultural forms *par excellence* for, in general, there is an extremely high consensus among the members of a speech community as to the defining characteristics and potential distribution of the phonemes, morphemes, tagmemes, etc., known to the group. These partially arbitrary understandings and expectations, most of them unconscious or pre-conscious, influence the verbal behavior of group members in predictable and dependable ways. Indeed, this "influence" is so regular that the linguist is able to formulate a description of the structure of a language on the basis of a relatively limited number of observations (a corpus).

The contrastive definition of a finite number of linguistic forms and the rigorous statement of their potentials for co-occurrence constitute an adequate description of the structure of a language.[2] I suggest, similarly, that the cultural forms influencing other than verbal behavior may be contrastively defined and their relationships stated systematically and economically. Furthermore, I would maintain that at least three types of units are necessary to such a description: I. social roles (and classes of roles), II. periods (and dimensions) of social time, and III. areas (and dimensions) of social space.

Like linguistic forms, social roles also constitute a sub-class of cultural forms. Each role consists of expectations regarding the behavior of classes of individuals or "actors". The partially arbitrary and inter-related behavioral expectations making up any given social role will be referred to as the *attributes* of that role (cf. Bruner *et al.* 1956, 25-49). One or more of these attributes will be "criterial" (Bruner *et al.* 1956, 30) or "pivotal" (Nadel 1957, 32) in the categorization of actors as legitimate performers of the role. Other associated or "entailed" attributes may be viewed as either free or conditioned behavioral variants. Finally, social roles may be grouped into *role-classes* on the basis of their shared attributes and/or their substitutability in some environment.

From this point of view, the linguistic analog of the social role is the morpheme with its free and conditioned allomorphs and its membership in distributional classes of morphemes. Let us now explore two aspects of these analogous units: their internal structure and their external distribution.

[2] This is a minimum requirement for an adequate description of a corpus. I accept, in principle, the further requirement that a description be generative; however, there is no need to burden the present paper with what would necessarily be a highly programmatic discussion.

Brown (Bruner *et al.* 1956, 263-264) has argued that morphemes are cognitive categories and that phonemes are their attributes: it is the unique *selection* and *arrangement* of these attributes (which are themselves categories on another level of analysis) which defines each morpheme. Every language system prescribes certain arrangements and proscribes others. According to most linguists, the phoneme-attributes are themselves meaningless, and it is only in certain traditional combinations that they carry meaning.

The similarity of these features to the internal structure of social roles may not be immediately evident, but I shall try to demonstrate the utility of the analogy. First of all, behavioral attributes – be they abstract (mild joking, exercise of jural authority) or concrete (speaks to audience, prepares food) – may pertain to many roles in a given culture, while some attributes have cross-cultural relevance. Thus it is the distinctive selection and arrangement of such attributes which makes possible the contrastive identification of any one role in a particular culture. Just as meaningless phonemes function to keep utterances apart, for purposes of structural description the manifestation (performance) of any behavioral attribute may be viewed as inherently meaningless *except* as it combines with other attributes to contrastively define a particular social role.

Specification of the attributes making up the *internal structure* of a role or morpheme is, of course, only one part of the analysis. Equally important is the statement of the potential *external distribution* of these units.

The external distribution of a social role consists, in the first instance, of its relationships with other social roles, i.e., its privileges of co-occurrence. Merton has dealt with this problem from a rather different perspective in his writings on the "role-set". Merton uses this concept to refer to "that complement of role-relationships in which persons are involved by virtue of occupying a particular social status" (1957, 110). He emphasizes that each social status involves "not a single associated role, but an array of roles", so that, for example, "the status of school teacher in the United States has its distinctive role-set, in which are found pupils, colleagues, the school principal and superintendent, the Board of Education, professional associations, and, on occasion, local patriotic organizations" (1957, 110-111).

Merton's theoretical interest in this concept focuses on the "functional problem of articulating the components of numerous role-sets . . . so that an appreciable degree of social regularity obtains" and status occupants are not subjected to "extreme conflict in their role-sets" (1957, 111). He discusses several social mechanisms which serve to articulate role-sets and thus mitigate the impact of diverse expectations upon a status occupant. But the fact remains that radically different behavioral expectations *are* attached to the role of "teacher" in connection with various members of the corresponding role-set. Phrased differently, the attributes of a role vary with – are conditioned by – the other roles with which it occurs, just as the phonemic shape of a morpheme may be conditioned by its occurrence with different distribution classes of morphemes.

The general principle may be stated as follows: the behavioral manifestation (or performance) of a particular allomorph or role variant is conditioned by its external distribution. Thus a structural statement describing which variants of the role "teacher" occur with which members of its associated role-set would be of the *same general form* as a statement describing which allomorphs of, say, the English plural morpheme [-S] occur with different phonological and morphological classes of noun stems (see Table I).

TABLE I
Isomorphism of Two Structural Statements

Role A, 'teacher':	Morpheme [-S], 'plural':
variant a_1 with B, 'pupil'	/-s/ with Class I noun stems
variant a_2 with C, 'colleague'	/-z/ with Class II noun stems
variant a_3 with D, 'principal'	/-əz/ with Class III noun stems
etc.	etc.

In Table I we see that a social role may be composed of several different subsets of behavioral expectations (variants a_1, a_2 ... a_n), and which of these is manifested depends (in part) upon which of the roles in its role-set (B, C ... J) it occurs with. Borrowing again from linguistic theory, we may say that these variants are in *complementary distribution* if they never occur in the same environments (i.e., in relation to the same member of the role-set), and thus we may speak of them as conditioned variants of the same structural unit: alloroles of the same roleme.

If no such environmental factors can be found which appear to condition the occurrence of different role variants, the latter may be said to be in free variation; but we must also consider the possibility that there are environmental factors other than the presence of other roles which may affect the manifestation of these units. It is in this regard that we now turn briefly to the notions of social space and social time.

SOCIAL SPACE AND SOCIAL TIME

The performance of a social role projects a definition of the situation, and this situation involves an ordered series of behavioral expectations – what Goffman has called a "plan for the co-operative activity that follows" (1959, 12-13). I would argue that recurrent social situations are themselves cultural forms having determinate distributions in social space and social time. I have defined a *situation* as "a *cultural form* consisting primarily of understandings concerning the scheduling of, and allocation of space for, the occurrence of *other* cultural forms" (Bock 1962, 158). In other words, a situation (as a unit of social structure) is here viewed as a kind of four-dimensional cognitive map within which social roles are located. For example, to say that a certain part of a building is a classroom is to imply that during certain socially defined periods of time ("classtime") the social roles of "teacher" and "pupil" are *expected* to occur within it. Such socially defined units of space and time may also condition the manifestation of social roles (and other cultural forms).

On closer investigation, it will appear that the "class" (or any other social situation) is *internally structured* in terms of social space and social time with varying expectations attaching to sub-areas of the classroom and sub-periods of class time. On the other hand, the "class" as a total situation is *externally distributed* into larger dimensions of social time (the school week or term) and areas of social space (the school building or campus) just as the component social roles are distributed into classes of roles.

Now if a role performance projects a situation, and if a situation implies a set of roles, it would appear that we are dealing with the kind of correlation between a functional "slot" and a class of "fillers" analogous to the unit of grammatical structure which Pike calls the *tagmeme* (Pike 1960, 121-122). Grammatical descriptions employing the tagmeme concept tend – like most descriptive statements in phonology and morphology – to be *linear* in form: they represent the obligatory or optional occurrence of tagmemes within a phrase, clause, or sentence as formulae which are isomorphic with the temporal sequence of these units in speech (Cf. Elson and Pickett 1962). Descriptions of social structure must, however, deal with the non-sequential or, broadly speaking, spatial relationships among social roles, as well as the linear and cyclical temporal sequences.

Thus the basic descriptive model (see Table II) which emerges from this approach is one which states the optional or obligatory occurrence of social roles (and their variants) within a situation-matrix bounded by a period of social time and an area of social space.

Given such a situation-matrix as a fundamental unit, it is possible to focus either upon its internal structure, spelling this out in considerable detail, or upon its external distribution, relating the component social roles, time periods, and spatial areas to more inclusive classes and dimensions. In these ways the structural relationship of the situation as a

TABLE II
The Descriptive Model

Situation: "Class"	Time: Class Meeting
Space: Classroom	Roles: +Teacher +Pupil ±Student-Teacher

\+ indicates obligatory occurrence
± indicates optional occurrence

whole to other recurrent situations in the system may be economically described.

AN EXAMPLE OF STRUCTURAL DESCRIPTION

A recurrent situation on the Micmac Indian Reserve studied by the author in 1961 will be used to illustrate how the method of structural description outlined above may be applied.[3] The structural description of any one situation occurring in a human community must, necessarily, refer to other situations; therefore, a notational system was devised to facilitate cross-referencing. The elements of this notation are given in Table III.

TABLE III
Notational System for Structural Description

Upper case letters (S, T, R. M) refer to cultural forms: areas of social space (S), periods of time (T), social roles (R), or matrices (M).
Integers following upper case letters label specific cultural forms.
Lower case letters (s, t, r) designate *variants* of cultural forms.
Decimals following lower case letters label variants of cultural forms.
Upper case clusters (SC, TC, RC) designate *classes* of cultural forms.
Letters following hyphens (e.g., RC-A) are used to label specific *classes* of cultural forms.
An integer preceding a letter, separated from it by a period, refers to a *matrix* other than the one under consideration.

Examples:	3.SC-A:	Space class "A" of matrix #3.
	4.R-B.1:	Role #1 from role class "B" of matrix #4.
	t-5.2:	Variant #2 of time period #5 (of the matrix under consideration).

[3] A narrative description of the wake, based upon participant-observation in four separate occurrences and several informant interviews, will be found in Bock (1962, 148-149).

The matrix to be presented (Table IV) describes the Indian-style wake, a situation which occurs nightly during the period between the death and the burial of an adult member of this Micmac Band. The external distribution of this period (14.TC-A: Time of Wake) is thus into the *life cycle* of individual Band members and into the night period of the daily cycle. The participating roles are contrastively defined in this and other situations. The reader should bear in mind that the matrix and its component cultural forms represent sets of expectations which influence the behavior of participating individuals; they do not represent the individuals themselves.

TABLE IV

Situation-Matrix # 14: Indian Wake

M-14		T-1	T-2	T-3	T-4	T-5
S-1: Bier Area	s-1.1: nucleus	R-1	R-1	R-1	R-1	R-1
	s-1.2: margin	±R-2			±R-2	
S-2: Front Area			R-3	R-4		r-2.1
S-3: Audience Area			R-2	R-2	±R-2 ±R-4	r-2.2 R-4
S-4: Marginal Area	s-4.1: kitchen				r-2.1	
	s-4.2: outside	r-2.2			±r-2.2 ±R-4	

14.SC-A: Place of Wake – External distribution into 9.S-A.1: House site (usually that occupied by deceased)

- S-1: Bier Area
  - s-1.1: nucleus – contains coffin
  - s-1.2: margin – area immediately surrounding coffin
- S-2: Front Area – focal region of performances during T-2, -3, and -5.
- S-3: Audience Area – seating area for R-2: Mourner
- S-4: Marginal Area – residual space, including
  - s-4.1: kitchen area
  - s-4.2: outside of house

14.TC-A: Time of Wake – External distribution (see discussion above).

TC-A = //T-1/T-2//:T-3/T-4://±T-5//:T-3/T-4://

- T-1: Gathering Time – participants arrive at SC-A: Place of Wake
- T-2: Prayer Time – saying of the Rosary by R-3: Prayer Leader
- T-3: Singing Time – several hymns sung with brief pauses in between
- T-4: Intermission – longer pause in singing
- T-5: Meal Time – optional serving of meal (about midnight)

14.RC-A: Participant Roles – External distribution noted for each:
R-1: Corpse – from 3:RC-A: Band Member
R-2: Mourner
r-2.1: Host – member of 9.RC-A: Household Group (of deceased)
r-2.2: Other – residual category
R-3: Prayer Leader
r-3.1: Priest – from 3.R-B.1.1: Priest
r-3.2: Other – from 14.R-4
R-4: Singer – usually from 11.R-A.4: Choir Member

The external distribution and internal structure (segmentation) of SC-A: "Place of Wake" are self-explanatory, though it should be noted that the precise physical arrangements may vary from one manifestation to the next. Thus, the structural description must be general enough to allow for non-structural variations (due, for example, to the different floor plans of Indian homes) while indicating the kinds of areas in terms of which the participants orient their behavior.

The internal structure of TC-A: "Time of Wake" is given in a linear notation with single or double slashes separating the component periods and colons including those periods which are repeated alternately; thus, //:T-3/T-4:// indicates the expected alternation of "Singing Time" with "Intermission" when the exact number of alternations is not structurally determined. The occurrence of periods of time or social roles is assumed to be obligatory unless marked as optional by the presence of the symbol ±. Separate treatment of the internal structure of the time dimension, though confusing at first, vastly simplifies the form of the matrix (which otherwise requires several identical columns) and makes possible independent consideration of the structure of social time.

For some of the more complex matrices, it is useful to set up several role classes; but in M-14, all the participants may be viewed as manifesting a single role class. The contrastive segmentation of RC-A into its component units may be accomplished in a number of ways. There is, at present, no motivation within the theory for the use of binary features; however, by pressing the linguistic analogy in this direction it is possible to differentiate the four members of this role class by means of three attributes, each of which has a positive and a negative pole: (a) Living/Dead; (b) Leads Prayers/Responds; and (c) Sings/Listens. Our social roles may then be contrastively defined as bundles or non-equivalent sets of these attributes; the structural statement may be made in tabular form or, as below, in linear form:

R-1: 'Corpse' = [–a] (Dead; other attributes irrelevant)
R-2: 'Mourner' = [a, –b, –c] (Living; Responds; Listens)
R-3: 'Prayer Leader' = [a, b] (Living; Leads Prayers)
R-4: 'Singer' = [a, c] (Living; Sings)

Given such a statement, natural classes or sub-classes of roles may be rigorously defined through the use of elementary logical notions. For example, RC-A may be defined as the intersection of sets containing *a* with those containing *–a*.

The role of "Mourner" (R-2) occurs in two variant forms (r-2.1; r-2.2), but as can be seen from the matrix these variants have different distribution potentials during only certain periods of the wake, while during T-2 and T-3 their distributions are identical. This may be viewed as a case of conditioned variation with neutralization occurring in some environments. The variants of R-3: "Prayer Leader" may be distinguished on the basis of their respective external distributions, but within M-14 they appear to be in free variation (i.e., either r-3.1 or r-3.2 occurs in the environment S-2 at T-2).

DISCUSSION

The goal of structural description in ethnography, as in linguistics, is the contrastive identification of cultural forms and the rigorous statement of their distribution. A situation-matrix such as that presented above does exactly this. It cannot do more, nor does it pretend to. Thus, M-14 does not explain or give the meaning of the Indian wake any more than a grammar of English explains a particular sentence-type. The "item and arrangement" (Hockett 1954) approach adopted in this example may be supplemented by more process-oriented (even transformational) statements (cf. Bock 1962, 225-226), but the aim remains strictly *formal.* Content enters the analysis only for the purpose of contrast.

Yet it is clear that a formal analysis which lacks all content is as meaningless as a grammar without an accompanying lexicon. How then are we to introduce cultural content into a structural description? One solution is to add to the contrastive role definitions what Nadel (1957) called the "entailed" attributes – the host of behavioral expectations that seem to follow from the assumption of a role. Here Merton's notion of the "role-set" again becomes useful since we may further specify (in our role lexicon) the variable attributes which are manifested only in certain relationships. Similarly, the recognition of classes of roles simplifies the specification of content since many normally non-contrastive attributes may be defined for some abstract role class (such as "citizen" or "adult male") and then allowed to carry over to all of its component roles.

One further example will indicate the way in which cultural content may be related to structural description. A central part of the Indian wake involves the singing (during 14.T-3) of certain traditional hymns for the dead. Though I personally lack the musicological and linguistic skills necessary to perform a structural analysis of these hymns, I feel quite certain that they constitute a class of cultural forms with distinctive formal features. And even if I am unable to analyze their internal structure, I am in a position to say something about their external distribution: they are manifested (i.e., expected to be performed) in the environment S-2 at T-3 of M-14. Furthermore, knowledge of these hymns and the ability to perform them are attributes of a particular social role (14.R-4: Singer), while the hymns themselves are members of a larger class of musical forms and might best be described as variants of the hymns used at other religious services. Finally, if material objects (such as the coffin) are treated as manifestations of still other cultural forms,[4] their internal structure, class membership, external distribution, and role correlates can be stated within the same type of structural framework, making possible the formal descriptive integration of most aspects of a culture.

The extensions of structure description suggested in the last two paragraphs are largely programmatic. The first attempt by the author to apply this approach to a body of field data (Bock 1962, 184-221) had more restricted aims and, even so, met with variable success in analyzing different situations. Ritual situations (such as the wake) yielded most readily to analysis, for in ritual, spatial and temporal boundaries are usually clear-cut, role-performances are carefully rehearsed, and the attributes which serve to contrast different roles are consciously emphasized and reinforced by highly visible and redundant cues. Indeed, it might be possible to define the process of *ritualization* in terms of the degree to which temporal, spatial, and role cues are made explicit and redundant for the purpose of insuring smooth and error-free interaction. A possible linguistic analog may be found in C. F. Voegelin's concept of "noncasual speech" (1960, 57-68).

Other types of situations are more difficult to describe in structural terms: units of social space or social time may overlap, resulting in indeterminate boundaries; the complex conditioning of roles by distributional factors may obscure the nature of the underlying units; and an insufficient or biased corpus of observations may lead to faulty analysis. But these difficulties are all similar to problems faced by the linguist in morphological analysis; and insofar as language is a part of culture, we may expect that equally complex patterning will be found in social structure.

[4] How one views the relationship of artifacts to culture depends, of course, on one's view of the nature of culture (cf. Osgood 1951). From the point of view expressed in this paper, the relationship is seen as analogous to that between speech and language: i.e., the material objects are expressions (manifestations) of cognitive units (expectations, etc.) which the ethnographer formulates as cultural forms. (Cf. Pike 1960, 115-118.)

In spite of the difficulties encountered, the attempt to formulate a structural description of some social group can be revealing; for by formalizing our conceptions of social structure we are led into a systematic search for the cultural forms in terms of which men orient their behavior in space, in time, and in relation to other actors.

BIBLIOGRAPHY

Bock, Philip K.
1962 "The Social Structure of a Canadian Indian Reserve". Unpublished Ph.D. dissertation, Harvard University, Cambridge, Mass.
Bruner, J. S., J. J. Goodnow and G. A. Austin
1956 *A Study of Thinking* (New York, John Wiley & Sons, Inc.).
Elson, B., and V. Pickett
1962 *An Introduction to Morphology and Syntax* (Santa Ana, Summer Institute of Linguistics).
Goffman, Erving
1959 *The Presentation of Self in Everyday Life* (Garden City, Doubleday Anchor Books).
Hockett, Charles F.
1954 "Two Models of Grammatical Description", *Word*, 10, 210-231.
Merton, Robert K.
1957 "The Role Set: Problems in Sociological Theory", *British Journal of Sociology*, 8, 106-120.
Nadel, S. F.
1957 *The Theory of Social Structure* (Glencoe, Free Press).
Osgood, Cornelius
1951 "Culture: its Empirical and Non-Empirical Character", *Southwestern Journal of Anthropology*, 7, 202-214.
Pike, Kenneth L.
1954-1960 *Language in Relation to a Unified Theory of the Structure of Human Behavior*, Parts I, II and III, Preliminary Edition (Glendale, Summer Institute of Linguistics).
Redfield, Robert
1941 *The Folk Culture of Yucatan* (Chicago, University of Chicago Press).
Voegelin, C. F.
1960 "Casual and Noncasual Utterances Within Unified Structure", in *Style in Language*, ed. by Thomas A. Sebeok (New York, Technology Press and John Wiley & Sons, Inc.), pp. 57-68.

From *Southwestern Journal of Anthropology*, 20 (1964), pp. 393-403. Reprinted with permission.

Section III

LANGUAGE IN SOCIAL STRATA AND SECTORS

B. Bernstein

SOME SOCIOLOGICAL DETERMINANTS OF PERCEPTION. AN INQUIRY INTO SUB-CULTURAL DIFFERENCES

Within the last thirty years in both the fields of sociology and psychology there has been an increasing awareness of sub-cultural and social class influences upon behaviour and in particular learning (1-31). Many workers have demonstrated correlations between sub-culture or class and educational attainments but there exists no unifying theory to explain the empirical relationships and found discrepancies between potential and actual attainment of working-class children.

While much of this work, especially that of the Chicago School (12, 13), has been the subject of severe methodological criticism it is widely agreed that these studies point to critical relationships between social class, behaviour and performance. J. Floud reports Professor P. E. Vernon as saying:

> It is argued that the influence of the environment is cumulative. At each stage in the child's life from birth to maturity its influence must be given increasing weight as a determinant of the differences between individuals and particularly of those differences which are measured by tests of intelligence and attainment, on which, in the main, we base our educational decisions about them (30).

Dr. H. Himmelweit (19) in a discussion of the relations between social class and education writes, "None of the facts mentioned here provides more than a hint as to the reasons for the different performance of children from the various social levels." It is with this gap in the existing knowledge of the relations between social class and educational attainment that this paper is primarily concerned.

It would seem important to understand what underlies "the complex of attitudes favourable to educational and social mobility" (29). That is, those factors which influence working-class children who do less well at grammar schools, leave early and fail to assimilate the grammar-school ethos; factors which influence those working-class children who tend to do less well on verbal tests of intelligence than on non-verbal tests, and those factors which influence educational attainment in basic subjects. A framework is also necessary within which much of the existing data can be re-examined and systematized and which would indicate new areas of research.

The purpose of this paper is to indicate a relationship between the mode of cognitive expression and certain social classes. The predisposition to form relationships with objects in a particular way is an important perceptual factor and may be distinguished from cognitive ability. Different terms, or the same term used to denote the same object, may imply different experiences, which are related to a more general method of ordering relationships. Two types of ordering of relationships will be proposed: that which arises out of sensitivity to the content of objects and that which arises out of sensitivity to the structure of objects. This division between structure and content is analytical and the two predispositions to perceive are not dichotomous but stages on a social continuum. The sociological determinants of these two stages and their implications will be examined in relation to certain formal educational institutions. It is necessary to examine the predisposition and resistance to certain educational processes. It is suggested that the lower the social strata the greater the resistance to formal education and learning and that this is a function of the social structure of the strata. This resistance is expressed in many different ways and levels, e.g. critical problems of discipline, non-acceptance of the values of the teacher, the failure to develop and feel the need for an extensive vocabulary, a preference for a descriptive rather than an analytical cognitive process. It is suggested that resistance is a function of a mode of perceiving and feeling which is characterized by a sensitivity to the content rather than to the structure of objects. It is contended that members of the unskilled and semi-skilled strata, relative to the middle classes, do not merely place different significances upon different classes of objects, but that their perception is of a qualitatively different order.

Sensitivity to the structure of objects is here defined as a function of learned ability to respond to an object perceived and defined in terms of a matrix of relationships. Sensitivity to content is a function of learned ability to respond to the boundaries of an object rather than to the matrix of relationships and inter-relationships in which it stands with other objects. This distinction it will be seen is wholly qualitative.

The basic requirements for the group termed "middle-class and associative levels" will be a family where the father is more likely to have received grammar school education, *or* some form of further education *or* certificated training for a skill, *or* one in which the mother is more likely to have received something more than elementary schooling *or* before marriage have followed an occupation superior to that of the father, *or* a non-manual occupation. Such a family may be found among certain wage-earning manual workers. Middle-class and associative levels include the occupational hierarchy above this base line. The base line is considered the transitional family structure which modifies social perception and orients it to sensitivity to the structure of objects. The term "working-class" includes all members of the semi-skilled and unskilled group except the type of family structure indicated as the base line for the middle-class and associative levels. The groups are fundamentally distinct because the first possesses:

(*a*) An awareness of the importance between means and long-term ends, cognitively and affectually regarded.
(*b*) A discipline to orient behaviour to certain values but with a premium on individual differentiation within them.
(*c*) The ability to adopt appropriate measures to implement the attainment of distant ends by a purposeful means-end chain.

Thus a major characteristic of the middle-class and associative levels is an instrumental attitude to social relations and objects, whilst for the second group the attitude is non-instrumental. Integral to this paper is the contention that sensitivity to the content or structure of objects varies in degree according to the extent and ramifications of the above factors.

The child in the middle-class and associative levels is socialized within a formally articulated structure. Present decisions affecting the growing child are governed by their efficacy in attaining distant ends, affectually and cognitively regarded. Behaviour is modified by and oriented to an explicit set of goals and values which create a more stable system of rewards and punishments, although the psychological implications of this may vary from one family to another. The future is conceived of in direct relation to the educational and emotional life of the child. Consequently, the child grows up in an ordered rational structure in which his total experience is organized from an early age. Within middle-class and associative levels direct expressions of feeling, in particular feelings of hostility, are discouraged. The word *mediates* between the expression of feeling and its approved social recognition, that is, a value is placed upon the verbalization of feeling. This is so in all societies but the important determining factor here is the nature of the words and the type of language-use, not necessarily the size of vocabulary, but the degree to which the social emphasis on an aspect of the language structure mediates the relation between thought and feeling. Language exists in relation to a desire to express and communicate; consequently, the mode of a language structure – the way in which words and sentences are related – reflects a particular form of the structuring of feeling and so the very means of interaction and response to the environment.

From this standpoint language facilities and language barriers are of the utmost importance and must be studied in their interplay with a host of other factors that make for ease or difficulty of transmission of ideas and patterns of behavior. Furthermore the sociologist is necessarily interested in the symbolic significance in a social sense of the linguistic differences which appear in any large community (Sapir) (32).[1]

Sapir goes on to say:

Peculiar modes of pronunciation, characteristic turns of phrase, slangy forms of speech, occupational terminologies of all sorts – these are so many symbols of the manifold ways in which society arranges itself and are of crucial importance for the understanding of the development of individual and social attitudes.

Again:

Language is heuristic . . . in the much more far-reaching sense that its forms predetermine for us certain modes of observation and interpretation (32).

When a middle-class mother says to her child, "I'd rather you made less noise, darling", the child will tend to obey because previous disobedience after this point has led to expression of disapproval or perhaps other punitive measures. The operative words in this sentence which the middle-class child responds to are "rather" and "less". The child has learned to become sensitive to this form of sentence and the many possible sentences in this universe of discourse. The words "rather" and "less" are understood, when used in this situation, as directly translatable cues for immediate response on the part of the middle-class child. However, if the same statement were made to a child from the family of an unskilled worker it would not be understood as containing the same imperative cues for response. "Shut up!" may contain a more appropriate set of cues. (Of course, the last statement is meaningful to a middle-class child, but what it is important to stress is the fact that the middle-class child has learned to be able to respond to *both* statements, and *both* are differentially discriminated within a finely articulated world of meaning. We are discussing two modes of language and the working-class child has only learned to respond to one, and so although he may understand

[1] In this paper the valuable work of Cassirer (33, 34), Whorf (35), and Sapir (32, 36) has been used to explore the social implications of language. See also H. Hoijer (36).

both, he will not differentiate effectually between the two.) Further, if the first statement is made by a middle-class person to a working-class child, the child will translate it into "Shut up" and will relate the difference between the statements to the different social levels. What he will not have, and what he cannot respond to *directly*, is the different language structure of the first sentence. The working-class child has to translate and thus *mediate* middle-class language structure through the logically simpler language structure of his own class to make it personally meaningful. Where he cannot make this translation he fails to understand and is left puzzled.

In an appendix to a *Study of Thinking* (37) the author considers that a range of experience may be differentiated in the lexicon of one language and undifferentiated in another. Although the context of the statements is in a discussion of distinctions within and between primitive languages the force of the comment is believed to hold here. Allison Davis made a contribution to the understanding of the importance of cultural usages and symbolic forms and means but he did not work out the consequences of his own statement, "The lower socio-economic groups have a different language structure than the higher groups. They speak various non-standard dialects" (13, p. 82). Similarly Eells and Murray (38) seem to be thinking in terms of a different dialect rather than the effects of different modes of language-use which differentiate different ranges of experience and thus modify what is actually responded to in an object. The difference in response between the children in the example involves a different structuring of receptivity to language cues and to relationships and symbolism implied by a language. It has been found by investigation that a value is placed on early verbalization in the middle-class child but this fact, in itself, is not so important as the mode of verbalization or the structure of the language and its functions. One of the aims of the middle-class family is to produce a child oriented to certain values but individually differentiated within them. The child is born into an environment where he is seen and responded to as an individual with his own rights, that is, he has a specific social status. This early process of individuation is accomplished by two important factors: the scrupulous observation of the child by the parents so that the very fine stages of development and the emergence of new patterns of behaviour are the object of attention and comment; together with recognition and communication in a language structure where personal qualifications are significantly used and which the child learns to use in response. The child's relation to the environment is such that his range and expression of discriminating verbal responses is fostered by the social structure from the beginning. A virtuous circle is set up which is continually reinforced, for the mother will elaborate and expand the embryo personal qualificatory statements that the child makes. It would follow that the greater the differentiation of the child's experience the greater his ability to differentiate and elaborate objects in his environment.

The next fact to consider is the way in which the order of communication, the mode of expression of language, modifies perception. It is necessary to make a distinction between non-verbal expressions of meaning and verbal expressions of meaning in any communication. The role of gesture, facial expression, bodily movement, in particular volume and tone of the speaking voice, will be termed "immediate" or direct expression, whilst the words used will be termed "mediate" or indirect expression. What *is* important is the emphasis placed upon one or the other and the nature of the form of the verbal communication. Now if the words used are part of a language which contains a high proportion of short commands, simple statements and questions, where the symbolism is descriptive, tangible, concrete, visual and of a low order of generality, where the emphasis is on the emotive rather than the logical implications, it will be called a *public* language.[2] Feelings which find expression in this language will themselves be affected by the form of the expressions used. Feelings communicated will be diffuse and crudely differentiated when a public language is being used, for if a personal qualification is to be given to this language, it can only be done by non-verbal means, primarily by changes in volume and tone accompanied by gesture, bodily movement, facial expression, physical set. Thus if the language between mother and child is a public one, as it is in the working-classes, then the child will tend to become sensitive to the quality and strength of feeling through non-verbal means of expression, for the personal qualification will be made through these means. And this has many implications for the structuring of experience and relationships with objects.

The language-use of the middle-class is rich in personal, individual qualifications, and its form implies sets of advanced logical operations;

[2] Characteristics of a public language are: short, grammatically simple, often unfinished, sentences with a poor syntactical construction; simple and repetitive use of conjunctions (so, then, and), thus modifications, qualifications and logical stress will tend to be indicated by non-verbal means; frequent use of short commands and questions; rigid and limited use of adjectives and adverbs; infrequent use of the impersonal pronoun (it, one) as subject of a conditional sentence; statements formulated as questions which set up a sympathetic circularity, e.g. "Just fancy?", "Isn't it terrible?", "Isn't it a shame?", "It's only natural, isn't it?" A statement of fact is often used as both a reason and a conclusion, e.g. "You're not going out", "I told you to hold on tight" (Mother to child on bus, as repeated answer to child's "Why?"). Individual selection from a group of traditional phrases plays a great part. The symbolism is of a low order of generality. *The personal qualification is left out of the structure of the sentence therefore it is a language of implicit meaning.*

volume and tone and other non-verbal means of expression although important take second place. It is important to realize that initially in the middle-class child's life it is not the number of words or the range of vocabulary which is decisive but the fact that he or she becomes sensitive to a particular form of indirect or mediate expression where the subtle arrangement of words and connections between sentences convey the feeling. It is the latter which the child originally strives to obtain in order to experience a full relationship with the mother and in so doing learns to respond to a particular form of language cues. Because of the importance of this type of mediate relation between mother and child a tension is created between the child and his environment such that there is a need to verbalize his relations in a personal, individual way. Thus the child at an early age becomes sensitive to a form of language-use which is relatively complex and which in turn acts as a dynamic framework upon his or her perception of objects. This mode of language-use will be termed *formal*. (It was stated earlier that the pressure within a middle-class social structure to intensify and verbalize an awareness of separateness and difference increases the significance of objects in the environment.) Receptivity to a particular form of language structure determines the way relationships to objects are made and an orientation to a particular manipulation of words.

The child in the middle-classes and associative levels grows up in an environment which is finely and extensively controlled; the space, time, and social relationships are explicitly regulated within and outside the family group. The more purposeful and explicit the organization of the environment with reference to a distant future, that is the greater the rationality of the connections and inter-relations between means and distant ends, the greater the significance of objects in the present. Objects in the present are not taken as given, but become centres for inquiry and starting points for relationships. The effect of this on the experience of the child is to make him more generally and specifically aware of a wide range of objects at any one time which will intensify his curiosity and reward his explorations. Here the critical factor is the mode of the relationship and this is a function of his sensitivity to structure. A dynamic interaction is set up: the pressure to verbalize feelings in a personally qualified way, the implications of the language learnt, combine to decide the nature of the cues to which he responds – structural cues. An orientation towards structure allows many interpretations or meanings to be given to any one object, which increases the area and intensity of the child's curiosity and receptiveness. This leads to an awareness of the formal ordering of his environment, notions of its extensions in time and space and so is the beginning of the formation of primitive interpretative concepts. This, of course, is part of the socializing process of any child but it is the mode of established relationships which is of decisive importance because the mode determines the levels of conceptualization possible. (Different children will be able to benefit more from this environment as a result of other factors, e.g. specifically psychological factors, but the means of utilizing and exploiting formal educational facilities are provided.)

The school is an institution where every item in the present is finely linked to a distant future, consequently there is no serious clash of expectations between the school and the middle-class child. The child's developed time-span of anticipation allows the present activity to be related to a future and this is meaningful. There is little conflict of values between the teacher and child and more importantly the child is predisposed to accept and respond to the language structure of communication. The school aims at assisting the development of consciousness of self, cognitive and emotional differentiation or discrimination, and develops and encourages mediate relationships. There is, in the child, a desire to use and manipulate words in a personal qualifying or modifying way and, in particular, a developing sense of tense (time) which together combine to reduce the problem of the teaching of English: reading, spelling, writing. The middle-class child is predisposed towards the ordering of symbolic relationships and more importantly, imposing order and seeing new relationships. His level of curiosity is high. There is a conformity to authority and an acceptance of the role of the teacher, irrespective of psychological relationships to his personality. This is not to say that at times feelings of rebellion will not appear. (The middle-class child is capable of manipulating the *two* languages – the language between social equals (peer groups) which approximates to a public language *and* a formal language which permits sensitivity to role and status.) This leads to appropriateness of behaviour in a wide range of social circumstances. Finally, the school is an important and socially approved means whereby the developing child can enhance his self-respect. Thus the social structure of the school, the means and ends of education, create a framework which the middle-class child is able to accept, respond to and exploit.

Before examining certain factors of the working-class environment which have a bearing on the mode of cognition the following study will be presented. The sample is of particular interest because of the class, educational and occupational homogeneity of the subjects. This study was carried out in a London day college on 309 male students with whom the writer had personal contact in the course of teaching. The sample consisted of boys between 15 and 18 with a mean age of 16 years all of whom were messenger boys (young postman grade) employed by the G.P.O. They came from unskilled and semi-skilled backgrounds

Stuff on England lang - class

"Soul on Ice"

Eldridge Cleaver
"Minister of Information"
Black Panther Party

Time Life - History
Series of War

and their homes were randomly distributed geographically in inner and outer London. Of this group 295 went to secondary modern schools, 5 to junior technical schools, 3 to central schools and 6 to grammar schools. All boys left at 15 years and have no recorded examination successes. They were given the Mill Hill vocabulary test 1948, Form I Senior and the Progressive Matrices 1938. It was predicted that the higher the score on the matrices the greater the difference between the matrices and the Mill Hill scores. That is, within this group of subjects there would not be a linear relation between the two scores. (16 points or more was taken as an arbitrary indication of a significant difference between the scores.)

In examination of the results 81 boys showed matrices greater than Mill Hill test discrepancy of 16 or more points, the differences ranging between 16-37 points. Of these, 19 boys falling within the matrices range 105-115 I.Q. pts. had Mill Hill I.Q. scores between 83-102, while the further 62 with a matrices range between 116-126 + I.Q. pts. had Mill Hill scores within the range 82-110 I.Q. pts. Of the total group only 18 boys with a matrices score of 116 I.Q. pts. or more showed a discrepancy of less than 16 pts. As predicted (see Table I), there is a

TABLE I

Results

Number of Subjects	3	23	77	64	104	38
Range of I.Q. Matrices	71-80	81-90	91-100	101-10	111-20	121-6
Matrices Mean	76	87	97	106	115	124
S.D.	1.41	2.11	2.73	3.03	3.17	2.15
Mill-Hill Mean	94	94	98	99	101	104
S.D.	10.2	7.9	5.78	6.37	7.63	7.5

non-linear relationship between the scores. There is a clear trend that the higher the matrices score the greater the discrepancy between the Mill Hill and the matrices scores. It will be seen that all Mill Hill means fall within the average range.

Where the matrices I.Q. is over 101 pts., Mill Hill means fall below this. Where the matrices I.Q. is below 100 pts., Mill Hill means rise slightly above this excepting the three lowest scores.

(It seems apparent that a great deal of potential ability is being lost as the greater proportion of these boys are functioning at an average or below average level of ability and educational attainment in formal subjects.) Their functioning ability in formal subjects is related to their Mill Hill scores. On matrices scores 80 of the subjects might have been potential candidates for grammar school; in fact only 6 went to grammar school, 5 to a technical school and 3 to central school and none of this group of 14 benefited in terms of attainment in examination. Of the total group 20.7% have potential ability for grammar school but would, and perhaps did, fail as a result of educational attainment and showing on verbal tests. (I.Q. of 116 considered the minimum required for grammar school entrance.)

The clustering of the vocabulary scores about the mean independent of matrices score indicates the discrepancy between the ability to solve certain non-linguistic *relational* problems involving logical addition and subtraction and purely linguistic problems of a conceptual or categorizing order. Although no evidence is offered here, the writer's experience with these boys indicates that the level of attainment in formal subjects is related to the vocabulary not the matrices I.Q. It is predicted on the basis of the theory that a comparative group of Mill Hill scores from subjects matched for similar age from middle-class strata would not show this non-linear relationship with the matrices. These results may have greater meaning in the context of the analysis of the working-class environment which follows.

The working-class family structure is less formally organized than the middle-class in relation to the development of the child. Although the authority within the family is explicit the values which it expresses do not give rise to the carefully ordered universe spatially and temporally of the middle-class child. The exercise of authority will not be related to a stable system of rewards and punishments but may often appear arbitrary. The specific character of long-term goals tends to be replaced by more general notions of the future, in which chance, a friend or a relative plays a greater part than the rigorous working out of connections. Thus present, or near present, activities have greater value than the relation of the present activity to the attainment of a distant goal. The system of expectancies, or the time-span of anticipation, is shortened and this creates different sets of preferences, goals and dissatisfactions. This environment limits the perception of the developing child of and in time. Present gratifications or present deprivations become absolute gratifications or absolute deprivations for there exists no developed time continuum upon which present activity can be ranged. Relative to the middle-classes, the postponement of present pleasure for future gratifications will be found difficult. By implication a more volatile patterning of affectual and expressive behavior will be found in the working-classes.

The language between mother and child is public: one which contains few personal qualifications, for it is essentially a language where the stress is on emotive terms employing concrete, descriptive, tangible and visual symbolism (11). The nature of the language tends to limit the verbal expression of feeling. The child learns only a public language from his mother and feeling is communicated by non-verbal means.[3] It must be emphasized that with the use of a public language the child will tend to make and respond to personal qualifications which are expressed by an immediacy of communication whether verbally or non-verbally expressed.

As the nature of the language-use limits the verbal communications of feelings the latter tend to be as undifferentiated as the language. Consequently the emotional and cognitive differentiation of the working-class child is comparatively less developed, and the cues responded to in the environment will be primarily of a qualitatively different order. He is sensitive to the content of objects. Because the language is public, with a corresponding emphasis on emotive content, the very vehicle of communication precludes the structure of objects as major referent points. Of critical importance is the type of language-use upon which value is placed, for once a value is so placed, then that language-use will reinforce the emotional disposition which resulted in the initial preference.

It must be seen clearly that the distinction between structure and content is one of degrees within a conceptual hierarchy. All that is implied is this: where there is sensitivity to content only the simplest logical implications or boundaries of the structure will be cognized. More definitely, certain aspects of an object will not register as meaningful cues; or if they do, the verbal response will be inadequately determined.

It is difficult to distinguish the complex of dynamic factors involved in this order of perception for the many relationships are mutually dependent and developmentally reinforce each other. The child is born into a world in which personal qualifications are established non-verbally in the sense that the personal qualifications are left out of the structure of the sentences. Relationships are made by the use of an individual selection from a public language, and by gesture, tone, change of volume and physical set, etc., that is, by *expressive symbolism*. Thus, the child early learns to respond and make responses to cues which are immediately relevant. Expressive symbolism of this order has no reference other than to itself. Through his relationships to this symbolism the child in turn learns to respond to immediate perceptions and does *not* learn a language other than a public language in his class environment. The

[3] It is relevant to quote here a finding of both G. Greenald (20) and J. Floud (21) that achievement in the grammar school was correlated with the social grading of the mother's occupation before marriage. This finding is of great importance as it indicates the order of the initial communication to the child.

stress on the present in the *means* of communication precludes the understanding of the meaningfulness of a time continuum other than of a limited order. Necessarily, the child lives in the here and now experience of his world, in which the time-span of anticipation or expectancy is very brief, and this is reinforced by the lack of a rigorous working out of connections between means and distant ends as discussed previously. One important consequence of this patterning of perception is that it produces a descriptive cognitive process, e.g. the recognition of events A, B, C, D as separate unconnected facts or at best crude causal connections are made. Sustained curiosity is not fostered or rewarded as answers to questions rarely lead beyond the object or further than a simple statement about the object. The social structure continues to reinforce the early patterning of perception.

It is now necessary to show how this mode of perceiving and the attendant structuring of receptivity conflicts with and induces a resistance to formal education. There is an initial conflict between the need to make and to be sensitive to the mediate responses which formal learning requires and the immediate responsiveness the child has learned from his social structure. This creates difficulties at many levels. The appropriate cues which enable a child to establish a personal relationship are absent; from the point of view of the working-class child the teacher's feeling is impersonalized through the language he uses. The public language is, in fact, a language to be used between equals (from a middle-class point of view) for it contains little reference to social status (i.e. a structured object) and the terms used to denote social status within the class environment are often judged unacceptable for use outside it. Thus the use of this language in a superior-inferior situation (to a doctor, teacher, etc.) may often be interpreted by the superior as a hostile or aggressive (rude) response. Because the working-class child can only use, only knows, a public language it is often used in situations which are inappropriate. The expressive behaviour and immediacy of response which accompany the use of this language may again be wrongly interpreted by the teacher. This may well lead to a situation where pupil and teacher each disvalues each other's world and communication becomes a means of asserting differences.

Fundamentally, it may lead to a breakdown of communications between teacher and child for two different languages are in fact being used. If the teacher is conscious of a deficiency of his own status this may exacerbate the existing difficulty of communication. In contrast to the middle-class child who is brought up to respond to the distinction between an office and its content, the working-class child confounds the two, so that if there is no personal relationship with the teacher his function and the subjects connected with it are together disvalued. Although the working-class child may still have at the same time a sense of unease and a recognition of failure.

The fact that the working-class child attaches significance to a different aspect of language from that required by the learning situation is responsible for his resistance to extensions of vocabulary, the manipulation of words and the construction of ordered sentences. Because he has previously learned to make personal qualifications through expressive symbolism he has little desire to acquire new words or order his existing vocabulary in a way which expresses this qualification. There is, in fact, from his own standpoint, no *need* to do this. The "I" of the child is adequately communicated by tone-volume-physical set, not in the language he uses. Unfortunately, within a formal learning situation, this means of communication is not recognized and must necessarily be disvalued. The attempt to substitute a different use of language and to change the order of communication creates critical problems for the working-class child as it is an attempt to change his basic system of perception, fundamentally the very means by which he has been socialized. The introduction of a new word, or a previously known word used differently, may not become a vehicle for future expression for there exists no emotional and thus cognitive framework in which it can find a place. A situation is created of mechanical learning, with its implication of forgetting when the original stimuli are removed. The working-class boy is often genuinely puzzled by the need to acquire vocabulary or use words in a way that is, for him, peculiar. It is important to realize that his difficulties in ordering a sentence and connecting sentences – problems of qualifying an object, quality, idea, sensitivity to time and its extensions and modifications, making sustained relationships – are alien to the way he perceives and reacts to his immediate environment. The total system of his perception, which results in a sensitivity to content rather than the structure of objects, applies equally to the structure of a sentence.

The mechanical understanding and manipulation of numbers according to elementary rules of addition, subtraction and multiplication may not show a discrepancy between the two classes except in speed. It is believed that the difficulty for the working-class boy will arise with the application of the underlying principles to the new symbols involved in fractions, decimals and percentages. He does not understand the underlying principles and so cannot generalize the operation to different situations. The principles and operations apply only to discrete situations. Further, verbal problems based upon this symbolism, which require an initial ordering of relationships, create difficulties. Finally, the understanding of a language, which for the working-class child has no content, e.g. algebra, transposition of formulae, etc., is a critical step in his understanding of number and often indicates a point in the gradient of difficulty which he is unable to pass.

These critical points of difficulty may not be directly the result of deficiency of intelligence, however this controversial term is defined; rather, because of the nature of an object and its symbolic relations (here the implications of number), much is lost to perception and not cognized. The working-class child will encounter difficulties with basic subjects that are of a different order from those encountered by the middle-class child, and these may inhibit learning, or the exploitation of what is learned, or both. (Simply, what is learned by a middle-class child will have a different significance to him from that which it has to a working-class child because of a differing perception of the items within a learning situation.)

(It has been pointed out that the level of curiosity of the working-class child is relatively low, and as compared with the middle-class child, differently oriented, and this removes a powerful stimulus from the classroom.) The working-class child has a preference for descriptive cognitive responses, and his response is an immediate one with only vague extensions in time and space, consequently his attention will be brief or difficult to sustain without punitive measures. Rather than pursuing the detailed implications and relations of an object or an idea, which at once create the problem of its structure and extensions, he is oriented towards the cursory examinations of a series of different items. Hoggart has described in his book, *The Uses of Literacy*, an attitude characterized by fragmentation and the need for logical simplicity (11).

There is no continuity between the expectancies of the school and those of the child. In the school an activity or a series of activities are meaningful in relation to a distant goal and the present has critical extensions in time and place. The working-class child is concerned mainly with the present, and his social structure, unlike that of the middle-class child, provides little incentive or purposeful support to make the methods and ends of the school personally meaningful. The problems of discipline and classroom control result not from isolated points of resistance or conflict but from the attempt to reorient a whole pattern of perception with its emotional counterpart. And this may create the disproportion between the intensity of any one response and the specific set of stimuli which occasion it. Finally it may be stated that the school provides an important means by which the middle-class child enhances his self-respect and that this is not so for the working-class child. His self-respect is in fact more often damaged (28). It is obtained elsewhere in the careful conformity to the symbols of his class.

An attempt has been made to show the social origins and some implications of two different orders of perception, characterized by sensitivity to structure or sensitivity to content. It must be emphasized that this is a distinction of general orientation. It has been stated that the middle-class child is aware of content through a structure of a different order from the working-class child and responds to qualitatively different perceptual cues. Cues which are meaningful to the middle-class child are not available to the working-class child. The way the receptivity of the working-class child has been structured is such, that that which is available to perception is determined by the implications of the language-use of his class environment. Fundamental to this paper is the assertion that the middle-class child is capable of responding to, manipulating and understanding, a public language, expressive symbolism and a formal language which is structured to mediate personal qualifications as a result of his class environment. It has been shown that a greater complexity of possible relationships is made available to him which permits a systematization of a high order. Because of the different structuring of the working-class environment the working-class child does not learn a language which is structured to mediate personal qualifications but is limited to expressive symbolism and a public language. This radically narrows the extent and type of his object relationships and has sociologically crucial implications for behaviour. The implications are very wide and only those relevant to formal education have been indicated in this paper.

The dynamics of sensitivity to structure "underlies the complex of attitudes favourable to educational and social mobility", whereas sensitivity to content, it would seem, is responsible for the poor showing in formal educational subjects by working-class children even if they have a high I.Q. This mode of perception (sensitivity to content) would explain some of the discrepancies between verbal and non-verbal tests (see study) and why working-class children tend to do less well on purely verbal tests. Although it has been found that working-class children do not become part of the social and cultural life of the grammar school (19, 40) this fact in itself is not explanatory nor need it necessarily lead to poorer educational performance. In fact it has been shown that often working-class children in grammar schools come from homes where there is little divergence between the aims of the school and those of the home (21). For the reasons given in this paper, the fact that many working-class parents apparently hold middle-class attitudes does not imply that the children are equipped affectually and cognitively to respond to the grammar school opportunity, despite the level of their measured intellectual potential. It is further important to consider the Hogben model (39) in the light of this paper, for in order to equate ability with opportunity it is necessary to understand precisely the variables which determine the *expression* of ability. This is necessary at the present moment, when the society in order to survive must be able to profit by the *expressed* potential of all of its members.

It is thought that many aspects of the present controversy relating to the concept intelligence might be seen differently within this conceptual framework. Specifically it might throw some light on the found discrepancies between potential ability and measured attainment of working-class pupils, by indicating how perception is patterned sociologically. A comparative study of middle-class and working-class nursery schools would be invaluable. The psychological causes of difficulties in the basic subjects is a different problem. What appears vital is the separating out of sociological and psychological factors in order that constructive methods may be worked out to prevent the wastage of working-class educational potential. If this theory is valid it is thought that it is possible to systemize many disparate hypotheses and much established data, relating to working-class and middle-class differences in attainment and behaviour.

Finally, although the low mobility rate of the unskilled and semi-skilled strata (31) may imply educational waste it is equally important to consider that as a result of the close relationship between education and occupation a situation may soon be reached when the educational institutions legitimize social inequality by individualizing failure. Democratization of the means of education together with the internalizing of the achievement ethic by members of the working-class strata may lead to an individualizing of failure, to a loss of self-respect which in turn modifies an individual's attitude both to his group and to the demands made upon him by the society. If the theory presented in this paper has practical value then it will also indirectly illuminate this dilemma inherent in present social policy.

REFERENCES

1. L. Wirth, *The Ghetto* (Chic. U. Soc. Series, 1929); *Community Life and Social Policy* (U. of Chic. Press, 1956).
2. W. H. Zorbaugh, *The Gold Coast and The Slum* (Chic. U. Soc. Series, 1944).
3. F. M. Thrasher, *The Gang* (Chic. U. Soc. Series, 1927).
4. W. F. Whyte, *Street Corner Society* (U. of Chic. Press, 1943).
5. C. F. Shaw and H. R. McKay, *Juvenile Delinquency and Urban Areas* (U. of Chicago, Behavioral Research Fund Monog., 1942).
6. Lloyd Warner *et al., Democracy in Jonesville* (Harper, 1944).
7. F. Zweig, *The British Worker* (Pelican Books, A.237).
8. N. Dennis, F. Henriques and C. Slaughter, *Coal is our Life* (Eyre and Spottiswoode, 1956).
9. T. Brennan, E. W. Cooney and H. Pollins, *Social Change in S.W. Wales* (Watts & Co., 1954).

10. B. M. Spinley, *The Deprived and the Privileged* (Routledge and Kegan Paul, 1953).
11. R. Hoggart, *The Uses of Literacy* (Chatto and Windus, 1957).
12. A. Davis *et al., Intelligence and Cultural Differences* (U. of Chic. Press, 1951).
13. A. Davis, *Social Class Influences upon Learning* (Harvard Univ. Press, 1955).
14. B. W. Estes, *J. Consulting Psych.*, 17 (1953), 58-62.
15. J. H. Boger, *J. Educ. Res.*, 46 (1952-3), 43-52.
16. H. M. Skodak and H. M. Skeels, *J. of Gen. Psych.*, 66 (1945), 21-58. H. M. Skodak and I. Harms, *J. of Gen. Psych.*, 32 (1948), 283-94.
17. A. H. Halsey and L. Gardner, *Br. J. of Soc.*, 4 (1953), 60-75.
18. W. J. Campbell, Unpub. Ph.D. Thesis, London U. (1951).
19. H. T. Himmelweit, *Social Mobility*, Ed. D. V. Glass (Routledge and Kegan Paul, 1954).
20. G. Greenald, Unpub. M.A. Thesis (Sociol.), London U. (1954).
21. J. Floud, Ed., *Social Class and Educational Opportunity* (Heinemann, 1957).
22. M. P. Honzik, J. W. Macfarlane and L. Allen, *J. of Exp. Educ.*, 17 (1948), 309.
23. N. Bayley, *Year Book Nat. Soc. Study Educ.*, 39 (1940), 11.
24. H. E. Jones, Carmichael's *Manual of Child Psychology* (1946), chapter XI.
25. N. Bayley, *J. of Gen. Psych.*, 75 (1948), 165.
26. A. D. B. Clarke and A. M. Clarke, *B. J. of Psych.*, xlv, Part III (1954).
27. A. D. B. Clarke, "How Constant is the I.Q.?" *Lancet*, 2 (1953), 877.
28. R. J. Havighurst, *Intelligence and Cultural Differences* (U. of Chic. Press, 1951), ch. III.
29. J. Floud and A. H. Halsey, *Year Book of Education* (1956).
30. A. V. Judges, Ed., *Looking Forward in Education* (Faber and Faber, 1955), ch. II.
31. J. R. Hall and D. V. Glass, *Social Mobility* (Routledge and Kegan Paul), 291-307.
32. E. Sapir, *Culture, Language and Personality* (U. of Calif. Press, 1956), 7, 70.
33. E. Cassirer, *The Philosophy of Symbolic Forms*, Vol. I (Yale U. Press, 1953).
34. E. Cassirer, *An Essay on Man* (Yale U. Press, 1944).
35. B. L. Whorf, *Language, Thought and Reality* (N.Y., Wiley and Sons, 1956).
36. H. Hoijer, Ed., *Language in Culture* (U. of Chic. Press, 1954).
37. J. S. Bruner, J. J. Goodnow and G. A. Austin, *A Study of Thinking* (Wiley and Sons, 1957), Append. on language.
38. K. Eells and W. Murray, *Intelligence and Cultural Differences* (U. of Chic. Press, 1951), 43.
39. L. Hogben, "Political Arithmetic" (1938).
40. A. N. Oppenheim, "Social Status and Clique Formation Among Grammar School Boys", *B. J. of Soc.*, 6 (1955), 228-245.

From: *British Journal of Sociology*, 9 (1958), pp. 159-174. Reprinted with permission.

William Labov

THE REFLECTION OF SOCIAL PROCESSES IN LINGUISTIC STRUCTURES

The procedures of descriptive linguistics are based upon the conception of language as a structured set of social norms.[1] It has been useful in the past to consider these norms as invariants, shared by all members of the speech community. However, closer studies of the social context in which language is used show that many elements of linguistic structure are involved in systematic variation which reflects both temporal change and extra-linguistic social processes. The following discussion presents some results of these studies which bring linguistics into close contact with survey methodology and sociological theory.

As a form of social behavior, language is naturally of interest to the sociologist. But language may have a special utility for the sociologist as a sensitive index of many other social processes. Variation in linguistic behavior does not in itself exert a powerful influence on social development, nor does it affect drastically the life chances of the individual; on the contrary, the shape of linguistic behavior changes rapidly as the speaker's social position changes. This malleability of language underlies its great utility as an indicator of social change.

Phonological indexes – based upon the elements of the sound system of a language – are particularly useful in this respect. They give us a large body of quantitative data from relatively small samples of speech: from only a few minutes' conversation, on any topic, we may derive reliable index scores for several variables. To a large extent, the variation on which these indexes are based is independent of the conscious

1 This paper is based upon a presentation given in a panel discussion on sociolinguistics, at a meeting of the Eastern Sociological Society, in Boston, April 12, 1964.

control of the subject. Furthermore, phonological systems show the highest degree of internal structure of all linguistic systems, so that a single social process may be accompanied by correlated shifts of many phonological indexes.

The examples to be cited below are drawn from a study of the social stratification of English in New York City, and particularly a linguistic survey of the Lower East Side.[2] This survey was based upon a primary survey of social attitudes of Lower East Side residents, carried out by Mobilization for Youth in 1961.[3] The original sample of the population of 100,000 consisted of 988 adult subjects. Our target sample was 195 of these respondents, representing about 33,000 native English speakers who had not moved within the previous two years. Through the assistance of Mobilization for Youth, and the New York School of Social Work, we had available a large body of information on the social characteristics of the informants, and we were able to concentrate entirely on their linguistic behavior in this secondary survey. Eighty-one per cent of the target sample was reached in the investigation of language on the Lower East Side.

New York City presents some exceptionally difficult problems for the study of linguistic systems: New Yorkers show a remarkable range of stylistic variation, as well as social variation, to such an extent that earlier investigators failed to find any pattern, and attributed many variables to pure chance.[4] To study social variation, it was first necessary to define and isolate a range of contextual styles within the linguistic interview. The context of the formal interview does not ordinarily elicit casual or spontaneous speech; the methods which were developed to overcome this limitation were crucial to the success of the investigation. The fact that we did succeed in defining and eliciting casual conversation is

[2] A complete report on this survey is given in "The Social Stratification of English in New York City", my Columbia University dissertation, 1964. The development of phonological indexes, and correlation with a complex set of social variables, represent continuations of techniques first developed in "The Social Motivation of a Sound Change", *Word*, 19 (1963), 273-309, which dealt with linguistic changes on the island of Martha's Vineyard, Massachusetts.

[3] Details on the sampling procedures and other methods utilized in this survey are provided in *A Proposal for the Prevention and Control of Delinquency by Expanding Opportunities* (New York, N.Y., Mobilization for Youth, Inc., 214 East Second St., 1961).

[4] "The pronunciation of a very large number of New Yorkers exhibits a pattern in these words that might most accurately be described as the complete absence of any pattern. Such speakers sometimes pronounce /r/ before a consonant or a pause and sometimes omit it, in a thoroughly haphazard fashion.... The speaker hears both types of pronounciation about him all the time, both seem almost equally natural to him, and it is a matter of pure chance which one comes to his lips." A. F. Hubbell, *The Pronunciation of English in New York City* (New York, Columbia University Press, 1950), 48.

shown in the convergence of these results with other studies which utilized anonymous observations, and also in the consistency of the patterns of stylistic variation which were found.

As one example we may consider the phonological variable (r) in New York City.[5] In the traditional New York City pattern, /r/ is not heard in final position, nor before consonants. The words *guard* and *god* are homonyms: [gɒ:d] and [gɒ:d]. So also, *bared* and *bad* are homonyms: "I [bɛ:ᵊd] my [a:m]; I had a [bɛ:ᵊd] cut." In recent decades, a new prestige form has appeared in the speech of native New Yorkers, in which /r/ is pronounced. The phonological index used to measure this variable is simply the percentage of words with historical /r/ in final and preconsonantal position, in which /r/ is pronounced. Thus we find a lower middle class man, 22 years old, using 27% /r/ in careful conversation: an (r) index of 27. In less formal contexts, in casual speech, he uses no /r/ at all: (r)-00. In the more formal direction, he shows (r)-37 in reading style, (r)-60 in reading lists of words, and (r)-100 in reading pairs of words in which his full attention is given to /r/: *guard* vs. *god, dock* vs. *dark,* etc. An upper middle class subject may show the same pattern at a higher level of (r) values; a working class speaker at a much lower level.

We may consider another variable, one which is not peculiar to New York City: the pronunciation of *th* in *thing, think, through, bath,* etc. The prestige form throughout the United States is a fricative, scraping sound: [θ]. In many areas, many speakers occasionally use stops, *t*-like sounds in this position: "I [tɪŋk] so; [svmtɪŋ] else." Even more common is an affricate, a blend of stop and fricative: "I [tθɪŋk] so; [svmtθɪŋ] else." The phonological index for (th) assigns "0" to the fricative, "1" to the affricate, and "2" to the stop; thus an index of (th)-00 would indicate the use of only fricatives, and an index score of (th)-200 only stops. A working class man, for example, might show an index score of (th)-107 in casual speech, -69 in careful conversation, -48 in reading style. A middle class woman might show a score of (th)-20 in casual speech, and -00 in all more formal styles.

Although there is a great range in the absolute values of these variables as used by New Yorkers, there is great agreement in the *pattern* of stylistic variation. Almost eighty per cent of the respondents showed patterns of stylistic variation consistent with the status of /r/ as a prestige marker, and stops and affricates for /th/ as stigmatized forms.

[5] The convention of notation which is adopted here is as follows: (r) represents the *variable*, as opposed to the phonemic unit /r/ or the phonetic unit [r]. A particular value of the variable is shown as (r-1) or (r-0), while an average index score is shown as (r)-35. In this case, (r-1) usually coincides with the phonemic unit /r/, and the more familiar notation /r/ is used instead of (r-1).

This pattern of stylistic variation is primarily of concern to linguists and to students of the ethnography of speaking. However, it is closely associated with the pattern of social stratification in New York City. The pattern of stylistic variation, and the pattern of social variation, enter into the complex and regular structure which is seen in Figure 1.

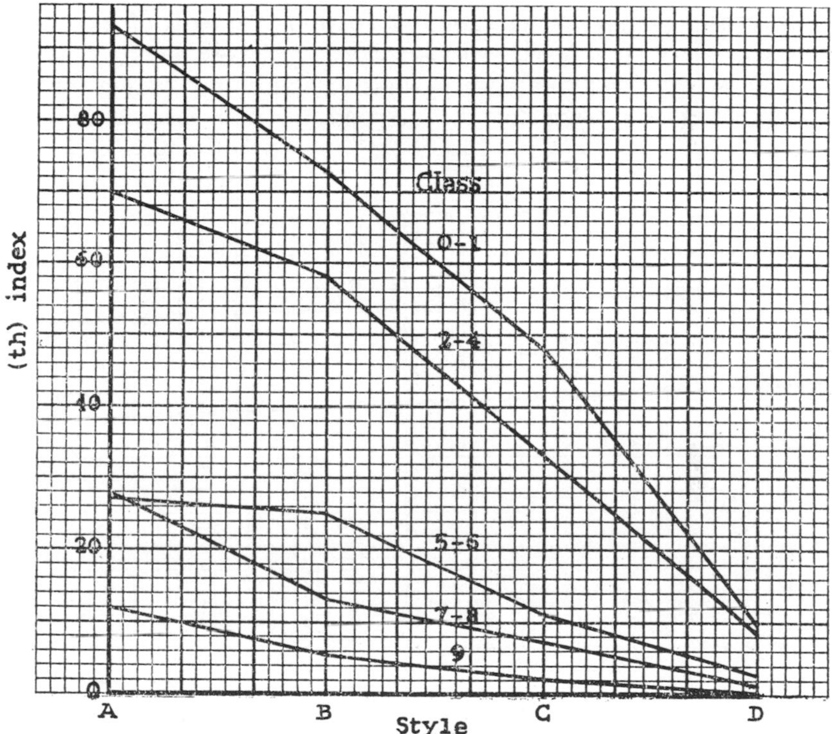

Figure 1. Class stratification of a linguistic variable with stable social significance: (th) in *thing, through*, etc.

Figure 1 is a class stratification diagram for (th), derived from the behavior of 81 adult respondents, raised in New York City.[6] The vertical axis is the scale of average (th) index scores. The horizontal axis repre-

[6] The main body of informants who were interviewed in detail with the linguistic questionnaire consisted of 122 subjects. Forty-one of these were residents of New York City who were born and raised outside of the city in the critical pre-adolescent years. These informants provided a valuable control in studying language changes and patterns peculiar to New York City. The high degree of regularity and agreement shown by the 81 New York City informants contrasted sharply with the irregular pattern of responses of the non-New Yorkers: in many cases, the trends shown by the New York informants were reversed by the others.

sents four contextual styles. The most informal style, casual speech, is shown at the left as A; B is careful conversation, the main bulk of the interview; C is reading style; D is the pronunciation of isolated words. The values on the diagram are connected by horizontal lines, showing the progression of average index scores for socio-economic class groups. These groups are defined as divisions of a ten-point socio-economic scale, constructed by Mobilization for Youth on the basis of their data in the primary survey. The socio-economic index is based on three equally weighted indicators of productive status: occupation (of the breadwinner), education (of the respondent), and income (of the family).[7]

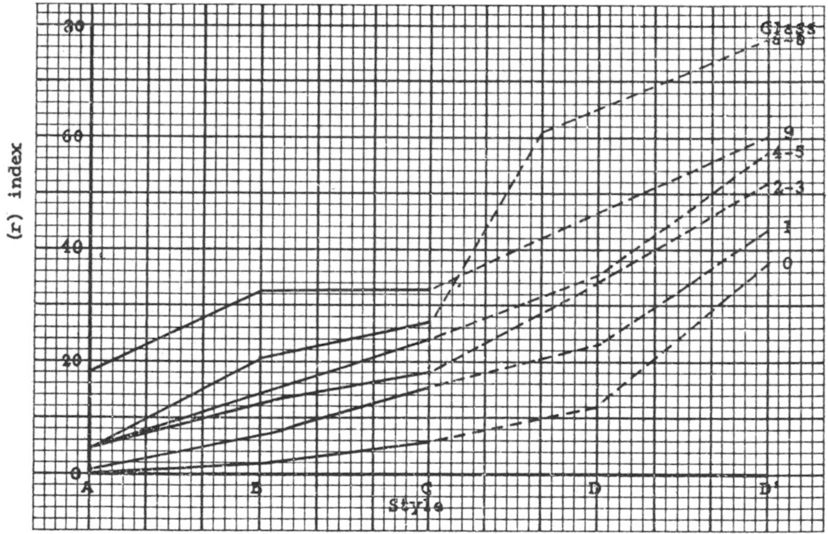

Figure 2. Class stratification of a linguistic variable in process of change: (r) in *guard, car, beer, beard, board,* etc.

Figure 1 is an example of what we may call *sharp stratification.* The five strata of the population are grouped into two larger strata with widely different use of the variable. Figure 2 is a class stratification diagram

[7] The original survey utilized the education of the breadwinner, rather than that of the respondent. It was felt that the linguistic survey should utilize the respondent's education as an indicator, since this might be more closely tied to language behavior than to other forms of behavior. However, the over-all correlations of linguistic behavior and socio-economic class were not affected by this change: there were just as many deviations from regular correlation produced by the change as eliminated by it.

which shows a somewhat different type of stratification. The vertical axis is the phonological index for (r), in which 100 represents a consistent *r*-pronouncing dialect, and 00 a consistent *r*-less dialect. The horizontal axis shows five stylistic contexts, ranging from casual speech, at A, careful speech at B, reading style at C, isolated words at D, and at D¹, the reading of word pairs in which /r/ is the sole focus of attention: *guard* vs. *god, dock* vs. *dark*. This structure is an example of what we may call *fine stratification*: a great many divisions of the socio-economic continuum in which stratification is preserved at each stylistic level. Other investigations of /r/ carried out in New York City support the following general hypothesis on the fine stratification of (r): *any groups of New Yorkers that are ranked in a hierarchical scale by non-linguistic criteria will be ranked in the same order by their differential use of (r).*

The status of /r/ as a prestige marker is indicated by the general upward direction of all horizontal lines as we go from informal to formal contexts. At the level of casual, every-day speech, only the upper middle class group *9* shows a significant degree of *r*-pronunciation. But in more formal styles, the amount of *r*-pronunciation for other groups rises rapidly. The lower middle class, in particular, shows an extremely rapid increase, surpassing the upper middle class level in the two most formal styles. This cross-over pattern appears at first sight to be a deviation from the regular structure shown in Figure 1. It is a pattern which appears in other diagrams: a similar cross-over of the lower middle class appears for two other phonological indexes – in fact, for all those linguistic variables which are involved in a process of linguistic change under social pressure. On the other hand, the social and stylistic patterns for (th) have remained stable for at least 75 years, and show no sign of a cross-over pattern. Thus the hyper-correct behavior of the lower middle class is seen as a synchronic indicator of linguistic change in progress.

The linear nature of the ten-point scale of socio-economic status is confirmed by the fact that it yields regular stratification for many linguistic variables, grammatical as well as phonological. The linguistic variables have been correlated with the individual social indicators of productive status – occupation, education and income – and it appears that no single indicator is as closely correlated with linguistic behavior as the combined index. However, an index which combines occupation and education – neglecting income – gives more regular stratification for the (th) variable. For education, there is one sharp break in linguistic behavior for this variable: the completion of the first year of high school. For occupation, there are sharp differences between blue-collar workers, white-collar workers, and professionals. If we combine these two indicators, we obtain four classes which divide the population almost equally, and stratify (th) usage regularly. This classification seems to be superior to the socio-economic scale for analysis of variables such as (th) which reflect linguistic habits formed relatively early in life. However, the combined socio-economic index, utilizing income, does show more regular stratification for a variable such as (r). Since /r/ is a recently introduced prestige marker in New York City speech, it seems consistent – almost predictable – that it should be closely correlated with a socio-economic scale which includes current income, and thus represents most closely the current social status of the subject.

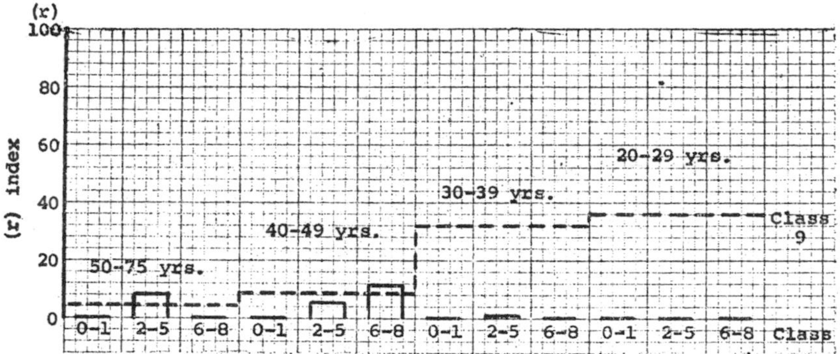

Figure 3. Development of class stratification of (r) for casual speech in apparent time.

Figure 3 shows the distribution of (r) by age levels, a distribution in *apparent time* which indicates a sudden increase in real time of the social stratification of (r) in every-day speech. The upper middle class usage is indicated by the horizontal dotted line. The usage of other class groups – 0-1, lower class; 2-5, working class; 6-8, lower middle class – is indicated by the series of vertical bars at each age level. For the two oldest age levels, there is little indication of social significance of /r/. But beginning with those under 40 years old, there is a radically different situation, with /r/ acting as a prestige marker of upper middle class usage only. This sudden change in the status of /r/ seems to have coincided with the events of World War II.

So far, we have been considering only one aspect of social stratification: the differentiation of objective behavior. In the recent studies of New York City, the complementary aspect of social stratification has also been examined: social evaluation. A subjective reaction test was developed to isolate unconscious social responses to the values of individual phonological variables. In these tests, the subject rates a number of short excerpts from the speech of other New Yorkers on a scale of occupational suitability, and cross-comparisons of these ratings enable us

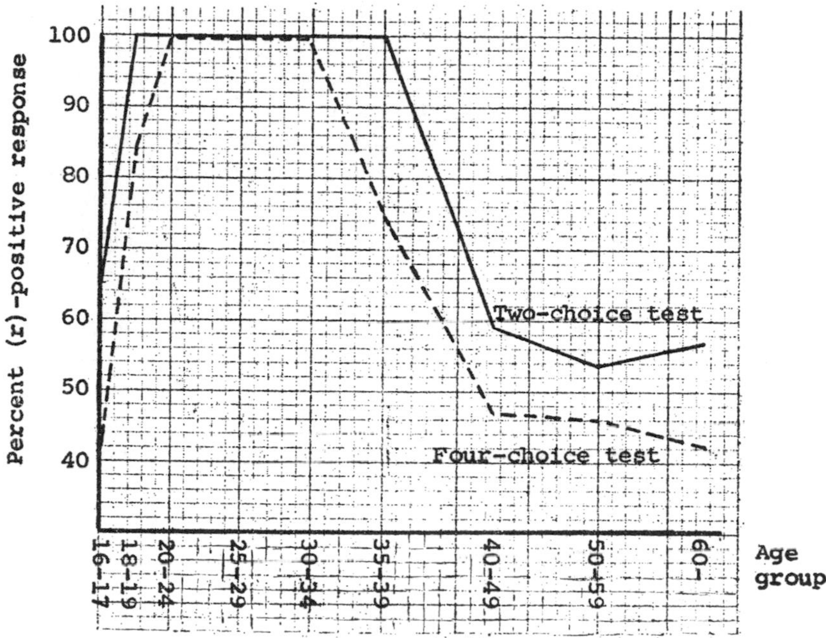

Figure 4. Development of social evaluation of (r) in two subjective reaction tests.

to isolate the unconscious subjective reactions of respondents to single phonological variables. Figure 4 shows the percentage of subjects who displayed reactions which were consistent with the status of /r/ as a prestige marker. We see that all subjects between 18 and 39 years old showed agreement in their positive evaluation of /r/, despite the fact (as shown in Figure 3) that the great majority of these subjects do not use any /r/ in their every-day speech. Thus sharp diversification of (r) in objective performance is accompanied by uniform subjective evaluation of the social significance of this feature. On the other hand, the subjects over 40 years old, who show no differential pattern in their use of (r), show a very mixed pattern in their social evaluation of /r/.

This result is typical of many other empirical findings which confirm the view of New York City as a single speech community, united by a uniform evaluation of linguistic features, yet diversified by increasing stratification in objective performance.

The special role of the lower middle class in linguistic change has been illustrated here in only one example, the cross-over pattern of Figure 2. When Figure 3 is replicated for increasingly formal styles, we see that in each age level, the lower middle class shows the greatest tendency towards the introduction of *r*-pronunciation, and in the most formal styles, goes far beyond the upper middle class level in this respect. A great deal of evidence shows that lower middle class speakers have the greatest tendency towards linguistic insecurity, and therefore tend to adopt, even in middle age, the prestige forms used by the youngest members of the highest ranking class. This linguistic insecurity is shown by the very wide range of stylistic variation used by lower middle class speakers; by their great fluctuation within a given stylistic context; by their conscious striving for correctness; and by their strongly negative attitudes towards their native speech pattern.

Another measure of linguistic insecurity was obtained by an independent approach, based on lexical behavior. The subjects were presented with eighteen words which have socially significant variants in pronunciation: *vase, aunt, escalator,* etc. Each word was pronounced in two alternate forms, such as [veɪz – vɑ:z], [æ'nt - ɑ'nt], [ɛskeleɪtə - ɛskjuleitə]. Respondents were asked to select the form they thought was correct. They were then asked to indicate which form they usually used themselves. The total number of cases in which these two choices differed was taken as the index of linguistic insecurity. By this measure, the lower middle class showed much the greatest degree of linguistic insecurity.

Social stratification and its consequences are only one type of social process which is reflected in linguistic structures. The interaction of ethnic groups in New York City – Jews, Italians, Negroes and Puerto Ricans – is also reflected in these and other linguistic variables. For some variables, New York City Negroes participate in the same structure of social and stylistic variation as white New Yorkers. For other variables, there is an absolute differentiation of white and Negro which reflects the process of social segregation characteristic of the city. For example, there is a Southern phonological characteristic which merges the vowels /i/ and /e/ before nasals: *pin* and *pen*, *since* and *sense*, are homonyms: "I asked for a straight [pɪn] and he gave me a writing [pɪn]." In New York City, this phonological trait has been generalized throughout the Negro community, so that the younger Negro speakers, whether or not they show other Southern characteristics in their speech, regularly show this merger. Thus this linguistic characteristic acts as an absolute differentiator of the Negro group, reflecting the social processes which identify the racial group as a whole. Similar phonological characteristics can be found which mark the Puerto Rican group.[8]

Segregation of Negro and white may be seen in aspects of linguistic behavior quite distinct from the phonological system. Our investigation

[8] Most New Yorkers differentiate the vowel of *can* as in "tin can" from that of *can* as in "I can". None of the Puerto Rican subjects interviewed showed a consistent use of this phonemic distinction.

of New York City speech includes a number of semantic studies: one of the most fruitful of these concerns the semantic structures which revolve about the term *common sense*. This term lies at the center of one of the most important areas of intellectual activity for most Americans. It is a term frequently used, with considerable affect; its meaning is often debated, and questions about common sense evoke considerable intellectual effort from most of our subjects. Negroes use the term *common sense*, but also an equivalent term which is not a part of the native vocabulary of any white speakers. This term is *mother-wit*, or *mother-with* [mʌðɝωɪθ]. For a few white speakers, mother-wit is identified as an archaic, learned term: but for Negroes, it is a native term used frequently by older members of the household, referring to a complex of emotions and concepts that is quite important to them. Yet Negroes have no idea that white people do not use *mother-wit*, and whites have no inkling of the Negro use of this term. Contrast this complete lack of communication in an important area of intellectual activity with the smooth and regular transmission of slang terms from Negro musicians to the white population as a whole.

The process of social segregation springs from causes and mechanisms which have been studied in detail. However, the opposing process of social integration is less obvious, and on the plane of linguistic structure, it is not at all clear how it takes place. Consider the semantic structure of *common sense*. When we analyze the semantic components of this term, its position in a hierarchical taxonomy, and its relation to coordinate terms in a semantic paradigm, we see great differences in the semantic structures used by various speakers.

This diversity can best be illustrated by contrasting two types of responses to our questions on common sense, responses which usually fall into two consistent sets. Respondent A may think of *common sense* as just "sensible talk". If he understands the cognitive content of an utterance, that to him is common sense. Respondent B considers common sense to be the highest form of rational activity, the application of knowledge to solve the most difficult problems. Do most people have common sense? A says yes, B says no. Who has a great deal of common sense? A thinks that doctors, lawyers, professors have the most. B thinks that uneducated people are more apt to have common sense, and immediately calls to mind some highly educated people with no common sense at all. If we say "two and two make four", is that an example of common sense? A says yes, B says no. Can we say that a person is intelligent, yet has no common sense? A says no, because intelligence is the same as common sense. B says yes, common sense and intelligence are quite different. A believes that if someone can be called *smart,* he would also have common sense; B sees no connection between smartness and common sense. Can one have *wisdom*, and yet no common sense? A says yes, B says no.

The extreme differences between types A and B, which are not independent of social stratification, lead us to question the possibility of semantic integration. Can such individuals, who have radically opposed semantic structures for *common sense,* be said to understand one another? Can the term *common sense* be used to communicate meaning between these speakers? Some writers (particularly the followers of General Semantics) feel that native speakers of English usually do *not* understand one another, that such opposing structures inevitably lead to misunderstanding. The results of our studies so far lead me to infer the opposite. People do understand one another: semantic integration seems to take place through a central set of relations of equivalence and attribution upon which all English speakers agree. With only a few exceptions, all subjects agree that *common sense* falls under the super-ordinate *judgment*: it is "good judgment". Equally high agreement is found in the collocation of *practical*, or *every-day,* with *common sense.* We have no simplex term to describe the quality of "not being learned from books", yet there is also a very high degree of agreement in this attribute of *common sense.*

If semantic integration takes place, it must be by a social process in which extreme variants are suppressed in group interaction at the expense of central or core values. The continuing studies of these semantic patterns are designed to throw light on the problem as to whether such a mechanism exists, and how it might operate.

This discussion has presented a number of aspects of language behavior in which linguistic structures are seen to reflect social processes. In the over-all view, there is a wide range of benefits which may be drawn from the interaction of sociological and linguistic investigations. These may be considered under three headings, in order of increasing generality:

1. Linguistic indexes provide a large body of quantitative data which reflect the influence of many independent variables. It does not seem impractical for tape-recorded data of this type to be collected and analyzed by social scientists who are not primarily linguists. Once the social significance of a given linguistic variant has been determined, by methods such as those outlined above, this variable may then serve as an index to measure other forms of social behavior: upward social aspirations, social mobility and insecurity, changes in social stratification and segregation.

2. Many of the fundamental concepts of sociology are exemplified in the results of these studies of linguistic variation. The speech community

is not defined by any marked agreement in the use of language elements, so much as by participation in a set of shared norms; these norms may be observed in overt types of evaluative behavior, and by the uniformity of abstract patterns of variation which are invariant in respect to particular levels of usage. Similarly, through observations of linguistic behavior it is possible to make detailed studies of the structure of class stratification in a given community. We find that there are some linguistic variables which are correlated with an abstract measure of class position, derived from a combination of several non-isomorphic indicators, where no single, less abstract measure will yield equally good correlations.

3. If we consider seriously the concept of language as a form of social behavior, it is evident that any theoretical advance in the analysis of the mechanism of linguistic evolution will contribute directly to the general theory of social evolution. In this respect, it is necessary for linguists to refine and extend their methods of structural analysis to the use of language in complex urban societies. For this purpose, linguistics may now draw upon the techniques of survey methodology; more importantly, many of the theoretical approaches of linguistics may be re-interpreted in the light of more general concepts of social behavior developed by other social sciences. The present report is intended as a contribution to this more general aim. It is hoped that the main achievements of linguistic science, which may formerly have appeared remote and irrelevant to many sociologists, may eventually be seen as consistent with the present direction of sociology, and valuable for the understanding of social structure and social change.

This study appears in this volume in published form for the first time. Printed with permission.

Roger Brown and Albert Gilman

THE PRONOUNS OF POWER AND SOLIDARITY

Most of us in speaking and writing English use only one pronoun of address; we say "you" to many persons and "you" to one person. The pronoun "thou" is reserved, nowadays, to prayer and naive poetry, but in the past it was the form of familiar address to a single person. At that time "you" was the singular of reverence and of polite distance and, also, the invariable plural. In French, German, Italian, Spanish, and the other languages most nearly related to English there are still active two singular pronouns of address. The interesting thing about such pronouns is their close association with two dimensions fundamental to the analysis of all social life – the dimensions of power and solidarity. Semantic and stylistic analysis of these forms takes us well into psychology and sociology as well as into linguistics and the study of literature.

This paper is divided into five major sections.[1] The first three of these are concerned with the semantics of the pronouns of address. By semantics we mean covariation between the pronoun used and the objective relationship existing between speaker and addressee. The first section offers a general description of the semantic evolution of the pronouns of address in certain European languages. The second section describes semantic differences existing today among the pronouns of French, German, and Italian. The third section proposes a connection between social structure, group ideology, and the semantics of the pronoun. The final two sections of the paper are concerned with expressive style by which we mean covariation between the pronoun used and characteristics of

1 Our study was financed by a Grant-in-Aid-of-Research made by the Ford Foundation to Brown, and the authors gratefully acknowledge this assistance.

the person speaking. The first of these sections shows that a man's consistent pronoun style gives away his class status and his political views. The last section describes the ways in which a man may vary his pronoun style from time to time so as to express transient moods and attitudes. In this section it is also proposed that the major expressive meanings are derived from the major semantic rules.

In each section the evidence most important to the thesis of that section is described in detail. However, the various generalizations we shall offer have developed as an interdependent set from continuing study of our whole assemblage of facts, and so it may be well to indicate here the sort of motley assemblage this is. Among secondary sources the general language histories (16, 48, 90, 142, 213, 275) have been of little use because their central concern is always phonetic rather than semantic change. However, there are a small number of monographs and doctoral dissertations describing the detailed pronoun semantics for one or another language – sometimes throughout its history (133, 139, 216, 353), sometimes for only a century or so (229, 401), and sometimes for the works of a particular author (55, 119). As primary evidence for the usage of the past we have drawn on plays, on legal proceedings (208), and on letters (89, 151). We have also learned about contemporary usage from literature but, more importantly, from long conversations with native speakers of French, Italian, German, and Spanish both here and in Europe. Our best information about the pronouns of today comes from a questionnaire concerning usage which is described in the second section of this paper. The questionnaire has thus far been answered by the following numbers of students from abroad who were visiting in Boston in 1957-1958: 50 Frenchmen, 20 Germans, 11 Italians, and two informants, each, from Spain, Argentina, Chile, Denmark, Norway, Sweden, Israel, South Africa, India, Switzerland, Holland, Austria, and Yugoslavia.

We have far more information concerning English, French, Italian, Spanish, and German than for any other languages. Informants and documents concerning the other Indo-European languages are not easily accessible to us. What we have to say is then largely founded on information about these five closely related languages. These first conclusions will eventually be tested by us against other Indo-European languages and, in a more generalized form, against unrelated languages.

The European development of two singular pronouns of address begins with the Latin *tu* and *vos*. In Italian they became *tu* and *voi* (with *Lei* eventually largely displacing *voi*); in French *tu* and *vous*; in Spanish *tu* and *vos* (later *usted*). In German the distinction began with *du* and *Ihr* but *Ihr* gave way to *er* and later to *Sie*. English speakers first used "thou" and "ye" and later replaced "ye" with "you". As a convenience we propose to use the symbols *T* and *V* (from the Latin *tu* and *vos)* as generic designators for a familiar and a polite pronoun in any language.

THE GENERAL SEMANTIC EVOLUTION OF *T* AND *V*

In the Latin of antiquity there was only *tu* in the singular. The plural *vos* as a form of address to one person was first directed to the emperor and there are several theories (55, 58) about how this may have come about. The use of the plural to the emperor began in the fourth century. By that time there were actually two emperors; the ruler of the eastern empire had his seat in Constantinople and the ruler of the west sat in Rome. Because of Diocletian's reforms the imperial office, although vested in two men, was administratively unified. Words addressed to one man were, by implication, addressed to both. The choice of *vos* as a form of address may have been in response to this implicit plurality. An emperor is also plural in another sense; he is the summation of his people and can speak as their representative. Royal persons sometimes say "we" where an ordinary man would say "I". The Roman emperor sometimes spoke of himself as *nos*, and the reverential *vos* is the simple reciprocal of this.

The usage need not have been mediated by a prosaic association with actual plurality, for plurality is a very old and ubiquitous metaphor for power. Consider only the several senses of such English words as "great" and "grand". The reverential *vos* could have been directly inspired by the power of an emperor.

Eventually the Latin plural was extended from the emperor to other power figures. However, this semantic pattern was not unequivocally established for many centuries. There was much inexplicable fluctuation between *T* and *V* in Old French, Spanish, Italian, and Portuguese (353), and in Middle English (229, 401). In verse, at least, the choice seems often to have depended on assonance, rhyme, or syllable count. However, some time between the twelfth and fourteenth centuries (133, 139, 229, 353), varying with the language, a set of norms crystallized which we call the nonreciprocal power semantic.

The Power Semantic

One person may be said to have power over another in the degree that he is able to control the behavior of the other. Power is a relationship between at least two persons, and it is nonreciprocal in the sense that both cannot have power in the same area of behavior. The power semantic is similarly nonreciprocal; the superior says *T* and receives *V*.

There are many bases of power – physical strength, wealth, age, sex, institutionalized role in the church, the state, the army, or within the family. The character of the power semantic can be made clear with a set of examples from various languages. In his letters, Pope Gregory I (590-604) used *T* to his subordinates in the ecclesiastical hierarchy and they invariably said *V* to him (291). In medieval Europe, generally, the nobility said *T* to the common people and received *V;* the master of a household said *T* to his slave, his servant, his squire, and received *V*. Within the family, of whatever social level, parents gave *T* to children and were given *V*. In Italy in the fifteenth century penitents said *V* to the priest and were told *T* (139). In Froissart (late fourteenth century) God says *T* to His angels and they say *V*; all celestial beings say *T* to man and receive *V*. In French of the twelfth and thirteenth centuries man says *T* to the animals (353). In fifteenth-century Italian literature Christians say *T* to Turks and Jews and receive *V* (139). In the plays of Corneille and Racine (353) and Shakespeare (55), the noble principals say *T* to their subordinates and are given *V* in return.

The *V* of reverence entered European speech as a form of address to the principal power in the state and eventually generalized to the powers within that microcosm of the state – the nuclear family. In the history of language, then, parents are emperor figures. It is interesting to note in passing that Freud reversed this terminology and spoke of kings, as well as generals, employers, and priests, as father figures. The propriety of Freud's designation for his psychological purposes derives from the fact that an individual learning a European language reverses the historical order of semantic generalization. The individual's first experience of subordination to power and of the reverential *V* comes in his relation to his parents. In later years similar asymmetrical power relations and similar norms of address develop between employer and employee, soldier and officer, subject and monarch. We can see how it might happen, as Freud believed, that the later social relationships would remind the individual of the familial prototype and would revive emotions and responses from childhood. In a man's personal history recipients of the nonreciprocal *V* are parent figures.

Since the nonreciprocal power semantic only prescribes usage between superior and inferior, it calls for a social structure in which there are unique power ranks for every individual. Medieval European societies were not so finely structured as that, and so the power semantic was never the only rule for the use of *T* and *V*. There were also norms of address for persons of roughly equivalent power, that is, for members of a common class. Between equals, pronominal address was reciprocal; an individual gave and received the same form. During the medieval period, and for varying times beyond, equals of the upper classes exchanged the mutual *V* and equals of the lower classes exchanged *T*.

The difference in class practice derives from the fact that the reverential *V* was always introduced into a society at the top. In the Roman Empire only the highest ranking persons had any occasion to address the emperor, and so at first only they made use of *V* in the singular. In its later history in other parts of Europe the reverential *V* was usually adopted by one court in imitation of another. The practice slowly disseminated downward in a society. In this way the use of *V* in the singular incidentally came to connote a speaker of high status. In later centuries Europeans became very conscious of the extensive use of *V* as a mark of elegance. In the drama of seventeenth-century France the nobility and bourgeoisie almost always address one another as *V*. This is true even of husband and wife, of lovers, and of parent and child if the child is adult. Mme. de Sévigné in her correspondence never uses *T*, not even to her daughter the Comtesse de Grignan (353). Servants and peasantry, however, regularly used *T* among themselves.

For many centuries French, English, Italian, Spanish, and German pronoun usage followed the rule of nonreciprocal *T-V* between persons of unequal power and the rule of mutual *V* or *T* (according to social-class membership) between persons of roughly equivalent power. There was at first no rule differentiating address among equals but, very gradually, a distinction developed which is sometimes called the *T* of intimacy and the *V* of formality. We name this second dimension *solidarity,* and here is our guess as to how it developed.

The Solidarity Semantic

The original singular pronoun was *T*. The use of *V* in the singular developed as a form of address to a person of superior power. There are many personal attributes that convey power. The recipient of *V* may differ from the recipient of *T* in strength, age, wealth, birth, sex, or profession. As two people move apart on these power-laden dimensions, one of them begins to say *V*. In general terms, the *V* form is linked with differences between persons. Not all differences between persons imply a difference of power. Men are born in different cities, belong to different families of the same status, may attend different but equally prominent schools, may practice different but equally respected professions. A rule for making distinctive use of *T* and *V* among equals can be formulated by generalizing the power semantic. Differences of power cause *V* to emerge in one direction of address; differences not concerned with power cause *V* to emerge in both directions.

The relations called *older than, parent of, employer of, richer than, stronger than,* and *nobler than* are all asymmetrical. If *A* is older than

B, *B* is not older than *A*. The relation called "more powerful than", which is abstracted from these more specific relations, is also conceived to be asymmetrical. The pronoun usage expressing this power relation is also asymmetrical or nonreciprocal, with the greater receiving *V* and the lesser *T*. Now we are concerned with a new set of relations which are symmetrical; for example, *attended the same school* or *have the same parents* or *practice the same profession*. If *A* has the same parents as *B*, *B* has the same parents as *A*. Solidarity is the name we give to the general relationship and solidarity is symmetrical. The corresponding norms of address are symmetrical or reciprocal with *V* becoming more probable as solidarity declines. The solidary *T* reaches a peak of probability in address between twin brothers or in a man's soliloquizing address to himself.

Not every personal attribute counts in determining whether two people are solidary enough to use the mutual *T*. Eye color does not ordinarily matter nor does shoe size. The similarities that matter seem to be those that make for like-mindedness or similar behavior dispositions. These will ordinarily be such things as political membership, family, religion, profession, sex, and birthplace. However, extreme distinctive values on almost any dimension may become significant. Height ought to make for solidarity among giants and midgets. The *T* of solidarity can be produced by frequency of contact as well as by objective similarities. However, frequent contact does not necessarily lead to the mutual *T*. It depends on whether contact results in the discovery or creation of the like-mindedness that seems to be the core of the solidarity semantic.

Solidarity comes into the European pronouns as a means of differentiating address among power equals. It introduces a second dimension into the semantic system on the level of power equivalents. So long as solidarity was confined to this level, the two-dimensional system was in equilibrium (see Figure 1a), and it seems to have remained here for a considerable time in all our languages. It is from the long reign of the two-dimensional semantic that *T* derives its common definition as the pronoun of either condescension or intimacy and *V* its definition as the pronoun of reverence or formality. These definitions are still current but usage has, in fact, gone somewhat beyond them.

The dimension of solidarity is potentially applicable to all persons addressed. Power superiors may be solidary (parents, elder siblings) or not solidary (officials whom one seldom sees). Power inferiors, similarly, may be as solidary as the old family retainer and as remote as the waiter in a strange restaurant. Extension of the solidarity dimension along the dotted lines of Figure 1b creates six categories of persons defined by their relations to a speaker. Rules of address are in conflict for persons in the upper left and lower right categories. For the upper left, power indicates *V* and solidarity *T*. For the lower right, power indicates *T* and solidarity *V*.

The asbtract conflict described in Figure 1b is particularized in Figure 2a with a sample of the social dyads in which the conflict would be felt. In each case usage in one direction is unequivocal but, in the other direction, the two semantic forces are opposed. The first three dyads in Figure 2a involve conflict in address to inferiors who are not solidary (the lower right category of Figure 1b), and the second three dyads involve conflict in address to superiors who are solidary (the upper left category in Figure 1b).

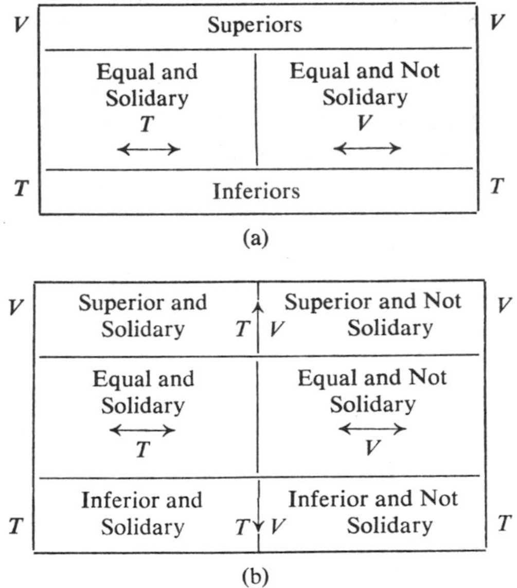

Figure 1. The two-dimensional semantic (a) in equilibrium and (b) under tension.

Well into the nineteenth century the power semantic prevailed and waiters, common soldiers, and employees were called *T* while parents, masters, and elder brothers were called *V*. However, all our evidence consistently indicates that in the past century the solidarity semantic has gained supremacy. Dyads of the type shown in Figure 2a now reciprocate the pronoun of solidarity or the pronoun of nonsolidarity. The conflicted address has been resolved so as to match the unequivocal address. The abstract result is a simple one-dimensional system with the reciprocal *T* for the solidary and the reciprocal *V* for the nonsolidary.

It is the present practice to reinterpret power-laden attributes so as to turn to them into symmetrical solidarity attributes. Relationships like *older than, father of, nobler than,* and *richer than* are now reinterpreted for purposes of *T* and *V* as relations of *the same age as, the same family as, the same kind of ancestry as*, and *the same income as*. In the degree that these relationships hold, the probability of a mutual *T* increases and, in the degree that they do not hold, the probability of a mutual *V* increases.

Customer $T\downarrow V \uparrow V$ Waiter	Officer $T\downarrow V \uparrow V$ Soldier	Employer $T\downarrow V \uparrow V$ Employee
Parent $T\downarrow T \uparrow V$ Son	Master $T\downarrow T \uparrow V$ Faithful Servant	Elder brother $T\downarrow T \uparrow V$ Younger Brother

(a)

Customer $\updownarrow V$ Waiter	Officer $\updownarrow V$ Soldier	Employer $\updownarrow V$ Employee
Parent $T\updownarrow$ Son	Master $T\updownarrow$ Faithful Servant	Elder Brother $T\updownarrow$ Younger Brother

(b)

Figure 2. Social dyads involving (a) semantic conflict and (b) their resolution.

There is an interesting residual of the power relation in the contemporary notion that the right to initiate the reciprocal *T* belongs to the member of the dyad having the better power-based claim to say *T* without reciprocation. The suggestion that solidarity be recognized comes more gracefully from the elder than from the younger, from the richer than from the poorer, from the employer than from the employee, from the noble than from the commoner, from the female than from the male.

In support of our claim that solidarity has largely won out over power we can offer a few quotations from language scholars. Littré, writing of French usage, says (251): "Notre courtoisie est même si grande, que nous ne dédaignons pas de donner du vous et du monsieur à l'homme de la condition la plus vile." Grand (139) wrote of the Italian *V:* "On commence aussi à le donner aux personnes de service, à qui on disait tu autrefois." We have found no authority who describes the general character of these many specific changes of usage: a shift from power to solidarity as the governing semantic principle.

The best evidence that the change has occurred is in our interviews and notes on contemporary literature and films and, most importantly, the questionnaire results. The six social dyads of Figure 2 were all represented in the questionnaire. In the past these would have been answered in accordance with asymmetrical power. Across all six of these dyads the French results yield only 11 per cent nonreciprocal power answers, the German 12 per cent, the Italian 27 per cent. In all other cases the usage is reciprocal, as indicated in Figure 2b. In all three of the languages, address between master and servant retains the greatest power loading. Some of the changes toward solidarity are very recent. Only since the Second World War, for instance, has the French Army adopted a regulation requiring officers to say *V* to enlisted men.

Finally, it is our opinion that a still newer direction of semantic shift can be discerned in the whole collection of languages studied. Once solidarity has been established as the single dimension distinguishing *T* from *V* the province of *T* proceeds to expand. The direction of change is increase in the number of relations defined as solidary enough to merit a mutual *T* and, in particular, to regard any sort of camaraderie resulting from a common task or a common fate as grounds for *T*. We have a favorite example of this new trend given us independently by several French informants. It seems that mountaineers above a certain critical altitude shift to the mutual *T*. We like to think that this is the point where their lives hang by a single thread. In general, the mutual *T* is advancing among fellow students, fellow workers, members of the same political group, persons who share a hobby or take a trip together. We believe this is the direction of current change because it summarizes what our informants tell us about the pronoun usage of the "young people" as opposed to that of older people.

CONTEMPORARY DIFFERENCES AMONG FRENCH, ITALIAN, AND GERMAN

While *T* and *V* have passed through the same general semantic sequence in these three languages, there are today some differences of detailed usage which were revealed by the questionnaire date. Conversations with native speakers guided us in the writing of questionnaire items, but the conversations themselves did not teach us the characteristic semantic features of the three languages; these did not emerge until we made statistical comparison of answers to the standard items of the questionnaire.

The questionnaire is in English. It opens with a paragraph informing the subject that the items below all have reference to the use of the singular pronouns of address in his native language. There are 28 items in the full questionnaire, and they all have the form of the following example from the questionnaire for French students:

1. (*a*) Which pronoun would you use in speaking to your mother?

T (definitely)	———
T (probably)	———
Possibly *T*, possibly *V*	———
V(probably)	———
V(definitely)	———

1. (*b*) Which would she use in speaking to you?

T (definitely)	———
T (probably)	———
Possibly *T*, possibly *V*	———
V(probably)	———
V(definitely)	———

The questionnaire asks about usage between the subject and his mother, his father, his grandfather, his wife, a younger brother who is a child, a married elder brother, that brother's wife, a remote male cousin, and an elderly female servant whom he has known from childhood. It asks about usage between the subject and fellow students at the university at home, usage to a student from home visiting in America, and usage to someone with whom the subject had been at school some years previously. It asks about usage to a waiter in a restaurant, between clerks in an office, fellow soldiers in the army, between boss and employee, army private and general. In addition, there are some rather elaborate items which ask the subject to imagine himself in some carefully detailed social situation and then to say what pronoun he would use. A copy of the full questionnaire may be had on application to the authors.

The most accessible informants were students from abroad resident in Boston in the fall of 1957. Listings of such students were obtained from Harvard, Boston University, M.I.T., and the Office of the French Consul in New England. Although we have data from a small sample of female respondents, the present analysis is limited to the males. All the men in the sample have been in the United States for one year or less; they come from cities of over 300,000 inhabitants, and these cities are well scattered across the country in question. In addition, all members of the sample are from upper-middle-class, professional families. This homogeneity of class membership was enforced by the factors determining selection of students who go abroad. The occasional informant from a working-class family is deliberately excluded from these comparisons. The class from which we draw shows less regional variation in speech than does the working class and, especially, farmers. At the present time we have complete responses from 50 Frenchmen, 20 Germans, and 11 Italians; many of these men also sent us letters describing their understanding of the pronouns and offering numerous valuable anecdotes of usage. The varying numbers of subjects belonging to the three nationalities result from the unequal representation of these nationalities among Boston students rather than from national characterological differences in willingness to answer a questionnaire. Almost every person on our lists agreed to serve as an informant.

In analyzing the results we assigned the numbers 0-4 to the five response alternatives to each question, beginning with "Definitely *V*" as 0. A rough test was made of the significance of the differences among the three languages on each question. We dichotomized the replies to each question into: (a) all replies of either "Definitely *T*" or "Probably *T*"; (b) all replies of "Definitely *V*" or "Probably *V*" or "Possibly *V*, possibly *T*". Using the chi-squared test with Yates's correction for small frequencies we determined, for each comparison, the probability of obtaining by chance a difference as large or larger than that actually obtained. Even with such small samples, there were quite a few differences significantly unlikely to occur by chance ($P = .05$ or less). Germans were more prone than the French to say *T* to their grandfathers, to an elder brother's wife, and to an old family servant. The French were more prone than the Germans to say *T* to a male fellow student, to a student from home visiting in America, to a fellow clerk in an office, and to someone known previously as a fellow student. Italians were more prone than the French to say *T* to a female fellow student and also to an attractive girl to whom they had recently been introduced. Italians were more prone than the Germans to say *T* to the persons just described and, in addition, to a male fellow student and to a student from home visiting in America. On no question did either the French or the Germans show a significantly greater tendency to say *T* than did the Italians.

The many particular differences among the three languages are susceptible of a general characterization. Let us first contrast German and French. The German *T* is more reliably applied within the family than is the French *T*; in addition to the significantly higher *T* scores for grandfather and elder brother's wife there are smaller differences showing a higher score for the German *T* on father, mother, wife, married elder bother, and remote male cousin. The French *T* is not automatically applied to remote relatives, but it is more likely than the German pronoun to be used to express the camaraderie of fellow students, fellow clerks, fellow countrymen abroad, and fellow soldiers. In general it may be said that the solidarity coded by the German *T* is an ascribed solidarity of family relationships. The French *T*, in greater degree, codes an acquired solidarity not founded on family relationship but developing out of some sort of shared fate. As for the Italian *T*, it very nearly equals the German in family solidarity and it surpasses the French in camaraderie. The camaraderie of the Italian male, incidentally, is extended to the Italian female; unlike the French or German student the Italian says *T* to the co-ed almost as readily as to the male fellow student.

There is a very abstract semantic rule governing *T* and *V* which is the same for French, German, and Italian and for many other languages we have studied. The rule is that usage is reciprocal, *T* becoming increasingly probable and *V* less probable as the number of solidarity-producing attributes shared by two people increases. The respect in which French, German, and Italian differ from one another is in the relative weight given to various attributes of persons which can serve to generate solidarity. For German, ascribed family membership is the important attribute; French and Italian give more weight to acquired characteristics.

SEMANTICS, SOCIAL STRUCTURE, AND IDEOLOGY

A historical study of the pronouns of address reveals a set of semantic and social psychological correspondences. The nonreciprocal power semantic is associated with a relatively static society in which power is distributed by birthright and is not subject to much redistribution. The power semantic was closely tied with the feudal and manorial systems. In Italy the reverential pronoun *Lei* which has largely displaced the older *voi* was originally an abbreviation for *la vostra Signoria* "your lordship" and in Spanish *vuestra Merced* "your grace" became the reverential *usted*. The static social structure was accompanied by the Church's teaching that each man had his properly appointed place and ought not to wish to rise above it. The reciprocal solidarity semantic has grown with social mobility and an equalitarian ideology. The towns and cities have led the way in the semantic change as they led the way in opening society to vertical movement. In addition to these rough historical correspondences we have made a collection of lesser items of evidence favoring the thesis.

In France the nonreciprocal power semantic was dominant until the Revolution when the Committee for the Public Safety condemned the use of *V* as a feudal remnant and ordered a universal reciprocal *T*. On October 31, 1793, Malbec made a Parliamentary speech against *V:* "Nous distinguons trois personnes pour le singulier et trois pour le pluriel, et, au mépris de cette règle, l'esprit de fanatisme, d'orgueil et de féodalité, nous a fait contracter l'habitude de nous servir de la seconde personne du pluriel lorsque nous parlons à un seul" (quoted in 49). For a time revolutionary "fraternité" transformed all address into the mutual *Citoyen* and the mutual *tu*. Robespierre even addressed the president of the Assembly as *tu*. In later years solidarity declined and the differences of power which always exist everywhere were expressed once more.

It must be asked why the equalitarian ideal was expressed in a universal *T* rather than a universal *V* or, as a third alternative, why there was not a shift of semantic from power to solidarity with both pronouns being retained. The answer lies with the ancient upper-class preference for the use of *V*. There was animus against the pronoun itself. The pronoun of the "*sans-culottes*" was *T* (133), and so this had to be the pronoun of the Revolution.

Although the power semantic has largely gone out of pronoun use in France today native speakers are nevertheless aware of it. In part they are aware of it because it prevails in so much of the greatest French literature. Awareness of power as a potential factor in pronoun usage was revealed by our respondents' special attitude toward the saying of *T* to a waiter. Most of them felt that this would be shockingly bad taste in a way that other norm violations would not be, apparently because there is a kind of seignorial right to say *T* to a waiter, an actual power assymmetry, which the modern man's ideology requires him to deny. In French Africa, on the other hand, it is considered proper to recognize a caste difference between the African and the European, and the nonreciprocal address is used to express it. The European says *T* and requires *V* from the African. This is a galling custom to the African, and in 1957 Robert Lacoste, the French Minister residing in Algeria, urged his countrymen to eschew the practice.

In England, before the Norman Conquest, "ye" was the second person plural and "thou" the singular. "You" was originally the accusative of "ye", but in time it also became the nominative plural and ultimately ousted "thou" as the usual singular. The first uses of "ye" as a reverential singular occur in the thirteenth century (229), and seem to have been copied from the French nobility. The semantic progression corresponds roughly to the general stages described in the first section of this paper, except that the English seem always to have moved more freely from one form to another than did the continental Europeans (213).

In the seventeenth century "thou" and "you" became explicitly involved in social controversy. The Religious Society of Friends (or Quakers) was founded in the middle of this century by George Fox. One of the practices setting off this rebellious group from the larger society was the use of Plain Speech, and this entailed saying "thou" to everyone. George Fox explained the practice in these words:

> Moreover, when the Lord sent me forth into the world, He forbade me to put off my hat to any, high or low; and I was required to Thee and Thou all men and women, without any respect to rich or poor, great or small (quoted in 116).

Fox wrote a fascinating pamphlet (122), arguing that *T* to one and *V* to many is the natural and logical form of address in all languages. Among others he cites Latin, Hebrew, Greek, Arabick, Syriack, Aethiopic, Egyptian, French, and Italian. Fox suggests that the Pope, in his vanity, introduced the corrupt and illogical practice of saying *V* to one person. Farnsworth, another early Friend, wrote a somewhat similar pamphlet

(118), in which he argued that the Scriptures show that God and Adam and God and Moses were not too proud to say and receive the singular *T*.

For the new convert to the Society of Friends the universal *T* was an especially difficult commandment. Thomas Ellwood has described (112) the trouble that developed between himself and his father:

But whenever I had occasion to speak to my Father, though I had no Hat now to offend him; yet my language did as much: for I durst not say YOU to him, but THOU or THEE, as the Occasion required, and then would he be sure to fall on me with his Fists.

The Friends' reasons for using the mutual *T* were much the same as those of the French revolutionaries, but the Friends were always a minority and the larger society was antagonized by their violations of decorum.

Some Friends use "thee" today; the nominative "thou" has been dropped and "thee" is used as both the nominative and (as formerly) the accusative. Interestingly, many Friends also use "you". "Thee" is likely to be reserved for Friends among themselves and "you" said to outsiders. This seems to be a survival of the solidarity semantic. In English at large, of course, "thou" is no longer used. The explanation of its disappearance is by no means certain; however, the forces at work seem to have included a popular reaction against the radicalism of Quakers and Levelers and also a general trend in English toward simplified verbal inflection.

In the world today there are numerous examples of the association proposed between ideology and pronoun semantics. In Yugoslavia, our informants tell us, there was, for a short time following the establishment of Communism, a universal mutual *T* of solidarity. Today revolutionary *esprit* has declined and *V* has returned for much the same set of circumstances as in Italy, France, or Spain. There is also some power asymmetry in Yugoslavia's "Socialist manners". A soldier says *V* and *Comrade General*, but the general addresses the soldier with *T* and surname.

It is interesting in our materials to contrast usage in the Afrikaans language of South Africa and in the Gujerati and Hindi languages of India with the rest of the collection. On the questionnaire, Afrikaans speakers made eight nonreciprocal power distinctions; especially notable are distinctions within the family and the distinctions between customer and waiter and between boss and clerk, since these are almost never power-coded in French, Italian, German, etc., although they once were. The Afrikaans pattern generally preserves the asymmetry of the dyads described in Figure 2, and that suggests a more static society and a less developed equalitarian ethic. The forms of address used between

Afrikaans-speaking whites and the groups of "coloreds" and "blacks" are especially interesting. The Afrikaaner uses *T*, but the two lower castes use neither *T* nor *V*. The intermediate caste of "coloreds" says *Meneer* to the white and the "blacks" say *Baas*. It is as if these social distances transcend anything that can be found within the white group and so require their peculiar linguistic expressions.

The Gujerati and Hindi languages of India have about the same pronoun semantic, and it is heavily loaded with power. These languages have all the asymmetrical usage of Afrikaans and, in addition, use the nonreciprocal *T* and *V* between elder brother and younger brother and between husband and wife. This truly feudal pronominal pattern is consistent with the static Indian society. However, that society is now changing rapidly and, consistent with that change, the norms of pronoun usage are also changing. The progressive young Indian exchanges the mutual *T* with his wife.

In our account of the general semantic evolution of the pronouns, we have identified a stage in which the solidarity rule was limited to address between persons of equal power. This seemed to yield a two-dimensional system in equilibrium (see Figure 1a), and we have wondered why address did not permanently stabilize there. It is possible, of course, that human cognition favors the binary choice without contingencies and so found its way to the suppression of one dimension. However, this theory does not account for the fact that it was the rule of solidarity that triumphed. We believe, therefore, that the development of open societies with an equalitarian ideology acted against the nonreciprocal power semantic and in favor of solidarity. It is our suggestion that the larger social changes created a distaste for the face-to-face expression of differential power.

What of the many actions other than nonreciprocal *T* and *V* which express power asymmetry? A vassal not only says *V* but also bows, lifts his cap, touches his forelock, keeps silent, leaps to obey. There are a large number of expressions of subordination which are patterned isomorphically with *T* and *V*. Nor are the pronouns the only forms of nonreciprocal address. There are, in addition, proper names and titles, and many of these operate today on a nonreciprocal power pattern in America and in Europe, in open and equalitarian societies.

In the American family there are no discriminating pronouns, but there are nonreciprocal norms of address. A father says "Jim" to his son but, unless he is extraordinarily "advanced", he does not anticipate being called "Jack" in reply. In the American South there are no pronouns to mark the caste separation of Negro and white, but there are nonreciprocal norms of address. The white man is accustomed to call the Negro by his first name, but he expects to be called "Mr. Legree". In America and in Europe there are forms of nonreciprocal address for all the dyads of asymmetrical power; customer and waiter, teacher and student, father and son, employer and employee.

Differences of power exist in a democracy as in all societies. What is the difference between expressing power asymmetry in pronouns and expressing it by choice of title and proper name? It seems to be primarily a question of the degree of linguistic compulsion. In face-to-face address we can usually avoid the use of any name or title but not so easily the use of a pronoun. Even if the pronoun can be avoided, it will be implicit in the inflection of the verb. "Dites quelque chose" clearly says *vous* to the Frenchman. A norm for the pronominal and verbal expression of power compels a continuing coding of power, whereas a norm for titles and names permits power to go uncoded in most discourse. Is there any reason why the pronominal coding should be more congenial to a static society than to an open society?

We have noticed that mode of address intrudes into consciousness as a problem at times of status change. Award of the doctoral degree, for instance, transforms a student into a colleague and, among American academics, the familiar first name is normal. The fledgling academic may find it difficult to call his former teachers by their first names. Although these teachers may be young and affable, they have had a very real power over him for several years and it will feel presumptuous to deny this all at once with a new mode of address. However, the "tyranny of democratic manners" (77) does not allow him to continue comfortable with the polite "Professor X". He would not like to be thought unduly conscious of status, unprepared for faculty rank, a born lickspittle. Happily, English allows him a respite. He can avoid any term of address, staying with the uncommitted "you", until he and his addressees have got used to the new state of things. This linguistic *rite de passage* has, for English speakers, a waiting room in which to screw up courage.

In a fluid society crises of address will occur more frequently than in a static society, and so the pronominal coding of power differences is more likely to be felt as onerous. Coding by title and name would be more tolerable because less compulsory. Where status is fixed by birth and does not change each man has enduring rights and obligations of address.

A strong equalitarian ideology of the sort dominant in America works to suppress every conventional expression of power asymmetry. If the worker becomes conscious of his unreciprocated polite address to the boss, he may feel that his human dignity requires him to change. However, we do not feel the full power of the ideology until we are in a situation that gives us some claim to receive deferential address. The American professor often feels foolish being given his title, he almost certainly will not claim it as a prerogative; he may take pride in being on a first-name basis with his students. Very "palsy" parents may invite their children to call them by first name. The very President of the Republic invites us all to call him "Ike". Nevertheless, the differences of power are real and are experienced. Cronin has suggested in an amusing piece (77) that subordination is expressed by Americans in a subtle, and generally unwitting, body language. "The repertoire includes the boyish grin, the deprecatory cough, the unfinished sentence, the appreciative giggle, the drooping shoulders, the head-scratch and the bottom-waggle."

GROUP STYLE WITH THE PRONOUNS OF ADDRESS

The identification of style is relative to the identification of some constancy. When we have marked out the essentials of some action – it might be walking or speaking a language or driving a car – we can identify the residual variation as stylistic. Different styles are different ways of "doing the same thing", and so their identification waits on some designation of the range of performances to be regarded as "the same thing".

Linguistic science finds enough that is constant in English and French and Latin to put all these and many more into one family – the Indo-European. It is possible with reference to this constancy to think of Italian and Spanish and English and the others as so many styles of Indo-European. They all have, for instance, two singular pronouns of address, but each language has an individual phonetic and semantic style in pronoun usage. We are ignoring phonetic style (through the use of the generic *T* and V), but in the second section of the paper we have described differences in the semantic styles of French, German, and Italian.

Linguistic styles are potentially expressive when there is covariation between characteristics of language performance and characteristics of the performers. When styles are "interpreted", language behavior is functionally expressive. On that abstract level where the constancy is Indo-European and the styles are French, German, English, and Italian, interpretations of style must be statements about communities of speakers, statements of national character, social structure, or group ideology. In the last section we have hazarded a few propositions on this level.

It is usual, in discussion of linguistic style, to set constancy at the level of a language like French or English rather than at the level of a language family. In the languages we have studied there are variations in pronoun style that are associated with the social status of the speaker. We have seen that the use of *V* because of its entry at the top of a society and its diffusion downward was always interpreted as a mark of good breeding. It is interesting to find an organization of French journeymen in the generation after the Revolution adopting a set of rules of propriety cautioning members against going without tie or shoes at home on Sunday and also against the use of the mutual *T* among themselves (308). Our informants assure us that *V* and *T* still function as indications of class membership. The Yugoslavians have a saying that a peasant would say *T* to a king. By contrast, a French nobleman who turned up in our net told us that he had said *T* to no one in the world except the old woman who was his nurse in childhood. He is prevented by the dominant democratic ideology from saying *T* to subordinates and by his own royalist ideology from saying it to equals.

In literature, pronoun style has often been used to expose the pretensions of social climbers and the would-be elegant. Persons aping the manners of the class above them usually do not get the imitation exactly right. They are likely to notice some point of difference between their own class and the next higher and then extend the difference too widely, as in the use of the "elegant" broad [a] in "can" and "bad". Molière gives us his "*précieuses ridicules*" saying *V* to servants whom a refined person would call *T*. In Ben Jonson's *Everyman in his Humour* and *Epicoene* such true gallants as Wellbred and Knowell usually say "you" to one another but they make frequent expressive shifts between this form and "thou", whereas such fops as John Daw and Amorous-La-Foole make unvarying use of "you".

Our sample of visiting French students was roughly homogeneous in social status as judged by the single criterion of paternal occupation. Therefore, we could not make any systematic study of differences in class style, but we thought it possible that, even within this select group, there might be interpretable differences of style. It was our guess that the tendency to make wide or narrow use of the solidary *T* would be related to general radicalism or conservatism of ideology. As a measure of this latter dimension we used Eysenck's Social Attitude Inventory (117). This is a collection of statements to be accepted or rejected concerning a variety of matters – religion, economics, racial relations, sexual behavior, etc. Eysenck has validated the scale in England and in France on members of Socialist, Communist, Fascist, Conservative, and Liberal party members. In general, to be radical on this scale is to favor change and to be conservative is to wish to maintain the status quo or turn back to some earlier condition. We undertook to relate scores on this inventory to an index of pronoun style.

As yet we have reported no evidence demonstrating that there exists such a thing as a personal style in pronoun usage in the sense of a tendency to make wide or narrow use of *T*. It may be that each item in the questionnaire, each sort of person addressed, is an independent personal norm not predictable from any other. A child learns what to say to each kind of person. What he learns in each case depends on the groups in which he has membership. Perhaps his usage is a bundle of unrelated habits.

Guttman (402) has developed the technique of Scalogram Analysis for determining whether or not a collection of statements taps a common dimension. A perfect Guttman scale can be made of the statements: (*a*) I am at least 5′ tall; (*b*) I am at least 5′ 4″ tall; (*c*) I am at least 5′ 7″ tall; (*d*) I am at least 6′ 1″ tall; (*e*) I am at least 6′ 2″ tall. Endorsement of a more extreme statement will always be associated with endorsement of all less extreme statements. A person can be assigned a single score – *a, b, c, d,* or *e* – which represents the most extreme statement he has endorsed and, from this single score, all his individual answers can be reproduced. If he scores *c* he has also endorsed *a* and *b* but not *d* or *e*. The general criterion for scalability is the reproducibility of individual responses from a single score, and this depends on the items being interrelated so that endorsement of one is reliably associated with endorsement or rejection of the others.

The Guttman method was developed during World War II for the measurement of social attitudes, and it has been widely used. Perfect reproducibility is not likely to be found for all the statements which an investigator guesses to be concerned with some single attitude. The usual thing is to accept a set of statements as scalable when they are 90 per cent reproducible and also satisfy certain other requirements; for example, there must be some statements that are not given a very one-sided response but are accepted and rejected with nearly equal frequency.

The responses to the pronoun questionnaire are not varying degrees of agreement (as in an attitude questionnaire) but are rather varying probabilities of saying *T* or *V*. There seems to be no reason why these bipolar responses cannot be treated like yes or no responses on an attitude scale. The difference is that the scale, if there is one, will be the semantic dimension governing the pronouns, and the scale score of each respondent will represent his personal semantic style.

It is customary to have 100 subjects for a Scalogram Analysis, but we could find only 50 French students. We tested all 28 items for scalability and found that a subset of them made a fairly good scale. It was necessary to combine response categories so as to dichotomize them in order to obtain an average reproducibility of 85 per cent. This coefficient was computed for the five intermediate items having the more-balanced marginal frequencies. A large number of items fell at or very near the two extremes. The solidarity or *T*-most end of the scale could be defined by father, mother, elder brother, young boys, wife, or lover quite as well as by younger brother. The remote or *V*-most end could be defined by "waiter" or "top boss" as well as by "army general". The intervening positions, from the *T*-end to the *V*-end, are: the elderly female servant known since childhood, grandfather, a male fellow student, a female fellow student, and an elder brother's wife.

For each item on the scale a *T* answer scores one point and a *V* answer no points. The individual total scores range from 1 to 7, which means the scale can differentiate only seven semantic styles. We divided the subjects into the resultant seven stylistically homogeneous groups and, for each group, determined the average scores on radicalism-conservatism. There was a set of almost perfectly consistent differences.

TABLE I

Scores on the Pronoun Scale in Relation to Scores on the Radicalism Scale

Group Pronoun Score	*Group Mean Radicalism Score*
1	5.50
2	6.66
3	6.82
4	7.83
5	6.83
6	8.83
7	9.75

In Table I appear the mean radicalism scores for each pronoun style. The individual radicalism scores range between 2 and 13; the higher the score the more radical the person's ideology. The very striking result is that the group radicalism scores duplicate the order of the group pronoun scores with only a single reversal. The rank-difference correlation between the two sets of scores is .96, and even with only seven paired scores this is a very significant relationship.

There is enough consistency of address to justify speaking of a personal-pronoun style which involves a more or less wide use of the solidary *T*. Even among students of the same socio-economic level there are differences of style, and these are potentially expressive of radicalism and conservatism in ideology. A Frenchman could, with some confidence, infer that a male university student who regularly said *T* to female fellow students would favor the nationalization of industry, free love, trial marriage, the abolition of capital punishment, and the weakening of nationalistic and religious loyalties.

What shall we make of the association between a wide use of *T* and a cluster of radical sentiments? There may be no "sense" to it at all, that is, no logical connection between the linguistic practice and the attitudes, but simply a general tendency to go along with the newest thing. We know that left-wing attitudes are more likely to be found in the laboring class than in the professional classes. Perhaps those offspring of the professional class who sympathize with proletariat politics also, incidentally, pick up the working man's wide use of *T* without feeling that there is anything in the linguistic practice that is congruent with the ideology.

On the other hand perhaps there is something appropriate in the association. The ideology is consistent in its disapproval of barriers between people: race, religion, nationality, property, marriage, even criminality. All these barriers have the effect of separating the solidary, the "in-group", from the nonsolidary, the "out-group". The radical says the criminal is not far enough "out" to be killed; he should be re-educated. He says that a nationality ought not to be so solidary that it prevents world organization from succeeding. Private property ought to be abolished, industry should be nationalized. There are to be no more out-groups and in-groups but rather one group, undifferentiated by nationality, religion, or pronoun of address. The fact that the pronoun which is being extended to all men alike is *T*, the mark of solidarity, the pronoun of the nuclear family, expresses the radical's intention to extend his sense of brotherhood. But we notice that the universal application of the pronoun eliminates the discrimination that gave it a meaning and that gives particular point to an old problem. Can the solidarity of the family be extended so widely? Is there enough libido to stretch so far? Will there perhaps be a thin solidarity the same everywhere but nowhere so strong as in the past?

THE PRONOUNS OF ADDRESS AS EXPRESSIONS OF TRANSIENT ATTITUDES

Behavior norms are practices consistent within a group. So long as the choice of a pronoun is recognized as normal for a group, its interpretation is simply the membership of the speaker in that group. However, the implications of group membership are often very important; social class, for instance, suggests a kind of family life, a level of education, a set of political views, and much besides. These facts about a person belong to his character. They are enduring features which help to determine actions over many years. Consistent personal style in the use of the pronouns of address does not reveal enough to establish the speaker's unique character, but it can help to place him in one or another large category.

Sometimes the choice of a pronoun clearly violates a group norm and perhaps also the customary practice of the speaker. Then the meaning of the act will be sought in some attitude or emotion of the speaker. It is as if the interpreter reasoned that variations of address between the same two persons must be caused by variations in their attitudes toward one another. If two men of seventeenth-century France properly exchange the *V* of upper-class equals and one of them gives the other *T*, he suggests that the other is his inferior since it is to his inferiors that a man says *T*. The general meaning of an unexpected pronoun choice is simply that the speaker, for the moment, views his relationship as one that calls for the pronoun used. This kind of variation in language behavior expresses a contemporaneous feeling or attitude. These variations are not consistent personal styles but departures from one's own custom and the customs of a group in response to a mood.

As there have been two great semantic dimensions governing *T* and *V*, so there have also been two principal kinds of expressive meaning. Breaking the norms of power generally has the meaning that a speaker regards an addressee as his inferior, superior, or equal, although by usual criteria, and according to the speaker's own customary usage, the addressee is not what the pronoun implies. Breaking the norms of solidarity generally means that the speaker temporarily thinks of the other as an outsider or as an intimate; it means that sympathy is extended or withdrawn.

The oldest uses of *T* and *V* to express attitudes seem everywhere to have been the *T* of contempt or anger and the *V* of admiration or respect. In his study of the French pronouns Schliebitz (353) found the first examples of these expressive uses in literature of the twelfth and thirteenth centuries, which is about the time that the power semantic crystallized in France, and Grand (139) has found the same thing for Italian. In saying *T*, where *V* is usual, the speaker treats the addressee like a servant or a child and assumes the right to berate him. The most common use of the expressive *V*, in the early materials, is that of the master who is exceptionally pleased with the work of a servant and elevates him pronominally to match this esteem.

Racine, in his dramas, used the pronouns with perfect semantic consistency. His major figures exchange the *V* of upper-class equals. Lovers, brother and sister, husband and wife – none of them says *T* if he is of high rank, but each person of high rank has a subordinate confidante to whom he says *T* and from whom he receives *V*. It is a perfect nonreciprocal power semantic. This courtly pattern is broken only for the greatest scenes in each play. Racine reserved the expressive pronoun as some composers save the cymbals. In both *Andromaque* and *Phèdre* there are only two expressive departures from the norm, and they mark climaxes of feeling.

Jespersen (213) believed that English "thou" and "ye" (or "you") were more often shifted to express mood and tone than were the pronouns of the continental languages, and our comparisons strongly support this opinion. The "thou" of contempt was so very familiar that a verbal form was created to name this expressive use. Shakespeare gives it to Sir Toby Belch (*Twelfth Night*) in the lines urging Andrew Aguecheek to send a challenge to the disguised Viola: "Taunt him with the license of ink, if thou thou'st him some thrice, it shall not be amiss." In life the verb turned up in Sir Edward Coke's attack on Raleigh at the latter's trial in 1603 (208): "All that he did, was at thy instigation, thou viper; for I thou thee, thou traitor."

The *T* of contempt and anger is usually introduced between persons who normally exchange *V* but it can, of course, also be used by a subordinate to a superior. As the social distance is greater, the overthrow of the norm is more shocking and generally represents a greater extremity of passion. Sejanus, in Ben Jonson's play of that name, feels extreme contempt for the emperor Tiberius but wisely gives him the reverential *V* to his face. However, soliloquizing after the emperor has exited, Sejanus begins: "Dull, heavy Caesar! Wouldst thou tell me..." In Jonson's *Volpone* Mosca invariably says "you" to his master until the final scene when, as the two villains are about to be carted away, Mosca turns on Volpone with "Bane to thy wolfish nature."

Expressive effects of much greater subtlety than those we have described are common in Elizabethan and Jacobean drama. The exact interpretation of the speaker's attitude depends not only on the pronoun norm he upsets but also on his attendant words and actions and the total setting. Still simple enough to be unequivocal is the ironic or mocking "you" said by Tamburlaine to the captive Turkish emperor Bajazeth. This exchange occurs in Act IV of Marlowe's play:

> Tamburlaine: Here, Turk, wilt thou have a clean trencher?
> Bajazeth: Ay, tyrant, and more meat.
> Tamburlaine: Soft, sir, you must be dieted; too much eating will make you surfeit.

"Thou" is to be expected from captor to captive and the norm is upset when Tamburlaine says "you". He cannot intend to express admiration or respect since he keeps the Turk captive and starves him. His intention is to mock the captive king with respectful address, implying a power that the king has lost.

The momentary shift of pronoun directly expresses a momentary shift of mood, but that interpretation does not exhaust its meaning. The fact that a man has a particular momentary attitude or emotion may imply a great deal about his characteristic disposition, his readiness for one kind of feeling rather than another. Not every attorney general, for instance, would have used the abusive "thou" to Raleigh. The fact that Edward Coke did so suggests an arrogant and choleric temperament and, in fact, many made this assessment of him (208). When Volpone spoke to Celia, a lady of Venice, he ought to have said "you" but he began at once with "thee". This violation of decorum, together with the fact that he leaps from his sick bed to attempt rape of the lady, helps to establish Volpone's monstrous character. His abnormal form of address is consistent with the unnatural images in his speech. In any given situation we know the sort of people who would break the norms of address and the sort who would not. From the fact that a man does break the norms we infer his immediate feelings and, in addition, attribute to him the general character of people who would have such feelings and would give them that kind of expression.

With the establishment of the solidarity semantic a new set of expressive meanings became possible – feelings of sympathy and estrangement. In Shakespeare's plays there are expressive meanings that derive from the solidarity semantic as well as many dependent on power usage and many that rely on both connotations. The play *Two Gentlemen of Verona* is concerned with the Renaissance ideal of friendship and provides especially clear expressions of solidarity. Proteus and Valentine, the two Gentlemen, initially exchange "thou", but when they touch on the subject of love, on which they disagree, their address changes to the "you" of estrangement. Molière (119) has shown us that a man may even put himself at a distance as does George Dandin in the soliloquy beginning: "George Dandin! George Dandin! Vous avez fait une sottise. . . ."

In both French and English drama of the past, *T* and *V* were marvelously sensitive to feelings of approach and withdrawal. In terms of Freud's striking amoeba metaphor the pronouns signal the extension or retraction of libidinal pseudopodia. However, in French, German, and Italian today this use seems to be very uncommon. Our informants told us that the *T*, once extended, is almost never taken back for the reason that it would mean the complete withdrawal of esteem. The only modern expressive shift we have found is a rather chilling one. Silverberg (378) reports that in Germany in 1940 a prostitute and her client said *du* when they met and while they were together but when the libidinal tie (in the narrow sense) had been dissolved they resumed the mutual distant *Sie*.

We have suggested that the modern direction of change in pronoun usage expresses a will to extend the solidary ethic to everyone. The apparent decline of expressive shifts between *T* and *V* is more difficult to interpret. Perhaps it is because Europeans have seen that excluded persons or races or groups can become the target of extreme aggression from groups that are benevolent within themselves. Perhaps Europeans would like to convince themselves that the solidary ethic once extended will not be withdrawn, that there is security in the mutual *T*.

From: *Style in Language*, Thomas A. Sebeok, ed. (Cambridge, Mass., Technology Press of M.I.T.; New York, John Wiley & Sons, Inc., 1960), pp. 253-276. Reprinted with permission. Consult original source for cited references.

Laura Nader

A NOTE ON ATTITUDES AND THE USE OF LANGUAGE*

Research which deals specifically with attitudes and beliefs that native speakers have about their language is scarce. Most reports on attitudes about language and their effect on the use of language have been discussed by linguists in studies of language borrowing or second language learning,[1] or else they are inserted (and often hidden away) by ethnologists as part of an ethnographic description.[2] This note will report some attitudes about Arabic, observed during a recent field trip to Lebanon.[3] The Lebanese materials as well as additional data from other areas suggest that the often discussed prestige factor in language borrowing, imitation or emulation may not always be associated with the social rank that an individual or group may have. The material suggests that there are many motives besides that of status enhancement which may influence speech imitation, and that these motives will vary with membership in a particular sub-group in society as well as with individual personality. It

* The ideas in this note have been discussed with Dell Hymes, Susan Ervin, John Gumperz, Richard Diebold, and Eugene Hammel. The author is grateful for their helpful comments.

1 See for example Susan Ervin, "The Verbal Behavior of Bilinguals; the Effect of Language of Report Upon the Thematic Apperception Test Stories of Adult French Bilinguals", University of Michigan Dissertation (Microfilm Publication 12,571); cf. *Dissertation Abstracts*, 15 (1955), 1664, or Einar Haugen, *The Norwegian Language in America* (Philadelphia, 1953), and Wallace Lambert, "Development of the Linguistic Dominance of Bilinguals", *Journal of Abnormal and Social Psychology*, 50 (1955), 197-200.

2 For example, see John Boman Adam's article, "Culture and Conflict in an Egyptian Village", *AA*, 59 (1957), 225-35.

3 Field research in Lebanon was sponsored by the Institute of International Studies, University of California, from June 1961 to September, 1961.

also appears that any one speaker may control several dialects or portions of several dialects apart from the one he knows best, and that the use he may make of other dialects will vary with different situations.

It has regularly been stated by some linguists and anthropologists that the prestige factor often leads to extensive borrowing from one language to another, or from one dialect to another.[4] The suggestion we glean from the examples that are usually given is that this speech emulation or imitation is undertaken by those in the lower ranks of society and that those whom they are emulating are of the higher echelons. This belief, however, has been modified in other quarters.[5] The counter suggestion

[4] There is an extensive discussion in E. R. Leach, *Political Systems of Highland Burma* (1954). On p. 50 he suggests, "If ... we find a political system which embraces several language groups and these language groups are ranked in a class hierarchy, superior and inferior, there is a prima facie probability that the language situation is unstable, and that the higher ranking groups are tending to assimilate the lower ranking groups ... it follows from very simple economic causes. It is advantageous for the individual to identify himself linguistically with those who possess political and economic influence."

Charles F. Hocket, in his book *A Course in Modern Linguistics* (1954), states (p. 404): "People emulate those whom they admire, in speech-pattern as well as in other respects. European immigrants to the United States introduce many English expressions into their speech, partly for other reasons, but partly because English is the important language of the country. Upper- and middle-class Englishmen, in the days after the Norman conquest, learned French and used French expressions in their English because French was the language of the new rulers of the country." The reverse question is rarely considered. To what extent did the Norman conquerors adopt English expressions? We can observe that in the long run the Norman conquerors not only adopted English words but the whole English language. "Bobby-soxers imitate in one way or another the latest and most popular radio or TV singer."

Martin Joos notes in his article "The Medieval Sibilants" (*Lg*, 28, 1952, 222-31), "... the dialects and idiolects of higher prestige were more advanced in this direction (of phonetic drift), and their speakers carried the drift further along so as to maintain the prestige-marking difference against their pursuers. The vanity factor is needed to explain why phonetic drifts tend to continue in the same direction; ..." Reprinted in M. Joos (ed.), *Readings in Linguistics* (Washington, 1957), 377-8.

[5] Weinrich, Uriel, "Research Frontiers in Bilingualism Studies", in *Reports for the Eighth International Congress of Linguists, Oslo, 5-9, August, 1957*, vol. I, p. 191: "It is probably safe to say that as the machinery of social science is brought to bear on problems of attitude and motivation in contact situations, it will become possible to deal with psychological and sociological factors in the regulation of interference which so far have eluded investigation. The linguist's oversimplified model of a 'prestige slope' on which innovations slide down will presumably be modified to allow for the diffusion of foreign material into national languages in a slangy, 'anti-prestige' direction."

See also John L. Fischer, "Social Influences in the Choice of a Linguistic Variant", *Word*, vol. 14 (1958), 56: "The grounds of prestige clearly vary according to individuals and societies. A variant which one man uses because he wants

is that, while prestige may be an important consideration, other factors such as the context of particular speech situations should not be ignored. It is also suggested that we should consider a more refined description of what constitutes prestige in particular cases.

The materials collected in Lebanon dealing with language attitudes were expressed about Arabic by Arabic speakers in Lebanon. During the summer, field time was spent among upper-class Christian Lebanese in Beirut, among middle-class Christians in Zahle, one of the larger more affluent Christian cities of Lebanon, and among Shia Moslems in a relatively small, humble village in the southern Bekka Valley. Recitations of various kinds were tape-recorded in the village and later were played back for people in Zahle and Beirut. Their comments were of the following order: "The people of the villages know how to use the Arabic language in a way in which we have forgotten." "I have an uncle who can speak like that; his father taught him." "Those people may have ragged clothes, but they have a rich language."[6] All of these responses struck me as unusual because of previous field experiences in Mexico. No Spanish speaker in Mexico City would express admiration of the Spanish spoken in the rural areas. Perhaps this is associated with the fact that many Mexican rural areas are in a state of transition from Indian to Spanish speaking. A similar situation, however, obtains in France. In Paris we would not expect to find Parisians wishing to emulate a French dialect spoken in the provinces. On the other hand upper-class male Spaniards might wish to imitate the Spanish spoken by the bull-herders

---

to seem dignified another man would reject because he did not want to seem stiff. . . ."

Also: Gumperz, John J., "Dialect Differences and Social Stratification in a North Indian Village", *AA*, 60, 668-82. Gumperz tells us (p. 679): "Among Sweepers, women devote most of the day to cleaning the houses and cattle compounds of the village, and much of that time is consumed in gossiping with and listening to the conversations of their employers. Men used to work in the cities. At present, most of them earn their living as occasional agricultural laborers, and few also do cleaning work similar to that of the women. Chamars and Sweepers thus seem to have the greatest amount of work contacts with other castes." Despite this contact, we are then told that these people are the most linguistically divergent of all the castes in the village. On p. 681 he states: "In examining intercaste communication, we find that linguistic differences have no correlation with work contacts. Bloomfield's concept of "density of communication" therefore needs some refinement. It becomes necessary to distinguish between several forms of communication. Not all of them have the same effect on linguistic diversity."

More recently Gumperz has discussed some of these questions in his article "Speech Variation in India", *AA*, 63, 976-88.

[6] It should be noted perhaps that all of these comments were made by bilingual French-Arabic speakers. This class of people often indirectly express guilt feelings about their inadequate knowledge of Arabic, which they attribute to the fact that they had to devote much of their time to the learning of French.

because this is considered more virile, or a young Boston Brahmin might be found imitating the language of the "beats". The general point to be made here is that the prestige factor which may encourage admiration, borrowing, or emulation in language need not be related to the affluent position of one group or another, or of one individual or another.

As a result of these comments on the village tapes I became interested in the way a Lebanese would rate the various dialects with which he is familiar. Ferguson has dealt with this subject previously in an article entitled "Myths About Arabic".[7] He states (pp. 79-80): "Sedentary Arabs generally feel that their own dialect is best, but on certain occasions or in certain contexts will maintain that the Bedouin dialects are better." The interesting part of this statement on dialect rating is the last half of the sentence, ". . . but on certain occasions or in certain contexts [they] will maintain that the Bedouin dialects are better." Ferguson goes on to tell of an experiment he tried: "I have repeatedly attempted to learn the place of origin of an Arab by asking him where the best Arabic is spoken, before I ask him where he comes from. So far the experiment has always succeeded. The Arab indicates, for example, that the best Arabic is spoken in Damascus; then a few minutes later when asked where he comes from he replies again 'Damascus'." If one wanted to refine Ferguson's experiment he might begin by posing two questions: where was the informant when the question was asked, and what would result if such a question were made more specific? In eliciting responses to Ferguson's question "What Arabic is best?", I found that the answer given depended in part on where the informant was. A man from Damascus visiting in Beirut would belligerently defend his dialect as the best, but in Damascus he would say that the Bedouin dialect was best. Under no circumstances did an informant suggest that the dialect of another town was best. Such a response would be considered as being disloyal to one's own dialect or town, whereas stating that Bedouin dialect was best was not being disloyal; it was expressing loyalty to a widespread cultural ideal – that the Bedouin speaks the purest of Arabic.

If we wanted to consider further under what situations attitudes about languages vary we could pose the second question and ask an informant a more specific kind of question, for example, "What Arabic speakers are capable of giving the best Arabic recitations at weddings, or what Arabic speakers are best at making up love poetry?"[8] We might get a picture of different dialects being best for specific language uses, or we might have a picture of different classes of people being best at different

[7] Ferguson, Charles A., "Myths About Arabic", in Georgetown University Press, *Languages and Linguistics Monograph Series*, No. 12 (1960), 75-82.

[8] Some people believe that the Iraqi dialect is especially good for creations in poetry.

uses of the language. In the process we would also discover some speech situations for which only a certain dialect would be used, and the question of best might not be central. Rather, appropriateness would be of importance. For example, no one would conceive of paraphrasing the Koran in colloquial Arabic. So we could say that colloquial Arabic and Koranic sayings are mutually exclusive.[9] On the other hand classical Arabic and scolding a child would be mutually exclusive (unless one digressed into classical proverbs), whereas bidding someone farewell could be done either in colloquial or classical Arabic, depending on such factors as the role relation between person(s) staying and the person(s) leaving. A Zahle dialect would be imitated if one were telling a joke.[10] The Beirut dialect would be imitated if one were putting on airs, or imitating those who do put on airs. We would need to distinguish whether a person imitated another dialect for reasons of identification with the group using that dialect or for situational reasons.

It would be very enlightening for a social anthropologist to have a refined description of these situations. An analysis of attitudes and beliefs about Arabic or any other language may tell us something about a kind of rank relationship which would not be apparent by analyzing what is often referred to as socio-economic positions of groups. Such description underlines the notion that there are many different factors at work in language interchange besides status enhancement, and that such factors may influence speech imitation, such as when a person wishes to be stiff or relaxed, honest, amusing, or ambivalent. These factors will vary with personality, with membership in a group, as well as with a broad range of cultural factors. Furthermore, it is important to recognize that any speaker may control several dialects or portions of several dialects, and change from one to another for situational reasons.[11] An analysis of the

[9] Charles Ferguson in his article "Diglossia", *Word*, 1959, 325-340, discusses the function of "High and Low" (classical vs. local Arabic dialect) in a variety of settings.

[10] It is interesting to note that in Lebanon the clown on various popular television shows was usually a man who spoke a dialect which is common to one middle-class section of the city of Zahle. The clown did not imitate the language of the rural peasant but rather a middle-class person from a major large city of Lebanon. A comparable example in the United States would be the imitation of a Brooklyn accent. In Egypt, however, the clown usually speaks a dialect of the rural peasant in Upper Egypt. Where one may be on the socio-economic ladder may not be the same place he would be on a dialect ladder.

[11] Note for example Angus McIntosh, *Introduction to a Survey of Scottish Dialects* (Edinburgh, 1952), p. 29: "At one end of the scale, there is in many places the 'broad' dialect speaker who is least affected by influence from the outside; at the other there may be someone whose speech has no perceptible regional characteristics at all. In between these extremes there may be intermediate types of speech and some people will have more than one at their command, each available for appropriate occasions."

special uses that an individual may make of other dialects, in what situations he may borrow words, style, accent, form, many tell us something about the range of prestige variants and the relative isomorphism of prestige scales that are involved in inter-dialect interchange.

From: *Anthropological Linguistics*, IV, 6 (1962), pp. 24-29. Reprinted with permission.

Clifford Geertz

LINGUISTIC ETIQUETTE

But the entire etiquette system is perhaps best summed up and symbolized in the way the Javanese use their language. In Javanese it is nearly impossible to say anything without indicating the social relationship between the speaker and the listener in terms of status and familiarity. Status is determined by many things – wealth, descent, education, occupation, age, kinship, and nationality, among others, but the important point is that the choice of linguistic forms as well as speech style is in every case partly determined by the relative status (or familiarity) of the conversers. The difference is not minor, a mere *du* and *Sie* difference. To greet a person lower than oneself (or someone with whom one is intimate) one says *Apa paḍa slamet,* but one greets a superior (or someone one knows only slightly) with *Menapa sami sugeng* – both meaning "Are you well?" *Pandjenengan saking tindak pundi?* and *Kowé seka endi?* are the same question ("Where are you coming from?"), in the first case addressed to a superior, in the second to an inferior. Clearly, a peculiar obsession is at work here.

Basically, what is involved is that the Javanese pattern their speech behavior in terms of the same *alus* to *kasar* axis around which they organize their social behavior generally. A number of words (and some affixes) are made to carry in addition to their normal linguistic meaning what might be called a "status meaning"; i.e., when used in actual conversation they convey not only their fixed denotative meaning ("house", "body", "eat", "walk", "you", "passive voice") but also a connotative meaning concerning the status of (and/or degree of familiarity between) the speaker and the listener. As a result, several words may denote the same normal linguistic meaning but differ in the status connotation they convey. Thus, for "house" we have three forms (*omah, grija,* and *dalem*), each connoting a progressively higher relative status of the listener with respect to the speaker. Some normal linguistic meanings are even more finely divided (*kowé, sampéjan, pandjenengan, pandjenengan dalem,* for ascending values of "you"), others less (*di-* and *dipun-*) for the passive voice; but most normal meanings, taking the vocabulary as a whole, are not divided at all. Thus the word for "table" is *medja* no matter to whom one is speaking.[1]

A further complication is that status meanings are communicated in speech not only intentionally in terms of word selection *within* the speaker's dialect but unintentionally in terms of the dialect he uses as a whole. Not only are there "levels" of speech within the dialect which are ranked in terms of their status (or *alus/kasar)* connotations; the various dialects in the community as a whole are also ranked in terms of the *alus* to *kasar* spectrum, this latter sort of ranking being characteristic, of course, of any stratified society.

In order to clarify the relationship between the intra-dialect and inter-dialect systems of status symbolization, one voluntary and one involuntary, I offer the accompanying three charts depicting paradigmatically how a single sentence alters within each of the dialects and among them. Table I shows the speech range in status terms for what I would call the non-*prijaji* but urbanized and at least slightly educated group, which would include the better educated *abangans,* most urban *santris,* and even some of the lower *prijajis*, particularly when they are mixing with people outside their own immediate circle. It is, then, the most common dialect in town. Table II shows the dialect of most peasants and uneducated townsmen, which is the most common style of all in terms of sheer numbers of users. Table III depicts the *prijaji* dialect, which, although spoken by a relatively small group of people, provides an ideal model of correct speech for the whole society.

The English sentence selected as an example is: Are you going to eat rice and cassava now? The Javanese words (low forms first) are as follows:

[1] Although in terms of the total Javanese vocabulary the number of words which show formal changes in terms of status connotations are relatively small in percentage, since they tend to be the most frequently occurring in actual speech, in word counts of common utterances the percentage of status-expression forms is quite high. In general it may be said that there is no set rule by which one can determine which words change in different status situations and which do not except a vague one that the commoner the word and the more it denotes something fairly closely associated with human beings, the more likely it is that it will have such forms.

TABLE I

Dialect of Non-Prijaji, Urbanized, Somewhat Educated Persons

<table>
<tr><th>Level</th><th>are</th><th>you</th><th>going</th><th>to eat</th><th>rice</th><th>and</th><th>cassava</th><th>now</th><th>Complete sentence</th></tr>
<tr><td>3a</td><td rowspan="2">menapa</td><td>pandjenengan</td><td rowspan="2">baḍé</td><td>ḍahar</td><td rowspan="3">sekul</td><td rowspan="2">kalijan</td><td rowspan="5">kaspé</td><td rowspan="2">samenika</td><td>Menapa pandjenengan baḍé ḍahar sekul kalijan kaspé samenika?</td></tr>
<tr><td>3</td><td rowspan="3">sampéjan</td><td rowspan="3">neḍa</td><td>Menapa sampéjan baḍé neḍa sekul kalijan kaspé samenika?</td></tr>
<tr><td>2</td><td>napa</td><td>adjeng</td><td rowspan="3">lan</td><td>saniki</td><td>Napa sampéjan adjeng neḍa sekul lan kaspé saniki?</td></tr>
<tr><td>1a</td><td rowspan="2">apa</td><td rowspan="2">arep</td><td rowspan="2">sega</td><td rowspan="2">saiki</td><td>Apa sampéjan arep neḍa sega lan kaspé saiki?</td></tr>
<tr><td>1</td><td>kowé</td><td>mangan</td><td>Apa kowé arep mangan sega lan kaspé saiki?</td></tr>
</table>

TABLE II

Dialect of Peasants and Uneducated Townspeople

<table>
<tr><th>Level</th><th>are</th><th>you</th><th>going</th><th>to eat</th><th>rice</th><th>and</th><th>cassava</th><th>now</th><th>Complete sentence</th></tr>
<tr><td>2</td><td>napa</td><td rowspan="2">sampéjan</td><td>adjeng</td><td rowspan="2">neḍa</td><td>sekul</td><td rowspan="3">lan</td><td rowspan="3">kaspé</td><td>saniki</td><td>Napa sampéjan adjeng neḍa sekul lan kaspé saniki?</td></tr>
<tr><td>1a</td><td rowspan="2">apa</td><td rowspan="2">arep</td><td rowspan="2">sega</td><td rowspan="2">saiki</td><td>Apa sampéjan arep neḍa sega lan kaspé saiki?</td></tr>
<tr><td>1</td><td>kowé</td><td>mangan</td><td>Apa kowé arep mangan sega lan kaspé saiki?</td></tr>
</table>

TABLE III

Dialect of the Prijajis

Level	are	you	going	to eat	rice	and	cassava	now	Complete sentence
3a	*menapa*	*pandjenengan*	*baḍé*	*ḍahar*	*sekul*	*kalijan*	*kaspé*	*samenika*	*Menapa pandjenengan baḍé ḍahar sekul kalijan kaspé samenika?*
3		*sampéjan*		*neḍa*					*Menapa sampéjan baḍé neḍa sekul kalijan kaspé samenika?*

Level	are	you	going	to eat	rice	and	cassava	now	Complete sentence
1b		*pandjenengan*		*ḍahar*					*Apa pandjenengan arep ḍahar sega lan kaspé saiki?*
1a	*apa*	*kowé*	*arep*	*neḍa*	*sega*	*lan*	*kaspé*	*saiki*	*Apa sampéjan arep neḍa sega lan kaspé saiki?*
1		*sampéjan*		*mangan*					*Apa kowé arep mangan sega lan kaspé saiki?*

Are:	*apa/napa/menapa*
you:	*kowé/sampéjan/pandjenengan*
going:	*arep/adjeng/bađé*
to eat:	*mangan/neđa/đahar*
rice:	*sega/sekul*
and:	*lan/kalijan*
cassava:	*kaspé*
now:	*saiki/saniki/samenika*

The numbers at the sides of the charts indicate the levels, and the sentences, on the right, derived by reading across the chart at each level, are those available to a speaker in the particular dialect concerned. This range of sentences does not represent a mere theoretical set of possibilities. All of these variations are used every day. Moreover the Javanese have names for each of the levels. Level 3a is *krama inggil;* level 3 is *krama biasa,* or just *krama;* level 2 is *krama madya,* or just *madya.* (These three highest levels are often referred to merely as *basa* or language, although by high *prijajis* only the first two would be so considered.) Level 1a is either *ngoko madya,* or just *madya*; and level 1 is *ngoko biasa,* or just *ngoko.* Level 1b, a *prijaji* specialty, is called *ngoko sae* ("fine *ngoko*") or *ngoko alus.*

Krama, madya, and *ngoko* – or high, middle, and low – are the three main levels expressing status and/or familiarity available to speakers in the language. They represent sets of linked conjugates (*menapa . . . badé . . . samenika*; *napa . . . adjeng . . . saniki*; *apa . . . arep . . . saiki*; etc.), the occurrence of one of which for any given meaning (e.g, *menapa/napa/apa*) will predict the occurrence of the other if the meaning concerned occurs (i.e., *bađé/adjeng/arep;* or *samenika/saniki/saiki*, etc.). In some cases the *madya* conjugate is the same as the *ngoko* (e.g., *lan*); sometimes it is the same as the *krama* (e.g., *sampéjan, neđa, sekul*); and of course, sometimes the conjugate is the same in all three cases (e.g., *kaspé*).

In addition to these sets of linked conjugates, there is a group of special words, mostly referring to people, their parts, possessions and actions, which occur independently of the first kinds of conjugates and which act to raise the level of speech indicated by the first, inevitable selection, one "notch" higher – or, better, one-half notch. *Dahar* and *pandjenengan* are such words in the above sentences, rasing level 3, *krama biasa* (literally: "usual" or "common" *krama)* to level 3a, *krama inggil* ("high" *krama*). In the *ngoko* level, the use of *krama* words (e.g., *sampéjan*, or *neđa* in the above) also has an honorific effect, lifting *ngoko biasa* (level 1) to *ngoko madya* (level 1a). As these *krama* words employed in *ngoko* sentences occur in the same meanings as the special honorifics, they might be called "low honorifics", in contrast to the special "high honorifics", such as *dahar, pandjenengan.* Finally, the use of high honorifics in a *ngoko* context yields level 1b, *ngoko sae.* As a result, the intra-dialect system of status symbolization consists, at the most, of three "stylemes" (high, middle, and low) and two types of honorifics (high and low). The honorifics occur, at least in the dialects described here, only with the high and low stylemes, never with the middle one.[2]

On the basis, then, of how many stylemes and how many types of honorific are customarily employed and what combinations occur, the three "class dialects" diagrammed in the charts are distinguished. In the dialect of the non-*prijaji*, urbanized, and at least somewhat educated group (Table I), all three stylemes are customarily used (high, middle, low) and both types of honorific (high and low). Since the high honorifics occur only with the high style and the low ones only with the low style,[3] a speaker of this dialect has five possibilities, represented by the five sentences: 3a, *krama inggil* (i.e., high styleme and high honorifics); 3, *krama biasa* (high styleme without honorifics); 2, *krama madya* (middle styleme without honorifics); 1a, *ngoko madya* (middle styleme with low honorifics); 1, *ngoko biasa* (low styleme, no honorifics).

In the peasant and uneducated townsman dialect or idiom (Table II), two stylemes (middle and low) and one type of honorific (low) customarily occur, the honorifics occurring only with the low styleme, to raise *ngoko biasa* to *ngoko madya.*[4] Thus the possibilities for the expression of "status meaning" for a speaker of this dialect are only three: 2, *krama madya* (middle styleme without honorifics); 1a, *ngoko madya* (low styleme plus low honorifics); 1, *ngoko biasa* (low styleme, no honorifics).

Finally, in the *prijaji* dialect, the middle styleme – considered to be vulgar – drops out. Thus, there are two stylemes (high and low) and both high and low honorifics, the high occurring with both high and low stylemes, the low, again, only with the high. This gives five possibilities: 3a, *krama inggil* (high styleme plus high honorifics); 3, *krama biasa*

[2] In utterances of more than minimal length the chance that at least one *krama/madya/ngoko* style marker will occur is nearly unity. I owe the suggestion to treat the "style" problem and the "high word" problem separately to Mr. Rufus Hendon, who has also suggested that the three linked conjugate sets be dissolved into a new unit, called a "styleme", which then occurs once in (nearly) every sentence, and that the high words, which occur sporadically, be called "honorifics". The formal parts of the above discussion are heavily dependent upon his analysis.

[3] As the two types of honorific are in complementary distribution, high ones occurring only with high Stylemes, low ones with low, the difference between them is redundant and could be eliminated in a more elegant analysis.

[4] As low honorifics are but high styleme "markers" occurring in low styleme contexts, a combination of high styleme and low honorifics is, of course, impossible for the honorifics could not be distinguished from the styleme markers.

(high styleme without honorifics); 1b, *ngoko sae* (low styleme, high honorifics); 1a, *ngoko madya* (low styleme plus low honorifics); and 1, *ngoko biasa* (low styleme, no honorifics).

It will be noted that sentences 3 and 3a are available to both *prijaji* and educated townsmen; sentence 2 to both educated and uneducated townsmen and to peasants; and 1 and 1a to all three groups (although, as mentioned, 1a tends to be omitted by the more *alus* among the *prijaji*); 1b is characteristically employed only by *prijajis*.

Given this brief and over-condensed formal analysis of the level problem, the sense in which Javanese linguistic behavior is but a part of their wider system of etiquette and, in fact, a simplified and summarizing model of it is more easily set forth. First, as already noted, the levels themselves reflect the *kasar* to *alus* continuum. *Ngoko,* level 1, is the basic language. People think in this, fall into it whenever the urge to express themselves overcomes the desire to maintain propriety, and generally regard it, like the peasant himself, as the rough, down-to-earth, and necessary foundation on top of which all the *prijaji* fancy work is erected. It is for this reason that all Javanese terms in this report have been given in their *ngoko* forms.

As one moves up the level ladder from *ngoko* toward *krama* (level 3) and *krama inggil* (level 3a), the manner of speaking shifts too: the higher the level one is using, the more slowly and softly one speaks – and the more evenly, in terms both of rhythm and pitch. As, on the whole, the "higher" conjugates tend to be longer than the lower ones (*kowé/sampéjan/pandjenengan* – and, for the *very* elevated, *pandjenengan dalem* – for "you"; *kéné/ingriki* for "here"), the high language levels, when spoken correctly, have a kind of stately pomp which can make the simplest conversation seem like a great ceremony. Like the forms of etiquette generally, the patterns of linguistic etiquette modulate, regularize, and smooth the processes of social interaction into an *alus,* unvarying flow of quiet, emotionally tranquilizing propriety.

It has already been pointed out how etiquette patterns, including language, tend to be regarded by the Javanese as a kind of emotional capital which may be invested in putting others at ease. Politeness is something one directs toward others; one surrounds the other with a wall of behavioral (*lair*) formality which protects the stability of his inner life (*batin*). Etiquette is a wall built around one's inner feelings, but it is, paradoxically, always a wall someone else builds, at least in part. He may choose to build such a wall for one of two reasons. He and the other person are at least approximate status equals and not intimate friends; and so he responds to the other's politeness to him with an equal politeness. Or the other is clearly his superior, in which case he will, in deference to the other's greater spiritual refinement, build him a wall without any demand or expectation that you reciprocate. This is, of course, but a restatement of the *andap-asor* pattern discussed more generally above. But in terms of language it is possible to state the exact nature of this pattern, the core of Javanese etiquette, in a rather more precise, abstract and formal manner.

If we take the six levels (or three levels and three half levels) of speech present in one dialect or another in Modjokuto, we can diagram them in terms of the "wall" metaphor as follows:

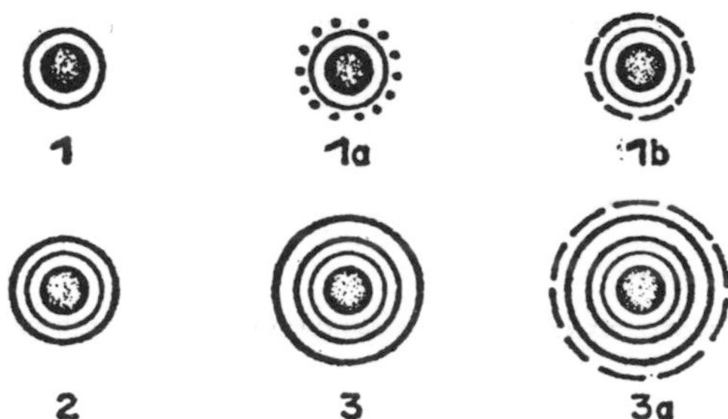

The solid center is intended to represent the *batin*, the inner life. The solid lines represent the stylemes – the low styleme taken as one "layer", the middle as two, the high as three. Low honorifics are represented by a dotted line, high by a dashed. The circles – solid, dotted, or dashed – around the solid center are thus intended to diagram the *lair*, the behavioral world of etiquette. The higher the level of language spoken *to* an individual, then, the thicker the wall of etiquette protecting his emotional life.

In such terms one can diagram nearly any relationship between two individuals of whatever rank or familiarity.[5] Thus, two close friends of equal rank (that two close friends will be of roughly equal rank is nearly a tautology for most Modjokuto Javanese) will both speak *ngoko* to one another:

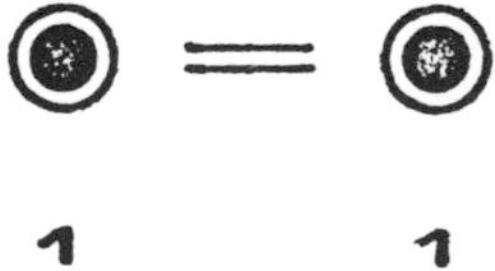

[5] One complication is that it is not entirely true that the status and/or familiarity relationship between speaker and hearer is the only determinant of status forms, because sometimes the status of a third person referred to, especially if he be quite high, may determine the form used: thus, in speaking to a lower-status person one will still use the high, *krama*, form of "house" when speaking of the one the District Officer lives in.

A high official, say the District Officer, and an ordinary educated urbanite will follow a sharply asymmetrical pattern:

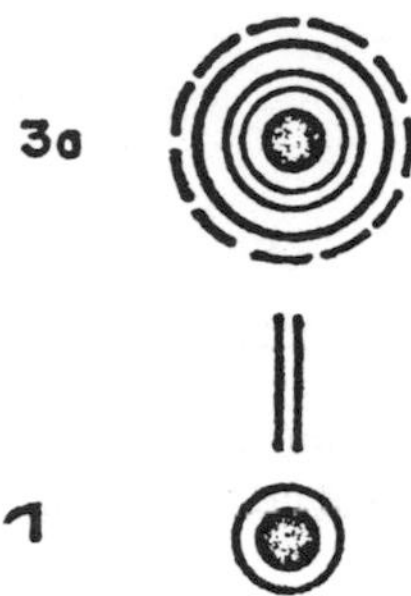

– i.e., the District Officer will speak *ngoko biasa,* the ordinary man, *krama inggil.*

Two ordinary townsmen who are not intimate friends tend to speak *krama madya* reciprocally:

Two *prijajis* who are not intimate friends tend to speak *krama biasa* (if particularly elevated, *krama inggil*) reciprocally:

A peasant speaking to a higher status person will use *krama madya,* for the most part, for he doesn't use *krama biasa* or *krama inggil:*

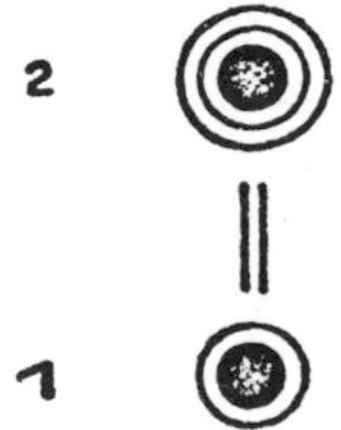

One might get a similar pattern if a "lower class" townsman were conversing with a "middle class" townsman, say a carpenter with a well-off storekeeper.

A peasant speaking to a fellow peasant with whom he is not intimate might use *krama madya,* but more commonly he will use *ngoko madya,* reciprocally:

1a 1a

Middle or lower ranking townsmen who are casual acquaintances might also use reciprocal *ngoko madya* or *krama madya,* depending mostly on the occasion, the content of what was being communicated, and so on.

Ngoko sae, the *prijaji* speciality, is used between *prijaji* who know one another fairly well and are of equal status but regard each other to be so elevated as to make the reciprocal use of *ngoko biasa,* or *ngoko madya,* which might sometimes be used in this context, unseemly:

1b 1b

The inclusion of this level in the dialect shows the *prijaji* reluctance to use very low language to anyone of much status. *Ngoko sae* is used to close friends and relatives whom one knows well enough to use familiar speech but to whom one wishes nevertheless to show proper respect. Thus sentences on this level resolve the conflict between familiarity and respect implicit in the Javanese etiquette pattern with a greater delicacy and subtlety than is possible in either the "urbanite" or "peasant" dialects.

A thorough semantic study of the contexts within which the different levels are employed would in itself be a complex and extended investigation, for the number of variables specifically determining the selection of a particular level are very numerous. They include not only qualitative characteristics of the speakers – age, sex, kinship relation,[6] occupation, wealth, education, religious commitment, family background – but also

[6] For a discussion of the selection of language levels within the kinship and family context see H. Geertz's volume *The Javanese Family*.

more general factors: for instance, the social setting (one would be likely to use a higher level to the same individual at a wedding than in the street); the content of the conversation (in general, one uses lower levels when speaking of commercial matters, higher ones if speaking of religious or aesthetic matters); the history of social interaction between the speakers (one will tend to speak rather high, if one speaks at all, with someone with whom one has quarreled); the presence of a third person (one tends to speak higher to the same individual if others are listening). All these play a role, to say nothing of individual idiosyncratic attitudes. Some people, particularly, it seems, wealthier traders and self-confident village chiefs, who tend to think the whole business rather uncomfortable and somewhat silly, speak *ngoko* to almost everyone except the very high in status. Others will shift levels on any pretext. A complete listing of the determinants of level selection would, therefore, involve a thorough analysis of the whole framework of Javanese culture.

In terms of the more general relationship between the Javanese language and Javanese culture, it is of interest to note how the three charts when taken together present a picture of how the three groups – "urbanites", "peasants", and *prijajis* – perceive the Modjokuto-wide status system, the varying form of their etiquette systems, and how they are related to each other – how, in essence, the ideal model set by the *prijajis* refracts through the rest of the social structure. The *prijaji* chart (Table III), with its excluded middle, shows the *prijaji* tendency to put people into two categories: those to whom one speaks respectfully, equals and superiors (i.e., other *prijajis*); and those to whom one speaks familiarly, inferiors (i.e., non-*prijajis)* and very close friends and relatives. As noted, level 1b, *ngoko sae*, forms a nice compromise between respect and familiarity, and among the more refined *prijajis* in the larger towns, the omission of *ngoko madya* (1a) in their dialect would even further strengthen the dichotomous nature of their model of the status system.

The peasant chart (Table II) shows both the peasants' lessened sense of internal differentiation of status within their own group and their view of the whole structure from the bottom, the upper reaches of the system being mostly beyond their ken. The chart, in fact, provides a concrete case in point of the relationship between gentry and peasant culture patterns outlined earlier. Gentry patterns are reflected dimly and in a somewhat distorted fashion in the peasant context, but they are reflected there. *Prijaji* speakers of (what they regard as) "correct" Javanese are continually making fun – to one another, or to the ethnographer – of "ignorant" villagers who use *tjinten* as the high form of *tjina* (Chinese), when "really" there is no higher form. Similarly for the village use of *konten* for *kori* (door) and, worst of all, their creation of high forms for place names which never should alter: *Kedinten* for *Kediri; Surobringo* for *Surabaja.*[7] For the *ubangan* peasants, at any rate, *prijaji* speech, like *prijaji* etiquette, religion, art, and style of life, is the ideal form, even though they may regard it as too difficult and restrictive for their own use. For the *santri* the religion and art drop out as patterns worthy of emulation, but the speech, etiquette, and style of life remain as models.

Table I shows the results of the jostling together of people from all walks of life in the urban context. Since the average middle rank urbanite mixes with everyone from *prijaji* to peasant, he employs whatever language level seems reasonable in the situation. To speak respectfully to a peasant, he will use *krama madya* (level 2); to a high *prijaji, krama inggil* (3a); and to people of his own rank or slightly higher he will use *krama biasa* (3). But he will have little use for the kind of subtleties represented by level 1b, *ngoko sae*. Thus, in place of the dichotomous (gentry versus the field) view of the status structure of the *prijaji* and the relatively speaking more equalitarian view of the peasant, the urbanite sees a more even gradation of status over quite a wide range.

Lastly, a word should be said about the increasing popularity of Indonesian, the national language based on Malay, among certain groups, particularly the urban youth and the political elite of the town. Indonesian appeals to those whose sense of political nationality as Indonesians rather than as Javanese is most developed, to those who are interested in the cultural products of the new Indonesia's mass media (newspapers, magazines, movies, radio), and those who wish to take leadership positions in government and business. But the use of Indonesian, now taught in all the schools, is spreading very rapidly beyond these somewhat special groups to nearly all townspeople and to a greater and greater number of peasants. As most available reading matter is now in Indonesian rather than Javanese, literacy more or less implies Indonesian, although a reading knowledge does not, of course, imply its use in everyday life. In any case, although the use of Indonesian for everyday conversation is still mostly confined to the more sophisticated urbanites, and its use suggests something of an air of "public speaking" for most Javanese, it is rapidly becoming more and more an integral part of their daily cultural life and will become even more so as the present generation of school children grows to adulthood. That it will, in the foreseeable future, en-

[7] These "mistakes" are based on false analogies to types of formal alteration which are common in moving from high to low Javanese. Though there are no specific rules for such changes, a few sorts of changes occur repeatedly (lower terms given first): (1) a shift of final vowel from *a* to *i*: *djawa/djawi*, "Javanese"; (2) a shift from *i* to *os: ganti/gantos*, "change"; (3) a kind of "pig-latin" form in the higher term involving, among other processes, various forms of medial or final nasalization: *kena/kenging*, "hit", "may"; *karep/kadjeng*, "wish", "want"; *kari/kantun*, "left behind"; (4) a complete change of form: *omah/grija*, "house".

tirely displace Javanese is, of course, entirely unlikely. Rather, it seems destined, at least in the short run, to become part of the general Javanese linguistic system, to become one more type of sentence among those available, to be selected for use in certain special contexts and for certain special purposes.

Before the meeting began, when they (the members of a mystical religious sect) were discussing language, Sudjoko said that one simply couldn't use Indonesian to discuss mystical philosophy. When I asked him why, he said: "Well, all the terms are in Javanese in the first place; and in the second place Javanese fits the kind of thought better. It would be very hard to express such thoughts in Indonesian; it just wouldn't feel right." Contrariwise, he said that giving a political speech in Javanese is one of the hardest things in the world to do; it just doesn't seem to have the expressions. Someone then noted that even when one goes to a political meeting in the village and they use Javanese, many of the words are Indonesian words which, although the people in the audience perhaps cannot use them or at least cannot make them into whole Indonesian sentences, they nevertheless understand quite well.

From: *The Religion of Java*, by Clifford Geertz (Glencoe, Ill., The Free Press, 1960), pp. 248-260. Reprinted with permission.

Marjorie S. Zengel

LITERACY AS A FACTOR IN LANGUAGE CHANGE

All language has been stated to change its lexicon at an approximately constant rate of speed when investigated by use of a test list of basic words selected for universality of incidence and minimal cultural notation and connotation. While written texts have of necessity been widely used in studies exploring languages no longer current, attention has been directed primarily to spoken language.

It has been implied (e.g., Herskovits 1955) that literacy is irrelevant and incapable of modifying the rate of language change. It has been more of a heuristic assumption than a demonstrated fact, however, that the trait of writing, universally understood and employed as a persistent and essential tool of communication by a sizable language community, will not alter the index of retention of lexical items. It would seem appropriate, therefore, to raise the question of the impact of effective mass literacy on the stability of the vocabulary of a language.

A casual sampling of modern languages suggests that a leaning toward conservatism correlates to some degree with a literate tradition. This correlation may be inferred from observations of the various effects of a literary language on its co-existing spoken counterpart. Affected facets of speech include grammatical forms, pronunciation, and vocabulary. The conservatism of orthography is too obvious to require comment; yet, in this connection, there would seem to be an additional correlation between the quantum of literate tradition among a given people at a given time and the degree of flexibility permitted in spelling.[1] If it is true, as

[1] Alongside the expansion of reading and writing skills in the Anglo-American world in recent years, the freedom of variation honored by Sam Weller has been on the wane. In contrast, random selection of written items in a language such as

these things would indicate, that literacy is attended by a linguistic conservatism, then the dynamics of vocabulary change among a wholly literate people should reflect this fact.

Mass literacy is a most recent and geographically limited feature in our world. No substantial language group can assert pretensions to universal literacy throughout a period of time long enough to fall within the time depth range considered sufficient for meaningful application of the techniques of glottochronology. Some additional centuries of universal compulsory education must elapse to provide conditions necessary for such testing. In the meantime, the problem, if it is to be attacked at all, must be approached less directly.

Among the peoples of the world, subgroups can be identified in which written language, through time, has been an essential tool to the functioning of the group. In accessible European history, one such group may be definitionally identified as that which specialized, at least to a substantial extent, in legal matters. Here, riding the tide of expansion and empire, accomplishing climactic feats of achievement, and coasting for centuries on cumulated prestige, the savants of the Roman law have left a wealth of documents.

Three of these documents, spanning 2,000 years, have been selected for study.

Several peculiarities setting them apart from literature as a whole should be noted. They are all in Latin: the first two in the idiom of the day, subject to the qualification that legalism of itself imposes conventional differences from ordinary speech; the third, from 16th-century France, when Latin may be said to have been a living language only esoterically within narrow areas of the total culture, such as law and religion. None is the work of an individual. All result from the combined efforts – in composition, critical scrutiny, debate and compromise – of many individuals. Thus, their language is not equatable with idiolect but must be considered as a kind of average of many idiolects. All were officially promulgated as law by sovereign authority and, as such, had an intimate and extensive significance in the societies from which they came.

The Twelve Tables of Rome date from 450 B.C., not long after the expulsion of the kings. No surely original text has survived. What exists of the *Twelve Tables* has been painstakingly reconstructed in text and arrangement from fragmentary quotations, recapitulations, and references in the works of later writers (Girard 1895; Ortolan 1884). In all, 53 texts or fragments of texts with a total vocabulary of about 252 different

---

Yucatecan Maya, which still lacks a substantial literate tradition, exposes unconventionalized practice, for example, *uinic* = winik.

words have been found. Grammarians suspect that in the process of survival by quotation some modernization of language has occurred. Its effect, if any, on this study would be to increase the rate of retention. To reduce this possible falsification, two reconstructions have been compared, and restored words or suspicious passages have been omitted. On terminal rechecking, other differences between the two versions have been found to be irrelevant to the lexical items selected for use here.

The Institutes of Justinian were enacted into law on December 30th, A.D. 533. The text is something over half a million running words (Sandars 1948).

The Custom of Brittany, with d'Argentré's commentaries, includes a Latin text of about 25,000 statutory words and around 1,000 double column folio pages of Latin glosses (d'Argentré 1621). The precise date is in some doubt. The document, published in 1621, is the third edition of a work relating to legislation enacted subsequent to 1580. A compromise target date of 1600 is treated here as the date of composition.

I have set up two test lists, checked them against the documents, and calculated rates of retention per 1,000 years.

In the operations of original selection and determination of persistence, considerations stated by Swadesh (1952, 1955), Gudschinsky (1956), and Hymes (1960) have been respected. There has been strict application of semantic criteria. Normal phonetic change, actually rarely affecting spelling, has, of course, been disregarded. Structural modifications, including accord and conjugational processes and other phenomena, have been excluded. Finally, attention has been centered on the stem morpheme, and, in two instances in the Legal List below, a single listing has been made to include more than one compound word.

Frequency of occurrence has been disregarded except in the few most patent instances. In other cases, where synonyms appear, the decision has been more difficult. In general, synonyms have not been regarded as displacing a word which also continues in use with unchanged meaning.

Where a term has not been found in the *Institutes*, but is used in the later document, it has been treated as continuously alive. In the commentaries to the *Custom,* frequent citation of Justinian and other sources of Roman law make it clear that we are dealing with a unilinearly transmitted body of knowledge, which would seem to justify such treatment.

My first or Swadesh List is of 32 words from the *Twelve Tables* text which appear on Swadesh's original 200 word List (Hymes 1960, 6).

By way of incidental comment, it can be said that the 100 word list shows no more validity for this type of unilineal study than the 200 word list. This may be explained by the fact that one of the controlling considerations in the development of the smaller list is the likelihood of worldwide incidence, a condition irrelevant here.

SWADESH LIST [2]

English	*Latin*	*Citations*	*First interval*	*Second interval*
all*	omnium	VI 3; I.pr.1; 1	+	+
and°	-que	V 7; —; —	—	0
bad	malum	VIII 25; I.2.6.3; 590	+	+
bone*°	ossa	X 5; I.4.4.7; —	+	0
burn*	urito	X 1; I.4.3.13; —	+	—
child	filium	IV 3; I.3.28.pr.; 75	+	+
cut	secanto	III 6; I.4.3.6; —	+	—
day	dies	II 2; I.1.20.1; 1	+	+
die*	moritur	V 4; I.1.12.pr.; 77	+	+
father	pater	IV 3; I.1.4.pr.; 132	+	+
five	quinque	VIII 4; I.1.14.2; 169	+	+
foot*	pedem	I 2; —; 462	(+)	+
fruit	fructus	XII 3; I.2.1.35; 76	+	+
give*	dato	I 3; I.1.2.7; 4	+	+
hand*	manum	I 2; I.1.3.3; 3	+	+
he	is	II 3; I.1.10.13; 9	+	+
if	si	I 1; I.1.1.2; 1	+	+
in	in+abl.	I 6; I.pr.1; 6	+	+
kill*	occisit	VIII 12; I.1.3.3; Intro.e iii	+	+
live	vivito	III 4; I.1.12.pr.; 155	+	+
night*	nox	VIII 12; I.4.1.2; 20	+	+
not*°	ne	I 3; —; —	—	0
other	alteri	VIII 4; I.1.1.3; 60	+	+
person*	hominem	X 1; I.1.2.1; 256	+	+
road*	viam	VII 7; I.4.3.5; 54	+	+
take (hold)	capito	I 1; I.1.3.3; 68	+	+
this*	hoc	X 2; I.1.1.2; 79	+	+
three	tres	XII 3; I.pr.6; 58	+	+
water*	aqua	VII 8; I.1.16.2; 365	+	+
with	cum	II 2; I.1.1.2; 49	+	+
woman*	mulieres	X 4; I.1.9.1; 77	+	+
year	biennium	VI 3; I.2.6.pr.; 65	+	+

[2] Only one occurrence of a word is cited in these lists. Citation to the *Twelve Tables* is by Orlotan's arrangement; the Roman numeral indicates table and the Arabic, article. Conventional citation to Justinian requires a capital letter indicating work, as I for *Institutes*, followed by three Arabic numbers, indicating, respectively, book, title and article. Citation to the *Custom* is by article number.

Word forms in these lists are as found originally; no attempt has been made to reduce them to a base form.

Parentheses around a survival symbol indicate that retention has been presumed because of later discovery. Otherwise, + means survival, — means replacement, 0 means that no sememe was found.

Items marked with ° were not used in the test list for the second time interval.

TABLE I

Findings from the Swadesh List

	Items from 100 word list	*Items surviving*	*Expected rate of retention*	*Rate of retention found*
First interval	32	30	81%	93.7%
Second interval	29	27	81%	93.4%

	Items from 100 word list	*Items surviving*	*Expected rate of retention*	*Rate of retention found*
First interval	15	14	86%	93.2%
Second interval	13	12	86%	92.8%

My second or Legal List has been conceived of as polar to the first. An essential criterion for presence on the glottochronology test lists is that a word shall be basic in the sense of being endowed with a minimal cultural content. The Legal List of this study is defined as a selection of words most heavily freighted with culture content. The area of applicability of this maximal cultural determination is reference to the law as one of the segments of human behavior peculiarly ascribable to culture. It is true that words on this list may have enjoyed popular use in the total speech community, but they all have clear and definite significance as technical legal terms.[3] It is in this sense that they have been handled.

LEGAL LIST

Latin	*English*	*Citations*	*First interval*	*Second interval*
adgnatus	agnate	V 4; I.1.15.pr.; 309	+	+
alienam	another's	VII 8; I.1.9.6; 94	+	+
arbitro	arbitrator	II 2; I.4.6.1; 18	+	+
arbitrium	decision	XII 3; I.4.6.31; 89	+	+
assiduo° (ads-)	substantial citizen	I 4; —; —	—	0
auctoritas	authority	VI 3; I.1.2.7; 104	+	+
causam	case, lawsuit	I 6; I.1.21.pr.; 8	+	+
clienti°	client	VIII 21; —; —	—	0
comitio	Comitium	I 6; I.2.10.1; —	+	—
confessi	acknowledged	III 1; —; 172	(+)	+

On the Swadesh list, * indicates items on the 100 word test list as well as on the 200 word list.

[3] Dr. Mitchell Franklin, W. R. Irby Professor of Law, Tulane University, has been kind enough to review and correct the writer's original selection of items for this list.

LEGAL LIST (*continued*)

Latin	*English*	*Citations*	*First interval*	*Second interval*
conserunt° (with manus)	fictitious judicial combat	VI 6; —; —	—	0
custos	curator	V 7; —; 42	(+)	+
damnum	damages	XII 3; I.4.1.pr.; 38	+	+
diffisus	postponed	II 2; I.3.15.4; 233	+	+
duplione	double	XII 3; I.2.1.29; 87	+	+
falsam	false	XII 3; I.1.6.6; 577	+	+
foro	forum	I 6; I.3.24.5; 7	+	+
fraude	fraud	III 6; I.1.6.pr.; 195	+	+
fundi	immovable property	VI 3; I.2.1.12; 10	+	+
furiosus	mad	V 7; I.1.10.pr.; 490 gloss	+	+
furtum	theft	VIII 12; I.2.1.16; 3	+	+
gentilis°	of same clan	V 5; —; —	—	0
haeredium	hereditary estate	VII 3; —; 301	(+)	+
haeres	heir	V 4; I.1.6.1; 2	+	+
hoste	alien	II 2; I.1.12.5; —	+	—
improbus	infamous	VIII 22; 1.2.10.6; 588 gloss	+	+
injectio (with manus)	legal seizure	III 2; —; 3	(+)	+
injuriam	injury	VIII 4; I.1.6.1; 45	+	+
intestabilis	incompetent to testify	VIII 22; I.2.10.6; —	+	—
intestato	intestate	V 4; I.1.9.2; —	+	—
judicatis (with rebus)	res judicata	III 1; I.4.13.5; —	+	—
judicatum	judicial settlement	III 3; I.4.9.1; 97	+	+
judici	judge	II 2; I.1.12.8; 1	+	+
jure	law, right, court	III 1; I.pr.; 37; 153	+	+
justi	lawful, just	III 1; I.2.1.35; 481	+	+
legassit	bequeath	V 3; I.2.4.1; 273	+	+
liber	free	IV 3; I.1.2.2; 337	+	+
libripens	balance-holder	VIII 22; I.2.10.1;; —	+	—
litem	suit	I 7; I.1.23.2; 19	+	+
mancipium	formal acceptance	VI 1; I.1.3.3; —	+	—
nexum	legal obligation	VI 1; I.1.12.4; —	+	—
nocet	injure	VII 8; I.2.10.8; 281	+	+
noxiam	injury	XII 2; I.4.8.1; 387	+	+
nuncupassit	declare formally	VI 1; I.2.10.14; —	+	—
orato° (adorat, perorant)	plead, argue	I. 5, 6, VIII 16; —; —	—	0
pacit	contract	VIII 2; I.2.8.1; 320	+	+
patronus	patron	VIII 21; I.1.16.1; 347	+	+
pecunia°	property	V 3; —; —	—	0
poenae	penalty	VIII 4; I.1.2.6; 1	+	+
potestas	power	V 7; I.1.2.6; 15	+	+
praesentes	present	I 6; I.1.5.3; 136	+	+
proletario°	commoner	I 4; —; —	—	0

LEGAL LIST (*continued*)

Latin	*English*	*Citations*	*First interval*	*Second interval*
rei	thing, affairs	V 3; I.2.2.pr.; 3	+	+
reo	litigant, party	II 2; I.3.16.pr.; 102	+	+
sacer	sacred	VIII 21; I.2.1.7; 265	+	+
servus	slave	XII 2; I.1.3.pr.;	+	—
talio	recompense in kind	VIII 2; I.4.4.7; —	+	—
tempestas°	term	I 8; —; —	—	0
testarier (antestator)	witness	VIII 22; I.2.10.3; 570	+	+
testimonium	testimony	II 3; I.2.10.9; 159	+	+
tutela	tutorship	V 3; I.1.13; 45	+	+
usus	use	VI 3; I.2.1.4; 75	+	+
venum	in sale	IV 3; I.1.3.4; 240	+	+
vindex°	surety for performance	I 4; —; —	—	0
vindiciam°	assertion of ownership	XII 3; —; —	—	0
vindicit	demand formally	III 3; I.2.1.26; 58	+	+
vitium	vice, defect	I 3; I.2.6.10; —	+	—
vocat	summon	I 1; I.1.15.2; 115	+	+

The apparent change of rate between the two intervals must be taken with a grain of salt. The rate for the first interval has been increased by the presumption of persistence applied to terms appearing in the *Custom* and not found in the *Institutes*. Had this not been done, the number of retained words would have been recorded as 54, resulting in a retention rate of 79.0 percent. It is believed that the higher rate of 85.1 percent more nearly approximates the truth.

For three reasons it is likely that the rate of retention of the second interval is too low. First, the material searched in the final document amounts in bulk to a small fraction of that of the *Institutes*. Second, consistent application of the presumption of survival by later discovery, applied to augment the *Institutes* list, has not been made to the *Custom* list. Such an operation would surely increase the persistences by those terms common in modern civil law jargon. Third, the *Custom* dates from a period in which the useful language relating to law outside the legal profession, and to a lesser extent even within it, was shifting from Latin to

TABLE II

Findings from the Legal List

	Number of items	*Items retained*	*Rate of retention*
First interval	68	58	85.1%
Second interval	58	46	80.5%

French. Thus, its language is no longer in full vigor, but existing in a reduction state which must inevitably have affected lexicon.

Comparative data for evaluation of the behavior of the Swadesh List has been tabulated in Table I. For the Legal List, the only comparative data found is Hymes' restatement of work by Lees (Hymes 1960, 9), in which he reports a retention rate in total vocabulary of 30 percent less than the 81 percent for the 200 word test list, and of 13 percent less than the 81 percent for vocabulary concerning body parts and functions. This last special semantic category is of such relative stability that a respectable portion of the glottochronology test lists has been drawn from it. The various retention rates may be summarized, for comparison, in Table III.

TABLE III
Summary

1.	General vocabulary	51% rate of retention
2.	Body parts and functions	68
3.	200 word basic	81
4.	Legal List* (Table II)	83
5.	100 word basic	86
6.	Swadesh List** (Table I)	93

* Average for the two time intervals.
** Average for the two time intervals of either 200 or 100 word list.

CONCLUSIONS

1. The generalization that lexical items with minimal cultural content are retained more persistently than other words is confirmed (Table III, items 1 and 3; 4 and 6).

2. The implication that vocabulary changes at different rates of speed in different semantic categories is confirmed (Table III, items 1 and 2; 1 and 4).

3. This differential rate of change may not, however, be equated with relative degree of attribution of cultural content to the semantic categories (Table III, items 2 and 4).

4. Some new factor must be recognized to account for the astonishing stability disclosed in this study (Table III, items 3 and 4; 3 or 5 and 6). Since these materials have been selected within an area where total literacy is a primary and integral necessity in the communicative process, it seems reasonable to conclude that it is to be reckoned with in language change through time and may be expected to retard the rate of vocabulary change.

REFERENCES CITED

d'Argentré, Bertrand
1621 *Comentarii in Patrias Britonum leges, seu Consuetudines generales antiquissimi Ducatus Britanniae.* In lucem editi cura et studio V. C. Caroli D'Argentré B. F. & in Senatu Armorico Praesidiis, etc. Editio tertia emendatissima ... (Paris, Nicolas Buon).
Girard, Paul Frédéric
1895 *Textes de Droit Romain,* publiés et annotés par ... 12 ed. (Paris, Arthur Rousscau).
Gudschinsky, Sarah
1956 "The ABC's of lexicostatistics", *Word,* 12, 175-210.
Herskovits, Melville J.
1955 *Cultural anthropology* (New York, Alfred A. Knopf).
Hymes, Dell H.
1960 "Lexicostatistics so far", *Current Anthropology,* 1, 3-44.
Ortolan, J.
1884 *Histoire de la Législation Romaine depuis son origine jusqu'à la législation moderne et généralisation du droit romain,* 12th ed., J. E. Abbé, ed., 3 vols. (Paris, E. Plon, Nourrit et cie, vol. 1).
Sandars, Thomas Collett
1948 *The Institutes of Justinian, with English introduction, translation and notes* (London, Longmans, Green and Co.).
Swadesh, Morris
1952 "Lexico-statistic dating of prehistoric ethnic contacts", *Proceedings of the American Philosophical Society,* 96, 452-63.
1955 "Towards greater accuracy in lexicostatistic dating", *International Journal of American Linguistics,* 21, 121-37.

From: *American Anthropologist,* 64 (1962), pp. 132-139. Reprinted with permission.

Uriel Weinreich

IS A STRUCTURAL DIALECTOLOGY POSSIBLE?

1. In linguistics today the abyss between structural and dialectological studies appears greater than it ever was. The state of disunity is not repaired if "phoneme" and "isogloss" occasionally do turn up in the same piece of research. Students continue to be trained in one domain at the expense of the other. Field work is inspired by one, and only rarely by both, interests. The stauncher adherents of each discipline claim priority for their own method and charge the others with "impressionism" and "metaphysics", as the case may be; the more pliant are prepared to concede that they are simply studying different aspects of the same reality.

This might seem like a welcome truce in an old controversy, but is it an honorable truce? A compromise induced by fatigue cannot in the long run be satisfactory to either party. The controversy could be resolved only if the structuralists as well as the dialectologists found a reasoned place for the other discipline in their theory of language. But for the disciplines to legitimate each other is tantamount to establishing a unified theory of language on which both of them could operate. This has not yet been done.

While the obstacles are formidable, the writer of this paper believes that they are far from insurmountable. The present article is designed to suggest a few of the difficulties which should be ironed out if the theories of two very much disunited varieties of linguistics, structural and dialectological, are to be brought closer together. A certain amount of oversimplification is inevitable, for the "sides" in the controversy are populous and themselves far from unified. The author would not presume to function as an arbitrator. He simply hopes, without a needless multiplication of terms, to stimulate discussion with others who have also experienced the conflict of interests – within themselves.

If phonological problems dominate in this paper, this is the result of the fact that in the domain of sounds structural and non-structural approaches differ most;[1] semantic study has (so far, at least) not equalled sound study in precision, while in the domain of grammar, specifically structural points of view have had far less to contribute.

2. Regardless of all its heterogeneity, structural linguistics defines a language as an organized system. It was one of the liberating effects of structural linguistics that it made possible the treatment of a language as a unique and closed system whose members are defined by opposition to each other and by their functions with respect to each other, not by anything outside of the system. But since organization must have a finite scope, one of the major problems in a structural linguistic description is the delimitation of its object, the particular system described. Only in ideal cases can the linguist claim to be describing a whole "language" in the non-technical sense of the word. In practice he must delimit his object to something less. One of the steps he takes is to classify certain items in his data as intercalations from other systems, i.e. as "synchronically foreign" elements (e.g. *bon mot* in an otherwise English sentence). Another step is to make certain that only one variety of the aggregate of systems which the layman calls a "language" is described. These steps are taken in order to insure that the material described is uniform. This seems to be a fundamental requirement of structural description.

To designate the object of the description which is in fact a subdivision of the aggregate of systems which laymen call a single language, the term "dialect" is often used. But if "dialect" is defined as the speech of a community, a region, a social class etc., the concept does not seem to fit into narrowly structural linguistics because it is endowed with spatial or temporal attributes which do not properly belong to a linguistic system as such. "Dialects" can be adjacent or distant, contemporary or noncontemporary, prestigious or lowly; linguistic systems in a strictly structural view can only be identical or different. It is proposed that the term "dialect" be held in reserve for the time being and that, for purposes of structural analysis as set forth here, it be replaced by "variety".

In deference to the non-structural sense of "dialect" as a type of speech which may itself be heterogeneous, some linguists have broken down the object of description even further to the "idiolect" level. This term has been used in the United States to denote "the total set of speech habits of a single individual at a given time". The term has been serious-

[1] Some of the phonological points made here were inspired by N. S. Troubetzkoy's article on linguistic geography, "Phonologie et géographie linguistique", *TCLP*, 4 (1931), 228-34; reprinted in his *Principes de phonologie* (Paris, 4, 1949), 343-50.

ly criticized on two grounds: 1. constancy of speech patterns may be more easily stated for two persons in a dialogic situation (a kind of *dialecte à deux*) than for a single individual; 2. there are differences even within an "idiolect" which require that it be broken down further (e.g. into "styles").

"Idiolect" is the homogeneous object of description reduced to its logical extreme, and, in a sense, to absurdity. If we agree with de Saussure that the task of géneral linguistics is to describe all the linguistic systems of the world,[2] and if description could proceed only one idiolect at a time, then the task of structural linguistics would not only be inexhaustible (which might be sad but true), but its results would be trivial and hardly worth the effort.

The restriction of descriptive work to homogeneous material has led to a paradox not quite unlike that proposed by Zeno about motion. A moving arrow is located at some point at every moment of time; at intermediate moments, it is at intermediate positions. Therefore it never moves. Rigidly applied, the typical elements of structural description – "opposition" and "function of units with respect to other units of the same system" – have come close to incapacitating structural analysis for the consideration of several partly similar varieties at a time. Fortunately, the progress of research no longer requires absolute uniformity as a working hypothesis.[3]

Structural linguistic theory now needs procedures for constructing systems of a higher level out of the discrete and homogeneous systems that are derived from description and that represent each a unique formal organization of the substance of expression and content. Let us dub these constructions "diasystems", with the proviso that people allergic to such coinages might safely speak of supersystems or simply of systems of a higher level. A "diasystem" can be constructed by the linguistic analyst out of any two systems which have partial similarities (it is these similarities which make it something different from the mere sum of two systems). But this does not mean that it is always a scientist's construction only: a "diasystem" is experienced in a very real way by bilingual (including "bidialectal") speakers and corresponds to what students of language contact have called "merged system".[4] Thus, we might construct a "diasystem" out of several types of Yiddish in which a variety possessing the opposition /i ~ ɪ/ is itself opposed to another variety with a single /i/ phoneme. Be it noted that a Yiddish speaker in a situation of dialect contact might find information in the confusion of /i/ and /ɪ/ of his in-

[2] Ferdinand de Saussure, *Cours de linguistique générale* (Paris, 4, 1949), 20.

[3] André Martinet, in preface to Uriel Weinreich, *Languages in Contact* (= *Linguistic Circle of New York, Publication no. 1*) (1953), vii.

[4] *Languages in Contact*, 8 f.

terlocutor, which is opposed, on the diasystem level, to his own corresponding distinction. It might tell him (in a "symptomatic" rather than a "symbolic" way) where, approximately, his interlocutor is from.

It may be feasible, without defining "dialect" for the time being, to set up "dialectological" as the adjective corresponding to "diasystem", and to speak of dialectological research as the study of diasystems. Dialectology would be the investigation of problems arising when different systems are treated together because of their partial similarity. A specifically structural dialectology would look for the structural consequences of partial differences within a framework of partial similarity.

It is safe to say that a good deal of dialectology is actually of this type and contains no necessary references to geography, ethnography, political and cultural history, or other extra-structural factors. In Gilliéron's classic studies, the typical (if not exclusive) interest is structural rather than "external". In the diasystem "French", we may very well contrast the fate of *gallus* in one variety where -*ll*- > -*ḍ*- with its fate in another variety where this phonological change did not take place, without knowing anything about the absolute or even relative geography or chronology of these varieties. Non-geographic, structural dialectology does exist; it is legitimate and even promising. Its special concern is the study of partial similarities and differences between systems and of the structural consequences thereof. The preceding is not to say, of course, that "external" dialectology has been surpassed; this subject will be referred to below (section 7).

Dialectological studies in the structural sense are, of course, nothing new. Binomial formulas like "Yiddish *fus*/*fis* 'foot' ", which are often condensed to $f^{u}_{i}s$ etc., have always been the mainstay of historical phonology. But it should be noted that structural dialectology need not be restricted to historical problems to the extent to which it has been in the past. Consequences of partial differences between varieties can be synchronic as well as diachronic. The following is an example of a "synchronic consequence". In one variety of Yiddish (we stick to Yiddish examples for the sake of consistency), the singular and plural of "foot" are distinguished as (*der*) *fus* vs. (*di*) *fis*, while in another variety, both numbers are *fis*. Now, in the number-distinguishing variety, the singular, *fus*, occurs also as a feminine (with *di*); even so, the distinction between singular and plural can still be made in terms of the vowel: *di fus* "sg." – *di fis* "pl.". In the other dialect, *fis* is invariably masculine, perhaps as a consequence of, or at least in relation to, the fact that there only a masculine could distinguish between sg. *der fis* and pl. *di fis*.[5]

[5] For an example of synchronic consequences in phonemics, see Anton Pfalz, "Zur Phonologie der bairisch-österreichischen Mundart", *Lebendiges Erbe; Fest-*

If structuralism were carried to its logical extreme, it would not allow for the type of comparisons suggested here: it could only study relations within systems; and since in a perfect system all parts are interrelated ("tout se tient"), it is hard to see how systems could even be conceived of as partially similar or different; one would think that they could only be wholly identical or different. Considerations of this nature prevented orthodox Saussureanism of the Geneva school from undertaking the study of gradually changing systems, since it was felt that languages could only be compared, if at all, at discrete "stages".[6] But a more flexible structuralism has overcome this hurdle by abandoning the illusion of a perfect system, and is producing notable results in the diachronic field.[7] We should now take the further step of asserting the possibility of a synchronic or diachronic dialectology based on a combined study of several partially similar systems.

This step in structural linguistic theory would, it seems, do much to bring it closer to dialectology as it is actually carried on.

3. We come next to dialectology's share in the proposed rapprochement. The main objection raised by structuralists against dialectology as usually practiced might be formulated thus: in constructing "diasystems" it ignores the structures of the constituent varieties. In other words, existing dialectology usually compares elements belonging to different systems without sufficiently stressing their intimate membership in those systems.

In the domain of sounds, this amounts to a non-phonemic approach. A traditional dialectologist will have no scruples about listening to several dialect informants pronounce their equivalents of a certain word and proclaiming that these forms are "the same" or "different". Let us assume four speakers of a language who, when asked for the word for "man", utter 1. [man], 2. [man], 3. [mån], and 4. [mån], respectively. On an impressionistic basis, we would adjudge 1 and 2 as "the same", 3 and 4 as "the same", but 1 and 2 as "different" from 3 and 4. Yet suppose that informant 1 speaks a variety in which vowel length is significant; phonemically his form is $_1$/măn/. Informant 2 does not distinguish vowel length, and has given us $_2$/man/. We can further visualize a variety represented by informant 3 where a vowel with maximum degree of opening has the positional variant [å] between /m /and /n/; phonemically, then,

---

schrift . . . Ernst Reclam (Leipzig, 1936), 1-19, which is at the same time one of the rare instances of German phonemics and of structural dialectology.

6 Albert Sechehaye, "Les trois linguistiques saussuriennes", *Vox romanica*, 5 (1940), 1-48, pp. 30 f.; H[enri] Frei, "Lois de passage", *Zeitschrift für romanische Philologie*, 64 (1944), 557-68.

7 Cf. the bibliography of diachronic phonemics by Alphonse G. Juilland in *Word*, 9 (1953), 198-208

we have $_3$/man/. In the fourth variety, no such positional variation exists; that form is perhaps $_4$/mon/. The structural analysis is thus different from the non-structural one: 2 and 3 now turn out to be possibly "the same" (but only, of course, if the systems are otherwise also identical), while 1 and 4 appear to be different. Structural linguistics requires that the forms of the constituent systems be understood first and foremost in terms of those systems, since the formal units of two non-identical systems are, strictly speaking, incommensurable.[8]

A similar requirement could be made about the units of content, or "semantemes". It would not do to say, for instance, that the word *taykh* in one variety of Yiddish is "the same" as *taykh* in another, if, in the one, it is opposed to *ózere* "lake", and hence means only "river", while in the other it is not so opposed and stands for any sizable "body of water". Similar structural cautions would be required with respect to "synonyms" in the diasystem. In the diasystem "Yiddish", *baytn, shtékheven*, and *toyshn* all signify approximately "to exchange", but they cannot be synonyms on the variety level if they do not all exist in any one variety.

A grammatical example might also be cited. In terms of function within the system, it would not be justified to identify the feminine *vaysl* "Vistula River" of two Yiddish varieties if in the one it is opposed to a neuter *vaysl* "eggwhite", while in the other it is completely homonymous with the (also feminine) word for "eggwhite". It is even doubtful whether any two feminines in these two varieties could be legitimately identified in view of the fact that one of the varieties does not possess a neuter gender altogether.

The dialectologist is used to comparing directly the "substance" of different varieties. The demand of the structural linguist that he consider the train of associations, oppositions, and functions that define linguistic forms seems to the dialectologist complicating, unreasonable, and unnecessary ("metaphysical"). To show up the disagreement most clearly, let us represent the phonic problem just discussed on a map and compare the traditional and the proposed structural treatments of it. Obviously the structural approach involves complications, but the dialectologist will become convinced of their necessity when he realizes that phonemics, like structural linguistics generally, represents not a special technique for studying certain problems, but a basic discovery about the way language functions to which structural linguists are completely committed.

Since, in the structural view, allophonic differences between sounds are in a sense less important than phonemic differences, the "substantial" isogloss (Fig. 2) which separates [a] from [å] in the overall /a/ area is structurally somehow less important than the purely formal isogloss

[8] *Languages in Contact*, 7 f.

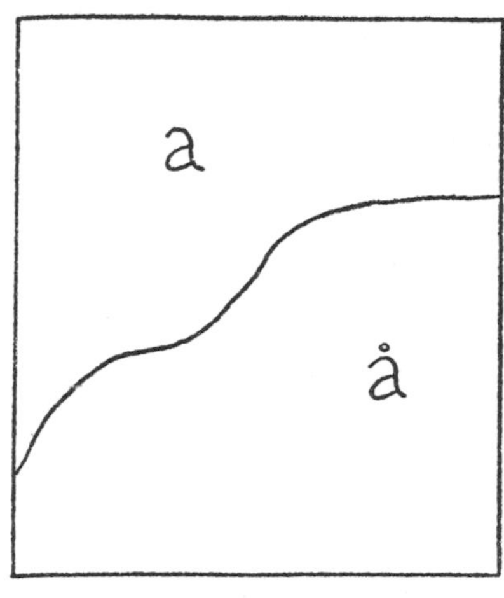

Fig. 1. Traditional

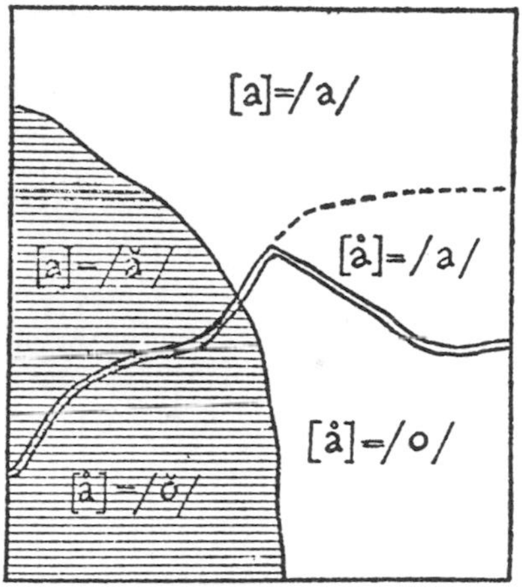

Fig. 2. Structural

THE VOWEL IN 'MAN' IN LANGUAGE *X*

On Fig. 2, a continuous single line divides areas with different phonemic inventories (shaded area distinguishing vowel length, unshaded area not distinguishing it). The double line separates areas using different phonemes in this word (difference of distribution). The dotted line separates allophonic differences.

which separates pronunciations of [mån] = /man/ from those of [mån] = /mon/; the latter isogloss may not reflect any difference in "substance" at all; it would not show up on the non-structural map (Fig. 1). The traditional dialectologist naturally wonders what he stands to gain by the drawing of such "metaphysical" lines. But if dialectological maps are considered diachronically as snapshots of change, and if it can be shown that the difference between phonemes and allophones can be material in determining sound change, it may be possible to convince the dialectologist that the structural map is after all more true to the reality of functioning language. Similar arguments, perhaps, could also be persuasive insofar as they are pertinent to grammatical and lexical matters.

If dialectologists would consider the functions of the elements which they use in their comparisons, their conception of a "diasystem" would come close to that proposed here for structural linguistics and might lead to the unified theory which is so badly needed.

4. The partial differences which are proposed as the specific subject matter of dialectologic study may be of two kinds: differences of inventory and differences of distribution. While the latter are the standard material of comparative study, the former have not received their due stress.

As an example of a difference in inventory, let us take a simple phonemic case first. In the following discussion, single slashes enclose sets of phonemes and single tildes designate phonemic oppositions in a variety identified by a preceding subscript number; oppositions in the constructed diasystem are characterized by double tildes, and the formulas for the diasystems are surrounded by double slashes. Given two varieties with identical five-vowel systems, we might construct the following diasystem: $_{1,2}//\mathrm{i} \approx \mathrm{e} \approx \mathrm{a} \approx \mathrm{o} \approx \mathrm{u}//$. Now let us assume that in one of the varieties, the front vowel of the intermediate degree of openness is more open than in the other; choosing a phonemic transcription which would reflect this fact, we might indicate the difference in the diasystem thus:

$$_{1,2}//\mathrm{i} \approx \frac{_1\mathrm{e}}{_2\varepsilon} \approx \mathrm{a} \approx \mathrm{o} \approx \mathrm{u}//.$$

Given two varieties, one of which (1) distinguishes three front vowels, the other (2) distinguishing four, we might formulate the corresponding part of the vowel diasystem thus:

$$_{1,2}//\frac{_1/\mathrm{i} \sim \mathrm{e} \sim \text{æ}/}{_2/\mathrm{i} \sim \mathrm{e} \sim \varepsilon \sim \text{æ}/} \approx \mathrm{a} \approx \mathrm{o} \ldots//.$$

Here is the actual vowel inventory of Yiddish considered as a diasystem of three dialects, 1. Central ("Polish"), 2. Southwestern ("Ukrainian"), and 3. Northwestern ("Lithuanian"):

$$_{1,2,3}//\frac{\dfrac{_1/\mathrm{i}\!: \sim \mathrm{i}/}{_2/\mathrm{i} \sim \text{ɪ}/}}{_3\mathrm{i}} \approx \mathrm{e} \approx \frac{_1/\mathrm{a}\!: \sim \mathrm{a}/}{_{2,3}\text{ɑ}} \approx \mathrm{o} \approx \mathrm{u}//$$

Similarly differences in inventory of grammatical categories might be stated, e.g. between varieties having two against three genders, three as against four conjugational types, and the like. All examples here are tentative and schematic; the possibilities of a more analytical statement of the diasystem, based e.g. on relevant features, remain to be investigated.

One thing is certain: In the study of language contact and interference (see section 5), a clear picture of differences in inventory is a prerequisite.[9]

Differences in distribution cannot be directly inferred from a comparison of the differences in inventory, although the two ordinarily stand in a definite historical relationship. For example, in the diasystem "Yiddish" described above, the phoneme $_3/\mathrm{i}/$ in variety 3 usually corresponds

9 *Ibid.*, 1 f.

to either $_2$/i/ or $_2$/ɪ/ in cognates of variety 2, and to either $_1$/i:/ or $_1$/i/ in cognates of variety 1 ($_3$/sine/ : $_2$/sɪne/ : $_1$/sĭne/ "enmity"). This is, as it were, a correspondence between the nearest equivalents. But many $_3$/o/'s correspond to /u/'s in variety 1 and 2, even though all three varieties today possess both /o/ and /u/ phonemes. Thus, /futer/ means "father" in varieties 1 and 2, but "fur" in variety 3; /meluxe/ means $_{1,2}$ "craft" and $_3$ "state"; /hun/ means $_{1,2}$ "rooster" and $_3$ "hen". For the tens of thousands of speakers for whom the contact of these varieties is an everyday experience, these "Yiddish" sound sequences are not fully identified until the particular variety of Yiddish to which they belong is itself determined. Now no one would deny that a form like Yiddish [fı̆ˇfl] ($_{1,2}$ "full", $_3$ "many") is identified fully only in conjunction with its meaning in one of the varieties, i.e. when account is taken of the differences in distribution of sounds in cognates occurring in the several varieties. The less obvious point made here is that the form is not fully identified, either, if relevant differences in *inventory* are not accounted for, i.e. if it is not rendered in terms of the phonemes of one of the concrete varieties: [fil] = $_1$/fĭl/, $_2$/fɪl/, $_3$/fil/.

Recent descriptive work on American English phonemics has come close to treating the language as a "diasystem" without, however, satisfying the requirements set forth here. The widely adopted analysis of Trager and Smith [10] provides a set of symbols by which forms of all varieties of American English can be described. It makes it possible for example, to transcribe Southeastern /pæys/ *pass* in terms of some of the same symbols used in /pæt/ *pat* of the same dialect or in /pæs/, /bəyd/ *bird*, etc., of other varieties. This violates the principle advocated here that the phonemic systems of the varieties should be fully established before the diasystem is constructed. We are not told whether in the phoneme inventory of Southeastern American English the /æy/ of *pass* does or does not correspond as an inventory item to the /æ/ of other varieties. We cannot tell if the [o] of *home* of Coastal New England is the same phoneme, or a different phoneme, from the [ow] in *go* in the same variety. For reasons of this type, the system has been criticized as providing not a phonemic description or a set of descriptions, but a "transcriptional arsenal".[11] Yet the remaining step toward the establishment of a phonemic diasystem is not difficult to visualize.

[10] George L. Trager and Henry Lee Smith, Jr., *An Outline of English Structure* (= *Studies in Linguistics Occasional Papers*, 3) (Norman, Okla. 1951), esp. pp. 27-9.

[11] Einar Haugen, "Problems of Bilingual Description", *Report of the Fifth Annual Round Table Meeting on Linguistics and Language Teaching* (= [Georgetown University] *Monograph Series on Languages and Linguistics* no. 7), 1959, 9-19.

5. We might now restate and specify the suggested position of structural dialectology in linguistics as a whole. Synchronic dialectology compares systems that are partially different and analyzes the "synchronic consequences" of these differences within the similarities. Diachronic dialectology deals (a) with divergence, i.e. it studies the growth of partial differences at the expense of similarities and possibly reconstructs earlier stages of greater similarity (traditionally, comparative linguistics); (b) with convergence, i.e. it studies partial similarities increasing at the expense of differences (traditionally, substratum and adstratum studies, "bilingual dialectology",[12] and the like).

The opposite of dialectology, which hardly needs a special name, is the study of languages as discrete systems, one at a time. It involves straight description of uniform systems, typological comparisons of such systems, and, diachronically, the study of change in systems considered one at a time.

6. It was stated previously that diasystems can be constructed *ad hoc* out of any number of varieties for a given analytic purpose. Constructing a diasystem means placing discrete varieties in a kind of continuum determined by their partial similarities. However, in passing from a traditional to a structural dialectology, the more pressing and more troublesome problem is the opposite one, viz. how to break down a continuum into discrete varieties. What criteria should be used for divisions of various kinds? Can non-technical divisions of a "language" into "dialects", "patois", and the like be utilized for technical purposes? [13]

Before these questions can be answered, it is necessary to distinguish between standardized and non-standardized language. This set of terms is proposed to avoid the use of the ambiguous word, "standard", which among others has to serve for "socially acceptable", "average", "typical", and so on. On the contrary, standardization could easily be used to denote a process of more or less conscious, planned, and centralized regulation of language.[14] Many European languages have had standardized varieties for centuries; a number of formerly "colonial" tongues are

[12] For an essay in bilingual dialectology, see Uriel Weinreich, "*Sábesdiker losn* in Yiddish: a Problem of Linguistic Affinity", *Word*, 8 (1952), 360-77.

[13] The possibility of introducing some scientific rigor into existing loose terminology has been explored by André Martinet, "Dialect", *Romance Philology* 8 (1954), 1-11. The article by Václav Polák, "Contributions à l'étude de la notion de langue et de dialecte", *Orbis*, 3 (1954), 89-98, which arrived too late to be utilized here as fully as it deserves, suggests that we call "language" a diasystem whose partial similarities are grammatical while its partial differences are phonologic and lexical.

[14] Cf. *Languages in Contact*, 99-103. An interesting book about standardization is Heinz Kloss, *Die Entwicklung neuer germanischer Kultursprachen von 1800 bis 1950* (Munich, 1952).

undergoing the process only now. Not all leveling is equivalent to standardization. In the standardization process, there is a division of functions between regulators and followers, a constitution of more or less clearcut authorities (academies, ministries of education, *Sprachvereine*, etc.) and of channels of control (schools, special publications, etc.). For example, some dialectal leveling and a good deal of Anglicization has taken place in the immigrant languages of the United States, and we might say that a word like *plenty* has become a part of the American Norwegian koinê.[15] But in the sense proposed here, there is no "standardized" American Norwegian which is different from Old-World Norwegian, and from the point of view of the standardized language, *plenty* is nothing but a regional slang term.

Now it is part of the process of standardization itself to affirm the identity of a language, to set it off discretely from other languages and to strive continually for a reduction of differences within it. Informants of standardized languages react in a peculiar way; moreover, it is much easier to deal with samples of a standardized language, to make generalizations about it and to know the limits of their applicability. On the level of non-standardized or folk lanugage,[16] a discrete difference between one variety and others is not a part of the experience of its speakers, and is much more difficult to supply. For example, it is easy to formulate where standardized Dutch ends and standardized German begins, but it is a completely different matter to utilize for technical purposes the transition between folk Dutch and folk German.

On the whole dialectologists have avoided dealing with standardized languages and have restricted themselves to folk language.[17] Consequently, in practice as well as in theory the problem of dividing and ordering the continuum of language is especially serious with respect to the folk level and not the standardized level. Time was when the continuum of folk language used to be divided on the basis of (usually diachronic) structural features, e.g. the geographic limits of a certain phonological development. Either one isogloss which the linguist considered important was selected (e.g. *k/x* as the line between Low and High German), or a bundle of isoglosses of sufficient thickness was used as a dividing line.

[15] Einar Haugen, *The Norwegian Language in America* (Philadelphia, 1953), 588.

[16] Interesting parallels could be developed between the sociolinguistic opposition "standardized" – "folk" and the social anthropologist's opposition between the cultures of complex (industrialized) and folk societies or strata of society; cf. e.g. George M. Foster, "What Is Folk Culture?", *American Anthropologist*, 55 (1953), 159-73.

[17] Some people are not averse to calling modern standardized languages "Indo-European dialects", or speaking of "literary dialects". Dialectology in the sense proposed in this paper need not restrict itself to the folk level, but such usage is one more reason why the term "dialect" ought to be held in abeyance.

In either case, the resulting divisions were not, of course, all of the same degree; they were major, minor, and intermediate, depending on the thickness of the bundle or the relative importance of the key isogloss. It is evident that no unambiguous concept of dialect could emerge even from this optimistic methodology any more than a society can be exhaustively and uniquely divided into "groups".

Classificatory procedures of this type are today virtually passé. Dialectologists have generally switched to extra-structural criteria for dividing the folk-language continuum. The concept of language area (*Sprachlandschaft*) has practically replaced that of "dialect" (*Mundart*) as the central interest in most geographic work,[18] and ever more impressive results are being obtained in correlating the borders, centers, and overall dynamics of language areas with "culture areas" in a broader sense. Instead of speaking, for instance, of the *helpe/helfe* and *Lucht/Luft* isoglosses as the border between the Ripuarian and Moselle-Franconian "dialects" of the German Rhineland, linguistic geographers now speak of the Eifel Barrier between the Cologne and Trier areas. This Eifel mountain range happens to be the locus not only of those two random isoglosses, but, among others, also the dividing line between *kend* and *keŋk* "child", *haus* and *hus* "house", *grumper* and *erpel* "potato", *heis* and *gramm* "hoarse"; between short-bladed and long-bladed scythes, grey bread in oval loaves and black bread in rectangular loaves, New Year's twists and New Year's pretzels, St. Quirin as the patron saint of cattle and the same as the patron of horses, two different types of ditty addressed to the ladybug, etc.[19] The line is meaningful as a reflex of a medieval boundary which can in turn be accounted for by more permanent climatic, orological, hydrographic, and other geographic factors.[20]

The search for ways to divide the folk-language continuum has also led to statistical correlation methods.[21] Rather than plotting the border lines of single selected structural features, which may be impossible in areas of amorphous transition, the following procedure is used. Inquiries are made at various points concerning the presence or absence of a whole list of test features; then the correlation between the results at

[18] This is particularly evident in the methodologically most advanced German Swiss work; cf. the publications series *Beiträge zur schweizerdeutschen Mundartforschung* edited by Rudolf Hotzenköcherle.

[19] Linguistic data from Adolf Bach, *Deutsche Mundartforschung* (Heidelberg, 2, 1950), 123 ff.; ethnographic data from Adolf Bach, *Deutsche Volkskunde* (Leipzig, 1937), 228.

[20] In the United States, Hans Kurath (*A Word Geography of the Eastern United States*, Ann Arbor, 1949) has successfully combined strictly linguistic with "external" criteria in breaking down the relatively undifferentiated American folk-language area.

[21] See David W. Reed and John L. Spicer, "Correlation Methods of Comparing Idiolects in a Transition Area", *Language*, 28 (1952), 348-60.

some reference point and at all other points is computed, and may be represented cartographically, points with similar correlation coefficients being surrounded by lines which have variously been called "isopleths" or "isogrades". Theoretically related to this procedure are the tests of mutual intelligibility between dialects.[22] All these procedures must depend on an arbitrary critical constant (or constants) for the drawing of a dividing line (or lines, of various degrees of importance), but they do yield an insight into the makeup of a continuously varying language area which supplements, if it does not supersede, the results derived by other methods.

In the domain of dialect sociology, where transitions are perhaps even more continuous and fluid than in dialect geography, the use of extra-linguistic correlations and statistical sampling techniques offers promising possibilities of research in an almost untrodden field.[23]

The use of the social-science tools of "external dialectology" can do much to supplement the procedures outlined for a structural dialectology. One problem for combined structural and "external" linguistic investigation is to determine what structural and non-structural features of language have in fact helped to break up the folk-language continuum into the non-technical units of "dialects", "patois", etc. This combined research might get to the heart of the question of diasystems as empirical realities rather than as mere constructs. One of its byproducts might be the formulation of a technical concept of "dialect" as a variety or diasystem with certain explicit defining features.

7. Finally a word might be said about the interrelationship of structural and "external" points of view applied to a specific dialectological problem. Given a map showing an isogloss, the "external" dialectologist's curiosity is likely to concentrate on the locus of that isogloss. Why is it where it is? What determines the details of its course? What other isoglosses bundle with it? What communication obstacle does it reflect?

The structural dialectologist has another set of questions, stemming from his interest in partial differences within a framework of partial similarity. To take up the semasiological example of Fig. 3 (which is schematized but based on real data), if *shtul* means "chair" in zone A,

[22] Cf. for example C. F. Voegelin and Zellig S. Harris, "Methods for Determining Intelligibility Among Dialects of Natural Languages", *Proceedings of the American Philosophical Society*, 95 (1951), 322-9.

[23] See the interesting paper by Stanley M. Sapon, "A Methodology for the Study of Socio-Economic Differentials in Linguistic Phenomena", *Studies in Linguistics*, 11 (1953), 57-68. A scheme for the classification of varieties of a language according to their function (ecclesiastic, poetic, scientific, etc.) to replace the unsatisfactory terminology of "styles" has been proposed by Yury Šerech, "Toward a Historical Dialectology", *Orbis*, 3 (1954), 43-56, esp. pp. 47 ff.

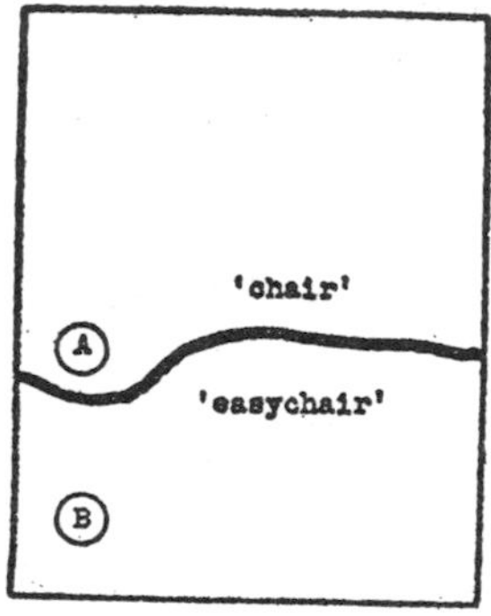

Fig. 3. Meaning of *shtul* in East European Yiddish (Schematized)

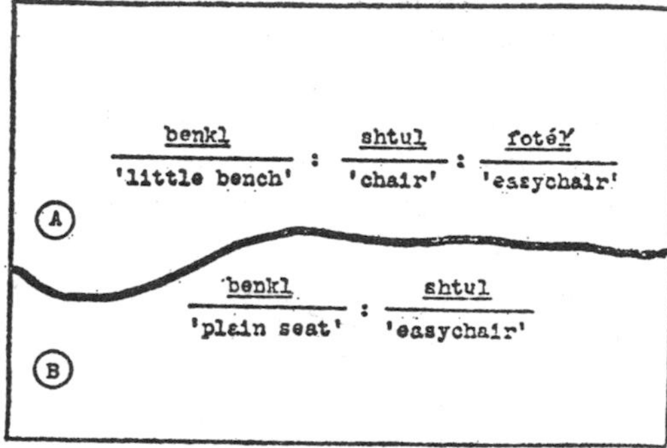

Fig. 4. Designations of Seats in East European Yiddish (Schematized)

but "easychair" in zone B, then what is the designation of "easychair" in A and of "chair" in B? Every semasiological map, due to the two-faceted nature of linguistic signs, gives rise to as many onomasiological questions as the number of zones it contains, and vice versa. If we were to supply the information that in zone A, "easychair" is *fotél',* while in zone B "chair" is *benkl,* a new set of questions would arise: what, then, does *fotél'* mean in B and *benkl* in A?[24] This implicational chain of questions could be continued further. The resulting answers, when entered on a map, would produce a picture of an isogloss dividing two lexical systems, rather than two isolated items (see Fig. 4). This would be the "structural corrective" to a traditional dialect map.

It is easy to think of dialectological field problems for the solution of which "external" and structural considerations must be combined in the most intimate manner. Such problems would arise particularly if the cartographic plotting of systems should produce a set of narrowly diverging isoglosses. Assume that an isogloss is drawn between a variety of a language which distinguishes short /u/ from long /u:/ and another variety which makes no such quantitative distinction. The structuralist's curiosity is immediately aroused about length distinctions in other vowels. Suppose now that the variety that distinguishes the length of /u/ does so also for /i/; but that the isoglosses, plotted independently, are not exactly congruent (Fig. 5). Some intriguing questions now arise concerning the dynamics of the vowel pattern of the discrepant zone. Nothing but an on-the-spot field study closely combining structural analysis and an examination of the "external" communication conditions in the area could deal adequately with a problem of this kind.

[24] The actual answer is that *fotél'* is not current in zone B, while *benkl* means "little bench" in zone A.

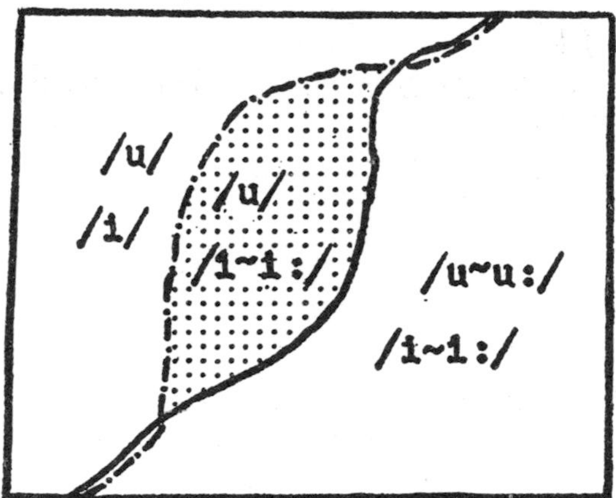

Fig. 5. Non-Congruent Vowel-Length Isoglosses in Language *Y*

8. In answer to the question posed in the title of this paper, it is submitted that a structural dialectology is possible. Its results promise to be most fruitful if it is combined with "external" dialectology without its own conceptual framework being abandoned.

From: *Word*, 14 (1954), pp. 388-400. Reprinted with permission.

Section IV
LANGUAGE REFLECTIONS OF SOCIO-CULTURAL ORGANIZATION

A. L. Epstein

LINGUISTIC INNOVATION AND CULTURE ON THE COPPERBELT, NORTHERN RHODESIA

This paper sets out to discuss some of the linguistic usages which have developed amongst Africans in the emerging urban communities of the Copperbelt of Northern Rhodesia.[1] Comparable data on those aspects of linguistic change considered here appear to be scanty in the literature: I hope therefore that the material I present may prove to have intrinsic linguistic interest. At the same time I wish to show how the use of such data may also be valuable in shedding light on the present way of life and social organization of urban Africans. Here I want to suggest tentatively that the study of linguistic innovation may have wider theoretical importance in providing a possible avenue for exploring the interrelations of structure and culture in situations of rapid social change.

Before turning to the theme of linguistic innovation itself, it is first necessary to sketch in the general linguistic situation on the Copperbelt. The region itself owes its present development almost entirely to the growth of a vast copper mining industry in the space of little more than a generation. The crude mining camps of the early thirties have transformed themselves into bustling, sprawling townships offering most of the amenities of larger and older Western cities. The population is of course entirely immigrant and is drawn from a welter of different ethnic

[1] This paper substantially reproduces one read before the meeting of the Australian branch of the Association of Social Anthropologists of the British Commonwealth held at Canberra in March 1959. The material itself was gathered in the course of field-work at Luanshya (August 1953-June 1954) and Ndola (October 1956-September 1957) when I was employed as a Research Officer of the Rhodes-Livingstone Institute, Lusaka. I am grateful to Dr S. Wurm and Prof. J. A. Barnes, both of the Australian National University, for a number of helpful suggestions.

and national groups. Mine managers and bureaucrats, engineers and geologists, skilled artisans and supervisors of labor are all "Europeans", but they include those who have come from the Union of South Africa (of whom a high proportion are Afrikaans-speaking), the United Kingdom, and, in the early days, Canada and the United States. The further diversification of the ethnic structure has gone hand in hand with the country's economic growth and the increased rate of White immigration after the last war. In addition to the Europeans, there is a relatively small Asiatic element which occupies an important role in the trading and commercial life of the towns. Finally there are the indigenous peoples themselves, the Africans, of whom there are now probably well over a quarter of a million living on the Copperbelt, and claiming membership of a hundred different tribes.[2] Africans participate in the economic life of the Copperbelt as casual, unskilled and semi-skilled workers, though an increasing number are now beginning to occupy posts which call for a greater measure of skill and responsibility. Socially, however, the practice of residential segregation whereby most Africans are bound to live in compounds or locations reduces to a minimum the extent of contact between Africans and Europeans outside the actual work situation.

This heterogeneity of population, with its accompanying diversity of custom and culture as well as wide differences in economic, political, and educational status, provides precisely the kind of polyglot setting in which one expects to find the emergence of "pidgin" and "creolized" languages. Thus on the mines it was imperative that there be some means of communication between European overseers and African laborers if instructions were to be understood and properly carried out. A high proportion of the early European miners came from South Africa, while many of the Africans who now came to the Copperbelt had previously worked on the Rand or at Wankie in Southern Rhodesia. Thus many were already well acquainted with Fanagalo or "Mine-Kafir", long well established in the south, and they introduced it to the Copperbelt. The term Fanagalo itself is rarely heard in Northern Rhodesia, where Europeans generally speak of "Kitchen-Kafir" and Africans of "*Chilapalapa*", presumably because of the continuous iteration of the term "lapa" which seems to recur with the same unwavering frequency as the words "long" and "bilong" in Melanesian pidgin. Fanagolo is a hybrid of Zulu, English, and Afrikaans. Its vocabulary is roughly 70% Nguni (mainly Zulu), 24% English, and 6% Afrikaans in origin, but it retains hardly any of the phonetical, morphological, or syntactical characteristics of the Nguni or other Bantu languages.[3]

[2] The records of African employees at the Roan Antelope Copper Mine listed 104 tribes in 1955.

[3] Cole, 1953.

Fanagalo is thus a "true" pidgin in that it is native to none, or virtually none, of those who speak it. Moreover, it is sharply reduced in structure and vocabulary as contrasted with the languages from which it is derived.[4] In these respects it is similar to Melanesian pidgin, and shares many of the defects, e.g. limited range of expression and lack of subtlety, frequently alleged against the latter. Unlike Melanesian pidgin, however, Fanagalo has never developed – and in Northern Rhodesia shows no sign of ever developing – into a native *lingua franca.* Undoubtedly the reasons for this lie in the very different linguistic situations obtaining in Africa and Melanesia. Africa, too, has its bewildering variety of languages and dialects but language groups, at least in Central Africa, are frequently measured in tens and sometimes hundreds of thousands and are never confined to a small cluster of neighboring villages as is often the case in New Guinea. In my experience it is only on very rare occasions when they can find no other common tongue that Africans resort to Fanagalo among themselves. Fanagalo tends therefore to be restricted to certain kinds of situations in which Africans interact with Europeans. Despite its many inherent limitations, Fanagalo is not a completely impoverished jargon. Among skilled speakers it lends itself readily to fluent and intelligent conversation on a wide variety of subjects. Nevertheless, in the eyes of Africans it remains essentially the language of command and direction, and by more educated Africans at least is invariably associated with European racialist attitudes, and the denial of African claims to full equality on the human plane.

If in the sphere of Black-White relations Fanagalo is the mark of social distance, English is the mark of social acceptance and even equality. For an African to address certain Europeans in English would be regarded as the height of "Kafir insolence".[5] Conversely, the use of English in the context of casual interaction between European and African indicates a more "personal" relationship, and even a degree of friendliness. On more formal occasions, such as at meetings of bodies in which Africans and Europeans participate jointly, it is now rare to hear an African speaking in the vernacular, and English has become the standard medium. The use of English in these circumstances has obvious advantages, but it is also a reflection of the prestige which is accorded the ability to speak English in the African section of the community. Nowa-

[4] Hall, 1955.

[5] The following incident, typical of its kind, was related to me by an African Education Officer who had studied in England. He was walking along the street of a Copperbelt town one day when it started to rain. He took shelter in a nearby building. Noting his smart dress and appearance a European accosted him and said in Fanagolo: "So you've left off wearing skins." The African replied in English that he did not understand Kitchen Kafir but the European merely got angry and told him to clear off.

days some command of English at least is indispensable to the African who aspires to urban leadership on the Copperbelt, although it should also be noted here that a too ready fluency in English may sometimes be bitterly denounced by other Africans who accuse their English-speaking fellows of "leaning too much to the side of the Europeans".

The use of English as a criterion of prestige among Africans is made possible only because adequate knowledge of the language is still confined to a small minority. What proportion of urban Africans speak English it is impossible to say. Any measure we might devise would be completely arbitrary and largely meaningless, for we have to deal with a continuum at one range of which is a very small number whose command of the language is well-nigh perfect and at the other are those whose efforts are fluent enough but frequently result in gibberish and almost complete incomprehensibility. In most cases the quality of English spoken merely reflects the poor standard of teaching in African primary schools, but even the best speakers employ usages deriving from the construction and idiom of their mother tongues. Nevertheless, there are circumstances when imperfection may become a source of virtue, for Copperbelt English often achieves a striking freshness and vividness of imagery which escapes the more orthodox idiom. One example must suffice here. On one occasion the African Urban Housing Board at Ndola was discussing the question of shop-rents in the location. One of the speakers, whose command of English was extremely good, was arguing against a proposed increase in shop-rents. He complained of the difficulties that beset the African store-keeper, and the heavy expenses he has to incur. Finally he exclaimed: "The result is that the shop-keeper remains with nothing. If these shops were our own we would be fighting for something. As it is we are fighting a goalless football."

The value that attaches to the speaking of English is best seen in the different kinds of social situation in which it is used. Among educated Africans the principal criterion appears to be whether their social status is involved. At meetings of associations and societies in which all the members enjoy equivalent educational status use of English is the general rule. Among close friends gathered in the privacy of the home the vernacular will probably be preferred; but if a less intimate acquaintance should join the company the talk will be continued in English. Similarly the parents of a girl who hope to marry her off to an educated young man will urge her to write her love-letters in English in order to make a good impression. Here I have been referring to those Africans who have achieved a moderate competence in the language. But the vast majority of urban Africans remain largely illiterate, having received the most rudimentary schooling. Nevertheless, there are few who have not acquired some smattering of English. Those who have the closest contact with Europeans outside a purely working context, such as house-boys and hotel waiters – and it is worth noting that domestic servants constitute the third largest labor category in the territory – often acquire quite an extensive English vocabulary, and their conversation is interlarded with English words and phrases even where the vernacular is fully adequate. The following perhaps is an extreme example, but it does reproduce fairly the distinctive flavor of much of everyday Copperbelt speech. Visiting one day a section of the Ndola location where we were working at the time, my research assistant found a man whom he had not seen before. Other people present – they were drinking beer at the time – introduced the stranger as Juwi Dick, and then explained to Juwi that my assistant was a newcomer from Lusaka engaged in social research. Juwi Dick at once greeted him:

> Welcome, Charlie,[6] to Ndola. Ndola Commercial Center for D.D.N.M. [Daily Drinker Never Miss]. The day I miss I will be in the grave.

He began to address the others:

> Uyu muntu umweni sana muno Ndola but ni well known pantu wa social kabili ni D.D.N.M. E member tufwaya mu Ndola. (This man is very much a stranger here in Ndola but he has become well known as a social worker and a daily drinker. These are the sort of people we want in Ndola.)

And then to display his largess, and to indicate that he was a man of some status, he added:

> Please, ba mayo, peni member uyu five cup pali two na six.... [To my assistant] O.K. my boy, I'll sign chaque for you. (Please, mother, give this chap five cups of beer for half-a-crown.... I'll pay for you.)

Thus, in a purely African context prestige is sought and conferred through the use of English. But according prestige is not its only or even perhaps its major function. The vernacular languages of Central Africa are often extremely rich in idiom, metaphor, and phrase; they are complex and subtle and particularly well adapted to the handling of personal relationships. However, they are not always fully adequate to cope with the varieties of experience of a modern urban and industrial society. English, on the other hand, at once offers a whole range of new concepts and ideas; it makes available to the African newspapers, journals, and the world of books. Secondly, it provides a means of communication which cuts across tribal linguistic barriers. Therefore when young men began to come together in meetings of the Welfare Societies, which were the earliest form of association to develop in the urban areas, and discussed the problems of the color-bar and of unemployment or complain-

[6] Charlie, of course, was just a name with which he greeted nearly everybody.

ed of the designation "boy" applied indiscriminately by Europeans to any African irrespective of his age or status, their insistence on the use of English was an expression of a growing awareness of themselves as Africans in a new multi-racial society. The new regimen was a source of much confusion and resentment, but their numerous grievances did not amount to a rejection of the system itself: rather they were now beginning to claim a proper place for themselves as Africans within that system. Their use of English was the expression of their desire to enter fully the modern world. And because they were aware of the many new problems of urban life, and were the natural intermediaries between the African urban populace and the European authorities, these young men gradually established themselves as leaders in the community.[7] Yet competence in English rarely goes by itself. Almost invariably it forms part of a complex which includes higher education, a more responsible job, better wages, and a standard of living and way of life which begins to approximate more closely that of the European. Over the years the rift within the African urban community has tended to widen and nowadays English has become on occasion the convenient symbol of the dominant cleavage within African society – a symbol marked by growing ambivalence.

It follows from the discussion above that the vast majority of Copperbelt Africans employ only the vernacular. Many speak a number of different languages, for in general Africans display a remarkable facility in picking up the speech of other tribes and areas. The principal languages spoken are Bemba, Nyanja, Lovale, and Lozi but many others are also heard. In linguistic classifications all of these are listed as belonging to Central Bantu, and they share many structural features in common such as the well known distribution of nouns into classes each with its own distinctive concordial prefixes. But in other respects they differ among themselves as much as do English, French, and German. However, the problems of communication are not as acute as might appear at first sight, for the numerical preponderance of Bemba-speaking Africans on the Copperbelt has led to the fairly widespread acceptance there of this language.[8] Together with English, which is used only in the upper standards, Bemba is now employed as the medium of instruction in the schools, and it is also generally used on those occasions when people of different tribes are gathered, as at church services[9] or public meetings,

7 For detailed discussion see Epstein, 1958.

8 Bemba is the language of the Bemba "proper", the largest and formerly one of the most powerful tribes in the territory, but it is also the mother tongue, with certain minor dialectical variations, of a number of other tribes, e.g., Aushi, Chishinga, Lunda, Tabwa, etc.

9 In one instance this led a group of Nyassaland Africans to break away and found an independent church, using another vernacular.

so that it has come to enjoy almost the status of a *lingua franca* on the Copperbelt.[10] The linguistic material I collected in the field relates solely to Bemba.

Urban Bemba differs considerably from the traditional language of the villages. Non-Bemba who have learned the language in the towns are not always punctilious in observing the strict grammatical forms, while among the Bemba themselves many of the nuances and finer points of the classical idiom have lost their relevance under urban conditions and are undoubtedly disappearing. I suspect, too, that a qualified linguist would also find evidence of considerable changes in phonetic structure and pronunciation.[11] The most obvious changes, however, are the innovations in words and phrases, and it is solely with these that I am concerned in this paper.

I have already noted how individual speakers frequently interlard their conversation with English words and expressions. In the example given above the speaker's remarks represented a purely personal idiom, something unique to himself. There are now, however, a large number of English words which have been adopted into Bemba and are now part of the language. A couple of typical examples, where the English words are assimilated to Bantu phonemic structure and adapted to the appropriate noun classes, are contained in the following verse from a popular song:

Ubu nindeta mubili obe mama
E *bulangeti* bwa kufimbana;
Mpumi yobe
E *kalashi* ndoleshamo.

This I have brought, your body my love,
Is a *blanket* for covering myself;
Your face
Is the *mirror* [glass] I look into.[12]

In a paper on Swahili borrowings from English, Gower[13] notes correctly

[10] I use the word "almost" advisedly. White (1951) reports, for example, that despite the large amount of migrant labor to the Copperbelt from the Balovale District very few from that area acquire any proficiency in speaking Bemba.

[11] See, for example, Comhaire-Sylvain, 1949.

[12] These examples show how two separate but coincident processes enter into the adoption of English words. In the first place the English word is assimilated to the phonemic structure of the Bantu language. Coincidently, the initial sound (or sounds) of the English word is assimilated to the class morpheme prefix most similar to it. In this way the loan word becomes a member of the class of nouns marked in Bemba by that particular prefix. Thus the nearest a Bemba speaker can get to saying "glass" is "*kalashi*" which thus becomes a noun of the class taking the prefix ka-.

[13] Gower, 1952.

that instances of such borrowing are to be sought in those spheres where contact with European culture impinges most widely and affects large numbers of Africans, and he lists examples which have derived from African experience of hospitals, transport, sport, and service in the army. But I have little doubt myself that the list could be multiplied extensively. For to the African the town represents a completely new kind of social environment which touches his life at nearly every point. The political, economic, social, and other institutions of the town provide a framework to which he has to adjust his behavior. Many of these institutions were wholly unknown to tribal society, and loan words now fill the linguistic gap, e.g. *amasukulu* (schools), *amachalichi* (churches), etc. Others did have their counterpart in the tribal system, but the divergence of function and practice is so marked that the vernacular provides no exact equivalent to the modern form, and the English term is again adopted. Thus Bemba has the abstract noun, *ubuteko*, government (from the verb *ukuteka*, "to rule") but this scarcely corresponds to the bureaucratic machinery of local (*Municipal*) or central government (*Kafulmende*) which are responsible for so many of the rules and regulations which control the lives of urban Africans. Similarly, there is a perfectly good Bemba word for court, *cilye*. This is also used when referring to the African Urban Courts,[14] but the loan-word *ikoti* is frequently preferred presumably because it suggests better the European character of much of the procedure in these courts where proceedings have to be initiated by the taking out of a summons (*ukushita saimoni*), where witnesses have to go into the box (*mbokoshi*), and are required to make a statement (*istatmenti*).

Above all what distinguishes urban society from the way of life of the villages is the need for employment. As in every urban community there are those who are able to survive by living on their wits or by sponging on kinsfolk (*amalofwa,* "loafers") but these are a minor exception to the general rule of wage-labor. Accordingly, we shall not be surprised to find a large number of loan-words associated with occupation (e.g. *bukalaliki*, office work from the English "clerk"; *bukalipenta,* "carpentry"; or *ukucita business*, "to run a store"), and pay[15] (e.g. *ukufola*, "to draw wages or earn" which derives from the command "Fall in" used at

[14] Described in Epstein, 1953.

[15] The Bemba terms for money are *ndalama* and *ulupya* (pl. *mypa*), both of which are loan-words of an earlier vintage. *Ndalama* is the same term as the Nyanja *ndarama* for which the standard Nyanja dictionaries give the derivation *ndala*, "whiteness", i.e. silver. But the correct etymology is probably the Arabic *dirhema*, a small coin, from the Greek *drachma*. See the Curator's note in Quiggin, 1949. *Ulupya* is the Indian rupee and presumably harks back to the days when Indian troops were used by Johnston in pacifying the Lake Nyasa region.

Army pay parades [16]; or *itiketi,* "ticket", i.e. the period to be worked before one becomes entitled to draw pay). Finally, there is a vast array of items of European material culture and technology which in the towns have become part and parcel of African daily experience. For obvious reasons these provide an enormously fertile source of loan-words which range from household goods as *ibeketi,* "bucket" or *machisa,* "matches" to motor-cars (sing. *mu-otoka* or *li-motoka*) and railway trains (sing. *istima*).

Most of the examples just given are cases of simple borrowing and adaptation of words from English and other languages in order to fill the inevitable gaps in the vernacular vocabulary. For the most part these words refer to a new social environment, in a sense external to the African, but impinging upon him at every point. Thus the choice of words has been largely pragmatic: the words themselves are morally neutral in the sense that they express little of the values and attitudes which Africans hold in regard to life in the towns. Of greater sociological interest, therefore, are those linguistic innovations which reflect directly the new customs, institutions, and modes of thought through which the towns are marked off as possessing for Africans today a wholly distinctive way of life. This vocabulary consists in the creation of completely new vernacular terms, or the investing of foreign loan-words with a significance unknown to the original, but often singularly appropriate for expressing the new categories of Copperbelt experience. The material I was able to collect on these new semantic creations is very far from complete, firstly because it was collected mainly in the course of casual conversation or in interviews directed to other matters and, secondly, because the terms themselves are being added to or dropped continuously. However, the tendency is for the terms to proliferate around certain areas of experience which have particular interest for urban Africans, and I have been able to group them loosely under a number of convenient headings.

To begin with there is the town itself, for which a number of alternatives are available. The Copperbelt proper is *Ku mikoti* which derives via Fanagolo from the Zulu word *umgodi* meaning "a hole of considerable size" and, by extension, a mine-shaft, while all line-of-rail towns are *Ku nyanji* (*Ku njanji*) from Bemba *nyanji,* "a railway line".[17] *Kalale* (from Harari, a Southern Rhodesia place-name) was first applied indiscriminately to all the mines of Southern Rhodesia, which provided cen

[16] The only other current expression deriving from army experience that I came across was *ukuya ku cuti,* "to go on leave", or, in its Copperbelt denotation, to go on a short visit to the rural areas. Picked up by African troops serving in the Far East, the expression derives from the Hindi word *chut,* "female genitalia".

[17] This is the meaning given in The White Fathers' *Bemba-English Dictionary,* but I have not been able to discover the derivation of the term.

ters of employment for Northern Rhodesian Africans before the opening of the Copperbelt, but is now used to refer to the urban areas in general, as is the English word "town", *itauni*, itself. However, these terms frequently express more than the idea of mere physical location. *Kalale* and *itauni* in particular suggest the ethos of urban life and in this sense are equivalent to the notion of "civilized" or sophisticated. Thus a young African who had spent some years working in Elizabethville in the Belgian Congo and had now returned to the Copperbelt once remarked with some feeling: "Ku Kongo ni ku *town,* kuno ni ku mushi" (In the Congo it's really "civilized"; here it's just as backward as a village).

In a context involving mere physical location Africans simply use the name conferred by the local authority when speaking of different parts of the African housing area. In other contexts, however, new terms are freely invented which express each section's special character in African eyes. While I was at Ndola a new device which was intended to serve the dual function of providing an overhead shower and flushing the latrine was introduced in one of the more recently completed sections of the location. The system did not appear to work very satisfactorily, and householders complained strongly of the public indignity they had to suffer in carrying a large tin of water with them on each visit to the latrine. The term *Ntapila* (from the verb *ukutapa,* "to draw water") was coined for the section, though many others preferred *ku mabeketi,* "the bucket section". More often it is the standard of housing which provides the distinguishing criterion. One large section of the Main Location at Ndola consists of semi-detached one-roomed houses of very poor quality. They were known invariably as *wayalezi,* "wireless", or *telefon,* "telephone", since everything that went on in the house was immediately broadcast to one's neighbors. Again, a new Suburb has gone up in the course of the last few years. The houses are much larger and much superior to anything in the adjoining Old Location. Typical of the urban scene is the way certain residents of the Suburb have come to designate themselves *fwe bamafour-roomed,* "we people who have four-roomed houses", in contradistinction to those lesser breeds in the Old Location, *Aba mu mabottle,* "those who live in bottles" – a reference to the rondavels which were among the earliest types of house provided for Africans in the town, but now being rapidly pulled down and replaced. These and indeed most other houses in the Old Location have only one room. There is little space for "proper" furniture even if the occupants had the means to buy it, and they generally present a bare appearance inside. Such houses are commonly known therefore as *ballroom* from the exclamation one might make on entry: "Kuti mwaba mu *ballroom.* Ng'oma shili kwi?" (You might be in the dance hall. Where are the drums so that we can dance?).

Semantic creation and innovation are at their richest in those areas of Copperbelt experience which diverge most sharply from traditional tribal custom and mores. Thus an entirely new vocabulary has grown up around the distinctive pattern of relations between the sexes that has developed in the urban areas. The social status and role of women in particular shows marked changes, and these are plainly reflected in the new terminology. Thus town life itself is epitomized in the person of the *town lady*, an expression which refers to an African woman who has become fully acquainted with urban customs and habits. One extremely popular song, *Cupo*, "Marriage", refers to the difficulties of a young wife newly arrived from the village who was a source of embarrassment to her more urbanized husband because she could not learn to serve tea properly when his friends came to visit him – she would insist on putting peas into the tea-pot. Emphatically not a *town lady!* Other terms specify more carefully the character of certain common Copperbelt types. Thus *championi* or *muchampioni* generally refers to a young woman who dresses smartly in the modern fashion. The term itself, the English derivation of which is obvious, appears to originate in the context of ballroom dancing competitions which have long been an established feature of African urban life. Apart from the skill of the dancers, great emphasis is laid on their immaculate grooming, the men wearing full evening dress and the women attractive evening gowns and long white gloves. But like so many aspects of life on the Copperbelt, the term is steeped in ambivalence for, on the one hand, it suggests excellence and standards to be emulated, while on the other it denotes sexual laxity. Young husbands will frequently object to their wives spending too much time in the company of other women, for it is thus that they learn *fya buchampioni*, "loose ways", and develop into *runners*. In the eyes of "respectable" married women *amachampioni* are equally suspect, for they do not know how to "keep their own marriages" and are a constant threat to everyone else's. Yet another, and somewhat similar category, is provided by the *bakapenta milomo* or more usually just *bakapenta*. The expression means literally those who paint the lips, adopting the English verb "to paint". The *kapenta* tends to be less sophisticated than the *championi*, but both terms are readily applied to young girls of easy virtue who hang around the location Beer Hall or Bottle Store in search of a good time. By extension, the word *kapenta* has also come to be applied to a tiny minnow-like fish (*mushipa*) which is used as a very cheap relish. It is so easy to prepare that a woman who has been occupying her day with a *boy-friend* instead of getting on with the housework can readily dash along to the market and buy some *kapenta* to prepare for her husband's meal when he comes back from work in the evening. One the other hand, such a meal might lead to awkward questions. A woman might say:

"Abalume bandi teti mbepikile ubwali pali *tukapenta* pantu twa cabe cabe, kabili nabo balakalipa nga basanga uto njipike abati pali kuntu waciya" (I wouldn't cook my husband a meal with *kapenta* relish for they are just rubbish, and besides he would get angry and say "so that's where you've been").

The term *ihuli*, from the Afrikaans word *hoer*, "whore", is also an accepted term in current use, but many Africans would deny that prostitution, in the sense of a purely commercial transaction, exists on the Copperbelt. To some extent they are correct, for the casual pick-up at the Beer Hall frequently develops into some kind of temporary union – even if it lasts only a matter of days – in which the man will buy food or give presents and the woman will cook and clean up the man's quarters. Most of these liaisons involve extra-marital relations for at least one of the parties, and the lover or mistress is designated by a whole host of terms, e.g. *cibamu, cikule, madear*, or *dali*, the latter two of English derivation but with a different nuance. The expression *spare wheel* aptly describes the woman a husband finds it convenient to have in reserve, so to speak. Some men do not enter into a "proper" marriage until quite late. If they are asked about it they will quickly dispel any reflection that might seem to be cast upon their manhood by explaining: "I married late because I have travelled a lot in foreign countries like the Belgian Congo or Southern Rhodesia. Of course I had many *abanakashi ba pleasure*, 'women of pleasure'," or again "I have never been married, but you know I have had many *piece-work* women."

Where extra-marital relations feature so prominently on the urban landscape it would be rather surprising if the art of love itself were linguistically ignored. *Amakiss* speaks for itself, but I think lacks the poetry of the verbal form *ukutomona* which in rural Bemba has as one of its meanings "to taste the first fruits". Highly admired in a girl-friend is the ability to perform a *dance du ventre*. The woman who does not know how to "dance" during intercourse, or as the Copperbelt African would express it, *ushaishiba double clutch*, is regarded as pretty poor game since the act then gives the man little satisfaction. To impregnate a woman is to *womb* her, while there are also a number of colloquialisms for the act of intercourse itself, including the rather unusual verb form to *coit*. In a matrimonial dispute that came before the Tribal Elders at Ndola, one of the Elders whose command of Bemba was limited but who had a flair for metaphor spontaneously produced a new word for the sexual act: *ukushanta*. This was a reference to the shunting of goods trains that goes on every night at Ndola, which is the railhead. The innovation was loudly acclaimed by all present, and I would not be surprised to learn that the word has now passed into common use.

Another major source of linguistic innovation centers round the institution of beer-drinking. Each town on the Copperbelt has its Beer Hall run by the local authority, the profits of which go towards providing African social welfare amenities. In addition, there is a vast amount of beer brewed privately and, for the most part, illicitly. Home-brewed beer offers greater variety than the Beer Hall. As well as typical village brews such as *cipumu*, the millet beer of the Bemba known on the Copperbelt as *hookworm* because it is said to cause diarrhea, or *katata,* a milder drink frequently referred to as *diesel* because of its thickness, there is a wide assortment of other concoctions such as *Seven Days, Pineapple*, or *Babitoni* (from Barberton, a Transvaal town), many of which have been introduced from Southern Rhodesia and South Africa. Such beers are often preferred by really heavy drinkers, *bacakolwa* (from the verb *ukukolwa*, "to be drunk"), because they are usually more potent than anything to be obtained at the Beer Hall and thus enable one to get drunk more quickly and at less cost. On the other hand, beer drinks in private houses are always likely to be interrupted and broken up by a police raid if the brewer has not taken the precaution of bribing the *kanyangu.*[18]

Despite the prevalence of private drinking, the Beer Hall remains the indisputable center of community life. It is the one part of the whole town which Africans regard in some way as unassailably and peculiarly their own. A large, open area laid out in chalets, the Beer Hall is the Africans' common rendezvous. Thus, far from being just a place where beer may be taken legally, the Beer Hall has come to serve as the public arena in which the struggle for prestige is ceaselessly waged. Thus the capacity of the *cakolwa* is greatly admired, but what one drinks is also relevant. "Kafir beer" – the Beer Hall brew – is the poor man's drink bought by *bacibombebombe*, "anyhow" laborers (from a form of the Bemba verb which means "to do something any old how") and others. On the other hand, the prestige which attaches to European bottled beer is evident in the remark of a young woman once overheard at the Beer Hall: "Teti nsumine kucito bucende pa mulandu wa kumpela *disilo* kwati ni Castle uyo banwa abasangu wa mpya shingi" (Do you think I can sleep with you because of the "diesel" you've given me as if it were Castle beer that Europeans drink and which costs such a lot?). All those who can afford it, therefore, buy European bottled beer, and always a quart in preference to a pint.[19] The quart is generally known as *maka*

[18] The *kanyangu* or compound policeman introduces yet another urban social personality. They are the "cow peas" boys. The expression originated on the mines where a food rationing system used to operate. The compound police who controlled the queues at the Feeding Store were believed to be in a position to get extra rations, of which cow peas, *nyangu*, were a prominent item.

[19] A girl who is offered a mere pint may even feel herself slighted. The following incident was reported by one of my assistants. A girl had seated herself be-

maka, the Nyanja word for "particularly" or "especially". The expression originated in the mine compounds where the "wealthy" miners, now frequently known as *BaNdalama*, literally "the moneyed ones", would buy quarts exclusively. During my stay at Ndola the term *maka maka CiMukume,* "especially Mukume's", was coined and soon found widespread acceptance. This was a reference to an African clerk called Mukume who was responsible for allocating houses in the location. It was generally believed that he had a very profitable income from the bribes he received which enabled him to visit the Beer Hall every day where he would surround himself with pretty girls and down innumerable quarts of Castle beer to show he was a *top guy*. A cheap winc which is also sold at the Beer Hall is known derisively as *ngungayi*. It sometimes happens that a *sugar boy* (one born or who has grown up in the towns) or other person accustomed to buy bottled beer will be temporarily short of cash. He will then buy the cheaper *ngungayi*, but promptly pour it into an empty Castle beer bottle. Similarly, Castle beer itself may be poured into an empty brandy bottle so that others are deceived into thinking it is a real *big boy*, i.e. genuine brandy, the sale of which is forbidden to Africans.

Nor does one go to the Beer Hall necessarily to drink. Leaders in the community, frequently known as *bameetingi*, will go to be seen by the people and to learn their problems; *bamambala* or *amacrook* will meet there to transact illicit dealings in diamonds, etc., while many others go simply to meet their friends and for the entertainment. As I mentioned earlier, the Beer Hall is the favorite haunt of the *kapenta*, and in themselves these provide an attraction. As one young man once expressed it: "You should know that people do not go to the Beer Hall just for beer alone, but to feed their eyes by looking at the *flowers of the country*." In order to attract attention, the *kapenta* will *ukupanga four*,[20] i.e. sit down with legs crossed and skirt raised so that young men nearby would be led to comment "ali na *mastanding yambi yambi*", an expression which seems to imply, long, straight legs just like those of a European woman. If the *kapenta* wished to further the acquaintance she might then add, "Nimkupela *Luna Park* isuma nganshi" (I have given you a real thrill, haven't I?). Not surprisingly, the combination of beer and provocative young women gives rise to innumerable fights and brawls in which newly

---

side a man at the Bottle Store, and he offered her a pint of bottled beer. She asked for a quart, remarking that pints were only given to skinny, unattractive women. The man went off and fetched two quarts for which she rewarded him with "lelo ndekupela *wonder tango, my dear*" (Today I will show you a really wonderful "dance").

[20] *Ukupanga four*, i.e. "to make four (legs)", is also sometimes used for the act of sexual intercourse.

acquired techniques are employed. "Namuteya *Chicago* awa na panshi" – I tripped him up – derives from the films, Chicago being associated with *amacowboy* and others given to fighting. *Ukuma bullet*, on the other hand, is to butt someone with the head, an effective way of knocking an opponent out with a single blow just as an animal is killed with one bullet from a gun.

One important source of linguistic innovation is provided by newspapers and magazines, especially in the sphere of politics. Here a large number of English words and expressions have been adopted, and are used in a vernacular context by the more sophisticated Africans, though often with a significant change of meaning. The term *amapolitics* itself has come into common use, generally to express the heightened political awareness that Africans have developed in recent years. For example, when Chitimukulu, Paramount Chief of the Bemba, visited the Copperbelt in 1956 he was received by Africans with little enthusiasm and a good deal of hostility. Discussing this one day with an educated but otherwise conservative Bemba he remarked, perhaps a trifle ruefully, "*Amapolitics* yafulisha ... umuntu uwacenjela ukwenda pakati" (There is so much politics today ... one has to be a very clever man to walk the middle path). Other terms are farther removed from the English original such as *left wings*, which simply means opposition, or *tactics* which means to find a line of argument that will convince people. Current events are themselves reflected in a number of expressions, though again not without some modification of meaning. Thus at one time the word *Korea* became synonymous with industrial strife, violence, and the strike weapon itself, for which however the English loan-word *listraka* remained the more usual. Similarly, Congress leaders at public meetings will speak of the Cold War, *nkondo yatalala*, when they refer to some political action, such as a *boycott*, which is to be carried out without violence.[21]

One development of particular interest is the growth of a new vocabulary of personal abuse, much of which has originated in a purely political context. Terms such as *Uncle Tom, informer, Capricorn*,[22] *Government tool*, etc. are in everyday use and are not confined to the political elite. Thus an ordinary spectator at a football match at which the Paramount Chief Chitimukulu was present was heard to remark "Takwaba mu calo mfumu yatumpa nge 'yi. Ishinankwe shonse shalingile mu Congress yena iyo-*Government tool*" (In the whole country there isn't a chief as

[21] References to current events are also sometimes found where we might least expect them. Thus at football matches a popular player setting off on a solo run would be cheered on with the cry *Mau Mau*. Again, at the time of the blocking of the Suez Canal, one young woman who had won herself a reputation because of her many lovers was promptly nicknamed Miss Suez Canal!

[22] Epstein, 1958, p. 174 fn.

stupid as this one. All his fellow chiefs entered Congress, but not he – Government tool!). Similar notions are expressed today in the use of such terms as *malinso* or *mbulu ne nsamba*, the monitor lizard and the iguana, the pertinence of which derive from folklore. The crocodile lays its eggs on shore: but the land is not its real home – its home is in the water. When the mother crocodile has hatched her eggs she trains her offspring so that they learn to follow her into the river. But there are some who have failed to follow her example, and so they have remained on the bank as lizards, out of their own proper environment. In the same way, all informers, Capricorns, etc., are *malinso* who have been left on the bank (i.e. with the Europeans) and are not with their own people. *Malinso* and *mbulu ne nsamba* are commonly used by speakers at Congress meetings to refer to African police or detectives present in the audience but they – or similar terms – would equally be cast at a woman at the water tap or in the butcher's shop whose husband, for example, had left the trade union to join the Salaried Staff Association. In times of social tension the use of such terms can be a powerful sanction in promoting social and ideological conformity.

We have now looked at *CiCopperbelti*,[23] the term by which Africans themselves now characterize the distinctive language of the towns, as it is used in a number of different social contexts. The picture of African urban culture that emerges in this way is of course a partial one; nevertheless, it mirrors vividly much that is characteristic of the new way of life in the towns – its humor and patience in the face of poverty and squalor, its uncertainties, ambivalence, and frequent intolerance, but above all its tremendous zest and gusto, its crude vigor and general restlessness. At the same time I think we may detect running through the various categories of semantic creation I have listed a single common thread which provides a major clue to the understanding of African urban social organization. Thus if we take the terms and expressions which are applied to the town itself and to its different parts, or those that are used in the context of beer-drinking and relations between the sexes, it will be seen that many of them involve, directly or indirectly, some evaluation in terms of prestige. Prestige, indeed, is a dominant concept in African urban thought: it remains now therefore to examine in closer detail some of the ways in which it is expressed.

The general notion of prestige itself is frequently conveyed by the terms *amastanding* or *ciheavy*, the English derivation of which requires no explanation. Thus one would say *takwata* (it doesn't have) *amastanding* of a cheap brand of cigarettes. Or again, when I once enquired the meaning of a Lamba word my informant said he did not know and

[23] In this context the prefix ci- is an index of language as, e.g., in Ci-Bemba, the Bemba language or language of the Ba-Bemba, the Bemba people.

added that anyway Lamba was not a language *lwa ciheavy*. At one time the English word "gentleman" itself served as a common index of status,[24] but today one is more likely to hear the expression *gentleman wa ciheavy* or even simply *umuheavy*. People of high repute in general are known as *bamashina*, literally "those with names", while particular individuals will be *big shot*, *top guy*, etc. Thus when a young Health Assistant employed by the Municipality was falsely charged with unlawful possession of a bicycle he demanded angrily of the policeman "Mulensebanya, tamwaishiba ukuti ndi *top guy*" (You are disgracing me. Don't you know I am a person of rank?). At the other end of the scale the notion of social distance is aptly conveyed by the adoption of the English word "far" as in the expression: Ine, nshifwaya ukulanda na mafala (I don't wish to speak with trash). Lack of sophistication and low social status generally are also suggested by the word *babuyasulo*, which is a compound of the Fanagolo *buya*, "to come" and the Nyanja *dzulo*, "yesterday". Synonymous with *kamushi*, "a villager or country bumpkin", it expresses the idea of the newcomer, crude, uneducated, and unacquainted with the ways of the town.

The importance of occupation in rating prestige is evident in daily speech. I have already referred to the *bacibombebombe*, who are also known categorically as *amaleba*, "laborers", while the expression *mwana leba*, "son of a laborer", is commonly used as a term of abuse, not least of all by women swearing at their ne'er-do-well husbands. Yet another term for casual and unskilled workers that has come into fashion is *bakapepala*. This derives from the practice on the mines whereby new employees work a short period without pay and receive only food rations, for which they have to produce a chit (*ipepala*, from the English "paper") daily at the Food Store. The office clerks there do not bother about their names, but simply call out "Imwe *bakapepala* iseni mupoke ifyakulya fyenu" (You chit-people, come and collect your food). It should perhaps be noted here that the use of these terms is not confined to clerks or others enjoying high prestige; they are equally accepted and used of themselves by those whom the terms designate. Wealth is an obvious component of prestige in this context, but it is not necessarily the major one. Reference has already been made to miners as *bandalama*, "the moneyed-ones", but for all their ability to buy quarts of beer they still remain *bachimba mabwe*, "diggers of stones". The notion of the parvenu is perhaps best conveyed by the term *kaboi*, "house-boy". Because of their contact with Europeans domestic servants are regarded as having achieved some of the more superficial marks of "culture", but in other respects are still unrefined and lacking in taste. An interesting

[24] See, for example, Wilson, 1941, p. 24.

illustration of this notion was provided for me by a young Government clerk who had received a bursary to go to University in South Africa. There he had had to learn European-style ballroom dancing to avoid the taunts of his new friends. In Northern Rhodesia he had never learned to dance because ballroom dancing is regarded as essentially *fya bukaboi,* the quintessence of the *kaboi* way of life.

In this paper I have been concerned simply to illustrate some of the linguistic innovations which mark the Africans' adjustment to modern urban life and conditions on the Copperbelt. Many, perhaps a majority, of those innovations I have called semantic creations center around the concept of prestige, but the material I have presented is obviously inadequate for a more detailed analysis of the role of this principle in social organization. But a few general observations may not be out of place. To begin with, it is apparent that there is scarcely a single aspect of social life or behavior to which the notion of prestige does not extend. I have described how drinking, sexual prowess, occupation, etc., provide measures of prestige, but these represent only a few of the criteria by which prestige is evaluated. I might have added physical appearance, as in the expression *ukukashika ni passport*, which stresses the value of a light complexion; or clothes, as in the term *simyamfule* (literally, "switch off the light while I undress") which refers to a cheap petticoat of such inferior quality that a girl would be ashamed to let her lover see it; or even membership of a particular tribe, as in the expression *Ba ku six o'clock*, a derogatory reference to the tribes of the far west, the land of the setting sun and, by implication, of darkness. In short, the criteria of prestige are many and varied. Some obviously run together, such as ability to speak English, white-collar occupation, smart dress, well-furnished home, etc., and this has enabled Mitchell [25] and myself [26] to speak of the "European way of life" as providing a scale in terms of which the African urban population is stratified. There is much in the present paper to confirm this view, but the evidence also suggests that we need to be much more careful and precise in the use of the concept of Europeanization, for as it stands it tends, I think, to over-simplify what is in fact a very complex process of selection. Secondly, given the existence of such prestige classes, it must be noted that the criteria of prestige may vary considerably from one stratum to another, and from group to group. Hence, in speaking of the Europeans as a "reference group",[27] we need to bear in mind that the "European way of life" in this context would have to include the behavior of Europeans living on the Copperbelt as it is perceived by Africans, patterns of behavior as they are ob-

25 Mitchell, 1956a.
26 Mitchell and Epstein, 1959.
27 Mitchell, 1956b.

served in Hollywood films or the novels of Peter Cheyney, and even aspects of the life of American Negroes as it is transmitted through popular African magazines published in South Africa. Finally, while the "European way of life" provides a valuable model of African social stratification in terms of structure, the very diversity of the criteria of prestige introduces great flexibility into the system. Such diversity allows of many different combinations and permutations which make "class placement" in practice extraordinarily difficult. In terms of social process, therefore, the variety of factors that may be employed in evaluating prestige serves to promote a continuous and unremitting struggle in which different and increasingly refined criteria may be variously invoked to advance one's claims to status, and leads to a bewildering assortment of rivalries, allegiances, and cross-cutting ties both within and between groups.

BIBLIOGRAPHY

Cole, D. T.
1953 "Fanagolo and the Bantu Languages in South Africa", *African Studies*, vol. 12, no. 1, 1-9.

Comhaire-Sylvain, S.
1949 "Le Lingala des enfants noirs de Leopoldville", *Kongo-Overzee*, vol. 15, 239-250.

Epstein, A. L.
1953 *The Administration of Justice and the Urban African* (= *Colonial Research Series*, no. 7) (London, H.M.S.O.).
1958 *Politics in an Urban African Community* (Manchester, Manchester University Press).

Gower, R. H.
1952 "Swahili Borrowings from English", *Africa*, vol. 22, no. 2, 154-156.

Hall, Robt. A., Jr.
1955 *Hands off Pidgin English* (Sydney, Pacific Publications).

Mitchell, J. C.
1956a *The Kalela Dance* (= *Rhodes-Livingstone Papers*, no. 27) (Manchester, Manchester University Press).
1956b "The African Middle Classes in British Central Africa", in *Development of a Middle Class in Tropical and Sub-tropical Countries*, Incidi (Brussels), 222-233.

Mitchell, J. C., and A. L. Epstein
1959 "Occupational Prestige and Social Status among Town Africans in Northern Rhodesia", *Africa*, vol. 29, no. 1, 22-40.

Quiggin, A. H.
1949 *Trade Routes, Trade and Currency in East Africa* (= *Occasional Papers of the Rhodes-Livingstone Museum*, no. 5) (Livingstone).

White, C. M. N.
1951 "Modern Influences upon an African Language Group", *Rhodes-Livingstone Journal*, no. 11, 66-71.

White Fathers
1947 *Bemba-English Dictionary* (Chilubula).
Wilson, Godfrey
1941 *The Economics of Detribalization* (= *Rhodes-Livingstone Papers*, no. 5) (Livingstone).

From: *Southwestern Journal of Anthropology*, 15 (1959), pp. 235-253. Reprinted with permission.

Werner F. Leopold

THE DECLINE OF GERMAN DIALECTS

1.1. DIALECTS AND STANDARD

It has been characteristic of the nations of Western Europe that their languages show a cleavage between geographically circumscribed dialects and standard forms of speech which enjoy higher social prestige and are current over the whole territory. In the tension and interaction between these two basic types, the standard forms have been gaining ground gradually over the dialects. As long as populations were generally stationary, the development was slow. It became accelerated in recent times by the progress of modern transportation and of means of mass communication like newspapers, radio, etc., all of which favored the standard language. But in German-speaking lands the position of the dialects was until recently still relatively strong.

1.2. POSTWAR MIGRATIONS

A radical change in the tempo of this development can be observed in postwar Germany. Migrations on an unprecedented scale took place and broke down the isolation of dialect areas. One has to go back to the great Germanic migrations at the dawn of history to find similar population movements. The geographical range of the postwar migrations was smaller than that of the demographic turbulence in Germanic antiquity, but by no means small, since German population groups from widely scattered regions of eastern Europe were dislocated, some by administrative resettlement during the war, many more by flight and forcible expulsion after the war. The numbers involved were undoubtedly very much larger. More than ten million expellees and refugees from the east have been crammed into the narrow space of West Germany, which is less than half of prewar Germany in area.[1] Among the more than 50 million inhabitants of West Germany, more than 20 percent are recent arrivals from the east; every fifth West German is an expellee or refugee. Among the 17 million inhabitants of the Russian Zone, 3.8 million are expellees,[2] an even higher percentage.

The literature on recent developments in the German language has until now hardly faced the consequences of these large-scale population movements. It has been felt that it is too early to draw conclusions from them, that their consequences can scarcely be gauged at this time, and that it would be premature to do more than "surmise" (*mutmassen*) their effect.[3] The following is an attempt to take a step toward an examination of this effect in broad outlines, on the basis of observations made and oral information gathered during a study trip through German-speaking lands in 1955. I found the effect to be very strong, but different from what I had expected.

1.3. EAST GERMAN DIALECTS

Almost one-third[4] of the population units (*Stämme*), those from the various eastern regions, lost their homelands and were deliberately scattered among the West Germans, not as transplanted communities, but as isolated individuals or families.[5] This process shattered the tradi-

[1] West Germany, with 50 million inhabitants, has the same area as the state of Oregon, with 1½ million inhabitants (M). Initials like (M) refer to informants listed at the end of this article. I must take the responsibility for reproducing their oral communications correctly. I am also indebted to many other informants, experts in various fields, who are not personally cited in this paper.

[2] Theodor Oberländer, *Die Überwindung der deutschen Not*, 2nd ed. (1954), 9. None of these statistical figures are entirely reliable because of the chaotic conditions in Germany at the end of the war; but they represent the best estimates of responsible West German sources.

[3] Walter Henzen, *Schriftsprache und Mundarten*, 2nd ed. (rev.) (Berne, Francke, 1954), 7, 209. References to this book, which digests the literature thoroughly, were added to the paper after the completion of the manuscript to provide some links with previous research. The purpose of the paper is to report on personal observations and informations, not to re-examine classifying principles.

[4] Alfred Karasek-Langer, "Volkskundlich Erkenntnisse aus der Vertreibung und Eingliederung der Ostdeutschen", *Jahrbuch für Volkskunde der Heimatvertriebenen*, Salzburg, vol. 1 (1955), 14.

[5] *Ibid.*, 11. Statistics about the deliberate scattering are given by Hugo Moser, "Umsiedlung und Sprachwandel", *Bildungsfragen unserer Zeit, Festschrift Theodor Bäuerle*, 2nd ed. (Stuttgart, 1956), 122-141, a very important study which

tional structure of their lives and destroyed the social frame for the survival of their dialects.

To be sure, after they were established in West Germany, a reaction set in. The expellees strove to renew the old ties. Homeland groups reassembled in flourishing social clubs. But this type of nostalgic association could not reconstitute the tightly knit community of living, which is lost lastingly. Here and there a vigorous spirit of enterprise gathered immigrants from the east in newly founded industrial establishments, even with their own living quarters in newly built settlements. But such enterprises did not reassemble workers from a single eastern area, nor did they exclude native West German workers, so that the new communities did not recreate the social communities of the past. In families and in the social homeland clubs, the home dialect was frequently cultivated, even by people from the cities who had not spoken dialect before the expulsion,[6] in an understandable desire to preserve the lost values, which were instinctively felt to be linked with the characteristic speech form of the homeland. But all public addresses and transactions in the clubs were carried on in standard German, as they had been at home, and the informal conversation around the tables, if in dialect, mixed a number of homeland subdialects. The dialects of the east are lost in their old form and will most likely disappear as the older generations die off. Even if a return to the old homeland, for which many of the expellees long and continue to hope, should become possible one day, the eastern dialects would no longer be the same.[7]

1.4. WEST GERMAN DIALECTS

The West German dialects also did not remain the same. The migration meant not only the dissolution of old social structures in the east but the formation of new ones in the west.[8] The traditional separation of German population groups in geographical compartments of homogeneous dialect speech ceased to exist. No community of the west remained unaffected by the influx of new eastern residents. This changed the social structure[9] and influenced the local dialect, which was no longer left to

agrees in many of its conclusions with my own observations and gives valuable supplementary data on several topics.

6 One of my informants (L) reported this situation for his own family.

7 K 1 has already heard arguments in families from the east about their former speech forms: "How did we use to say that?"

8 Eugen Lemberg and Lothar Krecker, *Die Entstehung eines neuen Volkes aus Binnendeutschen und Ostvertriebenen* (Marburg, 1950).

9 Sociologists are well aware of the radical changes in the social structure of

itself without outside interference (K 2).[10] Even in cases where Germans from the east moved back into areas from which their ancestors had emigrated centuries before, their customs and dialects were no longer identical. The long separation had led to divergent developments, and the individuals "returning" from the east did not fit easily in the ancestral social structure and speech form.

The thorough mixture of different populations in West Germany – no city or village being without its quota of expellees and refugees – and the clash of the newcomers' dialects with the local dialects did not, however, lead to a mixture of dialects as a rule. In my travels all over West Germany, Austria, and Switzerland, I had planned to collect evidence of the interaction of dialects. I found very little. If old settlers and newcomers had spoken only their dialects, a clash and eventual compromise might have resulted. In this struggle of dialects, to be sure, the settled dialects would have had an advantage. They had vested rights in their habitats and were not disturbed by the shattering experience of being uprooted from their soil. Also, the newcomers, although numerous in every community, were as a rule a minority, not homogeneous among themselves and in a socially depressed position, with little prestige, at least in the beginning. It would have been natural for the locally established dialects to resist interference from the outlandish intruding dialects, and for the speakers of eastern dialects to adapt themselves to a considerable extent to local speech in order to gain a foothold in the new home. Still, the influence could have been expected to work to some degree in both directions.

2.1. STRENGTHENING OF STANDARD

This, however, was not the case to any considerable extent. Germans, both those in the west and those from the east, had previously spoken

postwar Germany. The leading sociologist Helmut Schelsky lists, among the tasks of present-day sociological research, "eine sozialwissenschaftliche Tatbestandsaufnahme auf allen Gebieten unserer bis in die intimsten Strukturen erschütterten und veränderten sozialen Wirklichkeit", He mentions the expellees as the first element in the structural change ("Die Soziologie in der Praxis", in the symposium, *Deutscher Geist zwischen gestern und morgen,* Stuttgart, 1954, 262-280). Without emphasis on the newcomers, the very active sociologist K. Valentin Müller, himself an expellee from Prague, describes the erosion of the old middle class and the formation of a new middle class from technologically skilled workers. He says the social goal of laborers' sons is the middle layer of industrial employees, who have taken over the forms of the old middle class in modified shape (*Die Angestellten in der hochindustrialisierten Gesellschaft*, Cologne, 1957). The social rise is undoubtedly accompanied by a change of speech type.

[10] Around 1810, only the minister and the teacher spoke standard German in the village; all others spoke dialect (K 2). The situation changed slowly in favor of the standard since then, rapidly since the war.

not only their dialects but a form of standard German as well, which they had learned in school and used regularly for higher functions in life and in speaking with strangers not native to the soil in a narrower sense. In fact, in larger communities, in the west and particularly in the east,[11] a colloquial form of the standard, more or less tinged with local dialect features, had been used even in ordinary pursuits. When the old and the new elements of the population met, the natural way out of the difficulties which stood in the way of perfect communication was to resort to standard German, which was familiar enough to both, and was for both the natural form of speech to use with strangers. The result was a strengthening of colloquial standard German and a dwindling of the dialects.

The resistance of the dialects varies with the conservative or progressive attitudes of their speakers. In a rough division it may be said that the southern dialects have stronger vitality, whereas the northern dialects recede at an astonishing rate. A contributing reason is perhaps that Low German is too different from High German to be understood by those newcomers whose speech was not Low German. But the most striking impression in traveling through Germany today is that one hears everywhere, in the south as well as in the north, from adults and children, prevailingly standard German in the street, where one expects, on the basis of earlier experience, to hear dialect.

2.2. PROVINCIAL COLLOQUIAL STANDARDS

The gain of the standard does not so much affect the speech of educated people, who have long favored it on all levels of their lives, as that of the less educated ones, who used to cling to dialects or strongly dialect-tinged speech. Their standard speech is of course not the same as the intellectual standard German of the educated, which is close to the literary language, but a colloquial standard which retains a reduced dialectal tinge, now valid over wider areas than it used to be. The dialects are by no means extinct; but if the movement continues, severely restricted local varieties of dialects, and later the dialects in a larger sense, will give way to provincial colloquial standards of larger geographical scope.[12] This

[11] Cf. Erhard Riemann, "Die Ostvertriebenen und ihre Sprache", in: Richard Mehlem, *Niederdeutsch* (Hannover, 1956), 30: "Diese Auseinandersetzung war vor 1945 in Ostdeutschland viel weiter fortgeschritten als im deutschen Westen. In Ost- und Westpreusen wurde in den sozial gehobenen Schichten überhaupt nicht mehr Platt gesprochen . . . auch auf dem Lande."

[12] Mitzka's term "traffic dialects" (*Verkehrsmundarten*; cf. Henzen, 199) would cover leveled dialects valid over wider areas rather than local subdialects. As

development would probably have taken place without the influx of refugees, but their presence everywhere increased the tempo of the process greatly.

2.3. CITY AND COUNTRY

Big cities, drawing their population from various dialect areas of the surrounding country, started the trend long ago.[13] A more recent development is the reversal of the process: standardized city speech radiates into the surrounding countryside, even around smaller cities.[14] Around Villach (Carinthia), early in the present century, the farmers' dialect began at the city gates; now city speech is used there (Kr). Around Klagen-

---

Henzen (197 f.) states, there is no sharp boundary line between dialect and colloquial; the transition is gradual. A purely descriptive analysis of any speech type would not need to worry about assigning phenomena to either dialect or standard colloquial. It could simply state facts without tracing their provenience. In a larger conspectus which follows the lines of the linguistic development the difficulty must be faced. Henzen (201 f.) makes, for cities, a social distinction between two types of colloquial: a preponderant "lower" type, phonetically under the influence of dialect, which prevails in the south, and an as yet less common "upper" type, closer to the educated standard (*Hochsprache*), which predominates farther north. He states specifically (202) that the lower type is beginning to develop in and around Zürich, although in general Switzerland lacks the colloquial middle layer (199).

13 A good example outside of Germany is the city of London, which drew many of its speech features from neighboring West Saxon and Midland dialects, from medieval times. In German-speaking lands, the speech of big cities has long been a compromise from many sources, not so much a mixture of speech forms as a leveling off of the most striking features of the contributing dialects and a strengthening of the standard language. Examples are Berlin, Hamburg, the Ruhr district. (For the latter, see the publications of the sociologist Wilhelm Brepohl, especially the latest: *Industrievolk im Übergang; Wandel von der agraren zur industriellen Daseinsform, dargestellt am Ruhrgebiet*, Tübingen, 1957.) For Stuttgart, which retains so many dialect features that it appears to the north German as a citadel of Swabian, an informant (S) told me that his co-workers in the city recognize his Swabian as genuine, but an old woman in a village only 5 km away said to him contemptuously, "You are not even from Stuttgart": big city speech is not felt as genuine by real dialect speakers. In Vienna (Kr), the dialect mixture led to the abandonment of the striking features of all contributing dialects, and the numerically strong influx of non-German speakers (especially Czechs, 1848-1910), who learned to speak German in Vienna, promoted further leveling. See also Eberhard Kranzmayer, "Lautwandlungen und Lautverschiebungen im gegenwärtigen Wienerischen", *Zeitschrift für Mundartforschung*, XXI (1952/53), 197-239. For the debatable terms "Stadtmundart" and "Halbmundart" to designate city colloquials more or less affected by dialect, see Henzen, 203 ff., with literature (also his index).

14 Cf. Henzen, 208 ff.

furt (Carinthia) the country speech used to be Slovenian; now no native Slovenian speakers are found there any longer: the countryside speaks German (Kr). This movement has become vastly more important since the war. Because of the shortage of living quarters in the city, many factory workers, especially refugees, live in the villages around the city and commute daily or weekly between the city where they work and the village where their families live. For them the shop language becomes more important than the local speech, and the shop language is generally based more and more on standard German (K 1). Commuter speech is now an important ingredient of the language. There is, to be sure, a tendency for the workers to fall back into dialects as they approach home, as if subconsciously they desired to distinguish between the workaday speech and the relaxed home speech. It was reported several times that conversations on commuter trains would begin in the colloquial standard of the shop, but revert progressively to dialect as the travelers approached their homes. For the newcomers from the east the relaxed speech is likely to be the old home dialect of their parents rather than the local dialect of the new home, although the younger ones among them may have learned the latter in their schooldays – a temporary reversal in the process of assimilation. The gainer is the standard language, which penetrates the speech of the shop with its mixed group of workers as well as that of the village with its mixed population. The tendency to desert the country and to move to the city (*Landflucht*) is counteracted by a trend toward country residence and even country industry (K 1). The new settlements which have been built at the edge of a great many villages, primarily but not exclusively for refugees and expellees, have their center of gravity in the nearby city (K 2). Rivers and great highways were important arteries for the spreading of linguistic forms in olden times (Kr). Now the commuters' railroads have the same function (K 2), and with increasing motor traffic the roads begin to be important again.

2.4. VARIATIONS WITHIN THE STANDARD

Taking a closer look at the speech form which is gaining as the result of all these changes; we must keep in mind that the spoken form of standard German has not reached the same degree of uniformity as the written language, either in pronunciation or in vocabulary. Kretschmer [15] showed the great diversity of terms, particularly for matters of everyday life which are not effectively controlled by the written language, as of 1909-1915. At that time an impressive number of terms were geographically

[15] Paul Kretschmer, *Wortgeographie der hochdeutschen Umgangssprache* (Göttingen, 1918).

restricted in their currency, although the interpenetration had begun. In a recent collection of colloquial expressions by Küpper (1955) [16] the unity of colloquial speech could be assumed and provincial origins of expressions could be subordinated as historical background. Küpper (pp. 12ff.) emphasizes the leveling effect of large-scale interior migrations, especially since World War II. In a prospectus enclosed in the book, inviting volunteer contributions of readers, the expellees are mentioned as a separate category of speakers; but they do not yet figure in the book itself.

2.5. MEETING OF EASTERN AND WESTERN STANDARDS

When the eastern Germans came to settle among their western compatriots and both groups resorted to the colloquial standard language as a common denominator, their forms were not exactly alike in all details. There were certain differences in vocabulary and idioms, and dialect substrata had their effect on the pronunciation. Local coloring of the colloquial standard had not been an obstacle to communication as long as the speakers conversed mostly with speakers from the same area. Now however speakers from entirely different areas came to live together, and the differences became noticeable. They hardly affected communication as such; in most cases the speakers understood and were understood. Rather, the effect was psychological and sociological: the feeling that the others spoke somewhat differently was an obstacle to integration. The newcomers did not feel fully at home in the new environment, and the old settlers were not immediately ready to accept, as their own kind, people who did not speak just like themselves. The homogeneity for which any group strives had to be achieved with a struggle.

2.6. PROCESS OF COMPROMISE

The first things to go were differences in the newcomers' speech which gave the most striking impression of strangeness: definitely local expressions and conspicuous variations of pronunciation. Even in the speech of the highly educated, remnants of dialectal enunciation used to be common. Now it is often difficult or impossible to detect which region an educated speaker comes from. Among less well educated speakers, too, the differences of pronunciation become gradually less noticeable.

As to strikingly different regional words and expressions, it would

[16] Heniz Küpper, *Wörterbuch der deutschen Umgangssprache* (Hamburg, 1955). Although the aim of the book is not the same, it is strange that Küpper does not even mention Kretschmer in the list of his precursors.

sometimes happen as a consequence of the recent mingling of populations that an utterance containing one of them was not immediately understood and had to be explained. By this process the unfamiliar word became known among speakers who had not known it before. Many of the regional terms discussed by Kretschmer are now known over much wider and geographically separated areas; they are not necessarily used but at least understood. I have given examples of this dispersion in a previous article.[17] Where two synonymous terms met, one of them had to yield, unless a fully standard word was available on which the two groups could compromise. In the nature of things it was usually the word of the newcomers which gave way. The newcomer did not want to appear different. The entrance into a closely knit community was difficult enough without emphasis on differences in customs and speech. So the next time he avoided an expression if experience had taught him that it gave offense. Many of the newcomers were not willing to adopt the dialect of the new home; they had their pride and did not yield so easily to the ways of others; but to substitute a standard item, when one was available, did not mean giving up one's heritage, and perhaps even added prestige, because the standard language enjoys prestige everywhere. Nor was the standard version as offensive to the old settlers as a regional equivalent not current in the area. But hearing the local term constantly would eventually lead to its adoption, passively first, later actively. This is a facet of the slow, painful integration process. On the other hand even the local people, whose entrenched position gave their form of speech much more strength, occasionally came to use a word of the newcomers, if only in quotation marks, so to speak: "as you people say", "as the refugees say".[18] The grocer, who used to be asked for potatoes by one local term, now responds readily to six and more names for the potato, with which refugees and expellees ask for them (K 1). Of course, such multiplicity of terms cannot last. The motley variety of names for tools, for instance, becomes simplified and standardized (K 1) – a loss in color, but a gain in unity.

2.7. LEVELS OF COLLOQUIAL STANDARD

It is important to keep in mind that the standard speech even of the

[17] "Recent Developments in the German Language", *Journal of English and Germanic Philology*, LVII (1958), §§ 1.1, 1.2, and 5.

[18] Informant L reports two such experiences. His native east Swabian landlady told him, "Tante Anna [a refugee] bäckt heute *Nudla-Buchteln*" (the Austrian name for the yeast dish, of Czech derivation, added to the local name for L's benefit). A farmer speaking with a refugee woman used the local word *Stadel* "barn"; when she did not understand he added, "Ja, wie ihr sagt: *Scheune*."

same individual, in Germany and elsewhere, is not an invariable entity. It accommodates itself to the person or group spoken to. The colloquial standard of an individual has several layers suitable for a variety of social situations.[19] The intrusion of dialects is merely a special aspect of this condition. It is parallel to the intrusion of foreign languages into the English of immigrants in the United States (K 1). In Germany as in the U.S., the speech of the old settlers, into whose society the newcomers must fit themselves, is bound to win out, with only minor enrichments from the speech of the new arrivals. An important difference between the two situations, however, is the fact that in Germany the two groups do not speak two quite irreconcilable languages, but have as a common meeting ground the colloquial standard speech, which is strengthened by their intercourse and progresses on the way to unification. A colloquial standard which has its locus between the dialects of home life and the book-based speech of the educated has long been in the process of developing. It received a powerful boost by the mingling of populations in the wake of the second War. The old call for a respectable middle language [20] is beginning to be answered.

3.1. DIALECT SURVIVAL

Thus, a leveling of the colloquial standard was a consequence of the mingling of populations. Of course, where the position of the local dialect was still strong, complete integration on an intimate level required that the newcomers learn the dialect of the old settlers. Anyone who speaks differently, even though he is fully understood, is not felt to be a member of the group. Social and economic reasons often demanded full conformity. The rate of adaptation to dialects varied greatly with the psychological and social attitudes of the individuals. Older people are less given to learning new tricks than younger. Women have a tendency to be more conservative than men, and the tendency asserts itself strongly when they stay at home and do not mingle much with outsiders. On

[19] Cf. Henzen, 23, 197.

[20] Cf. Hugo von Hofmannsthal, preface to *Wert und Ehre deutscher Sprache* (1927): "Wir haben eine sehr hohe dichterische Sprache und sehr liebliche und ausdrucksstarke Volksdialekte, von denen die Sprache des Umgangs in allen deutschen Landschaften verschiedentlich angefärbt ist. Woran es uns mangelt, das ist die mittlere Sprache, nicht zu hoch, nicht zu niedrig. ... Unsere Nachbarn, Nord und Süd, Ost und West, haben sie. ... In dieser mittleren Sprache aber fasst sich allezeit das Gesicht der Nation zusammen." This observation echoes much older ones in his anthology, by Justus Möser, and Adam Müller (pp. 55, 74, 140 in the 1957 reprint, Fischer Bücherei). Adam Müller has the best formulation.

the other hand, if they go out to work, they often adapt themselves more readily and more successfully to the new surroundings, particularly the younger women. Young people are most likely to conform to their present environment. They have no strong attachment to the old home, which they remember only dimly and often unfavorably, because their memory reaches back only to the terminal stages of the old life, with its insecurity, persecution, and hardships. They do not share the nostalgic longings of their elders. They live in the present and the future. Besides, the groups of young people with whom they live are much less tolerant of differences than those of older people. The schoolyard community of children particularly enforces conformity subtly or crudely. There are many reports that children were forced to mend their speech ways by lickings or by ostracism. Thus, in strong dialect areas, the children of the expellees usually learned the new speech, half willingly and half under compulsion – sometimes even one dialect after another, if they were resettled several times, as often happened. The only mitigating element in this painful process of adaptation was the fact that the autochthonous population itself shifted at the same time more and more to standard colloquial speech, thus providing a more neutral meeting ground. In cases where the dislodged had to live successively in six or ten places, they naturally gave up learning each new dialect. Their speech became more and more standard without their being conscious of it (B, K 1).

3.2. CONFLICTS BETWEEN ADULTS AND CHILDREN

The differences in the attitudes of the generations led to many conflicts and psychological difficulties. In countless families, particularly those of rural origin, the parents insisted on maintaining the home dialect within the family and forbade their children to speak the dialect of the new homeland. It could happen that a child was punished by the parents for speaking the dialect of the new environment, and by the playmates in the schoolyard for not speaking it. The parents did not, however, object to the children speaking standard German,[21] and the playmates likewise felt a less strong aversion to a form of speech which for them, too, was an ideal cultivated by the school and basically recognized by them. The consequence was that many children of the newcomers became trilingual in the sense that they spoke the old dialect at home, the new dialect in the play group, and a form of standard in the classroom and elsewhere. The strongest of the three forms of speech was the standard, which radi-

[21] There were many cases of parents insisting that their children speak standard German rather than any dialect. (Cf. Lemberg and Krecker, 43; see note 8 above.) Thus standard German was reinforced in the families.

ated into both dialects. Even children willing to speak the parental dialect at home did not succeed in speaking it in pure form. Unconsciously they allowed it to be modified by the newly learned dialect or by the standard, and the parents themselves yielded to such influences without realizing it. This fact bears repetition: the dialects from the east are no longer the same, even where they are loyally preserved.

The conflict in a young speaker's mind is illustrated by the question of a seven year old boy to his father: "*Poppe, soll i schwätze, soll i sage, oder soll i spreche*?" The anecdote, reported from Swabia,[22] shows the child's consciousness of regional differences in the word for "to speak": *schwätzen* Swabian, *sɔgen* Bavarian, specifically a Lower Austrian dialect near Budapest (B), *sprechen* standard. It also shows the unconscious adaptation to Swabian, particularly in the dropping of the *-n* in all three infinitives, a feature which is characteristic not only of the dialect but of the easy colloquial standard of the region.

3.3. ADOLESCENTS

It is not possible to draw a simple picture of the process of linguistic assimilation. Too many personal and social variables enter into it.[23] What is given here is an average drawn from a great number of detailed observations made by me and my many informants. One complication is this: as mentioned before, young people who go to work every day learn the speech of their co-workers, which has greater authority for them than the home speech. After the stage of adolescence is over and the rebellion against parental authority subsides, the young newcomers often revert to more respect for the traditions and speech of the old homeland, and show more willingness to speak the home dialect in the family circle as well as they can. This creates a cross current retarding the assimilation. As long as the old folks are living, these young people waver between the homeland speech, which may be dialectal or a variety of the standard, and the shop speech, which is a different variety of the standard, influenced by a different dialect.

4.1. COLLECTION OF SOURCE MATERIALS

It is symptomatic that the scientific study of old customs and old dialects

[22] Hermann Bausinger, "Beharrung und Einfügung", *Jahrbuch für Volkskunde der Heimatvertriebenen*, Salzburg, vol. 2 (1956), 13.

[23] Perhaps the demonstration that linguistic changes are a complicated process is one of the values of a study showing a change in progress. For remarks about complexities in the development of the English standard language, cf. E. J. Dobson, *English Pronunciation 1500-1700* (Oxford, 1957), v.

is being undertaken energetically at this stage. Whenever extinction threatens a specimen, the museums become interested in it. There are numerous scholarly organizations which are eagerly at work to preserve the heritage of the dispossessed from the east.[24] The emphasis is on folklore, but several include the study of the waning dialects of the east. Their archives of tape recordings contain valuable source material, which can be exploited by dialectologists even after the dialects have ceased to exist. The feeling of urgency to preserve a record of dialects which are fast disappearing has led German scholars to assign priority to the recording of eastern speech, as long as individuals can still be found who have retained their native way of speaking relatively unimpaired. I heard several such recordings in different parts of Germany. What impressed me most was the fact that the choice of vocabulary and idioms even of good dialect speakers was to a considerable extent "tainted" by standard German, particularly in north Germany.[25] This, however, is not necessarily an effect of the postwar mingling of populations. The influence of the standard language on the dialects was under way before the recent upheavals.

One large scholarly enterprise embraces the old forms of speech in the west as well as those which have come from the east. Dr. Eberhard Zwirner's *Deutsches Spracharchiv* (founded in Brunswick, now located in Münster) is devoted to the ambitious plan of collecting tape recordings in 1200 localities of West Germany from six speakers in each: three old residents and three expellees; old, middle-aged, and young; rural and middle-class; dialect and colloquial speech. The aim is to catch the leveling of speech forms in the making as well as to preserve records of the old dialects. The project is well under way with the aid of public funds and the collaboration of local experts, Germanists and others, in the various regions; it is to be finished by 1959. Zwirner has begun to publish the records[26] and will evaluate them phonetically with his own phonometric method. Other scholars can use them for other linguistic purposes. The collection of materials from this period of transformation promises to be of lasting value. As yet little has been done by linguists to study the impact of the influx from the east on the language in the west – far less than by folklorists, who have found significant interpene-

[24] For names, addresses, and personnel as well as for accounts of their activities see part II of *Jahrbuch für Volkskunde der Heimatvertriebenen*, Salzburg, vol. 1 (1955) and vol. 2 (1956).

[25] Cf. Henzen, 193 ff., for infiltration of standard words, sounds, and forms into dialect, with literature.

[26] *Lautbibliothek der deutschen Mundarten* (Göttingen, 1957-). For an account of the plan and its precursors since 1899 see Eberhard Zwirner, "Lautdenkmal der deutschen Sprache", *Zeitschrift für Phonetik und allgemeine Sprachwissenschaft*, IX (1956), 3-13.

trations. Yet the opportunity for observing the linguistic effect of large-scale migrations in the making is unique, and the opportunity is passing rapidly with the progress of assimilation. Many observers in Germany and Austria feel that it is too early to study the effects, since nothing is as yet settled. I think, on the contrary, that the passing stage of turmoil ought to interest the linguist. Historical linguistics has always been handicapped by having only finished changes to study, being reduced to guesswork and arguments of plausibility for their explanation. Here for once we have a chance to observe changes as they are going on, and they prove to be much more complicated than the simplified abstractions of traditional formulations. Since little has been done by linguists during the period of transition, the recordings made during this time should prove to be very valuable in the future.

4.2. EXAMPLE: SWABIAN IN WÜRTTEMBERG

A few exact studies are available, which investigate the decline of the home dialects of eastern refugees and expellees in their new western abodes, and incidentally throw light on the strengthening of the colloquial standard.

Ulrich Engel, a student of Hugo Moser, has published a good examination of the speech of expellees as it has been affected by the encounter with Swabian speech in Württemberg.[27] He feels sure that there is a slight influence from the newcomers on the speech of their present environment, but he restricts his examination to the reverse influence.

Among the expellees (roughly one fifth of the population of the land Württemberg-Baden) the Sudeten Germans (from Bohemia) predominate with about 50%, followed by Germans from Hungary, 15%, and Silesians, 10%. The former homes of the remainder extend all the way from Yugoslavia to East Prussia and Russia. The newcomers were not settled as units but scattered over the land, and their home dialects were very different from each other. The Hungarian Germans alone, for example, spoke either Franconian or Swabian or Bavarian dialects. Württemberg-Baden itself has Swabish and Franconian dialects; but in this study we learn only about the clash with several Swabian dialects of the west, and with the Württemberg colloquial language, which is a compromise between Swabian and standard German.

[27] Ulrich Engel, "Die Sprache der Heimatverwiesenen und das Schwäbische", *Württembergisches Jahrbuch für Volkskunde*, 1956, Stuttgart, 90-111. The same annual contains, in a survey of the literature 1954-56 by Irmgard Hampp and Hermann Bausinger, an account of recent publications about the dialects and popular speech of Württemberg (140 f.).

Engel finds, as was to be expected, certain variations depending on age, social standing, residence, occupation, and individual attitudes, whereas the effect of sex and denomination is negligible. These variations are not stated in general terms but documented by concrete examples. He examines five cases in considerable detail. Two of them concern a single person. The others are families, one of them a large double family of eight related persons. All were village dwellers and dialect speakers in their former homes in various parts of Hungary (some of which later became parts of Yugoslavia). Their dialects differed from each other. In one case it was Swabian, in three cases varieties of Bavarian, and in one case Rhenish Franconian. Some now live in cities (Reutlingen, Tübingen, Stuttgart), others in a village, and one family was still (1954) in a refugee camp. Most of them went through a period of shifting residence in other dialect areas before becoming settled. In each case, salient features of the home dialect are stated briefly but adequately, with emphasis on sounds, but also some attention to forms and syntax. Then the changes in the speech of each individual are characterized. The results differ: some speakers preserve the home dialect, usually persons over 40; some speak both dialects, keeping them separate; some speak a dialect mixture. Engel observed that school children learn the new dialect to perfection, but does not state clearly whether any of them speak only the new dialect. The strengthening of the standard colloquial language is not directly evident in these cases of rural speakers. But going beyond these cases, Engel says that those who already spoke standard German in the old home (all Baltic Germans, nearly all north Germans, many Silesians, part of the Sudeten Germans) strive to acquire the colloquial standard in the form it takes in the new home, whereas dialect speakers (almost all Balkan Germans, most Sudeten Germans) incline toward the dialect of their new home.

Generalizing on the basis of his earlier, more comprehensive research (E), Engel examines the average reaction of speakers of different regional provenience. He finds that Low German dialects, which were already receding before the standard language in the old home, survived practically nowhere in South Germany. The Franconian speakers, intellectually flexible and adaptable, gave up their home dialects easily, because, as he says, their dialects differed least from the standard language; by implication this observation does testify to a strengthening of the standard. The Swabian dialects maintained themselves best, although they differed from the Swabian of the new home, having undergone a strong influence of neighboring Franconian dialects in the east. The speakers were not conscious of the minor differences between the old and the new forms of speech and therefore did not change their speech habits quickly.[28]

[28] Orally Engel remarked (E) that the old settlers noticed the difference in the

Bavarians, known for their conservative linguistic attitude, tended to retain some of their speech peculiarities, even the younger speakers who had otherwise switched to Swabian.[29] The result of these adaptations made by the newcomers was either bidialectism or dialect mixture, depending on circumstances and on the attitudes of the speakers.

4.3. EXAMPLE: SUDETEN GERMAN DIALECT

Another report, by Kurt Langer, a student of Ernst Schwarz, deals with the development of certain Sudeten German dialects transplanted from eastern Bohemia to West Germany.[30] The author, who had already made dialect studies in the old homeland, visited the expellees from his small home district now living in nearly all parts of West Germany, more than 1000 persons in about 100 localities. He, too, speaks repeatedly of the mutual influence of old and new dialects, but concentrates his attention on developments in the transplanted dialects.

The dialects of his homeland on the Oppa River, a tributary of the Oder, were better investigated than some other German dialects in the east. German settlers had been called to the area by local rulers in the 13th and 14th centuries to clear the land and bring it into cultivation.

Swabian of the newcomers but did not object to it, being used to the presence of refugees in their midst. Antagonism toward the newcomers was due to government favors extended to them rather than to dialect differences.

[29] Oral communication (E): Sudeten Germans with Bavarian dialect adapt themselves slowly to Swabian. Both forms of speech being conservative south German dialects, the need for adaptation is not urgent. Since the differences are considerable, however, a development takes place eventually. The speakers either learn Swabian, retaining their Bavarian as a separate entity, or Swabian elements intrude slowly into the Bavarian dialects. Refugees are only marginally considered in Engel's dissertation (E). Its chief topic is the demonstration that the area around every city in Württemberg speaks, in addition to the local dialect, two forms of the colloquial language: one which is close to the standard, the same in all of Württemberg, and another provincial one, which leans more heavily on local dialects.

[30] Kurt Langer, "Die Entwicklung der Mundarten der Vertriebenen des Oppalandes in der westdeutschen Umwelt", 1953 (typescript). The linguistically trained author, incapacitated by tuberculosis, undertook the study as occupational therapy. This paper, made available to me by the author, gives the general part of his studies concerning the dialects of his home district in Austrian (later Czechoslovakian) Silesia, as a specific example of the development of Sudeten German dialects in the west. Detailed studies are to follow. The Sudeten Germans in general were called to Bohemia and Moravia in the thirteenth century by local rulers and landowners to clear waste land around the edges of the then inhabited territory, toward the surrounding mountains (cf. Ernst Schwarz, *Sudetendeutscher Wortatlas*, Munich, 1954, vol. 1, 11).

By the criterion of dialect features, they must have come in two streams, some from Hesse, others from the eastern Main River, with an admixture of Bavarians. The leveling of the various Franconian (and Bavarian) dialects had been going on for seven centuries, to the time of the expulsion, 1945-46.

The expellees coming from Austrian (Czechoslovakian) Silesia were conservative in their attitude and liked to speak dialect. Even those with higher education or in better social position were not ashamed of it. But the scattering of the population (*Zersiedlung*) all over the west robbed the dialect of its sociological support in a coherent body of speakers. The newcomers felt more at home in the south of Germany than in the north; but here they collided with solidly conservative dialects which opposed themselves powerfully to their own form of speech. Yet, the dialects resisted assimilation better in the country than in cities, where the influence of the standard language militates against the retention of any pure dialect; only the old people (60-80 years), who lived in their small family circles, largely isolated from the environment, maintained their old dialect even in the cities. In the country the imported dialects maintained themselves for a time; but the fact that the newcomers did not all come from the same locality in the old eastern home district had the effect of leveling the differences between local varieties in favor of a district dialect which had not existed in this form before the expulsion.

Langer emphasizes that the dialects had been changing from generation to generation before the expulsion, in recent years especially through contact with other speakers in the labor service and in the army. The transplantation is reflected in speech as all previous vicissitudes of fate had been. The change of generations is decisive for the adaptation of the imported dialects to the new environment. Children up to the age of 14 no longer understand the most characteristic words of their parents' dialect. The score of youths up to age 20 in answering test questions is little better, although traces of the parental dialect in their speech show that they may retain more of it subconsciously. Langer questioned about 100 children and young people in the Allgäu district of Bavaria and found that the old characteristic equivalents for one noun ("potato") and two verbs ("toil" and "get drunk") were remembered only by speakers over 20 years of age. Speakers over 20 generally retain the home dialect, but speak a colloquial form of the standard language with the old settlers and with expellees from a different region. These are average conditions, which are subject to variation in individual cases, depending on occupation, character, crossmarriages, and other specific circumstances.

As the first sample of his specific observations in various regions of West Germany, Langer deals in this paper with some effects of the transplantation to the Memmingen-Mindelheim area of the Allgäu (western

Bavaria), where expellees from the Oppa land formed almost 30% of the population and lived mostly in rural surroundings. This produced a decided clash of dialects, with less influence of the standard language. The Franconian and Bavarian dialects of the old home collided with the Swabian-Bavarian dialect of the new habitat. Both parties were at first impressed by the fact that the other group spoke differently. A feeling of strangeness prevailed, which had to be overcome slowly, not without a stage of mutual mockery, distrust, even hostility. Linguistic misunderstandings occurred, because some expressions were not even mutually understandable. The children in school, more adaptable and more exposed to coercion from their playmates, switched to the dialect of the new home. Some parents tried to forbid the use of the new dialect in their house, but could not stem the tide. Through the children and through contacts of daily life the older people soon became acquainted with the differing speech forms of their new environment, learned to understand them, and eventually to use them.

The result among people over 20 was the elimination of dialect expressions from the old home which were strikingly different, and a slow adaptation to the vocabulary, idioms, and even sounds of the new home. However, as Langer emphasizes, these older people in the country chose to resort to the standard language as spoken around them rather than learn the new dialect. Wherever there was a choice in terms, the newcomers favored standard German. It is easy to see that the presence of standard speakers in large numbers in the villages and on the farms of a district where dialect had been the medium of normal everyday communication was bound to lead to a considerable strengthening of the standard, which had formerly been almost a foreign language learned in school and used rarely, with outsiders. In the cities, of course, the influence of the standard had been strong before. This study is valuable because it shows how the influx of expellees carried the process of linguistic standardization into rural speech, even in the conservative south.

Langer gives a considerable number of examples of old-home expressions which were lost and replaced, and a few instances of features of pronunciation (sounds) which were modified by a compromise between dialect and standard. Space does not allow citing many of them. *Vesper* "afternoon lunch" became *Brotzeit*; *Schwerbauch* (sic!) "fat stomach" became *Wambe* or *Ranzen*; *ein wenig* became *ein bissla Parapluie,* already receding in the old home before standard *Regenschirm* (in dialect pronunciation) was lost and largely replaced by local *Regadächla; Scheune* or *Scheuer* was superseded by the definitely Bavarian *Stadel;* [ropəʳ] *Radeber* "wheelbarrow" became *Schiebkarra* or standard *Schiebkarre; Erdäpfel* "potatoes" was displaced by various forms of *Bodenbirnen,* including this "standard" form. Velar [l] disappeared, and the east Bavarian vocalization [i] of /1/ before consonant (as in *Wald, Feld*), already recessive under standard influence in the old home, was given up. Local Swabian *woischt* "you know" was taken over by expellees in the half-standard form *waischt*. The most striking example of a newly learned word (by no means in standard meaning, to be sure) is *Hura* as a derogatory epithet of so general a meaning that it can be used good-naturedly in the Allgäu. We can imagine the shock which the expellees felt when they first heard themselves called *Huraflüchtlinge* or one of their girls *Huramensch*. The initial shock was an effective teaching device. They soon learned to use the word themselves. Coarse terms of the local dialect are learned easily by the newcomers because they are striking. The pleasant-sounding local word *Fiedle, Fiedla* "anus" was adopted even by older expellees. Otherwise the latter compromised by favoring the colloquial standard. This contributed to a weakening of both the old and the new dialects. At the meetings of compatriots the old-home dialects tended to emerge nostalgically from the semi-subconscious; but that is merely a retarding element, and even on these occasions the leveling of homeland subdialects took its course. While the educated generally leave dialects behind and speak a colloquial close to the written language, among the expellees there are some educated families which began to speak the old dialect in the new home although they had not used it before the expulsion. This is another retarding element without a future. It merely represents loyalty to memories of the lost homeland, which die with the older generations.

4.4. EXAMPLE: SOUTH AND NORTH

The difference between south and north German dialects in their resistance to the inroads of the standard language is well documented in a statistically fortified study by Otto Steiner,[31] which takes both native and immigrant children into account. All school children in the first four grades (ages 6-10) of the two districts Bamberg (northern Bavaria) and Northeim (Lower Saxony) were studied in 1954, their speech types being classified by their teachers. Steiner gives figures for eight categories of speech types including standard German, local dialect, imported dialect, and a number of transitional groups. Only his results for the major categories will be reproduced here. He finds that boys use the local dialect far more commonly than girls, who prefer High German (standard German). In both regions, for both sexes, the share of High German is much

[31] Otto Steiner, "Hochdeutsch und Mundart bei Einheimischen und Neubürgern der Kreise Bamberg und Northeim im Jahre 1954; Ergebnisse einer Schulkindererhebung", *Phonetica*, I (1957), 146-156.

larger in the cities than in the adjoining rural districts. Sole use of imported dialects is represented by a mere 1% of all cases. Adding speech noticeably influenced by imported dialects still yields only 5.7 to 8.3%.

More important for us is the difference between south and north. In and around Bamberg 80% of the native pupils still speak the local East Franconian dialect, including more than 50% in the city. The pull of the local dialect is still so strong that roughly half the children of newcomers have adopted it or speak it along with High German. Few speak only the imported dialect, more speak both it and either the local dialect or High German. Those from Berlin, the Russian Zone, and northeast Germany (Pomerania and East Prussia), whose home speech was very different from that of Bamberg, are not yet so well assimilated as those from Silesia and the Sudeten area, who form about half the contingent and whose home speech is more closely related.

The situation in and around Northeim is strikingly different. The local Low German dialect is spoken by fewer than 10% of the pupils, including only 11% of pupils from native families. High German is spoken by 60%; 20% use High German and the local dialect. In the city more than half the school classes speak High German exclusively. The imported dialects of the newcomers, here prevailingly Silesians and northeast Germans, are spoken by very few of the children, and few of them have learned the local dialect. The Northeim statistics show clearly that these children contribute significantly to the strengthening of High German. The figures for Bamberg show the same effect, although there the position of High German has not yet become so strong.

If the suspicion should arise that the teachers, whose professional duty is to cultivate High German, might be biased in favor of it in the data they supplied, Steiner invalidates the objection by quoting comments of the collaborating teachers. In and around Northeim the children speak High German during the recess, while playing, and in the street.[32] Those who speak both High German and Low German or another dialect re-

[32] Steiner's inquiry covered more than is contained in the published study. For example, he told me (St) that the teachers explored the play combinations of the various population elements by asking the pupils, "Who plays with whom?" The purpose of the question was not revealed to them; it was represented as a test to see whether they were good observers. The play groupings still showed complexes of strangeness in 1950. By 1954 the newcomers' children were integrated. Such sociological facts have of course a bearing on the children's speech. Individual differences also play a part. Gifted children are integrated more quickly than others because they are more popular as playmates, a fact which has been demonstrated statistically. The IQ distribution of the newcomers was about the same as that of the local population, as K. Val. Müller established statistically in 1946; the shocking disturbance of their environment had not affected it. For Müller's work, cf. in this connection especially: Karl Valentin Müller, *Heimatvertriebene Jugend*, 2nd ed. (Würzburg, 1956).

serve the dialect for conversation with their parents and grandparents, while among themselves they speak High German, adorned with occasional dialect expressions. Steiner is sure that the "unexpectedly radical turning away from Low German" is a fact, and my own observations in other Low German areas confirm its rapid decline. Steiner expects the imported dialects to die out in a few years and the "dramatic change" in the relationship between High German and the local dialects to continue, and this remark does not refer only to Low German provinces.

Steiner's study is of great interest because it does not deal with big cities, where the decline of dialects and the progress of the standard language is bound to be more rapid. My own observations were naturally made mostly in cities. Here however we have objective statistical evidence that the process goes on in small cities and in the country – at an amazing rate in the Low German-speaking north central part of Germany, more slowly on the Franconian-speaking northern edge of south Germany. Several typical aspects are confirmed by the study: the faster switch to High German in cities, even small ones, than in the country; the importance of the change of generations, children being ahead of the parents, who act as a retarding element; and the influence of evacuees, expellees, and refugees in strengthening the standard language.

5.1. SUMMARY: METHOD OF PRESENTATION

I have chosen to reproduce the results of three exact studies rather than to register the numerous details which I collected myself during my travels through Germany. My own observations gave me an overall view of developments in many dialect areas, the strong impression that the dialects were receding at a surprisingly fast rate before the standard language (especially in the Low German north, but not only there), and the conviction that the strengthening of the standard language is the most important linguistic development in the German-speaking lands today. I had not expected to find this as the salient feature of recent German.[33] My surprise provided the impetus for this report.

It is one thing, however, for the traveler to get a general impression based on a mosaic of a thousand details observed in contacts of daily life, and another to demonstrate the changes convincingly to the reader.

[33] I have reported about many other features in my article (see note 17). The victory of "dialect-free High German" in a new expellee settlement in Hessen, in a mountainous wilderness near the Spessart forest, over the dialects of speakers from 13 different home regions is impressively shown in a popular article by Siegfried Mauermann, "Hält sich die Mundart der Heimatvertriebenen?", *Muttersprache*, 1957, 249-252.

I decided that the presentation of a few concrete, objectively analyzed situations was more suitable for this purpose. Besides, no one can, of course, have an intimate knowledge of all the native dialects of the German-speaking lands in the west and all the dialects imported from the east. I had to leave the exact investigation of individual dialects to experts who concentrated their attention on limited sectors of the total situation. Even Langer, who restricts his study to expellees from his small home district in the Sudetenland, feels that the fate of their dialects in the various parts of West Germany is too comprehensive a topic for one man to investigate. Much less is it possible for one person to give the overall picture in exact detail. It must suffice to state, on the basis of my experience, that the selected cases are representative of the whole situation.

5.2. SUMMARY: EFFECT OF MIGRATIONS ON DIALECTS

The inroads made by the standard language into the domain of dialects, long in slow progress, have been greatly accelcrated by the vast population movements since the war. The eastern German dialects are dying out, the western are receding. The decline of dialects amounts to a rout in the Low German north.[34] It is slower but also unmistakable in the south. The extent of the change is masked by the survival of speakers of the older generations who were reared with dialect speech as the natural medium of easy, informal, intimate contacts and do not change their practice abruptly when they are among themselves. But they are no longer among themselves all day and every day. The presence of numerous newcomers of different home speech in every city and every village makes them use their second language, standard German, much more frequently than before. The decisive step forward is linked with the change of generations.[35] Not long ago children liked to relax from school discipline by reverting to the unconstrained easy speech of the locality.

[34] The amazing decline of Low German has not yet been recognized by the handbooks. In fact, Henzen (201) specifically exempts the Low German area from his statement that a colloquial close to the educated prevails more in northern cities than in southern. The situation is adequately described by Riemann (29; see note 11), who speaks about the recession of Low-German before High German among expellees from the northeast: "Was wir dort seit 70 Jahren registrieren konnten – nämlich das langsame Zurückweichen der Mundart der sozial Schwächeren vor der der sozial Überlegenen –, das vollzieht sich heute *in unvorstellbar schnellem Tempo* in den deutschen Westgebieten" (italics supplied). Cf. Moser, 138 (see note 5).

[35] The importance of the change of generations is stressed by Henzen (173 f., 210 f.).

Emotional values favored dialect, at least for children from families that did not cultivate High German at home. Even where they did, but High German was not yet completely natural, the speech of play would tend to emphasize features which were not favored by the home, to symbolize escape from restraint. It is striking to hear children in the street, all over the German-speaking lands, now use more or less pure standard German among themselves, when the observer who remembers former conditions expects to hear dialect.

5.3. SUMMARY: LEVELING OF COLLOQUIAL AND DIALECTS

The struggle between standard speech and dialect concerns the spoken colloquial form of the standard much more than the written form. Few individuals speak as they write on all occasions. For the ordinary pursuits of life most use a colloquial form of speech, in fact several forms depending on the nature of the contacts.[36] This colloquial speech still varies in different parts of the territory, depending on the strength of the regional dialect. It is typically a compromise between the standard language and the dialect. In the north the dialect elements are minor. In the south, particularly the southwest, dialect features in pronunciation and vocabulary are still much stronger but receding, and the provincial form of the colloquial speech tends to be uniform over larger areas than previously, the newcomers assisting in the leveling.

The leveling in the colloquial language is paralleled in the dialects. They used to vary from district to district, often from village to village, as the population units were largely self-contained. As the units were opened up by increasing intercommunication, the small subdialects combined into larger regional dialects with leveled-off features, at the same time as forms of standard speech made inroads into the dialects. Those among the newcomers who learned the new dialect learned it in leveled form and contributed to the leveling, strengthening the standard elements at the same time.

The development does not stop at political boundaries. Austria goes the same way as Germany. Switzerland, with fewer refugees and a linguistically very conservative attitude, applies strong brakes to the trend.

[36] The multiplicity of forms of the colloquial speech is emphasized by Henzen (20-25, 197-201), with a digest of the literature. Hugo Moser, in his inaugural address, *Mittlere Sprachschichten als Quellen der deutschen Hochsprache*, Nijmegen, 1955, makes the interesting attempt to prove that all forms of the German literary language, from Old High German and Old Saxon times on, were based on the colloquial speech of the circles which were successively the bearers of literature: nobility, clergy, monasteries, city patricians, and that leveling by regional compromises has always played a part in their development.

The Swiss have no real colloquial between the standard language and the dialects. Even the educated speak colloquially a German which remains dialectal at least phonetically. But Switzerland, too, is slowly going in the same direction.[37]

6. OUTLOOK

This seems to be the development in broad outline: even without the effect of the postwar migrations, small subdialects grow together into larger regional dialects. With powerful influence of the migrations, the dialects are affected more and more by the standard language. Along with the modified dialect, a colloquial standard is spoken which has not yet shed the influence of the underlying dialect, but settles into forms unified over wide areas. These regional colloquial languages tend to reduce their dialect features and to adapt themselves progressively to a countrywide standard. The trend is toward a single colloquial standard over the whole territory.

The whole process – let it be said again – promises to progress radically with the change of generations. Children are ahead of their elders in the switch to the standard language. They contribute powerfully to the strengthening of the standard and to the decline of the dialects.

INFORMANTS CITED

B — Hermann Bausinger, Ludwig-Uhland-Institut für Volkskunde, Tübingen. Interview 30 April 1955.

E — Ulrich Engel, Stuttgart, student of Hugo Moser, Ph.D. Tübingen 1955, dissertation (typescript) "Mundart und Umgangssprache in Württemberg; Beiträge zur Sprachsoziologie der Gegenwart". Interview Tübingen 30 April 1955.

K 1 — Alfred Karasek-Langer, folklorist, Berchtesgaden. Interview 12-13 May 1955.

K 2 — id., interview 11 July 1955.

Kr — Professor Eberhard Kranzmayer, Vienna, dialectologist. Native of Klagenfurt, Carinthia. Speaks Slovenian; has recorded the speech of the last Slovenian speakers around Klagenfurt. Interview 17 July 1955.

L — Kurt Langer, expellee from the east Sudeten area, Czechoslovakian Silesia. Interview in Ennepetal, Ruhr district, 15 August 1955.

M — W. Middelmann, Ministerialdirigent, Bundesministerium für Vertriebene, Bonn. Interview 14 April 1955.

[37] Cf. note 12 above. See also Henzen (who is Swiss) 191-193, for an interesting example of Swiss platform speech, which is really standard German with dialect sounds, and p. 193 for the progressing influence of the standard on Swiss dialect.

S Schreiber, buyer at Stuttgart's leading textile firm (2000 employees and workers), where the occupational speech is still "purely Swabian". Native Alsatian, but for 24 years at present place of employment. Speaks Swabian at work with ease; spoke cultured standard German with me. Interview 27 April 1955.

St Otto Steiner, Brunswick, expellee from Silesia; mathematician and physicist with training in statistics; collaborator of K. Val. Müller, sociologist. Interview 19 May 1955.

From: *Word*, 15 (1959), pp. 130-153. Reprinted with permission.

Paul L. Garvin and Madeleine Mathiot

THE URBANIZATION OF THE GUARANÍ LANGUAGE: A PROBLEM IN LANGUAGE AND CULTURE*

0. This paper is based on the assumption that Redfield's concepts of folk and urban[1] are applicable to language as well as culture. The linguistic equivalent of the distinction between folk cultures and urban cultures is the differentiation made by scholars of the Linguistic Circle of Prague and others between folk speech and the standard language,[2] which we here tentatively define as a codified form of a language, accepted by and serving as a model to a larger speech community. The Prague School has formulated a set of criteria for differentiating a standard language from folk speech, the latter of which, conversely, is characterized by the absence of these criteria.

These criteria are such that they presuppose the existence of an urban culture in the speech community using, or aspiring to use, a standard language. Consequently, we may consider a standard language a major linguistic correlate of an urban culture, and we may furthermore consider the degree of language standardization in this technical sense a measure of the urbanization of the culture of the speakers.

* The conceptual framework of this paper has been the major responsibility of the senior author, the Guaraní data and their systematization have been the major responsibility of the junior author.

[1] Cf. R. Redfield, *The Folk Cultures of Yucatán* (Chicago, 1941), *passim.*

[2] See Bohuslav Havránek, "Úkoly spisovného jazyka a jeho kultura" [The Functions of the Standard Language and its Cultivation], in Cercle Linguistique de Prague, *Spisovná čeština a jazyková kultura* [Standard Czech and the Cultivation of Good Language] (Prague, 1932), 32 ff. A portion translated as "The Functional Differentiation of the Standard Language", in *A Prague School Reader on Esthetics, Literary Structure, and Style*, Paul L. Garvin, Transl. (= *Publ. of the Washington Linguistic Club*, #1) (Washington, D. C., 1955), 1-18.

Conversely, since folk speech has been defined negatively, a low degree of standardization or its absence is here proposed as one possible diagnostic criterion of a near-folk or completely folk culture.

There are two possible scales of language standardization that can be applied here. In cross-cultural terms, different standard languages can be compared as to the degree to which they meet the formulated criteria, and one language can then be rated as more or less highly standardized than another, just as one culture can be called more urban or more folk than another. In intra-cultural terms, different segments of a speech community can be compared as to the degree to which the standard language has penetrated them, just as different subcultures of the same culture can be compared in terms of different degrees of penetration by urban elements.

This paper will be concerned with a concrete case of language standardization. The authors believe that by presenting some of the differential criteria for a standard language and applying them to their case, they can contribute to a further specification of the concept of urban, that is, non-folk-culture.

We have chosen the recent ethnolinguistic development of Guaraní in Paraguay as our test case.

Two languages are spoken in Paraguay: Guaraní and Spanish. In rural areas, Guaraní is spoken almost exclusively. In the Asunción metropolitan area which includes a large percentage of the country's population, both Guaraní and Spanish are used. Traditionally, Spanish has been the official language and the language taught in the schools, but in recent years there has been a developing movement in the metropolitan area to give Guaraní equal status with Spanish, which Paraguayans call the Guaraní renascence. This movement exhibits certain significant parallels with the nationalistic movements of the post-Enlightenment period of Europe (late 18th and early 19th centuries) to put some of the "lesser" languages on a par with the "great" languages. Unlike much of the European development, however, the desire in Paraguay is not to eliminate the "great" language, Spanish, as a competitor, but to have Guaraní and Spanish coexist as equals.

In view of the parallelism referred to above, the criteria developed by the Prague School in discussing the formation of the modern Czech standard language in competition with German, supplemented by some more recent thinking,[3] are considered by the authors to be applicable to the recent development of Guaraní in competition with Spanish, and we propose the hypothesis that there is now in the process of formation a

[3] Cf. Uriel Weinreich, *Languages in Contact* (= *Publ. of the Linguistic Circle of New York*, #1) (New York, 1953).

Guaraní standard language as part of an emergent bilingual urban culture.

To formulate our hypothesis in detail, and to prepare the ground for a procedure for its verification, we shall set forth the criteria for a standard language, and relate them to Guaraní data to the extent allowed by preliminary research at a distance.

We are proposing three sets of differentiative criteria for a standard language: 1. the intrinsic properties of a standard language, 2. the functions of a standard language within the culture of the speech community, 3. the attitudes of the speech community towards the standard language.

1. *Properties of a Standard Language.* – We shall here consider two differential properties of a standard language: flexible stability as originally stated by Vilém Mathesius,[4] and intellectualization as originally stated by Bohuslav Havránek.[5] Both of these properties are gradual and allow quantitative comparison.

1.1. *Flexible Stability.* This is by Mathesius discussed as an ideal property: a standard language, in order to function efficiently, must be stabilized by appropriate codification; it must at the same time be flexible enough in its codification to allow for modification in line with culture change.

There are two things involved in codification: 1. the construction of a codified norm, contained in formal grammars and dictionaries; 2. the enforcement of the norm by control over speech and writing habits through orthoëpy and orthography. The construction of the norm is entrusted to a codifying agency or agencies, the enforcement of the norm is achieved through the schools.

The flexibility of the norm is achieved by including in the normative code the necessary apparatus for modification and expansion, which includes provisions both for a systematic expansion of the lexicon, and an equally systematic expansion of stylistic and syntactic possibilities. This is the responsibility of the codifying agency or agencies.

In the case of Guaraní, the codifying agency is the recently founded Academía de Cultura Guaraní. Urban Paraguayans look upon the Academy as the final authority in language matters, to whom the language problem has been entrusted. The Paraguayan government has recently recognized the status of the Academy and accorded it a subsidy. The Academy is at present engaged in the preparation of normative orthographic, grammatical and lexical materials preparatory to an expected and hoped-for introduction of the teaching of Guaraní in the schools.

[4] Vilém Mathesius, in Havránek, *op. cit.*, fn. 1, pp. 14 ff.

[5] B. Havránek, *loc. cit.*

In these efforts, the Academía de Cultura Guaraní is continuing a normative tradition established by the Jesuit fathers of the 16th century (in their work on Língua Geral), and resumed informally during the Chaco War, when a military terminology was evolved to allow the use of Guaraní for communications understood by Paraguayans only.

In terms of the requirement of flexible stability, the revival of the interest in the normalization of Guaraní has not yet led to the achievement of this objective. But the conditions have been created for ultimately meeting this requirement, and there is a strong desire and expectation among Paraguayans to see it met.

1.2. *Intellectualization.* Havránek defines the intellectualization of a standard language as "its adaptation to the goal of making possible precise and rigorous, if necessary abstract statements",[6] in other words, a tendency towards increasingly more definite and accurate expression. This tendency "affects primarily the lexical, and in part the grammatical, structure".[7]

In the lexicon, intellectualization manifests itself by increased terminological precision achieved by the development of more clearly differentiated terms, as well as an increase in abstract and generic terms.

In grammar, intellectualization manifests itself by the development of word formation techniques and of syntactic devices allowing for the construction of elaborate, yet tightly knit, compound sentences, as well as the tendency to eliminate elliptic modes of expression by requiring complete constructions.

In essence, then, intellectualization consists in a tendency towards greater relational systematization and explicitness of statement. This is by Havránek summarized in a three-step scale of intellectualization, leading from simple intelligibility via definiteness to accuracy, to which correspond a conversational, workaday technical, and scientific functional dialects, respectively.[8]

Whereas folk speech is limited to the conversational and some phases of the workaday technical dialects, all three functional dialects are represented, at least as an ideal, in a standard language.

The degree of intellectualization of Guaraní remains to be tested. While there is a strong awareness on the part of our informants of the requirement of flexible stability, there is no comparable awareness of the requirement of intellectualization, beyond the expectation that Guaraní should develop into a language in which anything can be expressed adequately.

Our informants have made emphatic claims as to the precision and

[6] *Op. cit.*, fn. 2, p. 45; transl., *op. cit.*, fn. 2, p. 5.

[7] *Op. cit.*, p. 46; transl., *op. cit., ibid.*

[8] *Op. cit.*, p. 67 ff.; transl., *op. cit.*, p. 15 ff.

abundance of Guaraní terminology in certain limited areas. These claims will have to be checked. The work of the Guaraní Academy in reference to both terminology and syntax will have to be investigated and evaluated. No conclusions in this respect can be reached without a detailed linguistic analysis of Guaraní.

The entire question is thus still wide open.

2. *Functions of a Standard Language.* – We shall discuss three symbolic functions and one objective function of the standard language. The three symbolic functions are: 1. the unifying function, 2. the separatist function, 3. the prestige function; the objective function is 4. the frame-of-reference function.

2.1. *Unifying Function.* A standard language serves as a link between speakers of different dialects of the same language, and thus contributes to uniting them into a single speech community. A consequence of this is an identification of the individual speaker with the larger language community, in addition to, or instead of, the smaller dialect community.

In the case of Guaraní, not enough is known about the dialect situation to evaluate whether the Asunción form of speech serves as an interdialectal lingua franca or not. In terms of the group identification under the unifying function the situation is, however, clearcut: Paraguayans think of themselves as speakers of Guaraní, and not as speakers of any of its dialects; they even go so far as to deny the existence of dialect differences within Paraguayan Guaraní.

2.2. *Separatist Function.* Whereas the unifying function opposes the standard language to the dialects, the separatist function opposes a standard language to other languages as a separate entity rather than a subdivision of a larger entity. It thus can serve as a powerful symbol of separate national identity, and the individual's identification with his language community is then no longer a matter of course but becomes highly emotionally charged.

This is the case with Paraguayans. Guaraní is what makes them into a distinct Paraguayan nation, rather than just another group of South Americans. To all of them, those who speak Guaraní are fellow Paraguayans, those who speak only Spanish – although they may live in Paraguay – are not; they are foreigners and they are called "gringos". Even Paraguayans who speak mainly Spanish at home will speak Guaraní to each other when they meet abroad because, as one of our informants put it, "nos acerca más de nuestra tierra".

The identification is with the language and not with Indian ancestry. Immigrants, in order to be accepted as Paraguayans, will learn Guaraní. As Justo Pastor Benítez, a leading Paraguayan historian and writer, puts it: "La iniciación se realiza por el idioma guaraní, vehículo de la identificación nacional",[9] because "hablar Guaraní es ser dos veces paraguayo".[10] Thus, the President of the Republic, in spite of his German name, is "paraguayo" because he speaks Guaraní.

2.3. *Prestige Function.* There is prestige attached to the possession of a standard language: one of the ways of achieving equality with an admired high-prestige nationality is to make one's own language "as good as theirs", which in our terms means bringing it closer to the ideal properties of a standard language.

Making of Guaraní a"lengua de cultura" like Spanish is one of the major motivations of the work of the Academía de Cultura Guaraní. Although the achievement of a Guaraní lengua de cultura is so far only an ideal, Paraguayans take great national pride in being the only American nation possessing a language all of their own that is capable of such a development, and they think of themselves as a model for the other South American nations in their quest for national individualization. "La misión histórica que el Paraguay está destinado a cumplir en América", says Benítez, "es de dar algo propiamente americano, un destello del alma del Nuevo Mundo".[11]

The prestige function has thus been transferred from the possession of a functioning standard language to the possession of a potential standard language. This transfer of the prestige function has become possible because the functioning standard languages of South America, Spanish and Portuguese, are shared by several national units and thus are not capable of carrying the separatist function and serving as a vehicle of nationalist symbolism.

2.4. *Frame-of-Reference Function.* The standard language serves as a frame of reference for speech usage in general by providing a codified norm that constitutes a yardstick for correctness. Individual speakers and groups of speakers are then judged by their fellows in terms of their observance of this yardstick.

The standard language furthermore serves as a frame of reference for the manifestation of the esthetic function in language,[12] which by the Prague School is defined as the property of speech forms to attract attention primarily to themselves rather than to the message they convey. The esthetic function so conceived appears not only in literature and poetry, but also in humor, advertising, and any conspicuous linguistic usage in general. In a standard language community, routine standard usage is the culturally expected, and deviations from this usage have esthetic

[9] *El Paraguay y su Ciudadanía, América* (Buenos Aires), May-June, 1954.

[10] *El Solar Guaraní* (n. p., 1947).

[11] *Op. cit.*, fn. 10.

[12] Jan Mukařovský, *Jazyk spisovný a jazyk básnický* [Standard Language and Poetic Language], fn. 2, pp. 123 ff., transl., *op. cit.*, fn. 2, pp. 19 ff.

function in the above sense, since their cultural unexpectedness attracts attention irrespective of content. Thus the standard language is a frame of reference for the esthetic function.

In the case of Guaraní, the desirability of a frame of reference for correct speech is strongly felt, but the frame-of-reference function in this regard exists as yet only potentially.

The situation with regard to the esthetic frame-of-reference function is not clear-cut at all. On the one hand, Paraguayans claim that Guaraní is "marvelous for poetry and humor", which would indicate a strong occurrence of the esthetic function. On the other hand, whether this esthetic function manifests itself against the background of the incipient codified norm, against the background of informal folk usage, or even against the background of Spanish, is as yet an open question.

The only known factor in this problem is that present-day Guaraní poetry, of which there is a good deal, follows a European rather than a folkloric Indian esthetic canon as to its form, although the motifs are often aboriginal folkloric.

3. *Attitudes towards a Standard Language.* – The functions of a standard language discussed above give rise to a set of cultural attitudes towards the standard: the unifying and separatist functions lead to an attitude of language loyalty, the prestige function arouses an attitude of pride, and the frame-of-reference function brings about an attitude of awareness of the norm.

Language loyalty and pride are closely similar positive attitudes; we differentiate between them by assigning the intellectual and nationalistic attitudes to language loyalty, and the personal emotional attachments to pride.

3.1. *Language Loyalty.* This is the name given by Uriel Weinreich [13] to the desire of a speech community to retain its language and, if necessary, to defend it against foreign encroachment. Although language loyalty may be given to a form of folk speech, it becomes highly organized and articulate when it is given to a standard language, especially one that has not yet become sufficiently stabilized and generally recognized. Then language loyalty commonly manifests itself in attempts to justify the incipient standard language and to prove its worth.

This is dramatically true in Paraguay, as illustrated by Guillermo Tell Bertoni's comments quoted by Robustiano Vera in "La Defensa de la Lengua Guaraní": "La rica lengua del Paraguay puede disputar un puesto entre las lenguas cultas y dignas de un país civilizado." [14] Guaraní is worthy of preservation and improvement because, as Justo Pastor

[13] *Op. cit.*, fn. 3, pp. 99 ff.

[14] *Paraguay en Marcha*, vol. II, núm. 13 (January, 1949).

Benítez says, "el guaraní tiene tradición viva", it expresses "toda la gama del alma de una raza que vivía en contacto íntimo con la naturaleza".[15] Robustiano Vera attempts to prove the worth of Guaraní by attributing a high-prestige ancestry to it: "Hay muchas voces guaraníes que no solo son analógas, sino idénticas a sus similares egipcia, griega, y sanscrita ... gracias a la filología comparada ... quizás hallemos una primitiva lengua hablada por nuestra especie en una edad ignota." [16] Eloy Farina Nuñez in "El Idioma Guaraní" [17] sees the value of Guaraní in the understanding which its aboriginal character gives us of ancient cultures, including the Greek, and "un instrumento que, como el guaraní, en vez de alejarnos, nos aproxima más de la intimidad de la cultura helénica, hasta ponernos en contacto con el misterio de sus mitos y el milagro de su sensibilidad poética, bien merece la atención de los estudiosos del Nuevo Mundo".

Guaraní is, however, not merely worthy of improvement but capable of it. In Moisés S. Bertoni's words, "es un sistema filológico más único que raro, que posee en potencialidad miles de palabras jamás consignadas en ningún léxico, y probabilidades infinitas de formar cuantas se necesitan, aún para expresar lo que jamás se ha expresado, y siempre de una manera tan preciosa y clara que todos han de comprender".[18]

Throughout our interviews with Paraguayans runs a current of appreciation and love for Guaraní. They love to speak Guaraní because, as one informant put it, "uno se siente más dueño de sí mismo", or as another put it, "one has the feeling of having *said* something".

Guaraní finally plays an important part as an ingredient in Paraguayan patriotism. According to our informants, Paraguayan troops during the Chaco War, who would have reacted lethargically to Spanish commands, obeyed commands in Guaraní with enthusiasm and contempt for death.

3.2. *Pride.* As in the case of language loyalty, the possession of a form of folk speech as well as that of a standard language may be a source of pride for the speakers. Some positive attitude such as pride is a prerequisite for the desire to develop one's language into a standard. This attitude of pride will usually be focused on one or the other real or alleged property of the language. As with language loyalty, pride is often the more militant, the less recognized the status of one's language is by others.

There is no question but that Paraguayans are proud of having Guaraní. We have already discussed the significance they attribute to it under the prestige function further above.

[15] *Op. cit.*, fn. 14.
[16] *Ibid.*
[17] *Revista del Turismo* (Asunción), May, 1945.
[18] *Op. cit.*, fn. 14.

Only a very small segment of the population, the nouveaux riches of Asunción and some of the immigrants – so our informants tell us – show a contrary attitude: they look down on or are ashamed of Guaraní because it is an Indian language. But even in this group the negative attitude is not always permanent: one of our informants told us that his mother, a German immigrant, did not want him to learn this Indian language. Nevertheless, he could not help learning it, and his adult attitude is one of pleasure and pride in knowing it. It is, he says, not a mere dialect but a real language, and the more educated Paraguayans become, the more they appreciate Guaraní and make a conscious effort to improve their command of it.

What the Paraguayans appreciate most about Guaraní is that it is "la lengua del corazón". It is better suited, they say, for expressing emotions than Spanish – or, as one informant put it, than any other language he knows.

In Benítez' words, "son verdaderamente asombroses el número como del donaire de sus modismos; giros que hablan de una honda penetración; equivocos que se prestan a una sutil ironía; palabras que resumen todo un estado de alma; suaves y delicadas voces para el amor; expresiones de energía y afirmación como un grito de guerra . . .".[19] The flavor of Guaraní, they feel, is untranslatable – hence, even Paraguayan Spanish is studded with Guaraní loans.

3.3. *Awareness of the Norm.* This is an attitude more specifically limited to a standard language, since it is essentially a positive attitude towards codification. The codified norm is considered good and necessary.

In Guaraní, this attitude manifests itself primarily in a feeling for the desirability of a norm. Hence the high regard of literate Paraguayans for the work of the Academía de Cultura Guaraní which is expected to produce one.

The Paraguayan conception of a desirable norm for Guaraní is highly puristic. This purism is a correlate of their pride in Guaraní which we have discussed above. Many Paraguayans are bilingual and would like to speak both Spanish and Guaraní elegantly; they feel that mixing them, especially introducing unnecessary Spanish loans into Guaraní, is sloppy. We have already mentioned the conscious efforts to expand Guaraní vocabulary from native resources, which can be related to this puristic attitude.

4. Our preliminary survey of the Guaraní situation indicates that the conceptual framework which we have formulated is applicable to it at least in broad outline. As we see it, the descriptive aspect of the problem

[19] *Ibid.*

involves a multitude of questions of detail, some of them technical linguistic, some of them ethno-psychological, and some technical ethnographic. The broader ramifications of the problem – the relation of this linguistic phase of the culture to other phases of present-day urban Paraguayan culture – touch upon the core problem of the interpretation of modern cultures: what is a modern culture, as opposed to an aboriginal one? Even if one rejects the many proposed dichotomies of civilized versus primitive, Kulturvolk versus Naturvolk, or folk versus urban, there remains a strong impressionistic awareness that there is some difference.

We feel that a language-and-culture problem such as ours, which allows the introduction of certain quantitative technical criteria, constitutes a useful point of departure to throw further light upon the folk-urban problem.

From: *Men and Cultures; Selected Papers of the Fifth International Congress of Anthropological and Ethnological Sciences*, ed. A. F. C. Wallace (Philadelphia, Univ. of Pennsylvania Press, 1956), pp. 783-790. Reprinted with permission.

Charles A. Ferguson

MYTHS ABOUT ARABIC

In every speech community attitudes and beliefs are probably current about the language of the community as well as about other languages and language in general. Some of these are true, i.e. correspond very well to objective reality, others are involved with esthetic or religious notions the validity of which cannot be investigated empirically, and still others which purport to deal with facts are partly or wholly false. All these attitudes and beliefs, regardless of their truth-value, will be called here "myths".[1] This paper deals with the set of myths about Arabic current in the Arabic speech community today. The attempt will be made to give a fairly full picture, including all IMPORTANT myths whether true, false, or indeterminate.

Although the Arabic speech community is very large numerically, and spread over a vast EXPANSE spatially, the myths about the language are relatively uniform throughout the community and may safely be summarized without too much regard for local variations.[2] These myths may conveniently be discussed under four headings: the superiority of Arabic,

[1] This use adds one more meaning to an already overburdened technical term in folklore, but it has proved satisfactory in classroom discussions and may be followed until a more apt term is suggested.

[2] The attitudes and beliefs described here have been identified by the author in the course of over fifteen years of professional association with Arabs in connection with language problems. In some instances formal elicitation of reactions to language has been attempted but the bulk of the material is based on informal observation. Obviously this field calls for more precise research techniques which social psychologists or linguists might devise, but the author feels quite convinced that the picture given here will be confirmed, at least in its general outlines, by more carefully conducted investigations.

the classical-colloquial diglossia,[3] dialect rating, and the future of Arabic. These headings are in large part arbitrary, and apart from a few minor points Arabic language myths form a fairly well integrated single body of attitudes and beliefs.

SUPERIORITY OF ARABIC

The notion that one's own language is superior to other languages is quite widespread and may be regarded as a "normal" component of the language myths of any speech community,[4] but there is considerable variety in the attributes of superiority which are maintained by different countries. For example, speakers of a given language may regard their language as the most logical, or the best for singing, or the oldest, or the most highly developed, and so on, while speakers of another language may regard theirs as the most beautiful, or the language of the gods, or the most complicated, or the one easiest to pronounce. Accordingly, it is worthwhile to determine in just what respect Arabs feel their language to be superior.

First of all, Arabs feel that their language is beautiful, making its most direct appeal in the recitation of classical poetry and in formal or semi-formal oratory. There is no mistaking the emotional involvement of both the reciter or speaker and the audience on these occasions. It has been pointed out[5] that Arabs often seem to respond more deeply to the rhythms and phonetic symbolism of the classical language under these conditions than to the semantic content of the poem or the speech. It is easy to exaggerate this point for Arabic, or to underestimate its importance for other languages, but that it has a certain validity cannot be denied. For many purposes even the illiterate peasant will prefer a classical-sounding, highly literary Arabic which he only half understands to a pure conversational Arabic which he understands perfectly. In any case, the beauty of his language is important in the Arab's belief in the superiority of Arabic.[6]

Another feature of the superiority of Arabic which is felt by its native

[3] Since the author has already treated the classical-colloquial diglossia elsewhere, it will not be specifically discussed here. Reference is made to Charles A. Ferguson, "Diglossia", *Word*, Vol. 15, no. 2 (1959).

[4] There are, of course, speech communities which regard their primary language as inferior in important respects to some other language or languages. For example, in many Berber communities the speakers regard the native Berber as inferior to Arabic in most respects.

[5] P. K. Hitti, *History of The Arabs* (London, Macmillan, 1940).

[6] Again, it would be worth investigating the exact nature of the appeal. What particular phonetic features are associated with this attribute of beauty?

speakers, and often by others whose native language is not Arabic (e.g. Persian speakers), is its grammatical symmetry and "logical" structure. A real pride is felt in the root-and-pattern system and especially in the derived forms of the verb with the semantic ramifications of their formal differences, and in the ability of Arabic to provide just the right word for any concept, abstract or concrete. In some Arab circles today there is a feeling of impatience with some of the elaborate grammatical machinery of the classical language, and a lessening of the feeling of lexical adequacy of the language, but the admiration for the very complex but highly regular and symmetrical structure of the derivational system is still strong. The uneducated are relatively inarticulate about this, and it is the educated or half-educated who are most specific. The key word which comes up in their discussion is *ʾištiqāq*, which may be glossed "derivation" in the distinctive meaning which this has for Semitic languages.

Incidentally, another side of this picture usually goes unnoticed. Arabs are aware of the verb system and its related participles and verbal nouns, and are proud of it, but they seem completely unaware of the near chaos of the Arabic noun system. The fact that one cannot tell from the form alone whether a noun is singular, collective, or plural, the fact that one never knows whether a given singular has one plural, several plurals, or none, and if it has more than one whether there will be differences of meaning among them – these facts go unnoticed until an Arab is forced to teach his language to a speaker of another language. Many times after I have listened to an impassioned eulogy of Arabic grammatical logic and symmetry, I have replied with a few comments on the arbitrary "illogical" nature of gender and number categories in the noun and have watched the look of dawning realization of the fact on the Arab, reflecting the coming into awareness of a whole aspect of his language he had never thought about explicitly.[7]

Somewhat related to the preceding is the notion of the vastness and richness of the Arabic lexicon. Early in almost any discussion of the virtues of Arabic the word *wāsiᶜ* appears, which may be glossed "extensive", "spacious". The Arab feels his language has great reservoirs of lexicon, essentially inexhaustible – one can study for years and never approach the limits. That this might be simply the result of the long continued use of Classical Arabic and its constant enrichment from dialect borrowings and new coinages, or worse yet that this vastness of vocabu-

[7] Another feature of arbitrary complexity which can readily be labelled "illogical" is the syntax of the cardinal numbers. The reaction when these points are pushed is one of strong resentment and hostility, comparable to the reaction one gets from attacking at specific points the notion of "logical" structure current in the myths of certain other speech communities (e.g. discussion of irregular verbs in French, or the forms of the cardinal numbers in Sanskrit).

lary, if true, might even be a disadvantage, is not usually considered.[8]

Finally, under the heading of language superiority, certain *religious* aspects of the attitudes toward Arabic must be noted. In many speech communities the speakers feel that their primary language, or a superposed variety of it such as a literary standard, and even a special liturgical dialect or language, has a sacred character which sets it apart from all other languages. This is especially true where the dialect or language in question serves as the vehicle of a revealed body of scripture or as the language of essential rituals or prayers. In the Muslim world linguistic aspects of the Koran have always loomed large – the only miracle to which the Prophet pointed as evidence of the truth of Islam and the genuineness of the revelation was the beauty and effectiveness of the language of the Koran. Accordingly, the language of the Koran has been for some 1200 years a model for the classical language and this identification of Arabic with religion sometimes provides an important obstacle to deliberate efforts to make changes in the contemporary use of the classical language.

It is easy to imagine unanswerable arguments as to the superiority of any sacred language to all others. For example, the argument for Arabic could be phrased along these lines: God is all-knowing, all powerful; He knows and can utilize all languages; He chose Arabic as the vehicle of his ultimate revelations to the world; consequently, the Arabic language must be, in important respects, better than other languages. The arguer is rarely as explicit as this, but the feeling is there, and at least I have never heard a devout Muslim – no matter what his native language – dispute the fact that Arabic is the language of heaven, the means of communication of God and the angels.

It might be expected that Christian and Jewish Arabs would not share this feeling of the superiority of Arabic on religious grounds, and in fact some medieval Christian and Jewish literature in Arabic diverges sharply from the Classical language, showing a much weaker attempt to adhere to the norm of the Koran. But, interestingly enough, modern Christian Arabs at least often have a religious identification in this feeling of superiority of Arabic. In a few cases, I have even had Arabs point to the linguistic excellence of Arabic translations of the Christian Bible as EVIDENCE of the superior quality of this language – and this in spite of the fact that the Christian Bible translations in Arabic are not particularly distinguished by excellence of literary style.

[8] It would be a matter of considerably interest to determine which speech communities find this particularly visible in their language and to see what, if anything, correlates with it in the actual lexical structure of the language.

DIALECT RATING

We have seen that the speaker of Arabic regards the classical language as the best, or in some sense, the only *real* form of his language. What is his attitude toward the particular dialect he speaks vis-à-vis the dialects spoken by other Arabs? The answer is unequivocal – he regards his own dialect as the nearest to classical, the easiest to learn, and the most widely understood of the colloquial dialects.

For centuries, Arabs – or for that matter European scholars of Arabic – have been concerned with the question of which form of spoken Arabic is closest to the classical ideal. Generally two types of answers to this question have been in vogue, either the dialect of the bedouin or some particular tribe is regarded as best or the native dialect of the INVESTIGATOR has been so regarded. In the early centuries of the Muslim era the high regard for bedouin Arabic seems to have been the favorite answer, but as the number of *native* speakers of Arabic increased, the other answer attained the ascendancy. Today there is only a slight ambivalence left as a trace of the bedouin answer. Sedentary Arabs generally feel that their own dialect is best, but on certain occasions or in certain contexts will maintain that the bedouin dialects are better. This high rating of the bedouin dialects, however, is generally only given lip-service and in any actual test it seems clear that the speaker really feels his own dialect is superior.

This attitude is so strong that in testing it with speakers of Arabic from various areas and dialects over a period of fifteen years, I have found only two Arabs (apart from several with linguistic training) who expressly repudiated this notion. As a practical experiment, I have repeatedly attempted to learn the place of origin of an Arab by asking him where the best Arabic is spoken, before I ask him where he comes from. So far, the experiment has always succeeded. The Arab indicates, for example, that the best Arabic is spoken in Damascus; then a few minutes later when asked where he comes from he replies again "Damascus".

The question which dialect is closest to Classical is after all a question subject to empirical investigation. The structure of the various dialects can be examined and compared with that of Classical Arabic. It is difficult to establish appropriate weightings of the different aspects of language – sound, forms, lexicon, and their sub-system – but even with a satisfying qualification system, it would be very difficult to rate Arabic dialects on any linear scale of closeness to Classical. A dialect which is relatively close to Classical in certain respects may be quite far away in others.

As an indication of the strength of this feeling of the Classical quality of one's own dialect, I may cite a panel experience in a seminar on language problems. I had spent about two hours discussing this particular question in some detail with a group of intelligent Arab graduate students in an American university, and I felt that I had made the fundamental point that the rating of dialects was a difficult and not particularly useful task from the linguist's point of view. But at the conclusion of the discussion one of the students remarked "Yes, much of what you said is quite true, but the Arabic spoken in Jordan really *is* closer to Classical than the other dialects." The other students, who came from other parts of the Arab world, simply smiled. I would like to believe that they smiled because they saw the futility of making such judgments with a careful methodology, but I suspect that the smiles were because of the comfortable assurance each still felt that really *his* dialect was the closest to Classical.

THE FUTURE OF ARABIC

Very often a speech community has specific myths connected with the linguistic future of the community. But with the growth of modern nationalism and associated notions of the role of language in the nation, many speech communities have developed explicit sets of attitudes and beliefs about the future status of their language, and the Arab world is a good instance of this.

Speaking in general terms and avoiding the exceptions and modifications which would have to be made in special cases, the nationalist's ideal of the language situation in his country includes the following notions:

1. one national language per nation.
2. one standard form of the language as a norm for both spoken and written purposes, including a standardized orthography (often with preference for a unique national writing system).
3. Lexical and stylistic resources sufficiently developed for use of the national language in all kinds of literature: poetry, newspapers, technical literature in the sciences, etc.

It is clear from an inspection of these ideals that the present state of the Arabic language is far from being in accord with them, and many Arabs, especially among the educated leaders of public opinion, have fairly definite beliefs about future developments in the language. Sometimes these are regarded as *desirable* developments, to be brought about by activist means; at other times they are regarded as more or less inevitable developments. Often there is no clear realization of the difference between the two viewpoints.

Most Arabs seem to feel that the Arabic language of the future is going to be unified, standardized, universal in the Arab world, used for both speaking and writing, and appropriate for all kinds of literature. What is of interest is the nature of this ideal Arabic of the future, the way this new linguistic state will come into being, and the length of time which will suffice to bring it about.

On the first point, there is almost full unanimity. The Arabic of the future will not be a form of COLLOQUIAL Arabic. It will be a "modern", slightly streamlined form of Classical Arabic, purified of all regionalism or of excessive foreign vocubulary, and ignoring some of the subtleties of traditional Arabic grammar.

On the second point, the increase in the education of commoners and in the use of radio and the greatly increased mobility of Arabs are usually felt to be the decisive factors. It is generally felt that educated Arabs are actually beginning to use in communities a form of this future ideal Arabic, and that it will be a process of national development.

On the third point, opinions vary. Some believe it will take about ten years, others have estimates ranging up to fifty years. I have never heard a higher estimate than this.

From: *Languages and Linguistics Monograph Series, Georgetown University,* 12 (1959), pp. 75-82. Reprinted with permission.

Max Weinreich

YIDISHKAYT AND YIDDISH: ON THE IMPACT OF RELIGION ON LANGUAGE IN ASHKENAZIC JEWRY

0. Religion, as used in this paper with reference to Ashkenazic Jewry, is to be understood in its most inclusive sense. Today, there are many aspects of Jewishness that are not necessarily religious. But in traditional Ashkenazic Jewry, it must be firmly kept in mind, religion was no part-time job, no Saturday versus Sunday pastime, as it happens to be in some cases today. It was a way of life and, even more important, an outlook on life. I know of no word that would convey this idea of inclusiveness as cogently as the Yiddish term for Jewishness, *yi'dishkayt*.[1] That's why it was placed in the title.

The first "on" in the subtitle is a deficiency from the viewpoint of style; but it is needed for reasons inherent in the subject matter. The problems involved are complex and the material is vast and largely unexplored; a generalized presentation, encyclopedia style, therefore would have contained too many conjectures to serve a useful purpose. If there were no limitations of space and no apprehension as to the introduction of technicalities, the thing to do would be to submit in support of every statement as much evidence as available, to examine it and, if satisfactory, to interpret it in the light of the preceding discussion. Ultimately this would leave us with a newly acquired body of knowledge and with a set of tested methods as well. Such a procedure, however, was not feasible here. For this reason, only a very limited number of topics will be taken up with due allowance, however, for methodological questions, as they arise, and for the broader implications of the particular issues

[1] The all-embracing character of traditional *yi'dishkayt* is aptly rendered in the English phrase "Judaism as a civilization" coined by Professor Mordecai Kaplan. The term *yi'dishe kultur*, of modern origin, has a somewhat different connotation.

raised. It is hoped that in this way the paper will prove more helpful and that it will not only throw some light upon the specificness of Jewish language development, which is of substantial interest to linguistics, but also contribute to a greater general awareness of the language factor [2] in Jewish cultural history.

In the main, the discussion will be confined to three topics: the formation of the Yiddish language community; the fusion of the various components of Yiddish; and the relative position of Yiddish and Hebrew in traditional Ashkenazic society.

0.1. To make the page look less spotty, Yiddish examples and quotations are usually given in transcription. Present-day standard pronunciation is adhered to, except when attention is called to a different one. This applies to all parts of the language, regardless of the fact that Yiddish orthography retains the traditional spelling of words of Hebrew origin.

In the transcription, letters and letter combinations familiar to English are used as far as possible. *y* stands for the non-syllabic vowel as in *yid* "Jew", *boym* "tree". *ay* (as in *mayn* "my") and *ey* (as in *meynen* "to think") are pronounced approximately as in "shy" and "day", respectively. *sh* appears instead of the more technical symbols of the linguists, with *zh* signifying its voiced counterpart. *kh* stands for the voiceless velar spirant as in *khokhem* "wise man". The stress (ʹ) in polysyllabic words is indicated only if it does not fall on the penult. Length of vowel, if signalized at all, is marked by a colon (:). The symbol < means: derived from.

1. Though fascinating in itself and still unsolved, the question of when and why the name of the Biblical people of *Ashkenaz* became affixed to Germany is beyond the scope of this paper. In our present context we shall take it for granted that around the year 1000, somewhat indistinctly and hesitatingly at first, this designation for Germany made its appearance in Jewish writings and that within a few centuries it had become so firmly entrenched to the exclusion of all competitive terms that Ashkenazim has come to mean not only the German Jews but also their descendants in Eastern Europe and the world over.

1.1. The Ashkenazic branch of the Jewish people is older than its name. For the record, it must be recalled that Jewish settlements existed in Roman times in Cologne and, most probably, in Treves, Ratisbon and other urban settlements of what was later to become Germany; and though no record has come down to us on this matter, it is plausible that some of those "Samaritans" survived there in a state of suspended ani-

[2] I cannot think of an English equivalent for the handy abstract noun *shpra'khikayt* which we use in Yiddish to convey the twofold notion of language creation and actuality.

mation until Jewish individuals and settlements re-emerged in the ninth century. It is from that time on that the stream of tradition has been flowing uninterrupted for eleven hundred years or so.

Ashkenazic Jewry has undergone a most unusual development. Its history up to the Second World War, which ushered in a new and yet inscrutable stage, falls into two periods of almost equal length; if we do not take dates too exactly, the year 1500 may be considered the divide. It is convenient to speak of the western and the eastern periods, in that order. In the first period, our metropolises are in Central Europe: Mayence, Worms, Ratisbon, Prague. Later the center of gravity shifts to Eastern Europe, with Cracow, Lublin, Mezhbizh, Vilna, and Warsaw uppermost in one's mind when Ashkenazic Jewry is thought of. The name has become freed of its territorial connotations; geography, as it were, has been transformed into history.

For several more centuries the Jews of Germany, though lacking first-rate standing in the domain of intellectual achievements, attempted at least to keep pace with the main body centered in the East, until they started their dramatic cultural schism connected with Moses Mendelssohn and his school. Even this crisis, however, failed to block further geographical expansion; witness the Jewish communities in North and South America, Ashkenazic in their overwhelming majority, and the *yishuv* in Palestine before the latest waves of Oriental immigration.

1.2. Nor was the rise in numbers less spectacular. There is no mistaking the fact that in the incipient stage Ashkenazic Jewry hardly filled more than a handful of villages. In 1096, the fatal year of the first Crusade, the two largest communities in the area of the earliest settlement, Mayence and Worms, had a Jewish population of slightly over one thousand each. For 1650, the guesses about the number of the Jews in the world range, according to Ruppin, from one million to a million and three quarters, about equally split between Ashkenazim and Sefardim; the other branches of Jewry were rather negligible in numbers. In 1939, before the great German war of extinction against the Jews was unleashed, there were nearly seventeen million Jews in the world. Ninety-two percent of them were Ashkenazim; Ashkenazic, too, was the overwhelming majority of the leadership in every field of Jewish endeavor.

1.3. An inquiry into the differentials of the Ashkenazic and Sefardic branches of Jewry, both as to their ways of life and their respective place in Jewish culture as a whole, is of paramount importance to a realistic understanding of Jewish history for over one thousand years, and the fact that the topic has been so thoroughly neglected should in itself be made the subject of a study.

Obviously, no sweeping generalizations, even if adorned with some illustrative instances, will do. In order to arrive at valid conclusions, a painstaking analysis of minutiae is necessary, with equal attention paid to things material and spiritual. To mention but a few points of interest: population numbers as far as they can be ascertained or soundly estimated; occupational distribution at different times and in different localities; degree of contact with the non-Jewish surroundings for different strata of the Jewish population; sources of authority derived from antecedent centers (Babylonia vs. Palestine); degree of penetration of Talmudic learning into the great body of the people; impact of instant mass expulsions as against repeated reshuffling over an extended period; differences in the interpretation of religious laws and usages; differences in observance; the particular forms of Hebrew language and literature developed; and so on. As can be seen, only a liberal pooling of resources and methods of different disciplines will do justice to the subject.

Not until the evidence thus obtained is sifted will there be a reliable foundation for a correlative evaluation of the two main branches of the Jewish people.

2. By the same token, one should be on guard against drawing any easy analogies between the languages created by the Ashkenazim and Sefardim, i.e. Yiddish and Dzhudezmo (the name Ladino is incorrect; it should be reserved for an older variety of the written language, as it appears in religious literature). Different languages distribute their resources unequally, not only in their phonemes, morphology, and syntax but also in the domain of meaning: one of them may be capable of subtler distinctions in describing the inner world of thought and feeling while the other will excel in giving a most accurate account of changes in the weather. In what respect, formal or otherwise, do the languages of the Ashkenazim and the Sefardim resemble each other? The more we learn about any of the Jewish languages, the more we shall be able to ask pertinent questions about all of them (6.2-6.3); but actual knowledge can be gained only by thorough studies of each object.

2.1. The sets of differentials characterizing a language, to begin with, are studied as a system existing at the present time or at any given time, without reference to earlier stages in the language or to cultural currents that might have been operative in shaping or changing its course of development. But there is also another way of analysis, which we intend to follow here. Much of what characterizes a language today has its roots in the past, either in actual fact or in inherent potentialities, and concern for these roots is no less legitimate, though experience has made linguists wary of historical procedures applied without sufficient safeguards. In dealing with phonemics or morphology, the search primarily will be for the items from among which the choice was made and the way the system finally took shape out of the confusion that preceded it; extralinguistic (geographical, social, cultural) factors will be held responsible, in the main, for the circumstance that a particular item or combination of items was available as a possible object of selection. Where meaning is involved, extralinguistic factors may be expected to have played a much greater formative rôle, hence the desire to correlate them with the purely linguistic data will be more pronounced.

2.11. How far into the past are we to delve in analyzing a particular linguistic fact? There is no telling in advance. Research seems to show, for instance, that the modern dialectal system of Yiddish was not ready prior to 1600. But *a priori* this fact could not have been ascertained; moreover, subsequent ampler evidence may yet controvert this thesis, and single features that went into the making of the present-day dialects do go back to Old or even Earliest Yiddish.[3]

The rule to remember is that if we are making a study of the Hudson River it would be unwise to start at Yonkers or even at Poughkeepsie.

2.2. The present-day name of Yiddish, meaning "Jewish" in the language itself, does not seem to occur in texts until the fifteenth century. This is as we should expect it; no language is born in the limelight, nor was Yiddish. As long as the bulk of the Yiddish-speaking group dwelt among German speakers, Yiddish was considered just another variety of German, and in the Middle Ages, as is well known, German as a whole, like any folk language, did not enjoy any particular prestige. Ashkenazic writers in Hebrew refer to Yiddish as *leshonenu* "our language" or, if they become more specific, as *loshn a' shkenaz* "the language of Germany". In Yiddish itself, *taytsh* was the current name; it still lives in expressions like *tay'tsh-khumesh* "the Yiddish (version of the) Pentateuch", *fartaytshn* "to translate into Yiddish, to explain", *vos taytsh*? "what does it mean?", *staytsh*! "how is that! just think!"

Experience amply shows, however, that no linguistic inferences can be drawn offhand from the way a form of speech is designated by the group itself or by its neighbors. The fact that a separate name for a language becomes fixed is more often than not due to factors of an extralinguistic nature.[4] Linguistic reasons, applied in retrospect, call for the extension of the present-day name of a language over its whole history, regardless of how it was previously called. This has actually happened in the case of most European languages. Likewise, the language of Ashkenazic

[3] See footnote 5.

[4] For Dutch, in spite of its early rise, no other designations than *dietsch, duitsch* "German" were used until the sixteenth century, and the latter, though challenged by *Nederlandsch*, dragged on for two hundred years more. – The name *Ukrainian* completely superseded (*Little*) *Russian* or *Ruthenian* as recently as in our generation. – Provençal and Catalan are similar cases to consider.

Jewry has come to be called Yiddish since its inception, with the customary division into periods.[5]

3. The birthplace of Ashkenazic Jewry and of its language was the territory that extends from the left bank of the Middle Rhine toward the Franco-German language border. Until the fourteenth century, the territory frequently is designated in Jewish sources as *Loter*. This, of course, is but a variant of the name of the king after whom *regnum Lotharii,* or Lotharingia, Lorraine, was named. The kingdom of Lotharingia, though it lasted only a few decades as a political entity, may be said to have been a pivot in general history as well, what with the crucial importance of Franco-German relations to the western world ever since the Verdun treaty of 843. Still, there is significance in the specific Jewish name and it is worth preserving: it indicates that there are specific points in Jewish culture even in fields as neutral as geography. To begin with, the Jews had no scruples about "annexing" to their Loter such cities as Mayence and Worms which had never belonged to Lothair's kingdom. Furthermore, to the Jews this interstitial area was not one of tension, let alone of conflict; it was one of harmony, unshaken by power struggles of any kind.[6]

The Jews who formed the nucleus of Ashkenazic Jewry came to *Loter* from eastern France (*Tsorfas*, as the Jews called it) and, in smaller numbers, from northern Italy.[7] This influx is to be conceived of as a long-lasting process. As far as the Jews of France are concerned, there is direct evidence that they continued coming into Ashkenazic territory until there was no French Jewry any more, i.e., until the expulsion of 1394.

Up to that time, relations between the "old country" and the new were comparable to what was going on between Eastern-European Jews in America and Eastern Europe before the catastrophe of World War II: it was a most fruitful union of give-and-take. As time went on, the breach between *minhag tsorfas* and *minhag loter* (gradually developing into *minhag ashkenaz*) tended to widen, but the two remained infinitely closer

[5] The periodization of Yiddish which I submitted to the Fifth International Congress of Linguists and seems to have gained acceptance speaks of Earliest Yiddish (up to 1250), Old Yiddish (1250-1500), Middle Yiddish (1500-1750), and Modern Yiddish (since 1750). Cf. *Ve Congrès International des Linguistes, Bruxelles. 28 août-2 septembre 1939. Résumés des communications*, 49-51, and my article on Yiddish in *Algemeyne entsiklopedye, Yidn B* (Paris, 1940), 23-90.

[6] There are more examples of "Jewish geography". *Ashkenaz* was shown not to be synonymous with Germany. *Lite* is another case in point; it only roughly coincides with what is known as Lithuania.

[7] This statement is more definite than the ones usually encountered on the subject. I am reserving the proof for a further occasion.

to each other than, for instance, the *minhagim* of Ashkenaz and Sefard.[8] Italy, while more independent, also gravitates toward the northern group.

4. These basic facts of group genealogy were the determinants in the linguistic situation which ensued.

The languages spoken in France and Italy at the time Loter was "colonized" by the Jews were agglomerations of local Romance dialects now designated Old French and Old Italian. The varieties of Romance that the Jewish newcomers brought along (see 4.1) were one component that went into the formation of nascent Yiddish. Hebrew was another: though it had not been a spoken language for many centuries, it was the language of the sacred texts and of communion with God. The third component that entered the fusion was German of a local variety, or varieties, that the Jews encountered in the places of their new settlement. As far as raw material goes, this was the main component.

4.1. Neither in France nor in Italy was the Romance-based speech of the Jews identical with that of their non-Jewish surroundings. Hence, to avoid lengthy descriptions or misconceptions, separate terms are preferable for the "Judaized" versions of the two Romance languages in question. *Loez* being the customary designation of Romance among the Jews of the Middle Ages, I propose the terms *Western Loez* with French as its non-Jewish stock, and *Southern Loez* for its Italian counterpart. The characteristics of these two linguistic formations are but partly manifest; but their existence is beyond doubt.

4.2. The conditions of the Hebrew component are only seemingly less complex. In a sense, the English term *Hebrew* is a misnomer in our context, suggesting as it does either the language of the Bible or the new Hebrew revived before our very eyes. What traditional Jewry was concerned with was *loshn koydesh* "the sacred language" (originally: "the language of sacredness"), in which Biblical and Mishnaic Hebrew, Talmudic Aramaic, the post-Talmudic amalgamation of Hebrew and Aramaic all had converged into one linguistic entity. Perhaps, "Rabbinic Hebrew" would be the right designation; we shall omit, however, the qualifying adjective for the sake of brevity.

The Hebrew language, then, has a history. This history, however, has been studied but little for that crucial period between the completion of the Talmud and the rebirth in the nineteenth century, and as far as I can see, research has been confined chiefly to a study of the medieval grammarians who, incidentally, in the main belong to the Sefardic

8 The specialist in the field who would submit those resemblances and differences to a systematic scrutiny could be assured of the lasting gratitude of every student of Jewish culture.

group. Little has been produced by way of elucidating the antecedents and early phases of the Ashkenazic version of Hebrew, in its phonic as well as in its morphological, syntactical, and lexicological aspects. Only in part can the barrenness of the sources be blamed for this lack of scholarly interest. The problems remain and it may well be that further research into the history of Yiddish will provide many a hint to the students of post-Biblical Hebrew.

4.3. Amazingly, the German linguistic stock that the Jewish newcomers to Loter were exposed to and which they partly acquired is not so easy to identify either. This in spite of the fact that the scientific study of German has been conducted for well over a century. True, it is highly convenient to reach to the pigeonholes of Old High German (750-1100) and Middle High German (1100-1500), and the findings of German dialectology are, in a sense, even more instructive in the study of the early stages of Yiddish. Still, as soon as we get down to tasks of immediate significance, it turns out that much less has been found out about the realities of medieval German than we need for our purposes. Much more clarity will have to be achieved before the available material is put to proper use.

Suffice it to stress here one fundamental fact, never to be lost sight of and yet so often forgotten. It was not through study or through reading that the Jews got acquainted with the language of their new surroundings.[9] Whatever they took over, whole or modified, had to be acquired by oral contact, and by oral contact only. This compels us to ask about the kind of German that the Jews found in Loter not only with regard to period and region – intricate questions in themselves – but also with regard to its social level. A language without social dialects is hardly imaginable at all, but certainly there were conspicuous distinctions within language communities as thoroughly stratified as those of medieval Central Europe. With whom, then, were the main contacts of the incoming Jews? It was neither with the knights nor with the serfs. It is the language of the lower and middle classes of the urban settlements that the Jews were mainly exposed to. But the language of these strata is but

[9] Even if there had been in the Middle Ages a German literature in the modern sense of the word the Jews would have been unable to read it. The Latin alphabet was practically unknown among them and its very name in the Hebrew and Yiddish of the period, *galkhes*, reveals the reason; literally, the word signifies something belonging to the *galokhim* "the tonsured ones", i.e., the Catholic priests. The barrier between the alphabets, then, just as between the languages was of a religious nature (see 5.1), and until the emancipation the Jewish alphabet was practically the only one the Jews knew and used, including the signing of official (non-Jewish) documents. Even the German Jews who in the nineteenth century abandoned Yiddish for German continued well into the sixties and seventies to write their German in Jewish characters.

imperfectly and ambiguously represented in Middle High German grammars and dictionaries. To add to the difficulties, the critical editions upon which the grammars and dictionaries chiefly rest, differ materially from the actual texts they are presumed to reflect. This striving at uniformity can be explained in terms of the history of philology and unquestionably has its advantages, but not for our comparative purposes: we are offered carefully trimmed garden trees where we would welcome the thick foliage of a natural forest.

Because of the denatured character of what is known as "Middle High German" and the necessity of probing the Old High German period as well, strict adherence to the terms coined by German historical grammar is frequently misleading when the history of Yiddish is concerned. I believe that, on the whole, the less formalized term "Medieval German" is to be preferred in our context.

4.4. To have all the facts on the composition of the language assembled it must be added that with the eastward movement of Ashkenaz, a Slavic component also made its appearance and with the passage of time became rather potent; its earliest trace in vocabulary seems to be that untranslatable particle *nebekh* which as early as in the Old Yiddish period appears in Western Yiddish texts. And it is only now that the stage is set for examining what is most essential for understanding the specificness of the new language: namely, the material changes which all components experienced through reciprocal influences and through new phenomena that arose in, or even as the result of, the fusion.

5. What was the prime mover in all the developments that we have been dealing with so far? It is well known that tiny numbers of immigrants transplanted into a new environment tend to lose their identity within a few generations – unless there is a counterforce to offset the weight of sheer numbers and to maintain separateness.

The most commonly offered explanation for the separateness in our case is "ghetto". But this trite term is both meaningless, since it has so many meanings, and deceptive, since it feigns knowledge precisely where the inquiry should begin.[10] After all, the Jews who entered Loter, a terri-

[10] Little is gained by distinguishing between "compulsory" and "voluntary" ghetto because there is still the implication – highly questionable, to say the least, in our case — that it was a culture of higher rank from which the minority was excluded or withdrew. It is significant that in Yiddish, until the days of Hitler, *geto* was a foreign-sounding learned word, never much in vogue. The pre-emancipation restricted living quarters in the cities were invariably referred to, in a neutral way, as *yidishe gas*, sometimes simply *di gas* "the Jewish street, the street", and the idiom *af der yidisher gas* (literally: "in the Jewish street") to this very day conveys the idea: among Jews. I submit that the term ghetto is to be reserved for the Italian cities where it originated and for the German-made ghettos of Wolrd War II. Cf. my *Hitler's Professors* (New York, 1946), 92-4.

tory where German dialects were spoken, were sufficiently open to outside influences to adopt, albeit in a modified form, the speech of their new environment; on the other hand, Yiddish did not fail to leave traces on the vernacular of the environment either. Innumerable items such as names, legends, customs, folk beliefs made their way to and fro. Still, the Jews did not dissolve in that environment. This relative aloofness versus relative openness of traditional Ashkenazic society should be studied with much more devotion to detail and much more exactness in definition of concepts than has been done hitherto.[11]

5.1. What erected the linguistic barriers in Loter and made them stand was the difference between Jewish and non-Jewish culture; in turn, the cultures of the two communities were characterized by the disparate religions. Yiddish came into being as the linguistic vehicle of a community set apart from the outside world by its religion. Be it stressed again that we refer to a period in which religion was supreme; even cultural patterns that our age would tend to explain in economic or social categories at that time were conceived of as manifestations of religion and their exposition was couched in religious terms. It was shown above how slowly people in the past became conscious of the distinctive subtleties of their languages; it is therefore significant that what seems to be, in the fifteenth century, the first explicit statement by a naive observer on the difference in language between Jews and Germans concerns the use of religious terms.[12] In the sixteenth century and later both Jewish and non-Jewish sources put "Jewish German" in opposition to "Christian German".

But what about the obvious fact that Yiddish never was an outlet for religious expression only, that in recent centuries it frequently has been a medium of secular endeavors and that, as any other language, it can be used even in antireligious causes? The seeming contradiction resolves itself as soon as we recall the rule established by social science that forces may persist and continue operating even after the causes for their coming into being have partly or completely ceased to exist. Incidentally, religion as a formative agent of Ashkenazic culture by no means implies rigidity at any period; within mandatory limits, allowance was made from the very outset for all kinds of variations. It is this flexibility in the initial master pattern, I believe, which enabled Ashkenazic Jewry successfully to incorporate into the whole every new pattern as it devel-

[11] Some principles of research on this basic problem are outlined in my paper: "Ashkenaz: di yidish-tkufe in der yidisher geshikhte" [Ashkenaz: the Yiddish Era in Jewish History], read before the twenty-fifth annual conference of the Yiddish Scientific Institute and published in *Yivo-Bleter*, 35 (1951), 7-17.

[12] Isserlin (ca. 1390-1460), פסקים וכתבים, § 67 (Venice, 1519).

oped, and the language followed suit by constantly adapting and re-adapting itself to new needs of the community or any of its parts.[13]

6. Is this impact of religion on language an exclusive feature of Ashkenazic Jewry? Not at all. Is it specific in the case of Yiddish? Decidedly so.

The Polish Jewish scholar Matthias Mieses, a victim of the German war against the Jews, is to be credited with stressing the rôle of religion as a major language-forming factor among the Jews and correlating Jewish experience in this respect with analogous developments in most different societies.[14] To an English speaker, the consistent use of *thee* and *thine* for "you" and "yours" by the Quakers is familiar. Differences are reported to be much more pronounced between Greek Orthodox and Catholic Rumanians, between Greek Orthodox and Mohammedan Serbs, and in other comparable groups. Each of these variations in religion may be said to occasion some separateness in culture which, in turn, leaves its marks in the form of language differences.

Minimized or ignored when they were first so eloquently expounded, Mieses' ideas on the matter, as a whole, are no object of controversy any more. They fully agree with the broader theory of "special languages" that was developed by Arnold van Gennep about the same time.[15] Any group, it is now commonly accepted, tends to develop a linguistic "style" of its own; witness professional groupings (such as artisans, college students or, for that matter, thieves), in which vocabulary differences and other specific speech features are likely to arise. Small wonder then that the erection of religious barriers leads to the same consequences.[16]

6.1. A shift in emphasis, however, is needed to put Mieses' fertile ideas in their proper perspective. He does not distinguish between linguistic styles and distinct languages. While the Quakers exhibit a form of Christianity divergent from the prevalent types, their belief does not, so it seems, essentially differ from that of other Christian bodies. Their

[13] Cf. the discussion in my paper quoted in footnote 11.

[14] Matthias Mieses, *Die Entstehungsursache der jüdischen Dialekte* (Wien, 1915). It should be read together with Leo Spitzer's review in *Literaturblatt für germanische und romanische Philologie*, 42 (1921), 81-94, which also discusses K. Vossler's paper "Sprache und Religion", *Neuere Sprachen*, 28 (1920), 97-120

[15] A. van Gennep, "Essai d'une théorie des langues spéciales", *Revue des Études ethnographiques et sociologiques*, 1 (1908), 327-37. Van Gennep's ideas, adopted and developed by J. Vendryes, *La langage* (Paris, 1921), served as a point of departure for the penetrating research into Christian Latin which is discussed below.

[16] Some scholars even ascribe an exceptional power to religion. To quote Leo Spitzer: "We must acquiesce in the fact that transcendental ideas and wishes move the human mind — and, consequently, language — more vehemently than physical needs."

wide contacts with non-members may be another reason for the fact that their separateness is rather limited. Thus, in the linguistic field the difference in style is easily recognizable, but also easily surmountable.

The barriers between different denominations within the Rumanian or Serbian speech communities are higher, but still we deal with differences in language, not with different languages. The difficulty in providing a set of final criteria for a language may be as great as in establishing what constitutes "a people". But criteria have been agreed upon: transfer to a different ethnic group; decisive separation in territory; material changes in structure and cultural significance; adherence to different standard languages, and so on. Admittedly, there may be borderline cases, but an example from the Jewish field will show the point. There is definitely something that may be called Khasidic Yiddish. *Rebe* "Khasidic rabbi", *gabe* "the rebe's secretary", *hoyf* "the rebe's residence", *praven tish* "to maintain one's own position as a rebe", *shiraim* "the leavings of the rebe's meals", *kvitl* "written petition submitted to the rebe", *pidyen* "redemption money given to the rebe for his advice or blessing", *tikn* "purification of a sinful soul",[17] etc., belong to the mode of expression peculiar to the Khasidim; in Misnagdic speech, except with reference to Khasidim, the words mean different things or do not appear. On the other hand, *kat* "the (Khasidic) faction", *vayse khevre* "the scamps", literally "the fellows in white" were opprobrious names thrown by the Misnagdim at their opponents. But nobody would think of elevating this divergency in language to the degree of separateness of language.

6.2. Theoretically, with the passage of time any linguistic style can develop into a distinct language. But this potentiality is contingent upon certain conditions which materialize only every now and then. The more autonomous the community – and what counts is not how different it is but how different it *feels*[18] – and the longer the barriers are maintained, the greater the chances that a distinct language will come into being.

The analogies to Catholic Rumanian, Protestant French, etc., though illuminating as to details, therefore do not carry us far enough. In looking for help in methodology we might rather turn to the research into

[17] Then, by reinterpretation, "the brandy drunk on the anniversary of a person's death" and, finally, somewhat humorously, "brandy" pure and simple.

[18] There is much to learn from the sentences in which Tertullian, around the beginning of the third century, stressed the distance between the Christians and the pagans (*ethnici*) in spite of their physical closeness: "*Licet convivere cum ethnicis, commori non licet. . . . Convivamus cum omnibus; colaetemur ex communione naturae, non superstitionis. Pari anima sumus, non disciplina, compossessores mundi, non erroris.*" Compressed into a Yiddish formula, it is the difference between experiencing *di' velt* "this world" and *ye'ne velt* "that world, the world to come", definite emphasis being placed on the latter and its projections into earthly life.

those other Jewish languages to which Mieses' book is directly devoted. Care should be exercised in establishing equations since all these languages,[19] as compared with Yiddish, have much smaller numbers of speakers and are infinitely more limited in their literary use; but on the other hand, the paucity of material may make it easier to detect their specificness.

The general principle underlying a Jewish language (such as Judeo-Greek, Judeo-Italian, etc., as these linguistic entities are inadequately dubbed) may be said to be the presence of some non-Jewish "raw material" which has been permeated with a "Jewish spirit". As the raw material in the different cases is drawn from the most divergent sources: Persian in more than one variety, Arabic, Slavic,[20] Greek, several Romance languages, Teutonic, Jewish interlinguistics should prove the comparativist's delight. He would probably start with the hypothesis that, at least as compared with the linguistic material, the "Jewishness" of the languages involved was a more or less constant factor and then proceed to look for a uniform practice, if any, in the treatment of the raw material, in the application of "Judaizing" devices to structure, in the introduction of identical imagery ultimately stemming from the Jewish background, and so on. It is hard to overestimate the benefit that the student of Yiddish may derive from such comparative research.

6.3. Alas, the form "may" had to be used since there is not much at present to lead us beyond the general statement of aims. There are studies, varying in number, on almost any Jewish language, some of them highly commendable, such as Blondheim's or Spitzer's. But most of them lack perspective and the results of strenuous efforts are therefore often disproportionately small.

For the sake of illustration, let us take the case of Yevanic.[21] The Hellenization of the Jews set in as early as in the days of Alexander the Great and a kind of transformed Greek (whatever the degree and thoroughness of transformation) has been used by a portion of the Jewish people ever since. With the amount of knowledge accumulated on the history of Greek in general, on the Koine of the Hellenistic period,

[19] To simplify the argument, Hebrew and Aramaic are excluded from the discussion in this paragraph. One has become so accustomed to the fact of their being Jewish that little thought is given to the important question of how they have come to be it.

[20] In the case of medieval *leshon kna'an*, on which Professor Roman Jakobson of Harvard has been preparing an extensive study.

[21] A term proposed by Solomon A. Birnbaum in *Slavonic and East European Review*, 29 (1951), 420-43, for what is usually called "Judeo-Greek". Borrowed from Hebrew sources, the term emphasizes the differences from Greek rather than the resemblance to it; I wonder whether this is also the name, or one of the names, of the language in the language itself.

on the Septuagint, etc., we should expect to find here an excellent model for research into the younger Jewish languages. The few studies on Yevanic available, however, are haphazard and narrow. The questions of historic continuity, of dialectal diversity, of the degree to which the recorded texts reflect the spoken language of the period, of the existence of a semisacred variant used in the translations of the sacred writings, of the peculiar significance of each component, of the degree of fusion of the components, etc., have not even been posed. How, then, was it possible to give this casual enumeration of problems? Those are problems we are confronted with when dealing with Yiddish. And so it dawns upon us that it was a mistake on our part to look for comfort to quarters that could offer us but little. True, it is necessary to study the different Jewish languages along definite lines in order to achieve a maximum of comparability. But it is rather the insight gained from research into Yiddish, inadequate as it still is if measured by our ambitions, that opens new vistas of meaningful research into other Jewish languages, and not the other way around.

7. Greater help in recognizing our problems and improving our methods, therefore, can presently be expected from a field that is much more remote in its subject matter and that Mieses barely mentioned; it has the advantage of having been studied rather thoroughly. We are referring to the penetration of Christianity to pagan peoples and the linguistic effects that came in its wake. Among the languages so affected different types are discernible and each of them offers some clues for profitable comparison, as for instance the languages of Western and Central Europe, Old Slavic, the African or Australian languages of today. But here we shall limit ourselves to a few observations on "how Latin was baptized", as Christine Mohrmann puts it.

Christian (or ecclesiastical, as it was previously called) Latin, of course, has been the object of incisive research for decades. But it was church historians, not linguists, who were the pioneers in the field; this resulted in what we may call an atomistic approach to the problem. It was only after the Dutch school of Schrijnen, now best represented by Christine Mohrmann at Nijmegen, had taken over that new light was thrown on the subject. Where earlier scholars used to search in the main for "Christian words" introduced by the adherents of the new religion, Schrijnen insists upon the concept of a "special language", i.e. "a coherent system of differentiations of lexicological, semantic, morphological, syntactical, and even metrical nature".[22]

We shall see the significance of this approach for our subject in subse-

[22] Jos. Schrijnen, "Le latin chrétien devenu langue commune", *Collectanea Schrijnen* (Nijmegen, 1939), 335-56.

quent paragraphs. Still, to caution against taking analogies for identity, let us stress right here two essential differences.

7.1. In the case of Christian versus pagan Latin, there is a community in a given territory (T) speaking a given language (L), which is being attacked by a new religion (R); the result is the split of the language, formerly uniform in this respect, into two variants: pagan Latin (L_1), still representing the main trunk, and Christian Latin (L_2). Reduced to a formula, it looks like this:

$$R \rightarrow (TL) \begin{matrix} \rightarrow L_1 \\ \searrow L_2 \end{matrix}$$

With the Yiddish language (L), it did not work that way. Here two communities speaking differing vernaculars, which we designated as Western Loez (L_1) and Southern Loez (L_2), but adhering to the same religion (R) and possessing a common sacred language, Hebrew (L_3), came into a new territory and there created a new language, in which the raw material employed was chiefly German (L_4). The formula, therefore, is quite different: [23]

$$\begin{matrix} (L_1RL_3) \rightarrow \\ (L_2RL_3) \nearrow \end{matrix} (TL_4) \rightarrow L$$

This was a difference concerning the beginnings; the second reservation to be borne in mind concerns the end product. The cleavage between pagan and Christian Latin was only temporary. In the second century, Greek was still the official language of the Church even in the city of Rome. Three hundred years later there was no pagan Latin left; the Christians had become the sole carriers of a Latin which may be described as a compromise between the pagan and the Christian variants. Yiddish, on the contrary, had parted with German for good and the apartness became more and more marked as the centuries went by.

8. If there were today a chance to interview a *bokher* in Reb Gershom Meor Hagola's *yeshive* in Mayence in the first half of the eleventh century about linguistic conditions in his community, he would probably begin by insisting that the Jews spoke the same language as their non-Jewish environment. Pressed a bit further he might concede that there

[23] The usefulness of such symbolization need not be overestimated, but it does help to visualize different ways in which languages emerge. Incidentally, the formula for Yiddish does not necessarily cover all Jewish languages and by confronting their formulas a serviceable typology of Jewish languages, including Hebrew and Aramaic, can be worked out.

were some words used by the Jews exclusively, such as *toyre* "Tora", *mitsve* "commandment, good deed", *tfile* "prayer".

Would all those differentiating words be of Hebrew origin? The informant's first reaction would certainly be yes. Then he might yield a bit of ground by admitting that some Loez words such as *orn* "to pray" or *bentshn* "to bless" had also crept in. The interviewer might then point his finger at such expressions as *yi'dishn* "to circumcise", *rey'nikayt* "scroll of the Tora", *o'pgisn ne'gl-vaser* "to perform the (ritual) washing of one's hands in the morning", etc., which could hardly be considered German, because they had been coined by the Jewish group for its exclusive utterly Jewish needs. This might leave our *yeshi've-bokher* with a somewhat shattered belief in the "purely German" character of his language. But, unaffected as he is likely to be by the linguistic thinking of the mid-twentieth century, he might still claim to be essentially in the right: after all, only "some elements" had been traced; in his opinion, they did not alter his language as a whole. Were he endowed with the gift of citing later authorities, he could invoke Zunz, the greatest of them all, who had asserted that as late as in the sixteenth century the Jews, even those in Poland, "spoke a fairly correct German".

8.1. Zunz's statement just referred to [24] can be summarized as follows. There are four sets of Judaizing phenomena distinguishing "the German language customary among the Jews":

(a) Hebrew words for concepts concerning Judaism (*brokhe* "blessing", *yontev* "holiday"), Jewish life (*balebo's* "owner of a house, head of a household"), Jewish studies (*a'derabe* "on the contrary", *tomer* "if, maybe"), various aspects of everyday life (*akhile* "eating", *nekome* "revenge"); also as cryptic terms (*meshumed* "convert to Christianity", *bilbl* "frame-up").

(b) Combinations of Hebrew and German elements in four ways: the auxiliary verb *zayn* "to be" attached to Hebrew participles (*matsl zayn* "to rescue", *mekane zayn* "to envy"); non-Hebrew endings and prefixes added to Hebrew stems (*farkhi'deshn* "to amaze", *kho'metsdik* "having the qualities of leaven"); words compounded (*ho'lekra:sh* "the solemn act of naming the child"); abbreviations made into words (*rat*<*Ray'khs-Toler* "rix-dollar").

(c) Use of "uncustomary or faulty" German with reference to Jewish customs (*lernen* "to study", *oy'frufn* "to call up to the reading of the Law") and to Jewish peculiarities of all kinds (*shul* "synagogue", *yi'dishn*

[24] L. Zunz, *Die gottesdienstlichen Vorträge der Juden* (Berlin, 1832), 438-41. – In the summary, Zunz's own words are used as far as possible; but the number of examples has been reduced and the transcription is the one used in this paper throughout.

"to circumcise"); use of a considerable number of archaisms and provincialisms (*gevi'ner(i)n* "woman lying in", *haynt* "today").

(d) Use of words of foreign origin (*bentshn* "to bless", *milgroym* "pomegranate").

8.2. Errors of detail and crudeness of classification notwithstanding, Zunz's statement, although one hundred and twenty years old, is actually still to be admired for its compactness and discernment. It does take cognizance of the language-forming influence of religious philosophy, study, prayers, and ritual practices; it does quote terms pertaining to the autonomous Jewish communal organization which included the judiciary, training of the young, and social welfare in the widest sense.[25] It even shows that the differences reach into the domains of word formation and inflection and at least in passing mentions that "here and there" there was a difference in pronunciation.

In short, Zunz's well-known merits are here, too, displayed in full. But even he could not go beyond the limits set by the conceptual framework of his time. His, too, was the atomistic approach; he was looking only for single features of the Jewish speech form. Today, as has been alluded, linguists and social scientists are primarily concerned with the structure of a language as a whole. Consequently, when languages are compared with each other or the emergence of a new one is studied, interest centers not in lists of single items but rather in the "coherent system of differentiations", as Schrijnen put it.

8.3. Let us dwell for an instant upon that aspect of language which did not engage Zunz's attention and which is now a cornerstone of any linguistic analysis: the phonemic system. There can be no doubt that the variants of Loez which the Jews brought into Loter were characterized by peculiar speech habits. These inevitably were carried over into the new medium; as a matter of fact, there are phonic phenomena in later and even in contemporary Yiddish that go back to the pre-Yiddish stage. Thus our hypothetical Mayence *yeshi've-bokher* of the eleventh century, though convinced he spoke just the local variety of German, by his very pronunciation betrayed himself as a "foreigner" to the non-Jews; conversely, a non-Jew was easily identifiable as such even if he managed to intersperse his German with some "Jewish" words. At this distance, with the sources scanty and the spelling, as might be expected, far from accurate and consistent, the phonemics of the older stages of

[25] Curiously (and this refers not only to Zunz's listings but also to actual Jewish vocabulary) there are surprisingly few specific terms for what is assumed to have been the main occupation of the Jews in the period studied, i.e., money lending. This tends to prove that it is not so much the facts of life as such that affect language as the amount of psychic energy vested in them; in other words, what shapes language is not the occupation of its speakers but the preoccupation of their minds.

Yiddish is hard to detect; this also goes for the intonation.[26] But there are methods and techniques of overcoming the difficulties at least in part.

8.4. As the analysis proceeds, the formula of "German plus some additions" becomes even less tenable. We discover that an interpenetration of the different components took place in the language as a whole with the resultants afterwards undergoing an internal development of their own.

In many cases we can make use of Zunz's examples. Thus, in word formation, there are types like *mekane zayn* "to envy" (participle of Hebrew origin and auxiliary of German origin), *farkhi'deshn* "to amaze" (stem of Hebrew origin, prefix and ending of German origin), *ey'zlte* "she-ass" (stem of German origin, suffix of Hebrew – in the sense agreed upon in 4.3; more precisely, of Aramaic – origin), *kho'metsdik* "having the properties of leaven" (stem of Hebrew, suffix of German origin).[27] Compound nouns, needless to say, are formed freely regardless of the language stock of the parts and frequently in defiance of the rules governing compounding in the stock languages even if both parts are of the same stock; cf. *yeshi've-bokher* "yeshiva student", *da'm-soy'ne* "deadly enemy". In morphology, the type *pe'nimer* "faces" (plural of *ponim*, with the stem of Hebrew origin, to which umlaut and the ending *-er* of German origin are applied) stands against *bekhers* "goblets" (in which a suffix of Loez origin is added to a word of German origin) or *lates* "laths, lattice" (the stem of German and *-s* as the plural ending of nouns in *-e*, of Hebrew origin). The closer to our time, the more formants of different origin go into the fusion and the less dissoluble their union.

9. The preceding paragraph is not to be construed as an inventory: only specimens of fusion phenomena were offered.[28] A few more examples

[26] Presumably, it had something in common with what is presently called the *gemore-nign*. Other people's observations, I believe, will bear out my own that even after several generations of assimilation Westernized Jews sometimes, to their own dismay, relapse into so-called "Jewish intonation", particularly in affective states of mind. This fact, if a fact it be, can be explained along orthodox social-psychology lines, without having recourse to heredity.

[27] To be exact, *-dik* can be called a suffix of German origin only in a restricted sense; as such, it does not appear in German. The series of suffixes *-ik* (cf. German *-ig*), *-dik, -edik, -evdik* has no German parallel in either composition or application and is an excellent example of what was meant by internal development occurring even within the confines of one component.

[28] Syntax, in which fusion and convergence phenomena are prominent, has not been touched upon in the present discussion. – Cf. my paper: "Form Versus Psychic Function in Yiddish, A Study in the 'Spirit of Language' ", *Occident and Orient. Gaster Anniversary Volume* (London, 1936), 532-8.

follow to show what may be called a reinterpretation of formants. This, as will be seen, indicates our crossing into the field of meaning, where vocabulary is going to be our chief concern.[29]

9.1. The word *mefunik* "delicate, fastidious man" can easily be traced back to its Hebrew origin מפונק, of the root פנק. But with the passage of time, the word has been subject to metanalysis (cf. English *an apron* < *a napron, a nickname* < *an ekename*); instead of *me-funik*, it re-emerged as *mefun-(n)ik*, and was thus reassigned to the large group of nouns ending in *-nik* (such as *shlimezalnik, nudnik*, etc.). And now a chain reaction set in. The feminine form of *me-funik* to be expected is *me-funekes* (cf. *meshume'des(te)* "woman converted to Christianity" <*meshumed*), *tsadeykes* "pious woman" <*tsadik*, etc.).[30] But of *mefun-(n)ik* the feminine must be *mefu'n-(n)itse* (like *shlimeza'lnitse, nu'dnitse*), and that is the form actually in use. Further along the same lines, the well-known author Z. Shneour, who certainly knows his Hebrew, in his Yiddish writings rightly uses the adverb *mefu'nedik.*

9.2. *arba kanfes* (ארבע כנפות) "ritual four-cornered garment" literally means in Hebrew "the four corners". Since *arba* "four" appears in Yiddish in several connections, *kanfes* is clearly felt as a plural. The singular in Hebrew is כנף, which should have resulted in Yiddish **konef*, but such a word does not exist in Yiddish. Instead, it is *kanfe* for "one corner of the four-cornered garment". By virtue of its Yiddish pronunciation, *kanfes* was taken to have followed the Yiddish (and exclusively Yiddish) rule: nouns ending in *-e* form their plural in *-s*, and so a reconverted word, *kanfe* <*kanfes*, came into being.

tsitse "one of the tassels of the ritual four-cornered garment" also originated through reconversion from *tsitses*, with the additional peculiarity that the Hebrew etymon (צִיצִית, in Ashkenazic Hebrew pronunciation *tsitsis*) is no plural at all. It is a feminine singular; but in Yiddish, with its tendency for any vowel in unstressed syllables following the stressed one to become *-e*, the form *tsitses* developed, which was conceived of as a plural and led to the creation of a singular in accordance with the Yiddish pattern.

9.3. The noun *shem*, of Hebrew origin (שם), means "name", then "a good name, fame" and also, in some instances, "God's name". The plu-

[29] It is to be kept in mind that formants are no less carriers of meaning. In the English *cows, oxen, -s* and *-en* may be treated as synonyms, whereas *-s* in *the father's, the fathers, he fathers* may be said to be homonyms. Similarly, in *mouse – mice,* where in speech (as opposed to conventional spelling) the change in vowel constitutes the only difference between singular and plural, the vowels carry meaning.

[30] A learned stickler for correctness may go so far as to try that form but it would sound too affected to be acceptable. It is as if a contemporary English speaker would venture "specimina".

ral in Hebrew has the ending ות–, which is not the rule in masculine nouns. Yiddish has the same plural and on paper, since Yiddish keeps the traditional spelling, the Yiddish and Hebrew forms look identical. They are not. In Yiddish, the difference between an open and a closed stressed syllable has been essential for the development of its vowel; therefore, it is *shem* (singular) versus *sheymes* (plural). There is yet another deviation from Hebrew, a more conspicuous one. Stray leaves of a sacred book contain *sheymes* "God's names"; ultimately, such stray leaves themselves, which, traditionally, must not be used for any profane purpose nor even destroyed but must be solemnly buried in the cemetery, have come to be called *sheymes*. But now, in a further bold step, a singular form to denote one such stray leaf was formed, to wit, *sheyme*. Grammatically, the pattern is the same as in the previous cases of *kanfe* or *tsitse*. But something new has entered the picture: *shem*, with its meanings, continues to exist. The Yiddish dictionary now lists two separate nouns, *shem* and *sheyme*, of which the plurals, *sheymes,* just happen to be homonyms.

It is exactly the same with *kos* "cup, goblet". The difference between open and closed syllable produces a phonemic difference between singular and plural which is unknown to Hebrew: (*arba*) *koyses* "(four) cups" stands against (*der ershter*) *kos* "(the first) cup" at the Passover Seder. And there is also the second step. "To take a drink" is *makhn a koyse*. Apparently, for the habitual drinker the plural number is the point of departure; if he happens to consider a singular at all, he reconverts it from the plural. Again, the Yiddish dictionary has two nouns where Hebrew, the source, has only one.

9.4. If the stem vowel of a Yiddish noun is susceptible to umlaut, the umlaut usually does appear in the diminutive forms; *zak* "bag" – *ze'kele, kats* "cat" – *ke'tsele*; *ponim* "face" – *pe'niml, sod* "orchard" – *se'dele*. With regard to more recent words, however, the rule is usually broken: *zak* and *zok* "sock" are identical in their diminutive forms, but *shtot* "city" and *shtat* "state in the U.S." are not; Rhode Island is *a shta'tele*. Of *kart*(*e*) "invitation card" it is *kartl*, but the older "playing card" is *kort* and the diminutive *kertl*. On the basis of this divergence, the long established diminutive of *mantl* "cloak, overcoat" i.e. *me'ntele*, is nowadays reserved exclusively for the "mantlet of the scroll of the Law", whereas *ma'ntele*, the more recent variant, is the only word to denote a small overcoat.[31]

9.5. The Aramaic *knas* "payment of money imposed as punishment" is used in Yiddish with the same meaning, and a Yiddish verb *ka'nsenen* "to impose a fine" was derived from it. But the noun also signifies one

[31] Cf. the split as to meaning between "brethren" and "brothers" in contemporary English.

specific kind of fine, namely, the one imposed in olden days on the party that broke off an engagement. The *knas* to be paid in such contingency used to be stipulated in the engagement contract. Thus, Yiddish acquired a new verb *farknasn* "to betroth", and the terms *farknasn zikh* "to become engaged", *knas-mol* "engagement party" are the normal words even to people to whom the original legal connotations have become obsolete.

9.6. If only to call attention to a consistently neglected field, personal names also must be mentioned as an important reflection of linguistic development; no more than a few examples will be offered. Umlaut in names of Hebrew origin is traceable in *pelte* < *paltiel, shebsl* < *shabse*. Deviation from the non-Ashkenazic pattern can be shown in *nisn* versus *nisim*. Loez relics persist to this day in *bunem* (cf. *Bonhomme*), *shneyer* (cf. *Senior*), *an(t)shl* (cf. *Angelo*). Names such as *iser* (cf. *Israel*), *yente* (cf. *Gentile*), *rive* cf. רבקה have come into existence through a reinterpretation of stem elements as formants. *marem* has become a standing name while to begin with it was nothing more than an abbreviation מהר״ם. *alter*, *alte* are names born out of magic concepts. A conscientious study of Jewish names could fill a book culminating in far-reaching conclusions in the fields of linguistics and cultural history. What a pity that the last (and first!) ambitious attempt in this direction was made by Zunz in 1837, only slightly to be augmented in 1876!

10. The examples under 9.3-9.5, of course, were not chosen at random. Like the preceding ones, they are concerned with formants but, through changes in form peculiar to the language, new words with separate meanings, i.e., word oppositions existing in Yiddish only, were shown to have emerged. This has led us to the interplay of fusion phenomena in vocabulary proper. Here, as already noted in passing, the impact of extralinguistic factors will be greater or at least – one can never be too cautious – more patent than on formants. This is not to say, however, that the task of the student is less difficult in this case. The conceptual counterparts of linguistic items may be easier to identify; but the advantage is offset by the tremendous amount of potential material out of which the actual language system is built through an incessant process of selection.

10.1. Before we pass on to a review of selection phenomena in vocabulary, one vocabulary item will be used as a test case to show in some detail the tangle of meanings and connotations we encounter, with fusion phenomena in formants as additive complications that often have to be reckoned with. We choose the well-known word *shlimazl* "ill luck; unlucky, clumsy fellow".

If we dissect the word the conventional way, we arrive at *shlim* (of

German origin, cf. *schlimm*) plus *mazl* (of Hebrew origin, cf. מזל). As a whole, of course, it is Yiddish even in a technical sense, because it is here that the union of the two components was consummated.[32] But even more important is the frame of reference into which the word belongs.

mazl, to begin with, means "constellation". Old-style Jewish almanacs are still being published in which each of the twelve months is illustrated by the proper sign of the zodiac. The English *ill-starred* is also a reminder of better days for astrology; but in the Jewish sphere the belief in the influence of the stars on human fate has left much stronger linguistic traces. *ma'zltov!* to a contemporary Yiddish speaker is simply "congratulations!", but in its primary meaning it is a supplication for the aid of a good constellation. *dobre-mazl*, with a Slavic ingredient used but rarely on other occasions, means "good fortune".

The usual construction is *er hot shlimazl* "he has bad luck", but *er iz a shlimazl* "he is a (carrier of) bad luck" is also possible, *shlimazl* having been substituted for *shlimezalnik* "unlucky, clumsy, untidy fellow".[33] *harbe eynaim shlimazl in der shisl* "(with) many eyes, (there is) bad luck in the dish", i.e., too many cooks spoil the broth, is a proverb quoted in an eighteenth-century dictionary; *sheker un shlimazl* "lie and ill luck" is a popular saying referring to a pair of unlucky chums.

shlemi'l, the Western Yiddish equivalent for *shlimezalnik*, also belongs here. It is sometimes identified with the Biblical *Shelumiel* (Num. 1 : 6) but there is no reason whatsoever why this fleeting name, with no characteristics attached to its bearer, should have been charged with such significance. No less artificial is the attempt[34] to derive the word from a Hebrew שלא מועיל "(a person) who is not useful". There is no doubt that *shlemi'l*, with jocular leaning upon the Biblical name, was chosen as a gentler substitute in a milieu where *shlimazl* had become too offensive. Eastern Yiddish also has a "tenderized" version of the word in the form *shlimoy'z* (pronounced *shlimo:z*) that appears in the Polish dialect. It rests upon the pun *mazl* as opposed to *ma:zl* "small mouse"; in that dialect, the length of vowels is phonemic.

The sway of the *mazl* concept seems to have been so strong that the saying הכל תלוי במזל ואפילו ספר תורה שבהיכל "everything depends upon

[32] Inasmuch as we find the word in German – *Schlamasse(l), Schlamastik* – or in Polish – *ślamazarny* – it was borrowed from Yiddish. Cf. L. Spitzer, in: *Archiv für das Studium der neueren Sprachen und Literaturen*, 138 (1918), 234-6; idem, in: *Yivo-Bleter*, 2 (1931), 453; M. Altbauer, in: *Yivo-Bleter*, 2 (1931), 452-3.

[33] Here, with the suffix *-nik* added, the components become even more entangled. – The oldest sources of *shlimazl* and *shlimezalnik* that I know of are from 1654 and 1767, respectively.

[34] Cf. F. Lokotsch, *Etymologisches Wörterbuch der europäischen Wörter orientalischen Ursprungs* (Heidelberg, 1927).

mazl; even the scroll of the Law in the temple" [35] has become a popular proverb in Yiddish. However, it could not go uncontested since there is also a most authoritative statement in the Babylonian Talmud which contradicts it. This passage (Shab. 156a), while not dropping the idea of *mazl* entirely, seems to attempt a compromise between the ideas of fate and free will by stating אין מזל לישראל "there is no *mazl* (with regard) to the Jews", i.e. the Jews do not depend on the change of constellations, they are subject directly to God's authority. The *mazl* concept prevailed, however, and in later days the passage was reinterpreted to mean: "the Jews have no luck"; hence, the Yiddish proverb: *a yid hot nit keyn mazl* saying exactly this in so many words. Who, then, does have luck? Who but the Gentiles! Therefore, *a mazl fun a goy* "a Gentile's luck" is used to designate an exceptional degree of luckiness.

11. Language, we can now say on the basis of our evidence, is selective in essence; creation of and change in language can be described as an exertion of selective capacities on the part of its speakers. More often than not this selectivity affects a whole "field" of meanings simultaneously. No "Christian" language, for instance, possesses terms to match those which in traditional Yiddish have been chosen to denote, in ascending order, the rungs of the social ladder in Ashkenazic society, of which Talmudic studies were the mainstay: *an amhorets, a grober yung, a yid fun a gants yor, a sheyner yid, a yid a lamdn, a godl betoyre, a goen.*[36]

11.1. Hundreds of words can be picked out from any Yiddish dictionary to show that concepts from the domain of Jewish tradition and Jewish group life to a large degree are denoted in Yiddish by words of Hebrew origin.[37] But the qualifying "to a large degree" should be firmly kept in mind, as the expressions concluding the preceding paragraph easily show. Zunz, in the chapter referred to above (8.1), mentioned two categories of Hebrew-stock words that are used in Yiddish for other than *yi'dishkayt* purposes: first, cryptic terms and, second, "different expressions from the language of everyday life", in which two dozens of words were lumped together. Two more groups, overlooked by Zunz, easily suggest themselves to strengthen the evidence that the Hebrew component is not the carrier of *yi'dishkayt* only: euphemisms (e.g., *mashtn zayn* "to urinate", *tashmish* "sexual intercourse") and slangy parallels

[35] Zohar, פרשת נשא, 134.

[36] And how ineffective is the expression "Talmudic studies" as compared with the simple verb, unostentatious and yet so impressive, *lernen.*

[37] Cf. N. Shtif, "Di sotsiale diferentsiatsye in yidish" [Social Differentiation in Yiddish], *di yidishe shprakh*, 3., nos. 17-18 (1929), 1-22; Z. Kalmanovitch, in: *Literarishe Bleter* (1931), 8, and my "Vos volt yidish geven on hebreish?" [What Yiddish Would Have Been Without Hebrew], *Tsukunft*, 36 (1931), 194-205.

where the regular word is of non-Hebrew origin (e.g., *eynaim* "peepers" versus *oygn* "eyes", *yodaim* "paws" versus *hent* "hands").

This use of words of Hebrew origin for non-*yi'dishkayt* concepts is the first point of major interest in the study of the principles underlying selectivity in Yiddish vocabulary. More such points follow.

11.2. The Hebrew component is not the sole vehicle of tradition either. Many words of non-Hebrew origin serve for expressing *yi'dishkayt* concepts.[38] Some of them go back to the Loez stock: *bentshn* "to bless", cf. Latin *benedicere, ley'enen* "to read the Tora, to read (in general)", cf. Latin *legere, orn* "to pray" (used in Western Yiddish up to the present), cf. Latin *orare*. Words of German origin are, of course, much more numerous than Loez ones in this category as in any other: *yortsayt* "anniversary of death", *vakhnakht* "the night before circumcision", *fleyshik* "having the quality of meat", *milkhik* "having the quality of milk" [39] (both with reference to the dietary laws), *vo'khedik* "ordinary" (literally "pertaining to the weekdays", i.e., neither to the Sabbath nor to holidays), *farfastn* "to eat the meal preceding a fast", *o'pfastn* "to eat the meal following a fast", and so on, and so on. Note also the fixed combinations of verbs of non-Hebrew origin with Hebrew-stock nouns in expressions like *ley'enen krishme* "to read the shema", *zogn tilim,* "to recite the Psalms", *makhn a brokhe* "to say a blessing", etc.

11.3. A further aspect of fusion appears in phrases that, at first glance, seem to be built of material belonging to one component but at closer scrutiny turn out to be *calques* of or references to a different component. There are many expressions, for instance, which at face value contain no Hebrew but go back to Talmudic sayings: *es shitn zikh im perl fun moyl* "pearls pour from his mouth" i.e. he speaks beautifully (Kid. 39b); *af eyn fus* "(while standing) on one leg", i.e., cursorily (Shab. 31a); *vi a hor fun milkh* "like (removing) a hair from milk", i.e., with no effort at all (Ber. 8a), etc., etc.

11.4. It is no surprise to see that fusion has called into being new sets of synonyms. In addition to *got* "God" there are also substitute names for God of Hebrew origin with more or less learned overtones (*hakodesh borekh hu* "the Holy, blessed be He", *der riboyne shel oylem* "the Lord of the Universe", etc.) and one that seems to convey the greatest degree of reverence and intimacy at the same time: *der ey'bershter* "the Most High". Similarly, *shul* "synagogue", a carry-over from Loez, has more warmth about it than *beys-hakneses* which, though of Hebrew origin, sounds official and stiff. Another pair of synonyms denoting the house of prayer (and study) is *besmedresh* (cf. Hebrew בית המדרש) and *kloyz* (cf. Latin *clausa*). A chapter of the Mishna is called *a peyrik mishnayes;*

[38] See footnote 11.

[39] The older forms are *milkhding* and *fleyshding*.

peyrik is a word of Hebrew origin. But a Psalm is called ***a kapitl tilim*** and only that way (literally: "a chapter of the Psalms"; there is no singular of *tilim* "the Psalms"). *yi'dishn* is a very old word for "to circumcise", perhaps older in Yiddish than the synonyms of Hebrew origin *mal(e)n* or *mal(e) zayn.*[40] *rey'nikayt* "scroll of the Law" is no less reverential, though less technical, than its synonym derived from Hebrew, *seyfer-toyre*.

In some cases, where we can speak of synonyms only with regard to generic meaning, either specific applications or specific connotations must be taken into account. Thus, quotations from the Talmud are always given by *daf* "folio" (cf. Hebrew דף), but otherwise it is *a blat gemore*. In a German-Hebrew dictionary, *Stolz* is translated גאוה, but in Yiddish a differentiation took place: *shtolts* "pride" versus *gayve* "haughtiness, conceit".

11.5. Just as synonyms, homonyms indigenous to Yiddish, and only to it, have arisen out of the fusion of different stocks. Puns like the following result: *vos bistu beyz*? "why are you angry?" *ikh bin gornit beyz, ikh bin giml* "I am not angry at all, I am on good terms (with you)". Use is made of the double meanings of *beyz* ("angry", cf. German *böse*, and the name of the letter ב) and *giml* (the name of this letter, ג, in which the word *gut* begins, in colloquial Yiddish often signifies "good").

The crisscross resulting from the junction of meanings comes out nicely in the widely known proverb *kayen iz nit hevl*. On one level it concerns the Biblical brothers and may be taken to mean, "Cain is not Abel", i.e., disparate things should not be confused or, in a more generalized way: the evildoer should not be treated like his victim. But there is an alternate meaning which has taken precedence: "Eating (literally: chewing) is no trifle", i.e., material things cannot be dismissed lightly.

11.6. Folk etymology also belongs here. The custom of *tashlekh* (תשליך) "casting the sins into a river on Rosh Hashana", which originated in Ashkenazic Jewry, is associated with *teshlekh* "small pockets", because the pockets are turned inside out. *mern* "carrots" are eaten on Rosh Hashana because the same word, as a verb, means "to multiply". Among the western Ashkenazim there was established the custom of eating on Hoshana Raba *koul mit vaser*, "cabbage (cooked) with water" with reference to the Hebrew expression קול מבשר (pronounced *koul mevaser*) "the announcing voice", which appears in the liturgy of that day.

In the last two instances there took place what may be called reversed

[40] Probably coined with regard and in contrast to the medieval German *kristen(en)*, "to make a Christian". It is significant that neither the Hebrew מול itself nor the Yiddish terms derived from it suggest the crucial importance of the act of circumcision for becoming a Jew; only the word that uses German "raw material" stresses the point.

movement, i.e., a return effect of language upon behavior. The phenomena of this kind, branching out as they do into religious custom, superstitious practices, etc., merit a special study. It will prove particularly rewarding if the material will be confronted with the facts which testify to the incursions of Yiddish into the field of direct religious expression (see 14.1).

The very numerous cases of linguistic taboo also belong here.

11.7. Selectivity within one component has not been touched upon so far. The Hebrew dictionary lists two synonyms for "price": מחיר and מקח. The first is completely unknown in Yiddish, the second, *mekekh,* is most common. German has *rennen* and *laufen* "to run", *senden* and *schicken* "to send"; Yiddish has *loyfn* and *shikn* exclusively.

12. The last series of facts affords an opportunity of seeing the whole problem of selectivity from a new angle. It cannot be overemphasized that a language is characterized not only by what it takes and by the way it adapts its adoptions but also by what it rejects. The rule holds true in phonemics, morphology, etc., as well; but it is in vocabulary that it reveals itself most strikingly. Thus, traditional Yiddish has no words for concepts like Trinity, Holy Ghost, salvation,[41] purgatory, virtue, vice, etc., which are essential to Christian theology. No "Christian" language, no matter how divergent in other respects, can do without those words, but Yiddish had no use for them, and in this respect, as in many others, it resembles Hebrew, not German, with which it has a much greater part of the linguistic "raw material" in common.

12.1. If rejection is as indicative as acceptance, then the question of the why and wherefore imposes itself here, too. And while it is safe to assume that not every single item can be identified as to the motivating power behind it and that in many cases multiple factors were operative, the "no words" just as the "yes words" can be split up into definite categories. In other words, a deeper search will penetrate into what, at the present stage of knowledge, we are tempted to label arbitrariness.

12.2. In the present context, as we come back to the "yes words", only a few suggestions will be made. In the Hebrew component, there is both Biblical and post-Biblical stock, but the preponderance of the latter is unmistakable in the choice of words as well as in the imagery underlying similes and metaphors. That's why Yiddish frequently differs from the "Christian" languages even in what they took from Hebrew because their source is the Old Testament only. Yiddish, for instance, knows Korah not only as the leader of a rebellion against Moses (Num. 16), but also as fabulously rich (Pes. 119a); cf. the equally well known proverbial

[41] It was indeed a poor guess on the part of the translator to name one of Sholem Asch's novels *Salvation*. The title of the Yiddish original is *Der ti'limyid*.

phrases *ay'ngezunken vi koyrekh* "sunk down like Korah", said about sudden disappearance, and *raykh vi koyrekh* "rich as Korah".

As to selection from German stock, factors of time, place, and last but not least, social standing are to be considered. There is no doubt, however, that there was also reluctance to admit words signifying Christian concepts or otherwise negatively charged in an emotional sense, such as words relating to religious or superstitious practices, violent death, etc. To quote but one example out of many available, Old High German *sëganōn,* Middle High German *sëgenen* "to bless" did not fit because it still reminded of the original meaning of the Latin *signare* from which it stems, "(to bless by) making the sign – *signum* – of the cross". Therefore, *bentshn,* a word of Loez stock, was coined which for one thousand years has been leading an uncontested existence.[42]

But if the derivative of *benedicere* was chosen to the exclusion of any synonym, why wasn't its antonym, a derivative of *maledicere,* considered eligible and *(far)sheltn,* of German origin, is the Yiddish word instead? Why was *geze'genen zikh* "to take leave" not ostracized? Why was the term *yortsayt* "anniversary of death" not only adopted but made more important to the Jews than it ever was to the Church and transmitted to non-Yiddish Jews as far away as Persia? There are no ready answers to such questions except the metaphorical statement that the guards at the check points apparently not always displayed the same vigilance and that some "suspects" did slip through.

13. As the language of life from the cradle to the grave, Yiddish in no period was the medium of religious expression only. The oldest Yiddish manuscript bearing a date (1396) contains medical instructions; and it is well known that Yiddish long before the Haskala produced poetry, fiction, plays, etc. But since the eighteenth, and particularly in the nineteenth and twentieth centuries the "secular" sector of the Yiddish-speaking community has been growing rapidly. It goes without saying that the new ideological movements, the school systems up to the college level where all subjects were taught in Yiddish, the modern press, scientific research, etc., brought about profound changes in the language as a whole. This transition, with its blending of old and new features, has been repeatedly studied by Yiddish linguists. What interests us particularly in the present context, however, is the readjustment that took place, i.e., the adaptation of old material to new requisites of expression and

[42] Yiddish thus provides a rhyme, made use of at least as early as around 1500, to *mentshn* "people". German, as is known, has no rhyme to *Mensch.* This is but one of countless examples of specific Yiddish rhymes which begin appearing in the oldest Yiddish poetry that has come down to us; and it is obvious that peculiar rhymes, assonances, and alliterations are highly important in the establishment and development of linguistic separateness.

communication through the extension and reinterpretation of former meanings.

Thus, *nit milkhik nit fleyshik* "having the substance of neither milk nor meat" nowadays also means "dull, uninspiring" and can be applied regardless of whether or not the person in question observes the dietary laws. *klayzl* "a small synagogue", a diminutive of *kloyz*, still may denote, somewhat derisively, the house of prayer that a seceding part of a congregation sets up; but *klay'zldik* "factional" can be said of a dissenting group even in an organization of militant atheists. *shul* now denotes both "synagogue" and "school", which in ambiguous cases necessitates elaboration such as *shuln tsum da'v(e)nen* "synagogues", literally: *shuln* for praying, versus *ki'ndershuln* "schools", literally: *shuln* for children. *yontev* was a religious holiday as long as there was no other in the Jewish community – so much so that non-Jewish holidays are designated by a different word, *khoge*, also of Hebrew stock; but even an orthodox Yiddish newspaper today will naturally use *yontev* in connection with the Fourth of July. The idea of *goles* "Exile" has been the backbone of Jewish attitudes toward life throughout the centuries; a Jewish mother would comfort her boy hit by the stone of a non-Jewish attacker by saying *a yid iz in goles* "a Jew is in Exile (and thus has to suffer)", deploring their helplessness and yet sounding a hopeful note because ultimately the Messiah is bound to come. The concept of *goles*, very much related to the sense just given, is still a favorite topic of Jewish sociologists; but *go'les-regirung* is the standing term for any "government in exile" even if it is accused of being anti-semitic.

Long lists of such readjustments can easily be drawn up and instructive conclusions formed by arranging those phenomena into groups; here, however, we shall content ourselves with these few specimens in order to proceed to the last item of our discussion, the relative place of Yiddish and Hebrew as distinct linguistic entities in the "cultural economy" of Ashkenazic Jewry.

14. It is a curious reflection on nineteenth-century mentality that medieval Latin or Hebrew could be classed among the "dead" languages together with Phoenician or Numidian that have come down to us principally in inscriptions. To keep the issue clear, let us consider Hebrew only; Latin is a case apart.

True, ever since Hebrew ceased to be a spoken language (and, to a great extent, that had happened before the destruction of the Second Temple) it was no more that kind of an "immediate" language which people use in their everyday pursuits and in which they give vent to their emotions.[43] For those exigencies of life – we now know better than to

[43] Even today, Hebraists complain, full immediacy has not yet been obtained.

call them trivialities – Ashkenazic Jewry brought forth Yiddish. But the result of this far-reaching development was not a new monolingual condition but a state of peculiar bilingualism. Hebrew, as here consistently used in the sense of *loshn koydesh*, throughout the centuries has been the Jew's sacred language, that is the language of his intercourse with God and of the texts that contain or deal with God's Law. Communicating with God is certainly different from other functions of the language, yet it is inconceivable why it should be considered less alive.

14.1. But the fact that the Jews had a sacred language and called it that way does not mean that Yiddish, by contrast, was reserved for secular functions only. To begin with, there were no purely secular segments in the culture of traditional Ashkenazic Jewry; every nook and corner of life was permeated with *yi'dishkayt* and it has been shown how deeply this has affected the language as well. But even if we stay within the limits of more or less formalized direct religious expression, there are many things to account for, such as the *tkhines*, through which Jewish women for generations have been speaking to God,[44] the *got fun avroom* and similar "feminine prayers", the *raboysay mir veln bentshn* which is part of the after-meal ritual.[45]

14.2. Moreover, what may be called a semisacred variant of Yiddish emerged. The language used in the translation of the sacred texts gradually was disengaged from the spoken language and became rather rigidly fixed; eventually, this translation language itself became imbued with a measure of holiness.[46] Gradation of this kind, as Noble aptly remarks, is in line with the general Jewish concept of holiness typified, for instance, by the holiness of the Sabbath as contrasted with, but also complemented by, that of the holidays.

15. Ashkenazic bilingualism, definitely, is not founded on the dichoto-

---

Cf. S. D. Goitein in *Leshonenu*, 15 (1947-8), 57: "We are, all of us, strangers to our language; to some degree this applies even to *our children who know no other language, since Hebrew was not their mother tongue in the full meaning of the word* because their mothers, as a rule, spoke a foreign language too" (the italics are the author's).

44 Cf. Solomon B. Freehof, "Devotional Literature in the Vernacular", *Yearbook of the Central Conference of American Rabbis*, 33 (1923), 375-424.

45 The attempts to introduce Yiddish into the actual liturgy failed for psychological reasons that we can easily see but the mere fact that they were made is significant. Khasidism showed a particularly active interest in Yiddish.

46 Cf. Nechama Leibowitz, "Die Übersetzungstechnik der jüdisch-deutschen Bibelübersetzungen des 15. und 16. Jahrhunderts dargestellt an den Psalmen", *Beiträge zur Geschichte der deutschen Sprache und Literatur*, 55 (1931), 377-463, and Shlomo Noble, *Khumesh-taytsh. An oysforshung vegn der traditsye fun taytshn khumesh in di khadorim* (New York, YIVO, 1943). Noble's book is accompanied by an excellent summary in English.

my of sacred versus profane. The difference it stresses is that between the oral language and the language of recording.

Hebrew was the language of the sacred texts, of the immovable basis of study. Thus, whatever was to be committed to writing – in most cases it had to do with *yi'dishkayt* topics again – had to be in Hebrew. Hebrew was the language of the responsa, i.e., of scholarly correspondence on legal matters, but businessmen also used to write Hebrew or what they took for it. Incidentally, there was no puristic bias and the writers did not hesitate to insert Yiddish words or phrases wherever their Hebrew failed them. Moreover, the Hebrew itself was frequently peculiar. The fact that Ashkenazic Hebrew writers used to think in Yiddish makes medieval Hebrew a most interesting specimen of "a language with a substratum".

Just as Hebrew was the language of recording, Yiddish was the language of speech. As soon as the businessmen, or the rabbis for that matter, met and went on discussing the issues raised in their correspondence, the erstwhile Hebrew writers at once switched to Yiddish. Oral communication, except for passages from the sacred texts repeated verbatim, was firmly linked with the vernacular. Even in the responsa, if the witness is to be quoted, his testimony is offered in the vernacular, introduced by the abbreviation וז״ל.[47]

The coexistence of two languages differentiated in their functions was considered not merely inevitable, but natural. Only one of the languages, the oral one, had changed, but essentially it was the same situation as in Talmudic time with its coexistence of Hebrew and Aramaic. So natural, in effect, did this bilingualism appear that it was projected into the Biblical past.[48]

15.1. Had the two languages been equally well known, the ideal apportionment of functions might have been adhered to rigorously. As it happened, this was only the archetype of the actual relationship. Encroachments did take place, and while Hebrew did not have much of a chance as a spoken language except perhaps in a strained conversation with a casual visitor from a non-Ashkenazic community, the inroads that Yiddish made were deep and became deeper as the centuries rolled on.

The first Yiddish words that have come down to us are glosses in sacred texts. Out of them grew glossaries for the greater convenience of the *melamdim*. The next step was literal translation of an entire text. Literature of a more independent nature appeared but slowly. Occasionally it was frowned upon even when the contents was above reproach from the point of view of the opponent; to other rabbinical authorities, only contents counted and a learned author who was not too sure of his

47 Read: וזה לשׁונו

48 Cf., for instance, Noble's book, 14, 38.

proficiency in Hebrew was encouraged to write in Yiddish on the decisions and practices of his master.[49] As a rule, however, the superior position of Hebrew as the language of recording went practically unchallenged for centuries. Titles of Yiddish books sometimes were in Hebrew; one need only think of the "women's Bible" *Tsene Urene*, the most popular book of traditional Yiddish literature. Paragraphs used to start with a Hebrew phrase – first in translations, to refer to the corresponding paragraph in the Hebrew text, then as a stylistic device.[50] Words of Hebrew origin frequently were enclosed in parentheses within a current Yiddish text. It is only in the nineteenth century that the use of special Yiddish types, the so-called *vay'bertaytsh*, was generally discarded by the printers.

But with all this shown, professed, and no doubt sincere deference to the sacred tongue on the part of Yiddish writers, the position of Yiddish as a language of recording grew constantly stronger. The ideal pattern could not be sustained even within traditional Ashkenazic society, but it was at least adhered to theoretically. Then, with the rise of new social forces, with the advent of pro-Yiddish ideologies on the one hand and secular pro-Hebrew ideologies on the other, the centuries-old equilibrium was upset completely. This new period in Jewish cultural history is not necessarily within the compass of our present paper.

16. Without elaborating upon the broader implications and leaving aside the questions of methodology touched upon, the conclusions arrived at in our discussion can be summed up as follows:

(a) Yiddish originated and has been developing as the language of the Ashkenazic community which has been in existence for eleven hundred years or so.

(b) The set of historical events which led to the emergence and growth of the community and its language was the immigration of Jews from eastern France and northern Italy into Loter and the subsequent eastward movement of Ashkenazic Jewry.

(c) The linguistic corollary of those historical events was the availability of the main components that went into the formation of Yiddish: Rabbinic Hebrew, Loez in two varieties, the peculiar types of German which the Jews encountered, and different forms of Slavic spoken by the peoples among whom the Ashkenazim settled later.

(d) All components were subjected to a thorough process of accept-

[49] Cf. לקט ישר, J. Freimann, ed., 4 (Berlin, 1904). The author of this fifteenth-century text recalls: והם אמרו לי אם אינך תוכל לכתוב בלשון הקדש כתוב בלשון אשכנז.

[50] It can still be found as a standing feature in the numerous writings of as late an author as Ayzik Meyer Dik (ca. 1813-1893).

ance and rejection, based on both linguistic and extralinguistic reasons.

(e) Through interpenetration, readjustment, reinterpretation, etc., a unique fusion of the components took place; subsequently, the result of the fusion has been undergoing a uniform process of further development. Thus, all components of the language have become carriers of the same communicative and expressive purposes.

(f) The principal cultural determinant in the history of Yiddish is the fact that Ashkenazic Jewry came into existence as a community defined by *yi'dishkayt*. On the basis of evidence uncovered it can be firmly stated that *yi'dishkayt* shaped not only the conceptual world of the Ashkenazic community but its language as well. Moreover, although Yiddish never was a language of religious expression only and, in recent centuries, in growing measure has become a medium of "secular" endeavors, too, the master pattern of Yiddish as the language of a community defined by *yi'dishkayt* has not changed.

(g) Important results, both for linguistics and sociology, may be expected from further research in this area.

From: *Mordecai M. Kaplan Jubilee Volume* (New York, Jewish Theological Seminary of America, 1953), pp. 481-514. Reprinted with permission.

Harold C. Conklin

LEXICOGRAPHICAL TREATMENT OF FOLK TAXONOMIES*

0. INTRODUCTION

Many lexical problems are of considerable importance to linguists and ethnographers. With the interests of both groups in mind, I would like to discuss certain aspects of folk classification which I feel deserve more rigorous lexicographic attention than they have typically received.

An adequate ethnographic description of the culture (Goodenough 1957) of a particular society presupposes a detailed analysis of the communications system and of the culturally defined situations in which all relevant distinctions in that system occur. In this regard, accurate knowledge of both the grammar and lexicon of the local spoken language constitutes a minimum requirement. When the ethnographer works in an area for which adequate statements about the local language are unavailable in published sources, his first and often continuing task is the construction of a set of valid rules for the interpretation of the local language. In his phonological and grammatical analysis of new speech forms, he may find many helpful models in the descriptive linguistic literature. In attempting, however, to account for the obligatory semantic relations inherent in his lexical corpus, he may not be so fortunate. While extant dictionaries and vocabularies do provide glosses and

* The work on which most of this paper is based has been suported by the National Science Foundation. A number of students and other friends have offered constructive criticism of an earlier draft of this statement. For especially helpful and more detalied comments I am particularly indebted to Y. R. Chao, David Crabb, Arthur Danto, C. O. Frake, Paul Friedrich, W. H. Goodenough, J. H. Greenberg, Einar Haugen, P. F. Lazarsfeld, F. G. Lounsbury, and Volney Stefflre.

definitional information, many of the nontrivial, and often essential, semantic and contextual relationships obtaining among lexical items are often either neglected or handled in an imprecise and unsystematic manner (cf. Newman 1954, 86).

For formal linguistic analysis it is necessary that utterances be acceptable and interpretable grammatically. For ethnographic (including lexicographic) analysis utterances must also be acceptable and interpretable semantically. While an "appeal" to meaning does not improve grammatical analysis, neither does an intuitive appeal to morphosyntactic form yield the most appropriate analysis of meaning and reference (see 1.5. below). In fact, an adequate grammar may generate semantically unacceptable propositions (Chomsky 1955, 149; 1957, 103-4; cf. Landar 1960, 352; Frake 1961, 113). Results of some recent attempts to develop non-intuitive procedures for the evaluation of the grammaticalness and meaningfulness of sentences (e.g., Maclay and Sleator 1960; cf. Joos 1958) indicate that this difference is of considerable importance. The distinction between these two aspects of the analysis of speech is apparent even in the treatment of isolated forms.

In the course of several years of linguistic and ethnographic field work among the Hanunóo in the Philippines, it became abundantly evident that providing such segments as *sah, tabākuq, samparansisku-qalistun,* and *lāda. balaynun. tagnānam. qiruŋ-pādiq* each with the same gloss "(distinct) kind of plant" was – while adequate for certain syntactic purposes – most unsatisfactory for the task of semantic analysis. Had I not modified this procedure, I would have ended up with more than 2000 lexical items (including several hundred referential synonyms) each labeled identically. While employing glosses like "tea" and "tobacco" (in the first two cases above) proved useful in labeling familiar objects, the majority of these culturally significant Hanunóo designations referred to entities which to me were quite unfamiliar. In this type of ethnographic context one finds many instances where the problems faced traditionally by the compilers of bilingual dictionaries are considerably magnified (Nida 1958). For the ethnographer, the semantic structure of such folk classification is of paramount significance. Upon his analysis of it depends the accuracy of many crucial statements about the culture being described. Problems of analyzing and presenting such structures in a succinct fashion may be of interest even to lexicographers who work only in relatively familiar cultural surroundings.

1. FOLK CLASSIFICATION

In the lexicographic treatment of folk classification, we are concerned primarily with 1. the identification of relevant syntactic segments, 2. the identification of fundamental semantic units in specific contexts, 3. the delineation of significant sets of semantic units in particular domains, and 4. the translation (and marking) of these units so that important semantic relationships will not be obscured. In discussing different systems of classifying segments of the natural and social environment, the neutral term *segregate* (Conklin 1954) serves as a label for any terminologically-distinguished (i.e., conventionally-named) grouping of objects.

1.1. *Linguistic structure.* – The shape and combinatorial structure of the linguistic forms which designate folk segregates are irrelevant, in a strict sense, to the analysis of the system of classification itself; i.e., to the semantic structure (Conklin 1957). Labels and categories can change independently and therefore must be analyzed separately. On the other hand, a knowledge of the linguistic structure involved is essential for understanding the principles of folk *nomenclature*; and in working out this structure, clues for isolating folk segregate labels and for eliciting information about such segregates may be found.

1.2. *Lexical units and contexts.* – A full lexical statement (i.e., an adequate dictionary) should provide semantic explanation, as well as phonological and grammatical identification, for every meaningful form whose signification cannot be inferred from a knowledge of anything else in the language. It is convenient to refer to these elementary lexical units as *lexemes* (cf. Swadesh 1946; Newman 1954; Jorden 1955; Goodenough 1956), although other terms have been suggested, e.g., *idiom* (Hockett 1956; cf. Householder 1959, 508-24; Weinreich 1960, 337). So far as lexemic status is concerned, the morphosyntactic or assumed etymological relations of a particular linguistic form are incidental; what is essential is that its meaning cannot be deduced from its grammatical structure. Single morphemes are necessarily lexemes, but for polymorphemic constructions the decision depends on meaning and use (implying an analysis of the constraints imposed by the semantic structure, and the specification of relevant immediate contexts).

Formal segments such as *black bird* (vs. *blackbird*) or *in the old house* (vs. *in the doghouse*) can be excluded from the lexical statement because they are predictable, meaningfully, in that they can be considered *semantically endocentric* (Nida 1951, 12-3; 1958, 286; cf. Chao 1953, 385). Put another way, those constructions which are never *semantically exocentric* may be classed as *nonlexemic* forms (e.g., *sunburned face, long pink strand*). Problems do arise, however, in degrees of lexemic *exocentricity* (Nida 1958, 286) and, again, if caution is not exercised in distinguishing clearly between grammatical and semantic criteria. The compounds *firewater* and *silverfish*, for example, are endocentric morphosyntactically (either on an attribute-plus-head basis or on the perhaps stronger grounds of formal selection rules [Lees 1960, 128, 158]), but semantically they are as exocentric as *vodka* and *moth*.

In the study of segregate labels in folk classification, and despite some of the difficulties of technical definition noted, I find it useful to distinguish by explicit semantic criteria two kinds of lexemic units: *unitary lexemes* (no segments of which may designate categories which are identical with, or superordinate to, those designated by the forms in question) and *composite lexemes* (one or more segments of which, under specified conditions, may [a] designate the same categories as those designated by the forms in question [abbreviation], or [b] designate categories superordinate to those designated by the forms in question [generalization], see 2.-2.2). Unitary lexemes may be either *simple* (unsegmentable) or *complex* (segmentable). These distinctions are exemplified below:

Lexemes		
Unitary simple	*Unitary complex*	*Composite*
oak	poison oak	white oak
pine	pineapple	pitch pine
son	grandson	son-in-law
dart (an artifact)	darts (a game)	Baldwin apple
Jack	jack-in-the-pulpit	Port-orford cedar
dandelion	black-eyed Susan	black-crowned night heron
caterpillar (larva)	cat's-eye	caterpillar tractor

For contrast, consider a few similar but *nonlexemic* forms: *cheap pine, pine and oak, black-eyed Joe, darts* (plural of *dart* [Hockett 1956, 229]). For a native speaker, such distinctions cause little concern, but in new linguistic and cultural environs difficulties may arise.

For example, on first inspection, the following partially-identical Hanunóo forms (Cocklin 1954) might appear to belong to a simple paradigm (they could all be recorded during a conversation about rice cultivation and weeding problems):

1. *paray·paray*	"cattail"
2. *pāray· māyah*	"immature wild *pādaŋ* (plant)"
3. *pāray· qi kantuh*	"kind of wild sedge"
4. *pāray· bīhud*	"kind of rice"
5. *pāray· tāwuh*	"some one (else)'s rice"
6. *pāray· tīdah*	"that rice"

The glosses, however, indicate that several types of lexical units may be involved. Are there any formal linguistic clues?

Each of the six forms is easily segmented into two morphs, as I have indicated by the use of dots. Loose-joining, phonemically, is represented by a single raised period. Except for the closely-joined doubling in item number 1, the forms in this set provide no obligatory intonational or junctural contrasts. Furthermore, each form occurs in many identical frames such as *tūhay ŋāni ti* ______. " ______ is (are) certainly different." Thus, for most of the semantically distinct types of joining suggested by the glosses, there are no phonological clues and few, if any, immediate, formal indications. (A full syntactic statement covering the structure of compounds would separate out some of these forms on grammatical grounds [cf. Lees 1960].) Given the necessary semantic information, however, these distinctions can be noted easily for lexicographical purposes by rewriting the forms as follows:

1. *parayparay*
2. *pāray-māyah*
3. *pāray-qiŋkantuh*
4. *pāray. bīhud*
5. *pāray tāwuh*
   (5a) (5b)
6. *pāray tīdah*
   (6a) (6b)

This procedure clearly marks 1, 2, and 3 semantically exocentric, unitary lexemes; 4 as a composite lexeme; and 5 and 6 as non-lexemic, semantically endocentric constructions the initial lexeme of which is superordinately related to 4. Minimally, forms 1, 2, 3, 4, 5a, and 6a could be labeled "kind of plant", but by not attending to essential semantic distinctions this type of short cut would obscure such important contrastive relations as the mutual exclusion of coordinate categories (1 : [*pādaŋ*, implied – but not covered – by the specific growth stage term number 2] : 3 : 5a or 6a), and the possible total inclusion of subordinate categories (4 by 5a/6a; but *not* 1, 2, or 3 by 5a/6a). Statements about such relations, hinted at in some glosses and definitions, may be demonstrated only by systematic pairing in minimal, and relatively controlled, linguistic and semantic contexts.

1.3. *Lexical sets and domains.* – In many ways it can be said that the more discrete the phenomena referred to, the simpler the task of treating the associated terminology in a lexicographically adequate manner (cf. Wallace and Atkins 1960). If this is true for particular lexical items it is equally true for the semantically structured sets which such items may comprise (Frake 1961). Minimally, a *lexical set* consists of all semantically contrastive lexemes which in a given, culturally relevant context share exclusively at least one defining feature (Lounsbury 1956, 61-2). The semantic range of all such lexemes defines the *domain* of the lexical set. The initial establishment of domain boundaries, while widely recognized as an ideal goal, is often a very difficult task (cf. Voegelin and Voegelin 1957). Effective eliciting frames and procedural tests used to determine such boundaries, and convincing demonstrations of their intracultural reality, are subjects not often discussed in the linguistic or ethnological literature. Some of the essential factors involved in this type of analysis are treated briefly below under "levels" (2.) and "dimensions" (3.) of contrast. In general, the number and complexity of boundary problems increases as one moves from the investigation of lexical domains within a particular language to an attempt to "match" the domains of different languages (Öhman 1953; cf. Quine 1960, 26-79). This does not, however, preclude rigorous contrastive analysis.

1.4. *Translation and semantic structure.* – With few exceptions, the lexical items employed in systems of folk classification always comprise a segment of the everyday vocabulary of the particular language (Conklin 1957). The rules governing the obligatory semantic relations among the categories in such lexical sets are thus to be determined, evaluated, and described for each language. Such rules cannot be prescribed merely on the basis of familiarity *in another system* with the "concrete" denotata of the sets involved. In the case of folk botany, for example, this means that a local system of plant classification cannot be described accurately by attempting to obtain only vernacular "equivalents" for botanically recognized species. Translation labels (glosses) are frequently necessary, but they should be considered neither as definitions nor as exact equivalents (Lounsbury 1956, 163; for an attempt to use acronyms as a partial mnemonic solution to such translation problems, see Landar *et al.* 1960, 371). This well-established and perhaps obvious semantic principle is sometimes forgotten where the assumed absolute nature (in a cross-linguistic sense) of "scientific" names or of other long-established traditional distinctions in certain Western languages is involved (Öhman 1953; cf. Simpson 1961, 11).

1.5. *Syntactic vs. semantic structure.* – Implicit in the preceding remarks is the assumption that the relation between formal linguistic (syntactic, in the general, semiotic sense [Morris 1946]) structure and semantic structure need not be isomorphic (Lounsbury 1956, 189). If this assumption is taken seriously, a full dictionary should state explicitly the necessary and sufficient conditions for the unambiguous structural interpretation of each included lexeme in the context of the total lexicon as well as in that of the grammar. While such coverage has rarely been achieved, even for relatively small lexical domains, I feel that recognition of this goal has considerable relevance for this discussion. A brief illus-

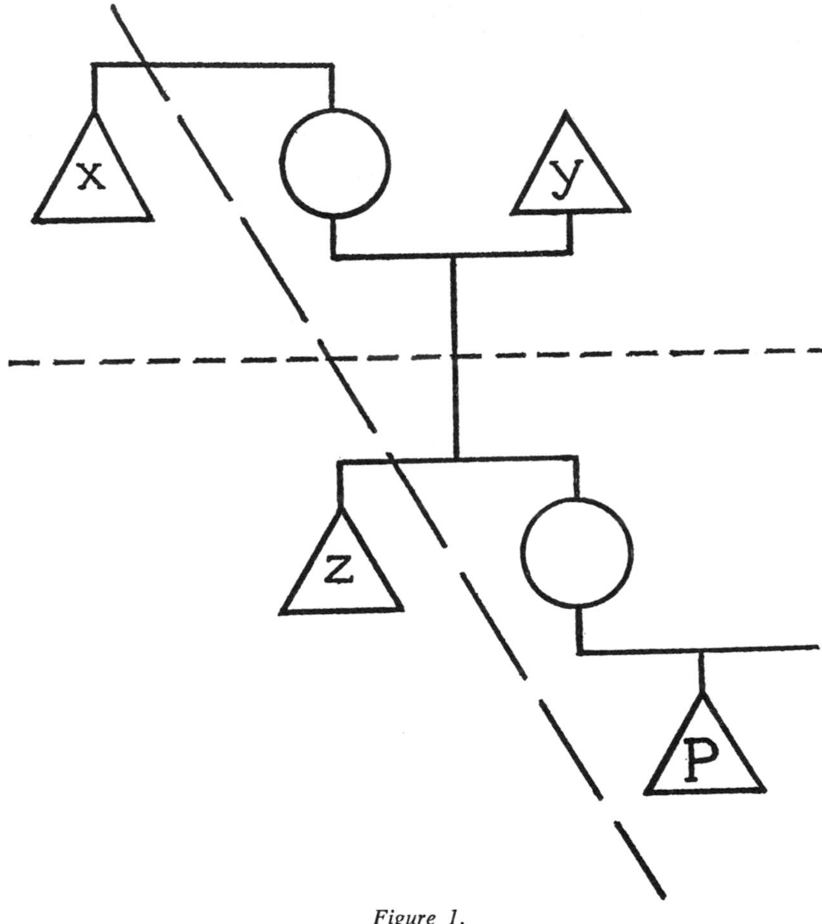

Figure 1.

A genealogical illustration of contrasting systems of kinship classification.

tration may help to indicate the kind of crucial lexical data that are often ignored, especially where meanings are either assumed on the basis of semantic patterning in a more familiar language, or where they are treated only partially (as in the derivation of definitional statements from translational labels).

Consider the following situation (which, with minor differences, I have encountered on a number of occasions): a woman, whose brother (x) and husband (y) are both named Juan, has a son, also named Juan (z) and a daughter who in turn has a son named Pedro (P). The genealogical situation is diagrammed in Fig. 1 (we can ignore the broken lines for a moment). Two fluent speakers of English, F, a Filipino whose first language was Tagalog, and A, a native speaker of a dialect of American English, both know Pedro and the specified members of his family. The fact that one of the Juans (x, y, or z) has died is known only to A (or F) who in turn wishes to relate this circumstance to his friend F (or A). A straightforward statement completing the sentence *P's* ______ *Juan died* would seem to do the trick; and, depending on the circumstances, one of two unitary lexemes (*grandfather, uncle*) might be used to fill the blank:

1. *Pedro's Grandfather Juan died.*
2. *Pedro's Uncle Juan died.*

However, if A uses *Grandfather*, F may ask *Which grandfather*?; if F uses *Uncle*, A may ask *Which uncle*? indicating a kind of two-way ambiguity which can only be resolved by recognizing that despite their unquestionable grammaticality and morphosyntactic identity, A's sentences 1 and 2, and F's sentences 1 and 2 differ semantically:

Sentence	*Kin term used*	*Kin type(s) included (Pr = parent's)*	
A1	*Grandfather*	y	(PrFa)
F1	"	x and y	(PrFa, PrPrBr)
A2	*Uncle*	x and z	(PrBr, PrPrBr)
F2	"	z	(PrBr)

This, of course, reflects only a small part of a very fundamental structural difference in Central Philippine and North American systems of kinship classification: universal terminological recognition of generation in the former vs. universal terminological recognition of degree of collaterality in the latter (these two "limits" to the lexical extension of kin class membership are indicated on the kinship diagram in Fig. 1 by the horizontal and diagonal broken lines, respectively). Although any careful investigator might learn this systematic distinction after a few days of field work, the principle goes unaccounted for in the relevant and extant bilingual dictionaries. The restrictions involved in this illustration are just as obligatory and inescapable within the respective semantic systems represented as is the distinction of singular vs. plural in English grammar.

2. LEVELS OF CONTRAST

Folk categories within the same domain may be related in two fundamentally different ways by *inclusion*, which implies separate levels of contrast, and by *exclusion*, which here applies only within single-level contrast sets. There may also be subcategoric, or componential, *inter-*

section (see 3. below). In studying semantic relationships, as among folk categories, it has often been demonstrated that likeness logically and significantly implies difference (Kelly 1955, 303-5). It is also pertinent, however, to note that total contrast (complete complementary exclusion) – which logically relates such segregates as *ant* and *ship* or *cough* and *pebble* – is less important than restricted contrast within the range of a particular semantic subset (compare the relations within and between the partial sets *robin – wren – sparrow; spaniel – terrier – poodle;* and *bird – dog*). When we speak of the category *dime* being included in the category *coin* we imply that every dime is also a (kind of) coin – but not necessarily the reverse. Furthermore, when we state (a) that the category *dime* contrasts with that of *quarter* and (b) that the category *coin* contrasts with that of *bill* we are speaking of two instances of relevant mutual exclusion at two different levels of contrast (Conklin 1955, 1957; Frake 1961). Such alignments of folk categories are common to all languages, though systematic indications of these relationships are rare even in the more detailed monolingual dictionaries.

2.1. *Hierarchic structure.* – Where the articulation between successive levels, each consisting of a set of contrastive lexical units, is ordered vertically by inclusion such that each mono-lexemic category at one level is totally included in only one category at the next higher level, we can speak of a lexical hierarchy. The two axes of such a structure involve the horizontal *differentiation* of contrastive but coordinate categories and the vertical increase of *generalization* or *specification* resulting from ascent to superordinate (including) or descent to subordinate (included) levels, respectively (Gregg 1954; Conklin 1957; Beckner 1959, 55-80; Frake 1961, 117). These axes are fixed and cannot be merged or interchanged, nor can the succession of levels be modified. *Dime* is not contrasted with *coin*, but at the same level with *nickel, quarter, penny,* etc. Subhierarchies of varying "depths" are often discernible within larger hierarchic structures. The depth (in levels) of the subhierarchy including the categories *hawk, pigeon,* and *starling* is less than that of the subhierarchy including *hawk, horse,* and *crocodile*; i.e., the first three segregates are included in a superordinate category at a lower level than that of the segregate ultimately including *hawk, horse,* and *crocodile*. The embedding of subhierarchies within increasingly deeper ones is characteristic of many systems of folk classification.

2.2. *Folk taxonomy.* – A system of monolexemically-labeled folk segregates related by hierarchic inclusion is a *folk taxonomy;* segregates included in such a classification are known as *folk taxa* (Conklin 1957; cf. Lawrence 1951, 53; Simpson 1961, 19). Some of the additional requirements of "model" or "regular" taxonomic systems (Woodger 1952, 201ff.; Gregg 1954; Beckner 1959, 55-8; Simpson 1961) are: 1. at the highest level, there is only one maximal (largest, unique) taxon which includes all other taxa in the system; 2. the number of levels is finite and uniform throughout the system; 3. each taxon belongs to only one level; 4. there is no overlap (i.e., taxa at the same level are always mutually exclusive). Folk systems vary widely with respect to these more specific "requirements", but the presence of hierarchically arranged though less "regular" folk taxonomies is probably universal. Most of the examples given here are taken from folk botany, but similar illustrations could be taken from other domains (Thomas 1957; Frake 1961).

Several important differences distinguish folk taxa from the taxonomic groups of biological systematics (Conklin 1957; Simpson 1961). The former usually relate only to locally relevant or directly observable phenomena. They are defined by criteria which may differ greatly from culture to culture. The number and position of levels of contrast may change from one sector of a folk system to another. There are no formal rules for the nomenclatural recognition or rejection of taxa (cf. Lawrence 1951, 213-5), though new groupings may be added productively with considerable ease. In respect to any particular local biota, there is no reason to expect the folk taxa to match those of systematic biology – either in number or in range. The Hanunóo classify their local plant world, at the lowest (terminal) level of contrast, into more than 1800 mutually exclusive folk taxa, while botanists divide the same flora – in terms of species – into less than 1300 scientific taxa.

2.3. *Special problems.* – Although they cannot be discussed here at length, a number of lexicographically important problems encountered in the analysis of folk taxonomies include:

1. Multiple and interlocking hierarchies. Unlike scientific taxa, folk segregates may belong simultaneously to several distinct hierarchic structures. The same segregates may be classed as terminal categories in a taxonomy based on form and appearance and also as terminal or non-terminal categories in another taxonomy based on cultural treatment (e.g., morphologically distinguished kinds of floral segregates vs. functional categories of plants as food cultigens, medicines, ornamentals, etc.) (Conklin 1954). Subhierarchies may be interarticulated in numerous ways (e.g., Joos 1956, 296-7) and there is always the potentiality of partial inclusion or domain overlap.

2. Extrahierarchic relations. Not all folk categories are directly related by class inclusion or contrast within the range of a particular superordinate category. For example, numerous difficulties may arise if lexemes designating separate ontogenetic stages or parts of members of particular segregates (see 1.2. above) are not distinguished from hierarchically arranged folk taxa (Chao 1953, 387-9; Conklin 1954, 1957; Frake 1961). *Part-of* (part-whole) relations are often complicated by ambigui-

ties (Nagel 1961, 381-3) not encountered in the analysis of *kind-of* (class inclusion) relations (e.g., the segregates *plant, stem, sap* are not related taxonomically like *plant, tree, elm*).

3. Synonymy and homonymy. When, within the context of a particular folk taxonomy, a single taxon may be labeled by phonemically distinct forms, as in the case of minor dialect variants or abbreviated terms (see 1.2.), we may speak of referential synonyms (or synonymous lexemes); e.g., *fin, finnif, five, fiver, five-spot, five-dollar bill.* In many such cases, it may be difficult to demonstrate taxonomic identity and the absence of categoric overlap. Alternative substructuring of the subhierarchy may be involved. Phonemically identical (homonymous) lexemes may designate separate taxa of different ranges of generalization at successive levels. Such situations (e.g., *animal* and *man* in the following partial contrastive sets: *animal*^{1} vs. *plant*, *animal*^{2} vs. *man*^{1}, *man*^{2} vs. *woman* [cf. Frake 1961, 117-9]) are not uncommon but they require careful contrastive pairing and testing for inclusion at each level involved. Similar steps must also be taken in working out problems concerned with distinguishing polysemy from homonymy (Wells 1958, 662-3; cf. Chomsky 1957, 95; Garvin 1960, 147).

4. Types of contrast. Paired folk taxa of some lexical subsets are related by simple, binary, segregate opposition. Many larger sets and some dyadic ones involve important types of semantic contrast other than antonymy (cf. Lyons 1960, 622). Structurally, for example, taxa may be contrasted in serial, complementary, or discontinuous arrays. (For subcategoric attribute relations, see 3. below.)

2.4. *Folk vs. botanical taxonomy.* – Ideally, in the study of interrelated lexical sets in folk taxonomies, priority and preference should be given to unanimously-agreed-upon, obligatory distinctions in specified contexts. When tested by means of what are essentially crucial experiments – by pairing and contrasting negatively and positively – one should be able to construct a model (i.e., a theoretical statement) of the hierarchic structure such that assertions of membership and inclusion in any of the implied taxa are unanimously and unambiguously denied whenever such assertions are incongruent (i.e., meaningless within the system) (cf. Joos 1958, 65). The assertion "Poodles, dogs, and animals are kinds of snails" would thus be rejected by speakers of my dialect of English – and on very easily specified semantic grounds. Within a particular universe of discourse (a taxonomic domain) how can one construct a nontrivial model by means of which only semantically acceptable, congruent propositions may be generated? An example from Hanunóo folk botany may serve as a partial answer.

In a situation where one Hanunóo farmer wishes to draw another's attention to a particular individual pepper bush Q, he may, of course, attempt to describe some of Q's unique attributes without naming the plant. Much more often, however, even in the course of a "unique" description, he will resort to the use of one or more of at least eight lexical units each of which might complete the frame *māluq, qinda pag* ______, "Hey, take a look at this______," but at different levels of contrast (allowing for different degrees of desired or required specificity):

I.	*kuwaq*	"entity" (i.e., something that can be named)
II.	*bāgay*	"thing" (not a person, animal, etc.)
III.	*kāyuh*	"plant" (not a rock, etc.)
IV	*qilamnun*	"herbaceous plant" (not a woody plant, etc.)
V.	*lādaq*	"pepper (plant)" (not a rice plant, etc.)
VI.	*lāda. balaynun*	"houseyard pepper (plant)" (not a wild pepper plant)
VII.	*lāda. balaynun. mahārat*	"houseyard chili pepper (plant)" (not a houseyard green pepper plant)
VIII.	*lāda. balaynun. mahārat. qūtin-kutiq*	" 'cat-penis' houseyard chili pepper (plant)" (not a member of any of five other terminal houseyard chile pepper taxa such as *lāda. balaynun. mahārat. tāhud-manuk,* the "cock's-spur" variety).

Within the domain of Hanunóo plant taxonomy, from level III down, and specifically within the range of *lādaq,* from level V down, conversations recorded during many similar situations would ultimately provide the lexicographer with fifteen unitary and composite lexemes (including a terminal set of eleven "pepper plant" names) arranged at four levels in the form of a discrete subhierarchy (Fig. 2). Specification below the level of the terminal taxa noted in the diagram (Fig. 2, 1-11), and

<table>
<tr><td colspan="11">kuwaq</td></tr>
<tr><td colspan="11">bāgay</td></tr>
<tr><td colspan="11">kāyuh</td></tr>
<tr><td colspan="11">qilamnun</td></tr>
<tr><td colspan="11">15 lādaq</td></tr>
<tr><td colspan="10">14 lāda. balaynun</td><td rowspan="3">lada. tirindukun-tigbayaq

11</td></tr>
<tr><td colspan="6">12 lāda. balaynun. mahārat</td><td colspan="4">13 lāda. balaynun. tagnānam</td></tr>
<tr><td>l. b. m. batūnis

1</td><td>l. b. m. hapun

2</td><td>l. b. m. pasītih

3</td><td>l. b. m. pinasyak

4</td><td>l. b. m. qūtin-kutiq

5</td><td>l. b. m. tāhud-manuk

6</td><td>l. b. t. mali-puŋkuk

7</td><td>l. b. t. pasītih

8</td><td>l. b. t. patuktuk

9</td><td>l. b. t. qarābaq

10</td></tr>
</table>

Figure 2. A segment of Hanunóo plant taxonomy. All folk taxa included in the taxon *lādaq*, are indicated.

hence outside this system of classification, may be provided only by semantically endocentric constructions describing individual plant variations, on which unanimous accord is rare and unpredictable. In this particular case, folk taxa 15, 14, and 11 happen to correspond rather closely with the scientific taxa *Capsicum*, *C. annuum L.*, and *C. frutescens* L., respectively; but the twelve remaining folk taxa involve distinctions not recognized as significant botanical subspecies by taxonomic botanists who have classified the same flora. Structurally speaking, however, some of the most important patterns of semantic contrast involve not only the hierarchic separation of these varied, lower-level, folk taxa (i.e. 1-10, 12-13), but also a large number of nonhierarchic relations governed by sublexemic class intersection (see 3.2.). Although such relations cannot be diagrammed with the taxonomic implications of Fig. 2, nor can they be treated effectively at all in terms of our hierarchic model, they should nevertheless be of considerable interest to linguists and others concerned with systems of folk classification.

3. DIMENSIONS OF CONTRAST

At any given level within a well-defined folk-taxonomic subhierarchy, the relations obtaining among three or more coordinate taxa may involve varying dimensions, or kinds of subcategory contrast. The conjunction of these dimensions, or more precisely, of the values (or specific attributes [cf. Bruner *et al.* 1956, 26-30]) along the several dimensions, define the categories involved within an essentially paradigmatic (i.e., nonhierarchic) subsystem (Lounsbury 1956; 1960, 27-8; for a discussion of the structurally similar though more typologically-oriented procedures of attribute space substruction and reduction see Greenberg 1957 and Lazarsfeld 1961).

3.1. *Nonhierarchic structure.* – Such multidimensional contrasts do not imply, and indeed do not allow, the ordering of the resultant categories by hierarchic inclusion. These features of nonhierarchic semantic structures, while not always sharply distinguished from the principles inherent in hierarchic systems, have been recognized and carefully analyzed in a number of domains, notably in kinship (Goodenough 1951, 92-110; 1956; Lounsbury 1956; Frake 1960; Wallace and Atkins 1960), color (Conklin 1955; cf. Lenneberg and Roberts 1956; Landar *et al.* 1960), orientation (Haugen 1957), disease (Frake 1961), and, beginning with Jakobson's pioneering efforts, in such partly modulational (Joos 1958, 70) paradigms as case and pronoun systems (Jakobson 1936; Sebeok 1946; Harris 1948; Lotz 1949; Wonderly 1952; Austerlitz 1959). The following example of multidimensional contrast in a regular paradigmatic structure will illustrate some of these points.

3.2. *Significant classification vs. cataloguing.* – If, omitting the high-level, wide-ranging *kuwaq* (see 2.4.), we list all the Hanunóo personal name substitutes occurring in various frames such as *māluq, qinda pag binwat ni* ____, "Hey, take a look at what ____ did (here)," we will invariably end up with an exhaustive and mutually exclusive lexical set consisting of just eight units (in each case representing a single morpheme). Arranged in the least meaningful type of catalogue, an alphabetical *index* (as in a dictionary), these lexical units are:

dah	"they"
kuh	"I"
mih	"we"
muh	"you"
tah	"we two"
tam	"we all"
yah	"he, she"
yuh	"you all"

The shapes provide little that is structurally suggestive, but the glosses do indicate that an ordering in terms of eight "traditional" distinctions along three quasi-semantic dimensions

1.	first person	: second person	: third person
2.	singular	: dual	: plural
3.	exclusive	: inclusive	

might be attempted. But the resulting applied structure is hardly elegant, economical, or convincing:

kuh 1s.	*tah* 1d.	*mih* 1pe.
---	---	*tam* 1pi.
muh 2s.	---	*yuh* 2p.
yah 3s.	---	*dah* 3p.

If a close examination is made of the distinctive contrasts involved, not in terms of labels but in terms of actual, minimal, obligatory differences, a more satisfactory, economical, and semantically verifiable solution is reached. The necessary and sufficient conditions for defining each of the eight categories depend on the regular intersection of six components which comprise three simple oppositions:

minimal membership	: nonminimal membership	$(M : \bar{M})$
inclusion of speaker	: exclusion of speaker	$(S : \bar{S})$
inclusion of hearer	: exclusion of hearer	$(H : \bar{H})$

These relations can be represented in list or diagrammatic form (Fig. 3). Even without further elaboration, the basic semantic structure of this

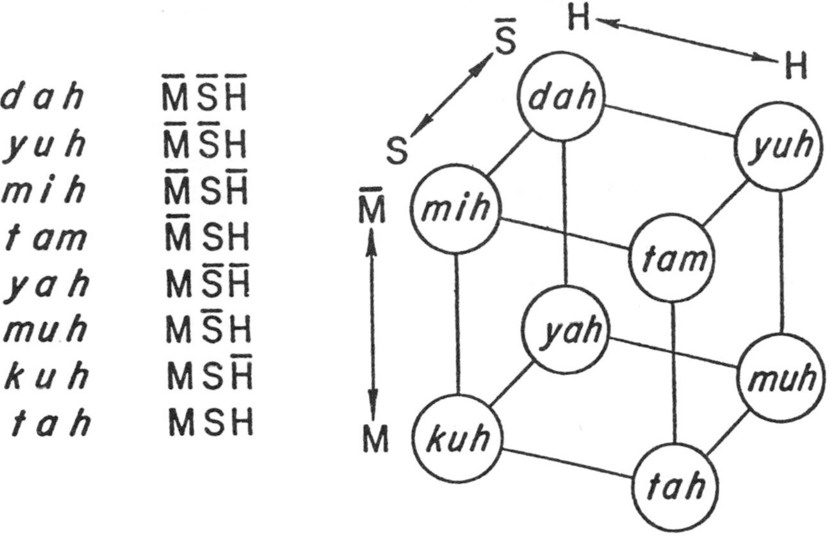

Figure 3. Paradigmatic structure of a Hanunóo pronominal set.

lexical set should now be clear. (In passing, it may be noted that pronoun systems in Tagalog, Ilocano [Thomas 1955], Maranao [McKaughan 1959], and some other Philippine languages exhibit very similar, if not identical, obligatory semantic relationships.)

This example also illustrates a very important, though perhaps less obvious, characteristic of paradigmatic relations at one level in a taxonomic subhierarchy in contrast to the noncommutative relations of class inclusion governing the larger taxonomic system. Within such a contrastive lexical set (as in Fig. 3), ordered by class intersection, the constituent categories cannot be arranged in a taxonomic hierarchy. Any arrangement (e.g., a circular, block, or branching diagram) superficially appearing to contradict this statement will prove on closer inspection either (a) to constitute what the biologists call a *key* (Mayr *et al.* 1953, 162-8; Simpson 1961, 13-6), essentially another kind of catalogue or finding list ordered by successive – but not necessarily taxonomically significant – dichotomous exclusion, or (b) to be based on some other artificially imposed, and hence semantically nonsignificant, classification.

4. LEXICOGRAPHIC TREATMENT

The ways in which the problems mentioned in this paper may be treated in bilingual dictionaries, especially ethnographic dictionaries, are practically unlimited. That very few of the possibilities have been explored to date is disappointing, but not discouraging. There have been a number of new attempts at expanding the analytic procedures of descriptive linguistics to include a more rigorous, thorough, and theoretically rewarding analysis of semantic structure (e.g., Goodenough 1956; Lounsbury 1956; Nida 1958; Frake 1961). Despite these more encouraging signs, I realize that most dictionaries will continue to be organized primarily as alphabetical indices. Suggestions regarding the ways in which structural semantic information (especially with reference to folk taxonomies) might be more adequately covered in such dictionaries would include, wherever possible: 1. consistent marking of each entry as to its status as a lexical unit and taxon, its immediately subordinate taxa and superordinate taxon, and all coordinate taxa included with it in this next higher taxon (simple diacritics and abbreviations can be devised for systematic use in compilation and checking); 2. differential marking of translation labels and of definitions; 3. concise indication of distinctive attributes which define categories belonging to analyzed lexical sets; 4. systematic cross-referencing to maximal taxa in all major subhierarchies, to referential synonyms, and to all units involved in categoric overlap; and 5. frequent use of structural charts and diagrams. Where only limited opportunities are available for accomplishing such tasks, priority might be given to those parts of the lexicon which, on the basis of non-intuitive and intracultural criteria, appear to involve semantic relations of an everyday, obligatory nature. In number of segregates, paradigmatic complexity, and hierarchic depth, certain lexical domains are likely to be more highly structured than others (Brown 1956, 307; Nida 1958, 283-4; Worth 1960, 277; Frake 1961, 121-2). For the student of folk taxonomy, focusing attention on these domains should lead not only to more interesting analytic problems but also to results of greater lexicographical and general cultural relevance.

5. REFERENCES CITED

Austerlitz, Robert, "Semantic components of pronoun systems: Gilyak", *Word*, 15 (1959), 102-109.

Beckner, Morton, *The Biological Way of Thought* (New York, Columbia University Press, 1959).

Brown, Roger W., "Language and categories" (Appendix) in *A Study of Thinking*, by Jerome S. Bruner *et al.* (New York, John Wiley and Sons, 1956), 247-312 (Appendix).

Bruner, Jerome S., Jacqueline J. Goodnow, and George A. Austin, *A Study of Thinking* (with an Appendix on Language by Roger W. Brown) (New York, John Wiley and Sons, 1956).

Chao, Yuen Ren, "Popular Chinese plant words, a descriptive lexico-grammatical study", *Language*, 29 (1953), 379-414.

Chomsky, A. Noam, "Semantic considerations in grammar", in *Georgetown University Monograph Series on Languages and Linguistics*, No. 8 (Washington, D. C., 1955), 141-150.

—, *Syntactic Structures* ('s-Gravenhage, Mouton, 1957).

Conklin, Harold C., "The relation of Hanunóo culture to the plant world". Unpublished Ph.D. dissertation in anthropology, Yale University. New Haven (1954).

—, "Hanunóo color categories", *Southwestern Journal of Anthropology*, Albuquerque, 11 (1955), 339-344.

—, "Ethnobotanical problems in the comparative study of folk taxonomy". Paper read at the Ninth Pacific Science Congress, Bangkok, 1957 [Published in *Proceedings, Ninth Pacific Science Congress*, 1957, 4: 299-301, Bangkok, 1962].

Frake, Charles O., "The Eastern Subanun of Mindanao", in *Social Structure in Southeast Asia*, ed. George Peter Murdock (Chicago, Quadrangle Books, 1960), 51-64.

—, "The diagnosis of disease among the Subanun of Mindanao", *American Anthropologist*, 63 (1961), 113-132.

Garvin, Paul L., "On structuralist method", *Georgetown University Monograph Series on Languages and Linguistics*, No. 11 (Washington, D. C., 1960), 145-148.

Goodenough, Ward H., *Property, Kin, and Community on Truk* (= *Yale University Publications in Anthropology*, No. 46) (New Haven, Conn., 1951).

—, "Componential analysis and the study of meaning", *Language*, 32 (1956), 195-216.

—, "Cultural anthropology and linguistics", in *Georgetown University Monograph Series on Languages and Linguistics*, No. 9 (Washington, D. C., 1957), 167-173.

Greenberg, Joseph H., "The nature and uses of linguistic typologies", *International Journal of American Linguistics*, 23 (1957), 68-77.

Gregg, John R., *The Language of Taxonomy: an application of symbolic logic to the study of classificatory systems* (New York, Columbia University Press, 1954).

Harris, Zellig, "Componential analysis of a Hebrew paradigm", *Language*, 24 (1948), 87-91.

Haugen, Einar, "The semantics of Icelandic orientation", *Word*, 13 (1957), 447-459.

Hockett, Charles F., "Idiom formation", in *For Roman Jakobson* (The Hague, Mouton, 1956), 222-229.

Householder, Fred W., Jr., Review of: *A course in modern linguistics*, by Charles F. Hockett, in *Language*, 35 (1959), 503-527.

Jakobson, Roman, "Beitrag zur allgemeinen Kasuslehre". *Travaux du Cercle Linguistique de Prague*, 6 (Prague, 1936), 240-288.

Joos, Martin, Review of: *Machine translation of languages: Fourteen essays*, ed. William N. Locke and A. Donald Booth, in *Language*, 32 (1956), 293-298.

—, "Semology: a linguistic theory of meaning", *Studies in Linguistics*, 13 (Buffalo, 1958), 53-70.

Jorden, Eleanor Harz, "The syntax of modern colloquial japanese", *Language*, 31 (1955), i-iv, 1-135.

Kelly, George A., *The Psychology of Personal Constructs*, Vol. 1: *A Theory of Personality* (New York, W. W. Norton, 1955).

Landar, Herbert J., "A note on accepted and rejected arrangements of Navaho words", *International Journal of American Linguistics*, 26 (1960), 351-354.

Landar, Herbert J., Susan M. Ervin, and Arnold E. Horowitz, "Navaho color categories", *Language*, 36 (1960), 368-382.

Lawrence, George H. M., *Taxonomy of Vascular Plants* (New York, Macmillan, 1951).

Lazarsfeld, Paul F., "The algebra of dichotomous systems", in *Studies in Item Analysis and Prediction*, ed. Herbert Solomon (Stanford, Stanford University Press, 1961), 111-157.

Lees, Robert B., "The grammar of English nominalizations", *International Journal of American Linguistics*, 26 (1960), i-xxvi, 1-205 (= *Publication 12, Indiana University Research Center in Anthropology, Folklore, and Linguistics*).

Lenneberg, Eric H., and John M. Roberts, *The language of experience, a study in methodology* (= *International Journal of American Linguistics Memoir No. 13*) (Baltimore, 1956).

Lotz, John, "The semantic analysis of the nominal bases in Hungarian", *Travaux du Cercle Linguistique de Copenhague*, 5 (Copenhague, 1949), 185-197.

Lounsbury, Floyd G., "A semantic analysis of the Pawnee kinship usage", *Language*, 32 (1956), 158-194.

—, "Similarity and contiguity relations in language and culture", *Georgetown University Monograph Series on Languages and Linguistics*, No. 12 (Washington, D. C., 1960), 123-128.

Lyons, J., Review of: *Language change and linguistic reconstruction*, by Henry M. Hoenigswald, in *Bulletin of the School of Oriental and African Studies*, 27 (1960), 621-622.

Maclay, Howard, and Mary D. Sleator, "Responses to language: judgments of grammaticalness", *International Journal of American Linguistics*, 26 (1960), 275-282.

Mayer, Ernst, E. Gorton Linsley, and Robert L. Usinger, *Methods and Principles of Systematic Zoology* (New York, McGraw-Hill, 1953).

McKaughan, Howard, "Semantic components of pronoun systems: Maranao", *Word*, 15 (1959), 101-102.

Morris, Charles W., *Signs, Language, and Behavior* (New York, Prentice-Hall, 1946).

Nagel, Ernest, *The Structure of Science: problems in the logic of scientific explanation* (New York and Burlingame, Harcourt, Brace and World, 1961).

Newman, Stanley, "Semantic problems in grammatical systems and lexemes: a search for method", in *Language in culture*, ed. Harry Hoijer (Chicago, University of Chicago Press, 1954), 82-91.

Nida, Eugene A., "A system for the description of semantic elements", *Word*, 7 (1951), 1-14.

—, "Analysis of meaning and dictionary making", *International Journal of American Linguistics*, 24 (1958), 279-292.

Öhman, Suzanne, "Theories of the 'Linguistic Field' ", *Word*, 9 (1953), 123-134.

Quine, Willard Van Orman, *Word and Object* (Cambridge, Mass., and New York and London, The Technology Press of M.I.T., and John Wiley & Sons, Inc., 1960).

Sebeok, Thomas A., *Finnish and Hungarian case systems: their form and function* (= *Acta Insittuti Hungarici Universitatis Holmiensis*, Series B, Linguistica, 3) (Stockholm, 1946).

Simpson, George Gaylord, *Principles of Animal Taxonomy* (New York, Columbia University Press, 1961).

Swadesh, Morris, "Chitimacha", in *Linguistic Structures of Native North America*, by Harry Hoijer *et al.* (New York, Viking Fund, 1946), 312-336.

Thomas, David, "Three analyses of the Ilocano pronoun system", *Word*, 11 (1955), 204-208.

——, "An introduction to Mansaka lexicography". 6 typescript pp. Nasuli, Philippines: SIL, 1957.

Voegelin, Charles F., and Florence M., *Hopi domains, a lexical approach to the problem of selection* (= *International Journal of American Linguistics Memoir No. 14*) (Baltimore, 1957).

Wallace, Anthony F. C., and John Atkins, "The meaning of kinship terms", *American Anthropologist*, 62 (1960), 58-80.

Weinreich, Uriel, "Mid-century linguistics: attainments and frustrations", *Romance Philology*, 8 (1960), 320-341.

Wells, Rulon, "Is a structural treatment of meaning possible?", *Proceedings of the Eighth International Congress of Linguists, Oslo, 1957* (Oslo, 1958), 654-666.

Wonderly, William L., "Semantic components in Kechua person morphemes", *Language*, 28 (1952), 366-376.

Woodger, J. H., *Biology and Language: an introduction to the methodology of the biological sciences including medicine* (Cambridge, Harv. University Press, 1952).

Worth, D. S., Review of: *Leksikologija anglijskogo jazyka*, by A. I. Smirnickij, in *Word*, 16 (1960), 277-284.

From: *Problems in Lexicography* (Fred W. Householder and Sol Saporta, eds.), *International Journal of American Linguistics*, 28 (1962), pp. 119-141. Also *Publication 21, Indiana University Research Center in Anthropology, Folklore, and Linguistics*. Reprinted with permission.

Charles O. Frake

THE ETHNOGRAPHIC STUDY OF COGNITIVE SYSTEMS *

WORDS FOR THINGS

A relatively simple task commonly performed by ethnographers is that of getting names for things. The ethnographer typically performs this task by pointing to or holding up the apparent constituent objects of an event he is describing, eliciting the native names for the objects, and then matching each native name with the investigator's own word for the object. The logic of the operation is: if the informant calls object X a *mbubu* and I call object X a *rock*, then *mbubu* means *rock*. In this way are compiled the ordinary ethnobotanical monographs with their lists of matched native and scientific names for plant specimens. This operation probably also accounts for a good share of the native names parenthetically inserted in so many monograph texts: "Among the grasses (*sigbet*) whose grains (*bunga nen*) are used for beads (*bitekel*) none is more highly prized than Job's tears (*glias*)." Unless the reader is a comparative linguist of the languages concerned, he may well ask what interest these parenthetical insertions contain other than demonstrating that the ethnographer has discharged a minimal obligation toward collecting linguistic data. This procedure for obtaining words for things, as well as the "so-what" response it so often evokes, assumes the objective identifiability of discrete "things" apart from a particular culture. It construes the name-getting task as one of simply matching verbal labels for "things" in two languages. Accordingly, the "problem-oriented" anthropologist, with a broad, cross-cultural perspective, may disclaim any interest in these

* In preparing this paper I have especially benefited from suggestions by Harold C. Conklin, Thomas Gladwin, Volney Stefflre, and William C. Sturtevant.

labels; all that concerns him is the presence or absence of a particular "thing" in a given culture.

If, however, instead of "getting words for things", we redefine the task as one of finding the "things" that go with the words, the eliciting of terminologies acquires a more general interest. In actuality not even the most concrete, objectively apparent physical object can be identified apart from some culturally defined system of concepts (Boas 1911, 24-25; Bruner *et al.* 1956; Goodenough 1957). An ethnographer should strive to define objects [1] according to the conceptual system of the people he is studying. Let me suggest, then, that one look upon the task of getting names for things not as an exercise in linguistic recording, but as a way of finding out what are in fact the "things" in the environment of the people being studied. This paper consists of some suggestions toward the formulation of an operationally-explicit methodology for discerning how people construe their world of experience from the way they talk about it. Specifically these suggestions concern the analysis of terminological systems in a way which reveals the conceptual principles that generate them.

In a few fields, notably in kinship studies, anthropologists have already successfully pushed an interest in terminological systems beyond a matching of translation labels. Since Morgan's day no competent student of kinship has looked upon his task as one of simply finding a tribe's word for "uncle", "nephew", or "cousin". The recognition that the denotative range of kinship categories must be determined empirically in each case, that the categories form a system, and that the semantic contrasts underlying the system are amenable to formal analysis, has imparted to kinship studies a methodological rigor and theoretical productivity rare among ethnographic endeavors. Yet all peoples are vitally concerned with kinds of phenomena other than genealogical relations; consequently there is no reason why the study of a people's concepts of these other phenomena should not offer a theoretical interest comparable to that of kinship studies.

Even with reference to quite obvious kinds of material objects, it has long been noted that many people do not see "things" quite the way we do. However, anthropologists in spite of their now well-established psychological interests have notably ignored the cognition of their subjects. Consequently other investigators still rely on stock anecdotes of "primitive thinking" handed down by explorers, philologists, and psychologists since the nineteenth century (Brown 1958, 256; Hill 1952; Jespersen 1934, 429; Ullman 1957, 95, 308). Commonly these anecdotes have been cited as examples of early stages in the evolution of

[1] In this paper the term *object* designates anything construed as a member of a category (Bruner *et al.* 1956, 231), whether perceptible or not.

human thought – which, depending on the anecdote selected, may be either from blindly concrete to profoundly abstract or from hopelessly vague to scientifically precise. A typical citation, purporting to illustrate the primitive's deficient abstractive ability, concerns a Brazilian Indian tribe which allegedly has no word for "parrot" but only words for "kinds of parrots" (Jespersen 1934, 429 ff.). The people of such a tribe undoubtedly classify the birds of their environment in some fashion; certainly they do not bestow a unique personal name on each individual bird specimen they encounter. Classification means that individual bird specimens must be matched against the defining attributes of conceptual categories and thereby judged to be equivalent for certain purposes to some other specimens but different from still others. Since no two birds are alike in every discernible feature, any grouping into sets implies a selection of only a limited number of features as significant for contrasting kinds of birds. A person learns which features are significant from his fellows as part of his cultural equipment. He does not receive this information from the birds. Consequently there is no necessary reason that a Brazilian Indian should heed those particular attributes which, for the English-speaker, make equivalent all the diverse individual organisms he labels "parrots". Some of this Indian's categories may seem quite specific, and others quite general, when compared to our grouping of the same specimens. But learning that it takes the Indian many words to name the objects we happen to group together in one set is trivial information compared to knowing how the Indian himself groups these objects and which attributes he selects as dimensions to generate a taxonomy of avifauna. With the latter knowledge we learn what these people regard as significant about birds. If we can arrive at comparable knowledge about their concepts of land animals, plants, soils, weather, social relations, personalities, and supernaturals, we have at least a sketch map of the world in the image of the tribe.

The analysis of a culture's terminological systems will not, of course, exhaustively reveal the cognitive world of its members, but it will certainly tap a central portion of it. Culturally significant cognitive features must be communicable between persons in one of the standard symbolic systems of the culture. A major share of these features will undoubtedly be codable in a society's most flexible and productive communication device, its language. Evidence also seems to indicate that those cognitive features requiring most frequent communication will tend to have standard and relatively short linguistic labels (Brown 1958, 235-241; Brown and Lenneberg 1954). Accordingly, a commonly distinguished category of trees is more likely to be called something like "elm" by almost all speakers rather than labelled with an ad hoc, non-standardized construction like, "You know, those tall trees with asymmetrical, serrated-edged leaves." To the extent that cognitive coding tends to be linguistic and tends to be efficient, the study of the referential use of standard, readily elicitable linguistic responses – or *terms* – should provide a fruitful beginning point for mapping a cognitive system. And with verbal behavior we know how to begin.

The beginning of an ethnographic task is the recording of what is seen and heard, the segmenting of the behavior stream in such a way that culturally significant noises and movements are coded while the irrelevant is discarded. Descriptive linguistics provides a methodology for segmenting the stream of speech into units relevant to the structure of the speaker's language. I assume that any verbal response which conforms to the phonology and grammar of a language is necessarily a culturally significant unit of behavior. Methodologies for the structural description of non-verbal behavior are not correspondingly adequate in spite of important contributions in this direction by such persons as Pike and Barker and Wright (Barker and Wright 1955; Pike 1954; cf. Miller *et al.* 1960, 14-15). By pushing forward the analysis of units we know to be culturally relevant, we can, I think, more satisfactorily arrive at procedures for isolating the significant constituents of analogous and interrelated structures. The basic methodological concept advocated here – the determination of the set of contrasting responses appropriate to a given, culturally valid, eliciting context – should ultimately be applicable to the "semantic" analysis of any culturally meaningful behavior.

SEGREGATES

A terminologically distinguished array of objects is a *segregate* (Conklin 1954, 1962; cf. Lounsbury 1956). Segregates are categories, but not all categories known or knowable to an individual are segregates by this definition. Operationally, this definition of a segregate leaves a problem: how do we recognize a "term" when we hear one? How do we segment the stream of speech into category-designating units?

The segmentation of speech into the grammatically functioning units revealed by linguistic analysis is a necessary, but not sufficient, condition for terminological analysis. Clearly no speech segment smaller than the minimal grammatical unit, the morpheme, need be considered. However, the task requires more than simply a search for the meanings of morphemes or other grammatical units. The items and arrangements of a structural description of the language code need not be isomorphic with the categories and propositions of the message. Linguistic forms, whether morphemes or larger constructions, are not each tied to unique chunks of semantic reference like baggage tags; rather it is the use of speech, the selection of one statement over another in a particular sociolinguistic context, that points to the category boundaries on a culture's cognitive map (Chomsky 1955; Haugen 1957; Hymes 1961; Joos 1958; Lounsbury 1956; Nida 1951).

Suppose we have been studying the verbal behavior accompanying the selection and ordering of items at an American lunch counter.[2] The following text might be typical of those overheard and recorded:

"What ya going to have, Mac? Something to eat?"

"Yeah. What kind of sandwiches ya got besides hamburgers and hot dogs?"

"How about a ham 'n cheese sandwich?"

"Nah . . . I guess I'll take a hamburger again."

- - - - - - - - - - - - - -

"Hey, that's no hamburger; that's a cheeseburger!"

The problem is to isolate and relate these speech forms according to their use in naming objects. Some, but apparently not all, orderable items at a lunch counter are distinguished by the term *something to eat*. A possibility within the range of "something to eat" seems to be a set of objects labelled *sandwiches*. The forms *hamburger, hot dog, ham 'n cheese sandwich*, and *cheeseburger* clearly designate alternative choices in lunch-counter contexts. A customer determined to have a "sandwich" must select one of these alternatives when he orders, and upon receipt of the order, he must satisfy himself that the object thrust before him – which he has never seen before – meets the criteria for membership in the segregate he designated. The counterman must decide on actions that will produce an object acceptable to the customer as a member of the designated segregate. The terminological status of these forms can be confirmed by analysis of further speech situations, by eliciting utterances with question frames suggested to the investigator by the data, and by observing non-verbal features of the situation, especially correlations between terms used in ordering and objects received.

In isolating these terms no appeal has been made to analysis of their linguistic structure or their signification. *Sandwich* is a single morpheme. Some linguists, at any rate, would analyze *hot dog* and even *hamburger* as each containing two morphemes, but, since the meaning of the constructions cannot be predicted from a knowledge of the meaning of their morphological constituents, they are single "lexemes" (Goodenough

[2] Because this is a short, orally presented paper, suggested procedures are illustrated with rather simple examples from a familiar language and culture. A serious analysis would require much larger quantities of speech data presented in phonemic transcription. For a more complex example, intended as an ethnographic statement, see Frake 1961.

1956) or "idioms" (Hockett 1958, 303-318). *Ham 'n cheese sandwich* would not, I think, qualify as a single lexeme; nevertheless it is a standard segregate label whose function in naming objects cannot be distinguished from that of forms like *hot dog*. Suppose further utterances from lunch-counter speech show that the lexically complex term *something to eat* distinguishes the same array of objects as do the single morphemes *food* and *chow*. In such a case, a choice among these three terms would perhaps say something about the social status of the lunch counter and its patrons, but it says nothing distinctive about the objects designated. As segregate labels, these three frequently-heard terms would be equivalent.

Although not operationally relevant at this point, the lexemic status of terms bears on later analysis of the productivity of a terminological system. In contrast, say, to our kinship terminology, American lunch-counter terminology is highly productive. The existence of productive, polylexemic models such as *ham 'n cheese sandwich* permits the generation and labelling of new segregates to accommodate the latest lunch-counter creations. However, the non-intuitive determination of the lexemic status of a term requires a thorough analysis of the distinctive features of meaning of the term and its constituents (Goodenough 1956; Lounsbury 1956). Such an analysis of the criteria for placing objects into categories can come only after the term, together with those contrasting terms relevant to its use, has been isolated as a segregate label.

CONTRAST SETS

In a situation in which a person is making a public decision about the category membership of an object by giving the object a verbal label, he is selecting a term out of a set of alternatives, each with classificatory import. When he asserts "This is an X", he is also stating that it is *not* specific other things, these other things being not everything else conceivable, but only the alternatives among which a decision was made (Kelly 1955). In lunch-counter ordering, "hamburger", "hot dog", "cheeseburger", and "ham and cheese sandwich" are such alternatives. Any object placed in one of these segregates cannot at the same time belong to another. Those culturally appropriate responses which are distinctive alternatives in the same kinds of situations – or, in linguistic parlance, which occur in the same "environment" – can be said to *contrast*. A series of terminologically contrasted segregates forms a *contrast set*.

Note that the cognitive relation of contrast is not equivalent to the relation of class exclusion in formal logic and set theory. The three categories "hamburger", "hot dog", and "rainbow" are mutually exclusive in membership. But in writing rules for classifying hamburgers I must say something about hot dogs, whereas I can ignore rainbows. Two categories contrast only when the difference between them is significant for defining their use. The segregates "hamburger" and "rainbow", even though they have no members in common, do not function as distinctive alternatives in any uncontrived classifying context familiar to me.

TAXONOMIES

The notion of contrast cannot account for all the significant relations among these lunch-counter segregates. Although no object can be both a hamburger and a hot dog, an object can very well be both a hot dog and a sandwich or a hamburger and a sandwich. By recording complementary names applied to the same objects (and eliminating referential synonyms such as *something to eat* and *food*), the following series might result:

Object A is named: *something to eat, sandwich, hamburger*
Object B is named: *something to eat, sandwich, ham sandwich*
Object C is named: *something to eat, pie, apple pie*
Object D is named: *something to eat, pie, cherry pie*
Object E is named: *something to eat, ice-cream bar, Eskimo pie.*

Some segregates include a wider range of objects than others and are sub-partitioned by a contrast set. The segregate "pie" *includes* the contrast set "apple pie", "cherry pie", etc. For me, the segregate "apple pie" is, in turn, sub-partitioned by "French apple pie" and "plain (or 'ordinary') apple pie". Figure 1 diagrams the sub-partitioning of the segregate "something to eat" as revealed by naming responses to objects A-E.[3]

	something to eat				
	sandwich		pie		ice-cream bar
	hamburger	ham sandwich	apple pie	cherry pie	Eskimo pie
OBJECTS:	A	B	C	D	E

Figure 1. Sub-partitioning of the segregate "something to eat" as revealed by naming responses to objects A-E.

[3] This example is, of course, considerably over-simplified. If the reader does not relate these segregates in the same way as our hypothetical lunch-counter speakers, he is not alone. Shortly after I completed the manuscript of this paper, a small boy approached me in a park and, without any eliciting remark whatsoever on my part, announced: "Hamburgers are more gooder than sandwiches." One could not ask for better evidence of contrast.

Again it is the use of terms, not their linguistic structure, that provides evidence of inclusion. We cannot consider "Eskimo pie" to be included in the category "pie", for we cannot discover a natural situation in which an object labelled *Eskimo pie* can be labelled simply *pie*. Thus the utterance, "That's not a sandwich; that's a pie", cannot refer to an Eskimo pie. Similar examples are common in English. The utterance, "Look at that oak", may refer to a "white oak" but never to a "poison oak". A "blackbird" is a kind of "bird", but a "redcap" is not a kind of "cap". For many English speakers, the unqualified use of *American* invariably designates a resident or citizen of the United States; consequently, for such speakers, an "American" is a kind of "North American" rather than the converse. One cannot depend on a particular grammatical construction, such as one of the English phrasal compounds, to differentiate consistently a single cognitive relation, such as that of inclusion (cf. Hockett 1958, 316-317). Because English is not unique in this respect (Frake 1961), the practice of arguing from morphological and syntactic analysis directly to cognitive relations must be considered methodologically unsound.

Segregates in different contrast sets, then, may be related by inclusion. A system of contrast sets so related is a *taxonomy* (Conklin 1962; Gregg 1954; Woodger 1952). This definition does not require a taxonomy to have a unique beginner, i.e., a segregate which includes all other segregates in the system. It requires only that the segregates at the most inclusive level form a demonstrable contrast set.

Taxonomies make possible a regulation of the amount of information communicated about an object in a given situation (compare: "Give me something to eat" with "Give me a French apple pie a la mode"), and they provide a hierarchal ordering of categories, allowing an efficient program for the identification, filing, and retrieving of significant information (Herdan 1960, 210-211). The use of taxonomic systems is not confined to librarians and biologists; it is a fundamental principle of human thinking. The elaboration of taxonomies along vertical dimensions of generalization and horizontal dimensions of discrimination probably depends on factors such as the variety of cultural settings within which one talks about the objects being classified (Frake 1961, 121-122), the importance of the objects to the way of life of the classifiers (Brown 1958; Nida 1958), and general properties of human thinking with regard to the number of items that the mind can cope with at a given time (Miller 1956; Yngve 1960).[4] Determining the precise correlates of

[4] At least in formal, highly partitioned taxonomic systems an ordering of superordinates according to the number of their subordinates appears to yield a stable statistical distribution (the Willis distribution) regardless of what is being classified or who is doing the classifying (Herdan 1960, 211-225; Mandelbrot 1956).

variations in taxonomic structure, both intra-culturally and cross-culturally, is, of course, one of the objectives of this methodology.

In order to describe the use of taxonomic systems and to work out their behavioral correlates, evidence of complementary naming must be supplemented by observations on the socio-linguistic contexts that call for contrasts at particular levels. One could, for example, present a choice between objects whose segregates appear to contrast at different levels and ask an informant to complete the frame: "Pick up that ____." Suppose we have an apple pie on the counter next to a ham sandwich. The frame would probably be completed as "Pick up that pie". If, however, we substitute a cherry pie for the ham sandwich, we would expect to hear "Pick up that apple pie". Variations on this device of having informants contrast particular objects can be worked out depending on the kind of phenomena being classified. Some objects, such as pies and plants, are easier to bring together for visual comparison than others, such as diseases and deities.

Another device for eliciting taxonomic structures is simply to ask directly about relations of inclusion: "Is *X* a kind of *Y*?" Since in many speech situations even a native fails to elicit a term at the level of specification he requires, most, if not all, languages probably provide explicit methods for moving up and down a taxonomic hierarchy:

"Give me some of that pie". "What kind of pie d'ya want, Mac?"

"What's this 'submarine' thing on the menu?" "That's a kind of sandwich."

Once a taxonomic partitioning has been worked out it can be tested systematically for terminological contrast with frames such as "Is that an X?" with an expectation of a negative reply. For example, we could point to an apple pie and ask a counterman:

1. "Is that something to drink?"
2. "Is that a sandwich?"
3. "Is that a cherry pie?"

We would expect the respective replies to reflect the taxonomy of lunch-counter foods:

1. "No, it's something to eat."
2. "No, it's a pie."
3. "No, it's an apple pie."

(Admittedly it is easier to do this kind of questioning in a culture where one can assume the role of a naive learner.)

In employing these various operations for exploring taxonomic structures, the investigator must be prepared for cases when the same linguistic form designates segregates at different levels of contrast within the same system ("man" vs. "animal", "man" vs. "woman", "man" vs. "boy") (Frake 1961, 119); when a single unpartitioned segregate contrasts with two or more other segregates which are themselves at different levels of contrast ("That's not a coin; it's a token." "That's not a dime; it's a token"); and when incongruities occur in the results of the several operations (terminological contrasts may cut across sub-hierarchies revealed by complementary naming; explicit statements of inclusion may be less consistent than complementary naming).

ATTRIBUTES

Our task up to this point has been to reveal the structure of the system from which a selection is made when categorizing an object. When you hand a Navajo a plant specimen, or an American a sandwich, what is the available range of culturally defined arrays into which this object can be categorized? Methodological notions of contrast and inclusion have enabled us to discern some structure in this domain of cognitive choices, but we still have not faced the problem of how a person decides which out of a set of alternative categorizations is the correct one in a given instance. How does one in fact distinguish a hamburger from a cheeseburger, a chair from a stool, a tree from a shrub, an uncle from a cousin, a jerk from a slob?

A mere list of known members of a category – however an investigator identifies these objects cross-culturally – does not answer this question. Categorization, in essence, is a device for treating new experience as though it were equivalent to something already familiar (Brown 1958; Bruner 1957; Bruner *et al.* 1956; Sapir 1949). The hamburger I get tomorrow may be a quite different object in terms of size, kind of bun, and lack of tomatoes from the hamburger I had today. But it will still be a hamburger – unless it has a slice of cheese on it! To define "hamburger" one must know, not just what objects it includes, but with what it contrasts. In this way we learn that a slice of cheese makes a difference, whereas a slice of tomato does not. In the context of different cultures the task is to state what one must know in order to categorize objects correctly. A definition of a Navajo plant category is not given by a list of botanical species it contains but by a rule for distinguishing newly encountered specimens of that category from contrasting alternatives.

Ideally the criterial attributes which generate a contrast set fall along a limited number of dimensions of contrast, each with two or more contrasting values or "components". Each segregate can be defined as a distinctive bundle of components. For example, the plant taxonomy of the Eastern Subanun, a Philippine people, has as its beginner a contrast set of three segregates which together include almost all of the more than 1400 segregates at the most specific level of contrast within the taxonomy. This three member contrast set can be generated by binary contrasts along two dimensions pertaining to habit of stem growth (see Table I).

TABLE I

Defining attributes of the constrast set of stem habit in the Subanun plant taxonomy

CONTRAST SET	DIMENSIONS OF CONTRAST	
	Woodiness	*Rigidity*
gayu "woody plants"	W	R
sigbet "herbaceous plants"	$\overline{W}$	R
belagen "vines"		$\overline{R}$

Applications of componential analysis to pronominal systems and kinship terminologies have made this method of definition familiar (Austerlitz 1959; Conklin 1962; Goodenough 1956; Lounsbury 1956; McKaughan 1959; Thomas 1955; Wallace and Atkins 1960). The problem remains of demonstrating the cognitive saliency of componential solutions – to what extent are they models of how a person decides which term to use? – and of relating terminological attributes to actual perceptual discriminations (Frake 1961; Wallace and Atkins 1960). As a case of the latter problem, suppose we learn that informants distinguish two contrasting plant segregates by calling the fruit of one "red" and that of the other "green". We set up "color" as a dimension of contrast with values of "red" and "green". But the terminology of "color" is itself a system of segregates whose contrastive structure must be analysed before color terms can serve as useful defining attributes of other segregates. Ultimately one is faced with defining color categories by referring to the actual perceptual dimensions along which informants make differential categorizations. These dimensions must be determined empirically and not prescribed by the investigator using stimulus materials from his own culture. By careful observation one might discover that visual evaluation of an object's succulence, or other unexpected dimensions, as well as the traditional dimensions of hue, brightness, and saturation, are criterial to the use of "color" terms in a particular culture (Conklin 1955).

Whether aimed directly at perceptual qualities of phenomena or at informants' descriptions of pertinent attributes (Frake 1961, 122-125), any method for determining the distinctive and probabilistic attributes of a segregate must depend, first, on knowing the contrast set within which the segregate is participating, and, second, on careful observations of verbal and non-verbal features of the cultural situations to which this contrast set provides an appropriate response.

This formulation has important implications for the role of eliciting in ethnography. The distinctive "situations", or "eliciting frames", or "stimuli", which evoke and define a set of contrasting responses are cultural data to be discovered, not prescribed, by the ethnographer. This structure does not limit the use of preconceived eliciting devices to prod an informant into action or speech without any intent of defining the response by what evoked it in this instance. But the formulation – prior to observation – of response-defining eliciting devices is ruled out by the logic of this methodology which insists that any eliciting conditions not themselves part of the cultural-ecological system being investigated cannot be used to define categories purporting to be those of the people under study. It is those elements of *our informants'* experience, which *they* heed in selecting appropriate actions and utterances, that this methodology seeks to discover.

OBJECTIVES

The methodological suggestions proposed in this paper, as they stand, are clearly awkward and incomplete. They must be made more rigorous and expanded to include analyses of longer utterance sequences, to consider non-verbal behavior systematically, and to explore the other types of cognitive relations, such as sequential stage relations (Frake 1961) and part-whole relations, that may pertain between contrast sets. Focussing on the linguistic code, clearer operational procedures are needed for delimiting semantically exocentric units ("lexemes" or "idioms") (Goodenough 1956; Nida 1951), for discerning synonomy, homonymy, and polysemy (Ullman 1957, 63), and for distinguishing between utterance grammaticalness (correctly constructed code) and utterance congruence (meaningfully constructed message) (Chomsky 1957; Joos 1958). In their present form, however, these suggestions have come out of efforts to describe behavior in the field, and their further development can come only from continuing efforts to apply and test them in ethnographic field situations.

The intended objective of these efforts is eventually to provide the ethnographer with public, non-intuitive procedures for ordering his presentation of observed and elicited events according to the principles of classification of the people he is studying. To order ethnographic observations solely according to an investigator's preconceived categories obscures the real content of culture: how people organize their experience conceptually so that it can be transmitted as knowledge from person to person and from generation to generation. As Goodenough advocates in a classic paper, culture "does not consist of things, people, behavior, or emotions", but the forms or organization of these things in the minds of people (Goodenough 1957). The principles by which people in a culture construe their world reveal how they segregate the pertinent from the insignificant, how they code and retrieve information, how they anticipate events (Kelly 1955), how they define alternative courses of action and make decisions among them. Consequently a strategy of ethnographic description that gives a central place to the cognitive processes of the actors involved will contribute reliable cultural data to problems of the relations between language, cognition, and behavior; it will point up critical dimensions for meaningful cross-cultural comparison; and, finally, it will give us productive descriptions of cultural behavior, descriptions which, like the linguists' grammar, succinctly state what one must know in order to generate culturally acceptable acts and utterances appropriate to a given socio-ecological context (Goodenough 1957).

From: *Anthropology and Human Behavior*, T. Gladwin and Wm. C. Sturtevant, eds. (Washington, D. C., Anthropological Society of Washington, 1962), pp. 73-85. Reprinted with permission. Consult original source for references.

Harold Basilius

NEO-HUMBOLDTIAN ETHNO-LINGUISTICS

The cross-fertilization of the sciences continues to develop from a desideratum to a necessity at an increasing pace owing obviously to the growing conviction that only by scientific teamwork can ultimate order be brought to the welter of data and tentative conclusions spawned by the individual sciences. Bertrand Russell refers to the matter as "the science to save us from science" (*New York Times Magazine*, 19 March 1950). As regards language, a consensus has developed which holds that language is the sole single characteristic which differentiates man from the other animals and which by that token alone affords the potential for relating man to the cultures which he has created. The realization of the potential requires scientific teamwork, as John Lotz only recently pointed out:

> Language exists mainly through speech, and thus only a cooperative effort of the various disciplines, such as communications engineering and physics, medicine and physiology, psychology and linguistics can achieve the solution of the problems of human speech.[1]

Almost a quarter of a century earlier Edward Sapir said much the same:

> It is peculiarly important that linguistics, who are often accused, and accused justly, of failure to look beyond pretty patterns of their subject matter, should become aware of what their science may mean for the interpretation of human conduct in general. Whether they like it or not they must become

[1] John Lotz, "Speech and Language", *Jour. Acoust. Soc. of Amer.*, 22 (Nov. 1950), 717.

[2] Edward Sapir, "The Status of Linguistics As a Science", *Language*, 5 (1929), 214.

increasingly concerned with the many anthropological, sociological, and psychological problems which invade the field of language.[2]

The virtually antipodal positions of anthropologists and sociologists on the one hand and linguists on the other to the question of the relationship between language and culture is all the more amazing. Even a cursory examination of sociological literature reveals a virtually complete consensus regarding the unique key position of language as related to culture.[3] The late culturist Ernst Cassirer summarized the matter thus:

> Language is neither a mechanism nor an organism, neither a dead nor a living thing. It is no thing at all, if by this term we understand a physical object. It is – language, a very specific human activity, not describable in terms of physics, chemistry, or biology. The best and most laconic expression of this fact was given by W. v. Humboldt, when he declared that language is not an *ergon*, but an *energeia*.[4]

In brief, anthropologists, culturists, psychologists, and sociologists look to the linguist for basic cooperative effort toward solving cultural problems. They welcome the development of the new science of ethnolinguistics.

Whereas some linguists, those particularly whose orientation is anthropological, because of their preoccupation with the languages of more primitive cultures, see eye to eye in the matter with the culturalists,[5]

[3] See for example: Burt W. and Ethel G. Aginsky, "The Importance of Language Universals", *Word,* 4 (Dec. 1948), 168 ff.; Ethel G. Aginsky, "Language and Culture", *Proceedings of the Eighth Amer. Scientific Congress,* Vol. II, 271-276; Stuart Chase, *The Proper Study of Mankind* (New York, 1948); Clyde Kluckhohn, *Mirror for Man* (New York, 1949), 159; H. D. Lasswell, Nathan Leites, and Associates, *The Language of Politics, Studies in Quantitative Semantics* (New York, 1949); Bronislaw Malinowski, *A Scientific Theory of Culture and Other Essays* (Chapel Hill, 1944), *passim*; Elton Mayo, *Social Problems of an Industrial Civilization* (Boston, 1945); Margaret Mead, "The Application of Anthropological Techniques to Cross-National Communication", *Transactions of the N. Y. Academy of Sciences,* (February 1947), *passim*; Pitirim A. Sorokin, *Social and Cultural Dynamics* (New York, 1941), Vol. 4, *passim*; E. B. Tylor, *Primitive Culture,* 1.1 (Boston, 1874); Ludwig Klages, *Die Sprache als Quelle der Seelenkunde* (Zurich, 1948).

[4] Ernst A. Cassirer, "Structuralism in Modern Linguistics", *Word,* 1 (1945), 110.

[5] See, for example, the well-known work of Franz Boas and Edward Sapir; Harry Hoijer, "Linguistic and Cultural Change", *Language,* 24 (1948), 335-345; Edgar H. Sturtevant, *An Introduction to Linguistic Science* (New Haven, 1947), pp. 2, 7; Eugene Nida, "Linguistics and Ethnology in Translation-Problems", *Word,* 1 (1945), 194-208: Charles F. Hockett, "Language 'and' Culture: A Protest", *American Anthropologist,* 52 (1950), 113, and the various articles of Benjamin Whorf collected as *Four Articles on Metalinguistics* (Washington, Foreign Service Institute, 1950).

the consensus among American linguists tends on the whole to want to leave the whole question of meaning and its cultural implications to the sociologists and psychologists.

The late and genuinely great Leonard Bloomfield's well-known resistance to "mentalistic" approaches to language persuaded him to a position seeming to avoid questions of meaning. He rationalized his position on the grounds of modesty. The following statement is typical:

> In order to give a scientifically accurate definition of meaning for every form of language, we should have to have a scientifically accurate knowledge of everything in the speakers' world. The actual extent of human knowledge is very small, compared to this.[6]

Bloomfield's apparent tendency to avoid the problem of meaning [7] and to focus linguistic science exclusively on the formal analysis of utterances was only recently raised to the level of positive and exclusive doctrine by Martin Joos before the Speech Communication Conference at M.I.T. The précis heading his paper states that:

> Physicists describe speech with continuous mathematics, such as Fourier analysis or the auto-correlation function. Linguists describe language instead, using a discontinuous or discreet mathematics called 'linguistics'. The nature of this odd calculus is outlined and justified here. It treats speech communication as having a telegraphic structure. (Non-linguists normally fail to orient themselves in this field because they treat speech as analogous to telephony.) The telegraph-code structure of language is examined from top to bottom, and at each of its several levels of complexity (compared to the two levels of Morse code) its structure is shown to be defined by possibilities and impossibilities of combination among the units of that level. Above the highest level we find, instead of such absolute restrictions, conditional probabilities of occurrence: this is the semantic field, outside linguistics, where sociologists can work. Below the lowest level we find, instead of such absolute restrictions, conditional probabilities of phonetic quality: this is the phonetic field, outside linguistics, where physicists can work. Thus linguistics is peculiar among mathematical systems in that it abuts upon reality in two places instead of one. This statement is equivalent to defining a language as a symbolic system; that is, as a code.[8]

[6] L. Bloomfield, *Language* (New York, 1933), p. 139. For a restatement of the same position in even more exaggerated terms see L. Bloomfield, "Meaning", *Monatshefte,* XXXV (1943), 101-106.

[7] That Bloomfield's tendency to avoid questions of meaning was more apparent than real is implicit in the above quotation from *Language.* From time to time Bloomfield himself corroborated this in conversation with friends, among them Roman Jakobson, and indicated that only lack of time had prevented him from tackling such highly important and pertinent questions as he would like to have done.

[8] Martin Joos, "Description of Language Design", *Jour. Acoust. Soc. of Amer.,* 22 (1950), 701.

That other linguists, however, continue to preoccupy themselves with the scientific formulation of relations between language and culture (in terms other than Joos' "structural semantics") is clearly shown by a recent article of M. B. Emeneau which suggests an addition to Bloomfield's Set of Postulates [9] in the following terms:

"Some forms are ordered in classes or sub-classes corresponding to systems or subsystems within the environment." [10]

Still other American linguists are programmatically rejecting the strict asseverance of meaning from sound and the exclusion of meaning from linguistic science, so, for example, Roman Jakobson [11] and John Lotz.[12]

Cassirer's apt summary of the bone of contention between the two schools of linguistics deserves quotation:

> We could use Plato's description of the great *gigantomaxia* as a very good formula for the struggle between the materialists and formalists in modern linguistics. The former 'maintain stoutly that alone exists which can be touched and handled.' And the only things in human speech that can be grasped in this way are sounds. If we have found the mechanical laws that govern the phenomena of sound-shift, of phonetic change, we have found the laws of language. The adversaries of this thesis – the structuralists – defend themselves 'with weapons derived from the invisible world above.' They emphasize that sounds, as mere physical occurrences, have no interest for the linguist. The sounds must have a meaning; the phoneme itself is a 'unit of meaning'. And meaning is not a visible or tangible thing.[13]

In Germany the work of a small group of linguists, sometimes called Neo-Humboldtians, proceeding from the dictum of Wilhelm von Humboldt that language is not an *ergon*, that is a mere means of exchange for purposes of communication, but instead an *energeia* which reconstitutes human experience ideally and makes this idealization overt, has been doing spadework in showing up specific manifestation of culture in several languages, notably German, and in some cases the manifestation of cultural differences in the variations between the vocabulary and grammatical structure of two or more languages. The stance of the Neo-Humboldtians is both mentalistic and psychologistic but their approach and method are nonetheless empirical. They are in conscious opposition to traditional linguistics including the contempo-

[9] *Language*, 2 (1926), 153-64.

[10] M. B. Emeneau, "Language and Non-Linguistic Patterns", *Language*, 26 (1950), 209.

[11] Roman Jakobson, "On the Identification of Phonetic Entities", *Travaux du Cercle Linguistique de Copenhague*, V (1949), 205-13.

[12] As cited above.

[13] Ernst Cassirer, as cited above, p. 113. The first two quotations are from the context and derive from Plato's *Sophist*.

rary American variety on the grounds that it has operated in a social vacuum by continuing to restrict itself exclusively to the formalogical analysis of languages.

Cassirer's interpretation and defense of von Humboldt's ideas from the point of view of modern structuralism aptly summarizes and evaluates the Neo-Humboldtian position:

But Humboldt was not only a friend and admirer of Goethe's; he was also a student of Kant and a pupil of Kant's philosophy. No other philosophical work had made such a deep impression upon his mind as Kant's *Critique of Pure Reason.* In his essay 'Ueber Schiller und den allgemeinen Gang seiner Geistesentwicklung,' Humboldt gave a general characterization of Kantian philosophy that, in spite of all the things that have been said and written about Kant, is in many respects still unsurpassed. But even in the work of Kant, Humboldt could not find an immediate inspiration for his own work. Kant was interested in mathematics, in physics, in ethics; but he was not interested in the problem of human speech. When Kant's *Critique of Pure Reason* appeared, Herder complained bitterly that in this work, the problem of human speech seemed to be entirely neglected. How is it possible, he asked, to criticize human reason without becoming a critic of human language? That was one of the principal objections raised by Herder. He became a fierce opponent of Kant; he wrote in 1799 his *Metkritik der reinen Vernunft.* Humboldt went the opposite way. He accepted Kant's theory of knowledge, but he tried to complete it; he applied the principles of Kant's critical philosophy to the study of human language. [See E. Cassirer, "Die Kantischen Elemente in Wilhelm von Humboldts Sprachphilosophie," *Festschrift für Paul Hensel*, Greiz, 1923, pp. 105-27.]

There was a time in which Humboldt's ideas seemed to be entirely forgotten in linguistics. The positivistic schools of the nineteenth century looked upon his theories with a certain suspicion. At best, they saw in them mere metaphysical speculations without empirical purport and value. In this respect, too, modern structuralism has done very much to revise and correct our historical judgment.

"Je me trouve d'accord", says Viggo Bröndal in his article "Structure et variabilité des systèmes morphologiques", "avec l'universalisme exigé et pratiqué il y a cent ans par le grand maître de linguistique générale qu'était Guillaume de Humboldt!" [14]

Some fifteen years earlier the eminent Professor M. V. Mathesius had said similar things before the Second International Congress of Linguists in Geneva in 1931. His chief interest was an assessment of the then new structural or functional linguistics. He observed that both the diachronic method of the neo-grammarians and Franz Bopp and the synchronic

[14] Ernst A. Cassirer, as cited above, 116-117.

method of the structuralists and Wilhelm von Humboldt had strong and weak points. A fusion of the good points of both, he thought, would contribute greatly to the development of general linguistics. He summarizes the positive and negative aspects of the Humboldtian position thus:

Si la linguistique Humboldtienne se distingue par une appréciation plus fine des faits compliqués de la langue et une conscience plus vive de leur interdépendance synchronique, elle ne réussit pas à élaborer des méthodes d'analyse définitives.[15]

In conclusion he states the hope and the possibilities of a fusion of the two positions:

Ce qui doit donner à la linguistique fonctionelle et structurale, remontant dans ses origines aux idées de Ferdinand de Saussure à l'Ouest et à celles de Jean Baudouin de Courtenay à l'Est, sa place dans le développement général de la linguistique, c'est la possibilité qui lui est propre de réunir la rigueur méthodique de l'école Boppienne à la fraîcheur de vue et à la notion de l'interdépendence des faits grammaticaux de l'école Humboldtienne.[16]

Leo Weisgerber [17] has become the recent unofficial spokesman of the Humboldtian view and has formulated a more or less comprehensive plan of linguistic research the ultimate objective of which is the discovery of the ethnic and national culture of German-speaking Europeans in contrast to that of other, mainly European, cultures. This is to be done by studying "the linguistic midway" (*die sprachliche Mittelwelt*) between reality and its conceptualization. Weisgerber's plan is studded with the results of many individual investigations by himself and others which bear on the interrelation of culture and language and these lend his plan

[15] M. V. Mathesius, "La place de la linguistique fonctionelle et structurale dans le développement général des études linguistiques", *Actes Du Deuxième Congrès International De Linguistes, Genève, 1931* (Paris, 1933), 145.

[16] *Ibid.*, 145-6. However, see J. v. Laziczius, "Das sog. dritte Axiom der Sprachwissenschaft", *Acta linguistica,* I (1939), 162-167, regarding the alleged incompatibility between de Saussure's *la parole/la langue* and von Humboldt's *energeia/ergon.*

[17] "Die Bedeutungslehre – ein Irrweg der Sprachwissenschaft", *GRM,* XV (1927), 161-183; *Die Entdeckung der Muttersprache im europäischen Denken* (Lüneburg, 1948); *Von den Kräften der deutschen Sprache,* Vol. I: *Die Sprache unter den Kräften des menschlichen Daseins* (Düsseldorf, 1949); Vol. II: *Vom Weltbild der deutschen Sprache* (Düsseldorf, 1950); Vol. III: *Die Muttersprache im Aufbau unserer Kultur* (1950); Vol. IV: *Die geschichtliche Kraft der deutschen Sprache* (1951). (See review of Volumes I and II by R. E. Saleski, *Language,* 26, 1950, 439-441.)

great plausibility.[18] Its ultimate validity remains to be shown by the results of the implementation of the entire plan.

Basic to the plan is the assumption of von Humboldt, derived in turn from Hamann and Herder, that language is the means by which men create their conception, understanding, and values of objective reality. Language is the intermediary world (*Zwischenwelt*) between subject and object. As a consequence the vocabulary, grammar, and syntax of a given language are no mere reflection of the culture of its users. They are that culture by virtue of their function of making overt the concepts, beliefs, and values of the culture. This assumption obviously denies Professor Bloomfield's oft cited opinion that a linguist's view of the psychology of language was not relevant to his function as a linguist.

The technique for investigating languages with a view to isolating their culture content is based on the structural concept of the "field". It is applicable to both the vocabulary and the grammar-syntax. Jost Trier defines the field concept as follows:

> Every language is a system of selection over and against objective reality. As a matter of fact every language creates a self-sufficient and complete image of reality. Every language structures reality in its own manner and thereby establishes the components of reality which are peculiar to this given language. The language-reality components of one language never recur in quite the same form in another, nor are they simply a straight forward copy of reality. They are instead the linguistic-conceptual realization of a view of reality proceeding from a unique but definite structuring matrix which continuously compares and contrasts, relates and distinguishes the data of reality. Implicit in the foregoing is, of course, the realization that nothing in language exists independently. Inasmuch as structuring constitutes the basic essence of language, all linguistic components are the result of structuring. The ultimate meaning of each is determined precisely and only by its relation to and function in the total linguistic structure.[19]

The structural concept is derived from von Humboldt's observation that "structuring is the most common and profound essential characteristic of all language", a point of view subsequently maintained by Ferdinand de

[18] Unfortunately Weisgerber's hieratic vocabulary and style are somewhat irritating and at times make one suspicious of the cultish character of his proposals. The repetition of words such as *Sehweise, Sicht, Herzwörter, Weltbild der Sprache, geistige Zwischenwelt, welterschliessend,* unfortunately convey the feeling of working magic, of ritual. They may be and probably are justifiable but they nonetheless lend his books a missionary tone which seems to argue a theology. He suggests the promise of a linguistic millennium but, although the documentation which he amasses is cogent, only an empirical beginning has been made.

[19] Jost Trier, "Das sprachliche Feld", *Neue Jahrbücher f. Wissenschaft u. Bildung,* 10 (1934), 428-449. Translation mine.

Saussure (*articulation*). By means of a typically German wordplay on *Glied* ('member, component') Trier expresses the structural whole-to-part and part-to-whole relationship between individual words and the total vocabulary thus: "The individual word is ordered or related structurally (*sich ergliedern*) on ascending levels to the whole of the structured and constructed vocabulary and conversely the total vocabulary is structurally reducible (*sich ausgliedern*) to its individual words." [20] This is hardly more than an expansion of Humboldt's statement that

In reality speech is not assembled from pre-existing words. On the contrary, words result from the totality of speech.[21]

Trier holds that the field or structural relationship of linguistic components constitutes the linguistic content of a language and that it is therefore the only empirical means for studying linguistic history in the highest sense of that term.[22]

With reference to vocabulary, Weisgerber illustrates the productive potential of the field concept as applied to the areas of 1) nature, 2) material culture, and 3) intellectual-spiritual culture.

P. Zinsli,[23] for example, reveals the remarkable differences between the mountain vocabulary of Swiss-German dialects and that of Standard German. The former show an amazing diversity and richness of words for specific aspects of the mountains which have no counterpart in Standard German. Zinsli has grouped the vocabulary under nine headings and shows convincingly that it is not a case of mere wealth of synonyms but rather that each word is expressive of a very definite and specific experience of some aspect of the mountains and that each word occupies its correlated niche in this vocabulary "field".

[20] *Ibid.*, p. 429.

[21] Wilhelm von Humboldt, *Über die Verschiedenheit des menschlichen Sprachbaus,* Akad. Ausg. VII, I, 72. Translation mine.

[22] Gunther Ipsen and Walter Porzig, somewhat to the contrary, contend that the field concept is a formal device and that a linguistic field may be said to exist only when it is based on purely linguistic relationships. Trier replies that his criterion of linguistic content is linguistic and not formalogical. The structural relationship is not an intellectual tongs superimposed on language and therefore formalogical in character. The structural relationship is a linguistic reality which can be approached empirically with the result of discovering the linguistic content of given languages.

See Gunther Ipsen, "Der neue Sprachbegriff", *ZDK*, 46 (1932), 14 ff.; Walter Porzig, "Wesenhafte Bedeutungsbeziehungen", *PBB*, 58 (1934), 70-97; Jost Trier, "Deutsche Bedeutungsforschung", *Germ. Philologie (Festschr. f. Behaghel)* (Heidelberg, 1937), 189-193.

[23] *Grund und Grat. Der Formaufbau der Bergwelt in den Sprachbegriffen der Schweitzer-deutschen Alpenmundarten,* diss. Zurich (1937) ["Ground and Grade. The Formal Structure of the Mountain World in the Linguistic Concepts of the Swiss-German Dialects"].

Zinsli's work is a dramatic illustration of the unique way in which groups of men experience inorganic nature and translate their unique experience into vocabulary. The dialect atlases of various European languages and of American English are a further corroboration of the fact established by Zinsli. The data which they collected deserve the kind of interpretation supplied by Zinsli.

Natural phenomena are classified in varying ways in different languages and Weisgerber quotes Karl Vossler regarding an interesting classification of the organic world in Argentinian Spanish:

It is already possible to read our predominant interests out of our vocabulary. In the tropics there are Negro languages which have 50 to 60 names for various kinds of palm trees but no generic term for palm tree. These Negroes live from the fruit of palm trees and have very precise vegetarian interests but lack botanical ones. The gauchos of the Argentine had about 200 expressions for the colors of horses but only four plant names: *pasto, paja, cardo, yuyos; pasto* was the name for all cattle fodder, *paja* for every variety of straw (for bedding down animals), *cardo* for all ligniform vegetation, *yuyos* for the remaining vegetable kingdom, lilies and roses, herbs and cabbage. Thus whatever the interest of the moment, it fixes itself like an aimed gun upon definite things and finds its thrusts in the vocabulary.[24]

A parallel to these four botanical categories of Argentine Spanish are the late middle and early modern High German zoological categories of fish, fowl, crawling animals, and running animals (*fisch, vögel, gewürm, thier*, as still used by Luther). A generic term like Modern High German *Tier* "animal" is conspicuously lacking although Luther does use *vieh* (Modern High German *Vieh* "cattle") referring to the species domestic animal. Modern zoology has changed this categorical scheme substantially, particularly through Linné's six classes of the quadrupeds, fowl, amphibians, fish, insects, worms, and sub-classes such as mammals, etc. The generic term *Tier* and its related concept of the animal kingdom is a development of the 18th century.

Weisgerber claims the most rewarding results of vocabulary field research in the area of man's conception of himself, for example, the vocabulary reflection of the function and achievement of the human sense-perception apparatus. The color controversy prior to 1900 provides a nice illustration:

The color controversy "arose from the difficulty encountered in translating the color words of the early Greeks, especially Homer. One gets into unexpected difficulties in trying to find the precise synonyms, for example, for Gr. *dzanthós, glaukós, ōchrós* and others of the commonest color words. In the one case *yellow* or *green* fits, in the next it doesn't. If

[24] Karl Vossler, "Volksprachen und Weltsprachen", *Welt und Wort* (1946), 98. Translation mine.

one considers all occurrences together, one arrives at amazing conclusions such as this: *ōchrós* sometimes has the meaning *greenish yellow*, sometimes the meaning *red; chlōrós* means *yellowish green* on occasion, but also *grayish brown*, etc. One has attempted to translate all of these words with *brilliant* on the assumption that the Greeks were less interested in the particular hue or tint than in the intensity (luster quality), particularly under the light conditions of the southern sky. This explanation was abortive, however, since Greek also has a well developed sequence of luster adjectives *lamprós, phaidrós, aiglēeís*, etc. The other alternative was to assume that this translation problem offered evidence for the study of the development of the color sense in the human race. From this point of view several observers seriously maintained that in our terms the Greeks must have been collectively color blind. But this conclusion also failed to hold water and thus the way remained open for the correct solution: If the observed discrepancies were attributable neither to the nature of the phenomena themselves nor to the structure of the human eye, then they must be grounded in the conceptual midway lying between reality and expression, that is, in the manner of human judgment." [25]

The vocabularies of taste and of smell in various languages reveal the same kind of translation difficulty and can be studied and explained intelligently only by the neo-Humboldtian assumption.

The objects of material culture are not given in the sense that nature is given. These objects are man-made and the linguistic means which express them are therefore related to the kinds of human activity which created them. The history of these activities, their objectives, the effects of fashion and taste, and many other similar considerations play an important part in developing the word-fields of material culture. As illustrations, Weisgerber refers to the German word-field for "container" (*Behälter*) and "piano" (*Klavier*) as listed by Dornseiff.[26]

In the realm of spiritual-intellectual culture the concept of the word-field is equally useful. Weisgerber cites and discusses numerous examples, notably Jost Trier's study of the German word-fields relating to the concept reason, its powers and qualities.[27]

Going from vocabulary to grammar-syntax, Weisgerber maintains that clarification of the ideological content of the parts of speech of sentence components, and of sentence patterns, as these reveal ways of experiencing reality, will contribute greatly to our understanding of ethnolinguistics.

[25] *Vom Weltbild d. deut. Spr.*, 141. Translation mine.

[26] F. Dornseiff, *Der deutsche Wortschatz nach Sachgruppen* (1933).

[27] Jost Trier, *Der deut. Wortschatz im Sinnbezirk d. Verstandes, die Geschichte eines Feldes* (Heidelberg, 1931).

The mass of the vocabulary of Indo-European languages consists of substantives, verbs, and adjectives. Fr. Mauthner had the idea that the world of substantives was "the world of mysticism, of mythology, of pure phenomenon, of abstraction", the adjectival world that of "sensualism, materialism, art, the so-called real world of matter and energy", and the verbal world the domain "of movement, effect, activity, with hidden purposes, with sense impressions which become energies and powers".[28] Regardless of the validity of the details of this observation, the point remains that the three parts of speech mentioned seem to reflect basically different views of experience. Empirical research in the matter promises rewarding results. So, for example, it has been possible to show that Modern High German expresses color reactions by means of adjectives (*farbig, rot, blau, bunt*, etc.) whereas the words for luster-quality are verbal in origin (*glänzen, leuchten, funkeln, glitzern*, etc.) and the adjectives for luster-quality are therefore participles. The conclusion is that color was experienced as a quality of the object whereas luster was felt as an energy radiating from an object. In older stages of German, however, the situation was not the same. In Early Modern High German the lilies "whitened", the saffrons "yellowed", and the balsams "blackened" (Meyfart). The color verbs were as common as, in Latin, *albere, livere* were, and the color adjectives were used side by side with them. Conversely, older Low and High German show a well developed category or field of luster adjectives (Old Saxon *berht, blēk, blīdī, hēdar, lioht, scīn, swigli, torht, whitig* by the side of only five verbs *blīkan, glītan, hēdron, liohtian, skīnan* of which the participles rarely occur). In Old High German the luster adjectives are also still very common (*beraht, glat, lioht, scīn, zorft, lougīn, blanc, glanz, glizīn*, etc.). Whatever the reasons for the shift, they appear to have had something to do with the way in which these phenomena were experienced. The cumulative effect of other similar researches dealing with the "meaning" of a part of speech would prove very productive.

The syntactic function of the various parts of speech also requires further investigation. Weisgerber points by way of example to the function of abstract nouns as that of "grasping the entire content of a sentence as an 'object' ".[29] Walter Porzig insists that the process of abstraction has created a new type of object by the side of visual and tactile objects, "objects of a higher order". Philosophical thinking becomes possible by attaching itself to these newly created realities. Thought is by definition *Gedankengang* (a course or sequence of ideas) and speech makes possible the expression of the relation of ideas to reality. Above

28 Fr. Mauthner, *Die drei Bilder der Welt* (1925); also referred to recently by Karl Jaspers, *Von der Wahrheit* (1946).

29 *Vom Weltbild d. deut. Spr.*, 178.

and beyond that, however, speech also makes possible the expression of the relation between relationships and this is its highest achievement.[30]

The syntactic functions of the form systems such as number, case, tense, aspect, also reveal the stance of the user toward objective reality and therefore need investigation from this point of view. The development of the tense system in German from the simple Germanic system of recognizing only present and past time actions is an example. H. Brinkmann has concluded on the basis of his study that people in the Old High German period had advanced from "the sensuously objective experience of action to temporal comprehension", and that "sensuous realism was gradually making way for an increasing rationalism".[31]

The redefinition in terms of functional syntax of the parts of speech suggests a similar redefinition of the functions of sentence components; for in the sentence, which is the matrix of the unity of speech, the parts of speech and the form systems acquire a new function and a new dimension as sentence components. The traditional concepts of subject, predicate, object, apposition, and the like have proved so unsatisfactory for speech analysis because they are either entirely formalogical or entirely extraneous and mechanical in character. Certainly they are not linguistic, that is, their referents are not the structuring devices of unified expressions. Erich Drach has contributed substantially to the investigation of German syntax from the functional and structural point of view.[32] Owing to lack of space, the discussion of the arresting results of his research must be postponed to another time and place.

The basic point of departure for the Neo-Humboldtians is always Wilhelm von Humboldt's idea that language is simply "the human being approaching the objective idea". That language is, in other words, not an independent reality but a relational one. That language is the midway between objective reality and man's conceptualization of it. As such it is the immediate overt expression of reality, and its word classes, and sentence patterns are structured meaning instead of being just vehicles for meaning. If this be valid, then Trier's insistence that linguistic fields are not mere formal devices but rather linguistic realities is likewise tenable. I have in my brief outline by no means exhausted the results of the empiric research which corroborates or at least supports the hypothesis. A good deal more *Kleinarbeit* is imperative. The available evidence is, however, sufficient to cause linguists to include the hypothesis within the compass of linguistic science. Unquestionably the hypothesis affords the most promising basis for relating the fruits of linguistic science to those of the other social sciences.

[30] Walter Porzig, *Das Wunder der Sprache* (Bern, 1950), p. 369.
[31] H. Brinkmann, *Sprachwandel und Sprachbewegung in ahd. Zeit* (1931).
[32] Erich Drach, *Grundgedanken der deutschen Satzlehre* (Berlin, 1937).

Although Weisgerber and the other Neo-Humboldtians speak a great deal about the ethnic or national character which individual languages express or rather are, they have attempted little in the way of conclusions based on their evidence. Weisgerber particularly has documented many peculiarities of German, and he compares these in broad terms especially with French. Rarely, however, does he attempt any generalizations beyond this.[33] To do so would require other kinds of evidence from psychology and anthropology-sociology. A basic method for correlating these differing kinds of evidence still remains to be developed. Although Weisgerber and others assume that the final proof of their pudding rests on a comparative procedure involving two or more languages, it seems that we are nowhere near having even the minimum of data for undertaking such comparisons.

As stated earlier, the great contemporary need is for scientific team work. It is quite apparent that neither linguists alone nor social scientists alone can crack the prize nut of the cultural secrets which languages appear to contain. It is barely possible that it just can't be cracked. Only empirical research can determine that. Science has, however, never prospered on the assumption that formalogical hypotheses were preferable to empirically grounded ones. When the evidence tends to support an hypothesis, the immediate obligation of science is to obtain and exhaust all further available evidence till a consensus can be established.

I respectfully submit that the Neo-Humboldtian hypothesis might constitute another assumption among Bloomfield's Postulates to the effect that it is possible "to have a scientifically accurate knowledge of everything in the speakers' world" (as cited above) by the scientific determination of its structural orientation which becomes overt and only so in language.

From: *Word,* 8 (1952), pp. 95-105. Reprinted with permission.

[33] So for example the cited study of Karl Bergmann, "Über eine wichtige bautümliche Verschiedenheit der deutschen und der französischen Sprache", *ZDK,* 47 (1933), 223-230, which purports to document the fact that French, as English, tends to form words by the addition of (Latin) suffixes, whereas German does it by compounding German words, e.g., French *sculpteur,* German *Bildhauer.* Bergmann concludes: "Valuable as the extraordinarily developed possibilities of compounding are in our language (i.e., German), there can be no doubt that the simple word or its extension (by suffixation) is superior in linguistic value to an equivalent compound: *Wäscherin* is linguistically superior to *Waschfrau, Nähterin to Nähmädchen, Vermieterin to Vermietsfrau.*" The criterion of linguistic value for Bergmann is obviously the economy of expression and the simplicity resulting from unity. Although Bergmann (and Weisgerber) conclude that these varying structural principles of French and German express the varying thought processes (*Denkweisen*) of the two linguistic communities, they do not venture to specify the how or the why of the matter.

John J. Gumperz

TYPES OF LINGUISTIC COMMUNITIES *

Comparisons of linguistic and social behavior have been impeded by the fact that linguistic and anthropological studies are rarely based upon comparable sets of data. While the anthropologist's description refers to specific communities, the universe of linguistic analysis is a single language or dialect, a body of verbal signs abstracted from the totality of communicative behavior on the basis of certain structural or genetic similarities. To be sure, studies of individual languages vary greatly in range. They may deal with the speech of a small band of hunters and gatherers, a village dialect, or a literary language spoken by several hundred million speakers. But on the whole, in selecting the data to be studied linguists give more weight to genetic relationships and structural homogeneity than to social environment. We think of English as a single whole, although a typical corpus may include texts stemming from rural England, urban United States, Australia, or even former colonial areas of Asia or Africa.

The process of linguistic analysis, furthermore, is oriented towards the discovery of unitary, structurally homogenous wholes (Hymes 1962). Stylistic variants, loans and the like are not excluded from grammars, but traditional interviewing techniques are not designed to measure their total range (Voegelin 1960, 65) and the tendency is to relegate them to the category of free variation. The effect of such procedures is the selection of one single variety (Ferguson and Gumperz 1960, 3) out of the complex of varieties which characterize everyday speech behavior.

* I am grateful to Catherine Callahan, Paul Friedrich, Dell H. Hymes and William Shipley for their helpful comments.

This one variety is then considered to be representative of the entire language or dialect.

Structural abstractions of this kind are quite adequate as long as interest is confined to language universals or typology and to comparative reconstruction. They have revolutionized our theories of grammar and in the field of language and culture they have disproved earlier naive notions which equated primitiveness of material culture with simplicity of language structure. But when we turn from a study of language as an institution to the analysis of speech behavior within particular societies, more detailed information is usually required. Thus views such as those of Linton who states that "there appears to be no correlation between the complexity of the language spoken by a people and the complexity of any other aspect of their behavior" (1936, 81) are valid only with respect to the internal structure of any one single speech variety. They should not be interpreted to mean, as they sometimes are, that it is impossible to distinguish between the speech habits of simple tribal groups and complex urban societies. European linguists of the Prague school as well as some American anthropological linguists have shown that the existence of codified standard languages as distinct from everyday casual speech is a "major linguistic correlate of an urban culture" (Garvin and Mathiot 1960, 283).

The subject of intra-language variation, which had been neglected in the early days of descriptive linguistics, is receiving renewed attention in recent years (Sebeok 1960). A number of scholars have called for a revision of the earlier "monolithic hypothesis of language structure". Instead they regard linguistic communication within a speech community in terms of an "interconnected system of subcodes" (Jakobson 1960, 352). If we accept this we might hypothesize that linguistic complexity within a particular society is not a function of internal patterning within a single homogeneous system, but can be understood in terms of the relation among diverse systems of different extent. A similar view of social complexity is presented in some of the recent anthropological work on "intermediate societies" (Cohn and Marriott 1958, 1, Casagrande 1959, 1). In order to deal adequately with such linguistic and social systems, the focus of linguistic enquiry will have to shift from simple descriptive analysis to analysis followed by comparative or contrastive study.

Although comparative analysis may be synchronic or diachronic in nature, scholars interested in the relationship of language to social environment have until now confined themselves primarily to diachronic comparison. The predominant view is that of Sapir (1951, 89), who tended to discount the effect of social environment and considered "drift" as the major factor in determining the structural peculiarities of a language. This view has also had considerable effect on synchronic studies, as can be seen from a paper by Triandis and Osgood dealing with the cross-cultural application of the semantic differential:

> Greek belongs to a subgroup of the Indo-European family of languages that is quite distinct from all other members of the family. Our present findings, then, support the assumption that the same general semantic structure will be found in all Indo-European languages. (Triandis & Osgood 1957, 192)

Sapir's views on language change have never been completely accepted by all linguists and anthropologists. The work of Boas as well as that of European linguists concerned with *Sprachbund* phenomena has long since pointed to the limitations of the genetic approach (Hymes 1961, 23). In recent years Weinreich's studies on structural borrowing in Switzerland and in the Yiddish-speaking areas of Eastern Europe have further emphasized the importance of social environment (1952, 360; 1953). The areal approach to linguistic relationships was further developed by Emeneau (1956, 3; 1962) in a number of carefully documented studies. Emeneau takes as his point of departure the South Asian culture area which he treats as a "single linguistic area". He points out the existence of numerous structural parallels among languages of Indo-Aryan, Dravidian and Munda stocks in Central India, as also between the Dravidian Brahui and the surrounding Indo-Aryan and Indo-Iranian language groups in the Northwest. Similar area-wide cross-language influences have been noticed in the California Indian language region, the very area from which Sapir draws his most striking examples of the lack of relationship between language and social environment. Catherine Callahan (1961) demonstrates the existence of a series of glottalized stops in Lake Miwok which seem to be borrowed from the surrounding Indian languages. William Shipley (1960) shows some striking differences in the sentence structure of Northern and Southern Maidu which also suggest the influence of environment.

The above studies in area linguistics, however, are historically oriented, and are of more interest to students of culture history than to the social anthropologist. While the concept of structural borrowing refers to the end result of a process of change, it does not provide an insight into the dynamics of this process. Its synchronic correlates, speech diversity and code-switching among different dialects, styles or languages will probably hold more interest for scholars oriented towards functional analysis. Such studies must however begin with a specific community, not with a linguistically defined entity (Gumperz 1951, 94).

In his recent paper, "The Ethnography of Speaking", Hymes (1962) reviews the literature on speech behavior and relates it to the more traditional types of linguistic and anthropological endeavor. He calls for a new approach to the "descriptive analysis of speaking" and suggests that "the speech activity of a population should be the primary object of attention". The present paper is an effort in this direction.

Linguistic distribution within a social or geographical space is usually described in terms of speech communities (Bloomfield 1933, 42). We find a number of instances of the use of extra-linguistic criteria in defining such communities. Frings and his group of German dialectologists have adopted techniques from geography for the determination of cultural regions on the basis of marketing and traffic patterns, distribution of items of material culture and the like and have used these regions as the focus for their study of speech distribution (Gumperz 1961a). American linguists have dealt with small urban groups (Putnam and O'Hern 1955), while Einar Haugen's monumental *The Norwegian Language in America* is an example of an exhaustive study of an immigrant group (1953). In all these studies, however, speech communities are considered coterminous with a single language and its dialects and styles. Bilinguals are said to "bridge speech communities" (Hockett 1958). Some writers have gone so far as to liken them to the sociologist's "marginal man" (Soffietti 1955).

There are no a priori grounds which force us to define speech communities so that all members speak the same language. Total bi- or multi-lingualism is the rule rather than the exception in a wide variety of societies including the nineteenth-century Russian urban elite, the ruling groups of many modern Asian and African nations, the American immigrant groups mentioned above as well as many others. Weinreich as a matter of fact also speaks of "bilingual speech communities" in describing the Yiddish speakers of Eastern Europe (1953). Furthermore, from the point of view of social function, the distinction between bilingualism and bidialectalism is often not a significant one (Gumperz 1961a, 13; Martinet 1954, 1).

The present paper will therefore employ the term "linguistic community" by analogy with Emeneau's term "linguistic area". We will define it as a social group which may be either monolingual or multilingual, held together by frequency of social interaction patterns and set off from the surrounding areas by weaknesses in the lines of communication. Linguistic communities may consist of small groups bound together by face-to-face contact or may cover large regions, depending on the level of abstraction we wish to achieve.

Social communication within a linguistic community may be viewed in terms of functionally related roles, defined according to Nadel (1957, 31ff.) as "modes of acting allotted to individuals within a society". Nadel's approach to the analysis of role is couched in terms familiar to the linguist. He regards each role as characterized by certain perceptual clues or "attributes" consisting of "diacritics" implicit in role behavior such as dress, etiquette, gestures, and presumably also speech behavior; and by role names such as priest, father, or teacher which serve to provide advance information regarding the nature of the role behavior to be expected. A particular diacritic is considered as peripheral if its presence or absence does not change the native's perception of the role and relevant if it does change role perception. Role behavior is further said to vary in accordance with the "inter-actional setting", a term which seems to correspond to the linguist's "context of situation" (Firth 1957, 32) or "environment".

The totality of communication roles within a society may be called its "communication matrix". There are as yet no generally agreed-upon procedures for isolating individual roles, although correlations between language use or style and like behavior have been noted in a number of recent studies (Fischer 1958, 47; Chowdhury 1960, 64; Ferguson 1959, 2). For our purposes it will be sufficient to isolate only those roles or role clusters which correlate with significant speech differences. We assume then that each role has as its linguistic diacritic a particular code or subcode which serves as the norm for role behavior. We speak of the "code matrix" as the set of codes and subcodes functionally related to the communication matrix.

The nature of the components of the code matrix varies from community to community. In some all components are dialects or styles of the same language. These we will refer to as subcodes. In others the matrix also includes genetically distinct languages, in which case we will use the term codes. The distinction between code and subcode is largely a linguistic one, however; it does not necessarily correspond to a difference in social function. The peasant in Southern France uses his patois as the language of the home and employs a regional variant of standard French towards outsiders. In Brittany, Breton serves as the home language while communication with outsiders is maintained through a second variant of Standard French. Both Breton and the patois are used in roughly equivalent contexts of situation and have similar social function within the peasant community.

The criterion for inclusion of a code in a study of a linguistic community is that its exclusion will produce a gap in the communication matrix. English is an important part of the communication matrix of urban India while it could be omitted from an ethnography of a remote tribal community. Similarly, Sanskrit is relevant for the description of certain Hindu communities in India but not for certain Muslim groups. The distinction between uniformity and diversity of dialects or monolingualism and bilingualism thus becomes less important than the distinction between the individual and the societal.

Subcodes of the same language within the code matrix also show varying degrees of linguistic differences. Local dialects may be either linguistically different or very similar to the other superposed forms of speech. The same is true for styles. Ferguson has recently pointed to some important linguistic differences between the formal and informal media (1959, 2) of certain urban populations. We will use Weinreich's term, languages distance (1952), to refer to the totality of differences in phonology, grammar or lexicon within the code matrix as measured by contrastive study.

Societies also vary in the way in which roles cluster within the communication matrix. In rural India the role of the religious preacher is closely associated with that of the social reformer, while in American society, we would consider the two quite separate (Gumperz 1961b). Another characteristic feature of some societies is the distinction between behavior within the home and peer group and behavior towards outsiders. In South Asia this distinction in roles corresponds to sharp difference between local dialects and superposed forms of speech. The sanctions against mixing the two types of behavior have been long so strong that some Indians have an almost insurmountable aversion to writing down informal speech. Possibly such socially enforced distinctions in role behavior are a major factor in the preservation of local dialects. We will use the term role distinctness to refer to the degree to which role behavior is kept separate.

An examination of linguistic communities in various parts of the globe reveals a definite relationship between the overall characteristics of the code matrix and certain features of social structure. Connections of this type have often been noted (Greenberg 1956, 109). Nineteenth century European dialectologists, for instance, have demonstrated the relation between political and societal boundaries and present-day dialect isoglosses (Gumperz 1961a). Other dialectologists have pointed to the contrast between relative homogeneity of speech in recently settled areas such as the American West and diversity in longer-settled areas on the East Coast. It is assumed that this homogeneity is the result of processes of change resulting from resettlement of populations of different origin under conditions favoring fluidity of roles and statuses. This conclusion is also supported by our own experience with foreign language settlements in the United States where the language tends to be preserved as long as the settlers remain a distinct social group, as is the case in some rural settlements but will disappear when the settlers are merged into urban society.

We have already referred to the work of the Prague school linguists and of Garvin on the relationship between urban societies and standard languages (1960, 283). Garvin and Mathiot define a standard language as a "codified form of a language accepted by and serving as a model to a larger speech community". They list a number of criteria as characteristic of a standard language. Two of these, codification and language loyalty are of special interest. Codification relates to the fact that rules of pronunciation and grammar are explicitly stated (e.g. in the form of standard grammars and dictionaries), while language loyalty, a concept introduced by Weinreich (1953, 106), is the attitude which lends prestige to a language and leads people to defend its "purity" against "corruption" in pronunciation or "foreign" loans.

The above and similar references to the relation between speech distribution and social environment are all limited to specific cases. More generalized formulations should become possible through the application of concepts such as code matrix, role distinctness, language distance and language loyalty to linguistic communities of different degrees of social complexity. Such classifications might show rough parallels between speech distribution and social groups of the type now classified by social scientists as bands, larger tribal groups and modern urbanized communities. Any formulations of this kind will of necessity be extremely tentative, especially since social scientists themselves do not seem to agree on the theoretical basis for distinguishing between simple and complex societies (Schneider 1961) and since reliable cross-cultural information on speech behavior is almost non-existent. They are offered here only in the hope that they may stimulate further research.

We begin with the least complex communities, consisting of small bands of hunters and gatherers such as we find among American Indians of the Great Basin. Social contacts in these groups are limited to face-to-face communication, there is a minimum of social stratification and contacts with outsiders are relatively infrequent. Speech is not completely uniform, however; perceptible differences may be observed between what has been called casual every-day speech and non-casual styles used in singing, recitation, myth-telling and similar ritually defined situations. There are some cases in such societies, where ritual formulas contain words, sentences or songs in a language which is unintelligible to the natives themselves. In general, however, the language distance between casual and non-casual speech is relatively small and control of the non-casual style does not seem to be confined to a particular group (Hymes 1958, 253; Yegerlehner 1953, 264; Voegelin 1960, 57ff.).

Diversity may be somewhat greater in the case of larger, economically more advanced tribal communities which, although not integrated into larger societies, maintain some trade relations with the outside. There, to the extent that ritual activities requiring the use of non-casual language become specialized, these styles may become associated with particular groups. Trade with other tribes speaking other languages requires bilingualism but speaking in these languages tends to be confined to certain roles only. In many societies, trade relations are limited and superficial and surrounded by ritual intended to keep the trader from trespassing on tribal society. As trading activities expand in scope and specialized groups of traders arise, one or the other tribal language may spread over wide areas as a trade language, as in the case of Hausa in Africa. The forms of language used in trade situations tends to be quite distinct from that used within the tribal group. They differ from standard languages in that they usually lack codification and tend to have no special prestige outside the trading situation. So-called pidgin or mixed languages are not as a rule found in purely tribal societies but are the result of contact between an economically developed society and a tribal group or groups.

Tribal societies may have outside relations other than trade through intermarriage or religious ritual. In such situations, there is evidence to show that bi- and multi-lingualism is much more common than most linguistic and ethnographic studies would lead one to believe. Such bilingualism, however, is rarely of the societal type. Within the community only the tribal language is spoken. In certain California Indian tribes (the Yurok, Karok and Hupa) living in the same general area and maintaining regular contact, this is carried to such an extreme that each tribe has a different name for the same physical landmark. Evidently the tribal language is the symbol of communal identity, although it does not show the formal characteristics of a standard language. We may say that for such tribes, language loyalty applies to the tribal language, although the communication matrix may also include certain trade languages.

Community bilingualism, speech stratification or major stylistic variance seems to become possible only as the economic base expands to allow economic stratification. One common type of variation found in societies which, although relatively advanced, still preserve some tribal characteristics, is that between "high" and "low" language styles (Garvin and Riesenberg 1952, 201; Uhlenbeck 1950). One characteristic of such societies is the existence of a ruling group representing conquerors from the outside who maintain considerable social distance from the rest of the population. High and low styles tend to vary in lexicon, morphophonemics and allomorphy but not in phonology. They also utilize different borrowing sources: high Javanese borrows from Indo-Aryan languages while high Balinese, it is said, borrows from Javanese. Regardless of the difference between high and low forms, both seem to be regarded as part of the same language by local populations.

Diversity tends to reach a maximum in the more typical intermediate societies characterized by the existence of peasant, herder or even tribal strata or population in various degrees of integration in the socially dominant groups. Social systems in these societies exhibit a high degree of social stratification and occupational specialization. Social behavior is characterized by role distinctness, so that individuals act differently in different contexts. These distinctions are emphasized by elaborate ritual and behavioral conventions (i.e. etiquette) as well as by differences in dress, food habits, and the like. An extreme example of this is the Indian caste society, which gives the impression of a multitude of distinct populations living side by side and communicating only with respect to a limited portion of their total activities. Other less complex intermediate societies tend to differ in degree of complexity, not in kind. The code matrix in such societies may include several distinct languages and, in addition, the language distance between subcodes varies from purely lexical and phonetic variances to important structural divergences. One interesting phenomenon is the occurrence of deliberate speech disguise of the type found in modern "Pig Latin". This type of disguise, while rendering the subcodes mutually unintelligible, is describable in terms of relatively simple transformation rules (Chomsky and Halle, 1967).

In discussing speech distribution in these societies we will distinguish between the vernacular form of the language learned at home and argots or special parlances learned after childhood and used only in certain limited situations (Gumperz 1961a, 12). Geographic diversity of speech forms is greatest in the case of the vernaculars used among the rural populations. This diversity may take the form of variant dialects or of genetically distinct local languages. In both cases the social functions are similar; they serve as in-group languages and co-exist with superposed codes used for communication with strangers. In medieval Europe, for example, we find islands of Celtic speech in the Alpine regions interspersed among Romance and Germanic dialect continua. Slavic languages alternate with Germanic dialects in the East while Basque occurs with Romance in southwestern Europe. Similarly in India the North Dravidian tribal languages and Munda languages such as Korku are found deep in the Indo-Aryan territory.

Argots or special parlances are of several types. The first, which we may call subregional or regional dialects, serve for communication in the market place and as media of inter-group communication. They resemble the trade languages of tribal areas in that they show little codification and carry no great prestige. The language distance between these codes and local forms of speech may be small if both are dialects of the same language. If local populations speak a genetically distinct language, those local residents whose business requires contact with the outside tend to be bilingual.

The second set of argots is that employed by certain social and occupational groups in the pursuit of their special activities. We may include here the special parlances spoken by commercial groups, thieves' argots, and literary and recitation styles of popular storytellers. The social function seems to be that of maintaining group exclusiveness. They tend to be guarded and preserved from outsiders in somewhat the same way that craft guilds guard their craft skills. Codes in this set may on occasion be written; and to the extent that proper pronunciation and grammar serve as a means of group identification, they may be said to show some codification, but their prestige as a rule is limited.

The third category includes the sacred and administrative codes which are distributed over wider and geographically and socially more diverse regions than the previous set. Thus, in medieval Europe, Latin was used as both administrative and sacred language in Germanic, Romance and Slavic speech areas. Sanskrit and Persian in medieval India had similar functions. These codes serve as the language of special administrative and priestly classes but they are not necessarily spoken by the actual rulers. They share some of the characteristics of occupational codes in that they function to maintain group exclusiveness; they are characterized by extreme codification, symbolized by the necessity for a large investment of time in the study of grammar and rhetoric and, of course, by the existence of schools for this, with their complements of scholars. When administrative and sacred codes differ, the sacred codes are accorded the greatest amount of prestige. Intermediate societies, then, in contrast to tribal societies, tend to show language loyalty to codes which may be quite distinct from the vernacular.

Extreme diversity and language distance between the administrative and sacred codes and other codes in the code matrix is maintainable only as long as government remains in the hands of a small ruling group (Havranek 1936, 151). As a greater proportion of the population is drawn into the national life and becomes mobilized, the old administrative code may be replaced by one drawn from the regional strata. The new administrative subcodes characteristic of this type of society are as a rule not quite identical with the spoken idiom of the urban mobilized groups; considerable language distance may be maintained in a number of instances (Ferguson 1959). In general, however, the tendency is for the code matrix to become less and less diverse as local populations are integrated into the dominant groups or "mobilized" as Deutsch (1953) has called it and as role distinctness decreases.

Language distances within the code matrix are lowest in some highly urbanized communities such as we find in parts of modern Europe and in the United States. In these communities, the distinction between standard and local dialects has almost disappeared. It is reflected only in the form of regional standards such as we have in the American

Midwest, Southwest, or West. Some social speech distinctions persist. In addition there are a number of distinct formal and informal subcodes, as well as technical and scientific parlances. In contrast to what we find in intermediate societies, however, language distances among these forms tend to be confined to the syntactical and lexical levels. We rarely find two or three different sets of inflectional allomorphs or function words such as characterize stylistic differences in some of the Asian languages. A large portion of the differences that do occur are justified by special requirements for technical terminology. It almost seems that shallow linguistic contrast in styles is a direct correlate of the fluidity of roles symbolized by the distinction between caste and class. Language loyalty in these societies is bestowed on the standard, which now closely reflects the majority speech.

WORKS CITED

Bloomfield, Leonard
1933 *Language* (New York).

Callahan, Catherine
1961 "Phonemic Borrowing in Lake Miwok". 17 pp. typescript.

Casagrande, Joseph B.
1959 "Some Observations on the Study of Intermediate Societies", in *Intermediate Societies, Social Mobility and Social Communication. Proceedings of the 1959 Annual Spring Meeting of the American Ethnological Society,* 1-10.

Chomsky, Noam, and M. Halle
1967 *The Sound Pattern of English* (New York).

Chowdhury, Munier
1960 "The Language Problem in East Pakistan", in C. A. Ferguson and John J. Gumperz, eds., *Linguistic Diversity in South Asia,* (= RCAFL, 13) (Indiana University), 64-78.

Cohn, Bernard S., and McKim Marriott
1958 "Networks and Centers in the Integration of Indian Civilization", *Journal of Social Research,* Ranchi Bihar, 1.

Deutsch, Karl W.
1953 *Nationalism and Social Communication* (New York and Cambridge, Mass.).

Emeneau, M. B.
1956 "India as a Linguistic Area", *Lg,* 32, 3-16.
1962 *Brahui and Dravidian Comparative Grammar* (Berkeley).

Ferguson, C. A.
1959 "Diglossia", *Word,* 15, 2.

Ferguson, Charles A., and John J. Gumperz, eds.
1960 *Linguistic Diversity in South Asia, op. cit.*

Firth, J. R.
1957 "A Synopsis of Linguistic Theory, 1930-1955", in *Studies in Linguistic Analysis* (Special Volume of the Philological Society), 1-32.

Fischer, John L.
1958 "Social Influences on the Choice of a Linguistic Variant", *Word*, 14, 47-61.

Garvin, Paul, and Madeleine Mathiot
1960 "The Urbanization of the Guarani Language – A Problem in Language and Culture", in *Man in Culture* (Philadelphia), 783-90.

Garvin, Paul, and S. H. Riesenberg
1952 "Respect Behavior on Ponape", *AA*, 54, 201-220.

Greenberg, Joseph
1956 "The Measurement of Linguistic Diversity", *Lg*, 32, 109-115.

Gumperz, John J.
1961a "Speech Variation and the Study of Indian Civilization", *AA*, 63, 976-88.
1961b "Religion and Social Communication in Village North India". Typescript of talk presented to Seminar on Hinduism, August 1961, University of California, Berkeley.

Gumperz, John J., and C. M. Naim
1959 "Formal and Informal Standards in the Hindi Regional Language Area", in *Linguistic Diversity in South Asia, op. cit.*

Haugen, Einar
1953 *The Norwegian Language in America* (Philadelphia).

Havranek, B.
1936 "Zum Problem Norm in der heutigen Sprachwissenschaft und Sprachkultur", International Congress of Linguists, 4th, *Actes* ..., (Copenhagen), 151-57.

Hockett, Charles F.
1958 *A Course in Modern Linguistics* (New York).

Hymes, D. H.
1958 "Linguistic Features Peculiar to Chinookan Myths", *IJAL*, 24, 253-57.
1961a "Alfred Louis Kroeber", *Language*, 37, 1-28.
1962 "The Ethnography of Speaking", in *Anthropology and Human Behavior*, T. Gladwin and W. M. C. Sturtevant, eds. (Washington, D.C.), 13-53.

Jakobson, Roman
1960 "Linguistics and Poetics", in *Style in Language*, Thomas A. Sebeok, ed. (New York), 350-377.

Linton, Ralph
1936 *The Study of Man* (New York).

Martinet, André
1954 "Dialect", *Romance Philology*, 8, 1.

Nadel, S. F.
1957 *The Theory of Social Structure* (London).

Putnam, George N., and Edna M. Hern
1955 "The Status Significance of an Isolated Urban Dialect", *Lg*, 31 Supplement.

Sapir, Edward
1951 "Language and Environment", in *Selected Writings of Edward Sapir*, David Mandelbaun, ed. (Berkeley), 9-103.

Schneider, David M.
1961 "Comments on Studies of Complex Societies", *Current Anthropology*, 2, 215.

Sebeok, Thomas A.
1960 *Style in Language* (New York).
Shipley, William
1961 "Maidu and Nisenan: A Binary Survey", *IJAL*, 27, 46-51.
Soffietti, James P.
1955 "Bilingualism and Biculturalism", *Journal of Education Psychology*, 46, 222.
Triandis, H. C. and C. E. Osgood
1958 "A Comparative Factorial Analysis of Semantic Structures in Monolingual Greek and American College Students", *Journal of Abnormal and Social Psychology*, LVII, 187.
Uhlenbeck, E. M.
1950 *De Tegenstelling Krama: Ngoko, Haar Positie in het Javaanse Taalsystem* (Djakarta).
Voegelin, C. F.
1960 "Casual and Non-Casual Utterances within Unified Structure", in *Style in Language*, Sebeok, T. (ed.), *op cit.*, 57-68.
Weinreich, Uriel
1953 *Languages in Contact* (= *Publications of the Linguistic Circle of New York*, Number 1) (New York).
1952 "Sabesdiker Losn in Yiddish: A Problem of Linguistic Affinity", *Word*, 8, 360.
Yegerlehner, John
1958 "Structure of Arizona Tewa Words, Spoken and Sung", *IJAL*, 24, 264-67.

From: *Anthropological Linguistics*, 4 (1962), pp. 28-40. Reprinted with permission.

Section V

MULTILINGUALISM

W. E. Lambert, R. C. Gardner,
R. Olton and K. Tunstall

A STUDY OF THE ROLES OF ATTITUDES AND MOTIVATION IN SECOND-LANGUAGE LEARNING

When viewed from a social-psychological perspective, the process of learning a second language takes on a special significance. From this viewpoint, one anticipates that if the learner is appropriately oriented, he may find that by learning another social group's language he has made the crucial step in becoming an acculturated part of a second linguistic-cultural community. Advancing toward bi-culturality in this sense may be viewed as a broadening experience in some cases, or it can engender "anomie", a feeling of not comfortably belonging in one social group or the other. With a different orientation, a language learner may look on his learning task as making him better educated or more cultured, or as equipping him with a useful skill for his future occupation, with little regard for the culture or the people represented by the other language. In other circumstances, one might consider learning another group's language as a means of getting on the "inside" of a cultural community in order to exploit, manipulate or control, with clearly personal ends in mind.

A series of studies carried out at McGill has been concerned with such topics, and various findings have increased our confidence in a social-psychological theory of language learning. This theory, in brief, holds that an individual successfully acquiring a second language gradually adopts various aspects of behavior which characterize members of another linguistic-cultural group. The learner's ethnocentric tendencies and his attitudes toward the other group are believed to determine his success in learning the new language. His motivation to learn is thought to be determined by his attitudes and by his orientation toward learning a second language. The orientation is "instrumental" in form if the purposes of language study reflect the more utilitarian value of linguistic achievement, such as getting ahead in one's occupation, and is "integrative" if the student is oriented to learn more about the other cultural community as if he desired to become a potential member of the other group. It is also argued that some may be anxious to learn another language as a means of being accepted in another cultural group because of dissatisfactions experienced in their own culture while other individuals may be equally as interested in another culture as they are in their own. However, the more proficient one becomes in a second language the more he may find that his place in his original membership group is modified at the same time as the other linguistic-cultural group becomes something more than a reference group for him. It may, in fact, become a second membership group for him. Depending upon the compatibility of the two cultures, he may experience feelings of chagrin or regret as he loses ties in one group, mixed with the fearful anticipation of entering a relatively new group. The concept "anomie", first proposed by Durkheim (1897) and more recently extended by Srole (1951) and Williams (1952), refers to the feelings of social uncertainty or dissatisfaction which sometimes characterize not only the bilingual but also the serious student of a second language.

The first studies (Gardner & Lambert, 1959; Gardner, 1960) were carried out with English-speaking Montreal high school students studying French who were examined for language learning aptitude and verbal intelligence as well as attitudes toward the French community and their intensity of motivation to learn French. Our measure of motivational intensity is conceptually similar to Jones' (1949 and 1950) index of interest in learning a language which he found to be important for successful learning among Welsh students. A factor analysis indicated that aptitude and intelligence formed a factor which was independent of a second comprising indices of motivation, type of orientation toward language and social attitudes toward French-Canadians. A measure of achievement in French was reflected equally prominently in both factors. In this case, then, French achievement was dependent upon both aptitude and intelligence as well as a sympathetic orientation toward the other group. This orientation apparently sustained a strong motivation to learn the other group's language. In the Montreal setting, it was clear that students with an integrative orientation were the more successful in language learning in contrast to those instrumentally oriented. (We have not concentrated on the manipulative orientation mentioned earlier and we are aware that a certain degree of error in classifying students may occur until attention is given to this form of orientation.)

Gardner's 1960 study confirmed and extended these findings. Using a larger sample of English-Canadians and incorporating various measures of French achievement, the same two independent factors were revealed, and again both were related to French achievement. But whereas aptitude and achievement were especially important for those French skills stressed in school training, the acquisition of French skills whose development depends on the active use of the language in communicational settings was determined solely by measures of an integrative motivation to learn French. Further evidence indicated that this integrative motive was the converse of an authoritarian ideological syndrome, opening the possibility that basic personality dispositions may be involved in language learning efficiency.

Information had been gathered about the students' parents' orientation toward the French community. These data supported the notion that the proper orientation toward the other group is developed within the family. Students with an integrative disposition to learn French had parents who also were integrative and sympathetic to the French community. The students' orientations were not related to parents' skill in French nor to the number of French acquaintances the parents had, indicating that the integrative motive is not due to having more experience with French at home but more likely stems from a family-wide attitudinal disposition.

A study by Anisfeld and Lambert (1961) extended the experimental procedure to samples of Jewish high school students studying Hebrew at parochial schools in Montreal. They were administered tests measuring their orientation toward learning Hebrew and their attitudes toward the Jewish culture and community, as well as tests of verbal intelligence and language aptitude. These tests were correlated with measures of achievement in the Hebrew language at the school year's end. The results support the generalization that both intellectual capacity and attitudinal orientation affect success in learning Hebrew. However, whereas intelligence and linguistic aptitude are relatively stable predictors of success, the attitudinal measures vary from one social class school district to another. The measure of a Jewish student's desire to become more acculturated into the Jewish tradition and culture was sensitive for children in a district of Montreal where socio-psychological analysis of the nature of the Jewish population's adjustment to the American Gentile culture suggested that these particular Jews were concerned with problems of integrating into the Jewish culture. In another district made up of Jews more recently arrived in North America who were clearly of a lower socio-economic class level, the measure of desire for Jewish acculturation did not correlate with achievement in Hebrew, whereas measures of pro-Semitic attitudes or pride in being Jewish did.

More recently, students undergoing an intensive course in French at

McGill's French Summer School were examined for changes in attitude during the study period (Lambert, Gardner, Barik and Tunstall, 1961). Most were American university students or secondary school language teachers who referred themselves more to the European-French than the American-French community in their orientations to language learning. In this study, it became apparent that feelings of anomie were markedly increased during the course of study. As students progressed to the point that they "thought" in French, it was noted that their feelings of anomie also increased. At the same time, they tried to find means of using English even though they had pledged to use only French for the six-week period. The pattern suggests that American students experience anomie when they concentrate on and commence to master a second language and, as a consequence, develop stratagems to control or minimize such feelings.

The most recent study (Peal and Lambert, 1961) compares 10-year-old monolingual and bilingual students on measures of intelligence. Of relevance here is the very clear pattern that bilingual children have markedly more favorable attitudes towards the "other" language community in contrast to the monolingual children. Furthermore, the parents of bilingual children are believed by their children to hold the same strongly sympathetic attitudes in contrast to the parents of monolingual children, as though the linguistic skills in a second language, extending to the point of bilingualism, are controlled by family-shared attitudes toward the other linguistic-cultural community.

These findings are consistent and reliable enough to be of more general interest. For example methods of language training may be modified and strengthened by giving consideration to the social-psychological implications of language learning. Because of the possible practical as well as theoretical significance of this approach, it seemed appropriate to test its applicability in a cultural setting other than the bicultural Quebec scene. The present series of studies was therefore conducted in various regional settings in the United States, two of them also bicultural and a third more representative of "typical" urban American cities. The bicultural settings permitted an examination of attitudes working two ways: attitudinal dispositions of American students toward linguistic minority groups in their immediate environment and the attitudes of members of the cultural minority group toward the general American culture about them.

METHOD AND PROCEDURE: ENGLISH-SPEAKING AMERICAN STUDENTS

Subjects. – Three samples of native English-speaking high school students were administered a battery of tests designed to measure French achievement, language aptitude, and various attitudinal and motivational characteristics. The samples consisted of students from Louisiana, Maine and Connecticut.

Materials. – Fifty-seven measures were obtained for each student.

(1) Rating of Integrative Orientation.
(2) Rating of Instrumental Orientation.
(3) Anomie Scale.
(4) California F Scale.
(5) Ethnocentrism Scale.
(6) Preference for America over France.
(7) Attitudes to Franco-Americans.
(8) Attitudes to Franco-American Acquaintances.
(9) Motivational Intensity.
(10) Desire to Learn French.
(11) Social Inquisitiveness Scale.
(12) Sensitivity to Others Scale.
(13) Parental Encouragement to Learn French.
(14) Student's Orientation.
(15) French vs. Franco-American Orientation.
(16) Parents' French Friends.
(17) S's French Acquaintances.
(18) S's French Friends.
(19) Orientation Index.

Variables 20-24 are the five sub-scales from the Carroll-Sapon *Modern Language Aptitude Test* (1959).

(20) Number Learning.
(21) Phonetic Script.
(22) Spelling Clues.
(23) Words in Sentences.
(24) Paired Associates.
(25) Sex.

Variables 25-29 are the four sub-scales from the *Cooperative French Listening Comprehension Test, Form A* (1955).

(26) Part I – Phonetic Discrimination.
(27) Part II – Answering Questions.
(28) Part III – Completion of Statements.
(29) Part IV – Comprehension of Passages.

(30) Parents Favor S Learning French.

Variables 31-33 are the three sub-scales from the *Cooperative French Test, Elementary Form, Q* (1940).

(31) Reading.
(32) Vocabulary.
(33) Grammar.
(34) Other than School Experiences in French.
(35) Self Rating of French Skills.
(36) Rating of Mother's French Skills.
(37) Rating of Father's French Skills.
(38) IQ.
(39) Mid-term French Grade.

Variables 40-45. Each student was asked to rate the following concepts on 23 7-point evaluative scales. *S*'s score for each concept was his mean evaluation. The concepts were:

(40) French People.
(41) Me.
(42) Americans.
(43) Me, as I'd like to be.
(44) Franco-Americans.
(45) My French Teacher.

Variables 46 and 47. Comparative Evaluation of French and English Speakers. Ss listened to tape recordings of nine "speakers" reading a 2½ minute passage of philosophical prose. Ss rated the personality of each guise on 20 6-point evaluative scales.

(46) Comparative Evaluation of European French and English Speakers.
(47) Comparative Evaluation of French-Canadian and English Speakers.

Variables 48-52. Each student was asked to read a short prose passaage and his oral production was recorded on tape. The tapes were later heard and scored by the same judge, a linguist. The total Reading Score was obtained by combining sub-scores on the following variables:

(48) Phonetic Accuracy.
(49) Linking.
(50) Stress.
(51) Rhythm.
(52) Absence of Nasalization.
(53) Correctness and Complexity of Free Speech.
    Complexity of pattern.
    Correctness.
(54) Number of French Acquaintances.
(55) Reading Fluency.
(56) Pronunciation Accuracy.
(57) Type of Accent.

INTEGRATING SUMMARY OF AMERICAN SAMPLES

If we compare the results obtained from the analyses of the three samples of English-speaking American students, a clear and interesting picture emerges of the roles played by two independent determinants of achievement in French study. These two determinants represent an aptitude-intelligence dimension on the one hand and an attitudinal-motivational dimension on the other. In the previous studies conducted in Montreal's bicultural and bilingual setting, the same two dimensions were found to be equally effective as predictors of French achievement and they were also found to be independent of one another. This independence means that there is little or no correlation between aptitude and social motivational variables. That is, one could not predict from a knowledge of a student's aptitude what his attitudes or motivation might be, and vice versa. However, one could make a better prediction from a knowledge of both the student's aptitude and his attitudinal disposition toward the other group as to how well he would do in language study, than from a consideration of one of these elements alone. We have become especially concerned with the attitudinal factor because it offers an intriguing opportunity to ameliorate the language learning process by changing students' orientations toward particular linguistic-cultural groups and thereby modifying their motivation to learn a second language. Although it is far from being settled, psychologists tend to regard intellectual capacity as fairly permanently fixed by heredity. On the other hand, attitudes and motivations are malleable and amenable to remarkable changes. Consequently we were encouraged to find in our Montreal studies that these more changeable characteristics played so important a role.

This study was of particular importance because of the feeling that the Canadian results might be limited to the Montreal bicultural scene and have little relevance for other communities. It is of special interest to note a basically similar pattern appearing in all three of the American settings, two bicultural and one monocultural. Hartford, Connecticut, is a large eastern city where various cultural groups, including Franco-Americans, very likely have their own neighborhoods, but where no predominantly French communities would be found as in the Maine and Louisiana areas studied. The same two dimensions found in Montreal again show themselves as independently associated with achievement in French study, even though the specific attitudinal component takes on different forms in each setting. From a technical point of view, the correlation method, including factor analyses, will not permit an unambiguous determination of whether these dimensions, especially the attitudinal disposition, are determinants of or are determined by achievement, but we feel confident that our decision to interpret them as determinants is logically consistent with the design of the study and the overall findings which have emerged. To decide for certain whether these dimensions are cause or effect will demand strictly experimental investigations, and such an approach becomes a logical sequel to a correlational study such as this one.

The Role of Aptitude and Intelligence in French Achievement

It is clear from these analyses that the subtests of the Modern Language Aptitude Test (MLAT) are generally highly correlated with intelligence. These two measures of intellectual capacity are strong predictors of achievement in the reading, vocabulary and grammar aspects of the Cooperative French Test (CFT) in two of our settings but not in the third (Maine). We argue that skill in these subtests calls for intellectual quickness in the learning and storing of vocabulary items and grammatical rules. The Otis test of intelligence is particularly strong as a predictor and is generally as efficient as the MLAT in this respect whereas the Primary Mental Abilities (PMA) measure of intelligence is somewhat less efficient.

In addition to predicting CFT scores, intellectual capacity is also a reliable determiner of grades received in French, of accuracy in French speech, and also the proper use of rhythm in French speech for the case where more attention is given to the oral-aural features of French in school training (i.e. Connecticut).

The subtests of the MLAT, without the pure intelligence component being involved, are differentially sensitive as predictors of various facets of French achievement. The findings support Carroll's conceptualizations of language aptitude and tend to validate the Carroll-Sapon Modern Language Aptitude Test. Thus the Number Learning subtest in the Louisiana study was a determinant of reading fluency and the development of a good accent in French. The Phonetic Script and Spelling Clues subtests of the MLAT are strong determinants of the various linguistic measures of oral skill in both the Maine and Connecticut studies. Spelling Clues, along with an index of the number of French friends a student has, also predict one's skill in comprehending complex passages of French as measured by the French Listening Comprehension Test (FLCT), part IV, in the Maine study.

The Role of Attitudes and Motivation in French Achievement

A clear and consistent pattern emerges in all three settings indicating that students who have a strong motivation and desire to learn French obtain good grades in the language. In each setting there is apparently a different foundation for this motivation. In Louisiana, the motivation appears to derive from strong parental encouragement and personal satisfaction in the student's attempt to learn the language. In Maine, the motivation apparently is fostered by the students' (especially the girls') identification with their French teachers, and depends in part on the student being sensitive toward the feelings of other people. In Connecticut the strong motivation to learn French seems to come from the students' own integrative orientations toward the study of the language as well as their realization of the language's potential usefulness for them.

In two settings it was found that an ethnocentric syndrome (made up of high scores on the F scale, Ethnocentrism scale, Anomie, and Preference for American over French Culture scales) contributes to poor French grades in both instances as well as to poor comprehension in one case and poor oral reading skills in the other. In the third setting (Maine), low F scale scores interact with measures of intellectual capacity to determine French grades.

The other findings are specific to regions. In Louisiana it was found that stereotyped negative feelings toward Franco-Americans contribute to poor achievement in comprehension of complex French passages and in vocabulary skill. Also, an integrative orientation toward learning French and favorable attitudes toward Franco-Americans contribute to vocabulary skill and, to a lesser extent, to one measure of French comprehension. In Maine it was noted that the number of French friends the student has determines in part (along with measures of intellectual capacity) his comprehension of complex French passages. Furthermore, students from families who have developed many friendships with French-speaking people and who are instrumentally oriented in their study of French are likely to develop good oral skills.

Finally, an important (but incidental) trend was noted for French grades to be independent of oral and often aural skills. That is, teachers are apparently not grading students for achievement in oral-aural aspects of French. If we assume that the grade assigned reflects the teacher's overall estimate of a student's progress, we find that the teachers' estimates are at variance with the student's own estimate of his skill in the language which is generally related to how well he can speak and understand the language.

INTEGRATING SUMMARY, FRANCO-AMERICAN SAMPLES

When we shift attention from the American to the Franco-American student learning French, several distinctive changes appear in the roles played by a student's intellectual capacity and his social attitudes in language learning. The most important difference is the manner in which social attitudes and, in some cases, intellectual capacity affect the degree and form of bilinguality of the Franco-American students who have had opportunities to become competent in both French and English. The evidence indicates that the social attitudes of these individuals towards their two cultures determine whether they will capitalize on the opportunities available to them to become bilingual, or psychologically align themselves with one or the other cultures and consequently develop a linguistic dominance. The study, therefore, elucidates the various strategies which linguistic minority group members develop in adjusting to the bicultural demands of living in the United States. This topic is of wide interest to many behavioral scientists, but has only been given systematic attention by a small number, notably Child (1943), Spoerl (1946), and Soffietti (1955).

In view of their limited experience with French at school, the Louisiana Franco-American students show some characteristics similar to the American students studying French for the first time and in other respects they reveal their bicultural background. This dual pattern indicates that the Louisiana Franco-Americans look on the learning of French as do the American students on the one hand and on the other hand in a manner similar to the genuinely bicultural students. Thus, students with high aptitude and a preference for French culture excel in aural and written French skills. A strong motivation to learn French for integrative reasons leads to a feeling of competence in French and skill in French grammar. Furthermore, students who hold favorable stereotypes toward French people show good oral skills in French while those with unfavorable stereotypes are poor in French oral skill, as though stereotypes determine their oral skills. These patterns are generally similar to those revealed by American students encountering French for the first time at school.

The problem of adjusting to a bicultural social setting also becomes apparent in the analysis. Louisiana Franco-American students for whom the French language is dominant have trouble with the learning of English. Possibly as a consequence of this linguistic imbalance, they stress their preference for the American over the French culture, as though they were striving to dissociate themselves from their French background in order to make a more satisfactory adjustment to the American culture and its English language. Incidentally, boys are more bothered than girls by their French background and this affects their skills in French, the boys being deficient in contrast to girls. Franco-Americans from the Louisiana region who are highly authoritarian reveal a dominance in English skills. On the other hand, students with low authoritarian tendencies coupled with favorable attitudes towards their own cultural group develop bilingual skill. Finally a strong desire for French identity is reflected in a dominance of French over English, suggesting that a very strong desire for a rejuvenation of French culture in Louisiana can retard bilingualism.

Concerning the Franco-American students from Maine, substantial evidence indicates that their attitudes toward their own linguistic cultural group can affect their adoption or rejection of their own native language. In other cases, linguistic minority group members in the Maine community studied face a conflict of cultural allegiances which affects their skill in both their languages.

In the Maine setting, two contrasting approaches to the development of bilingualism became apparent. In one case, students who are intellectually bright and who have a non-ethnocentric outlook profit from their language training in both English and French and thus develop into bilinguals. An alternative route to bilingualism is apparent. Students with a strong instrumental orientation toward learning French which is reinforced by parental encouragement develop good oral and aural skills in French, show competence in English grammar and feel they are doing well in both languages.

Furthermore, there are apparently two alternative routes for these students to maintain a dominance of French over English. Franco-American students from this Maine setting who have a strong desire for French identity, who prefer and constantly think in French rather than English reveal a dominance of French over English and a special competence in French comprehension. In contrast, students who express a strong motivation and desire to learn French, especially for integrative reasons, show a dominance of French and particularly good phonetic skill in French while at the same time they are poor in English grammar.

Certain attitudinal patterns promote a dominance of English over French for the Franco-Americans from Maine. English is dominant for those who express a clear preference for the American over the French culture and who negate the value of knowing French. They show poor oral skill in French and express an anxiety about their progress in English. This pattern reflects a rejection of French background, similar in many respects to the rebel reaction of Italian-Americans described by Child (1943).

Finally, those Franco-Americans who apparently face a conflict of cultural allegiances – showing an authoritarian preference for the

Franco-American culture and a preference for American over European French culture – are poor in aural tests in French, feel they are poor in French and show signs of being poor in English vocabulary. Apparently, those students who face an unresolved conflict of cultural allegiances are held back in their progress in both languages.

It is felt that these relations of attitude dispositions and bilingual skill can be of interest and use to those studying bilingualism or America's linguistic minority groups.

COMPARISONS OF FRANCO-AMERICAN SUBJECTS FROM LOUISIANA AND MAINE

Several lines of evidence have suggested that fundamental differences exist between our two samples of Franco-American students in terms of their experience with French, their degree of bilinguality, and their adjustment to the American society as ethnic minority groups. We were able to compare the Louisiana and Maine samples of Franco-American students on various measures. It is certain that the Maine French students have a great deal more formal instruction in French than have the Louisiana students. The Maine students have had training in French from their first years of school in a parochial school system while the Louisiana students in their public school system have the opportunity to study French at the high school level only, making a difference of nine years of training. The Maine students also have more opportunities to learn and use French with their families. Comparisons 19, 20 and 51 indicate that both parents of the Maine students are typically better skilled in French and give more encouragement to their children to learn French. The two samples do not differ on the number of French-speaking friends they have (Comparison 55), but it is virtually certain, as will be evident later, that more French is spoken among Franco-Americans in Maine than in Louisiana. It is clear that the Maine students particularly enjoy being with other Franco-Americans (Comparison 52) although there is no difference in attitudes to Franco-Americans in general (Comparison 45) nor toward American culture (Comparison 44). Furthermore there are no regional differences in terms of authoritarianism, ethnocentrism or anomie (Comparisons 41-43). The samples do not differ with respect to their desire and motivation to learn French (Comparisons 47 and 48) or their preference for French over English (Comparison 32). Apparently the fundamental difference stems from being or not being a part of a real French community. The Maine students feel a part of a living French community where the instrumental value of knowing the language is very clear to them, much more so than for the Louisiana students (Comparison 40). They are moreover encouraged and offered enough opportunities to permit them to feel they have actually learned the language (Comparison 18) and to think in French rather than English (Comparison 31). Their basic stereotypes toward French-speaking people are more favorable than is the case with the Louisiana students (Comparison 46 and a similar trend in 54). Comparison 53 is of particular interest. It indicates that the Louisiana Franco-American is more concerned than his counterpart in Maine about his identity as a French person, as though he nostalgically would like to be part of a vital French community. Other evidence makes it very clear that this feeling reflects a desire and not a reality. The Louisiana students are markedly less prone than those in Maine to think of themselves as French when asked about their ethnic background by either English-speaking or French-speaking people (Comparisons 34 and 35). Their style of French speech is markedly less French than is the case for the Maine group. That is, their accent has no French characteristics whereas the Maine group has a distinctive French-American accent (Comparison 21) and, linguistically considered, the Louisiana students' French speech is markedly poorer in phonetic accuracy, proper linking, stress, rhythm and nasalization (Comparisons 17, and 23 to 26).

But it is not only the speech style that differentiates the two groups. The free speech and reading fluency of the Maine students (Comparisons 8 and 13), their comprehension of spoken French (Comparisons 14-16) are all markedly superior to those of the Louisiana French students. This highly superior skill in French among the Maine Franco-Americans has not, however, made them comparatively deficient in English. They feel as skilled in English as do the Louisiana students (Comparison 27) and comprehend the value of knowing English equally well (Comparisons 37 and 38). They apparently are more balanced in their bilingual skills than is the case in Louisiana, where the students show a dominance of English skills in one of our measures of bilinguality (Comparison 29). In fact, the Maine students' varied experiences in languages: standard French at school, American French at home and English in the community, may well have contributed to their superior skills in making phonemic distinctions and in sensing grammatical differences, as noted in Comparisons 7, 3 and 5.

These comparisons indicate that the Franco-American students from Maine are participants in a decidedly more dynamic French community, one which transmits its linguistic and cultural heritage more effectively than does the French community in Louisiana. In fact, the pattern of variables suggests that the French tradition in Louisiana is merging much more rapidly with the general American culture than is the case for the Maine community studied. It is possible that both the Franco-American and English-speaking communities in Maine respect this desire for linguistic-cultural transmission and encourage the teaching of French in school for a much greater number of years. Family support for this transmission is noted in the greater use of French at home by the parents of Franco-American students in Maine. As a consequence of this comparatively extensive experience with French at home and at school, the Maine students are more skilled in all aspects of French and are more ready to perceive themselves as French as though they were more proud of their linguistic and cultural background than are the Louisiana students. Yet they are apparently equally competent in English.

It is of incidental interest to note the clear step-wise increases in performances on the oral and aural tests for the American students at various stages of training in French. However, we did not test these for significance.

In summary, these comparisons have highlighted the similar attitudinal dispositions of the Franco-American students when contrasted with American students. The Franco-Americans are more anomic, authoritarian and ethnocentric than American students, and, although more sympathetic to Franco-American culture than are the Americans, they are nevertheless much more favorable to the American than to the European French way of life. This pattern strongly suggests that Franco-American students are caught in a very meaningful cultural conflict which presents them with problems regarding their allegiances to each of their cultural heritages. Other evidence indicates that they are comparatively reserved in social situations and possibly embarrassed about their Franco-American style of French.

Both groups of Franco-Americans are decidedly poorer on the MLAT, indicating the difficulty of ascertaining their language potential with a test standardized for monolingual American subjects.

Both groups also are generally superior to American students in the ability to comprehend spoken French as measured by the FLCT but the Maine sample of Franco-Americans is superior to the Louisiana group in this respect. On measures of oral skill in French, the Maine group is markedly superior to American students while the Louisiana group of Franco-Americans is no better than or even inferior to the American students. The superiority in oral skill for the Maine sample of Franco-Americans is restricted to measures of linguistic aspects of proper French speech. Neither group of Franco-Americans excels in a test of free speech in French which measures accuracy and complexity of oral output.

It is hoped that these comparisons will be valuable for those who would like to develop the latent potential of American linguistic minority groups and encourage Franco-Americans to enter the language teaching profession. Any attempts made to develop this potential should include a very sensitive appreciation for the social-psychological implications of being a Franco-American in this culture.

SUMMARY AND CONCLUSIONS

American students of English-speaking backgrounds who are in the process of studying the French language have a generally negative set of stereotypes about the basic personality characteristics of French-speaking people. The general pattern is to look on the European French speaker as being less thoughtful, less intelligent, clearly less honest and dependable, less generous, less kind, less reliable, less stable, and having less character than the same person when speaking in English. At the same time he is seen as being more humorous and entertaining, very likely in the sense that he is somewhat ridiculous.

These students have different but clearly negative stereotypes about the Franco-American person. He is perceived as comparatively shorter, less honest, less generous and less kind, while at the same time he is viewed as more leaderlike, somewhat more intelligent, more self-confident, more entertaining, clearly more nervous, more ambitious and somewhat more stable and sociable. In general the stereotype is that the Franco-American is a cruel, dishonest, short person who is nervous, self-confident, bossy and ambitious while at the same time being entertaining, perhaps in the sense of being a ridiculous person rather than a threatening one.

The Franco-American students from Louisiana have very similar reactions to those of the American students, suggesting that they have adopted community-wide stereotypes about their own group, a characteristic reaction of various minority groups (see Lambert, et al., 1960). They behave as though they are rejecting their cultural background and actively identifying with and finding value in the purely "American" culture. This pattern of over-identification with the American culture is not found among the Franco-American students in the Maine communities studied. In fact there is strong evidence in their case of a basic pride in their French background, although "American" standards of physical and social traits do seem more valuable to them. There is no certain explanation for this difference between Louisiana and Maine Franco-Americans. It may well be due to the greater experience the Maine students have had in the French language and in French folkways. This point itself would be worthy of further investigation.

These findings vividly indicate the difficulty most students in these regions have in orienting themselves favorably to the other cultural-linguistic group whose language they are supposed to learn. It is apparent that teachers of French also work at a great disadvantage in trying to teach the language in the face of these stereotypes of French people. It would certainly be worth the effort to develop research plans to systematically *change* these stereotypes in certain communities, if possible. It is our contention that the learning of foreign languages would be greatly facilitated if negative stereotypes of foreign groups were modified to favorable and friendly dispositions.

In summary

This examination of various value orientations of American high school students has led to a potentially useful set of facts about students' orientations to life in general and to the study of language in particular. Achievement in French is not generally a central goal for American students. Rather, it is incidental to the more demanding purpose of trying to find one's way in the future. To the extent that students are intellectually bright and have a strong achievement drive, they tend to do well in all school work and more or less incidentally do well in French. This achievement motivation coupled with intelligence promotes good performance in all school work, including not only French grades but also those aspects of French performance not likely stressed in school (Factor I). These intellectually bright, achievement-oriented students are good estimators of how much they will have to do to succeed in school work and they apparently do not feel they have to work strenuously in order to succeed.

In general, value orientations do not play an important role in predicting who will or will not do well in French (Factors I and II). That is, students who value pleasure are no more or less likely to do well in French than are those who value intellectual matters. However, students who *value* success, but who are not clearly *motivated* to succeed, tend to obtain good school grades but do not excel in related work which is usually not stressed in class, such as oral and aural training in French. The comparison of Factors III and I suggests that success value is less important for *general* competence than is success motivation coupled with intellectual ability. The point here is that the intelligently motivated student has a lively interest and a broad competence, extending beyond school requirements, which can be capitalized on by skilled teachers.

Certain components of French skill were found to be independent of intellectual capacity. These skills depend on a strong desire to do well in French, a favorable feeling toward French study and a competence in habits of study (Factor IV). Thus, regardless of intellectual ability or achievement drive, the student can, in certain cases, do well in French if he is favorably motivated to French study itself.

The other factors do not include references to language achievement. They were discussed because of the patternings of values which were revealed.

This monograph describes a series of exploratory research studies carried out to determine the bases of skill in language learning. In particular, we were interested in comparing the importance in the language learning process of intellectual ability and language learning aptitude, on the one hand, and social attitudes toward the "other" language group and motivation to learn the language, on the other hand. Our attention was first directed to an examination of how these variables affect the language learning of American students who come from homes where only English is spoken. In order to compare the results of the present investigation with earlier studies carried out with English-speaking students learning French in Montreal, we chose two samples of students from bicultural American communities in Louisiana and Maine. A third sample of American students was drawn from the public school system of Hartford, Connecticut, which was considered representative of most large city school systems along the Eastern coast of America. The Connecticut setting did not have a distinctive sub-community of Franco-Americans in its immediate environment comparable to those in the Louisiana and Maine districts studied. Thus, the Hartford students would not be expected to have a clear linguistic cultural group in their immediate experience toward which favorable or unfavorable attitudes would have developed through direct contact.

A large battery of tests was administered to these students early in the year, and near the end of the year, tests of achievement in French were given, and grades in French were obtained from teachers. The tests were inter-correlated and factor analyzed. The resulting patterns of inter-relations were studied and interpreted. The results indicate that, similar to the Montreal studies, two independent factors underlie the development of skill in learning a second language: an intellectual capacity and an appropriate attitudinal orientation toward the other language group coupled with a determined motivation to learn the language. The details of this major finding were discussed.

The second phase of the investigation was concerned with the role of aptitudinal, attitudinal and motivational variables in the linguistic development of potentially bilingual Franco-American students – those coming from homes in which primarily French was spoken. Two samples of Franco-American high school students were chosen from the Louisiana and Maine settings. The analysis indicated the manner in which social attitudes toward their own linguistic group and the American culture around them influence their progress in becoming bilingual, retaining the dominance of French or developing dominance of English. The manner in which the Franco-American student faces and resolves the cultural conflict he is likely to encounter in the American society was found to determine his linguistic development in French and English.

The third phase of the study focused on a comparison of Franco-American students from the Louisiana and Maine settings. The results make it very clear that whereas the Louisiana French culture is rapidly merging into the general American culture, the Maine community of Franco-Americans enjoys a comparatively dynamic and distinctive existence.

The fourth phase compared the Franco-American and American students in their various competences in French and in their attitudinal dispositions. The results reinforce the finding mentioned above of the cultural conflicts faced by Franco-American students. Furthermore, the Maine Franco-Americans show a decided superiority over the American students in their French skills whereas the Louisiana Franco-Americans show little or no advantage in French over American students.

The fifth phase of the study examined the stereotypes both American and Franco-American groups of students hold toward French people. The analysis makes it very clear that all groups except the Maine Franco-Americans hold unfavorable stereotypes of French people. The Maine Franco-Americans give evidence of a basic pride in their French heritage. The consequences of holding negative stereotypes toward the very people whose language one is supposed to learn become apparent in this analysis.

The sixth and final phase deals with the role of students' values in the language-learning process. The results indicate that achievement in foreign language training is not a central goal for American students. Rather it is apparently incidental to the more challenging goal of trying to find and prepare one's way for the future. Intelligence coupled with a value placed on achievement are major determiners of success in most school work, including the study of language.

These findings not only supply needed information about the student learning languages, they also point the way to a large number of next steps to be taken in the fascinating study of language learning and bilingualism.

This study was sponsored by the Language Development Section of the U.S. Office of Education under Title VI of the National Defense Education Act, Section 602, Public Law 85-864. We extend our gratitude to many colleagues for valuable suggestions offered with regard to the design and analysis of this work, notably Professors William W. Lambert (Cornell), John Carroll (Harvard),

George A. Ferguson (McGill), Vernon J. Parenton (Louisiana State University), Dr. Bruce Gaarder, Alfred Hayes and Loretta Wawrzyniak of the U.S. Office of Education.

Mrs. Irène Vachon-Spilka from the University of Montreal was responsible for the linguistic analysis of the samples of oral production in French obtained from each student and for the construction of the phonetic discrimination test used with the Franco-American students. Mme. Janine Lambert and Dr. Nicole Deschamps rated each student for accuracy of pronunciation, reading fluency and type of accent.

Mr. Roy Miles of Lafayette, Louisiana, and Dr. Dean Allen of Bowdoin College, Maine, helped us greatly in carrying out the testing in their regions and advising us on local matters. The sympathetic encouragement of the superintendents, principals and teachers of a large number of high schools in Louisiana, Maine, and Hartford, Connecticut, finally permitted this study to be undertaken. We sincerely thank them for their cooperation.

These excerpts appear in published form for the first time in the present volume. Printed with permission. Consult original source for references.

Simon R. Herman

EXPLORATIONS IN THE SOCIAL PSYCHOLOGY OF LANGUAGE CHOICE *

Although social psychologists have been giving increasing attention in recent years to the subject of language,[1] the field is still relatively unexplored by them. One of the problems which thus far has not received systematic attention relates to the choice by a bilingual speaker of one language rather than the other in situations where either language could serve as the medium of conversation.

In a multilingual society instances are readily observable of choice of language which is determined by considerations other than the requirements of the particular conversation. These considerations would appear generally to be related to the speaker's reference to groups in the wider social milieu. It seemed to us that the determinants of this choice merited exploration. And if group identifications were, indeed, found to play a significant part, it would permit an approach from the opposite angle:

* This preliminary paper is part of a wider study in preparation on the social psychology of language choice. I am grateful to Dr Ben Halpern, of the Harvard Center for Middle Eastern Studies, and to Mr Erling O. Schild, of the Hebrew University, for their helpful suggestions in the discussion of the study. The collation of the data was carried out by Sarah Molcho and Freda Sosnowski, graduate students in the Department of Sociology. This study was made possible by a research grant from The James Marshall Fund.

[1] A reflection of this interest is to be found in the third edition of *Readings in Social Psychology* (Maccoby, Newcomb & Hartley, 1958) which for the first time has a special section devoted to researches on language. Linguists in their turn have become increasingly aware of the importance of the social-psychological context in the study of language behaviour, as, for instance, in the investigation of "interference" (deviations from the norms of a language which occur in the speech of a bilingual as a result of his familiarity with the other language). A notable example of this awareness is the work of Weinreich (1953).

the choice of language could be used as a behavioural index to group preferences and to the direction of social adjustment – particularly among immigrants and other newcomers in a society. An analysis of the determinants of language choice might conceivably also shed light on problems of motivation associated with the learning of a new language.

Although our paper is concerned with the choice between two languages, the discussion may also have some pertinence within the realm of a particular language to the adoption of a form of slang or the imitation of an accent that is the distinctive mark of a class or clique and sets it apart from other groups in that society speaking the same language.

LANGUAGE CHOICE AS AN OVERLAPPING SITUATION

Personal needs, background, and immediate situations

As a starting-point to such analysis, it is useful to look at the speaker who is in the position of having to choose between two (or more) languages as a person in an overlapping situation, i.e. he is located in the common part of two psychological situations that exist simultaneously for him.

(a) One situation may correspond to the person's own need or desire to speak a particular language (e.g. the language in which he is most proficient); the other may correspond to the norms of his group, which may demand of him the use of another language (e.g. the national tongue, which he may speak with difficulty). There may be a conflict between personal needs and group demands.[2]

(b) In the determination of which language he will use the forces operating may arise not only from the immediate face-to-face situation but also from the situation at large. Barker, Dembo, and Lewin (1941) have stressed the importance of the general problem of how the background of a situation influences behaviour in an immediate situation. In seeking to define background and immediate situation, they write:

> The regions of the life space which constitute the background are, according to our definition, not a part of the activity regions in which the individual is

[2] "The effect of group belongingness on the behaviour of an individual can be viewed as the result of an overlapping situation: one situation corresponds to the person's own needs and goals; the other to the goals, rules and values which exist for him as a group member. Adaptation of an individual to the group depends upon the avoidance of too great a conflict between the two sets of forces" (Lewin, 1951, pp. 271-2).

involved at the time. . . . On the other hand the background still influences the behaviour in some way. It cannot be omitted from the life of space, if one is to be able to derive the actual behaviour. The individual behaves as if he were in an overlapping situation consisting of both the immediate and the background situation, the background usually having less relative potency [3] (*op. cit.*, pp. 138-9).

Barker, Dembo, and Lewin were concerned in their study with the influence of a *background of frustration* – caused by the inaccessibility of the attractive toys with which the children had played in the earlier part of the experiment – on an immediate play situation in which the children had to content themselves with less attractive toys. In their experiment the background is a mood or psychological state which impinges on the ongoing activity. But the concept of a background situation overlapping with an immediate situation may also be used to cover the intrusion on the psychological field of other forces from the wider context of an activity. An illustration is provided by a recent study by Campbell and Yarrow (1958), who view the behaviour of children in an interracial summer camp as that of persons in an overlapping situation: the children are exposed to the influences of their immediate environment (the desegregated camp), but at times influences obtrude from the background situation (in this case, the home and neighbourhood environments).

The less the background obtrudes, the more likely is the person to be responsive to the demands of the immediate situation. One of the merits of what Lewin has termed the "cultural island" as a medium of change lies precisely in the fact that this represents a situation from which background influences are largely excluded.[4]

The group factor to which we have referred above may be embedded either in the background situation or in the immediate situation. And so our discussion can be limited to forces arising from three sources: (i) personal needs, (ii) the immediate situation, and (iii) the background situation.

We shall discuss background situation principally in terms of *groups*

[3] In this paper we shall concern ourselves largely with cases where the background has the higher relative potency.

[4] "Sometimes the value system of this face-to-face group conflicts with the values of the larger cultural setting and it is necessary to separate the group from the larger setting . . . The effectiveness of camps or workshops in changing ideology or conduct depends in part on the possibility of creating such 'cultural islands' during change. The stronger the accepted subculture of the workshop and the more isolated it is the more it will minimize that type of change which is based on the relation between the individual and the standards of the larger group" (Lewin, 1951, pp. 231-3).

in the wider social milieu that are not directly involved in the immediate situation but yet may influence the behaviour – "hidden committees", so to speak. Though a group factor may also be operative in the immediate situation, the reference then is to the face-to-face group actually participating in the activity. Under personal needs we subsume a number of personal variables, such as relative proficiency in the languages, emotional attachment to a particular language (e.g. to the mother-tongue), level of aspiration in regard to the use of languages.

The relative potency of the situations – general principles

In a particular instance the forces arising from these three situations may operate in the same direction, i.e. all point to the use of the same language. The problem in which we are interested exists when the overlapping situations are antagonistic. The question then arises which situation has the higher potency, i.e. which decisively determines the language behaviour.

In a recent paper, Herman and Schild (1960) have analysed the relative potency of a situation as a function of its relative valence (attractiveness or repulsiveness) *and* its relative salience (prominence in the perceptual field).[5]

The factor of salience is of special importance in analysing the influence of a background situation. In order that this influence may be exercised, the background situation – which from its very nature is usually less salient than the immediate situation – has to gain in salience; it has, as it were, to move momentarily into the foreground.

Our hypothesis is that a background situation or, more specifically – in the sense in which we are using the term – a "background group" gains in salience under the following conditions:

1. When the activity takes place in a public rather than a private setting.
2. When the behaviour in the situation may be interpreted as providing cues to group identifications (including social status) or conformity to group norms.
3. When the person involved in the activity wishes to identify (or to be identified) with a particular group or to be dissociated from it, or desires (or feels obliged) to conform to the norms of a reference group.

[5] An example from the present study of the effect of changing salience: the parents of a young child – newly arrived immigrants to Israel from Poland – told in the interview with them how the child speaks only Polish to them at home and continues to do so when they take him to nursery school. But when the school comes into view (and even before he enters its gates), he switches over to Hebrew.

When these three conditions co-exist, the relative salience of a background situation is likely to be high. If the background situation which thus gains in salience also has higher valence for the person than the immediate situation, it will determine his behaviour, i.e. it will have the higher relative potency. If the valence of the group is positive, the person will act in accordance with its norms. If it is negative, he will act in a way that dissociates him from the group.

Our hypothesis is that personal needs or desires are likely to be dominant under any of the following conditions:

1. Where the setting is private rather than public.
2. Where the situation provokes insecurity, high tension, or frustration.
3. Where it touches the central rather than the peripheral layers of the personality.

From the analysis of the conditions under which the background situation and personal needs are likely to have high potency, it can be deduced in what circumstances the immediate situation has high potency. This is likely to be so under one or other of the following conditions:

1. When the person is not concerned about group identifications.
2. When the behaviour is task oriented.
3. When well-established patterns of behaviour characterize a relationship.

After formulating these general hypotheses about the relative potency of the three situations, we proceeded to derive from them a series of hypotheses relating more specifically to the language behaviour of the bilingual speaker. We shall provide illustrations from our empirical material indicating the kind of support there is likely to be for a particular hypothesis. The hypotheses obviously still require systematic testing.

We shall furthermore outline a characteristic pattern in the language development of a new immigrant at various stages in his adjustment, indicating the fluctuations in the potency of personal needs, the background situation, and the immediate situation. In observing this pattern we shall also see in what circumstances – once the determinants of language choice are known – we can use the choice of a language as a behavioural index of group preferences and of social adjustment.

AN EXPLORATORY STUDY

A multilingual society such as that of Israel provides rich material for a study of language choice. Although Hebrew has won for itself a secure place as the national language, some 60 per cent of the population (according to a survey undertaken in 1954) reported the use of more than one language in daily life. This is not surprising when it is realized that the greater part of the population is composed of immigrants who arrived in the years following the establishment of Israel as a State in 1948. A large majority of the immigrants of these years knew no Hebrew when they arrived. They came from a variety of countries and brought with them a great diversity of languages.

The empirical material to which we refer in this paper was gathered (for the purposes of the more extensive study in preparation on the social psychology of language choice) from the following sources:

(a) Case histories by students (including a number of officials from government and other institutions attending university courses) describing their use of Hebrew and other languages.
(b) Interviews with immigrants and visiting students.
(c) A brief questionnaire (dealing mainly with questions relating to the prestige of various languages) administered to 84 students in four classes at the Hebrew University.
(d) Surveys of the use of languages in a variety of situations in the collective settlement of Tsora in the Judaean hills (with a population of settlers from South Africa and local-born Israelis) and in a stratified sample of the population of an immigrant township, Kiryat Gat (with immigrants from Britain, Poland, Hungary, Morocco, Egypt).[6]

We also had available the data of an extensive statistical investigation undertaken by Bachi (1956), who has analysed the extent of the use of Hebrew among various sections of the population classified on the basis of length of stay in Israel, country of birth, sex, age, occupation, education, and place of residence in Israel. Included in his material is a special survey carried out in 1950-51 of a stratified sample of 12,500 immigrants (from among the 237,000 immigrants who arrived in 1948-49).

THE RELATIVE POTENCY OF THE SITUATIONS – APPLICATION OF PRINCIPLES TO LANGUAGE BEHAVIOUR

Of particular interest to the social psychologist are the circumstances in which the relative potency of the background situation is likely to be

[6] The material relating specifically to languages was gathered in the course of a more general survey of Kiryat Gat conducted by Eric Cohen under the direction of Professor S. N. Eisenstadt of the Department of Sociology of the Hebrew University.

high. Indeed, the study of language choice provides a strategic vantage point for the exploration of the influence of a background situation on behaviour.

Conditions under which the background situation may have high potency

When the language is used in a setting that is public rather than private

To the extent that the immediate situation is public, it is more exposed to the impingement of the background situation. Immigrants who use their native tongue at home often switch to Hebrew in a bus, at a concert, and in other public places. In the collective settlement studied, South African settlers used English when in their own rooms, but switched to Hebrew in the communal dining-room. This tendency is even more pronounced where the foreign language is subject to public derogation. Some of our subjects who spoke German unreservedly with their German-speaking parents at home told of their feelings of shame if the parents addressed them in this language outside the home (during the period when the use of German was looked upon askance in Israel).

When the language spoken may be interpreted as providing cues to group identifications (including social status) or conformity to group norms

(*a*) *Where the relative prestige of the languages differs markedly.* There are likely to be differences in the measure of prestige accorded to languages spoken in a multilingual community. We found such differences in the evaluations accorded to languages by the groups we studied. The four groups of 84 students were presented with a list of the major languages spoken in Israel and were asked to indicate beside each language whether it had "very high", "high", "medium", "low", or "very low" prestige in their eyes. The order which emerged was as follows: [7] (1) Hebrew, English – 94; (3) French – 91; (4) Russian – 76; (5) German – 72; (6) Arabic – 64; (7) Spanish – 58; (8) Yiddish – 54; (9) Polish – 51; (10) Ladino, Hungarian – 44; (12) Turkish – 41; (13) Roumanian – 40 (14) Persian – 33.

When they were asked in similar terms to indicate how they thought the languages were rated by the public, the rank-order correlation between their own rating and that attributed by them to the public was .89. The students are, of course, a selected group, and their rating will

[7] The scoring is such that if a language was unanimously rated "very high" it would receive 100; if all students rated it as "very low" it would have received 20. Cf. the scoring of ratings of job prestige by Bendix and Lipset (1953, p. 412).

not necessarily correspond to that of a sample of the population. When, however, the same question on "the prestige of the languages in your eyes" was given to a group of 56 nurses attending a country-wide seminar, a rating closely similar to that of the students was obtained, the rank-order correlation between the ratings of the two groups being .93.

The students were also presented with a list of settlers from various countries, groups using the languages on the list, and were asked to rate their prestige. A rank-order correlation of .84 was found between prestige of the languages and prestige of settler groups speaking these languages. Although it appears that a relationship exists between the prestige of the language and that of the group speaking it, the nature of that relationship has still to be studied. Indeed, the general question as to what the determinants of prestige are remains to be investigated.[8] When asked to indicate which of a number of factors had influenced them in rating the prestige of three of the languages Arabic, English, Hebrew, students gave reasons differing from language to language.

Because of its high prestige, many of our subjects from English-speaking countries use English in circumstances where immigrants with languages of low prestige pass over to Hebrew.

When in our studies a group of settlers from North Africa were asked what languages they knew, they replied, in almost all cases, "Hebrew, French, Arabic", placing Arabic last, although this was the language in which they were most proficient.

(*b*) *When there is public derogation of certain languages.* There may be an opposition in a community to the use of certain languages for political and other reasons. During the period of the British Mandate in Palestine, the critical attitude towards the Mandatory Power's policy produced in some circles an aversion to the study and use of English that some of our subjects now bitterly regret in view of the current importance of English in a professional career. The memory of Nazi persecutions has resulted in a revulsion in sectors of the Israel population against German.

Within Israel society there are sharply conflicting attitudes to a language such as Yiddish. In some circles it is highly cherished; in others it is derided as a symbol of the unpleasing aspects of a Diaspora existence.

(*c*) *Where language tolerance is low.* The freedom of language choice will be determined by the degree of language tolerance in the particular society. In a country of immigration such as Israel, this tolerance refers not only to permissiveness toward the use of foreign languages but also to the attitude toward a faulty use of the national tongue. Because the

[8] The term "prestige" was left undefined in the question. Cf. Weinreich (1953, p. 79), where he proposes the restriction of the term to a language's value in social advance.

larger part of the population arrived within the last decade since the founding of the State and since there are constant accessions of new immigrants, a high degree of language tolerance has perforce to exist. As Hebrew has become more firmly established as the language of Jews in Israel, protagonists of that language have tended to treat with greater leniency the use of foreign tongues by immigrants who cannot be expected to have mastered Hebrew. The erstwhile negative attitude towards the publication of newspapers in foreign languages has also been modified. The faulty use of Hebrew is widely tolerated, and oldtimers will frequently help out an immigrant speaking a halting Hebrew by suggesting the proper word or phrase or even correcting his mistakes.

When visiting American students were asked – at the end of six months in Israel – whether Israelis were tolerant or intolerant toward their use of English, 39 of the 40 students replied that the Israelis were tolerant. The tolerance was apparently highest for English [9] and differed from language to language.

To the extent that a wide range of deviation from the use of the national language is tolerated, speakers will be freer to choose languages in terms of the requirements of the immediate situation or personal needs.

Where the speaker wishes to identify (or be identified) with a particular group or to be dissociated from it, or desires (or feels obliged) to conform to the norms of a reference group

(*a*) *Where the speaker is a marginal man.* The more marginal a person is in a particular society, the more salient for him becomes the question of language as an indicator of group affiliation and the less free he is to respond merely in terms of the demands of the immediate situation. The interviews we gathered show that newcomers anxious to be accepted in Israel society speak Hebrew on occasions in which persons more firmly entrenched feel themselves free to choose the language in which they are most at ease or to act in terms of the immediate situation. Immigrants from Arabic-speaking countries often eschew Arabic in public lest they be identified as belonging to immigrant groups of low prestige. On the other hand, local-born Israelis have no such hesitation in using Arabic when occasion demands.

(*b*) *Where there is strong loyalty.* Language loyalty [10] will cause a

[9] English is also the language of the largest group of tourists, and the importance of civility to tourists is constantly stressed through press and radio.

[10] "A language, like a nationality, may be thought of as a set of behaviour norms; language loyality, like nationalism, would designate the state of mind in which the language (like the nationality), as an intact entity, and in contrast to other languages, assumes a high position in a scale of values, a position in need of being defended" (Weinreich, 1953, p. 99).

person to use the particular language in a wide variety of situations and he will be impervious to the requirements of the immediate situation or to his personal needs. Thus, when Hebrew was battling to establish itself as the language of the Jews of Palestine before the establishment of the State of Israel, protagonists of the slogan "Hebrew, speak Hebrew" insisted on extending the use of the language to all situations.

Conditions under which the situation corresponding to personal needs may have high potency

When the language is used in a setting that is private rather than public

We have seen earlier that when the setting is public, background factors may intrude more easily. Conversely, when the situation is private – emphasizing the personal character of the interaction – the salience of background factors is low and they play little or no part.

Where husband and wife are immigrants with a common country of origin, the language of that country continues to be used by them in private conversation. Bachi (1956), in his survey of new immigrants who entered Israel in 1948-49 and were studied in 1950-51, found that the percentage reporting use of Hebrew between husband and wife was only 3.7 (op. cit., p. 209). In our studies of Tsora and Kiryat Gat, where the settlers had already been in Israel for a period of some years, the language between husband and wife was still that of the country of origin.

When the situation provokes insecurity, high tension, or frustration

(*a*) *When the situation is new or threatening.* Speaking an unfamiliar language is equivalent to entering into a new psychological situation. Directions are uncertain – the improper use of an idiomatic phrase, for example, may hold the speaker up to derision. He feels himself on unstable ground. If, furthermore, the immediate situation in which he is called upon to use this or that language is itself new (e.g. he is not well versed in the subject-matter of the conversation, or he is addressing a superior whose attitude to him is undefined and whom he is anxious to impress), he will be hesitant to use a language in which he is not proficient and will prefer the familiar tongue. On the other hand, if he is an expert in the subject or is addressing someone on whom he is not dependent and whom he does not need to impress, he may more readily use the language in which he is less proficient if the requirements of the situation demand it. (For example, an immigrant nurse reported how much more confidently she used her halting Hebrew when speaking to patients under her care.)

The immigrants among our subjects reported greater ease in using Hebrew when speaking to children – the situation was seen as less threatening.

The situation is generally more threatening for the immigrant who needs Hebrew in the job he is seeking than for the visiting student who, in terms of his different time perspective, requires the language for the period of his stay but not necessarily beyond it.

Government officials and social workers among our subjects reported how tension was sometimes eased when they began speaking to the immigrant in the language familiar to him.

(*b*) *Where the speaker is deprived of the aid of gestures and other clues to the meaning being conveyed.* A telephone conversation sometimes has the advantage of anonymity – and is in this sense less threatening – but generally our subjects reported greater hesitancy in the use of the new language in a conversation of this kind. One is without the aid of gestures, pauses to find the correct word are less tolerated, clues provided by facial expression as to the meaning of the other person's words are not available, and, furthermore, he may abruptly terminate the conversation. Tension is also heightened when there is any reduction in audibility in a telephone conversation.

(*c*) *When the state of the person is one of extreme fatigue or excessive excitement, or in cases of severe frustration.* Our subjects reported that in moments of fatigue – as at the end of a hard day's work – or at times of great exitement they tended to revert to the language most familiar to them.

Learning a new language involves a process of differentiation. It would seem that excessive fatigue or tension results in dedifferentiation and temporary regression.[11] In such circumstances recourse is had to the more familiar language, the use of which is more automatic and which does not require the conscious effort demanded by the new language.

(*d*) *When the level of aspiration in regard to the correct usage of language is very high* (as with a writer and a lawyer among our subjects), a person will not easily venture forth in a language in which he is not proficient. Similarly, persons with high sensitivity to criticism will not readily use a new language in which they are not proficient unless there are other compelling circumstances. So, too, persons with low frustration tolerance will easily be deterred from the use of the new language.

[11] "If the regression is caused by dedifferentiation of the individual, the dedifferentiation is probably brought about by the emotional tension" (Barker, Dembo & Lewin, 1941, p. 217).

When the situation touches the central layer rather than merely peripheral layers of personality

Thus, when the function of language is primarily self-expression, personal needs will be dominant. As Sapir has pointed out: "In spite of the fact that language acts as a socializing and uniformizing force, it is at the same time the most potent single known factor for the growth of individuality" (1956, p. 19). A new, not completely familiar, language does not allow for the free and full expression of personality. Immigrants among our subjects stated that they were not their "old selves" in the new language, that it seemed to stunt their personalities, and that others remarked how "different" they were when they returned to the familiar tongue. In circumstances where there is strong need for the untrammelled expression of personality, where the person feels the need to be "himself", he will tend to choose the language in which he can best express that self.

Conditions under which the immediate situation may have high potency

From what has been written above about the potency of the background situation and of personal needs, it can be deduced when the immediate situation has high potency.

1. The person who is not concerned about group identifications can act more freely in terms of the demands of the immediate situation. Thus, whereas marginality results in high potency of the background situation, the person who is not in a marginal position may respond more easily to the stimuli of the immediate situation.

2. The more task-oriented the behaviour, the less likely are personal needs or group identifications to enter. Thus where the function of language is purely instrumental – as when asking a fellow-workman to pass a tool – the more likely is the person to use the language which the immediate situation requires.

3. When well-established patterns of behaviour characterize a relationship it is more resistant to background influences and changing personal needs.

Thus, where the relationship between the persons has been previously structured and a particular language used by them, it is difficult to pass over to a new language. The language has become an intrinsic part of the structured relationship, and our subjects in such cases felt that to use another language would be "artificial". Immigrants reported that they continued to use the language of the country of origin with friends they had known before immigration, whereas they may have used

Hebrew with immigrants from that country whom they met for the first time in Israel itself.

Social intercourse would generally be facilitated if a speaker were free to choose that language demanded by the immediate face-to-face situation. But this, as we have seen, can often only be so where there are no compelling contrary demands arising from the background situation or personal needs.

Once it has been determined which situation is dominant, it may still be necessary as a second step to analyse conflicting alternatives within the high-potency category itself. Where the background is dominant, the question may arise as to which of two competing reference groups will have the determining influence. Again, the language actually chosen where the immediate situation is dominant will depend on such factors as the languages known in common by the bilingual speaker and his interlocutor, by the power relations between the two, by the subject-matter of the conversation (certain subject-matters that have been learned in one language rather than the other are more easily discussable in that language).

Where an element in the ongoing activity changes it may affect the balance and be reflected in a change in the language used. Thus when a group is conversing in a particular tongue they may switch over to another language in deference to a new arrival into their circle. It was observed that the South African settlers at Tsora would converse in English among themselves, but as soon as a local-born Israeli joined the circle they would switch to Hebrew. The composition of the group had changed – indeed the situation itself had changed.

FLUCTUATIONS IN THE POTENCY OF THE SITUATIONS – A DEVELOPMENTAL PATTERN

From our analysis of the interviews with immigrants several developmental patterns are discernible in regard to the use of a new language. The following pattern is common to a number of immigrants from North American and British Commonwealth countries who come to Israel of their own volition and who have strong emotional ties with the English language and culture. It is illustrated from the case history of an immigrant from England.[12]

[12] Differences in some of the earlier stages of the pattern are observed where the immigrant arrives and settles as a member of a compact group speaking the language of the country of origin. All our observations show that for a considerable time he continues to speak that language within the confines of the group.

A different pattern is also observed in regard to immigrants with weak ties to

STAGE 1. A PERIOD OF 'ANTICIPATORY SOCIALIZATION'

The study of Hebrew in anticipation of their immigration to Israel is often undertaken by Zionists.

After leaving school, my thoughts turned more and more to Israel and plans for the possibility of visiting the country and possibly settling there. I began to interest myself in the modern language by reading, and more recently before coming, by taking lessons and attempting to pick up radio broadcasts in Hebrew.

STAGE 2. A PERIOD OF OVER-CONFORMITY—DOMINANCE OF BACKGROUND

On arrival there are the difficulties of using a new language in a new environment; but also satisfaction in being able to take the first steps in Hebrew. Frequently the newcomer arrives with the belief that the prevailing norm about using Hebrew to the exclusion of other languages is more rigidly observed than is actually the case.[13] Moreover, he is anxious to be accepted into Israel society and believes Hebrew is the key to this acceptance.

In spite of my stumbling efforts, I was complimented and encouraged. I was told that it was incredible that I had been in the country for so a short time. I naïvely accepted these compliments at their face value and continued undaunted in my efforts to speak. I sought out every opportunity for hearing Hebrew being spoken and avoided as much as possible English-speaking people. My reading matter, I decided, would be exclusively Hebrew, and I made a firm resolution to avoid every English printed word.

STAGE 3. A PERIOD OF VACILLATION—FLUCTUATING POTENCY OF BACKGROUND AND PERSONAL NEEDS

Soon, however, the newcomer becomes aware of the wide range of deviations from the norm. The limitations in his knowledge of Hebrew also tend to become more apparent. He begins to feel the need for English-speaking company, and conformity to the norm of Hebrew usage becomes less strict.

The fact that so many Israelis spoke English and made use of their knowledge in conversing with me became a great source of irritation. I felt I was being held back in my progress, and, in addition, I was disappointed that

---

the languages of the country of origin. Bachi has pointed to the greater ease with which such immigrants abandon that language (1956, pp. 230-2).

13 Cf. Merton's analysis of the "visibility" of norms (1957, pp. 341-53).

English held such a prominent place in the country. It seemed to testify to an inadequacy and lowering of the status of Hebrew.
My initial enthusiasm began to wane. My rate of progress began to slow down, and I was becoming more and more aware of my deficient knowledge. I decided to take an *Ulpan*[14] course. During this period I was beginning to feel a little discouraged. I began to appreciate my English conversationalists, and spent more time with them.

As he moves into the life of the country and enters on an occupation the demands on him in regard to Hebrew increase. He is now not always treated with the indulgence accorded the complete stranger. At his place of work his colleagues, often possessing a superior knowledge of the language, serve as a source of comparative reference, and he becomes even more aware of his linguistic weakness.

During this period I began to consider the possibility of staying and investigated the possibilities of work. These considerations had repercussions on the attitude of those with whom I came into contact, who were no longer so indulgent or sympathetic. I was told over and over again, in no uncertain terms, that my Hebrew was inadequate for most types of work.
In my field work it was essential not only to understand, but also to make myself understood, in order to be able to function with any degree of adequacy. I was probably making some progress in my knowledge of Hebrew, but at the same time was becoming more and more unsure of my abilities, and only spoke Hebrew when it was absolutely essential.

In speaking a new language, the person is usually making certain comparisons: (a) with the facility attained by himself in the other languages known to him; (b) with the standards in society at large; and (c) with his colleagues or friends or others in the immediate situation.

In regard to (a): it takes a long time and much effort before the immigrant can attain a proficiency in Hebrew comparable to that gained by him in the languages he brings with him. He is constantly irked by the comparison, and his frustration may find expression in "attitudinal aggression" directed against Hebrew.[15]

In regard to (b): to the extent that he uses Israel society at large as his comparative reference group, he finds some encouragement in the fact that there are so many others in the same boat as he.

In the stage which we are presently discussing, it is (c) which has the greatest salience, and our subject – and other subjects who are im-

[14] *Ulpan* is the Hebrew term for the intensive – usually residential – seminars for the study of Hebrew by immigrants.
[15] Cf. the discussion by Zajonc (1952) of the aggressive attitudes of the "stranger" as a function of conformity pressures.

migrants – report considerable chagrin in finding themselves at such a disadvantage in their place of work compared to colleagues who are fluent in Hebrew.

STAGE 4. RETREAT AND WITHDRAWAL—DOMINANCE OF PERSONAL NEEDS

If the newcomer came alone – as did our subject – the more serious crisis that develops now is in the social, cultural sphere. In the new environment he is often without the prestigeful status he enjoyed in his country of origin and he is very much in need of recognition. If at such time he cannot express himself adequately the crisis is acute. He feels that the limits on his range of expression result in a poverty of thought and that he is not his "old self". At this stage he tends to compare his relatively meagre Hebrew with his mastery of English. The need for the support and the opportunities of self-expression which English-speaking company affords becomes urgent.

I was conscious of a constant sense of irritation at being unable to express myself adequately and precisely, and gradually realized that my general level of thinking was being affected by this state of affairs. It seemed as though I was adjusting my thinking within the capacity range of my ability to express myself, in other words to an infantile level.
I withdrew from contact with Israelis as much as possible, and began to mix more and more with English-speaking people. Among such company some of my self-confidence was restored. It was exhilarating to be able to discuss and converse without strain and effort.

The need at this stage to have recourse to English-speaking society is also seen in subjects less sensitive than the subject of the case history from which we are quoting.

STAGE 5. ADJUSTMENT AND INTEGRATION—DOMINANCE OF IMMEDIATE SITUATION

If the crisis is weathered, and the immigrant feels his position in Israel society more secure, he begins to use the two languages more freely in accord with the demands of the immediate situation.

During the latter few months of my stay in Israel, there seems to be an almost imperceptible change in the direction of a relaxation of resistances towards the use of Hebrew, and a consequent easing of anxieties connected with its use. Although I still feel seriously handicapped in my work and social contacts through my lack of proficiency, I am more ready to accept this limitation, and attempt to compromise, regarding it as inevitable.

It never occurs to me to speak Hebrew with English people or with anyone whose command of English is superior to my command of Hebrew.

When he has attained some mastery of Hebrew the immigrant sometimes experiences an unexpected setback in regard to his expectations for social contact with Israelis. He had perceived the lack of knowledge of Hebrew as the barrier in the way of acceptance into Israel society. But now when this barrier no longer exists, he finds to his dismay that acceptance is still incomplete. Gradually he may begin to understand that a complete submersion of his identity is not possible, perhaps not even desirable. He cannot become an Israeli such as the local-born Israeli is, but he can become an Israeli of English background who recognizes that he is unable to shed what he has acquired in the course of a long socialization process.

Being regarded as English no longer disturbs me, as it did at the beginning of my stay. I have no particular desire to preserve my English accent, but, in the meantime, it seems to make my mistakes legitimate, by testifying to my "foreign" status, and thus is not inconvenient.

The choice of language at the various stages in the above case history reflects the passage from a position of marginality – with oscillation between attempts to submerge identity in a general Israel environment and withdrawal into the English-speaking group – to a position of adjustment as a member of Israel society retaining the elements of identity derived from socialization in another culture. In the first stages the background situation is dominant; then follows a period of alternating potency of background and personal needs; thereafter personal needs become dominant, and eventually an equilibrium is reached where the subject is more freely responsive to the requirements of the immediate situation.

SOME IMPLICATIONS OF THE ANALYSIS

Language Choice as a Behavioural Index

We began our discussion with an analysis of the conditions under which one or other situation has the higher potency in determining the choice of language. In this discussion the language chosen has been the dependent variable. The choice of language may in its turn serve as a subtle behavioural index to the direction of acculturation and to the vagaries in social adjustment.

Immigrants are, for at least an initial period, in the position of marginal men. In this position the choice of language is often a significant indication of the group with which they wish to identify. But it would obviously be a misleading oversimplification to say that the more frequently the immigrant speaks the new language the more certain it is that he wishes to remain permanently in the land of adoption, and that, conversely, the frequent use of the language of the country of origin indicates a disinclination to enter the new society. We would submit that the analysis has to take into account the criss-crossing factors we have analysed in the preceding sections of this paper. It will be more clearly understood then why, instead of a regular progression, there are sometimes fluctuations in the use of the new language by the immigrant.

Our material supplies suggestive examples, in addition to those illustrated by the specimen case history, of how the choice of language may be a significant clue to the direction of social adjustment. Let us quote one further example:

Immigrants from countries such as the U.S.A. and Britain are often questioned as to whether they intend to remain permanently in Israel or whether there is a possibility of their return to the country of origin. Frequently they find it difficult to answer such questions – even to themselves. Our material would suggest the hypothesis that those immigrants who elect to speak only Hebrew to their children have thereby indicated a decision to make Israel their permanent home. This does not mean that immigrants who choose to speak English with the children have taken a different decision about their future in the country. It simply means that, in their case, indices other than that of language would have to be sought.

We have referred mainly to the position of immigrants, but the implications of the study are not limited to them. In a society where distinct linguistic groups live side by side, language choice may indicate the trends in the assimilation of members of one group by the other. It may – subject to the necessary qualifications – be used as a reflector of marginality.

Language and the Personality of the Newcomer

Our analysis implies a cautionary note for the attitude of a host society to newcomers. The host society may legitimately wish to encourage the use of its language by the newcomers, but it may aggravate the problem of adjustment if it insists too strictly on the adherence to its language norms. The transition from one language to another is fraught with deep implications for the personality of the immigrant or other newcomer, and there are occasions when he needs to speak the language with which he is familiar, in which he can fully express his own self.

If, as our analysis would indicate, group references play an important part in the choice of a language, it would follow that the readiness of a person to learn and use a second language may depend in part on the measure of his willingness to identify with the group with which the language is associated – or, at any rate, on his desire to reduce the social distance between himself and that group.[16]

SUMMARY

The position of a bilingual speaker required to choose one language rather than the other in situations where either could serve as the medium of conversation may usefully be analysed as that of a person in an overlapping situation. He may be influenced by factors in the background situation or by personal needs or by the demands of the immediate situation. The choice depends upon the relative potency of these situations. Potency is regarded as a function of valence *and* salience, and the factor of salience is seen to be of particular importance in determining the influence of a background situation on behaviour.

The present preliminary paper sets out a number of hypotheses in regard to the determinants of the relative potency of the situations in language behaviour. A case history of an immigrant is presented, illustrating a pattern in regard to the fluctuations in the potency of background, personal needs, and immediate situation at various stages in the immigrant's adjustment.

In this analysis the language chosen has been the dependent variable. It is suggested that the choice of language may in its turn serve – subject to certain qualifications – as a behavioural index of group preferences and social adjustment. It is furthermore suggested that the analysis of the determinants of language choice may have implications for the policy of the host society in regard to the use of its language by immigrants and other newcomers. The analysis may also have relevance to problems of motivation in the learning of a second language.

[16] The function of social-psychological factors in the learning of foreign languages is increasingly recognized. An example is the following conclusion about the learning of Spanish by North Americans working in the Latin-American countries. "A strong psychological identification with the other people and culture may more than make up for below-average language learning ability whereas a man of superior language ability may fail to make the necessary psychological identification and make poor progress" (Whyte & Holmberg, 1956, p. 13).

REFERENCES

Bachi, R.
1956 "A statistical analysis of the revival of Hebrew in Israel", *Scripta Hierosolymitana,* 3 (Jerusalem, Magnes Press).
Barker, R. G., Dembo, T. and Lewin, K.
1941 *Frustration and regression: An experiment with young children* (= *Univ. of Iowa Studies in Child Welfare,* 18, No. 1).
Bendix, R. and Lipset, S. M.
1953 *Class, status and power* (Glencoe, Ill., Free Press).
Campbell, J. D. and Yarrow, M. R.
1958 "Personal and situational variables in adaptation to change", *J. soc. Issues,* 14, 29-46.
Herman, S. N. and Schild, E. O.
1960 "Ethic role conflict in a cross-cultural situation", *Hum. Relat.,* 13, 215-28.
Lewin, K.
1951 *Field theory in social science,* ed. by D. Cartwright (New York, Harper; London, Tavistock Publications).
Maccoby, E. E., Newcomb, T. M. and Hartley, E. L. (Eds.)
1958 *Readings in social psychology,* 3rd ed. (New York, Holt).
Merton, R. K.
1957 *Social theory and social structure,* revd. and enlarged ed. (Glencoe, Ill., Free Press).
Sapir, E.
1956 *Culture, language and personality,* ed. by D. G. Mandelbaum (Univ. of California Press).
Weinreich, U.
1953 *Languages in contact* (= *Publications of the Linguistic Circle of New York,* No. 1).
Whyte, W. F. and Holmberg, A. R.
1956 "Human problems of U.S. enterprise in Latin America", *Hum. Organisation,* 15, 11-15.
Zajonc, R. B.
1952 "Aggressive attitudes of the stranger as a function of conformity pressures", *Hum. Relat.,* 5, 205-16.

From *Human Relations,* 14 (1961), 149-164. Reprinted by permission.

Joan Rubin

BILINGUAL USAGE IN PARAGUAY

The description of Paraguayan bilingualism presented thus far has pointed to an unusually highly bilingual area with a slowly increasing degree of bilingualism; ambivalent feelings toward Guarani but not toward Spanish; and, in restricted circumstances (the rural areas, schools, and formal public functions in Asunción), rigid patterns of usage. Apart from these two circumstances, determinants of usage have not yet been defined. It is the purpose of this chapter to analyze usage behavior where the determinants are not as clear-cut and to determine what variables operate in patterning usage.

In a description of Javanese respect behavior, Geertz, 1960, lists the variables which determine choice of a particular linguistic level:

> They include not only qualitative characteristics of the speakers – age, sex, kinship relation, occupation, wealth, education, religious commitment, family background – but also more general factors: for instance, the social setting (one would be likely to use a higher level at a wedding than in the street); the content of the conversation (in general, one uses lower levels when speaking of commercial matters, higher ones if speaking of religious or aesthetic matters); the history of social interaction between the speakers (one will tend to speak rather high, if one speaks at all, with someone with whom one has quarreled); the presence of a third person (one tends to speak higher to the same individual if others are listening). (p. 257-8)

Hasselmo, 1961, in his description of Swedish-American code-switching, attributed switching to: the participants, the topic and the location. He, like Geertz, lists the variables without indicating the linguistic behavior which results from the different variables, alone or in combinations.

Brown and Gilman, 1960, isolated two dimensions, power and solidarity, to explain pronoun usage in several European languages. The power relation is an asymmetrical and non-reciprocal one. The more powerful individual uses "tu" and receives "vous" from the less powerful individual. Among power equals in the Middle Ages they note that among the upper classes, the custom was to use a mutual "vous" form and among the lower classes, the custom was to use a mutual "tu" form. In more modern times, the solidarity relation enters "as a means of differentiating address among power equals". (p. 253) With individuals with whom one had greater solidarity, one used "tu" and with those with whom one had lesser solidarity, one used "vous". As a result of the interaction of these two dimensions, "tu" comes to have a common definition as a pronoun of condescension or intimacy and "vous" has the semantic characteristics of respect or formality.

By considering only these two dimensions, Brown and Gilman set up a table of six possible relationships.

TABLE 1A

(After Brown and Gilman, 1960, p. 259) *

Superior	V	Superior	V
Solidary	T	Not Solidary	V
Equal		Equal	
Solidary	T	Not Solidary	V
Inferior	T	Inferior	T
Solidary	T	Not Solidary	V

* This table should be read as follows: Column I, cell 1, represents a conflict situation in which the dimension of power demands the use of "vous" whereas the dimension of solidarity demands the use of "tu", e.g., younger to elder brother. Column I, cell 3, represents an equilibrium situation in which "tu" is required by both the dimensions of power and solidarity, e.g., child to parent. Column II, cell 2, represents an equilibrium situation in which the dimension of solidarity alone determines the form of address, ("vous"), e.g. between non-solidary acquaintances.

Brown and Ford, 1961, found the two variables defined in Brown and Gilman, 1960, also determined usage in direct address in American English. They renamed these the degree of intimacy and status. Status in the United States, they find, is based on two criteria: age and occupational status. If these two dimensions are in conflict, then occupational status takes priority. Applying these variables to the data, the authors found that in self-reciprocal address, degree of intimacy determined usage; in non-self-reciprocal address, status was the determiner. In moving from a non-self-reciprocal to a self-reciprocal pattern, the authors observed that it is always the person of higher status who initiated the change.

The Brown and Ford analysis is based upon a consideration of the relationship between two persons. In any dyadic relationship, there is always room for and, in fact, expectation of change in usage. In the self-reciprocal pattern, change occurs as intimacy grows from last name reciprocity to first name reciprocity; change also occurs in the progression from non-self-reciprocal toward self-reciprocal.

Another approach to analysis of linguistic usage variables is suggested by Stewart, 1962. Stewart isolated two variables in the speech situation. Each variable has a binary opposite, i.e., public-private, formal-informal. Stewart defined the term "public" as impersonal or representative and "private" as personal and non-representative. Since all behavior is representative in some sense, it may be assumed that Stewart meant conscious representation of a particular status relationship. This is observable in statements by high officials who preface a conversation by: "Speaking for myself alone." Stewart defined formal behavior as prescribed behavior, whereas informal behavior was defined as non-prescribed behavior. Again, since all behavior is, in some sense, prescribed, it may be assumed that he meant prescribed within rigid bounds or with no variation permitted.[1]

The formality-informality opposition which Stewart suggests, may, in some societies, not be an opposition but rather a reflection of a scale of increasing formality.

The literature discussed above has suggested several variables which are operable in linguistic choice. These may be grouped as follows:

1. The relationship between two or more persons involved in conversation. This would be considered from the speaker's point of view and his estimate of the relationship. In this group, one could include Brown and Ford's intimacy and status variables. I would add that sex might be a separate variable. Regardless of intimacy or status, members of the opposite sex might with each other use forms different from those used with members of the same sex.

2. The attributes of either the speaker or the addressee. Here one might list class level and origin. ("Origin" specifies the area a person comes from – specifically, rural, town or urban.) Even though great intimacy exists, certain classes might prefer different reciprocal forms.

3. The aspects of the situation. Here one could include Stewart's

[1] Other analyses of linguistic usage include those of Barker, 1947, and Ferguson, 1959. Barker, in his thesis on Spanish-English usage in Tucson, Arizona, used dimensions similar to Stewart's. Ferguson described linguistic usage in situations in which only the formal-informal variable was applicable.

formality-informality and public-private variables. Another variable might be the location of the situation, i.e., rural, town or urban. A final variable might be the degree of seriousness of the situation. Many informal situations may obviously be quite serious.

In attempting to predict when each language would be used and under what circumstances code-switching would be permissible or expected, the technique of componential analysis (cf. Lounsbury, 1956, Goodenough, 1956) appeared to be relevant. In componential analysis one has a term, or name or label and a referent(s) to which it is applied. Dimensions common to the referent(s) are then isolated. In a bilingual situation, the particular language used might be considered the term. In Paraguay, there are three terms – Spanish, Guarani and Code-Switching/Alternate Use of Both Languages. The situations, not the referents, are the instances of use of these languages. The dimensions would be derived from the common elements in each situation. I encountered difficulty in applying this technique to bilingual usage in Paraguay. Whereas its application to kinship terminology leads to a relatively neat dimensional definition with each term and its contexts definable in unique combinations of the variables, such was not the case in the bilingual situation. In no situation did all the informants use exactly the same term. Also, situations defined by the same dimensions brought forth different terms.

It would appear that there are three possible explanations for the difficulties encountered in applying componential analysis to the study of bilingual usage. (1) In kinship analysis what is defined by the dimensions is the referential content of forms. The label used applies to a specific, clearly definable referent. In language usage, what is defined by the dimensions is the situational content. This situational content may have many aspects to it and is much more illusive and difficult to define. (2) Kinship terms apply to the entire universe to which they are appropriate. Linguistic usage, however, is limited by the fact that some members of the group are proficient in both languages, whereas others are not. Usage may vary depending on the expected proficiency, rather than on the social dimensions which might be relevant if the universe were similar in its linguistic proficiency. (3) Kinship terminology is definable on a purely formal basis, the dimensional definition is extractable from the particular referent without reference to other social pressures. In linguistic usage, in addition to the social dimensions operative in defining a particular situation, other pressures, not immediately apparent in the situation, color the choice and the results are not as sharp as we might desire.

Additionally, componential analysis as it is applied to kinship data usually operates on an unordered basis. While it might be possible to isolate the dimensions operating in linguistic choice, these dimensions are not unordered but rather ordered. The situation is similar to the operation of a computer which may state a sequence such as the following: if a, stop and choose 1; but if *b*, then ask: if *b'*, stop and choose 2, but if *b''*, then ask ... Computer analysis operates in a completely binary fashion. Some of the dimensions I found applicable seem to operate in a scale fashion, however. This may be expressed as a series of binary oppositions.

In the analysis of linguistic usage in Paraguay, my concern has been with group usage rather than with individual usage. At any one time, an individual may vary from the expected pattern or there may be several choices equally available and open to individual choice. My concern has been with describing only those dimensions which seem to set the pattern for the group. As a result predictability will not be perfect because of the factor of individual variation.

There is a third difficulty preventing the completely accurate prediction of usage. While the ideal situation might be defined by an ordered series of dimensions, manipulation of the system may occur for stylistic reasons. This is apparent in Goodenough's paper, "Formal Properties of Status Relationships" (American Anthropological Association, 1961), which illustrated the usual deference required in certain kin relationships and then demonstrated the purposeful shock value of violating this deference order. That is, individuals aware of ideal behavior patterns will manipulate these patterns for stylistic purposes. This is not too frequent in this case. Nonetheless, I did find some conscious manipulation. One woman reported that when a drunk man approached her, she used Spanish to put him in his place. Another type of manipulation, although rare in Luque (a town in which much of my data was collected), is the use of language to achieve higher social status. Some upwardly mobile individuals insist on using Spanish even though Guarani would normally be expected.

Initially, an attempt was made to use Brown and Gilman's two dimensions of power and solidarity to predict whether Spanish or Guarani would be used in a given discourse. It seemed reasonable to expect that Spanish would be used with persons with greater power or those with whom one had little solidarity for the same reasons that Europeans would use the "vous" form. Similarly, it might be expected that Guarani would be used with persons of lesser power or those with whom one had high solidarity. The language used with those who were one's power equals would then be determined on the basis of solidarity (Rubin, 1962).

TABLE 1B
(After Brown and Gilman, 1960, p. 259)

Superior Solidary	Spanish Guarani	Equal Solidary	Guarani
Inferior Solidary	Guarani Guarani	Equal Not solidary	Spanish
Superior Not solidary	Spanish Spanish	Inferior Not solidary	Guarani Spanish

Although the Brown and Gilman chart appeared at first to define the usage of Guarani and Spanish in Paraguay, on further consideration the 2 × 3 matrix seemed inadequate to define the criteria for choice of language.

(1) Between individuals of high solidarity, status was not an important criterion. Usage was defined rather by the location of the discourse or the formality of the occasion.

(2) Between individuals of low solidarity, again status did not really seem to be an important criterion in the choice of language. In the first place, the self-reciprocal usage between persons of inferior and superior status fostered suspicion that the model was inadequate and secondly, other factors such as location, first language acquisition, predicted language proficiency, seemed much more adequately to explain the choice of language and the resulting usage. (See analysis of interviews below.)

(3) Even though some usage patterns were explained by the model, many of the questionnaire results obtained were not consistent and this 2 × 3 model did not help to clarify these "mixed" results.

The questionnaire used [2] defined situations and asked which language would normally be used. The questionnaire had deficiencies which may have had a bearing on the results. Some of the questions were ambiguous. For example, Number 26 (What language do you use when angry?) does not indicate with whom one is angry. Informants frequently raised this question before answering. Another difficulty was that not everyone could answer all questions. Some people did not have spouses or children; some claimed they never drank or got angry. A third difficulty was that the answer Spanish/Guarani was ambiguous. It could mean code-switching or it could mean alternation according to a particular situation. I have taken this response to mean here a bilingual response and will not clarify this ambiguity except when additional data is available.

[2] Available as Appendix IV of the dissertation.

The questionnaire was given to bilinguals in a rural area and in a town area. The results of these interviews follow. A double asterisk will indicate responses which are in a majority.

ITAPUAMI

(number interviewed – 40)

Unambiguous questions

	Guarani	*Spanish*	*Both*
1. With your spouse daily	28**	0	1
2. With your spouse when angry	27**	0	1
3. With your parents	34**	6	0
4. With your spouse when your children are present	20**	6	2
5. With your sweetheart in the street	9	6	3
6. With your sweetheart making love	8	5	4
7. With your children	19**	11	4
8. With your friends drinking tea	28**	0	7
9. With your friends in the streets of Luque	14	9	12
11. With your boss	9	4	7
12. With your employees	0	0	0
14. With the doctor	7	25**	7
15. With the *curandero*	32**	2	2
17. With your servant daily	0	0	0
18. With your grandparents	32**	0	1
19. With your godmother	22**	13	5
20. With the police chief or mayor	13	19	8
22. To confess	15	15	4
23. With the mother of your sweetheart or spouse	27**	2	1
24. With your servant when angry	0	0	0
28. With your schoolteacher	0	37**	3
29. With the authorities in Asunción	4	33**	2
32. In the "country"	40**	0	0
34. With your neighbors	38**	0	2
35. Drinking alcoholic beverages	22**	2	5
36. With your friends in the streets of Asunción	5	25**	6
37. With the bus fare collector	13	22**	5
39. With your siblings	32**	2	5

Ambiguous Questions (Ambiguous as to location, intimacy)

	Guarani	*Spanish*	*Both*
10. With your "marchante" (term applies to both patron and client)	22**	3	10
13. To make jokes	25**	1	6
16. With an unknown man wearing a suit	7	17	15
21. With a woman wearing a long skirt and smoking a big black cigar	37**	1	2
25. At a dance	11	7	20**
26. When angry	33**	0	6
27. With an unfamiliar well-dressed person	4	24**	11
30. With a bare-foot woman	35**	0	5
31. With a stranger	5	9	18**
33. In town or in Asunción	4	23**	11
38. When you want to say something intimate	22**	6	10

LUQUE
(number interviewed – 66)

Unambiguous Questions

	Guarani	*Spanish*	*Both*
1. With your spouse daily	16	10	27**
2. With your spouse when angry	28**	8	11
3. With your parents	37**	10	18
4. With your spouse when your children are present	14	22	14
5. With your sweetheart in the street	15	34**	9
6. With your sweetheart making love	13	34**	9
7. With your children	6	34**	18
8. With your friends drinking tea	25	7	23
9. With your friends in the streets of Luque	12	8	9
11. With your boss	8	16**	7
12. With your employees	4	3	7
14. With the doctor	1	56**	8
15. With the *curandero*	43**	0	5
17. With your servant daily	9	3	6
18. With your grandparents	39**	6	6
19. With your godmother	20	28	8
20. With the police chief or mayor	2	55**	9

	Guarani	Spanish	Both
22. To confess	12	29**	16
23. With the mother of your sweetheart or spouse	28**	5	11
24. With your servant when angry	9**	1	5
28. With your schoolteacher	0	58**	8
29. With the authorities in Asunción	0	56**	6
32. In the "country"	52**	0	12
34. With your neighbors	32**	11	20
35. Drinking alcoholic beverages	13	4	12
36. With your friends in the streets of Asunción	6	29	23
37. With the bus fare collector	25	21	12
39. With your siblings	29	10	21

Ambiguous Questions

	Guarani	Spanish	Both
10. With your "marchante"	35**	3	16
13. To make jokes	38**	2	22
16. With an unknown man wearing a suit	0	40**	12
21. With a woman wearing a long skirt and smoking a big black sigar	52**	1	8
25. At a dance	5	24	31**
26. When angry	30**	9	17
27. With an unfamiliar well-dressed person	0	44**	5
30. With a bare-foot woman	32**	0	14
31. With a stranger	0	11**	6
33. In town or in Asunción	0	18	19**
38. When you want to say something intimate	30**	12	16

Analysis

1. The first and most important variable to be considered in predicting language usage in Paraguay is the *location* of the interaction. If it occurs in the rural area, Guarani is the rule. Indicative of this are the following answers:

> – The majority of answers to Question 32 (in the country) was Guarani.
> – The majority of the people living in the rural area and speaking to people living there, too, answered Guarani. (See questions 1, 2, 3, 4, 7, 8, 15, 18, 19, 23, 34, 35, 39.) Exceptions to these answers

usually indicated that the person did not live in the rural area.
– The majority of townspeople answered that Guarani was used with a person living in the country. In question 15, the *curandero* usually lives in the rural area and, therefore, Guarani is the rule.

The great exception to this rule was the answer "Spanish" to Question 28 (With your schoolteacher). This is due to the extraordinary pressure on students and teachers to use Spanish in the school. Teachers try to insist on the use of Spanish at all times even in rural areas.

As noted earlier, the rural area was the place where the strongest sanctions against use of Spanish were applied and where people were said to be "putting on the dog" if they did use Spanish.

Outside the rural area, the rule is not as clearcut. In the town of Luque, the situation is completely ambiguous and each situation must be considered according to variables other than location. Since much more Spanish is spoken than in Itapuami the situation is more bilingual. When in Asunción (even though the highest number of bilinguals in the country live here) people of Luque feel they should speak Spanish because they consider it the only language of Asunción. One would never be out of place using Spanish in Asunción, but on many occasions in Luque, Guarani would be more appropriate.

The clearest example of this contrast of usage between Luque and Asunción is seen in the following:

The contrasting answers to Question 9 (with one's friends in the streets of Luque) and to Question 36 (with one's friends in the streets of Asunción) show a clear trend toward greater use of Spanish.

Itapuami Answer

	Guarani	*Spanish*	*Both*	*Total*
9. Luque	14	9	12	35
36. Asunción	5	25	6	37

Luque Answer

	Guarani	*Spanish*	*Both*	*Total*
9. Luque	6	8	9	29
36. Asunción	12	29	23	58

– In the response to Question 33 (at a dance) many informants said that they considered the location of the dance. If in the "country", then Guarani would be in order, if in the town, then both languages would be acceptable, if in Asunción, then Spanish would be expected.

2. The second variable which is important, after the location is known, is the formality-informality of the interaction. Formality (as defined by Stewart and modified in this study) refers to "a limited set of expected behavior" whereas informality refers to "the normal range of permitted behaviors within a group". Formality relates to a number of factors: certain *social identities* (see Goodenough 1961)[3] may require formal behavior; some occasions require formal behavior. The dimension formality-informality seems better defined on a scale than as a single binary opposition. In Paraguay, one would expect that Spanish would be required on formal occasions, while choice might be anticipated as one moves toward greater informality. The choice situation may be further determined by other variables or it may be completely free.

The number of social identities in Paraguay which appear to place a limitation on expected behavior are the following:

- a doctor-patient relationship
- teacher-student relationship
- authority-ruled relationship
- lawyer-client relationship
- speaker-audience relationship
- boss-employee relationship
- priest-parishioner relationship
- sweetheart-sweetheart relationship
- merchant-customer relationship

The questionnaire results showed that Spanish was used overwhelmingly for the following identities:

- Question 14 patient-doctor relationship
- Question 28 student-teacher relationship
- Question 29 ruled-authority relationship

However, in the patient-doctor relationship of the *curandero* we have already noted the priority of the dimension of location. Medical doctors do not usually go out or live in rural areas. If they did, they would be expected to use Guarani, if possible.[4]

Again the importance of location is seen in the contrast between the results of Question 29 (With the authorities in Asunción) and Question

[3] *Social identity* according to my understanding of Goodenough, 1961, refers to the interrelationship of the two positions in a status situation.

[4] An interview with a medical doctor indicated that he took into consideration the linguistic proficiency of his patient and would, if necessary, use Guarani. Many physicians from Asunción reported that they had to learn Guarani in order to practice.

20 (With the police chief or mayor). The police chief or mayor is situated in Luque. As we noted, there is greater choice in Luque than in Asunción, where Spanish is predominant.

Initially a sweetheart relationship is formal. Many young men indicated that when they first started courting a young lady they used Spanish. As the courting progressed, the formality seemed to decrease and some young men indicated they used Guarani. Unfortunately Questions 5 and 6 do not reflect the change in behavior required through time and the results are therefore not significant.

Question 11, the employee-boss relationship, showed a small majority spoke Spanish in Luque. I feel that this relationship is less formal than the doctor-patient one because of the frequent interaction. But since the relationship is a restricted one, the trend is toward Spanish.

The parishioner-priest relationship reflected in Question 22 (to confess) is an extremely formal one. In Luque, a majority uses Spanish. However, results in Itapuami are divided and I do not have an adequate explanation for this.

Some situations are more formal than others. In Paraguay, dances tend to be formal but there are a number of criteria which dictate the degree of formality. If the dance floor is brick, then the dance is more formal than if the floor is packed earth. If the dance takes place in the center of town, it is more formal than if it is held in the suburbs.

Some topics are more formal. In Paraguay, school subjects, legal and business affairs are often discussed in Spanish. There is an obvious relation between these topics and the most formal social identities.

3. A third dimension bearing on linguistic choice is the degree of intimacy of the speakers. This dimension is relevant only in town or urban informal discourse since rural and formal discourse are fairly clearly defined.

According to Brown and Ford, certain factors are predisposing to intimacy. These are "shared values (which may be derived from kinship, from identity of occupation, sex, nationality, etc., or from some common fate) and frequent contact". (p. 377)

For most Paraguayans, Guarani is the language of intimacy, indicating solidarity or identity with the addressee, whereas Spanish indicates mere acquaintance. Clearest indication of this is the practice of Paraguayans overseas who tend to use more Guarani with their country-men even though they may have used more Spanish at home in Paraguay. This seems to indicate that when abroad Paraguayans establish their identity by use of the more unusual and intimate language.[5]

Degree of intimacy may influence a formal social identity. In speaking

[5] Through interviews and other observations in the United States, I have found that Paraguayans frequently use Guarani among themselves.

to an authority or a doctor, in his role as authority or doctor, a friend might use both languages in a conversation although generally Spanish would tend to dominate the conversation.

In social identities which are not highly formal, a shift from formal to informal behavior is more likely. This shift may occur as intimacy progresses. This is demonstrated in the remarks of young men who said they used Spanish when they first started courting (formal situation). As they proceeded in the courtship and intimacy grew (informal situation), many informants said they switched to Guarani. One young man indicated: "It seems as though when we speak Guarani, we are saying something more intimate and something which is sweeter to us."

While Spanish is the language of non-intimacy, linguistic usage in intimate situations depends to some extent on the first language learned. I was told that rural medical students tend to speak Guarani among themselves in Asunción, while students from Asunción usually tend to use Spanish among themselves. Thus intimacy is expressed by different language usage, depending on the first language learned.

However, the large majority of the population associate intimacy with Guarani. Even at the most formal dances in Luque, male comments about female behavior were always in Guarani.

Luque answers to Questions 16 and 27 (with strangers) indicate that with people with whom one is not intimate, one tends to use Spanish. I often found this to be true, even in the rural areas where, upon arrival, the bilingual was shoved forward to greet me in Spanish. However, I feel that the responses to these questions are not clearly indicative of lack of intimacy because the location of the encounter is not specified.

4. A fourth dimension which enters into informal town-urban usage is the degree of seriousness of the discourse. In general, jokes are in Guarani in all spheres. (Cf. Question 13.) Many informants said that jokes were more humorous in Guarani or that Guarani lent itself to the expression of humor.

Angry discourse is usually conducted in the first language acquired. This is clear from our data on Question 2 in Luque (with your spouse when angry). Those whose first language was Guarani felt that "se rete mejor" (one scolds better) in Guarani whereas those whose first language was Spanish preferred Spanish to indicate the seriousness of the matter. In response to Question 24 (with your servant when angry) I feel that the majority used Guarani because it was the first language of the addressee and the speaker wanted to impress the addressee on his own terms with the importance of the matter.

Either language is possible among bilinguals in a completely informal situation in Luque. An example is the situation between friends in a moderate atmosphere (not angry or funny). Compare, for example, the results of Question 35 (Drinking alcoholic beverages), Question 34 (With your neighbors) and Question 8 (Drinking tea) where the situation is eminently informal. The results are quite divided.

The set of ordered dimensions in the choice of language may be put into a chart which indicates the order of the decisions and the resulting language used. The left side of the chart always results in a resolution of the binary opposition and indicates a clear choice of one particular language. (See Chart I)

In addition to the immediate social setting, certain additional factors tend to influence linguistic usage and cause deviation from expected linguistic behavior.

1. School pressures. The strongest pressure to use Spanish comes from the schools. Parents are urged to use Spanish with their children at home to provide more practice. Some informants used Spanish with their children until their offspring had passed school age and then they changed to Guarani or bilingual usage.

This pressure is seen by a comparison of the answers to Questions 1, 4 and 7.

LUQUE

	Guarani	*Spanish*	*Both*	*Total*
1. Spouse	16	10	27	43
4. Spouse, child present	14	22	14	50
7. Children	6	34	18	58

ITAPUAMI

	Guarani	*Spanish*	*Both*	*Total*
1. Spouse	28	0	1	29
4. Spouse, child present	20	6	2	28
7. Children	19	11	4	34

Thus, in Luque, parents tend to use more Spanish and less Guarani in the presence of and in speaking to their children. Even in Itapuami some effort is made to use more Spanish when speaking to children.

2. Estimate of linguistic proficiency. People often consider the ability of the addressee in choosing between the languages. Indications are:

– Answers to Question 21 (With a woman in a long skirt smoking a big black cigar) were overwhelmingly Guarani. Responses included the additional information that the addressee was probably from the country or was probably monolingual. The predictability of her linguistic ability made the responses unanimously Guarani even though the question did not state this.

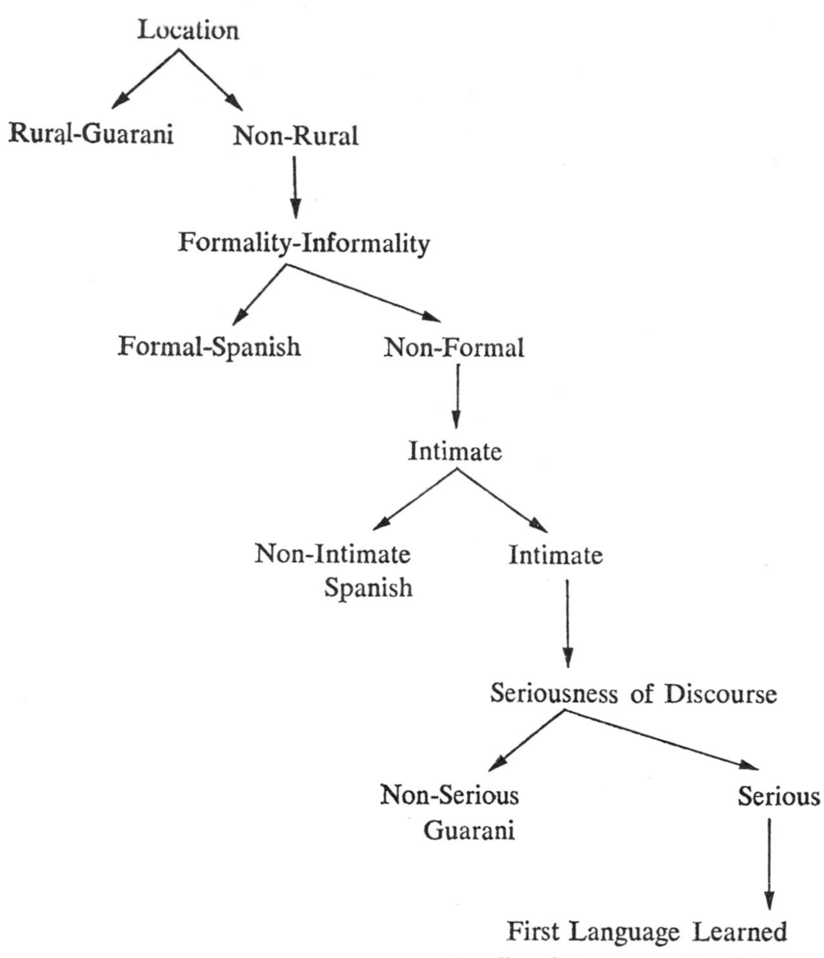

– In response to Question 30 (With a bare-foot woman) informants said they thought such a woman might know Guarani better.
– The head doctor of the Luque hospital said that in selecting a language in which to address his patients, he considered which language they might be more comfortable in and tried to encourage them to use it, too.
– The response to Questions 3, 18 and 23 was, in the majority, Guarani. (With your parents; With your grandparents; With the mother of your sweetheart or spouse.) This, I feel, is directly attributable to the linguistic ability of the ascending generation. Number 19 (With your godmother) produced divided responses.

Since godparents are usually in the ascending generation and often selected from the more affluent members of the community, (also those with greater education and more proficiency in both languages) the divided response is not unexpected. Informants indicated that some godparents lived in the rural area and it was with these that the response was usually Guarani.

3. Trend toward bilingualism. As indicated in the chapter on Stability, a slow increase in bilingual ability is indicated in Luque. This is also reflected in an increased willingness to use both languages in informal situations. Comparison of data on usage with different generations demonstrates the trend toward frequent alternate use of both languages rather then greater use of Spanish.

Luque		*Guarani*	*Spanish*	*Both*	*Total*
1. Spouse	G^0	16	10	27	53
39. Siblings	G^0	29	10	21	60
3. Parents	G^1	37	10	18	65
18. Grandparents	G^2	39	6	6	51

4. First language acquisition. In Luque there is, in informal situations with friends, some trend to use the first language acquired. This is, at the same time, countered by the pressure toward greater alternate use of both languages. Examples of this trend toward first language usage can be noted in the following responses:

Question 39 (With your siblings)

Language Used		*First Language*	
Spanish	9	Spanish	4
		Guarani	1
		Both	5
Guarani	29	Spanish	1
		Guarani	26
		Both	2
Both	21	Spanish	4
		Guarani	8
		Both	9
Total	59		

Out of 59 responses, 39 (approximately 66% of the informants) used their first language with their "intimates".

Again in Question 8 (With friends drinking tea) a correlation between first language acquisition and usage is seen.

Language Used		*First Language*	
Spanish	7	Spanish	2
		Guarani	3
		Both	2
Guarani	25	Spanish	0
		Guarani	20
		Both	5
Both	23	Spanish	6
		Guarani	9
		Both	8
Total	55		

Out of 55 answers, 30 (approximately 54%) used their first language with their "intimates".

5. Sex. There is a tendency for men whose first language was either Spanish (or both) to use more Guarani with other men, but to use Spanish with women who are their intimates. Women, on the other hand, whose first language was either Spanish or both, tend to use Spanish to both male and female intimates.

SUMMARY

This study represents an attempt to determine the factors making a particular language appropriate in a specific situation within the general context of Paraguayan bilingualism. The dimensions isolated were: location, formality, intimacy, seriousness of the situation and sex. The dimensions intimacy and sex refer to the relationship between the two individuals engaging in a discourse. The seriousness of the occasion and the location refer to the setting. The dimension of formality may refer either to the setting or to the type of social identity between the dyad in a discourse. The dimensions do not combine in an additive fashion to determine usage but rather operate in a priority order.

These dimensions, which are found in any discourse, have been shown to be somewhat skewed by further pressures. Two refer to individual attributes: the estimated linguistic ability of the addressee and the first language acquired by the speaker. The third pressure is that which comes from school orientation.

Finally, the dimensions are skewed by changes in the social situation in the course of time. As more education becomes available and the numbers of bilinguals increase, I observed a trend toward greater bilingual usage, or fairly unrestricted choice, at least in informal situations.

Linguistic usage in Paraguay reflects the history of Paraguayan cultural contact and settlement. In the administrative center, Asunción, which had the most contact with the outside, there is the greatest use of Spanish. In the more rural areas, which historically had little contact with Asunción or the outside, Guarani is the language most generally used. Increasing contact with Asunción does not seem to have altered this. Since Spanish has, throughout Paraguayan history, been used for administrative purposes, it is in such formal situations and in discussing related topics that Spanish would be expected and is, in fact, used. Since Paraguay did not develop a sharply defined class system, usage in non-rural, non-formal situations falls back on the equalitarian criteria of intimacy and the seriousness of a situation.

Stewart's public-private dimension does not seem to have predictive value in Paraguayan linguistic usage. Consideration seems to be given instead to the social identity of the dyad and the degree of formality. If the situation is extremely formal, little variation is permitted in linguistic usage. If it is not too formal, considerations of intimacy and seriousness may prevail.

Brown and Ford's criterion of status was not employed in this study because in Paraguay only the dimension of intimacy was found relevant. This does not imply that status awareness is non-existent (cf. Chapter III "la gente" and "la sociedad") but status does not seem to be a determining factor in linguistic behavior. The language used in a superordinate-subordinate relation is reciprocal and no status difference is revealed. Here the choice of language is usually based on how well acquainted the two participants in a discourse are.

The free variation in usage between the two languages corresponds with the relatively elastic social class structure (cf. Chapter III). As indicated, while the extremes of the social class structure are well marked, there is a continuous gradation between these extremes. In oral discourse, certain situations which might be compared to the extremes in the class structure required a particular language. Between these extremes there existed a series of language choices which did not always reflect exactly the changing social situation. While this free variation does compare with the continuous gradation in the social structure, there is no necessary causal relationship between linguistic usage and class structure. Rather, in both linguistic usage and social class there is a wide area of indeterminacy which in the case of linguistic usage, may be determined by a system of ordered priorities.

This study also indicates that Luque is moving toward a greater degree of bilingualism as reflected in both the increasing bilingual ability of its citizens and the increasing free variation of usage in informal situations. If Luque represents the direction of bilingualism in Paraguay, then we may expect an equilibrium between the two languages to remain so long as the distribution of usage continues to be both mutually exclusive in certain situations and in free variation in others.

REFERENCES

Barker, George C., "Social Functions of Language in a Mexican-American Community", *Acta Americana,* V (1947), pp. 185-202.

Brown, Roger and Marguerite Ford, "Address in American English", *Journal of Abnormal and Social Psychology,* LXII (March, 1961), pp. 375-385.

Brown, Roger and Albert Gilman, "The Pronouns of Power and Solidarity", in Thomas A. Sebeok, ed., *Style in Language* (New York; The Technology Press of the Massachusetts Institute of Technology and John Wiley and Sons, 1960), pp. 253-276.

Ferguson, Charles A., "Diglossia", *Word* XV (1959), pp. 325-340.

Geertz, Clifford, "Linguistic Etiquette", in *The Religion of Java* (Glencoe, Illinois; The Free Press, 1960), pp. 248-260.

Goodenough, Ward H., "Componential Analysis and the Study of Meaning", *Language,* XXXII (1956), pp. 195-212.

——, "Formal Properties of Status Relationships". Unpublished paper read before the 1961 Meetings of the American Anthropological Association.

Hasselmo, Nils, "American Swedish: A Study in Bilingualism". Unpublished doctoral dissertation, Department of Linguistics, Harvard University, 1961.

Lounsbury, Floyd G., "A Semantic Analysis of the Pawnee Kinship Usage", *Language,* XXXII (1956), pp. 158-194.

Rubin, Joan, "Bilingualism in Paraguay", *Anthropological Linguistics,* IV (1962), pp. 52-58.

Stewart, Wm. A., "Creole Languages in the Caribbean", in Frank A. Rice, ed. *Study of the Role of Second Languages in Asia, Africa, and Latin America* (Washington; Center for Applied Linguistics, 1962), pp. 34-53.

From *National Bilingualism in Paraguay* by Joan Rubin. Doctoral dissertation, Yale University, 1963, Chapter 7: "Usage", pp. 200-235. Revised. This study appears in published form for the first time in the present volume. Printed by permission.

William A. Stewart

A SOCIOLINGUISTIC TYPOLOGY FOR DESCRIBING NATIONAL MULTILINGUALISM [1]

Of the various social and technical problems which beset the new and developing nations in particular, a sizable number turns out to be directly related to language in some way. Problems which are of a linguistic nature include widespread illiteracy, the lack of a standardized national language, the need for pedagogical tools in locally-adapted language teaching, and the lack of modern technical vocabularies in languages which must suddenly be employed for communicating scientific knowledge. Of course, problems such as these may occur both in linguistically uniform and linguistically diverse nations, but it is especially in the latter that they may take on greater complexity and require more difficult solutions.

National multilingualism – that is, the use within a single policy of more than one language – exists to some extent in all the major areas of the world.[2] It is especially in Asia, Africa, and Latin America, however,

[1] This is a revised version of the author's "Outline of Linguistic Typology for Describing Multilingualism" in Frank A. Rice, editor, *Study of the Role of Second Languages in Asia, Africa, and Latin America* (Washington, D.C., Center for Applied Linguistics, 1962), pp. 15-25.

[2] As will become clearer when sociolinguistic function is discussed, the precise nature of the "use" of various languages will have to be taken account of before this definition of national multilingualism can have any practical meaning. For example, the fact that in the United States, French may be used in the classroom and Latin or Hebrew in religious worship will not in itself qualify the nation to be considered a multilingual one in anything like the same sense that India, Nigeria, and Switzerland are considered multilingual nations. As used here, the term *polity* refers not only to nation-states, but also to non-sovereign colonies and territories, particularly if these are geographically separated from the parent state.

that multilingualism – often as the linguistic aspect of a still-vigorous ethnic or cultural pluralism – has given rise to communication problems of a serious enough nature to have prompted a number of national governments to initiate remedial programs. Although these programs have varied greatly in their details, they have usually been oriented in terms of one of two fundamentally different policies:

1. The eventual elimination, by education or decree, of all but one language, which is to remain as the national language.
2. The recognition and preservation of important languages within the national territory, supplemented by the adoption of one or more languages to serve for official purposes and for communication across language boundaries within the nation.

The first of these policies clearly aims at eliminating linguistic diversity, and is usually part of a more general policy which has as its goal the eventual assimilation to a "national" culture of all ethnic minorities. This policy is the one usually followed by a majority of the Latin American governments. The second approach is more tolerant of multilingualism, and usually represents an official policy of recognizing cultural pluralism as a fundamental characteristic of the nation. This policy is the one usually adopted by the newly independent African states. The extent to which either of the two policies proves to be the more suitable one will depend largely upon the nature of the particular cultural, linguistic, and political situation being dealt with. What the two approaches have in common, however, is that they both of necessity involve a certain amount of direct language manipulation.

Virtually every program involving language manipulation has, at one time or another, met with unpredicted reactions either for or against changes in the linguistic status quo. For example, there have been cases where people have resisted being taught a new language because of their feeling that it was, for some reason, an inappropriate one for them to use. Conversely, there have been cases where total language replacement has occurred, with a speed which has surpassed all previous estimates, due in large part to high receptivity for the new language as being more "worthy" than the languages previously spoken. Or, there have been cases where a new language has been accepted, but only for use in certain social situations. Where reactions of this type have caught language planners unawares, it has not necessarily been because they were totally unpredictable, but rather because not enough information was sought in advance about the ways in which languages may interact with other aspects of society. One way such information could be obtained would be through the description and comparison of different national multilingual situations.

The present typology is intended to contribute to the development of a comparative framework for describing national multilingualism by suggesting a technique for describing national sociolinguistic situations. In particular, it will emphasize the kinds of social, functional, and distributional relationships which different linguistic systems may have within (and to some extent across) national boundaries, and it will develop both a conceptual framework and a system of notation for identifying these.[3]

THE SPECIFICATION OF LANGUAGE TYPES

In specifying the relationships which may exist between various linguistic systems in a multilingual society, it is important to take account or the fact that linguistic systems may differ, not only in their structures, but also in their histories, their relationships to other linguistic systems, the extent to which they have acquired codified norms of usage, and in the manner of their transmission from generation to generation. Such social and technical characteristics can have an effect on the role which a particular linguistic system may assume in the linguistic makeup of a multilingual polity, so that linguistic systems characterized by different configurations of such attributes will tend to fall into different categories of intrinsic social value, insofar as their use in a particular polity is concerned. Such categories will be referred to as *language types*.[4] Language type can be an important factor in determining whether or not a particular linguistic system is likely to be accepted by the members of a national society (including its language planners) as suitable for some specific role, such as for use as an official language.

The number of attributes which can be isolated as determining language type can be expected to vary with the degree of analytical refinement employed in the description of language-society interaction. At the level of generalization assumed for the practical goals of a typology

[3] As used here, the term *linguistic system* is intended to include only those language-like codes which show enough structural stability, social spread, and consistency of usage to make them relevant in terms of the present typology's focus on multilingualism at the national level. Thus the term will specifically exclude ad hoc and/or highly unstable codes of the type which, under certain circumstances, may develop as private media of communication between small aggregates of individuals, such as between master and servant, or the members of a nuclear family. For the same reasons of focus, specialized styles and registers, as well as argots, jargons, and secret languages, will not be treated independently from the more general linguistic systems of which they constitute sub-varieties.

[4] In the cover terms *language type* and *language function,* the word *language* is used as a practical equivalent of the more technical term linguistic system (see note 3). Later, it will acquire a more specialized meaning.

specifically intended for describing national multilingualism, the classification of linguistic systems into language types can be made on the basis of the presence vs. the absence of four attributes. These are:

1. *Standardization*, i.e., the codification and acceptance, within the community of users, of a formal set of norms defining "correct" usage.[5]

The standardization of a given language may be *monocentric*, consisting at any given time of a single set of universally accepted norms, or it may be *polycentric*, where different sets of norms exist simultaneously.[6] When a language has come to be used in more than one country and has, in addition, developed multimodal standardization, the form of standardization prevalent in any one country may be either *endonormative*, when it is bases upon models of usage native to that country, or *exonormative*, when it is based upon foreign models of usage.[7] Finally, conventions for the writing of the language may be an important characteristic of standardization.[8]

[5] Throughout this typology, the term *standardization* is used to indicate *formal standardization,* in which language behavior is codified by the community of users. So far, very few of the world's several thousand languages have been standardized in this sense. However, many more languages show evidence of at least some *informal standardization,* which may occur when there is a certain amount of normalization of language behavior in the direction of some linguistic usage with high social prestige (such as the speech of local élites, etc.). Although the two kinds of standardization are alike in that they both serve to bring about increased uniformity of usage through dialect leveling, in formal standardization this leveling comes about through deliberate conformity to codified rules, while in informal standardization it comes about through more or less automatic adjustments which are made in terms of uncodified but socially preferred norms of usage.

[6] In polycentric standardization, the different sets of norms may represent independent codifications of dialectal or other linguistic differences (such as the use of different alphabets for writing the language) which are related to differences in political or religious identity or in geographic location, or they may be the result of incomplete replacement of an older set of norms by a newer one.

[7] There is no necessary correlation between polycentric standardization and a language's use in more than one country. Some languages which are used in only one country have polycentric standardization (e.g. Serbo-Croatian in Yugoslavia), while others which are used in more than one country have monocentric standardization (e.g. French and Dutch). However, there are cases where languages which are used in more than one country have developed polycentric standardization which may reflect political divisions (see note 6). Where this is the case, the differences between the sets of norms may be slight, cf. the British and American norms for English and the Continental and Brazilian norms for Portuguese, or they may be more marked, cf. the Rumanian and Moldavian norms for Daco-Rumanian and the Indian and Pakistani norms for Hindi-Urdu.

[8] In a strict sense, formal standardization is probably independent of writing, since there appear to have been cases where unwritten languages have developed norms defining "correct" (i.e. prescribed) usage, in the form of orally trans-

2. *Autonomy*, i.e., the function of the linguistic system as a unique and independent one.

Under most conditions, a linguistic system will be autonomous in terms of any other linguistic system with which it is not historically related. Where two historically related linguistic systems exist, but where structural differences are fairly marked and there is no sociolinguistic interdependence, each will be autonomous in terms of the other. Even in cases where, within a series of historically related forms of speech, there is no true linguistic boundary evident (i.e., where, over a geographic expanse, dialect change is gradual rather than abrupt), the standardization of two fairly different dialects is likely to produce two centers of autonomy, with the remaining dialects becoming heteronomous in terms of either one or the other standardized form.[9] Because of this, the total linguistic area may come to be regarded as one neatly divided between two different languages.[10] Accordingly, in situations where two or more historically related linguistic systems are involved, the presence vs. absence of autonomy can serve as a useful criterion for distinguishing between *language* and *dialect*.[11]

3. *Historicity*, i.e., the linguistic system is known or believed to be the result of normal development over time.

---

mitted conventions and models. Also, any linguistic system lacking formal standardization can be technically reduced to writing for certain specialized purposes (such as for linguistic description or for the publication of educational or religious tracts) without the writing system becoming established as a normal device in the language community. However, writing can be considered a part of formal standardization when it constitutes an established system, together with its orthographical conventions, which is accepted and used by the particular language community.

[9] A linguistic system will be *heteronomous* in terms of another, historically related one when the former functions in the linguistic community as a dependent variety of the latter, and is consequently subject to "correction" in its direction, i.e., is subject to regular structural readjustment so that it will come to resemble the other more closely.

[10] The confrontation of Dutch and German as "distinct" languages in the linguistic area including present-day Holland, Germany, Austria, and Switzerland represents a case of precisely this kind.

[11] A linguistic system which is heteronomous in terms of another, autonomous system will constitute a *dialect* of that system. By extension, two or more historically related linguistic systems which are heteronomous in terms of a single autonomous system will be considered to stand in a dialect relationship to each other, and the field of heteronomy around a single focus of autonomy will represent a single *language*. For a more technical formulation of essentially the same definition of *language* and *dialect*, see the Introduction to Charles A. Ferguson and John J. Gumperz, eds., *Linguistic Diversity in South Asia: Studies in Regional, Social and Functional Variation* (= *IJAL*, 26.3 [1960] and Publication Thirteen of the Indiana University Research Center in Anthropology, Folklore and Linguistics).

What gives a language historicity is its association with some national or ethnic tradition. Although some cultures have myths about a sudden or miraculous origin for their (or some other) language, this will not necessarily have an effect on practical attitudes about the "normalcy" of such systems unless it is held to have occurred at some remote time in the past. There are, however, certain factors which do tend to bring about the view that a particular linguistic system is somehow "unnatural" or "abnormal" in origin. One obvious factor of this kind is a knowledge of the fact that the linguistic system has been contrived or invented by some individual. Another is the knowledge or belief that the linguistic system represents a recent and relatively ad hoc development. Such a knowledge or belief can arise through direct observation of an ad hoc system in the process of development or, in the case of pidginized languages, from an impressionistic reaction to the marked grammatical deviation between the pidginized system and some other, well-known language with which it has a close lexical relationship. Once such views about the non-spontaneous origin of a linguistic system become current, they may continue on in the form of stereotyped attitudes and clichés.[12]

4. *Vitality*, i.e., use of the linguistic system by an unisolated community of native speakers.

Although this attribute probably has less effect upon the potential social importance of a linguistic system than any of the preceding ones, the existence of a community of native speakers does tend to contribute to it in proportion to such factors as the number and geographic distribution of such speakers, and the impact of non-linguistic aspects of their culture on others. A community of native speakers is also likely to serve as a source for standardization and new vocabulary, as well as for spoken and written models of usage.

The various ways in which the foregoing attributes can combine to characterize a number of relevant language types is indicated by the table on page 537.

Some well-known examples of *standard* (symbol: S) type languages are the official languages of modern Europe, such as English, French, German, Hungarian, and Russian. Where it is desirable to indicate a case of multimodal standardization, this can be done by modifying the symbol S with a numeral indicating the number of norms, e.g.

S_2, S_3, etc.

[12] For a discussion of the nature of impressionistic reactions to pidginized languages, as well as some examples of clichés embodying them, see William A. Stewart, "Creole Languages in the Caribbean" in Frank A. Rice, *op. cit.* (see note 1 for reference), particularly pp. 42-44.

ATTRIBUTES *				TYPE	SYMBOL
1	2	3	4		
+	+	+	+	Standard	S
+	+	+	—	Classical	C
+	+	—	—	Artificial	A
—	+	+	+	Vernacular	V
—	—	+	+	Dialect	D
—	—	—	+	Creole	K
—	—	—	—	Pidgin	P

* 1 = standardization, 2 = autonomy, 3 = historicity, 4 = vitality.

In cases where there are specific names for each of the norms, these can be indicated parenthetically, e.g.

Serbo-Croatian: S_2 (Serbian; Croatian)

Furthermore, when a language is used in a particular situation with exonormative standardization, this can be indicated by modifying the Symbol S with an *x*, and indicating parenthetically the model followed, e.g., English as used in Jamaica and Nigeria would be:

S_x (British norm)

and English as used in the Virgin Islands and Liberia would be:

S_x (American norm) [13]

Although *classical* (symbol: C) type languages are less numerous than S-types, they often play a very important role in a society in which they

[13] It should be remembered that such indications refer to formal standardization only. Even where formal standardization is exonormative, such as has been pointed out to be the case for English in Jamaica, Nigeria, the Virgin Islands, and Liberia, the norms of informal standardization are likely to be characteristically endonormative.

are used. Latin and Sanskrit are examples of C-type languages, however the C which is probably the most widely used one at present is Classical or Literary Arabic. Outside of Malta, which has an Arabic S (i.e. Maltese), the Arabic C is the only standardized form of the language. In Greece, two varieties of Modern Greek are used, an S (called *dhimotiki*) and a modern C (called *katharevousa*), the latter to be distinguished from Ancient Greek, which is an archaic C. Where necessary, an archaic C can be indicated by modifying the symbol C with an *a*:

Ancient Greek: C_a

The essential difference between an S and a C is that the former has native speakers (i.e. vitality) while the latter does not. However, it is possible for a C to become or give rise to an S by acquiring a community of native speakers, as in the case of Israeli Hebrew, an S which developed from a C through this process.

Examples of *artificial* (symbol: A) type languages are Esperanto, Ido, Volapük, and Interlingua. This type of language is primarily designed to meet the needs of international communication, and consequently will rarely if ever have an important function exclusively within a single national territory. However, such languages sometimes acquire a large following of committed supporters, societies for their propagation, etc. In particular, this has happened in the case of Esperanto.

Vernacular (symbol: V) type languages are usually learned as first or native languages, although there are cases where some have become media of wider communication and thus acquired significant numbers of secondary speakers. Most tribal languages of Africa and the Americas are V's. Due to their lack of formalized grammars and lexicons, V's are generally accorded less prestige than either S's or C's.[14] However, a V may become an S through the codification and acceptance of its grammar and lexicon, cf. the case of Tagalog in the Philippines.

Both S's and V's normally subsume a certain amount of linguistic variation, much of it in the form of a number of structurally identifiable subsystems of the *dialect* (symbol: D) type, which may correlate with differences between speakers, or with differences in use for particular situations. In these cases, D's need not normally be treated independently from the S's or V's of which they form a part. However, it sometimes happens that a particular D may enjoy special status in a national

[14] Of course, linguists hold that all linguistic systems have a grammatical structure, just as they have a vocabulary, and that these are subject to scientific analysis and description. The question here is merely whether or not the culture with which the linguistic system is traditionally associated has developed a formally accepted set of rules about the way the system is supposed to behave.

situation (e.g., it may be associated with a special function, or, used by a special group, and perhaps have a special name), or it may be isolated politically from what would normally be its superordinate system. Examples of the former are Schwyzertütsch in Switzerland and Neapolitan in Italy. Examples of the latter are Accadian in the northeastern United States (where standard French is generally absent) and the local variety of English used in the Leeward Island group of the Netherlands Antilles (where Dutch, rather than standard English, is the official language). In these and similar cases, it will generally be useful to specify such D's in a sociolinguistic profile of the nation.

Both the *creole* (symbol: K) and *pidgin* (symbol: P) types represent a particular kind of linguistic development which can occur in certain kinds of social and linguistic contact situations, where media of wider communication come into existence which derive their vocabularies from one source, but their grammatical structures from another. The early stage of such a development is characteristically a P, which has no native speakers. At times, however, a P may acquire native speakers and undergo further development, and so become a K. P's and K's are most often designated in terms of the language from which they derive their vocabulary. Thus one usually speaks of different varieties of Pidgin English (spoken in parts of Asia and West Africa), Pidgin Fula, and Pidgin Sango (both pidginized varieties of West African languages), referring to linguistic systems which utilize the vocabularies of English, Fula, and Sango respectively, even though in their grammars the P's may differ considerably from those languages. In the same way, one usually speaks of varieties of French Creole or Creole French (spoken in parts of the Caribbean and the Indian Ocean), and English Creole or Creole English (spoken, for example, in Jamaica and Sierra Leone). Of course, P's and K's, like V's, may undergo standardization and thereby become S's, cf. Bahasa Indonesia, a standardization of "Bazaar Malay", a Malay-based pidgin.[15]

[15] There are P's which are currently acquiring native speakers and thus in the process of becoming K's, e.g. Neo-Melanesian (= Melanesian Pidgin English), and some P's and K's are undergoing standardization, and becoming S's, e.g. Neo-Melanesian, Papiamentu, and Sranan. P's and K's usually function sociolinguistically as special kinds of dialects of their lexical-source languages. However, they are likely to have markedly different grammatical systems, and hence to qualify as distinct languages from a purely structural point of view. Thus, the English-based K which is widely used in rural Jamaica is traditionally regarded there as merely a substandard, dialectal variety of English. Yet it is structurally different enough from English in some ways to have prompted linguists to classify it as a separate, though obviously related, language.

THE SPECIFICATION OF LANGUAGE FUNCTIONS

Another factor of importance in describing cases of national multilingualism is the specification of the *function* of each of the linguistic systems within the national communities. The specification of sociolinguistic function serves as an answer to the question. For what purpose is a particular linguistic system used as a medium of communication in the nation? Of course, differentiation between various possible sociolinguistic functions can be made as refined as the descriptive goals warrant. However, the following functional categories seem to be adequate for the purposes of general description and comparison:

1. *Official* (symbol: o); [16] function as a legally appropriate language for all politically and culturally representative purposes on a nationwide basis. In many cases, the o function of a language is specified constitutionally.

2. *Provincial* (symbol: p); function as a provincial or regional official language. In this case, the official function of the language is not nationwide, but is limited to a smaller geographic area.

3. *Wider communication* (symbol: w); the function of a linguistic system (other than one which already has an o or p function) predominating as a medium of communication across language boundaries within the nation.

4. *International* (symbol: i); the function of a linguistic system (other than one which already has an o or p function) as a major medium of communication which is international in scope, e.g., for diplomatic relations, foreign trade, tourism, etc.

5. *Capital* (symbol: c); the function of a linguistic system (other than one which already has an o or p function) as the primary medium of communication in the vicinity of the national capital. This function is especially important in countries where political power, social prestige, and economic activity are centered in the capital.

6. *Group* (symbol: g); the function of a linguistic system primarily as the normal medium of communication among the members of a single cultural or ethnic group, such as a tribe, settled group of foreign immigrants, etc. So strong can the association between linguistic behavior and group identity be, that at times a linguistic system with a g function may serve as an informal criterion for ascertaining group membership.

7. *Educational* (symbol: e); the function of a language (other than one which already has an o or p function) as a medium of primary or secondary education, either regionally or nationally.

[16] Lower case symbols are used for coding language functions, just as upper case symbols were for coding language types.

8. *School subject* (symbol: s); the language (other than one which already has an o or p function) is commonly taught as a subject in secondary and/or higher education.

9. *Literary* (symbol: l); the use of a language primarily for literary or scholarly purposes.

10. *Religious* (symbol: r); the use of a language primarily in connection with the ritual of a particular religion.

Under various conditions, the same linguistic system may occupy more than one functional slot (and indeed the o function generally includes uses which are otherwise classified as w, i, c, e, and s functions). Furthermore, although the possibilities of co-occurrence of a given language function with a given language type are varied enough so that both need to be specified for each case, there is nevertheless a certain correlation between the two in that the o, p, l, s, and r functions will almost always be associated with S or C types, the i function with S, C, or A types, and the g function with S, V, or K types.

Multilingual situations may be considered stable when the different linguistic systems are geographically, socially, and functionally noncompetitive. For example, there may be two languages in a given nation which both have a p or g function. But as long as there are the languages of different local administrative units, or of different social or ethnic groups, then no linguistic conflict is involved. At the same time, two different linguistic systems may be used by the same people, but if they occupy different functional slots (e.g. one has an o function and the other an r function) then there is no conflict. However, language conflicts can occur if this complementary relationship is upset, either by a natural historical process or by direct administrative intervention.

Lastly, account should be taken of a special kind of functional relationship that can hold between two forms of speech which, although they may be structurally alike in some ways, are still unalike enough in others to constitute different systems from a linguistic point of view. One of these is usually autonomous, while the other is heteronomous in terms of it to at least some extent, and the two are used as alternatives of each other in a way which is reminiscent of the alternation between formal and informal style levels within a single language or dialect. The appropriate term for this kind of complementary relationship between two, closely related linguistic systems is *diglossia* (symbol: d).[17] Where a diglossia situation exists, the linguistic system which is used for more

[17] For a fuller discussion of diglossia, see Charles A. Ferguson, "Diglossia", *Word*, 15, 325-340 (1959) and William A. Stewart, "The Functional Distribution of Creole and French in Haiti", *Georgetown University Monograph Series on Languages and Linguistics*, Number 15, 149-159 (1963).

formal purposes (usually the autonomous one) can be designated as the *high* (symbol: H) variety, while the one which is used for informal purposes can be designated as the *low* (symbol: L) variety. A diglossia relationship can accordingly be indicated as follows, e.g. the situation in Haiti:

French So (d: L = Creole)
Creole K (d: H = French)

THE SPECIFICATION OF DEGREE OF USE

A final factor of importance in describing cases of national multilingualism is the specification of the *degree of use* of each of the linguistic systems within the national communities. Of course, this information could be presented by listing the total number of speakers after each entry. However, it seems more useful for comparative purposes to provide such information in the form of a number of classes denoting degree of use in terms of the percentage of users (not necessarily native speakers) within the polity. For this typology, a rating in terms of six such classes has been devised, as follows:

Class	*Percentage*
Class I	75% +
Class II	50% +
Class III	25% +
Class IV	10% +
Class V	5% +
Class VI	Below 5%

It should be clear that this classification rates linguistic systems according to degree of use only, and cannot be taken by itself as an index of relative sociolinguistic importance.

National Multilingualism

With the concepts of linguistic type, function, and degree of use established, it is now possible to arrive at a more suitable working definition of national multilingualism than the tentative one given toward the beginning of this typology. The most obvious modification which should be made in the earlier definition of national multilingualism is the exclusion from it of linguistic systems having highly restricted functions of a kind which makes them marginal to the patterns of communication within the polity. The i, e, s, l, and r functions are of this nature. Linguistic systems with these functions can be listed in national sociolinguistic descriptions, but they should not be taken as determiners of national multilingualism. With this modification, national multilingualism can be defined as *the established use within a single polity of more than one linguistic system with an o, p, w, c, or g function.* In some cases, it may prove more practical to list only those linguistic systems belonging to Class V or higher. In others, however, the listing of Class VI members as well may be desirable.

A Sociolinguistic Profile: Netherlands America

In order to illustrate how the sociolinguistic notation suggested in the preceding pages may be used in describing specific situations, this typology will close with a profile of the sociolinguistic situation in Netherlands America – one which exhibits most of the sociolinguistic types and functions discussed above. Administratively, Netherlands America is comprised of two units: Surinam, a territory on the South American mainland, and the Netherlands Antilles, consisting of six islands in the Caribbean Sea. The latter unit is further split administratively into the so-called Curaçao island group (consisting of Curaçao, Aruba, and Bonaire), and the Leeward island group (consisting of St. Martin, St. Eustatius, and Saba). Surinam and the Netherlands Antilles are linked politically by their affiliation with the Kingdom of the Netherlands, and linguistically by their sharing a single official language – Dutch. Yet, the official linguistic unity is merely a veneer covering what is undoubtedly one of the most complex language situations in the Western Hemisphere. For the total language situation is quite different in Surinam and the Netherlands Antilles. Moreover, there is within the latter unit a difference in language usage between the Curaçao island group and the Leeward island group. Accordingly, the three areas will be treated separately.

SURINAM

Class II	Sranan	Kcw	
Class III	Hindustani	S_2g	(Hindi, Urdu)
Class IV	Dutch	So	
	Javanese	Dg	
Class V	Aukan	Kg	
	Saramakkan	Kg	
Class VI	Arabic	Cr	

	,,	Dg	(Lebanese colloquial)
	Arawak	Vg	
	Calinya	Vg	
	Chinese	Dg	(Hakka)
	English	Sis	
	French	Ss	
	Hebrew	Cr	
	Latin	Crs	
	Oiana	Vg	
	Sanskrit	Cr	
	Trio	Vg	

NETHERLANDS ANTILLES

1. *Curaçao Island Group*

Class I	Papiamentu	K	(d: H = Spanish)
Class IV	Dutch	So	
	English	Sigs	
Class V	Spanish	Sisl	(d: L = Papiamentu)
Class VI	Hebrew	Cr	
	Latin	Crs	

2. *Leeward Island Group*

Class I	English	D
Class IV	Dutch	So
	Papiamentu	Kg

From the preceding list, it is apparent that a number of other languages are used besides Dutch in Netherlands America. In Surinam, these include three creoles, as well as a number of Amerindian and Asiatic languages. It will also be noted that no less than four religious languages are used – another indication of Surinam's social diversity.[18] In the

[18] Sranan (also known as Taki-Taki) is an English-based creole which is spoken along the coast, particularly in and around Paramaribo. That it does not stand in a diglossia relationship with standard English (Surinam's most important international language) is probably due in great part to the fact that historical developments have brought about such a marked structural difference between the two languages that their lexical relationship has become obscured for all but the specialist. Aukan and Saramakkan are Portuguese/English-based creoles (the latter more Portuguese in vocabulary than the former) which are spoken by the two main Bush Negro groups. Hindustani, Javanese, Chinese, and colloquial Arabic are the principal languages of various immigrant groups. Neither Javanese nor Chinese are used in their standardized forms to any appreciable

Netherlands Antilles, the total number of languages used is considerably less than in Surinam, but the degree of permanent multilingualism is still striking, considering the size of the islands and their populations.[19] One very interesting difference between the two units is that in Surinam, no one language is used by more than 75 percent of the total population, while such a language does exist in each of the subdivisions of the Netherlands Antilles.

This revision appears in published form for the first time in the present volume. See footnote 1. Printed by permission.

---

extent. Classical Arabic, Hebrew, Latin, and Sanskrit are, of course, the religious languages of Moslems, Jews, Roman Catholics, and Hindus respectively. There appears to be another religious language, Koromanti, which is used by officiants of the Winti cult, but its linguistic nature has not yet been determined.

[19] Papiamentu is a Spanish/Portuguese-based creole which, as the list indicates, stands in a diglossia relationship with Spanish. Because of the proximity of Venezuela, Spanish is an important language of trade and tourism in the Curaçao island group and still shows traces of the fact that it was once used as a full-fledged literary alternate for Papiamentu. English, besides being an important international language in the Curaçao island group, is the native language of a colony of American residents on the island of Aruba. In the Leeward island group, a non-standard dialect of English is the native language of most of the inhabitants. There, Papiamentu is restricted to groups of immigrants from Curaçao.

Stanley Lieberson

AN EXTENSION OF GREENBERG'S LINGUISTIC DIVERSITY MEASURES

1. In 1956, Greenberg proposed eight measures of linguistic diversity designed to determine the possibilities of communication among the population of some delimited area.[1] Taking note of the considerable variance between areas of the world in their linguistic diversity, Greenberg's measures allow us to quantify this diversity on a continuum ranging from complete diversity such that no two people speak a mutually intelligible language or dialect to the other extreme where all inhabitants share a common tongue. By going beyond mere verbal descriptions of an area's linguistic diversity, these quantitative measures enable us to correlate language usage with social, economic, political, and geographic factors.

Although Greenberg refers only to the linguistic diversity of spatially delineated population aggregates such as nations, states, and cities, his measures are equally applicable to any socially meaningful population delimited on a non-areal basis. Thus, for example, we could apply his measures to the civil service of India, the Ukrainian ethnic population of the U.S.S.R., teen-agers in Brussels, Negroes in Chicago, and the like.

Greenberg's measures are all confined to diversity or communication *within* some defined population. In this paper, we extend Greenberg's measures to linguistic diversity or communication *between* two or more spatially delineated populations or between socially defined subpopulations of a larger aggregate. The measures proposed here are extensions of the probability-type indexes of Greenberg which have

[1] Joseph H. Greenberg, "The measurement of linguistic diversity", *Language*, 32, 109-15 (1956).

merited commendation from the statisticians Goodman and Kruskal.[2] Thus, there is no difficulty in using Greenberg's measures of diversity within an area jointly with the measures proposed here for diversity between areas or populations. That is, the results obtained by these procedures are fully compatible and may be compared without further adjustment.

A solution is offered for measuring interaction between groups which is applicable to all eight of the measures proposed by Greenberg. However, we will only illustrate its application with two of these measures since the procedure is basically the same for all eight indexes.

2. Algeria prior to the exodus of the French provides us with an illustration of the application of H, the *Index of Communication* between groups. H within groups is "the probability that if two members of the population are chosen at random, they will have at least one language in common." [3] Based on the language(s) spoken by the population 10 or more years of age shown in Table 1, we find H is .669 for the total population, .801 for the Moslem population, and 1.000 for the European population. What we find then is fairly high communication probability for the total population of Algeria, higher communication within the Moslem segment, and maximum communication within the European segment. We may be somewhat suspicious of the latter figure since apparently not a single European is unable to speak French. We will not consider the computational procedure for these indexes since it is based on the formula described by Greenberg.[4]

TABLE 1

Language Distribution, Algeria 1948,
Population 10 Years of Age and Over

	Arabic	*Berber*	*French and Arabic*	*French, Arabic, and Berber*	*French and Berber*	*French*	*Sum*
Total population	.676	.097	.064	.041	.006	.116	1.000
Moslem	.780	.112	.053	.047	.007	.001	1.000
European	—	—	.135	.003	.001	.860	.999

[2] They refer to Greenberg's paper as "one of the few instances we know in which descriptive statistics are constructed so as to have operational interpretations in the sense that we have discussed". Leo A. Goodman and William H. Kruskal, "Measures of association for cross classifications. II: further discussion and references", *Journal of the American Statistical Association,* 54, 155 (1959).

[3] Greenberg, 112.

[4] Greenberg, 112.

The conventional H index fails to provide us with a measure of the potential communication between the two major ethnic segments of the population, Moslem and European. That is, if we randomly select a Moslem and if we randomly select a European, what is the probability that they will be able to communicate in a mutually intelligible language? It is necessary to introduce a new measure to obtain this communication potential between groups. First, let us consider why H for the total population is inadequate. The H of .669 for the entire population is weighted by the relative numbers of the component segments we are interested in. In the case of Algeria, there are 5.4 million Moslems and only .8 million Europeans ten years of age or older. To the extent that there is a numerical difference, H will be weighted in the direction of the larger group. Second, H within the entire population is influenced by the communication probabilities within each segment of the population and not solely between the segments of the population. Thus, if we have a nation composed of two groups, A and B, all members of A speaking only language X and all members of B speaking only language Y, computation of Greenberg's H for the entire population would give us a measure of the communication possibilities within the entire population but would tell us nothing about the linguistic possibilities between the ethnic groups.

Both of these objections can be avoided by means of the following procedure. Taking the linguistic distribution of each population as shown in Table 1, we determine the cross-products between members of the two groups who have one or more common languages. We do not take the cross-products of common language among members of the same socially or spatially defined group such as we would if we were computing the value of H within a population. Let A, B, and F represent respectively Arabic, Berber, and French languages. Further, let subscript 1 represent Moslem speakers and subscript 2 represent European speakers. The between-group H index is: $A_1 (A_2 + FA_2 + FAB_2) + B_1 (B_2 + FAB_2 + FB_2) + FA_1 (A_2 + FA_2 + FAB_2 + FB_2 + F_2) + FAB_1 (A_2 + B_2 + FA_2 + FAB_2 + FB_2 + F_2) + FB_1 (B_2 + FA_2 + FAB_2 + FB_2 + F_2) + F_1 (FA_2 + FAB_2 + FB_2 + F_2)$. In the case of communication between Moslems and French, the data in Table 1 yield: .780(0+.135+.003) + .112(0+.003+.001) + .053(0+.135+.003+.001+.860) + .047(0+0+.135+.003+.001+.860) + .001(.135+.003+.001+.860). In this case, H between the two ethnic groups is .216.

As indicated earlier, the proposed measure is based upon the same type of analysis as that of Greenberg and therefore the different computational procedure does not prevent us from interpreting the results along with that obtained for H within the populations. Algeria prior to the revolution was a society with a fairly high degree of over-all communication, .669, but in which the ethnic segments are highly split. That is, communication is rather high within the groups, but is low between them. If we randomly select a Moslem and randomly select a European, in little more than 2 out of 10 times will they possess a common language.

3. The between-group application of Greenberg's measures is not restricted to two groups, but can be applied to as many groups as desired. We have divided Belgium into three areas: the predominantly French speaking area (composed of Hainault, Liege, Luxembourg, and Namur); the predominantly Dutch speaking area (Antwerp, West Flanders, East Flanders, and Limburg); and Brabant, which includes Brussels, in the center. Again using the H index, we can determine the probabilities of communication within each area by means of Greenberg's procedure. We find H fairly high within each area, although it is lowest within Brabant (Table 2). By computing intergroup H along the lines suggested earlier, we find communication is fairly high between Brabant and the Dutch and French areas, being .695 and .639 respectively. However, H between the Dutch and French speaking areas is very low, .249. It is noteworthy that H within Brabant is lower than H within either the French or Dutch areas. Thus we find that a population with a relatively lower communication level within may have considerably higher communication levels with other areas than do linguistically more uniform areas. Finally, the use of both within- and between-area measures indicates that communication for residents of Brabant is nearly as great with residents of the Flemish and Waloon areas of Belgium as it is with fellow residents of Brabant (.695 and .639 compared with .748).

TABLE 2

Language Distribution, Belgium 1949, Population All Ages

	F	D	G	FD	FG	DG	FDG	None	Within-Group H
Brabant	.293	.309	.001	.318	.010	.002	.036	.030	.748
French Areas	.837	.007	.018	.056	.023	.001	.012	.046	.866
Dutch Areas	.019	.753	.002	.152	.001	.005	.030	.040	.893

F = French
D = Dutch
G = German
FD = French and Dutch
FG = French and German
DG = Dutch and German
FDG = French, Dutch, and German

4. The application of our between-groups approach to all of the measures of diversity proposed by Greenberg can be readily summarized. In

each case, we need the linguistic distribution of the subpopulations that are to be examined. Second, we obtain the cross-products between the proportions of the two social groups using the same language(s) such that we never multiply within a subcategory but always across subpopulations. If the method is to be weighted by some resemblance factor such as that based on the glottochronology as in the B, D, and F measures,[5] then the between-group application is similarly weighted. In each instance we obtain a measure of diversity between subgroups which is independent of linguistic homogeneity within the subgroups and which is not distorted by the relative sizes of the groups. Rather, these measures describe the diversity existing between the two subpopulations in the form of a probability statement.

5. The procedure as well as the substantive potential may be illustrated with the A index of linguistic diversity. Called the MONOLINGUAL NON-WEIGHTED METHOD, it is described thusly: "If from a given area we choose two members of the population at random, the probability that these two individuals speak the same language can be considered a measure of its linguistic diversity." [6] Our conversion into a between-groups measure of A is essentially as before, namely the probability that an individual randomly drawn from one population and an individual drawn from a second population will speak the same language. This we will consider a measure of linguistic similarity between groups. If we have the mother tongue distributions of two or more populations and, for example, wish to measure their linguistic diversity in a manner analogous to the within-group A measure, then we obtain the cross-products of the same tongue in each group. Using data for the Norwegian first and second generations in the United States, shown in Table 3, we can compare the linguistic diversity between generations for 1940 in the following manner: (.924) (.502) + (.051) (.477) + (.012) (.008) + (.013) (.013) = .488.[7] Since Greenberg's indexes, except for H discussed earlier, are stated in the form of probability of diversity, we will follow this procedure by subtracting the cross-products from 1, thus A = 1-.488 = .512. The range of our index runs from 0 (where pairing of members of the two groups would always yield speakers of the same language) to 1.000 (which would occur when such a pairing would always yield speakers of different languages).[8]

[5] Greenberg, 110-12.

[6] Greenberg, 109.

[7] For convenience we assume that the small proportion in the "all other and not reported" category all speak the same tongue in both generations.

[8] In monolingual populations, A = 1 — H.

TABLE 3

Mother Tongue Distribution, Norwegian Foreign White Stock in the United States, 1940

	Norwegian	*English*	*Swedish*	*All Other and Not Reported*	*Total*
Foreign Born	.924	.051	.012	.013	1.000
Second Generation	.502	.477	.008	.013	1.000

The potentialities of using our between-group measure of linguistic diversity in conjunction with Greenberg's measure for within-group diversity may be illustrated with the data shown in Table 4. The first two columns give the A measure within the first and second generations of various foreign white groups in the United States. We observe some fairly sharp rises in diversity within generations of the same foreign born group. This is particularly the case for foreign born groups that were relatively homogeneous in their mother tongues, such as the Norwegians, Swedes, Germans, and Greeks. For example, the probability is .124 that two randomly selected German-born immigrants will have different mother tongues; the probability is .524 that two randomly selected second generation Germans will have different mother tongues. In all cases there is less linguistic unity within the second generation than the first. This is due to the generally sharp rise in English as a mother tongue in the second generation accompanied by a declining but still substantial segment of the second generation with the old-world mother tongue such as was shown for Norwegians in Table 3. Applying our between-group measure of A, we see in the last column of Table 4 the probability of mother tongue diversity between randomly selected members of the two generations of the same national origin. These figures are strikingly higher than those for diversity within the first generation. In other words, we find inter-generational linguistic unity of nationality groups is less than the unity within the immigrant groups themselves.[9]

6. Shown in Table 5 above the diagonal are the A indexes between foreign born groups computed in the manner suggested earlier. We find very high diversity between different immigrant groups. For example, the probability is .998 that a Norwegian and a German immigrant will

[9] The close relationship between the learning of English and immigrant residential segregation has been described elsewhere. See: Otis Dudley Duncan and Stanley Lieberson, "Ethnic segregation and assimilation", *American Journal of Sociology*, 64, 366-74 (1959); Stanley Lieberson, "The impact of residential segregation on ethnic assimilation", *Social Forces*, 40, 52-7 (1961); Stanley Lieberson, *Ethnic Patterns in American Cities* (New York, 1963).

TABLE 4

Mother Tongue A Indexes among and between First and Second Generation Groups, United States, 1940

	A Index Among		*A Index Between Generations*
	Foreign Born	*Second Generation*	
Norway	.143	.520	.512
Sweden	.122	.513	.589
Switzerland	.495	.531	.739
Germany	.124	.524	.535
Greece	.113	.529	.468
Poland	.407	.485	.476
U.S.S.R.	.603	.690	.762
Lithuania	.430	.583	.555

have different mother tongues. Below the diagonal are the inter-group diversity indexes for second generation members of these groups. With the one exception of the Swiss-German comparison, the diversity index is always higher for the foreign born than the second generation. For example, the probability that a second generation German and Norwegian will have different mother tongues is reduced to .763.

On a substantive basis, these data, in conjunction with those reported in Table 4, suggest that European immigrant groups in the United States were mostly very distinct from one another in their mother tongues. Differences between first and second generations in mother tongue

TABLE 5

Mother Tongue A Indexes Between Foreign White Groups, United States, 1940

(First Generation Above Diagonal)

	Norway	*Sweden*	*Switzerland*	*Germany*	*Greece*	*Poland*	*U.S.S.R.*	*Lithuania*
Norway		.980	.996	.998	.999	.999	.998	.999
Sweden	.725		.997	.998	.999	.999	.998	.999
Switzerland	.711	.659		.353	.999	.984	.949	.984
Germany	.763	.721	.548		.999	.971	.921	.978
Greece	.808	.774	.756	.800		.999	.999	.999
Poland	.892	.872	.859	.875	.909		.887	.952
U.S.S.R.	.797	.761	.710	.738	.829	.872		.918
Lithuania	.865	.840	.825	.854	.886	.904	.855	

composition are in the direction of breaking down the initially high linguistic barriers between nationality groups accompanied by a drop in mother tongue unity within the nationality groups. Moreover, we have seen that the mother tongue diversity between generations of the same foreign group were fairly substantial and far greater than the diversity within the first generation. In other words, the process of assimilation involved a rise in foreign mother tongue diversity within nationality groups and a drop in mother tongue diversity between different origin groups.

7. On a methodological basis, we have tried to demonstrate that the inter-group measures proposed provide us with a means for studying ethnic and regional linguistic separation and their influence on such broad problems as nationalism and assimilation. Thus, by means of Greenberg's indexes, it is possible to determine the linguistic communication within areas or socially significant populations. By means of the indexes proposed here, it is possible to get at questions of linguistic communication between segments of a given population. These measures, used in tandem, provide an instrument for a quantitative approach to a basic sociolinguistic problem, namely, the degree language sets populations apart such that communication or unity within social components of a population is greater than that between the components. These measures can be readily applied to such subpopulations as social classes, juvenile delinquents, racial, ethnic, and tribal populations, age groups, regions, and occupational groups.

From *Language*, 40 (1964), 526-531. Reprinted by permission.

William F. Mackey

THE DESCRIPTION OF BILINGUALISM*

INTRODUCTION

Bilingualism is not a phenomenon of language; it is a characteristic of its use. It is not a feature of the code but of the message. It does not belong to the domain of "langue" but of "parole".[1]

If language is the property of the group, bilingualism is the property of the individual. An individual's use of two languages supposes the existence of two different language communities; it does not suppose the existence of a bilingual community. The bilingual community can only be regarded as a dependent collection of individuals who have

* This framework of description is based on the conclusions of my article on the definition of bilingualism in the Journal in 1956 (see note 6 below). During the 1960 International Seminar on Bilingualism in Education, I had an opportunity of discussing this with students of bilingualism in different parts of the world who encouraged me to elaborate this into a general framework for the description of bilingualism. I am grateful to the members of this seminar for their encouragement, criticism, and helpful suggestions. I also thank the Canadian National Commission for UNESCO for making it possible for me to attend this seminar, which was held in Aberystwyth in August 1960.

[1] It is important not to confuse bilingualism – the use of two or more languages by the individual – with the more general concept of language contact, which deals with the direct or indirect influence of one language on another resulting in changes in "langue" which become the permanent property of monolinguals and enter into the historical development of the language. Such foreign influences may indeed be due to past periods of mass bilingualism, as in the case of the Scandinavian element in English. But bilingualism is not the only cause of foreign influence; the presence of words like *coffee* and *sugar* in English does not argue a period of English-Arabic bilingualism. Language contact includes the study of linguistic borrowing.

reasons for being bilingual. A self-sufficient bilingual community has no reason to remain bilingual, since a closed community in which everyone is fluent in two languages could get along just as well with one language. As long as there are different monolingual communities, however, there is likelihood of contact between them; this contact results in bilingualism.

The concept of bilingualism has become broader and broader since the beginning of the century. It was long regarded as the equal mastery of two languages; and this is the definition still found in certain glossaries of linguistics, e.g., "Qualité d'un sujet ou d'une population qui se sert couramment de deux langues, sans aptitude marquée pour l'une plutôt que pour l'autre".[2] Bloomfield considered bilingualism as "the native-like control of two languages".[3] This was broadened by Haugen to the ability to produce "complete meaningful utterances in the other language".[4] And it has now been suggested that the concept be further extended to include simply "passive-knowledge" of the written language or any "contact with possible models in a second language and the ability to use these in the environment of the native language".[5] This broadening of the concept of bilingualism is due to realization that the point at which a speaker of a second language becomes bilingual is either arbitrary or impossible to determine. It seems obvious, therefore, that if we are to study the phenomenon of bilingualism we are forced to consider it as something entirely relative.[6] We must moreover include the use not only of two languages, but of any number of languages.[7] We shall therefore consider bilingualism as the alternate use of two or more languages by the same individual.

What does this involve? Since bilingualism is a relative concept, it involves the question of DEGREE. How well does the individual know the languages he uses? In other words, how bilingual is he? Second, it involves the question of FUNCTION. What does he use his languages for? What role have his languages played in his total pattern of behaviour? Third, it includes the question of ALTERNATION. To what extent does he alternate between his languages? How does he change from one language to the other, and under what conditions? Fourth, it includes the question of INTERFERENCE. How well does the bilingual keep his languages apart? To what extent does he fuse them together?

[2] J. Marouzeau, *Lexique de la terminologie linguistique* (Paris, Geuthner, 1951).
[3] L. Bloomfield, *Language* (New York, Holt, 1933), p. 56.
[4] E. Haugen, *The Norwegian Language in America: a study in bilingual behaviour*, 2 vols. (Philadelphia, University of Pennsylvania Press, 1953). Vol. 1 (The Bilingual Community), p. 7.
[5] A. R. Diebold, Jr., "Incipient Bilingualism", *Lang.*, 37 (1961), p. 111.
[6] W. F. Mackey, "Toward a Redefinition of Bilingualism", *JCLA* 2 (1956), p. 8.
[7] W. F. Mackey, "Bilingualism", *Encyclopædia Britannica* (1959 ed.).

How does one of his languages influence his use of the other? Bilingualism is a behavioural pattern of mutually modifying linguistic practices varying in degree, function, alternation, and interference. It is in terms of these four inherent characteristics that bilingualism may be described.[8]

DEGREE

The first and most obvious thing to do in describing a person's bilingualism is to determine how bilingual he is. To find this out it is necessary to test his skill in the use of each of his languages, which we shall label A and B. This includes separate tests for comprehension and expression in both the oral and written forms of each language, for the bilingual may not have an equal mastery of all four basic skills in both languages. He may indeed be able to understand both languages equally well; but he may be unable to speak both of them with equal facility. Since the language skills of the bilingual may include differences in comprehension and expression in both the spoken and written forms, it is necessary to test each of these skills separately if we are to get a picture of the extent of his bilingualism. If, however, we are only interested in determining his bilingualism rather than in describing it, other forms of tests are possible: word-detection tests, word-association and picture vocabulary tests, for example, have been used for this purpose.[9]

The bilingual's mastery of a skill, however, may not be the same at all linguistic levels. He may have a vast vocabulary but a poor pronunciation, or a good pronunciation but imperfect grammar. In each skill, therefore, it is necessary to discover the bilingual's mastery of the phonology (or graphics), the grammar, the vocabulary, the semantics, and he stylistics of each language. What has to be described is proficiency in two sets of related variables, skills and levels. This may be presented as in Table 1.

If we consider Table 1, it is easy to see how the relation between skills and levels may vary from bilingual to bilingual. At the phonological-graphic level, for example, we have the case of the Croatian who understands spoken Serbian but is unable to read the Cyrillic script in which

[8] We must not confuse "bilingual description" with the "description of bilingualism". "Bilingual description" is a term which has been used to denote the contrastive analysis of two languages for the purpose of discovering the differences between them. This is also known as "differential description". Differential description is a prerequisite to the analysis of one of the most important characteristics of bilingualism – interference.

[9] E. Peal and W. E. Lambert, "The Relation of Bilingualism to Intelligence", *Psychological Monographs*, 1962, 76.

TABLE 1
Degree

Skills	*Levels*									
	Phonological-Graphic		Grammatical		Lexical		Semantic		Stylistic	
	A	B	A	B	A	B	A	B	A	B
Listening										
Reading										
Speaking										
Writing										

it is written. At the grammatical level, it is common to find bilinguals whose skill in the use of the grammatical structures of both languages cannot match their knowledge of the vocabularies. At the lexical level it is not unusual to find bilinguals whose reading vocabulary in Language B is more extensive than it is in Language A, and far beyond their speaking vocabulary in either language. At the semantic level a bilingual may be able to express his meaning in some areas better in one language than he can in the other. A bilingual technician who normally speaks Language A at home and speaks Language B indifferently at work may nevertheless be able to convey his meaning much better in Language B whenever he is talking about his specialty. Finally, a bilingual's familiarity with the stylistic range of each language is very likely to vary with the subject of discourse.

To get an accurate description of the degree of bilingualism it is necessary to fill in the above framework with the results of tests. Types and models of language tests are now being developed.[10] On these models it is possible to design the necessary tests for each of the languages used by the bilingual in the dialects which he uses.

FUNCTION

The degree of proficiency in each language depends on its function, that is, on the uses to which the bilingual puts the language and the conditions under which he has used it. These may be external or internal.

External functions. – The external functions of bilingualism are determined by the number of areas of contact and by the variation of each in duration, frequency, and pressure. The areas of contact include all

[10] For a study of test making, see R. Lado, *Language Testing* (London, Longmans, 1961).

media through which the languages were acquired and used – the language-usage of the home, the community, the school, and the mass media of radio, television, and the printed word. The amount of influence of each of these on the language habits of the bilingual depends on the duration, frequency, and pressure of the contact. These may apply to two types of activity – either comprehension (C) alone, or expression (E), as well. These variables plotted against the areas and points of contact give Table 2.

If we examine Table 2 we note that it lists a number of contact areas and points, each of which appears opposite a number of columns of variables. Let us first consider the contacts.

Contacts. – The bilingual's language contacts may be with the languages used in the home, in the community, in the school, in the mass media of communication, and in his correspondence.

Home languages. – The language or languages of the home may differ from all or any of the other areas of contact. Within the home the language of the family may differ from that of its domestics and tutors. Some families encourage bilingualism by engaging a domestic worker or governess who speaks another language to the children. Others send their children as domestic workers into foreign families for the purpose of enabling them to master the second language. This is a common practice in a number of bilingual countries. Another practice is the temporary exchange of children between families speaking different languages. There are even agencies for this purpose.[11] Some families who speak a language other than that of the community insist on keeping it as the language of the home.

Within the family itself the main language of one member may be different from that of the other members. This language may be used and understood by the other members; or it may simply be understood and never used, as is the practice of certain Canadian Indian families where the children address their parents in English and receive replies in the native Indian language of the parents.

In families where one of the parents knows a second language, this language may be used as one of two home languages. Studies of the effects of such a practice have been made by Ronjat,[12] Pavlovitch,[13] and

[11] Examples of this are the Canadian "visites interprovinciales", a description of which may be found in "French or English – with Pleasure!" in *Citizen*, 7.5 (1961), pp. 1-7.

[12] J. Ronjat, *Le développement du langage observé chez un enfant bilingue* (Paris, Champion, 1913).

[13] M. Pavlovitch, *Le langage enfantin: l'acquisition du serbe et du français par un enfant serbe* (Paris, 1920).

<table>
<tr><th rowspan="5">Contacts</th><th colspan="44">Variables</th></tr>
<tr><th colspan="4">Duration</th><th colspan="4">Frequency</th><th colspan="36">Pressure</th></tr>
<tr><th colspan="4"></th><th colspan="4"></th><th colspan="4">Economic</th><th colspan="4">Administrative</th><th colspan="4">Cultural</th><th colspan="4">Political</th><th colspan="4">Military</th><th colspan="4">Historical</th><th colspan="4">Religious</th><th colspan="4">Demographic</th></tr>
<tr><th colspan="2">A</th><th colspan="2">B</th><th colspan="2">A</th><th colspan="2">B</th><th colspan="2">A</th><th colspan="2">B</th><th colspan="2">A</th><th colspan="2">B</th><th colspan="2">A</th><th colspan="2">B</th><th colspan="2">A</th><th colspan="2">B</th><th colspan="2">A</th><th colspan="2">B</th><th colspan="2">A</th><th colspan="2">B</th><th colspan="2">A</th><th colspan="2">B</th><th colspan="2">A</th><th colspan="2">B</th></tr>
<tr><th>C</th><th>E</th><th>C</th><th>E</th><th>C</th><th>E</th><th>C</th><th>E</th><th>C</th><th>E</th><th>C</th><th>E</th><th>C</th><th>E</th><th>C</th><th>E</th><th>C</th><th>E</th><th>C</th><th>E</th><th>C</th><th>E</th><th>C</th><th>E</th><th>C</th><th>E</th><th>C</th><th>E</th><th>C</th><th>E</th><th>C</th><th>E</th><th>C</th><th>E</th><th>C</th><th>E</th><th>C</th><th>E</th><th>C</th><th>E</th><th>C</th><th>E</th><th>C</th><th>E</th></tr>
<tr><td>1. Home</td><td colspan="44"></td></tr>
<tr><td>Father</td><td colspan="44"></td></tr>
<tr><td>Mother</td><td colspan="44"></td></tr>
<tr><td>Siblings</td><td colspan="44"></td></tr>
<tr><td>Other relatives</td><td colspan="44"></td></tr>
<tr><td>Domestics, etc.</td><td colspan="44"></td></tr>
<tr><td>2. Community</td><td colspan="44"></td></tr>
<tr><td>Neighbourhood</td><td colspan="44"></td></tr>
<tr><td>Ethnic group</td><td colspan="44"></td></tr>
<tr><td>Church group</td><td colspan="44"></td></tr>
<tr><td>Occupation group</td><td colspan="44"></td></tr>
<tr><td>Recreation group</td><td colspan="44"></td></tr>
<tr><td>3. School</td><td colspan="44"></td></tr>
<tr><td>Single medium</td><td colspan="44"></td></tr>
<tr><td>Dual media:</td><td colspan="44"></td></tr>
<tr><td>Parallel</td><td colspan="44"></td></tr>
<tr><td>Divergent</td><td colspan="44"></td></tr>
<tr><td>Subjects:</td><td colspan="44"></td></tr>
<tr><td>__________</td><td colspan="44"></td></tr>
<tr><td>__________</td><td colspan="44"></td></tr>
<tr><td>__________</td><td colspan="44"></td></tr>
<tr><td>Private tuition</td><td colspan="44"></td></tr>
<tr><td>Group</td><td colspan="44"></td></tr>
<tr><td>Individual</td><td colspan="44"></td></tr>
<tr><td>Self</td><td colspan="44"></td></tr>
<tr><td>4. Mass media</td><td colspan="44"></td></tr>
<tr><td>Radio</td><td colspan="44"></td></tr>
<tr><td>Television</td><td colspan="44"></td></tr>
<tr><td>Cinema</td><td colspan="44"></td></tr>
<tr><td>Recordings</td><td colspan="44"></td></tr>
<tr><td>Newspapers</td><td colspan="44"></td></tr>
<tr><td>Books</td><td colspan="44"></td></tr>
<tr><td>Magazines</td><td colspan="44"></td></tr>
<tr><td>5. Correspondence</td><td colspan="44"></td></tr>
</table>

Leopold[14] to test the theory that two languages can be acquired for the same effort as one. Each experiment used Grammont's formula "une personne: une langue",[15] whereby the same person always spoke the same language to the child, the mother limiting herself to one of the languages and the father to the other.

Community languages. – These include the languages spoken in the bilingual's neighbourhood, his ethnic group, his church group, his occupation group and his recreation group.

1. Neighbourhood. A child is surrounded by the language of the neighbourhood into which he is born, and this often takes the place of the home as the most important influence on his speech. A corrective to this has been the periods of foreign residence which bilinguals have long found necessary in order to maintain one of their languages.

2. Ethnic group. The extent to which the bilingual is active in the social life of his ethnic group is a measure of the possibility of maintaining his other language. This may be the most important factor in a community with no other possible contact with the language.

3. Church group. Although church groups are often connected with ethnic groups, it is possible for the bilingual to associate with one and ignore the other. Although he may attend none of the activities of his ethnic group, he may yet bring his children to the foreign church or Sunday school, where sermons and instructions are given in a language which is not that of the community.

4. Occupation group. The bilingual's occupation may oblige him to work with a group using a language different from that which he uses at home. Or, if he lives in a bilingual city like Montreal, the language of his place of work may be different from that of the neighbourhood in which he lives. Or, if he is engaged in one of the service occupations, he may have to use both his languages when serving the public.

5. Recreation group. A bilingual may use one of his languages with a group of people with whom he takes part in sports, in music, or in other pastimes. Or he may attend a club in which the language spoken is not that of his home or his neighbourhood. Or the foreign children in a unilingual school may be in the habit of playing together, thus maintaining the use of their native language.

School languages. – A person's language contact in school may be with a language taught as a subject or with a language used as a medium of instruction. Both may be found in three instructional media: single, dual, and private.

[14] W. F. Leopold, *Speech Development of a Bilingual Child.* 4 vols. (Chicago and Evanston, Northwestern University Press, 1939-1949).

[15] M. Grammont, "Observation sur le langage des enfants", *Mélanges Meillet* (Paris, 1902).

1. Single medium. Some parents will go to a lot of trouble and expense to send their children to a school in which the instruction is given in another language – schools in foreign countries, foreign ethnic communities, or bilingual areas.[16]

In bilingual areas, the language of single medium schools must be determined by the application of some sort of language policy. This may be based on one of the four following principles: nationality, territoriality, religious affiliation, ethnic origin.

According to the principle of nationality, a child must always take his schooling in the language of the country, regardless of his ethnic origin, religious affiliation, or of the language which he speaks at home. This is the policy of most of the public school systems in the United States.

According to the principle of territoriality, the child gets his schooling in the language of the community in which he happens to be living. This is the practice in Switzerland, for example.

The principle of religious affiliation may be applied in countries where linguistic divisions coincide to a great extent with religious ones. A sectarian school system may take these language divisions into account. In Quebec, for example, there are French Catholic schools, English Protestant schools, and English Catholic schools. The French Protestants in some areas may not be numerous enough to warrant a separate school system, in which case a French Protestant family might send their children to an English Protestant school rather than to a French Catholic one.

The principle of ethnic origin takes into account the home language of the child. In countries where bilingual communities are closely intermingled the policy may be to have the child do his schooling in the language which he normally speaks at home. This is the policy, for example, in many parts of South Africa.

2. Dual media. The bilingual may have attended schools in which two languages were used as media of instruction. Dual media schools may be of different types. In their use of two languages they may adopt a policy of parallelism or one of divergence.

Parallel media schools are based on the policy that both languages be put on an equal footing and used for the same purposes and under the same circumstances. The parallelism may be built into the syllabus or into the time-table. If it is part of the syllabus, the same course, lesson, or teaching point will be given in both languages. This has been the practice in certain parts of Belgium. If the parallelism is built into the time-table, the school makes exclusive use of one of the languages during

16 W. F. Mackey, "Bilingualism and Education", *Pédagogie-Orientation*, 6 (1952), pp. 135-147.

a certain unit of time – day, week, or month – at the end of which it switches to the other language for an equal period, so that there is a continual alternation from one language to the other. This is the practice of certain military and technical schools in Canada.

Another type of dual media school is governed by a policy of divergence, the use of the two languages for different purposes. Some subjects may be taught in one language, and some in the other. This is the practice in certain parts of Wales. In describing the influences of such practices on a person's bilingualism it is important to determine which subjects are taught in which language. If one of the languages is used for religion, history, and literature, the influence is likely to be different than it would if this language were used to teach arithmetic, geography, and biology instead.[17]

3. Private tuition. Schooling may be a matter of private instruction, individually or in small groups. This may be in a language other than that of the community. The second language may be used as a medium of instruction or simply taught as a subject.

Some people may prefer to perfect their knowledge of the second language by engaging a private tutor in the belief that they thus have a longer period of direct contact with the language than they would otherwise have.

Finally, there is the bilingual who tries to improve his knowledge of the second language through self-instruction. This may involve the use of books and sound recordings (see below).

Mass media. – Radio, television, the cinema, recordings, newspapers, books, and magazines are powerful media in the maintenance of bilingualism. Access to these media may be the main factor in maintaining one of the languages of a bilingual, especially if his other language is the only one spoken in the area. Regular attendance at foreign film programmes and the daily reading of foreign books and magazines may be the only factors in maintaining a person's comprehension of a foreign language which he once knew. Reading is often the only contact that a person may have with his second language. It is also the most available.

Correspondence. – Regular correspondence is another way by which the bilingual may maintain his skill in the use of another language. He may, for business reasons, have to correspond regularly in a language other than the one he uses at home or at work. Or it may be family

[17] W. F. Mackey and J. A. Noonan, "An Experiment in Bilingual Education", *English Language Teaching*, 6 (1952), pp. 125-132.

reasons that give him an occasion to write or read letters in one of his languages. The fact that immigrants to the New World have been able to correspond regularly with friends and relatives in Europe is not to be neglected as a factor in the maintenance of their native languages.

Variables. – Contacts with each of the above areas may vary in duration, frequency, and pressure. They may also vary in the use of each language for comprehension (C) only, or for both comprehension and expression (E).

Duration. – The amount of influence of any area of contact on the bilingualism of the individual depends on the duration of the contact. A 40-year-old bilingual who has spent all his life in a foreign neighbourhood is likely to know the language better than one who has been there for only a few years. A language taught as a school subject is likely to give fewer contact hours than is one which is used as a medium of instruction.

Frequency. – The duration of contact is not significant, however, unless we know its frequency. A person who has spoken to his parents in a different language for the past twenty years may have seen them on an average of only a few hours a month, or he may have spoken with them on an average of a few hours a day. Frequency for the spoken language may be measured in average contact-hours per week or month; for the written language it may be measured in average number of words.

Pressure. – In each of the areas of contact, there may be a number of pressures which influence the bilingual in the use of one language rather than the other. These may be economic, administrative, cultural, political, military, historical, religious, or demographic.

1. Economic. For speakers of a minority language in an ethnic community, the knowledge of the majority language may be an economic necessity. Foreign parents may even insist on making the majority language that of the home, in an effort to prevent their children from becoming economically underprivileged. Contrariwise, economic pressure may favour the home language, especially if the mastery of it has become associated with some ultimate monetary advantage.

2. Administrative. Administrative workers in some areas are required to master a second language. A bilingual country may require that its civil servants be fluent in the official languages of the country. Some countries may require that foreign service personnel be capable of using the language of the country in which they serve. A few governments have been in the practice of granting an annual bonus to the civil

servant for each foreign language he succeeds in mastering or maintaining; this is the case in some branches of the German Civil Service.

3. Cultural. In some countries, it may be essential, for cultural reasons, for any educated person to be fluent in one or more foreign languages. Greek and Latin were long the cultural languages of the educated European. Today it is more likely to be French, English, or German. The quantity and quality of printed matter available in these languages constitute a cultural force which an educated person cannot afford to ignore.

4. Political. The use of certain languages may be maintained by the pressure of political circumstances. This may be due to the geographical contiguity of two countries or to the fact that they are on especially friendly terms. Or the pressure may be due to the influence of the political prestige of a great world power. Political dominance may result in the imposition of foreign languages, as is the case for certain colonial languages. After many years of such dominance the foreign colonial language may become the dominant one, develop a regional standard, and be used as the official language of the country.

5. Military. A bilingual who enters the armed forces of his country may be placed in situations which require him to hear or speak his second language more often than he otherwise would. People serving in a foreign army must learn something of the language which the army uses. The fact that two countries make a military treaty may result in large-scale language learning such as that witnessed in Allied countries during the Second World War. Military occupation has also resulted in second language learning, either by the populace, by the military, or by both.

6. Historical. Which languages the bilingual learns and the extent to which he must learn them may have been determined by past historical events. If the language of a minority has been protected by treaty, it may mean that the minority can require its children to be educated in their own language. The exact position of the languages may be determined by the past relations between two countries. The important position of English in India is attributable to the historical role of Great Britain in that country.

7. Religious. A bilingual may become fluent in a language for purely religious reasons. A person entering a religious order may have to learn Latin, Greek, Coptic, Sanskrit, Arabic, or Old Church Slavonic, depending on the religion, rite, or sect of the particular order into which he enters. Some languages, also for religious reasons, may be required in the schools which the bilingual may have attended; Latin and Hebrew are examples of such languages.

8. Demographic. The number of persons with whom the bilingual

has the likelihood of coming into contact is a factor in the maintenance of his languages. A language spoken by some five hundred million people will exert a greater pressure than one used by only a few thousand. But number is not the only fact; distribution may be equally important. Chinese, for example, may have a greater number of native speakers than does English; but the latter has a greater distribution, used, as it is, as an official and administrative language in all quarters of the globe.

Internal functions. – Bilingualism is not only related to external factors; it is also connected with internal ones. These include non-communicative uses, like internal speech, and the expression of intrinsic aptitudes, which influence the bilingual's ability to resist or profit by the situations with which he comes in contact.

Uses. – A person's bilingualism is reflected in the internal uses of each of his languages. These may be tabulated as in Table 3.

TABLE 3
Internal Uses

Uses	*Auto-Language*	
	A	B
Counting		
Reckoning		
Praying		
Cursing		
Dreaming		
Diary writing		
Note taking		

Some bilinguals may use one and the same language for all sorts of inner expression. This language has often been identified as the dominant language of the bilingual. But such is by no means always the case. Other bilinguals use different languages for different sorts of internal expression. Some count in one language and pray in another; others have been known to count in two languages but to be able to reckon only in one. It would be possible to determine these through a well-designed questionnaire.

Aptitude. – In describing bilingualism it is important to determine all those factors which are likely to influence the bilingual's aptitude in the use of his languages or which in turn may be influenced by it. These may be listed as follows:

1. Sex
2. Age
3. Intelligence
4. Memory
5. Language attitude
6. Motivation

Sex. – If sex is a factor in language development, as past research into the problem seems to indicate, it is also a factor in bilingualism (see note 9).

Age. – Persons who become bilingual in childhood may have characteristics of proficiency and usage different from those who become bilingual as adults. Studies of cases where two languages were learned simultaneously in childhood have given us some indication of the process (see notes 12, 13, 14, above). Although Leopold's study reveals an effort on the part of the child to weld two phoneme systems into one, it does not indicate any lasting effect on either language (see note 14). But it does show a great deal of forgetting on the part of the child. Indeed, the child's reputed ability to remember is matched by his ability to forget. For him, bilingualism may simply mean a transition period from one native language to another. Children can transfer from one mother-tongue to another in a matter of months. This has been demonstrated by Tits in his experiment with a six-year-old Spanish girl who was suddenly placed in a completely French environment and, after only 93 days, seems to have lost her Spanish completely; in less than a year, she had a knowledge of French equal to that of the neighbourhood children.[18]

The child's adaptability has been related to the physiology of the human brain. Penfield and other neurologists have put forth theories to explain the child's linguistic flexibility.[19] Before the age of nine, the child's brain seems particularly well suited to language learning, but after this age the speech areas become "progressively stiff" and the capacity to learn languages begins to decrease. Some experienced teachers and psychologists, however, have claimed that there is no decline in language-learning capacity up to the age of twenty-one.[20]

Intelligence. – We are here concerned more with the relation of intelligence to bilingualism than with the influence of bilingualism on intelligence.[21] A number of testable mental traits such as figure-grouping ability, number, space and pattern perception, and others have already been tested on groups of bilinguals (see note 9).

Although it seems safe to include intelligence as a factor in bilin-

[18] D. Tits, *Le mécanisme de l'acquisition d'une langue se substituant à la langue maternelle chez une enfant espagnole âgée de six ans* (Bruxelles, Veldeman, 1948), p. 36.

[19] W. Penfield and L. Roberts, *Speech and Brain-Mechanisms* (Princeton, Princeton University Press, 1959).

[20] M. West, "Bilingualism", *English Language Teaching*, 12 (1958), pp. 94-97.

[21] N. T. Darcy, "A Review of the Literature on the Effects of Bilingualism upon the Measurement of Intelligence", *Journal of Genetic Psychology*, 82 (1953), pp. 21-57.

gualism, we have as yet been unable to discover its relative importance. Experimental research into the problem has mostly been limited to selected samples of persons of the same intellectual level and has often been based on the assumption that the ability to speak is simply a motor-skill which can be measured by tests of imitation and reading aloud. One would expect intelligence to play some sort of role, nevertheless, in such a skill as comprehension, where a bilingual's reasoning ability and general knowledge should help him guess meanings from context.

Memory. – If memory is a factor in imitation, it is also a factor in bilingualism; for the auditory memory span for sounds immediately after hearing them is related to the ability to learn languages. An analogy may be taken from the learning of sound-codes like those used in telegraphy. It has been demonstrated that the span of auditory comprehension is the main difference between the beginner in telegraphy and the expert; whereas the beginner can handle only one word at a time, the expert can deal with ten, keeping them all in his memory before interpreting them.[22] As his degree of proficiency increases, the bilingual keeps more and more words in his memory before deciding on the meaning of an utterance. There is conflicting evidence, however, on the exact role of rote memory in language learning.

Attitude. – The attitude of a bilingual towards his languages and towards the people who speak them will influence his behaviour within the different areas of contact in which each language is used. It may in turn be influenced by his hearer's attitude towards him as a foreign speaker. In certain situations he may avoid using one of his languages because he is ashamed of his accent. In other situations he may prefer to use his second language because his first language may be that of an unpopular country or community. It has been said that some speakers of minority languages even harbour an attitude of disrespect toward their first language and an admiration for their second.

Because of such influences as these, the attitude of the speaker may be regarded as an important factor in the description of his bilingualism. The attitudes of bilinguals towards their languages have been tested directly by questionnaire and indirectly by having the bilinguals list traits of speakers whose recorded accent reveals their ethnic origin.[23]

Motivation. – It seems obvious that the motivation for acquiring the first language is more compelling than the motivation for learning a second. For once the vital purposes of communication have been achieved, the reasons for repeating the effort in another language are

[22] D. W. Taylor, "Learning Telegraphic Code", *Psychological Bulletin*, 40 (1943), pp. 461-487.

[23] W. E. Lambert et al., "Evaluation Reactions to Spoken Language", *Journal of Abnormal and Social Psychology*, 60 (1958), pp. 44-51.

less urgent. In the case of simultaneous childhood bilingualism, however, the need for learning both languages may be made equally compelling. Not so for the person who becomes bilingual as an adult. Yet a need or desire of the adult to master a second language may be strong enough to enable him to devote the necessary time and energy to the process of becoming bilingual.

ALTERNATION

The function of each language in total behaviour and the degree to which the bilingual and his hearers have mastered both languages determine the amount of alternation which takes place from one language to the other.

The readiness with which a bilingual changes from one language to the other depends on his fluency in each language and on its external and internal functions. There seems to be a difference in alternation, for example, between bilinguals brought up on Grammont's "une personne : une langue" formula and bilinguals conditioned at an early age to speak two different languages to the same person.[24]

Under what conditions does alternation from one language to another take place? What are the factors involved? The three main factors seem to be topic, person, and tension. Each of these may vary both the rate of alternation and the proportion of each language used in a given situation – oral or written. We may present the variables as in Table 4.

TABLE 3
Alternations

	Topics				*Persons*				*Tensions*			
	1	2	3	4	1	2	3	4	1	2	3	4
Rate												
Oral												
Written												
	A B	A B	A B	A B	A B	A B	A B	A B	A B	A B	A B	A B
Proportion:												
Oral												
Written												

If we examine the alternation in the speech or writings of bilinguals we notice that it may vary in both rate and proportion. The switch may

[24] M. E. Smith, "A Study of the Speech of Eight Bilingual Children of the Same Family", *Child Development*, 6 (1935), pp. 19-25.

occur only once, or it may take place every few sentences, within sentences, or within clauses. The rate may be measured by establishing a ratio between the number of units in the stretch of text examined and the number of switches which take place.

Alternation in the speech or writings of a bilingual will also vary in proportion. For example, a French-English bilingual when speaking English may, in a given situation, switch from time to time to French. But the amount of French used may be less than 5 per cent of the entire text. On the other hand, his interlocutor, who switches less often, but for longer stretches, may use as much as 50 per cent French in his replies.

Rate and proportion of alternation may vary greatly in the same individual according to the topic about which he is speaking, the person he is speaking to, and the tension of the situation in which he speaks. A German-English bilingual speaking in English to a close friend who he knows understands German may permit himself to lapse into German from time to time in order to be able to express himself with greater ease. On the other hand, when speaking to a person with whom he is less well acquainted he may avoid the use of German switches except when forced to speak about topics which his English does not adequately cover. Or his control of English may break down and he may switch frequently to German only when speaking in a state of tension due to excitement, anger, or fatigue.

INTERFERENCE

The foregoing characteristics of degree, function, and alternation determine the interference of one language with another in the speech of bilinguals. Interference is the use of features belonging to one language while speaking or writing another.

The description of interference must be distinguished from the analysis of language borrowing. The former is a feature of "parole"; the latter of "langue". The one is individual and contingent; the other is collective and systematic. In language borrowing we have to do with integration;[25] features of one language are used as if they were part of the other. These foreign features are used by monolingual speakers who may know nothing of the language from which such features originated. The loans, however, may be integrated into only one of the dialects of the language and not the others. If loan-words are integrated

[25] E. Haugen, *Bilingualism in the Americas: a bibliography and research guide* (University of Alabama, American Dialect Society 1956), p. 40. (See review by W. F. Mackey in *JCLA*, 4, pp. 94-99)

into the French of Switzerland, for example, they do not necessarily become part of the French of Belgium. And the loan-words of Belgium are not necessarily those of Canada; and in Canada, the loans current in Acadian are not necessarily those of the French of Quebec. Indeed, the integration of borrowed features may be limited to the language of a village community. A good example, of this may be found by studying the varieties of German spoken in the multi-lingual Banat, where German ethnic groups are scattered among non-German language groups speaking Hungarian, Serbian, and Rumanian. If we look at the use of the article among the Banat Germans we find that it may vary from village to village. One German village may use *die Butter*, while another village may use *der Butter*; one village may use *das Auto*, while another may use *der Auto*. In some cases, the borrowed feature may be integrated into the language of a section of a village. No matter how small the area concerned, a borrowed feature may be distinguished by its integration into the speech of the community.

In contradistinction to the consistency in use of borrowed features in the speech of the community is the vacillation in the use of foreign features by its bilingual individuals. In the speech of bilinguals the pattern and amount of interference is not the same at all times and under all circumstances. The interference may vary with the medium, the style, the register, and the context which the bilingual happens to be using.

The medium used may be spoken or written. Bilinguals seem to resist interference when writing to a friend more than they do when speaking to him.

Interference also varies with the style of discourse used – descriptive, narrative, conversational, etc. The type and amount of interference noted in the recounting of an anecdote may differ considerably from that noted in the give-and-take of everyday conversation.

Interference may also vary according to the social role of the speaker in any given case. This is what the Edinburgh School has called REGISTER.[26] A bilingual may make sure that all his words are French if he is broadcasting a French speech over the radio; but at the same time he may be quite unconscious of many cases of syntactic interference which have crept into his speech. If, however, he is telling the contents of the speech to his drinking partner, he may be far less particular about interlarding his account with non-French words; yet the proportion of syntactic interference may be considerably less.

Within each register, there are a number of possible contexts, each of which may affect the type and amount of interference. The bilingual

[26] I wish to thank M. A. K. Halliday and J. C. Catford for introducing me to this term and to the important variable it represents in language description.

may be speaking to the above drinking partner in the presence of his superiors or in the company of his colleagues.

In each of these contexts the interference may vary from situation to situation. A French-Canadian business man just back from a sales conference in Atlantic City will tell his friends about it with more English interference immediately upon his return than will be noticed when he recounts the same events three months later.

In the last analysis, interference varies from text to text. It is the text, therefore, within a context of situation used at a specific register in a certain style and medium of a given dialect, that is the appropriate sample for the description of interference. Since each text may vary in length, this also must be taken into account if, in addition to the different sorts of interference, we are to get an idea of the proportion of each sort and the total percentage of interference.

In each text, or sample of speech, we analyse the interference of only one of the languages with the predominant language or dialect. If the predominant language is French, we look for elements which are foreign to the particular dialect of French used. We look for the elements which have not been integrated into the dialect.

The first thing to do, therefore, in analysing a case of interference in a text is to identify its model[27] in the dialect of the language from which it comes. This model may be from the cultural, semantic, lexical, grammatical, phonological, phonetic, or graphic levels of the dialect. At each of these levels, what is imported may be a separate item or an arrangement of items; in other words, it may be a unit or a structure. By discovering whether the imported form is a unit or a structure and then identifying the level to which it belongs, we are able to locate the TYPE of interference. This may occur once in the text; or it may recur many times; each time it recurs it is a TOKEN of interference and should be indicated as such.

After having identified the model in the interfering language we compare it with its replica in the text. This enables us to determine the sort of substitution which has taken place. It may be a substitution in level or in structure. A substitution in level takes place when, for example, the foreign word is modified at the phonological level by an adaptation of its phonemes to those of the text. A substitution in structure takes place when a structure in the model becomes a unit in the replica, or a unit in the model becomes a structure in the replica.

These interrelated factors appear in Table 5 in tabulated form.

If we examine Table 5 we notice that it distinguishes two main treat-

[27] The terms "model" and "replica" were established by Haugen to distinguish the feature introduced from the other language (the model) from its rendition into the language being used (the replica). See Haugen, *Bilingualism* ..., p. 39.

TABLE 4

Interference

Language ....

Dialect ....

Medium g..............................

Style ....

Context ....

Situation ....

Length of Text ....

A—B ....√

B—A ....

Levels	*Importation*				*Substitution*										*Proportion*	
	Unit		Structure		Units					Structures					Percentages	
	Type	Token	Type	Token	C	S	L	G	P	C	S	L	G	P	Units	Structures
1. Cultural																
Phenomena																
Experience																
2. Semantic																
3. Lexical																
4. Grammatical																
Parts of Speech																
Grammatical categories																
Function																
Forms																
5. Phonological																
Intonation																
Rhythm																
Catenation																
Articulation																

ments of interference: the sort of material which the bilingual imports into his speech (importation) and what he does with it (substitution).[28]

The importation columns list only the units and structures of the text which are attributable exclusively to the bilingual's use of another language. In each case it is necessary to identify the model and to compare it, not with the replica, but with all possible equivalents in the dialect of the monolingual community to which the text under analysis belongs. If the text is in the French of Quebec, any English elements are compared with equivalents in the French of the same area, including English loans that have already been integrated into the speech of the area. Only in this way can we distinguish between integration and interference, between the foreign elements existing in the dialect and those attributable to the speaker, between the influences of language contact in "langue", and the effects of bilingualism on "parole".

The description of interference requires three procedures: (1) the discovery of exactly what foreign element is introduced by the speaker into his speech; (2) the analysis of what he does with it – his substitutions and modifications; and (3) a measurement of the extent to which foreign elements replace native elements.

The first of these procedures consists in identifying the foreign element, checking it with its counterparts in the monolingual speech of the area, and discovering the model in the foreign language responsible for the interference. This procedure depends on an accurate and complete description of the two languages involved and on an analysis of the differences between them. Unfortunately there are very few differential descriptions available;[29] most of those in existence are far too sketchy for the sort of analysis of the cultural, semantic, lexical, grammatical, and phonological levels which we shall now exemplify.

Cultural interference. – Although cases of interference may be found in the speech of the bilingual, their causes may be found, not in his other language, but in the culture which it reflects. The foreign element may be the result of an effort to express new phenomena or new experience in a language which does not account for them.

Phenomena include the result of the introduction of unfamiliar objects, obliging the bilingual speaker to use whatever resources his two languages put at his disposal. He may have to talk about such things as hot-dogs and cornflakes, for which the dialect he is speaking may have no equivalent. Such unit phenomena are to be distinguished from the structure or patterning of phenomena occasioned, for example, by the

[28] Here again I am following Haugen's terminology. See also his "Analysis of Linguistic Borrowing", *Lang.*, 26 (1950), p. 212.

[29] W. W. Gage, *Contrastive Studies in Linguistics: a bibliographical checklist* (Washington, Center for Applied Linguistics, 1961).

introduction of a new technology such as a railway system, or a culture pattern based on the automobile, with its motels, filling stations, and curb-service.

In addition to new phenomena, cultural interference includes new types of experience such as the introduction of the custom of greeting and thanking into the speech habits of Amerindian bilinguals. Here again we must distinguish between the units of experience and their structure. For example, both German and English have behaviour units for greeting and thanking; but these are patterned differently. The German *Bitte*, for instance, includes not only English *Please* but parts of English *Thanks*, *Not at all*, *Pardon*, or silence. A case of cultural interference in the behavioural structure of experience might consequently appear as follows in the speech of X, a German-English bilingual:

	English Counterpart	German Model	English Replica
X.	*Here's a seat.*	*Bitte.*	*Please.*
Y.	*Thanks!*	*Danke!*	*Thanks!*
X.	(silence)	*Bitte.*	*Please.*

Semantic interference. – Cultural interference due to new phenomena or experience is to be distinguished from semantic interference, which is due to familiar phenomena and experience being classified or structured differently in the other language. The classic example here is the division of the colour spectrum into units. The bilingual speaker has a single experience of colour, but his two languages may have a different number of colour units, some of which may overlap. If the speaker is a Welsh-English bilingual, he will have one unit in Welsh but two units in English for blue and green (= Welsh *glas*) and grey and brown (= Welsh *llwyd*).[30] If he is a French-English bilingual he may use *pain brun* (E. *brown bread*) for *pain bis*, and *papier brun* (E. *brown paper*) for *papier gris*.[31] And if he is an English-Spanish bilingual he may be tempted to use *oficina* (E. *office*) for a doctor's office (*consulta*), a lawyer's office (*bufete*), an individual office (*despacho*), and a group office (*oficina*).

In addition to the incorporation of new units of classification into the speech of bilinguals, there is the introduction of new semantic structures. Even though the semantic units may be the same in both languages, a foreign way of combining them may be introduced as a new semantic structure. Both English and French, for example, have com-

[30] J-P. Vinay and J. Darbelnet, *Stylistique comparée du français et de l'anglais* (Paris, Didier; Montréal: Beauchemin, 1958), p. 261.

[31] J. Darbelnet, "La couleur en français et en anglais", *Journal des Traducteurs*, 2 (1957), pp. 157-161.

parable units for hat (*chapeau*), talk (*parler*), and through (*à travers*); but when the bilingual speaker uses the figurative *Il parle à travers son chapeau* he introduces into his speech a foreign semantic structure based on the English model *He's talking through his hat*. Similarly, when the German-English bilingual says that *Winter is before the door*, or *He was laughing in his fist*, he is using in his English speech semantic structures based on the German models *Winter steht vor der Tür* in place of the English *Winter is around the corner*, and *Er hat sich ins Fäustchen gelacht* in place of the English *He was laughing up his sleeve*.

Lexical interference. – Lexical interference involves the introduction of foreign forms into the speech of the bilingual, either as units or as structures. We must here distinguish between lexical items which have been integrated into the dialect (loan words) and those which occur in the utterances of a particular bilingual. A Belgian using the word *goal-keeper* in a French-language sports broadcast, or a Frenchman using *goal* (for the same person) may be using an integrated English loanword; while a Canadian French-English bilingual who listens to his hockey broadcasts in French might prefer the term *gardien de but*, although his compatriot who listens to the same broadcasts in English might from time to time use the word *goalie*, with an anglicized pronunciation. It is this latter case that would constitute an instance of interference.

Resistance to lexical interference results in the elimination of integrated loans, since the bilingual is not always able to make the distinction between what is "accepted" and what is not. It is in this way that bilinguals contribute to the "purification" of the language. The monolingual, on the other hand, being unable to identify the foreign loans is unable to eliminate them. The use of *gardien de but* and *fin de semaine* for integrated loans like *goal* and *week-end* may be instances of resistance to interference. A study of the vocabulary of French sports broadcasts on the national radio networks of France and Canada might well reveal that the latter's conscious resistance to lexical interference results in a sports vocabulary which is less anglicized.

What applies to isolated lexical units also applies to the grouping of such items into collocations. Here again we must distinguish between integration and interference. An English-French bilingual who does all his shopping in French may, when speaking English at home, use such lexical structures as *gigot d'agneau* instead of *leg of lamb*. Yet this French collocation may never enter the speech of the English-speaking community; indeed it may never be used by any other English-French bilingual.

Grammatical interference. – Grammatical interference includes the introduction into the speech of bilinguals of units and structures of foreign parts of speech, grammatical categories, and function forms.

The interference may involve the creation of new items belonging to a different part of speech. For example, when the French-Englihs bilingual says *Je n'ai pas pu le contacter* he is making a new verb out of the French noun *contacte* on the model of the American *I wasn't able to contact him.*

Two languages often have the same parts of speech, but they may differ considerably in the way they put them together into structures. This is one of the domains of interference of which bilingual speakers are most unconscious. And the extent of such interference varies greatly from region to region. Thus Acadian bilinguals tend to put more adjectives before the noun in French than do French speakers in other parts of Canada. Some Acadians who can identify these English structures may tend to resist them. But the more complex structures will escape the notice of even the most perceptive Probus. The bilingual who says *une des plus grande jamais vue dans la région* may not notice that he is using the English model *one of the biggest ever seen in the area.*

Grammatical interference also includes the introduction of features from different grammatical categories. The simplest of these is in the category of gender. The bilingual speaker may tend to carry over the gender of one language into that of another, as when the Serbian-German bilingual uses *der* or *dieser Zwiebel* on the model of the Serbian *taj luk.*

Structural interference in grammatical categories has to do with the use of concord and government. When an English-French bilingual says *Vos montagnes sont beaux*, his indifference to concord is influenced by the fact that English has no system of agreement between noun and adjective.

The third type of grammatical interference concerns the function forms of the two languages. Function forms may be free or bound. Free forms include such units as prepositions, conjunctions, determinatives, and so on. A French-English bilingual who says *sur le comité, dans quinze jours*, and *sous étude* is probably modelling these prepositions on those of English, as they appear in such expressions as *on the committee, in fifteen days*, and *under study.* Free forms appear in a number of compulsory structures in some languages which require such things as the marking of classes of nouns by determinatives. This is the case for English, the use of whose function forms differs from that of French. So that when a French-English bilingual uses the article in such expressions as *on the page five*, he is applying the French model *à la page cinq.* Whereas when the Russian-English bilingual leaves out the article in an English sentence like *Where is meeting of committee?* his model is the Russian *Gdje sobranie komitjeta?*

Bound function forms, which result from such inflectional and derivational processes as affixation, internal change, zero modification, and reduplication, are also subject to bilingual interference. When a French-English bilingual says *Those Sunday driver there block my way and I couldn't see*, he is being influenced by the lack of inflected /-s/ for plurals in spoken French. The structure of bound forms may also be carried over by bilingual speakers from one language to another, both in their order and in their boundness.[32] Hungarian-German bilinguals, for example, tend to carry over the patterns of the structure of the Hungarian prepositional prefixes into their German, as the following attested individual instance will illustrate:

German Counterpart

1. *Hat er es zerbrochen? Ja.*
2. *Haben Sie es gesagt? Ja.*
3. *Hat er es bekommen? Ja.*

Hungarian Model	German Replica
1. *Megmondta? Meg.*	1. *Hat er es zerbrochen? Zer.*
2. *Kiment? Ki.*	2. *Haben Sie es gesagt? Ge.*
3. *Bejött? Be.*	3. *Hat er es bekommen? Be.*

Phonological interference. – Phonological interference affects the units and structures of intonation, rhythm, catenation, and articulation.

Intonation. – Of all phonological features, intonation is often the most persistent in interference and the most subtle in influence. Welsh and Anglo-Indian bilinguals may often be identified as such only by their intonation, since both the range of their tone units and their patterns are carried over into English.

The tone-groups, or structures of intonation, are more readily identified as causes of interference than are the individual tone units. When the English-French bilingual suggests *C'est ˈtrès ˈutil*, he is carrying over into his French the implicative intonation structure of English as used suggestively in such sentences as *It's ˈvery ˈuseful.*

Rhythm. – Not all languages have the same number of stress levels. A speaker of a language with no tertiary level is likely to leave this out of his speech in other languages. Identification of interference at this level, however, is hampered by lack of research findings into the nature and number of stress units.

More is known about rhythm structures, or stress-patterns, as they

[32] W. F. Mackey, "Bilingualism and Linguistic Structure", *Culture*, 14 (1953), pp 143-149.

are often called. Interference in stress patterning can readily be spotted. A French-English bilingual who uses *I think ˈso* (for *I ˈthink so*) and *examinaˈtion paˈper* or *examiˈnation ˈpaper* (for *examiˈnation pˈaper*) is obviously transferring his French stress-pattern into English. If interference in stress-patterning is easy to identify, it is not always easy to explain. When the above bilingual also pronounces *deveˈlopment* for *deˈvelopment*, the replica is as far removed from the model as it is from the counterpart.

Catenation. – Catenation has to do with the linking together of speech sound into the chain of speech. This includes the units specially used for linking and separating sounds – units of junction and syllabation; it also includes the structures used for this purpose. These differ from language to language.

Like other phonological features, catenation is subject to interference in the speech of bilinguals. This includes interference in junction and syllabation.

Junction. – Interference in junction may take the form of the incorporation of foreign junction units into the chain of speech. When a German-English bilingual says /meʔ ai ʔ ask hau ʔ its dʌn./ (*May I ask how it's done?*) he is introducing into his English the glottal junction unit of his German, that is, the German "Grenzsignal" (Trubetzkoy). Conversely, if an English-German bilingual says /viliʲ ist grauʷ abə niçt alt/ (*Willi ist grau, aber nicht alt*) he is placing into the German junction points the palatal and velar glides of his English.

Interference in the mechanism of junction involves the changes which take place when two units are linked. It also involves the direction of such changes. For example, both French and English use assimilation as a linking mechanism, but not in the same direction; so that when a French-English bilingual speaks English he tends to introduce the regressive assimilation of French while ignoring the progressive assimilation of English. Thus he pronounces the sentence *Take this bag, not those ones*, as /teg ðɪz bæg, nəd ðoz wʌns/ instead of /tek ðɪs bæg, nət ðoz wʌnz/.

Syllabation. – The division of the chain of speech into syllable units may not be the same in both of the languages spoken by the bilingual. A French-English bilingual may tend to make two syllables out of the English monosyllable *tire* /taiɚ/ and pronounce it /tajœ:r/. When such adaptations become loanwords, however, they sometimes are phonematically homophonous with native words. In such cases the bilingual may endow certain allophonic differences with the distinctive function of phonemes, so that *tire* is pronounced /tajœ:r/ and *tailleur* is pronounced /tɑjœ:r/ or /tɔjœ:r/.

In syllabic structure the extent of interference depends on the degree of difference between the languages spoken by the bilingual. This may be small, as it is between English and French; or it may be a much wider difference, as it is between English and Japanese. So that when a Japanese-English bilingual says /gurando/ for English *ground*, he is replacing the English syllabic structure /CCVCC/ by the more familiar Japanese /CVCVCV/; similarly, when he says /sisutema/-/CVCVCVCV/ for English *system* /CVCCVC/.

Articulation. – This includes many of the features of interference, popularly identified as comprising a foreign accent. The foreign element may be a unit of articulation, as when a German-English bilingual uses the German velar fricative or uvular trill /R/, as in *ready* pronounced /Redi/, instead of the English retroflex. Or the interference may be in the structure of these units of articulation, as when the /-gst-/ structure of English phonemes is replaced by /-gɛst-/ in the speech of certain Spanish-English bilinguals who pronounce *drugstore* as /drɔgɛstɔr/.

Allophones as well as phonemes may be responsible for cases of interference. This is the case when English [ɫ] is introduced into post-vocalic positions in French. An allophone may exist as such in both the languages; or it may exist as an allophone in one and as a phoneme in the other. These may differ, however, in the position in which each may occur. Thus the nasal trio /m, n, ŋ/ occurs in both English and Spanish; the difference is that, while they all occur finally in English, only /-n/ occurs finally in Spanish. This difference produces interference in the speech of Spanish-English bilinguals which results in a tendency to reduce to /rʌn/ or /rɔn/, for example, the pronunciation of the three English words *rum*, *run*, and *rung*. Haugen has elegantly formulated such transfers as E/-m, -n, -ŋ > -n/S.

The identification of foreign units and structures is one thing; the description of what the bilingual does with them is something else. This is the second procedure in the description of interference. It involves the analysis and classification of the different types of substitution made by the speaker.

In introducing a foreign element into his speech, a bilingual may use it exactly as he would in the foreign language, or he may modify it in two ways: (i) by changes in structure, (ii) by changes in level.

The change in structure may consist in taking a structure from one language and using it as a unit in the other, or it may consist in taking a unit from one language and using it as a structure in the other. For example, Sicilian-Americans may use the English collocation *son of a gun* as the unit adjective *sonamagonga* in their Italian speech, or reduce highly frequent sentences like *I don't know* and *What's the matter* to units like *aironò* and *vazzumàra.*[33] Contrariwise, a unit in one language may be used as a structure in the other. For example, a unit like the monosyllabic English word *club* may be rendered by a Chinese-English bilingual as three units /$kü_1$-$lö_4$-pu_4/, which, if used in Chinese, would be a structure of three signs meaning "all-joy-section".[34]

Second, the bilingual may change the characteristics of the foreign item at one or more of the following levels: cultural, semantic, lexical, grammatical, or phonological. Only a few examples of the many possibilities may be given here. Let us take the most obvious – the modification of the foreign words. Their introduction into the text (spoken or written) is accounted for under the "importation" column; it now remains for us to list their modifications under the "substitution" column.

The bilingual may modify the foreign word or collocation by changing its cultural content, its meaning, its grammatical role, or its pronunciation. An example of a change in cultural content is the use of cursing and other such expressions as ordinary nouns or content words in the other language, as when the English expression *God damn it* is used as a French verb *godamer.* This is to be distinguished from a modification in semantic content such as takes place when a Canadian French-English bilingual uses the English word *sport* in French only in the sense of agreeable, cordial, or fair-dealing as when he says *Il est bien sport!* But the same speaker is altering the foreign word at the grammatical level when he says *Il faut bien que je le toffe encore quelques semaines* (I'll just have to put up with it for another couple of weeks), where the English adjective *tough* is used as a French verb (*toffer*).

Finally, the foreign word may undergo changes at the phonological level. This occurs regularly in the speech of certain types of bilinguals. Like other sorts of interference, this is often the result of what Weinreich has called interlingual identification,[35] the practice of bilinguals of equating features of one language with those of the other. English speakers of French, for example, will tend to equate the French /e/ with their native /ei/. This equation is applied whenever words like *cours d'été* are pronounced /ku:ɚ dei tei/. The bilingual speaker, however, will not necessarily modify the pronunciation of all the foreign words he introduces. The above bilingual who introduced *sport* and *tough*

[33] A. Menarini, "L'italo-americano degli Stati Uniti", *Lingua Nostra*, 1 (1939), pp. 154-156.

[34] H. Frei, "Monosyllabisme et polysyllabisme dans les emprunts linguistiques", *Bulletin de la Maison franco-japonaise*, 8 (1936), p. 79.

[35] U. Weinreich, *Languages in Contact: Findings and problems* (New York, Linguistic Circle of New York, 1953), p. 7.

into his French may well pronounce the first as in English, complete with vocalic *r*, and the second as in French, as [t̪ɔf].

The phonological analysis of foreign words must not be confused with the analysis of foreign accents. This latter begins at the phonological level. When speaking his second language, the bilingual may treat all or some of the foreign phonetic features in terms of those of his first language. In describing what he does we must determine how many of these are changed and the extent to which each is modified. The modification may take the form of equating two distinctive elements of the second language with one distinctive element in the first, as when a French-English bilingual pronounces both English /ʌ/ and English /ɑ/ as /ɔ/, making both *nut* and *knot* homophonous; or he may classify both /d/ and /ð/ as /d̪/, reducing *udder* and *other* to the same pronunciation. The modification may also take the form of the introduction into one language of distinctions which are necessary only in the other, resulting in such effects as the staccato impression created by certain German bilinguals. Third, he may rearrange the features of the second language on the model of his first, as when the German-English bilingual aspirates and devoices all his initial plosives, pronouncing *building* as [p^hildiŋ]. These three types of substitution have been variously called dephonemization, phonemization, and transphonemization (Jakobson) or under-differentiation, overdifferentiation, and reinterpretation (Weinreich).

For the ultimate analysis of what constitutes interference in pronunciation, however, we must go deeper than the phonological level. We can only get a complete picture of what happens by resorting to the use of instrumental phonetics. For such features as the lack of synchronization and variations in muscular tension noted in the speech of certain bilinguals may well be attributable to the habitual use of two languages.

It seems likely that the measurable differences in range of articulatory movement, latitude of variation, distribution of articulatory energy, and synchronization of phonetic variables may become basic elements in the study of interference. A person, for example, whose first language is one with a narrow range of articulatory movement – a language like English, for instance, is likely to narrow the wider articulatory range of a language like German whenever he attempts to speak it. Similarly with the relative latitude of variation, distribution of articulatory tension, and synchronization of different speech movements.[36]

[36] I am grateful to Georges Straka for giving me evidence of mutual French-Czech interference which could be resolved only by the use of instrumental techniques. During his term as visiting professor in the experimental phonetics laboratory of Laval, he demonstrated techniques of analysis which will permit the realization of our plans for an instrumental study of phonetic interference.

The synchronizing of voicing and closure seems to differ from language to language. An example of the extent to which languages may differ may be seen by comparing the amount of voicing of the /b/ in German, English, Spanish, French, and Russian. A bilingual who has a /b/ in his first language which is voiced during only half of the closure time may tend to devoice part of the /b/ of his second language which monolinguals pronounce almost entirely voiced. This sort of interference may be illustrated thus:

	Russian Counterpart	German Model	Russian Replica
Closure:	————————	————————	————————
Voice:	————————	————	—————

If the text analysed, however, is based not on the spoken but on the written form of the language, we will have to look for evidence of another sort of interference – graphic interference, the transfer of writing habits from one language to the other. This may take the form of differences in script and differences in spelling. A Serbian-German bilingual with no knowledge of the Roman alphabet may be faced with the alternative of writing his second language in Cyrillic. The use of a foreign writing system may become standardized, however, as is the case when Yiddish is written in Hebrew characters.

The most usual form of graphic interference seems to be in the realm of spelling. The presence of a great number of cognate words in English and French encourages bilinguals to transfer the spelling from one language to the other or to adopt spellings which appear in neither language. Some bilinguals will confuse such pairs as *homage* and *hommage*, *rhythm* and *rythme*, *development* and *développement*.

The third procedure in the analysis of interference is a quantitative one. For it is necessary to know, not only the sort of interference which takes place, but also the extent of such interference.

If 10 per cent of a text is constituted of imported elements, it obviously represents a degree of interference greater than that of a text which reveals only 2 per cent. To determine such proportions, we count all cases of interferences (total tokens) and calculate what percentage of the total text these represent. This gives us our first, rough picture of the amount of interference in the text. But this is not sufficient and may even be misleading. A text dealing with some subject where the same foreign technical term comes up again and again – say 20 tokens – indicates less interference than does a text in which different foreign terms, 20 different types, occur each only once. We must therefore calculate, not only the total tokens, but also the total types.

Finally, we want to know not only the total amount of interference, but where it predominates. We therefore must calculate the type-token figures for each level, distinguishing the units from the structures. This is indicated in the final column of the interference table. Other relationships within the text may be discovered by the application of mathematical procedures for type-token calculations, which have now been developed for the use of linguists.[37]

CONCLUSION

Bilingualism cannot be described within the science of linguistics; we must go beyond. Linguistics has been interested in bilingualism only in so far as it could be used as an explanation for changes in a language, since language, not the individual, is the proper concern of this science. Psychology has regarded bilingualism as an influence on mental processes. Sociology has treated bilingualism as an element in culture conflict. Pedagogy has been concerned with bilingualism in connection with school organization and media of instruction. For each of these disciplines bilingualism is incidental; it is treated as a special case or as an exception to the norm. Each discipline, pursuing its own particular interests in its own special way, will add from time to time to the growing literature on bilingualism (see bibliographies in Haugen, note 25, Weinreich, note 35, and Jones.[38] But it seems to add little to our understanding of bilingualism as such, with its complex psychological, linguistic, and social interrelationships.

What is needed, to begin with, is a perspective in which these interrelationships may be considered. What I have attempted in this study is to give an idea of the sort of perspective that is needed. In order to imagine it, it was necessary to consider bilingualism as an individual rather than a group phenomenon. This made possible a better and more detailed analysis of all that it entails; and the object of our analysis appeared as a complex of interrelated characteristics varying in degree, function, alternation, and interference. By providing a framework of analysis for each of these, we hope to have contributed to a more accurate description. For this to be complete, however, there are three remaining steps.

First, we have to test our frameworks through extensive use in the description of a variety of cases of individual bilingualism. I plan to

[37] G. Herdan, *Type-Token Mathematics: A Textbook of Mathematical Linguistics* (The Hague, Mouton, 1960).

[38] I. Jones, *Bilingualism: A bibliography with special reference to Wales* (Aberystwyth, University College, 1960).

provide samples of these in the near future; but I hope that others may also be tempted to do the same so as to be able to criticize, modify, and perhaps expand the present versions until we arrive at some recognized procedure for treating each framework. Second, we must discover the extent to which factors in each framework need to be correlated with factors in the others. Finally, we must quantify those factors which remain unquantified so as to arrive at a method for the complete description of bilingualism.

From *Canadian Journal of Linguistics*, 7 (1962), 51-85. Reprinted by permission.

Section VI

LANGUAGE MAINTENANCE AND LANGUAGE SHIFT

Roman Jakobson

THE BEGINNING OF NATIONAL SELF-DETERMINATION IN EUROPE

The origins and the development of the national idea in Europe have been in recent years, particularly since the first World War, a favorite topic of culturo-historical studies. These studies have traced the gradual movement of European peoples toward national self-determination, and have described as normal the development from a vague feeling of warring tribal solidarity to a more conscious patriotism which customarily crystallizes around the prince, the king, in brief, the sovereign. According to these studies, during the twelfth and thirteenth centuries national culture was more and more emphasized; the claims of national language increased and finally reached a culmination in the Reformation.

This historical schema is usually considered as the common European pattern for the birth and growth of the national idea. But, in reality, such a Pan-European evolutional scheme is a pure fiction, a hasty generalization which is in accord with the facts only in the history of those European peoples who belong entirely to the occidental political and cultural world. This one-sided schema has to be substantially revised in dealing with the history of the peoples who were at least temporarily influenced by the French Empire, by the Byzantine cultural radiation.

Only by taking account of such cardinal differences between these western and eastern European influences, can we understand the dynamics of European national and linguistic problems and their historical consequences. National and linguistic problems have been among the most pertinent and vital motive forces of European history, and it is necessary to understand their roots if we are to comprehend the foundations of the old and the new Europe. In this connection we have to grasp and to keep in mind the peculiarity of the eastern European culturo-historical development. We must do this not merely for the study of this branch in itself but because the east of Europe is not a unit hermetically sealed and isolated; it is an integral part of the whole European continent. There were and are many interrelations and interpenetrations between the east and west which are of great consequence for both. A clear knowledge of each with its distinctive features is really indispensable for a serious, capable approach to the history of Europe in general.

It is a difficult task to fix exactly the boundaries of two related cultural areas. Generally they are tied by intermediate links. After the beginning of the Middle Ages we may envisage all the European peoples east of Charlemagne's empire as peoples of eastern Europe. Thus the eastern European area comprises all the Slavic and Baltic peoples, all the Finno-Ugrian peoples of Europe, and, besides the southern Slavs, the other peoples of the Balkan peninsula as well.[1]

Among the new peoples who did not participate in the ancient culture and who still are on the historical scene, the Slavs were the first in eastern Europe to join the Christian culture and to create a written literature in the vernacular. In eastern Europe the Slavs were the first and the only ethnic unit to start a new national cultural language in the early Middle Ages.

In this respect the Slavic case is so peculiar and so different from the usual occidental pattern of cultural history that it really merits a special, unprejudiced examination, the more so as until recently there persisted a tendency artificially to fit the Slavic case into the western scheme. Let us recall certain cardinal facts, which for the most part remain undervalued or misunderstood.

In the ninth century, when with the downfall of Charlemagne's supranational empire the first outlines of the later national states loomed in Europe, there arose also the first historic Slavic empire governed by Slavs, the first Czechoslovak state known under the name of Great Moravia. Toward the second half of the ninth century this empire attained a period of high political, economical and cultural prosperity. Great Moravia embraced not only the domain of modern Czechoslovakia, that is Moravia proper, Bohemia and Slovakia, but also a considerable part of modern Austria and Hungary, which then also were inhabited by Slavs. To the southeast Great Moravia reached to the boundaries of Bulgaria, at that time a large Turco-Slavic state; to the north she dominated some Polish and Sorbian regions. Great Moravia proper and particularly the borderland between modern Moravia and

[1] As to medieval Scandinavia, its cultural position and its attitude in relation to the Roman and the Byzantine world is so peculiar that the question would demand quite a special study.

Slovakia was the scene where, for the first time in Czechoslovak and in all Slavic history, there arose in the sixties of the ninth century a prose and poetry and even a liturgy using the national language. The sixties of the ninth century brought not only the birth of Slavic literature, but also the first formulation of the national idea in Czechoslovak and in all Slavic history.

About 863 Saint Constantine-Cyril and his brother Methodius began their apostolic work in Great Moravia. First of all, Constantine made a Slavonic translation of liturgic texts and of the Gospel for the use of his Moravian parish. To this he appended a poetic foreword, also in Slavonic. Besides some fragments, this foreword of about a hundred verses is the only remnant of Constantine's poetic work. Thus the history of Slavic and particularly Czechoslovak literature is initiated with an exalted eulogy glorifying national letters:

Now hear with your understanding!
Thus hear, Slavic people!
Hear the Word, for it came from the Lord:
The Word, which feeds human souls,
The Word, which strengthens the heart and the mind,
This Word, ready for the cognition of God!
As without light there will be no joy,
For the eye sees all God's creation
But all appears without beauty–
So every soul deprived of letters
Who is ignorant of the Scriptures,
The Law revealing divine paradise!
What ear, dumb
To thunder-peal can fear God?
How can nostrils, which smell not flowers,
Sense the divine miracle?
And the mouth, which tastes not sweetness,
Makes man like unto stone.
And moreover, a soul, deprived of letters,
Grows numb in human beings!
And in considering all this, brethren,
We bring you counsel
Capable of freeing all humanity
From bestial life and iniquity.
Ye, who list the Word in foreign tongue,
Unreasonable to reason,
Ye have to hear more than the mere voice of a copper bell.
And therefore Saint Paul has taught:
I had rather speak five words with my understanding
That I might teach others also,
Than ten thousand words in an unknown tongue. . . .

The great Slavic poet, Constantine the Philosopher (Cyril), develops his subject further. He says that people without books in their own language are naked; he compares them to a body which, deprived of its proper food, rots and infects everything about it. In a subtle play on words, the poet deplores the inexpressible misery of peoples who, speaking with the Lord in a tongue meaningless to them, cannot tell Him of their distress.

We look in vain for a similar work in western mediaeval literatures. This poem, by eloquently asserting the leading role of comprehension in the spiritual life of every people, would directly impose its vernacular upon every people as a sacred right and duty. It contains in brief the pivotal ideology of Czechoslovak and even all Slavic mediaeval literature; it is a striking expression of the spirit of this literature. Particularly in the first, the Old-Church-Slavonic, period of Czechoslovak culture – from the ninth to the eleventh century – are the views mentioned by Constantine-Cyril thoroughly developed.

How is it that this beautiful and original poem, preserved in several old manuscripts and printed in some philological publications, has nevertheless remained almost unknown even to students of Slavic history and literature? How is it that neither this poem nor other similar Slavic documents of the Early Middle Ages have been utilized for the study of mediaeval ideology? It is a strange case, but unfortunately such paradoxical instances are frequent enough in Slavic historiography; foreign schemes were borrowed to interpret the Slav's own past. If the facts of this past did not fit into the scheme, so much the worse for the facts: discordant facts often were kept in the shadow. Thus, in particular, the ninth century declarations of the rights of peoples contradicted sharply the conventional history of nationalism and were so treated. Moreover, it was inadmissible to suppose Slavic initiative in cultural advance because, according to the unvarying German viewpoint, the historic role of the Slavs was merely to strive to imitate their western neighbors and to be completely in their tow. For instance, only some fifteen years ago, even a Czech philosopher, E. Rádl, wrote: "I cannot believe that Constantine and Methodius advanced the revolutionary principle that it is necessary to understand the liturgy. . . . Thus they would be Luther's forerunners," – the philosopher remarks ironically.[2] But such unfounded and tendentious reasonings do not stand against the authentic historical sources. It is sufficient to recall, for instance, Constantine's diatribe against the revilers of Slavic worship which was

[2] "It is not easy to comprehend the psychology of this *Don Quixote of Czech philosophy*", the eminent Belgian mediaevalist, H. Gregoire, truthfully observes: "Would it be a Protestant mysticism which does not dare to take something away from the glory of Luther as an original innovator?" (*Renaissance* I, [New York, 1943], p. 666.)

reproduced in his reliable *Life*, written in Great Moravia shortly after his death – probably by his brother Methodius.

Constantine the Philosopher (Cyril) reasoned thus: "Does not the rain sent by the Lord fall equally on everyone? Does not the sun shine equally for the whole world? Do we not all equally breathe the air? Do you not feel shame at authorizing only three languages and condemning other peoples to blindness and deafness? Tell me, do you think that God is helpless and cannot bestow equality, or that he is envious and will not give it?" But there are those who do not want to understand this simple truth, Constantine argues, and for them he adds numerous quotations from the Holy Scripture, particularly from Saint Paul who became the mainstay for the doctrine of the Slavic apostles and their followers. Constantine was the first to recognize with acute penetration the vital importance of the first Epistle to the Corinthians for the idea of equality.

Equal rights – both of nations and of languages – is the leading principle of the Great Moravian spiritual heritage. As a Czech legend of the tenth century relates, Constantine posed the polemic question to the western adversaries of the Slavic liturgy: "If everybody has to glorify the Lord, why do you, select fathers, prevent me from saying mass in Slavic whereas God created this language perfect alike as the other tongues?" And because the Mass and the Church were considered as most sacred in the mediaeval hierarchy of values, so the national language, too, became consecrated by entering into the Mass – and the nation unified by this language was consecrated in its turn. Liturgy and church became national – not in a way opposing the Universal Church – and nation was raised to a sublime sacred value; and the struggle for a national liturgical language naturally became a struggle for national culture in general, and for national rights in general.

In this movement initiated by the Moravian Apostles, equal rights to the highest of values, namely the Divine Word, was claimed for every nation and for all people. Thus the *national* trend here is bound up with a *democratic* trend. And according to another Czech legend of the tenth century, Constantine defended the national language as the most effective means of abolishing people's ignorance. On the other hand, the adversaries of the Czech fighters for the heritage of Constantine and Methodius sharply rejected all concessions to the lower strata (*mediocribus*) on the grounds that comprehension of the Sacrament by them meant its profanation.

The idea of nation and national language as high cultural values, the equality of all languages – all this ideology, typical of the Slavic and particularly the Czech Middle Ages from first to last, evidently was ahead of its time; and historians of occidental thought are inclined to assign the period of such ideas to the decline of feudalism and to the

Reformation. Two problems suggest themselves: first, the reason for the early advent of these innovatory ideas in the Slavic world, and secondly, the consequences of this early advent.

The Old-Church-Slavonic *Lives of Constantine and Methodius*, written in Great Moravia in the seventies and eighties of the ninth century, clearly relates what had happened there at the beginning of the sixties:

> Rastislav, the Moravian prince, moved by God, took counsel with his elders and the Moravian people and sent to the Byzantine emperor Michael (III) the following message: Our people have rejected paganism and they observe the Christian law, but we Slavs are simple folk and have no teacher who can explain to us in our own language the right Christian faith so that other countries too may see it and imitate us. So send us, sovereign, such a bishop and teacher, for the good law always proceeds from thee to all lands.

The Emperor sent Constantine the Philosopher (Cyril), professor of the Constantinople University and expert missionary, with his brother Methodius. "You are Salonikian natives," said the Emperor, "and all Salonikians speak the pure Slavonic language."

It is worthy of note that in the ninth century the linguistic differentiation in the Slavic world was still very slight. For instance, the difference between the Moravian and the Macedonian dialects was much less than the difference between British and American English. Constantine adapted his vernacular dialect to the literary and liturgical use of the Moravians and devised a special alphabet. Thus the first literary language in the Slavic world, known in philology as Old-Church-Slavonic, came into being. It was modeled on Greek; it was carefully patterned after the language of a great and ancient culture; and both Old-Church-Slavonic and its inheritors, particularly standard Russian, derived great advantage from this high model.

But not only the internal form, not only the style of the first Slavic cultural language was borrowed from Byzantium, but also the idea itself of one's own spiritual, lofty language was a Byzantine suggestion. This idea could hardly be embodied in the sphere of occidental Europe, but the foreign policy of the Byzantine church did not *a priori* forbid so-called barbarian peoples to glorify the Lord in their vernacular – *voce publica*.

The newest historical and archeological researches reveal a great Byzantine influence in the Czech country during the early Middle Ages. Byzantine imports prevailed in Moravia and Bohemia until the end of the tenth century. In the eleventh century German industry began to compete little by little: earlier, only the German manufacture of arms had penetrated. Cultural, economical, and political gravitation of Great Moravia to Byzantium is indisputable.

Of course, had the Czechoslovak country belonged completely to the Byzantine cultural world, there would have been merely a new satellite, a new province of this splendid culture. But the Czechoslovak country, situated on the great watershed, on the cross-road of Europe, was face to face not only with the Byzantine, but likewise with the western world. The Great Moravian empire and subsequently the Czech principality – or later Czech kingdom – were interested in their western neighbors, and, above all, these neighbors were interested in the Czech country. These neighbors, the Germans, were interested in taking possession of this prosperous domain. The message of the Great Moravian sovereign, Rastislav, to the Byzantine emperor cannot be considered a simple and casual episode. Moravia looked for Byzantine good-will and assistance against the danger of aggression from Louis the German. Recent historical works have proved there were two great coalitions: the German empire gaining the support of Bulgaria and seeking to be upheld by Rome, found on the other hand its counterpoise in the collaboration of Byzantium and Great Moravia.

The German clergy, infiltrating into Great Moravia through various ways, attempted to seize the commanding positions in the land. Fighting against this fifth column was an important task of Saint Constantine and Saint Methodius. The latter's *Life* narrates: "Moravians recognized that the German priests, who lived among them, did not wish them well, but plotted against them, and the Moravians banished them all. . . . And the Moravian country began to grow in all directions and fight its enemies successfully." Nevertheless, the German clergy continued by hook or crook to intrude; and, when both apostles were no longer alive, the German priests and their mercenaries resorted to bloody reprisals against the partisans of the Slavic church whom they then imprisoned, robbed, tortured, humiliated in every possible way, enslaved and exiled. A Slavic eyewitness's report, preserved in a Greek version, adds that "these mercenaries were barbarous for they were Germans, cruel by nature and still more so when acting under orders".

Amid conditions of vigilant defense against the constant menace of aggression, the question of national rights came to the fore in an entirely different manner. The country was too much tied up with the occident to be in position to content itself with assistance from Byzantium, and the German danger was too immediate to allow unconcern about the attitude of Rome. The leaders of the Moravian mission as well as their followers had continually to maneuver between East and West. There was a deep divergence of interests and tendencies between the Holy See and the Germans.[3] These latter endeavored slyly to substitute their selfish policy of predatory rule for Papal universalism. Essentially this German imperialistic tradition was beyond comparison further removed from a truly universalistic ideology than the Moravian bent toward the universal equipollence of nations and languages. The Slavic Apostles were quite aware of this latent conflict, and they curried the favor of Rome by suggesting the possibilities of expanding the influence of Rome to the Slavic world. Rome reciprocally supported Saint Constantine's bold initiative and then helped Methodius in establishing the historic claim of the Slavic church.

This church became legally linked with the Apostolic Church. Thus, it was said that the Apostle Paul had preached in Illyricum, the ancient region to the east of the Adriatic. According to this legendary conception, Paul preached in the vicinity of Great Moravia; he nominated Saint Andronicus as his successor; and the latter incorporated Moravia into his mission. Thus Methodius appears as the legal inheritor of Andronicus; and, the Great Moravian propaganda adds that already in St. Paul's time, Illyricum was Slavic, and consequently the Slavic church has an ancient Apostolic continuity.

This historic (or quasi-historic) right, however, was too shaky as a base for persuading the adversaries of the Slavic party. And if it were only a simple question of historic privilege, the whole problem would be devoid of general interest. But in Great Moravia the assertion of a Slavic national right met an implacable German opposition, and in this stubborn struggle a new, militant ideology arose and transformed the Byzantine model. While Constantine, as a diplomat of the Byzantine school, skillfully juggled with the historic and juridical privileges of the Slavic church, of the Slavic language and of the Slavic nation, the same Constantine, as philosopher and representative of the new-born Slavic ideology, rejected any idea of privileged nations or languages. With an unprecedented sharpness he proclaimed the sacred principle of equality for all nations and all national languages and equal title to the supreme spiritual goods. The corollary of this principle was the imprescriptible sovereignty of one's own nation, language, and church. And the defense of these three goods became an indivisible and sacred task involving resistance against the enemy and even against one's own sovereign

[3] This cardinal and chronic tension has been judiciously elucidated in historical literature from the appearance of the pioneer monograph of A. Lapôtre, S.J., *L'Europe et le Sainte-Siège a l'époque carolingienne* (Paris, 1895), to the basic book of Abbé Fr. Dvorník, *Les Légendes de Constantin et de Méthode vues de Byzance* (Prague, 1933), and the instructive study of P. J. Alexander, "The Papacy, The Bavarian Clergy, and The Slavonic Apostles", *The Slavonic Year-Book* (American Series, I, 1941).

if he proved untrue to the nation, to its language and to its church.[4]

The significance of these ideas for the development of Slavic cultures was decisive. When at the end of the ninth century, the Slavic church in Great Moravia was crushed under German pressure, the tradition survived in the western province of this state, Bohemia, which after the downfall of Great Moravia remained as an autonomous principality and continued to cultivate the Slavic church and literature during the tenth and eleventh centuries. Moreover, when at the end of the ninth century the Slavic church in Great Moravia was abolished, the vast diffusion of this church and culture began. The influence of this diffusion has led us more closely to examine the Moravian chapter in the international history of the national idea.

Some leading representatives of the Moravian Church took refuge in Bulgaria and this country preserved and developed the legacy of the Slavic Apostles and, from the end of the tenth century, made Russia a beneficiary of this legacy. This Church-Slavonic culture penetrated early from the Czechs to Croatia and later from the Bulgarians to Serbia.

Particularly in Bulgaria, Bohemia and Russia the Church-Slavonic culture quickly reached a high degree of development. The use of a national language and the close connection with Byzantine culture, which took supreme place in the European and Near-Eastern world of the Early Middle Ages, were both factors having here a salutary effect. We could, for instance, mention the high level of education received by some of the sovereigns in the enumerated countries in comparison with many of their compeers in the German empire at that time: the Bulgarian czar Simeon studied in the Constantinople University at the end of the ninth century; Saint Venceslaus, the Czech sovereign who was killed in 929, read Slavonic, Greek and Latin. Of various Russian princes in the eleventh century mentioned in a contemporary Russian chronicle, one spoke six languages, another founded many schools – even a special school for translators – and a public library at the Kiev cathedral, a third in 1086 opened the first school for girls. A Russian princess, married to the French king Henry the First, wrote French in Slavonic letters. There was a Russian princess known as a capable scribe of religious literature and another had studied philosophy, rhetoric, grammar and geometry.

[4] This fidelity to the sacred national idea, often in direct opposition to the opportunism and the prevarications of the sovereign's policy, is especially emphasized in the various legends about Prokop, the great Czech saint of the eleventh century, and this feature sharply contrasts with the court allegiance of the mediaeval national trends in western Europe.

In one of the oldest monuments of Slavic painting, the Novgorod icon of Sophia-Wisdom, the Bible is placed on the top above the image of Christ. From the time of the Slavic Apostles the Bible has been highly venerated in Church-Slavonic tradition, and according to the same tradition, the Bible must use the national language in order to be understood.

What an outlook for the development of national culture! Nevertheless, it seems almost miraculous to us that already in the first decades of its penetration into Bulgaria on the threshold of the tenth century, this culture gave birth to a genuine golden age of Bulgarian literature: many Greek theological, philosophical, grammatical and rhetorical treatises were translated or imitated, and the whole terminology of these sciences was carefully translated into the Slavonic language. All this activity was brilliantly continued in Russia where a literature rich in original values sprang up, in the eleventh and twelfth centuries. The ideological trends of the Slavonic culture, trends already engendered in Great Moravia, continued.

As has been mentioned, Byzantium considered the supreme rights of a national language as a magnificent privilege. This privilege could be granted to a great nation. But it was not a matter of necessity, and the Byzantine imperialistic tendency to thrust out Slavonic from the Church and replace it by Greek repeatedly manifests itself in the history of Slavic peoples. The Slavic world changed this Byzantine conception of the select few into a negation of privileged nations and privileged languages. In the case of Bulgaria, the conflict between the two conceptions was clearly brought out. Byzantium considered Bulgaria a sphere of direct influence and endeavored to spread there the Greek church with Greek worship and Greek clergy, but the Church-Slavonic ideology helped Bulgaria to preserve its national individuality. The means of defense used by Great Moravia against the western onsets was also employed by Bulgaria against the East. As early as the beginning of the tenth century, a prominent Bulgarian writer of Moravian tradition, the monk Khrabr, insists that the Slavic language is the equal of Greek, Latin and Hebrew because all languages arose at the same time, the time of the Tower of Babel; and if Slavic has no ancient letters, it is all the better because its creators were Christian saints while Greek and Latin letters were invented by unknown pagans. The great Russian author of the eleventh century, Metropolitan Illarion, goes still further in defending unhistoric languages: the new faith demands new words and letters just as new wines require new skins.

In the particular Russian situation, that of a nation spread over a large area, the united ideas of national church, national language and national culture nurtured a conscious patriotism which finds its eloquent expression in the oldest Russian literature, an expression without parallel in mediaeval western literatures.[5]

The dynamism of this tradition did not stop with the ethnic and linguistic limits of the Russian people. The contagion went further. Thus, in the fourteenth century, a North-Russian learned monk, Stefan of Perm, following, as his contemporary biographer set forth, in the steps of the Slavic Apostles, put forward the maxim that new languages have to be cultivated for the glorification of God. He invented letters for the Ziryani language, translated church books into this tongue and successfully christianized the Ziryani people by preaching and teaching in their vernacular. Thus, this tribe, dwelling in the northeastern corner of European Russia near the Arctic Ocean and today numbering around four hundred thousand persons, was the first of the numerous Finno-Ugrian peoples to possess a vernacular translation of the Gospel. The Finns in Finland made their first modest attempts to write in their mother-tongue only in the middle of the sixteenth century, almost two centuries later than the Arctic tribe which had been stimulated by the mighty Church-Slavonic tradition.

But what befell the Czechoslovak world which was the starting point of this tradition? North and south of the Czechs their ancient Slavic neighbors had been enslaved and Germanized if they accepted German clergy or exterminated if they defended their paganism. Neither a Christian capitulation to German invaders, nor a pagan defense against them, but a Christian defense was the Czech solution – the way of a national Christian culture based on national language, on national clergy, and on the sacred idea of national equality.

It is true that repeated pressure from without destroyed the Slavic church in the Czech state toward the end of the eleventh century but some of its effects persisted, such as the power of historical precedent and of several Czech propaganda manuscripts in Latin defending the national church, the national language and national equality. Without these reminders, without these traditional and still effective slogans, we should be unable to explain the mighty Czech national renascence, with its national language, in artistic and scientific literature in the thirteenth and especially in the fourteenth century. For the Latin-Czech dictionary compiled in the second half of the fourteenth century, including about seven thousand words and rendering into the vernacular the whole terminology of contemporaneous Latin culture, or for the remarkable Czech attempts of that time to give the whole system of scholastic

[5] On the far-reaching significance of the Byzantine ferment for the vitality and power of the Russian state and culture, see the excellent study of S. H. Cross, "The Results of the Conversion of the Slavs from Byzantium", *Annuaire de l'Institut de Philologie et d'Histoire Orientales et Slaves*, VII (New York, 1944).

philosophy and theology, not in Latin but in the national language, there is no parallel in western mediaeval history. Linked with the ancient Moravian and Czech precedents there naturally arose also in Prague of the fourteenth century new tenacious strivings for a liturgy in the vernacular.

The fifteenth century, the Hussite epoch, which represents both the first steps of the Reformation in Europe and the first modern social movement in Europe, is the culmination of the old Czech history; and the native Church-Slavonic reminiscences find a new and striking expression in the ideology of the Hussite movement. Such leading representatives of this movement as Jerome of Prague frankly acknowledge their tie with the old tradition. The pivotal, contagious problems of Hussite ideology – equality, self-determination, the right of every nation to the supreme goods, the sovereign rights of the vernacular, national and linguistic diversity considered as a splendid and blessed treasure – all these ideas seize upon, strengthen and deepen the traditional views we have examined.

The radiation of Hussite ideas was especially widespread. One may mention here only the effect of their creative initiative on the emancipation of national languages. An intensive influence of Czech culture, language, ideology over neighboring Poland began with the Christianization of this country in the tenth century. In the fifteenth century, as Polish investigators have shown, we find particularly numerous and striking traces of the Czech model in every field of Poland's cultural and social life. The first translations of the Gospel or of the rudiments of Polish poetry in the fifteenth century offer merely a retouching of Czech originals. The Hussite ferment appears in Poland, and all these impulses, particularly the idea of a national language with full rights, favor the extraordinarily energetic development and flowering of Polish culture in the sixteenth century and particularly the sudden and world famous achievements of Polish poetry.

The Church-Slavonic culture doubtless touched the Hungarian people, as historic data and Church-Slavonic elements in the Hungarian vocabulary testify, and here we discover ancient Czech and perhaps still older Great Moravian traces. It was Czech missionaries inspired by the Church-Slavonic tradition who founded and organized the Hungarian diocese. Likewise the Hussite epoch influenced Hungarian cultural growth. Apart from the scanty and unimportant fragments of the thirteenth and fourteenth centuries, the history of the written vernacular begins here with the Hungarian translation of the Gospel made in the fifteenth century in Transylvania under the influence of Czech-Hussite emigration. In the same region, at the same time and under the same influence, parts of the Gospel and Psalms were translated into Rumanian in a Hussite surrounding, possibly even by a Czech; these translations were the first and, for a long while, they remained the only texts written in Rumanian.

Already in the ninth century one of the oldest German authors, Otfried von Weissenburg, had turned the attention of his countrymen to the instructive example of the Moravians who glorified the Lord in the vernacular. But the Latin idea of privileged languages had taken root so deeply among the Germans, that many centuries and the advance of the Reformation were required to make them recognize the sovereign rights of a national language. Moreover, we know Luther's initial hesitations, his previous criticism of the Czech Hussites on this question, and then his adhesion to their viewpoint. The new investigations of the roots of Luther's reform essentially confirm the old statement of Pietists who saw a sinuous thread of continuity from the Eastern Church tradition to the work of Luther. Thus, the new European literary languages which the Reformation stirred into life in the sixteenth century, for instance, the Finnish, the Lithuanian, the Lettish and the Slovenian, are a late reflex to the same current which had its source in Byzantium and which in the ninth century had awakened the self-consciousness and national movement of the Slavs.

It is true that the idea of national self-determination and of the full-valued national language comes intensively to the fore during the epoch of the Czech Reformation and was one of its keynotes. This idea, however, has neither arisen nor become extinct with the epoch in question, but passed through the whole of Czech history: it was rooted deeply in the ninth century in the stirring times of the Great Moravian empire, and it did not lose its vitality and fertility with the downfall of the Czech Reformation (1621). The legacy of the Slavic Apostles still persisted and was realized both by Comenius, the great spiritual leader of Czech Protestant emigration, and by Balbín, the outstanding writer of the Czech Counter-Reformation. Balbín asked: what could raise our language higher than the vernacular liturgy of the Slavic Apostles, for the few words of the priest which accompany the Holy Sacrament "have such an infinite power that they go far beyond the words '*let there be*' by which the world has been created" (1672).

Thus the sacramental character of national language and, hence, of the national idea has remained from century to century an unyielding ground for the ideology of Czechs and most of the Slavic peoples in spite of the great spatial and temporal variations in their life and faith. Finally, these tenets could not help leaving their impress on the other nations of Europe.

From *The Review of Politics*, 7 (1945), 29-42. Reprinted by permission

Karl W. Deutsch

THE TREND OF EUROPEAN NATIONALISM – THE LANGUAGE ASPECT

In recent years, public opinion in the democratic countries has become increasingly aware of the dangers inherent in the unlimited competition of a host of rival nationalistic movements and sovereign nation-states. Having recognized it as a danger to be overcome, many liberal thinkers, like the experts of the Royal Institute of International Affairs, or Mr. Max Lerner,[1] are prone to assume that the trend toward nationalistic disintegration has already reached its peak. Many consequent suggestions of policy are based on the assumption that nationalism is declining, or about to decline.

The following inquiry into some of the evidence as to the actual direction of the general trend of European nationalism will be limited in two respects. First, it will be concerned at this stage with the surface trend alone, irrespective of its causes. Second, the evidence examined will be limited primarily to the language aspect of nationalism, that is, to the assimilation or diversification of national languages. It should be borne in mind, however, that the other major elements of nationality, such as political and educational institutions, literature, territory, group loyalties, and nationalistic movements, and frequently even sovereign states and customs areas, are all closely interconnected with the language factor. There is hardly a national language in all Europe for which there could not also be shown the existence of many of the other political and economic factors of nationality. In different nations, the proportions of these factors may vary; there will be border-line cases. But a view of the

[1] *Nationalism; A Report by a Study Group of Members of the Royal Institute of International Affairs* (London, 1939), p. 336; Max Lerner, "The War as Revolution", *The Nation*, Vol. 151, pp. 68-71 (July 27, 1940).

evidence over a longer period of years is likely to show how closely the language factor is linked with the rest of the picture.

I

Do Europe's nations tend to coalesce, to become one, and to accept one written language for their intercourse, administration, business, and literature? If so, and if in consequence we have been getting fewer and larger language areas in Europe, then the many political proposals for fewer and larger states would seem to have also the forces of nationalism itself on their side. Evidence of increasing willingness to accept economic competition and political rule from other language groups would point in the same direction. What are the facts?

Throughout European history, we find former common languages splitting up into increasingly different local dialects. But the speakers of these dialects accept economic coördination around the common centers of market, town, and capital city. They accept political subordination under a wider territorial administration, and social subordination under an upper class around a central élite. In the process they accept as their common standard language above their dialects the speech of the capital or of the economically central region, as spoken by the élite. Usually it is accepted at first in written intercourse; later, given sufficient intensity of education and daily communication, it becomes the standard for the daily speech of the nation.

Villages become subordinated to towns and states. Dialects become subordinated to standard languages. But what of the number of economic centers, what of the number of social and political élites, what of the number of standard languages themselves?

In the hundred years between 1800 and 1900, the number of full-fledged national languages in Europe increased from 16 to 30, that is, at a faster rate than in any of the preceding ten centuries.[2] And in the 37

[2] In 950 A.D., there were in Europe six full-fledged written languages, i.e., languages with a grammar, literature, and some employment in business and public administration – Latin, Greek, Hebrew, Arabic, Anglo-Saxon, and Church Slavonic (Old Bulgarian). See G. Sarton, *Introduction to the History of Science* (Baltimore, 1927-1931), Vol. I. In 1250 A.D., two languages, Anglo-Saxon and Provençal, had become submerged, but there were 17 languages flourishing in Europe, as noted in Sarton's survey: Latin, Greek, Hebrew, Arabic, Church Slavonic, High German, Low German, French, Icelandic, Russian, Spanish, Catalan, Portuguese, Italian, Norwegian, Swedish, and Danish. Sarton, *op. cit.*, Vols. II and III. ("... a deeper study would introduce other languages; I speak only of those [outstanding] ... by their exceptional vitality or by the creation of masterpieces", *ibid.*, Vol. II, p. 293). In 1800, five of the languages of 1250 had become submerged or relatively inactive: Hebrew, Arabic, Low German, Catalan, and Norwegian; and a survey published in 1809 showed only 16 languages flourishing in Europe: Greek, Church Slavonic, German, French, Icelandic, Rus-

years between 1900 and 1937, Europe's standard languages further multiplied to 53, adding almost as many to their number as in the entire thousand years that went before.[3]

The 15 nations that awakened to national language and literature between 1800 and 1900 comprise today a population of more than 80 millions.[4] Eleven of them have since attained, at one time or another, some form of statehood: Bulgarians, Czechs, Croats, Esthonians, Finns, Latvians, Norwegians, Rumanians, Serbs, Slovaks, and Ukrainians. Two others, the Slovenes and the Flemings, have reached a degree of political autonomy; and the last two of the 15, the Welsh in Great Britain and the Yiddish-speaking Jews in the U.S.S.R., have (as of the late 1930's) considerable autonomy in matters of language and education. Among all of these the sense of group loyalty has found expression in nationalistic or patriotic movements.

The 23 smaller nations which awakened between 1900 and 1937 contain today a population of more than 30 millions.[5] Seven of these reached some form of statehood between 1900 and 1941: Albanians, Irish, Byelo-Russians, Karelians, Moldavians – the three last-named

---

sian, Spanish, Portuguese, Italian, Swedish, Danish, English, Dutch, Polish, Magyar, and Turkish (Osmanli). J. Ch. Adelung – J. S. Vater, *Mithridates* (Berlin, 1809). In 1900, a century later, 15 of the above-mentioned languages were flourishing, Church Slavonic being the only one to have dropped out; and to their number had been added Welsh, Flemish, Norwegian (Riksmaal and Landsmaal), Finnish, Rumanian, Czech, Slovak, Serbo-Croatian (a common literary standard language with two sharply different alphabets, traditions, literatures, and loyalties), Slovene, Bulgarian, Ukrainian, Yiddish, Esthonian, and Latvian. See F. N. Finck, *Die Sprachstämme des Erdkreises* (Leipzig, 1911); A. Meillet, *Les Langues du Monde* (Paris, 1925); W. L. Graff, *Language and Languages* (New York and London, 1932); L. Bloomfield, *Language* (New York, 1933); and works on the individual languages.

[3] In 1937, all of the thirty national languages of 1900 were flourishing, and still more were joining their number with new literatures and educational or political institutions or movements: Lithuanian, Irish, Scottish Gaelic, Basque, Breton, Catalan, Rheto-Romance, Lusatian Serb, Albanian, Hebrew (modern), Karelian, Byelo-Russian, Moldavian, Georgian, Ossete, Bashkir, Cheremiss, Chuvash, Mordvin, Samoyede, Syryen (Komi), Tartar, and Votiak. Sources as above. The data for 1900 and 1937 have been checked with the survey of Biblical translations in E. M. North, *The Book of a Thousand Tongues* (New York and London, 1938). Nationalities in the European part of the U.S.S.R. of 1937 are listed in accordance with the language map of Europe by A. Drexel and R. Wimpissinger in their *Atlas Linguisticus* (Innsbruck, 1934). Exclusion of the territory of European Russia from consideration would not materially change the picture of the basic trend.

[As philologists disagree in many cases as to what to count as standard languages and what as dialects, the different surveys have been taken in conjunction and their testimony verified, wherever possible, against evidence from sources within the disputed language group.]

[4] Sources as above, and current statistics.

[5] Sources as above.

only as "Union Republics" within the federal framework of the U.S.S.R., whose constitution grants them, theoretically, the "right to secede" – and the Georgians and Lithuanians, who each formed a sovereign state before becoming Soviet "Union Republics". Of the 13 remaining nationalities, nine have formed administrative units on a national, linguistic basis with various degrees of political self-government within the European part of the U.S.S.R.: the Bashkirs, Chuvashs, Cheremiss, Mordvins, Ossetes, Samoyeds, Syryens, Tartars, and Votiaks.[6] The process was not dissimilar in the rest of Europe; Lusatian Serbs enjoyed some autonomy in education in their own language in Germany from 1918 to 1937; Gaelic-speaking Scotsmen found increased rights for their language in education as well as a number of administrative concessions to the special problems and to the separate identity of Scotland stressed by the Scottish nationalists; Basques and Catalans obtained full political autonomy under the Spanish Republic and played an important part in the Spanish civil war; Rheto-Romans found their ancient language introduced on a basis of full equality into the administration of Switzerland; Hebrew-speaking Jews found a large measure of economic and political autonomy in Palestine, and many of them believe that this will eventually change the position of the "Jewish nationality" all over Europe; a million Bretons in France saw the revival of their old language with a new nationalistic movement in their midst.

Most of these nationalistic movements, new states, and new autonomous districts have grown up from already existing language groups, among people who were already speaking some old vernacular in their families and in their simple, mostly rural, life. These now, on becoming commercialized, industrialized, and literate, are elevating their idiom to the status of a written standard language with its own grammar, literature, and claims for social recognition. If this process should continue, we may expect, with the spread of literacy and industrialization, the rise of nationalistic movements all over the world. In order to visualize the possible scope of this process alone, one should recall the estimate that there are more than 2,700 spoken idioms or dialects in the world,[7] while not more than half of mankind is as yet literate.[8]

[6] See note 3, second paragraph, above. On the Moldavian language and nationality, see *Eleven Union Socialist Soviet Republics* (Moscow, 1938), p. 33 (in Russian); and H. Kloss, "*Sprachtabellen*", in *Vierteljahresschrift für Politik und Geschichte,* Vol. 1 (7) (Berlin, 1929), pp. 111-112.

[7] "The actual number of languages recently computed by officers of the French Academy is put at 2,796." *World Almanac,* since 1929. A more recent survey by E. Kieckers lists almost 3,000 living languages: *Die Sprachstämme der Erde* (Heidelberg, 1931), pp. 237-257.

[8] F. C. Laubach, *Toward a Literate World* (Columbia University Press, 1938); quoted in North, *op. cit.*, p. 18, note 3.

II

If this were the entire story of the rise of modern nationalism, we could then at least also expect that this increase of new nationalistic movements would eventually stop, first in Europe and later in the rest of the world, as the supply of historically inherited language groups became exhausted. Actually, however, the rise of standard national languages is a more complex process, and no simple limitation upon the number of existing dialects can be hoped for.

First of all, a standard language is not merely a standardized single local idiom. It may be regarded rather as a combination of several idioms in that it is usually a language accepted as a common standard by the speakers of several different dialects. It may be a combination of several different elements of speech, such as the Greek Koiné. It may be the language of the capital or central city or central region around which some social, economic, cultural, and often, though not always, political integration has taken place, and where an élite has been assembled, whose composition is to some extent reflected in the language.[9] English, the language of London; Danish, the language of Copenhagen; French, the language of Paris, the Ile de France, and the Champagne; standard Italian, the language of educated Florence – all these show that the national standard language is itself the result of economic, cultural, and political coöperation and affiliation.

These elements of affiliation, in their turn, are subject to change. In the twelfth and thirteenth centuries, the Netherlands were united with Cologne and Lower Germany by a chain of wholly fluid transitions in their written languages. Netherlands writers, such as Jacob van Maerlant and Heinrich von Veldeke, have their place in both Dutch and German literature. In the sixteenth century, the Netherlands broke away from the rest of the German dialect area, and the speech of Brabant was regarded as standard. In the seventeenth century, with the decline of Flanders and the rise of the northern provinces, the speech of Amsterdam became the standard for what is today modern Dutch. At present, the speakers of the Lower Saxon, Plattdeutsch vernacular of Gelderland, of Frisian in Friesland, and of genuine Lower Frankish, Dutch dialects are all united in using Dutch as the language of school and church and as the medium of their common national allegiance. On the other hand, the continuous area of Germanic dialects, mutually intelligible from

[9] While standard languages are evolved in the capital cities, they are not necessarily dominated by the original dialect of the metropolitan region. Rather, they will be based on the speech of the new urban population, and particularly of its most important social group, even if its members have been recruited from all over the country. O. Jespersen, *Mankind, Nation, and Individual from a Linguistic Point of View* (Oslo and Cambridge, Mass., 1925), p. 65.

village to village without a break, is now split into three standard languages, Flemish,[10] Dutch, and German, with another offshoot in a fourth national language, Afrikaans, across the sea. It was not at first these languages that made history; it was history that made these languages.

The acceptance of a common national language contains an element of choice. Macedonians, speaking an intermediate range of dialects, may equally well accept integration into the Serb or into the Bulgarian nation, or else hold out for a nationhood of their own.[11] Slovaks may break away from their common written language with the Czechs, as they did in 1845; later, they may join them in a state based on the idea of a common Czechoslovak nationality, as they did in 1918; and again later their nationalists may protest against attempts of any of their own Slovak countrymen to reduce the relatively small grammatical differences between the two mutually intelligible languages, as they did in the disputes about the new Slovak grammar in 1932.[12]

There is, then, room for new changes and new combinations among the local idioms and ways of speech integrated into the national languages of any given time. Serb and Croat, Russian and Ukrainian, Danish and Norwegian, may be brought closer together or forced farther apart. Provençal, Frisian, Plattdeutsch, and Schwyzerdütsch have all had their literary renaissance in the nineteenth century and form today potential instruments for future new political alignments in case such should come to be desired by strong groups among the populations involved. Thus the elevation of Schwyzerdütsch to a political language of equal rank with standard German was actually suggested in March, 1938, in the Swiss legislature. In considering the possibilities of future national differentiation, we should bear in mind, therefore, not only the present number of dialects and of their present groupings under national standard languages, but also their possible new combinations in times of exceptional change and stress.

III

In the second place, we find a new development since the middle of the nineteenth century, and particularly strongly in the twentieth: a tendency to increase deliberately the differences between kindred, and particularly

[10] "Gradually the language of the Dutch Republic began to be considered in Belgium as that of the enemy and the heretic, and an opposition was created between Dutch and Flemish. ..." G. Duflou, "The Flemish Language", in *Encyclopedia Britannica* (14th ed., 1937), Vol. IX, p. 371.

[11] "... the movement for an autonomous Macedonia ... tends to wean away from the main national body one-fifth of the total Bulgarian population and set it up as a separate nation." S. Christowe, in *An American Symposium on the Macedonian Problem* (Indianapolis, Ind., 1941), p. 21.

[12] C. A. Macartney, *Hungary and Her Successors* (London, 1937), pp. 88, 127.

between neighboring, languages. The rise of the Slavic written languages and literatures in the first half of the nineteenth century had been characterized by the ideas, if not of Pan-Slavism, at any rate of "Slavic mutuality", of a broad give-and-take among Slavic languages and literatures. Less than a century later, in 1937, the Czech philologist, M. Weingart, found that the old give-and-take of the romantic period had been replaced by "an evident distaste for the influence of the other Slavic literary language, particularly of the neighboring one. Thus the Ukrainian language is struggling against Polonisms as well as Russisms, Slovene against Serbo-Croatisms, and ... Slovak against Bohemisms, not infrequently only imaginary ones. There is in this a visible turning away from the ideas of romanticism and the direct opposite of what then was demanded by Jan Kollar." [13]

Under favorable circumstances, the new trend has gone even farther. Considerable population groups begin here and there to mark themselves off more sharply from their neighbors by accepting *new languages* which they themselves never spoke, but which are derived from some language used at one time by some of their actual or reputed ancestors. Scottish and Irish nationalists struggling with their unfamiliar varieties of modern Gaelic; [14] young Zionist Jews diligently learning modern Hebrew; Norwegian patriots changing their historical written language, Dano-Norwegian, for a mixture of Norse peasant dialects, Landsmaal or Folkemaal [15] – all these are examples of a new trend to increase consciously, indeed even to *create*, new linguistic differences by an act of the political will. It can be done; the languages of whole communities, in time of whole nations, can be changed to suit the desire for nationalistic separation. That seems to be the evidence of Palestine, Norway, and Ireland.

The development of modern philology and modern education has made it possible to revive, modernize, and utilize any ancient language sufficiently known to history, if it should so suit any group's desire for separate identity. At the same time, new ways of speech are formed through the changing and splitting up of old languages into new accents and idioms under the influence of time and geographic separation. With

[13] M. Weingart *et al., Slovanské spisovné jazyky v době přítomné* (Prague, 1937), p. 5.

[14] Cf. the section on Scotland in A. J. Aucamp, *Bilingual Education and Nationalism* (Pretoria, 1926); also M. C. Brogan, "Linguistic Nationalism in Eire", in *Review of Politics,* Vol. 3, pp. 225-242 (1941).

[15] "It does not often happen that a language form created by conscious deliberation and planning wins the warm support and widespread acceptance which has fallen to the lot of New Norse, the creation of Ivar Aasen." E. I. Haugen, "The Origin and Early History of the New Norse Movement in Norway", repr. from *Publications of the Modern Language Association,* Vol. 48, No. 2, p. 558.

the possibility of changing alignments and combinations between all of these elements, the national languages of today appear not only as a cause, but also as a result, of national differentiation. So far as the linguistic factor is concerned, the nationalistic disintegration of mankind may go on with hardly any limit so long as the economic possibilities and the political desires for it remain effective.

IV

For each of the 53 European language groups, we found some form of political organization or movement. Further powerful nationalistic loyalties have developed in Europe which are not bound to a separate language of their own: one long before 1800, the Swiss; a second in the nineteenth century, the Belgian; a third at the beginning of the twentieth century, the Macedonian; [16] and a fourth, a border-line case, the nationalism of those Scottish nationalists whose loyalties are attached to Lowland Scots.[17] Non-linguistic nationalistic organizations claim members from among the speakers of four languages in Switzerland, of two languages in Belgium, from members of the whole kaleidoscopic language map of Macedonia. In all these cases, there are at least two loyalties open to the members of many language groups. The Bulgar-speaking Macedonian may follow the Macedonian IMRO or the Bulgarian government; there have been Flemish separatists and Belgian patriots among the Flemish-speaking Belgians, often in intense conflict during the first World War and ever since; there are regionalistic Bretons and Provençals who are ardent French patriots – and there are those who were accused of separatism; [18] there are patriotic, and there are Pan-German, Swiss in German-speaking Switzerland; and in Austria, Chancellor Engelbert Dollfuss died in 1934 for what he conceived to be his patriotic duty to Austrian independence and the "Austrian spiritual character", while the Austrian storm-trooper who killed him went to the gallows for what he had been taught was his duty to Greater Germany. The enumeration is by no means complete. More hopeful features for a possible solution are to be found in that British loyalty which today unites the overwhelming majority of Englishmen, Welshmen, and Scotsmen. But elsewhere there is a considerable list of cases where within the

[16] The Macedonian movement calls for the support of "all Macedonians regardless of nationalities, religion, sex, or political convictions . . . for the establishment of Macedonia as an independent Republic within her geographical and economic boundaries". Cf. Ch. Anastasoff, *The Tragic Peninsula; A History of the Macedonian Movement for Independence since 1878* (St. Louis, 1938), pp. 308-310.

[17] W. A. Craigie *et al., The Scottish Tongue* (London, 1924), pp. 3-46.

[18] P. Pansier, *Histoire de la Langue Provençale à Avignon* (Avignon, 1927), Vol. IV, pp. viii-ix.

same communities of language the loyalties of nationalism are in intense conflict on both sides, demonstrating their disintegrating power.

V

The growth of linguistic diversity in Europe from 16 languages in 1800 to 30 in 1900 and to 53 in 1937 has been paralleled to some extent since 1871 by the growth in the number of modern sovereign states in Europe from 15 in 1871 to 21 in 1914 and to 29 in 1937,[19] as well as by the steady rise in the height of the tariff walls and other economic controls separating their national economies from each other. So far, the second World War has shown little indication of a reversal of the trend. The great European powers have been careful to reckon with the vitality of nationalistic feelings, trying to utilize them wherever practicable. By the spring of 1941, Hitler's armies had created two new states, Slovakia and Croatia, and had tried for a time to foster a movement for a third new state among the Bretons in France.[20] The Soviet government had set up, largely along linguistic lines, two new "Union Republics", the Finnish-Karelian and the Moldavian.[21] Iceland, under British occupation, dropped her last tie of personal union with Denmark in order to emerge in full legal sovereignty. For the Allied nations in particular, the liberation of small nations has become both a major war aim and an important political weapon.

So far as the language factor is concerned, the bulk of the evidence shows for the years from 1800 to 1941 a steady increase in the diversity and strength of nationalistic feeling. In the long run, the peaceful unification of Europe may have to be brought about against this very current. To deal with it democratically and constructively, our understanding of the functioning of nationalism, already advanced by the pioneering work of scientists like Carleton J. Hayes and Hans Kohn, and of statesmen like Dr. Eduard Beneš and the late T. G. Masaryk, will have to be further developed and extended.

19 F. Martin (ed.), *The Statesman's Year-Book, 1871* (London, 1871), pp. v-ix; also *1914*, pp. xix-xxix; and *1937*, pp. ix-xiii.

20 *New York Times*, July 14, 1940, p. 21: 1-3; July 26, p. 3: 7; July 27, p. 6: 3.

21 A representative of still another European nationality – the 54th – spoke at the "All-Slav Conference" in Moscow on Aug. 10 and 11, 1941. According to the report, he represented 400,000 Slonzaks or Lakhs, a Slav people on the borders of Czech and Polish Silesia. *The Slavic Peoples Against Hitler* (New York, 1941), pp. 20-21.

From *American Political Science Review*, 36 (1942), 533-541. Reprinted by permission.

Douglas Taylor

NEW LANGUAGES FOR OLD IN THE WEST INDIES

It is usually assumed that most if not all "natural" languages spoken today are the products of slow but continual change, obsolescence, innovation and borrowing; and that divergence among members of a clearly related group, like the Romance languages, can be fully accounted for by the gradual fragmentation of what once was, to all intents and purposes, a single linguistic community. This assumption, though well founded, is rarely susceptible of positive proof, even in the comparatively rare case of languages with a long written record; for writing is always more conservative than speech, and especially so at times and places in which this skill is acquired only by a small minority; so that the presumably gradual transition from late Latin to, let us say, Old French is largely undocumented. On the other hand we know of some languages, like Sabir or Lingua Franca (once used in the Levant), that began – and often ended – as nobody's mother tongue, but serve or served to facilitate communication between members of different speech communities who became – often rather suddenly as the result of some historical accident – interdependent. Such most likely had been (but no longer was) the so-called "men's speech" of the 17th-century Island Carib, which largely consisted of Karina (Cariban family) lexemes articulated by means of phonemes, inflexion and syntax belonging to the indigenous Arawakan language; for if it be true, as tradition had it, that the Carib conquerors of the Lesser Antilles killed all the indigenous males and took the women to wife, some sort of linguistic compromise must have been an urgent necessity.[1] In what follows I shall attempt to discuss the occur-

[1] See, s.v. "Galíbi" (p. 229) et passim: Raymond Breton, *Dictionnaire caraïbe-*

rence and development of other such languages in the West Indies subsequent to the introduction of Negro slaves, and the part that they play or played in the life of the communities concerned.

In Guiana, the Caribbean and Louisiana various new languages such as Sranan (Negro English), Saramakkan, Papiamentu, Negro Dutch and several forms of French Creole have emerged within the past three hundred years, and, for the most part, prospered. At first "pidgins" or jargons employed only between African and European, and between Africans of different provenance, all of them later became "creolized" – adopted, that is to say, as the first and in general only language of whole communities; and with the exception of Negro Dutch (formerly spoken in the Virgin Islands, but probably now extinct), they remain that to this day. These languages are peculiar in combining rather similar grammatical structures of a non-Indo-European and seemingly West African type with vocabularies that are preponderantly of English, Portuguese or Spanish, Dutch and French ancestries respectively. By far the most widespread and diversified of them is French Creole, whose four main dialects (excluding those of Mauritius and Réunion in the Indian Ocean), each containing an indeterminate number of mutually intelligible subdialects, are spoken in French Guiana, certain of the Lesser Antilles (Trinidad, Grenada, St. Lucia, Martinique, Dominica, Guadeloupe and dependencies and St. Thomas), Haiti and Louisiana. Sranan is spoken mainly in Surinam, as the name implies; but as a second or trade language it is also used to some extent, by Amerindians and others, in the neighbouring French and British territories to the east and west. Saramakkan is spoken only by the Bush Negroes on the upper reaches of the Surinam or "Saramakka" river. It has not yet been thoroughly investigated; but appears to be a tone language containing Portuguese, English and African elements. Papiamentu is confined to the three Dutch islands of Curaçao, Aruba and Bonaire. It is usually assumed to be the only Spanish Creole in the Americas; but Tomás Navarro and, more recently, H. L. A. van Wijk have shown that the many Portuguese items in its lexicon are basic, and that its hispanicization must have taken place at a time long after the Spaniards and other Spanish speakers had left Curaçao for the mainland.[2]

A *pidgin* may then be defined as a linguistic compromise that is nobody's mother tongue; and a *creole* as a mother tongue that began in a pidgin, and has not come to be identified with any previously existing

français (Auxerre, 1665); réimprimé par Jules Platzmann, édition fac-simile (Leipzig, 1892).

[2] Tomás Navarro, "Observaciones sobre el papiamento", *NRFH*, VII (1951), p. 188 ff., and H. L. A. van Wijk, "Orígenes y evolución del papiamentu", *Neophilologus*, XLII (1958), p. 169 ff.

traditional language (see now footnote 14). I think it was Voltaire who said that while a foreign language may be learnt in two or three years, it takes half a lifetime to master one's own; and in the same sense it seems obvious that the process of creolization presupposes and entails considerable enrichment and regulation of the original pidgin, whose formation for the requirements of a rapidly learnt second language necessarily involved a notable reduction of two or more speech communities' means of expression and communication. All creoles are therefore "regular" languages in that each has its own pattern of distinctive units of sound, its own grammatical signs and conventions, and a vocabulary adequate for the cultural demands of its native speakers. Moreover, such languages evolve, once creolization has taken place, in much the same ways as do other idioms, and in accordance with their native speakers' changing needs of communication. But they differ from languages with a longer tradition in having basic grammars whose source cannot clearly be identified with that of their basic vocabularies, and in being comparatively free from such fossilized historical débris as result in our own irregular noun plurals and verbal conjugations.

Of these creolized languages' short history little, unfortunately, is known; for few writers of the past took any serious interest in them, and the slaves themselves were, almost without exception, illiterate. However, we know that the first French settlers and missionaries employed a sort of *petit-nègre* in their attempt to make themselves understood by the slaves; for toward the middle of the 17th century, Father Chevillard wrote: "Les nègres . . . se familiarisent rapidement avec le langage de l'européen, langage volontairement corrompu pour faciliter sa compréhension"; and at about the same time Father Pelleprat remarked: "Nous nous accomodons à leur façon de parler qui est ordinairement par l'infinitif du verbe, comme par exemple: 'moi prier Dieu, moi aller à l'Eglise, moi point manger'; et y ajoutant un mot qui marque le temps à venir ou le passé, ils disent: demain moi manger, hier moi prier, et ainsi de suite." Moreover, both these priests have left us samples of the language in which religious instruction was given to slaves in their time.[3] So, from Chevillard:

Toy sçavoir qu'il y a un Dieu: Luy grand Capitou, luy sçavoir tout faire sans autre l'aider: luy donner à tous patates; luy mouche manigat pour tout faire,

[3] Citations from Chevillard and Pelleprat are both taken from L. Calvert, "Histoire de la formation du language créole", *Martinique*, December 1944. The latter author himself took them from, respectively: C. A. Banbuck, *Histoire politique, économique et sociale de la Martinique* (Paris, 1935), and Pierre Pelleprat, *Relation des missions des pp. de la Cie. de Jésus dans les isles, et dans la Terre Ferme de l'Amérique méridionale* (Paris, 1656). Calvert does not say what edition of the latter he used; but the spelling – evidently modernized in the case of Pelleprat, and not (or less) in that of Chevillard – is as given by him.

non point comme luy. Vouloir faire maison, non faire comme homme, car toy aller chercher hache pour bois, puis couper roseaux, prendre mahoc et lianes et ainsi pequins faire case. Or Dieu mouche manigat, luy dit en son esprit, moy vouloir homme, luy preste miré homme. Enfin luy envoyé meschant en bas en enfer, au feu avec maboya et autres sauvages qui n'ont vouloir vivre en bons chrétiens. Mais tous bons chrétiens, luy bons pour mettre en son paradis où se trouve tout contentement, nul mal, nul travail, et nulle servitude ou esclavage, mais une entière joye et parfaite liberté.

And from Pelleprat:

Seigneur, toi bien savé que mon frère lui point mentir, point lui jurer, point dérober, point lui méchant. Pourquoi toi le voulé faire mourir!

Mon frère, toi te confesser, toi dire comme moi: Seigneur, si moi mentir, moi demander à toi pardon; si moi dérober, si moi jurer, si moi faire autre mal à toi, moi bien faché, moi demander pardon.

But this is something very different – apart from a couple of resemblances such as the absence of a copula (*luy grand Capitou*) and the employment of *moi, lui,* etc. as subject (*moi demander, lui envoyé*) – from the language used a hundred years later as portrayed in the first French Creole texts, and which differs little from that current at the present time.[4] So, for example, no French Creole employs the objective personal pronouns *me, te, le* or *se* (*toi te confesser, toi le voulé, où se trouve*), the auxiliary verb *avoir* (*qui n'ont vouloir*), or the conjunction que (*toi bien savé que*); while Chevillard's *toi savoir* and *moi vouloir* vs. Pelleprat's *toi bien savé* and *toi le voulé* suggest a jargon in the making rather than one already established.

Then was this incipient jargon a model, as is usually assumed, imitated and modified by the African slaves; or itself a kind of imitation of these Africans' speech, as we are told ("We adapt ourselves to their manner of speaking . . .")? Most probably both. Surely Fr. Pelleprat was not claiming, for himself and others who had never before come into contact with Negroes, a familiarity with West African languages. But the first French settlers and missionaries got their slaves from the Spaniards and, more especially, from the Dutch; who in their turn got them from

[4] On p. 234 of her *Du français aux parlers créoles* (Paris, 1956), Élodie Jourdain gives the text of a message sent by a Guianese Amerindian, pupil of the Jesuits, to the French Governor d'Orvilliers in 1744; and which she believed to be the oldest monument of French Creole: *Anglai pran Yapok, yé méné mon père allé, toute blang foulkan maron dans bois* "(the) English have taken (the) Oyapok (post), they have carried off (the) priest, all (the) white (people) have cleared out (and) taken refuge in (the) woods". The same message would be conveyed in the same words in the Guianese dialect of today.

the Portuguese settlements or "factories" on the west coast of Africa, where a Portuguese pidgin had been in use since the 15th century. And as Van Wijk has shown, slaves bought or captured in the interior usually remained in these "collecting centres" quite long enough to learn the pidgin, which served henceforth not only in their dealings with Europeans of whatever nationality engaged in the slavetrade, but also as a lingua franca between fellow slaves whose mother tongues were not mutually intelligible. It was, I suggest, this "façon de parler" to which the first French settlers and missionaries sought to adapt themselves, and whose vocabulary they sought to gallicize.

There can be no doubt that they succeeded in the latter part of this enterprise; for few words of Ibero-Romance ancestry are to be found in modern French Creole, except in the Guianese and Haitian dialects, where they are a little more common (*cf.* Guianese *briga* "to fight" and *fika* "to be in a situation or state", from Ptg. *brigar, ficar*; and Haitian *kachimbo* "pipe" and *mantèg* "lard", from Ptg. *cachimbo, manteiga* – or Sp. *manteca*). However, Portuguese *pai, compai* and *mãe*, which have been naturalized in the "normal" Spanish dialects of Trinidad, Puerto Rico and probably other of the Spanish-speaking Antilles,[5] are also employed – though only as friendly or endearing terms of address, without any reference to kinship – in French Creole of the Lesser Antilles, whose *iche* (French spelling) "son(s), offspring" apparently derives from an early dialectal form (with hushing sibilant but no *f* or aspirate *h*) of Sp. *hijo, -ja* or Ptg. *filho, -lha*. And had the slaves arrived in the French islands speaking nothing but their native African languages, it is most unlikely that Frenchmen there should have taught them words like: *capitou* (cf. Ptg. *capitão*) "chieftain, leader", *pequins* (cf. Ptg. *pequeno*) "little ones", *miré* (cf. Ptg. & Sp. *mirar*) "look at" and *mouche* (cf. Sp. *mucho*, Ptg. *muito*) "very, much, many".[6]

The importance of the Portuguese elements in Papiamentu, beginning with the name of the language itself (*papia* "speak" < Ptg. *papear* "chat" + nominalizing *-mentu*, a fully productive suffix, < Ptg. *-mento*), has never been denied; but their presence has usually been attributed to the Sephardic Jews who sought refuge in Curaçao in the second half of the 17th century and later. Van Wijk argues that these refugees were not at that time either numerous or powerful enough to have exerted

[5] See: Robert Wallace Thompson, "A Preliminary Survey of the Spanish Dialect of Trinidad", *Orbis*, VI (1957), p. 353 ff., and Manuel Álvarez Nazario, *El arcaísmo vulgar en el español de Puerto Rico* (Mayagüez, Puerto Rico, 1957).

[6] It is true that *mouche manigat* "very skilful" is said to have occurred also in the jargon used between Europeans and Island Caribs; and some have attributed *manigat* to the latter's language. Breton denies this; but if he was mistaken, these Indians must have had a peculiar sense of humour; for the most similar word in their language, *manikati*, means "unable or not disposed to do (something)".

such an influence; although they most probably helped to de-Africanize the Portuguese pidgin spoken by the incoming slaves. Moreover, he has found in the vocabulary of Curaçao: "more than 70 Portuguese words that occur also in the Negro English of Surinam [Sranan] in the same characteristic shapes as in Papiamentu". This is not the place to argue either for or against such a hypothesis; but if a Portuguese pidgin or creole spoken in a Dutch island could be hispanicized to the extent that is seen in modern Papiamentu by visiting missionaries and others coming from the adjacent mainland of South America, it would not be surprising if an originally Afro-Portuguese pidgin left still fewer remnants of its vocabulary in creolized languages that emerged among slaves belonging to English and French masters. Finally we may mention, as not irrelevant to our discussion, Whinnom's opinion that the Spanish Creole dialects now spoken in the Philippine Islands evolved from the imitation, by Spanish soldiers, of a Portuguese pidgin that was widely used as a trade language in the Eastern Seas during the 16th, 17th and early 18th centuries, not only by the Portuguese themselves, but also by the Dutch and English.[7]

The West Indian slave-owners' precautionary policy of mixing together Africans belonging to different tribes must have led to general use of the local pidgin, and to its creolization in the second or third generation born in the American colonies. But the importation of African slaves continued, with some interruptions, throughout the 18th and early 19th centuries; and in Martinique, where 5,435 individuals of African birth were reported to be living as recently as 1905, it was renewed between 1857 and 1860 under the new label of "indentured labour (engagés)".[8] It therefore seems justified to say that these new West Indian languages have been throughout most of their history the mother tongue of some, but a second language for other of their speakers.

Understandably, their importance has varied enormously with time and place. Father Labat, who was in the islands (principally Martinique) between 1693 and 1705, appears not to have considered them worthy of mention; though he discusses the speech of the Island Carib, and tells us that he learnt the African language of his "Arada" slaves. A hundred years later ("Paris, 17 Brimer, an 10 Répiblique francé, yon et indivisible"), Bonaparte and Leclerc considered French Creole important enough to have their proclamation "a tout zabitans Saint-Domingue" translated into it; and during the second half of the 19th century, the

[7] Keith Whinnom, *Spanish Contact Vernaculars in the Philippine Islands* (Hong Kong-London, 1956). In a review of this book, in *Word*, 13 (1957), p. 489 ff., I have mentioned some similarities between the languages therein described and the West Indian creoles.

[8] L. Calvert, *op. cit., Martinique,* June 1944.

indigenous (Island-Carib) Indians of Dominica gradually gave up their own language for it. At the present time, French Creole is the mother tongue of more than 95% of the population in Dominica and St. Lucia (not more than a third of whom can express themselves in English) and Haiti (where less than a third can express themselves in French); while it is rapidly dying out in Trinidad and Grenada, where it is probably not understood by more than 10% of the inhabitants. It is probably safe to say that in French Guiana and the French islands every native inhabitant (excepting perhaps some Amerindians in the former) is now more or less bilingual in French and Creole; a circumstance which tends to bring their dialects of Crcole much closer to "normal" French than they were even fifty years ago. And owing to the prestige of Spanish, something of the same sort appears to be happening – or to have already happened – to Papiamentu; which is, according to Van Wijk:

> casi el único idioma criollo – más exactamente idioma semi-criollo – que tiene además valor cultural, pues en él se escriben no sólo diarios y revistas, sino también novelas, cuentos y hasta poesía. Lamentable es que el papiamentu carezca de una ortografía uniforme, ya que las distintas ortografías basadas en argumentos etimológicos vacilan entre la transcripción española y la holandesa de los sonidos.

The first part of this statement, if not altogether exact, shows that the social aspects of the several creoles are very different. Some stories and more poems have been written and published, during the past two hundred years, in various dialects of French Creole and in Sranan; though the earlier writings were not – understandably, in view of the slaves' enforced illiteracy – produced by what we should call native speakers. They employ, for the most part, an inconsistent spelling that leans heavily on the conventional orthography of one or another "national" language. This also is understandable; for only in Haiti and within the past decade, so far as I know, have the schools begun to teach reading and writing in a creole mother tongue; and even there the standardized orthography based on a phonological analysis of Haitian Creole has had to be abandoned under pressure from people who think that their language should at least "look like" French!

But native speakers of French Creole (of whatever dialect) who also possess a modicum of French or English have come to regard the use of their mother tongue in much the same light as speakers of standard French do the use of *tu* instead of *vous* – with this difference, that the former will often change from the "intimate" to the "polite" form with the same interlocutor when coming within earshot of "respectable" strangers. Some years ago, in Dominica, a very good variety show, composed and performed in Creole by local talent, was rather widely deplored as being "unprogressive". I myself have served, by request, as interpreter between a Dominican and a Martiniquais whose mother tongues, always employed in the family circle, differed less than those of a Bostonian and a Baltimorean; but who, being hitherto unacquainted, both felt it incumbent on them to converse only in their respective "national" languages. And from Guadeloupe to St. Lucia, if not elsewhere, many people who themselves habitually speak Creole are wont to chide any children whom they hear using it in the street.

The antecedents for this attitude are sufficiently clear. The various pidgins arose, persisted and became creolized under conditions in which social status was determined mainly by racial identity; the ratio of "white" to "black" was constantly decreasing;[9] and the former, once they themselves had become bilingual, actively discouraged the latter from learning the "masters' language". The abolition of slavery brought no immediate change in these conditions; but with the decline of the old plantation system (Fr. *habitation*) it soon became evident that these coloured populations would be a burden on the mother country unless and until they became literate and learnt the national language. It was hoped to accomplish this end by the introduction, several generations ago, of public schools (whose numbers and equipment are still inadequate). But the attainment of bilingualism in a community where there is little opportunity of practising the second language in contacts with its native speakers is always and everywhere a difficult task; and it has been rendered particularly arduous in English islands like St. Lucia and Dominica, where children have been – and are – taught that their mother tongue is "only a monkey language" – or no language at all, that it "has no grammar", cannot be written and is a mark of social inferiority.[10] Poorly trained and poorly paid local teachers might be excused for spreading such false doctrine; but as recently as 1945 the Educational Adivser to the Comptroller for Development and Welfare in the West Indies published a report in which he stated his opinion that: "The aim should be not to make the children bilingual, but ultimately to make English the mother tongue." I cannot conceive how a shift of language without an interim period of bilingualism might be achieved

[9] L. Calvert (*op. et loc. cit.*), citing Martineau & May, *Trois siècles d'histoire Antillaise,* says: "Les noirs sont moins nombreux en 1652, avec Pelleprat. Ils tendent à l'égalité en 1658, avec Rochefort; ils sont supérieurs en nombre en 1660, d'après la relation des îles. C'est donc entre 1658 et 1660 que la population noire dépasse la blanche pour suivre un mouvement continuellement ascendant. Elle la double en 1720, la quadruple en 1740, époque à laquelle les blancs étaient eux-mêmes cinq fois plus nombreux qu'en 1660. Le nombre des noirs augmentait sans cesse: Il atteignait 70.000 en 1763 et 90.000 en 1789."

[10] See: Pierre Vérin, "The Rivalry of French Creole and English in the British West Indies", *De West-Indische Gids,* 38 (1958), p. 163 ff.

– except by removing all infants from their homes and parents, and taking full charge of them until the age of puberty! Moreover, most educationalists are now agreed that children who learn to read and write first in their mother tongue subsequently make better progress in the second language than those others whose schooling is in the latter from the start.[11]

Some readers may ask why it is that no pidgin or creole is current in the Spanish-speaking Antilles, or in English islands such as Jamaica, Barbados and St. Vincent. So far as the former territories are concerned, R. W. Thompson has answered the question as follows: [12]

> In addition, a more serious effort was made by the Spaniards and Portuguese to plant their New World territories with peasants of European stock. As a result, their subjects of African descent did not greatly overwhelm in numbers those who spoke a European language in conformity with native usage, as happened in the English, French and Dutch colonies of the West Indies. Today there is no Spanish *creole* dialect in the New World, where the Negroes of Cuba, of the Dominican Republic and of Porto Rico pronounce the voiced dental fricative δ every bit as well as their white or mulatto compatriots.

On the other hand, Cromwell did make a serious effort to provide the English planters (no island south of Montserrat other than Barbados was at that time in English hands) with the enforced labour of as many "convicts, vagabonds and light women" of British stock as he could lay his hands on; the last two categories designating, in the main, Catholic priests, boys and girls. "In four years", we are told, "sixty-four hundred white slaves rounded up in Ireland and Scotland were sent out to the West Indies. The population of Jamaica seven years after its conquest was fifteen thousand." [13] But though black slaves proved more efficient than white, and gradually replaced the latter in the English islands, the Africans had time to learn from their British fellow sufferers, and to pass on, a dialect which, though far from standard English, is not in my opinion a creole.[14] Nevertheless, there are some remarkable correspond-

[11] See: UNESCO, *The Use of Vernacular Languages in Education* (= *Monographs on Fundamental Education,* No. VII) (Paris, 1953).

[12] Robert Wallace Thompson, "The 'th-Sounds" and Genetics", *Phonetica* I, 3/4 (1957).

[13] Germán Arciniegas, *Caribbean Sea of the New World* (New York, 1946), p. 213 ff.

[14] *Pāce* Professor Robert Le Page formerly of the UCWI (and others), who holds that "broad Jamaican Creole stands in much the same relationship to English as does Haitian Creole to French" (personal communication). The clue to what I regard as an essential difference is the qualification, "broad". So far as I could ascertain, there is a continuous gradation in the speech of Jamaicans –

ences between the Negro English creole of Surinam (Sranan) – which colony the Dutch received in compensation for the theft of New Amsterdam, alias New York – and the English dialects of Barbados and Jamaica.[15]

The linguistic history of St. Vincent is another story. Until 1763 this island was, like Dominica, in the hands of the Caribs; and its language was Island Carib. But in 1635 (the year in which the French occupied Guadeloupe and Martinique), the living cargoes of two wrecked slave-ships had sought refuge there; and been joined in the course of the years by numerous fugitives from neighbouring islands, particularly Barbados. These Negroes soon adopted the language and customs of their Indian hosts, and stole as many of their women as possible; the more readily, no doubt, because only identification with the indigenous Caribs preserved them from recapture. After the Treaty of Paris in 1763, the English moved in, bringing their own slaves; and ten years later the Caribs, "red" and "black" alike, were confined to the northernmost quarter of the island. But the black outbred the red to such an extent that after the unsuccessful Carib war of liberation (1795-96), very few pure Indians were left in St. Vincent; and the modern descendants of the 5000-odd Caribs who were deported to Central America in 1797, now numbering some 30,000, are of preponderantly negroid stock, although they alone today have retained the Island-Carib language.[16]

Though prediction is impossible, it seems likely that the future fortunes of the West Indian creoles will largely depend on their speakers' ability to adapt them to new requirements of communication – with regard to both speech and writing – in a changing world. So far as speech is concerned, this should offer little difficulty in places where the present national or official language is a later stage of that from which

---

such as exists within perhaps most fairly large speech communities – from the broadest dialect to the local variety of standard English; and everybody normally uses the nearest approximation to the latter with which he or she is familiar. But there is not and cannot be any such gradation from a French Creole to any dialect of French because of great differences in basic grammar; and it is always clear which language is being spoken, even though it be a variety of Creole that is full of gallicisms or a variety of French that is full of creolisms. I do not doubt that "broad" Jamaican (or Barbadian) began in a pidgin that became the mother tongue of some; but this mother tongue has evolved continuously in the direction of "normal" English, as which it should now be identified for the reasons stated above.

[15] For some examples of such correspondences, see: Merville J. Herskovits, *The Myth of the Negro Past* (New York, 1941), p. 282.

[16] For further details of this people's history, see the Introduction to my monograph, *The Black Carib of British Honduras* (= *Viking Fund Publications in Anthropology*, No. 17) (New York, 1951).

the creole's basic vocabulary was drawn, as in the French territories and in Haiti. But elsewhere, lexical borrowing is apt to be replaced by "code switching" – by the use, that is to say, of whole phrases or sentences lifted from the source-language. In Dominica, this is particularly common among chauffeurs, truck-drivers, clerks, typists and salesmen; while the introduction of such things as fertilizers, spraying and contour draining have made it not infrequent even among peasants. On the other hand, fishermen, hunters, sawyers and other woodsmen, sugar-cane workers in field and factory, bakers, carpenters, coopers and others who practise a conservative handicraft usually have, pertaining to their occupation, a rich Creole vocabulary that has been passed on without change throughout many generations, and that differs little – and if at all, then only by greater conservatism – from its counterpart in Martinique or Guadeloupe. Moreover, native speakers of Dominican Creole are not given to extending the meaning of a word as they know it; so, *hwazwè* (Fr. rasoir) "razor" is replaced by *réza* (Eng. *razor*) when a "safety razor" is referred to, *vè* (Fr. *verre*) "glass drinking-vessel" and *vè butey* (Fr. *bouteille*) "broken glass" are replaced by *glas* (Eng. *glass*) in any other reference, and *dis nwè* (Fr. *dix noirs*) "sixpence" has not been extended to "ten cents" of the new currency, which is called *tensens*.

The net result of numerous such changes and innovations, which have been gaining ground during the past forty – and especially the past fifteen – years, is that conversation between native speakers of French Creole belonging, respectively, to the English and to the French islands (of the Lesser Antilles) is today much more hampered and restricted than was the case only a generation ago; hampered because, in the French islands, the phonology is becoming closer to that of French (introduction of front rounded vowels, loss of the aspirate *h* and its replacement by velar *r;* whereas in the English islands *h* has been retained and velar *r* merged, for most speakers, in a non-distinctively velarized *w*); restricted because there is not and has never been a common vocabulary pertaining to things and institutions unknown in the islands before the present century, but which have recently become commonplace.

As for writing, so long as only those who have first become literate in another language can attempt to write and read a creole mother tongue, there will continue to be some wavering between an "etymological" spelling (mainly where the second or school language was the source of the creole's lexicon) and one that is "phonetic" – not in a scientific sense, but in terms of the second language's conventional orthography (mainly where the second language was not the source of the Creole's lexicon). So perhaps, for Papiamentu: *gaap* or *haap* from Dutch *gapen*, *loer* or *lur* from Dutch *loeren, yuda* or *joeda* from Spanish *ayudar, joven* or *hoben* from Spanish *joven, bij* from Dutch *bij* but *bai* from Portuguese *vai.* And in the case of a French Creole dialect some of whose speakers have French and others English as the language of literacy, the situation is much more serious. So, one and the same utterance, which might be transcribed phonematically: *se joomu yon ki sav fòs kuto ki ã cè-y* "it's the pumpkin alone that knows the strength of the knife in its heart", would be likely to appear, when written by a Martiniquais, as: *c'est geo'omon yonne qui save fò'ce couteau qui en tchoeu'-y*; and when written by a Dominican or a St. Lucian ignorant of French as: *say zhowomoo yon kee sahv force cootow kee ahn chair ee.* But were a Creole word of English ancestry to be recorded, "etymologist" and "phonetician" would most probably change places, the one writing, for example, *saïbòte* and the other *sideboard* for what is, phonologically, *saybod.*

Under the circumstances, it is hardly surprising that even personal correspondence is usually written – often by the intermediary of an interpreter scribe – in what passes for the national language. But a better and more general knowledge of the latter, spoken and written, could, I suggest, be achieved most rapidly and painlessly by way of literacy in the creole mother tongue; for writing which some adequate, consistent and simple orthography should be agreed upon. Conventional French spelling clearly has none of these qualities; but since the vast majority of those who speak a French Creole have or wish to acquire French as a second language, some concessions should be made by the others; and it would be wise for the educational authorities of the W. I. Federation to adopt such digraphs and trigraphs as are or may be used to represent similar distinctive sounds of both English and French; for example *ou* as in *you* and *vous, tch* as in *clutch* and *tchèque.* Thus the Creole proverb cited in the preceding paragraph would appear as orthographic: *se joomou yon ki sav fôs kouto ki ã tchê-y.*

In conclusion I should perhaps apologize for having given what may be a disproportionate place in my discussion to French Creole. But though I have done so mainly because I know most about it, having spoken one of its dialects almost daily for the past twenty years, there are reasons why it may be considered more important than some of the others of its kind, in respect to the rôle that it has played in the past, and may still play in the future. French Creole as a whole is more widespread and diversified and has a greater number of native speakers (between three and four million in Haiti alone) than any other creole language. However, size is no guarantee of longevity when the ability or the will to adapt is lacking; and there can be little doubt that, thanks to encouragement from Holland and to native speakers' own volition, the creoles now spoken in Dutch territories have made most progress in that direction. In token of which I shall end with a poem by Trefossa, written in Sranan (Negro English), and for whose translation I must plead guilty.[17]

wan tru puëma na wan skretji-sani.
wan tru puëma na wan stree te f'dede.
wan tru puëma na wan tra kondre,
pe ju kan go
te ju psa dede fosi.

wan tru puëma na den wortu d'e tan abra
te ala trawan n'in ju libi wasi gwe;
wan koko soso,
ma wan di kan sproiti
njun libi

lon na mi abra dan,
Arusubanja fu grontapu
kande wandee, wandee
mofo fu mi sa broko opo
fu tatji dji onoosruwan tu wortu
di, te den gro, sa trowe lepi stari,
di mi suku noo.

a real poem is a frightening thing.
a real poem is a strife with death.
a real poem is another land,
where you can go
once death has been outrun.

a real poem is the words that stay
when others from your life are
a naked kernel [washed away;
but one that can put forth
new life

then let pour over me
the world's Arusubanya.
perhaps one day, one day
my mouth will open up
to tell for simple souls a double tale
which, when it grows, will cast ripe
that now I seek. [stars

From *Comparative Studies in Society and History*, 3 (1961), 277-288. Reprinted by permission.

[17] From: Trefossa (puëma fu), *Trotji*; p. 19. Published for the Bureau of Linguistic Research in Surinam (University of Amsterdam) (Amsterdam, 1957). Arusubanja is the name of a rapid in the Surinam river; and means, literally "shakes the ribs loose".

John E. Hofman *

THE LANGUAGE TRANSITION IN SOME LUTHERAN DENOMINATIONS

From the time of the Protestant Reformation, Lutheran churches had been ethnic in character, and the meeting of mother tongue and faith proved mutually reinforcing. It was, therefore, natural that many Scandinavians and Germans should continue the use of Norwegian, Swedish, Danish, and German in their newly-founded American parishes. E. Haugen writes: "In the case of the Norwegians, as apparently among most immigrants, the church is the primary institution which provides the immigrants with a justification for the use of the language" (Haugen 1953, p. 238). Time and the total environment, however, were on the side of Anglification. Gradually the use of English entered the church services of these immigrant Lutherans, and the ethnic mother tongue retreated surely and inexorably. Yet the transition has been far from even in different places and at different times.

The general trend toward gradual Anglification is well illustrated by such indices as the relative use of ethnic- and English-language church publications. Table 1 compares the circulation of three types of English- and German-language organs read in The Lutheran Church-Missouri Synod. Here we see clearly the steady advance of the English media. Of special interest is the comparatively steep decline of German in the 30's. Whether this is due to a turnover of generations twenty-five to thirty years after the end of mass immigration, to political factors such as a

* The main source of my data is the Statistical Yearbook of the Missouri Synod of the Lutheran Church published by the Concordia Publishing Co. in St. Louis. Similar material has been gleaned from publications of the Wisconsin Synod and the Norwegian Lutheran bodies. Information on ethnic and religious concentrations was taken from publications of the U.S. Bureau of the Census.

TABLE 1
Circulation in % of Church Publications in Missouri Synod between 1923 and 1947

Year	*Lutheraner* (German)	*Witness* (English)	*Kinder und Jugendblatt* (German)	*Young Lutherans Magazine* (English)	*Amerikanischer Kalender* (German)	*Lutheran Annual* (English)
1923	52	48	50	50	63	37
1925	51	49	44	56	60	40
1927	51	49	44	56	60	40
1929	51	49	44	56	60	40
1931	51	49	44	56	60	40
1933	39	61	44	56	60	40
1935	25	75	36	64	44	56
1937	23	77			35	65
1940					35	65
1945					21	79
1947	7	93				

Source: Adapted from Statistical Yearbook of Missouri Synod. Missing data unavailable.

revulsion against German during the rise of Hitler, to a natural breakthrough of English, or to a combination of all of these and other factors remains open to question.

The relatively greater decline of the *Lutheraner* as compared to the children's *Kinder und Jugendblatt* and the *Kalender* invites speculation. It is reasonable to assume that the children's magazine continued to be ordered by the Lutheran Day Schools of the Synod, which persisted in using German in the 30's for reading instruction. The *Kalender*, which incidentally became bilingual in the 30's, may have enjoyed similar institutional favors.

Table 2 summarizes the information available on parochial schools during a ten-year period. Clearly, while some use of German continued to be made in the 30's within the schools, especially in reading instruction, the language was rapidly yielding to English.

In Figure I, the general trends for German and Norwegian show a close similarity in the curves of language transition. It is interesting that the use of Norwegian in church services underwent an unusually sharp decline at the onset of World War I. Evidently, the political currents engendered by the war with Germany forced a "premature" rise in the

TABLE 2

The Use of Language in Lutheran Day Schools of the Missouri Synod, between 1923 and 1935

Year	In Religious Instruction			In Reading Instruction	
	German %	English-German %	English %	English-German %	English %
1923	17	38	45	59	41
1925	—	—	—	—	—
1927	4.7	34.8	60.5	47.5	52.5
1929	3.7	29.1	67.2	43.3	56.7
1931	2.2	24.4	73.4	37.7	62.3
1933	0.8	20.1	79.1	31.4	68.6
1935	1.7	15.7	82.6	27.6	72.4

Note: No data available for 1925.

Source: Adapted from Statistical Yearbook of Missouri Synod, 1923, 1925, 1927, 1929, 1931, 1933, 1935.

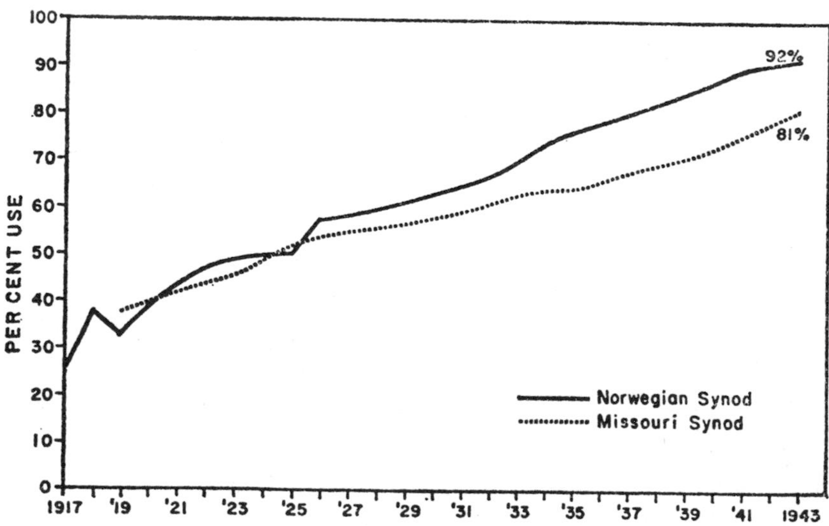

Figure I: Use of English in Services of Missouri Synod and Norwegian Lutherans.

Sources: E. Clifford Nelson; *The Lutheran Church Among Norwegian Americans,* II, p. 251. Paul T. Dietz, "The Transition from German to English in the Missouri Synod from 1910 to 1947", *Concordia Historical Institute Quarterly,* XXII (October, 1949), No. 3, p. 126.

use of English which subsided with the return of normal times. After 1925 the Anglification of the Norwegian church proceeded at a faster pace than that of the Missouri Synod, and the notion of a greater conservatism in the German-speaking denomination could easily suggest itself. But here care should be exercised against drawing any hasty conclusions. An inspection of immigration data may throw some light on the question of why German showed greater retentiveness. Table 3, which presents comparisons of the immigration of German and Norwegian settlers into the United States, shows that the German immigration began earlier, remained more sustained for a longer period, and was always much larger numerically. This indicates that the most crucial variable in the relatively greater persistence of German may well be the greater numerical concentration of Germans. More German was heard by more Germans in more places. Conservatism is an unnecessary assumption in order to account for the somewhat greater retentiveness of German.

Not only was the persistence of German as a vehicle of instruction somewhat greater than that of Norwegian, but the enrollment in Missouri Synod schools was larger than that in the Norwegian Lutheran Church of America. "The three Synods which united to form the Norwegian Lutheran Church in America in 1917 reported that week-day or vacation instruction was being given by 1,796 teachers to 41,716 children" (Haugen 1953, p. 101). In 1920, the elementary schools of the Missouri Synod reported enrollment of 73,063 students (Report of Board 1961, Cumulative Tables, Table I). Nevertheless the language transition in these two Lutheran churches has been monotonously steady in the direction of Anglification as both German and Norwegian have gradually yielded to the constant environmental pressure exerted upon them.

REGIONAL TRENDS

Our study of regional differences in the language transition utilizes data of the Missouri Synod exclusively. The districts can be roughly grouped as follows: (See Figure II)

1. *Most heavily shaded*: Those at or near 30% Anglification in 1920 (base line) and reaching the vicinity of 70% (1940 ceiling), representing an annual increase of 2%. These districts comprise Minnesota, Wisconsin, Michigan, northern and southern Illinois, North Dakota, Texas, Kansas, and northern Nebraska.

2. *Less heavily shaded*: Districts which resemble the first group in most respects except that their base line and ceiling are about 5% to

TABLE 3
Immigration of Germans and Norwegians between the years 1880 and 1960

Years	*German Immigrants*	*% of Total (1871-1960)*	*Norwegian Immigrants*	*% of Total (1871-1960)*
1871-1880	718,182	16.9	95,323	13.2
1881-1890	1,452,970	34.3	176,586	24.5
1891-1900	505,152	11.9	95,015	13.2
1901-1910	341,498	8.1	190,505	26.4
1911-1920	143,945	3.4	66,395	9.2
1921-1930	412,202	9.7	68,531	9.5
1931-1940	114,058	2.7	4,740	0.7
1941-1950	226,578	5.3	10,100	1.4
1951-1960	326,423	7.7	13,607	1.8
Total	4,241,008	100.0	720,802	100.0

Source: Adapted from the Statistical Abstracts of the U.S. 1940 and 1960.

10% higher, comprising Iowa, southern Nebraska, southern Dakota, and central Illinois. The districts in these first two groupings constitute the "heartland" of the Missouri Synod.

3. *Least heavily shaded:* Districts whose 1920 base line is near 50% use of English and whose 1940 ceiling is near or above 75%. In this group are the Western, Atlantic, Central, Eastern, Oregon-Washington, California-Nevada, Oklahoma, and Colorado districts. All except Central are at the periphery of the "heartland". They are, generally, areas of secondary migration and considerably more exposed to the inroads of Anglification than is the "heartland".

4. *Not included in Figure:* Districts outside the United States, viz., the Canadian districts of Alberta, Ontario, British Columbia, and Manitoba-Saskatchewan. The development in Canada appears to have been different from that in the United States.

5. *Not shaded in Figure:* The Southern District, high in Anglification from the start, and almost completely Anglicized by 1950.

The geographic aspect of differences in the language transition becomes immediately apparent. It follows then, that differences in the institutional retentiveness of the ethnic language are a function of varying situations as they have come about in different localities. Most German Lutherans settled originally in certain Midwestern states where, at least till the 30's, they maintained their greatest relative ethnic, religious, and occupational continuity. Hence, their linguistic "retentiveness". In the more peripheral Western regions, the greater mobility and heterogeneity of the popula-

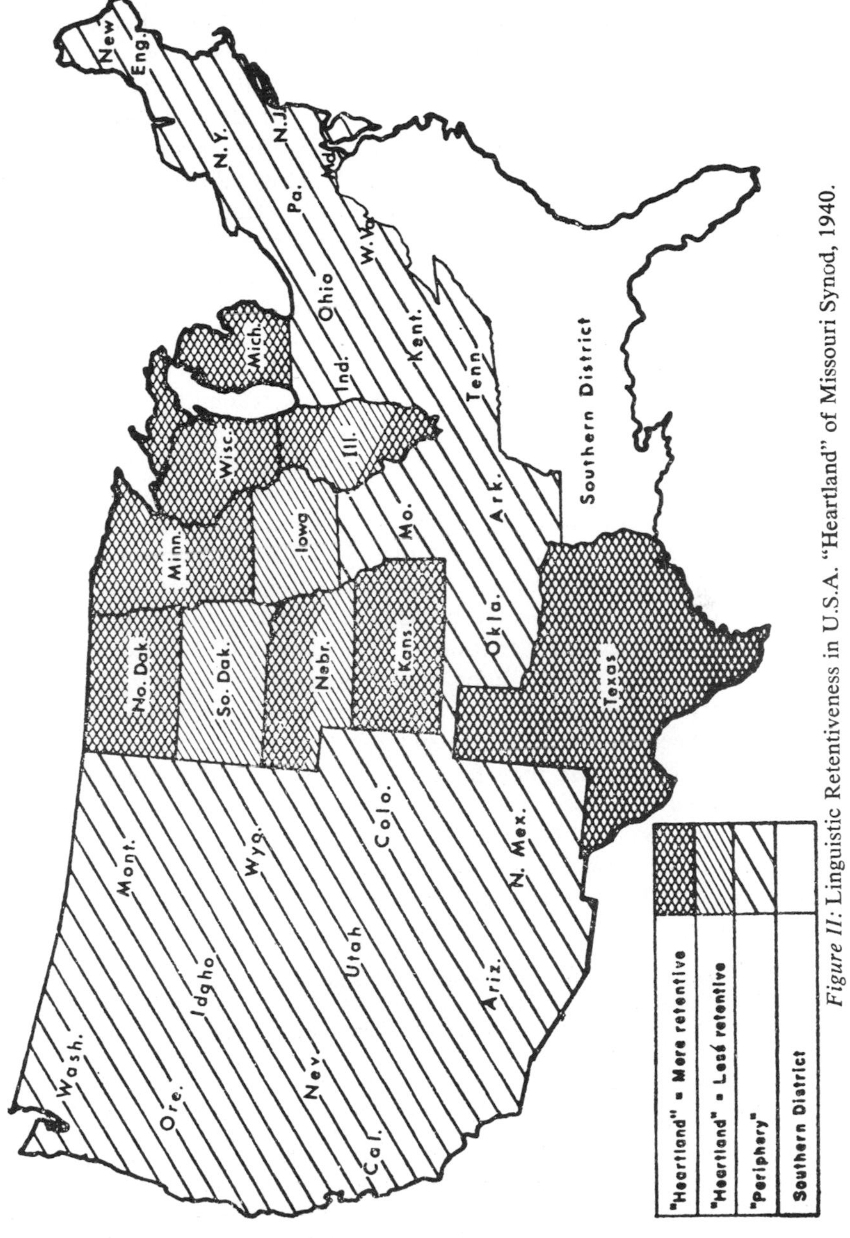

Figure II: Linguistic Retentiveness in U.S.A. "Heartland" of Missouri Synod, 1940.

tion made the task of preserving the ethnic mother tongue quite difficult, regardless of intention. Hence, a more rapid pace of Anglification.[1] We may thus advance the hypothesis that *whenever religio-ethnic concentrations coincide with other factors, such as occupational and residential stability and a traditional frame of reference, a situation is created which enhances the ideological climate suitable for the retentiveness of the ethnic mother tongue in the religious service*. In our discussion of certain Minnesota counties, we shall try to adduce further evidence for the plausibility of such situational factors underlying linguistic retentiveness.

Tables 4 and 5 illustrate the presence of both similarities and differences in regional development. The linguistic transition in Minnesota, like that in North Dakota-Montana on the one hand and in Manitoba-Saskatchewan on the other, points to the overall advance of the use of English in church services. But, differences are readily seen. The existence of hundreds of parishes in Minnesota probably favored a great variety of solutions as reflected in the prominence of the part-German, part-English approach. Such compromise solutions were practical only in the larger, better organized parishes of the Missouri Synod, and do not seem to have been as readily adopted in Canada or North Dakota-Montana. These latter communities were apparently forced into "either-or" alternatives. For them, the presence of older members in a parish may have prolonged the retention of "German-only" beyond the point of usefulness with younger members. Then, since the parish was too weak to try a bilingual solution, a switch to "English-only" became inevitable. The fact that these states lagged behind the national average in membership increase may have been in part a consequence of this organizational weakness.

It is within the local community, however, that we must look for the interplay of forces making for one linguistic solution or another. Thus in examining our hypothesis that whenever religio-ethnic concentrations

[1] Haugen anticipated these observations in his analysis of the language situation in the Norwegian Lutheran Church services: "As late as in 1930 there was still a wide variation between different districts. In Canada there were 70.6% Norwegian services in 1930 compared to only 12.3 in the Rocky Mts. district. In the latter area the Norwegians were scattered and largely urban, while in Canada they lived in compact rural settlements in the prairie provinces. The farming areas of North Dakota and Northern Minnesota were also notably higher in their retention than South Dakota and Southern Minnesota. East Coast and West Coast show almost identical distributions, close to the national average. The so-called Eastern district included such Midwestern States as Wisconsin and Illinois, but also urban communities like Chicago and Brooklyn. As the years passed, however, the difference between the districts was rapidly disappearing. Norwegian appeared to be approaching extinction at about the same time everywhere" (Haugen, 1953, p. 268).

TABLE 4
Distribution of German and English Services in Lutheran Church, Missouri Synod, 1923-1941

Year	*District*	*All German*	*More German*	*Half & Half*	*More English*	*All English*	*Total*
1923	Minnesota	46	120	100	27	58	351
1925	„	37	109	117	39	81	383
1927	„	21	97	119	50	77	364
1929	„	17	84	137	46	123	407
1931	„	15	60	147	60	134	416
1933	„	9	43	148	63	151	414
1935	„	6	30	127	90	147	400
1937	„	1	22	114	94	165	396
1939	„	2	12	113	106	179	412
1941	„	4	9	95	93	192	393
1923	North Dakota and Montana	42	30	54	14	48	188
1925	„	36	29	54	20	51	190
1927	„	20	23	61	17	51	172
1929	„	32	22	67	29	63	213
1931	„	26	16	61	32	69	204
1933	„	25	10	58	36	72	201
1935	„	26	8	46	38	84	202
1937	„	15	11	44	38	91	199
1939	„	17	12	38	39	102	208
1941	„	15	10	37	39	113	214

Source: Stat. Yearbooks of the Evangelical Lutheran Synod of Missouri, Ohio, and other States. St. Louis, Mo., Concordia Publishing House.

and certain other factors coincide, a situation is created which enhances the ideological climate suitable to retentiveness of the ethnic mother tongue, we are led to seek confirmation on the local level.

LOCAL FACTORS IN LINGUISTIC RETENTIVENESS

First, let us briefly trace the process of linguistic concentration. In Figures III, IV, and V, all bilingual parishes in the districts of Michigan, Minnesota, and North Dakota are plotted for 1940 and 1950. The white circles represent bilingual parishes in which at least some German was used in 1940, but in which no German was used in 1950. The black circles designate parishes that maintained the use of some German into 1950. Thus the distribution of circles provides a picture of the direction of linguistic retreat. Bilingual parishes, already concentrated in 1940,

TABLE 5

Distribution of German and English Services in Lutheran Church, Missouri Synod between 1923 and 1941

Year	*District*	*All German*	*More German*	*Half & Half*	*More English*	*All English*	*Total*
1923	Alberta and British Columbia	57	2	20	1	27	107
1925	„	49	6	16	4	62	137
1927	„	47	5	25	4	63	144
1929	„	48	4	30	11	51	144
1931	„	55	11	36	3	53	158
1933	„	58	12	36	5	58	169
1935	„	46	11	32	5	58	152
1937	„	51	9	36	9	75	180
1939	„	37	23	23	11	101	195
1941	„	29	14	21	9	108	181
1923	Manitoba and Saskatchewan	57	13	17	8	27	122
1925	„	58	16	15	5	13	107
1927	„	68	12	13	3	22	115
1929	„	63	16	17	7	39	142
1931	„	75	18	22	7	42	164
1933	„	63	18	24	7	53	165
1935	„	52	25	24	27	50	178
1937	„	52	21	29	6	60	168
1939	„	39	21	32	4	61	157
1941	„	38	20	34	6	87	185

Source: Stat. Yearbooks of the Evangelical Lutheran Synod of Missouri, Ohio, and other States. St. Louis, Mo., Concordia Publishing House.

became even more concentrated by 1950. The linguistic transition can, therefore, be described as a whittling away toward one or more core areas, that is, an "in-gathering" rather than a "thinning-out" process. This is especially apparent in the case of Minnesota. The process of concentration makes good sense if we can demonstrate that the areas toward which it moves display the characteristics of religio-ethnic concentration and continuity posed in our hypothesis. Globally, this can be shown by a mere inspection of the ethnic tables in the Paullin-Wright Atlas. Areas such as the Michigan Bay area, known as "the Thumb", and the region south-west of the Twin Cities in Minnesota are traditionally "German". In areas more sparsely settled by Germans, the language transition would yield a pattern of "thinning-out" rather than "in-gathering", since no one subregion would be strong enough to form a central core.

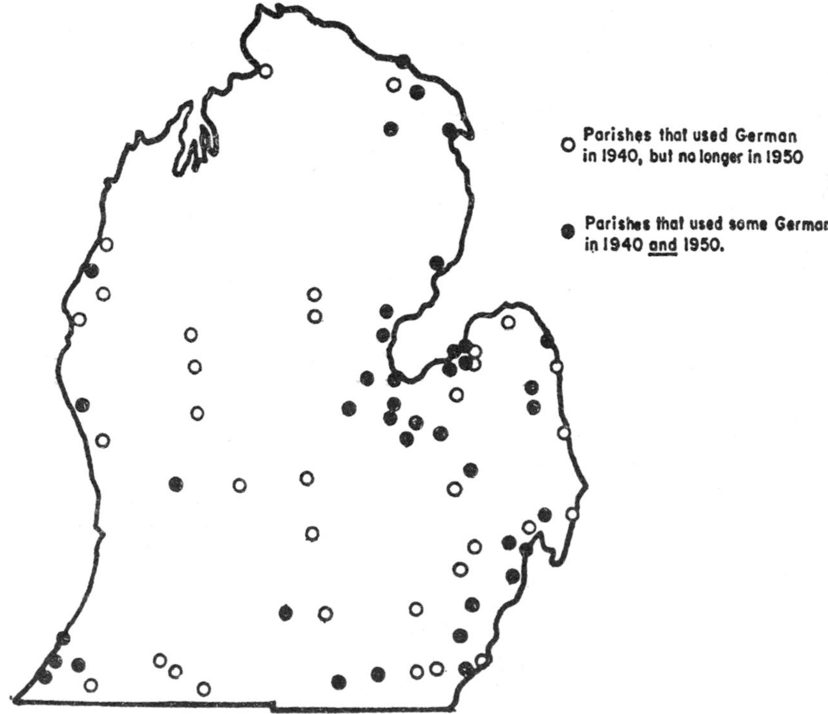

Figure III: The use of German in Michigan parishes of the Missouri Synod.

Source: Adapted from Statistical Yearbooks of Missouri Synod, 1940, 1950.

Einar Haugen, in his study of the Norwegian language in America, has made a similar point (Haugen 1952, pp. 5-6):

These areas where Norwegian has survived the longest in popular speech are not necessarily those areas where the number of persons born in Norway is largest nor those which were settled most recently. . . . Of course, such factors as continued immigration have played an important role, since much of the recent immigration has gone to the same areas as did the earlier, thereby reinforcing the use of the language. But, immigration which is dispersed in the cities or in marginal rural areas is more quickly Anglicized than that which maintains its solid neighborhood core. In the latter, people speak Norwegian simply because everybody else does without reflecting much about it. For them it is not a cultural duty or a program of behavior. If you ask why they do so, it is difficult for them to find an answer.

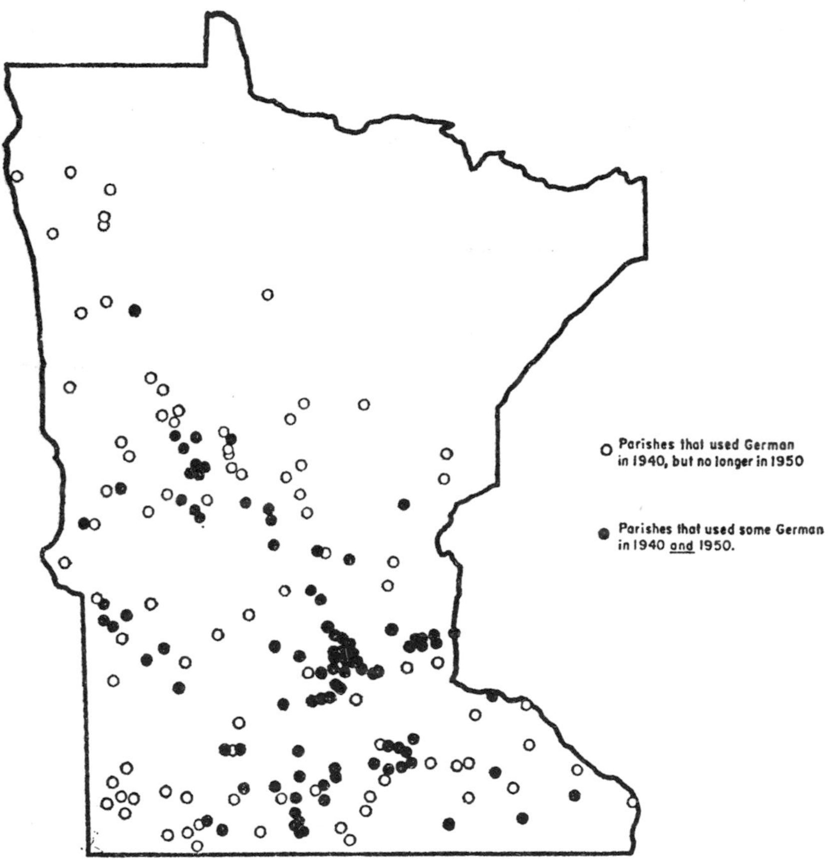

Figure IV: The use of German in Minnesota parishes of the Missouri Synod.

Source: Adapted from Statistical Yearbooks of Missouri Synod, 1940, 1950.

The core areas are characterized by both early concentrated settlement and continued immigration. If, in addition to what we have observed about the process of concentration in Michigan, Minnesota, and North Dakota, we realize that a considerable organizational effort must have been involved in the maintenance of bilingual parishes, it follows that the more retentive parishes should also be the better established and more populous ones. Indeed, Table 6 shows this to be the case with respect to a number of parishes picked at random from Yearbooks of the Missouri and Wisconsin Synod. Similar results were obtained when retentive parishes, those using German in 1940 and 1950, were com-

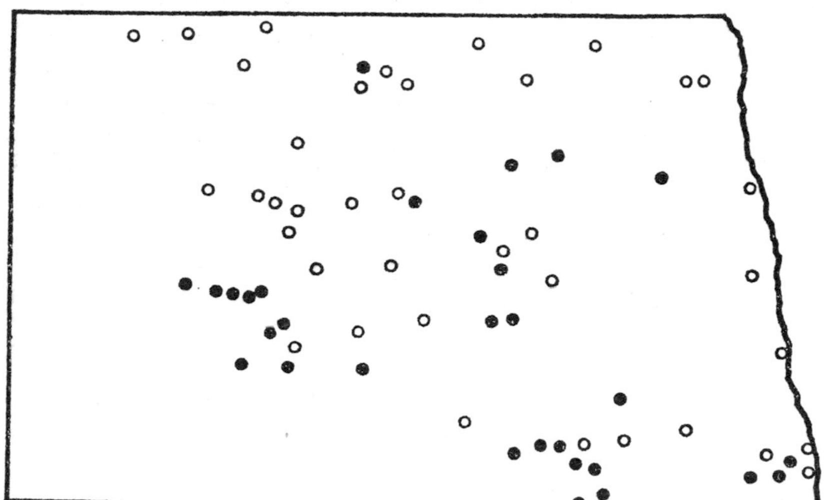

Figure V: The use of German in North Dakota parishes of the Missouri Synod.

Source: Adapted from Statistical Yearbooks of Missouri Synod, 1940, 1950.

pared with non-retentive parishes, those using German in 1940 but no longer in 1950 (Table 7). Thus in Table 7 we see that the linguistically more retentive parishes were larger, had a greater church-going ratio (a fact that holds for other samples as well), and supported more parochial schools.

The available data do not tell us whether the larger parishes became so as a result of internal growth or of external consolidation, i.e., merges between parishes. The weight of circumstantial evidence is on the side of organic, internal growth inasmuch as the total number of parishes in the most retentive areas remained rather stable over many years. Still, a certain amount of absorption of the smaller parishes by the larger, especially in rural areas, cannot be ruled out.

A picture has emerged of the linguistically retentive parish in the Missouri Synod as a typically larger, older, and possibly better organized unit than its "non-retentive" counterpart. In our consideration of regional trends, we hypothesized that church-associated retentiveness of the ethnic tongue prevails in areas where the ethnic and/or religious group is relatively concentrated over time. We also hypothesized that other conditions, such as occupational stability and a traditional frame of reference,

TABLE 6

Size and Age of Average Linguistically Retentive Parish 1950, 1958

	Missouri Synod						*Wisconsin Synod*	
	Minnesota 1950		*Michigan 1950*		*Iowa 1950*		*Wisconsin, West 1958*	
	Same G	*None*	*Same G*	*None*	*Same G*	*None*	*Same G*	*None*
Number of Parishes	99	78*	76	63*	26	225	89	68*
Average Founding Date	1888	1916	1880	1916	1889	1906	1878	1897
Souls per parish	432	250	647	287	448	210	303	589

Source: Adapted from Statistical Yearbooks of Missouri and Wisconsin Synods.

* Random sample.

TABLE 7

Linguistically Retentive vs. Non-Retentive Minnesota Parishes in Missouri Synod, 1940, 1950

	Institutional Retentiveness 83 Parishes Using German in 1940 and *in 1950*	*Institutional Non-Retentiveness 129 Parishes Using German in 1940, but* not *in 1950*
Souls per Parish, 1940	544	289
Communicants per Parish, 1940	394	196
Ratio of Communicants to Souls	.72	.67
Number of Parochial Schools	44	40
Pupils per Parish	2766/83 = 33.3	1158/129 = 9.0

Source: Statistical Yearbooks of Missouri Synod, 1940, 1950.

would reinforce religio-ethnic homogeneity as conditions of linguistic retentiveness.[2] Minnesota was chosen as the locale for testing this

[2] Today, no occupation serves as a surer basis of family-centered continuity than agriculture. When this rural bias is seen in conjunction with membership in the most conservative of Lutheran denominations, the traditional frame of reference should be obvious. At the same time, any statement of this kind has to be quite tentative until more direct figures on the actual occupational distribution of parishioners from both kinds of parishes can be ascertained.

hypothesis, inasmuch as it has passed through many of the phases typical of other districts; it has one of the largest memberships in the Missouri Synod; and, being predominantly rural, it does not present some of the special problems of more urbanized districts.

TWELVE MINNESOTA COUNTIES: AN AREA STUDY

Twelve counties, six of them containing the most "retentive" parishes and six of them the least, were selected for a comparison of ethnic and religious concentration (Table 8). Church-associated (institutional) linguistic retentiveness served as a basis for assigning the twelve counties to the two categories. The main criterion of retentiveness was *stability* of bilingualism rather than absolute number of parishes at any one time. Only Carver, Sibley, and McLeod Counties, however, can be classed as really retentive. Blue Earth, Watonwan, and Martin are rather wobbly cases of linguistic retentiveness, and should be regarded as intermediate in position.

Table 8 illustrates ethnic and denominational indices, based on census data, for the twelve counties. The table appears to confirm the major hypothesis. The linguistically retentive counties are characterized, generally, by larger concentrations of German-Americans organized in their own national church. Here the retention of the German language has the benefit of relatively greater secular and sacred reinforcement. The picture is particularly clear in the case of the three most retentive counties, Carver, Sibley, and McLeod, especially when these are contrasted with the six least retentive counties. In Ottertail, Lac Qui Parle, and Morrison counties, the presence of many Scandinavian-Americans organized in parishes of their own denominations have provided competition and ample opportunity for intermarriage. Warner and Srole (1954, pp. 290-293) have pointed to the affinity between these two ethnic groups. Their coexistence should Anglify both groups at a quicker rate, with English taking the role of common denominator. As Haugen has observed (Haugen 1953, p. 280): "We may also assume that no one learned English and began using it because they wanted to, but only because practical necessity forced them to. . . . Any facts we can find out about linguistic retentiveness are thus in large measure bound to reflect the degree of social isolation of the group." In Todd and other counties, the presence of many Catholics who are not committed to national churches and probably not as motivated to maintain any ethnic mother tongue would create a situation similarly conducive to more rapid Anglification. Todd, Faribault, and Pipestone counties, in addition, comprise large segments of other competing sects and nationalities.

TABLE 8
Denominational and Ethnic Configuration in Selected Counties, Minnesota, 1930

	German Lutherans	*Scandi-navians*	*Roman Catholics*	*Others*	*German Stock**	*Scandi-navian Stock**
	%	%	%	%	%	%
Carver	48	8	32	12	33	7
Sibley	61	9	18	12	34	11
McLeod	45	1	32	22	32	6
Blue Earth	33	12	27	28	23	10
Watonwan	22	49	15	14	19	29
Martin	38	13	13	36	25	14
Most Retentive Counties	26.1	13.0	24.2	36.7	26.4	11.7
Ottertail	28	36	17	19	15	32
Lac Qui Parle	10	63	16	11	24	40
Morrison	8	75	5	12	22	15
Tod	21	9	41	50	19	16
Faribault	13	27	24	36	18	17
Pipestone	22	4	21	75	19	18
Least Retentive Counties	16.2	26.8	32.6	24.8	17.6	23.8

* Foreign born and Native of Foreign and Mixed Parentage.

Source: U.S. Census, 1930: Report on Religious Bodies, 1936.

On the whole, the more retentive counties appear to be higher in percentage of church-going. This may be circumstantial evidence of greater conservatism, but it may also be the result of many other variables. It could also be argued that "conservatism", if it can be thus identified, is associated with agriculture. The more retentive Missouri Synod parishes typically are more rural than the less retentive ones. The rural parish, however, is not necessarily located in a predominantly rural county. While it is true that Carver and Sibley counties are completely rural, the same can be said for Lac Qui Parle. If occupational pursuit does indeed discriminate between the more and the less retentive parish, this does not necessarily characterize the county as a whole in which the parish is located. Thus the degree of rurality of a county does not help to discriminate between counties of more or less linguistic retentiveness.

Ethnic and denominational homogeneity remain as the only independent sociological variables that can be isolated on an extensive, county-wide basis as having probable bearing on the linguistic retentiveness within the parish.

A SAMPLE PARISH STUDY

A small sample (N=60) of pastors of Minnesota parishes was selected to include all 35 parishes reported by the Missouri Synod to be using some German as late as 1958; of the other 25 parishes, all but two had been bilingual until at least 1950.

On the basis of previous findings, we expected the retentive parishes to be more homogeneous in ethnic and occupational makeup, to be somewhat older and larger, and to display other signs of greater organizational strength. By and large, the earlier findings were sustained. Again the "ethnic predictor" emerged as most clear-cut of all. The retentive parish of 1962 was more homogeneous (76.5 German stock) than the non-retentive (66.4). The extent of interethnic marriages was also smaller for the former, with intermarriage cited by several pastors as a factor in the Anglification of the parish. Correspondingly, ingroup marriages were recognized to favor retention of the ethnic tongue. As one pastor put it: "In the last 25 years the lines of demarcation [between the ethnic groups] became less and less distinct. Little attention is paid to it now. Yet, when marriage takes place, most are within one language group."

Most of the differences between the two types of parish were exceedingly slight. However, the present comparison is an extremely rigorous test of our hypothesis. Our present subdivision may be said to classify *retentive* parishes as more retentive or less retentive, rather than as retentive or non-retentive. Still we may ask why the differences between retentive and non-retentive parishes are not any more clear-cut than they are.

For one thing, these concepts have become relative to a generally high level of Anglification so that the distinction is just the least bit arbitrary. After all, a parish which gives one monthly service in German, or fewer, is not really much more retentive than one in which German has been altogether discontinued. Moreover, by this time, at a point near the end of the language transition, the forces of religio-ethnic-occupational homogeneity and organizational strength that originally combined to generate greater linguistic retentiveness can no longer be clearly operative inasmuch as they have very little left to operate on. As the curve of the linguistic transition approaches its asymptote of complete Anglification, the possibilities of orderly fluctuations become increasingly limited, and a rising share of the variance in observable linguistic phenomena may be "error" variance. Stating it differently, "chance" factors become of increasing importance in determining the retentiveness and non-retentiveness of a particular parish. Chance factors, in the context of this study, should be understood to refer to factors other than statistically measurable sociological variables, e.g., the presence of a German-speaking pastor (twice as many pastors in retentive as in non-retentive parishes were reported as having a very good knowledge of German), the activities of an energetic group of elders, the relative recency of German instruction in Lutheran day schools, subtle differences in attitudes among certain segments of the parish membership, and so on, singly or in any combination.

The approach throughout the study has been to focus on sociological variables rather than motivational ones. The composition of a population was held to set the conditions for whatever attitudes underlay institutional retentiveness. Undoubtedly there was a time when this pre-eminence of demographic factors was not so clear-cut, when attitudes of religious conservatism and ethnic identification did play a major role. As Nelson (1960, p. 243) writes:

> Moreover, the arguments which were to be repeated in other foreign language groups were articulated there [among German-speaking parishioners]: (1) the use of English must be promoted in order to save the second and succeeding generations for the Lutheran Church; and (2) the use of German must be continued in order to (a) preserve the true faith which was diluted when Anglicized, and (b) to conserve the cultural heritage.[3]

Indeed, it would not have been surprising had the Missouri Synod, known to be one of the most conservative Lutheran bodies, persisted in an ideology of church-associated linguistic retention. Such a development has precedents in the history of religions. The fact is that this did not happen. On the contrary, there are a number of indications that, if anything, the Synod shifted to an ideology of non-retention. Ethnicism, once a pillar of the church, came to be viewed as a deterrent to expansion. As one of the pastors put it: "It became apparent that restricting the church to German would stifle further growth." Haugen (1953, p. 238) makes this point quite clearly:

> ... eventually the rebellion against the immigrant language reared its head in the church also. Faced with this problem, the church compromised its lesser goal for the sake of its larger one. To stay alive and carry on its spiritual message, the church had to yield and become first bilingual, then increasingly English.

[3] See also Dietz (1949).

The questionnaire data suggest that the 1962 *home* may actually have been more retentive than the church. This strengthens the impression that the prime mover of retentiveness has been non-institutional and non-ideological during the last few decades. Many statements made by pastors in reply to a variety of questions indicate that the last institutional prop was removed when Lutheran schools ceased to teach the German language in the 30's and 40's. The very naturalness of the language transition is reflected in the type of reason given again and again to account for the remaining persistence of German: "To serve older folks and recent immigrants." The matter-of-factness with which the transition is viewed comes out very clearly in the following: "Originally the majority were of German extraction. For a certain period they endeavored to preserve that language as long as they could, somewhat for sentimental reasons and somewhat because they enjoyed the services made in the language in which they had been brought up. The majority, however, soon prevailed who were interested in helping the people spiritually as much as possible and thought that this could be done best in the language which all understood."

One might even speculate that it is precisely this apolitical non-ideological, unconscious inertia of old habit that has made the long persistence of German possible. For had there been a strong movement of retentiveness subsequent to the First World War, formidable counter-currents might have generated opposition and smothered the use of German in a hail of politics. (This may hold for other ethnic tongues as well.) As it was, German was rarely actively threatened from the outside because it did not itself constitute a threat. It may be the innocuous naivete of its popular use that, ironically, has kept the language alive so far.

REFERENCES

Auvray, P., P. Poulain, and A. Blaise, *Sacred Languages* (New York, Hawthorn, 1960).

Brady, M. F., "Why American Catholics Conduct Schools", in *The Role of the Independent School in American Democracy* (Paper delivered at a Conference on Education, Milwaukee, Marquette University Press, 1956).

Dietz, P. T., "The Transition from German to English in the Missouri Synod from 1910 to 1947", *The Concordia Historical Institute Quarterly*, XXII (St. Louis, Mo., Concordia Publishing House, Oct. 1949), 97-121.

Fichter, J. H., *Dynamics of a City Church* (Chicago, University of Chicago Press, 1951).

Fichter, J. H., "Conceptualizations of the Urban Parish", *Social Forces*, 31, (1952), 31, 43-46.

Fichter, J. H., *Parochial School* (Notre Dame, Ind., Univ. of Notre Dame Press, 1958).

Handlin, O., "The Church and the Modern City", *Atlantic Monthly,* 210 (1962), 2, 101-05.

Haugen, E., "The Struggle over Norwegian", in *Norwegian-American Studies,* XVII (Northfield, Minn., Norwegian-American Historical Association), 1952.

Haugen, E., *The Norwegian Language in America,* Vol. I (Philadelphia, Univ. of Pennsylvania Press, 1953).

Nelson, Clifford, *The Luthern Church among Norwegian-Americans,* II (Minneapolis, Augsburg Publishing House, 1960).

Paullin, C. O. and J. K. Wright, *Atlas of the Historical Geography of the United States* (New York, Carnegie Institute and American Geographic Society, 1932).

Report of Board of Parish Education, *The Lutheran Church-Missouri Synod* (St. Louis 2, Mo., 210 N. Broadway, 1961).

Statistical Yearbooks of the Evangelical Lutheran Synod of Missouri, Ohio, and other States (St. Louis, Mo., Concordia Publishing Co.).

Warner, L. and L. Srole, *The Social System of America* (New Haven, Yale University Press, 1954).

From *Language Loyalty in the United States* by Joshua A. Fishman *et al.* (The Hague, Mouton, 1966), pp. 139-155. Reprinted by permission.

Heinz Kloss

DAS NATIONALITÄTENRECHT DER VEREINIGTEN STAATEN VON AMERIKA

RÜCKSCHAU

Das amerikanische Nationalitätenrecht war entgegen einer außerhalb Amerikas allgemein verbreiteten, aber auch innerhalb Amerikas vorherrschenden Meinung außerordentlich reich entwickelt. Die sprachliche Angleichung, der die nichtenglischen Gruppen auf dem Festland fast durchweg verfallen sind, ist bisher meist als das Ergebnis einer zielbewußten staatlichen Assimilierungspolitik aufgefaßt worden. Angesichts der zahlreichen nichtenglischen Einwanderergruppen hätten, so heißt es, die Amerikaner ja nicht umhin gekonnt, auf der Alleingeltung des Englischen in allen Volksschulen zu bestehen – und das Ergebnis sei eben die fast allgemeine Verenglischung der Einwanderernachkommen.
Aber wie unsere Darstellung erweist, sind die nichtenglischen Volksmassen in den USA nicht *durch* ein ihren Sprachen *ungünstiges*, sondern *trotz* eines ihnen *günstigen* Nationalitätenrechts verenglischt worden. Nicht durch juristische Bestimmungen und behördliche Maßnahmen, nicht auf dem Wege über den Staat sind die Nationalitäten assimiliert worden, sondern durch die Absorptionskräfte der ungemein hochentwickelten amerikanischen Gesellschaft. Man mochte den Nationalitäten noch so viele Möglichkeiten zur Selbstbehauptung geben, die Leistungen der angloamerikanischen Gesellschaft und die Bewährungs- und Aufstiegsmöglichkeiten, die sie bot, waren so groß, daß sich die Abkömmlinge der "Fremden" ihr früher oder später freiwillig eingegliederten.

Gewiß haben sich Rechtsbuchstabe und Rechtswirklichkeit, haben sich Inhalt und Anwendung der Rechtsnormen nicht immer und überall entsprochen. Aber wo sie voneinander abwichen, da war nicht selten die Rechtswirklichkeit sogar noch günstiger als das geschriebene Recht. In Ohio z. B. war 1840 Deutsch (in Cincinnati) ein Unterrichtsmittel der öffentlichen Grundschule geworden. Das Schulgesetz von 1870 beschränkte es auf die Stellung eines Unterrichtsfaches. Trotzdem hat es sich in Cincinati bis in den Ersten Weltkrieg als Unterrichtsmittel behauptet. Und wo umgekehrt das geschriebene Recht günstiger aussah als die Rechtswirklichkeit, da lag es nicht selten daran, daß die Amerikaner eine Gesetzesvorschrift zugunsten einer Minderheitensprache beibehielten, obgleich die Volksgruppe schon lange keinen Wert mehr auf sie legte und keinen Gebrauch mehr von ihr machte. In Louisiana war die französische Volksgruppe, was sprachliche Wünsche auf dem Gebiet von Schulwesen, Gesetzesveröffentlichungen usw. angeht, schon von 1890 herauf fast vollständig gleichgültig und in gewissen Sinne abgestorben. Aber erst die Verfassung von 1921 und ein Gesetz von 1922 z. B. trugen im Schulwesen dem veränderten Zustand der französischen Volksgruppe endgültig Rechnung. In Pennsylvanien wurden deutsche Ausgaben der Gouverneursbotschaften nach 1850 kaum mehr, nach 1880 gar nicht mehr von der bodenständigen Bevölkerung verlangt, wurden aber bis in die neunziger Jahre hinein bewilligt. Die deutsche Presse Ostpennsylvaniens hat nach (etwa) 1890 vielfach geradezu von den amtlichen Bekanntmachungen gelebt. die ihr auf Grund älterer Gesetze zustanden; obwohl die Herausgeber englischer Blätter sich beschwerten, wurden diese Rechte nicht beseitigt, bis die Blätter trotz dieser künstlichen Ernährung an innerer Entkräftung gestorben waren.

In zwei Bereichen vor allem haben wir wahre Großleistungen der amerikanischen Nationalitätenpolitik kennengelernt: einmal die schöpferische Handhabung des Selbstbestimmungsrechtes und daneben im Bereich der Sprachpolitik die sorgfältige, dabei aber rein pragmatisch erfolgte und nie theoretisch unterbaute Entwicklung eines Altsiedler- und eines Zuwandererrechtes.

Was zunächst das Selbstbestimmungsproblem angeht, so sei besonders die selbständige Art hervorgehoben, auf die es in Puertoriko gelöst worden ist. Es ist ja ein elementarer Fehler, den Sinn einer Ausübung des Selbstbestimmungsrechtes in der Änderung der staatsrechtlichen Zugehörigkeit zu erblicken. Wie die Entscheidung der Tessiner für die Schweiz im Jahre 1798 und die der Puertorikaner für die USA im Jahre 1952 verdeutlichte, kann das Selbstbestimmungsrecht auch in dem Sinne ausgeübt werden, daß sich eine Volksgruppe dafür entscheidet, unter ehrenvolleren, freiheitlicheren Bedingungen als bisher im gleichen Staatsverband zu bleiben.

Dieser Beitrag der Amerikaner zur Praxis des Selbstbestimmungsrechtes hat schon in mehreren VN-Dokumenten seinen Niederschlag gefunden. Die Vollversammlung der VN hat am 27. November 1953, d. h. am gleichen Tage, wo sie anerkannte, daß durch den Commonwealth-Status Puertorikos die Vereinigten Staaten der Pflicht enthoben seien, die Insel weiterhin in ihre Jahresberichte über abhängige Gebiete aufzunehmen, auch den Grundsatz der Assoziierung als eine der Möglichkeiten zur Verwirklichung des Selbstbestimmungsrechtes anerkannt. Die damals noch undeutliche Grenzziehung zwischen den Begriffen "Assoziierung" und "Integrierung" wurde 1960 wesentlich verbessert,[1] so daß seither von den VN endgültig drei Möglichkeiten anerkannt werden, dem Selbstbestimmungsrecht Genüge zu tun: Unabhängigkeit, Integrierung (was im Falle Puertorikos Gliedstaatlichkeit – statehood – bedeutet hätte) und Assoziierung. Dabei ist zu beachten, daß sich zwei zwar untereinander verwandte aber doch deutlich voneinander verschiedene Konzeptionen der "Assoziierung" herausgebildet haben. Die eine, im Falle Puertorikos verwirklichte und in der VN-Entschließung von 1960 ausgesprochene faßt association auf als die staatsrechtliche Beziehung zwischen zwei Partnern, von denen einer dem anderen deutlich übergeordnet bleibt, so daß association hier eine Alternative zur independence (oder zu integration d. h. im Falle Puertorikos zur Gliedstaatlichkeit) bleibt. Demgegenüber beruht z. B. Griechenlands 1961 erfolgte Assoziierung mit der EWG und beruhten de Gaulles einstige Pläne für eine Assoziierung Algeriens mit Frankreich auf der Voraussetzung, daß beide Partner unabhängige Staaten und als solche Völkerrechtssubjekte sind.

Man kann die beiden Formen der Assoziation als Binnenassoziation (internal association, Typ USA – Puertoriko) und Außenassoziation (external association, Typ EWG – Griechenland) unterscheiden. Gemeinsames Merkmal beider Assoziationsarten ist, daß zwei Gemeinwesen auf der Grundlage der Freiwilligkeit und der Gleichberechtigung einen Vertrag abschließen, durch den sich der eine Partner dem anderen in einer Weise beiordnet, die diesem anderen ein Mehr an Verantwortlichkeit und Entscheidungsbefugnis auf dem den Gegenstand des Vertrages bildenden Aufgabenbereich überläßt.

Als "Außenassoziation" kann z. B. die durch den Freundschaftsvertrag vom 1. August 1962 zwischen Neuseeland und West-Samoa hergestellte Beziehung bezeichnet werden.[2] Eine mit der Beziehung zwischen Puertoriko und den USA vergleichbare "Binnenassoziation" finden wir im früheren Verhältnis Eritreas zu Äthiopien (1952-1962) und im heutigen der Faroer zu Dänemark (seit 1948). Andere Fälle sind

[1] Dok. A/2630, Suppl. 1017, 21-23. Dok. A/RES/1541 (XV) vom 21. Dezember 1960. Vgl. Kloss in Zs. "Vereinte Nationen", H. 3, 1962, 75-78, 93-94.

[2] New Zealand Treaty Servies 1962 No. 5 (= Dept. of External Afairs, Wellington, Publ. No. 256).

weniger eindeutig.[3] Die Beziehung Surinams und der Niederländischen Antillen zum niederländischen Gesamtstaat ist gedacht als Integration; sie treten als zwei Gliedstaaten neben die europäischen Niederlande als den dritten Gliedstaat.[4] Doch weist das sorgfältig durchdachte Gefüge dieser Beziehungen auch deutliche Wesensmerkmale der Binnenassoziation auf,[5] was an dieser Stelle nicht näher ausgeführt werden kann. Immerhin besitzen Surinam und die Niederländischen Antillen mehr Mitbestimmungsrecht im niederländischen Gesamtstaat als Puertoriko im amerikanischen. Übrigens ist auch bei der heutigen Stellung Puertorikos nicht einzusehen, warum es nicht einigen Nebenorganisationen der VN als "assoziiertes" Mitgleid beitreten könnte, etwa der UNESCO, wo heute schon mehrere nicht unabhängige Gebiete vertreten sind.[6]

Über dem Beitrag zum Selbstbestimmungsrecht, den Amerika im Falle Puertorikos gegeben hat, darf keinesfalls der nicht weniger wichtige vergessen werden, den die Freisetzung der Philippinen bedeutete, dieser erste Fall von Entkolonialisierung eines Gebietes, das vorher weder Mandatsgebiet (wie Irak) noch Protektorat (wie Ägypten), sondern eine Voll-Kolonie gewesen war. Wie durch den Unabhängigkeitskrieg der Vereinigten Staaten zum erstenmal das Selbstbestimmungsrecht einer in kolonialer Abhängigkeit lebenden weißen Nation verwirklicht worden war, so bedeutet die Unabhängigkeit der Philippinen einen entscheidenden Durchbruch auf dem Wege zur Entkolonialisierung der farbigen Nationen.

Ebensogroß ist die amerikanische Leistung auf dem Gebiet des Sprachenrechtes. In den Vereinigten Staaten ist das Sprachenrecht in erster Linie eine Funktion des Grades der Bodenständigkeit einer Volksgruppe. Alle anderen Faktoren, wie vor allem die Kopfstärke oder der Anteil an der Gesamtbevölkerung, die Siedlungsdichte, die Ähnlichkeit mit oder Verschiedenheit von der rassischen oder konfessionellen Zu-

[3] C. J. Friedrich, *Puerto Rico: Middle Road to Freedom* (N.Y., Rinehart, 1959), 16-17, hat als erster auf eine gewisse Analogie im Status von Puertoriko und West-Berlin hingewiesen; West-Berlin nimmt demnach in seiner Beziehung zur Bundesrepublik zwar de jure die Stellung eines Gliedstaates („Landes"), de facto aber die eines binnenassoziierten Gemeinwesens ein.

[4] Vgl. M. W. H. van Heldingen, *Het Statuut voor het Koninkrijk der Nederlanden* (Den Haag, 1957). *De Rechtsorde in het Koninkrijk der Nederlanden* (Den Haag, 1960 [2]) (= *Schakels,* S 32 NA 32; 1. A. S 31 NA 26).

[5] Als Assoziierung wird die Beziehung der überseeischen Reichsteile zu Holland aufgefaßt von E. J. Sady, *The U. N. and Dependent Peoples* (Washington, D.C., Brookings Institution, 1957 [2]), 97.

[6] Im Juli 1961 waren assoziierte Mitglieder der UNESCO u. a. Mauritius, Ruanda-Urundi, Singapur, Tanganjika, der Westindische Bund – alles damals noch nicht souveräne Gebilde; im März 1963 waren es Katar, Mauritius und Singapur. Mit der Ernährungs- und Landwirtschaftsorganisation (FAO) der VN waren im März 1963 assoziiert: Britisch-Guyana, Jamaika, Mauritius, Rhodesien und Nyassaland.

sammensetzung des staatsführenden Volkes, die größere oder geringere sprachliche Verwandschaft, die Siedelweise (Sprachinseln!) erweisen sich demgegenüber als sekundär.

Das wird deutlich, wenn man auf Hawaii das Sprachenrecht der alteingesessenen Althawaiier vergleicht mit dem der zahlenmäßig weitaus stärkeren Japaner, oder wenn man gegenüberstellt das Sprachenrecht der nur rund 200.000 alteingesessenen Sprachspanier in Neu-Mexiko dem der 2 Millionen mexikanischen Neueinwanderer in Kalifornien und Texas oder der zugewanderten 800.000 Puertorikaner in Neu-York. Charakteristisch ist auch die Großzügigkeit, mit der die Sprachen winziger ozeanischer Sprachgemeinschaften in Mikronesien und auf Samoa gefördert werden.

Es lassen sich da im einzelnen noch sehr viel feinere Abstufungen nachweisen als die zwischen Altsiedlern und Zuwanderern.

Das duldende Nationalitätenrecht ist allen sprachlichen Minderheiten, auch den "*Mitzuwanderern*", gleichmäßig zugute gekommen. Das gleiche gilt von gewissen Zweigen des fördernden Nationalitätenrechtes, vor allem der Berücksichtigung der nichtenglischen Sprachen im öffentlichen Büchereiwesen und in dem amtlichen Bekanntmachungen.

Andere Formen der Förderung blieben den "*Alleinzuwanderern*" vorbehalten, d. h. den aus der Einwanderung der Jahre 1830-1850 hervorgegangenen deutschen Gruppen oder jenen Minderheiten, die zwar vom Bund her gesehen Zuwanderer (und zwar Mitzuwanderer) waren, von ihrem jeweiligen Gliedstaat her gesehen aber Erstsiedler wie die Skandinavier der Mittelwestens und die Tschechen in Texas. Hierher gehören die Pflege der Nationalitätensprachen an öffentlichen Schulen sowie die Veröffentlichung gewisser für die breite Öffentlichkeit bestimmter amtlicher Dokumente, z. B. Gouverneursbotschaften oder neuer Staatsverfassungen in den Minderheitensprachen; das alles ist vor allem für Deutsch, aber auch für Tschechisch, Skandinavisch, Französisch und Niederländisch bezeugt.[7]

Weiter noch geht der Staat in der Förderung solcher Gruppen, die zu den Altsiedlern gehören, die aber nicht Allein-Altsiedler, sondern zusammen mit den Angelsachsen ins Land gekommene *Mitaltsiedler* sind. Solche Gruppen, wie z. B. die Deutschen in Pennsylvanien und in Ohio, erringen sowohl das Recht auf die nichtenglische oder zweisprachige Staatsschule wie das auf den Druck fachlicher Regierungsdokumente – z. B. Behörden-Jahresberichte, in Pennsylvanien auch Parlamentsakten – in ihrer Sprache. Und endlich die *Allein-Altsiedler* die *vor* den Angelsachsen seßhaft gewordenen Spanier von Neu-Mexiko

[7] Es ist eine ausgesprochene Ausnahme von dieser Regel, wenn kurz vor 1914 an den öffentlichen Schulen von Milwaukee Mitzuwanderersprachen wie Polnisch und Italienisch zugelassen wurden, siehe S. 106 (*Das Nationalitätenrecht* ...).

und Franzosen von Louisiana, erringen in wichtigen Bezirken sogar die volle nationale Gleichberechtigung, vor allem für das Parlament, aber zum Teil auch in Verwaltung und Rechtspflege.[8] Das trifft in verstärktem Maße zu für diejenigen *Allein-Altsiedler,* die in Außengebieten ohne nennenswerte angloamerikanische Zuwanderung wohnen. In Puertoriko führte die nominelle Gleichberechtigung von Altsiedlersprache und Englisch praktisch zur Vorherrschaft der ersteren; die Angelsachsen auf Puertoriko spielen die Rolle einer sprachenrechtlich der Mehrheit nicht in jeder Hinsicht voll gleichgestellten Minderheit. Fast unbeschränkt ist auch die Alleinherrschaft des Japanischen in Riukiu.

Ausschlaggebend aber bleibt die Grundunterscheidung zwischen Altsiedlern und Zuwanderern; sie bilden das eigentliche Gegensatzpaar, wobei dann Mitzuwanderer und Allein-Altsiedler jeweils die extremste Möglichkeit verkörpern. So eng schließt sich das vereinsstaatliche Nationalitätenrecht an die verschiedenen Einwurzelungsgrade der Volksgruppen an, daß man geradezu darangehen kann, an Hand seiner Entwicklung eine Art organischen oder natürlichen Sprachenrechtes für Einwanderervolksgruppen zu entwerfen. Grundlage einer organischen nationalitätenrechtlichen Ordnung ist der Satz, daß alle Einwanderergruppen Anspruch auf ein sehr hohes Ausmaß von Duldung ihrer Sprachen im privaten, im staatsfreien Raum haben. Solches duldendes Nationalitätenrecht ist zu gewähren, wo nur immer eine Volksgruppe ihre Sprache und Art zu pflegen wünscht und bereit ist, hierfür durch Unterhaltung privater Einrichtungen die nötigen Opfer zu bringen. Diese Regel hat man in den Vereinigten Staaten mit nur geringen Unterbrechungen immer befolgt.

Hingegen kann nicht der Satz aufgestellt werden, daß allen Volksgruppen förderndes Nationalitätenrecht zuteil werden müsse. Zunächst einmal wird es, die Geschichte der Vereinigten Staaten hat das bewiesen, immer wieder große Volksteile geben, die eine Erhaltung ihrer Sprache gar nicht wünschen. Es wäre ein Unding, wollte der Staat sie gegen ihren Willen am Leben erhalten. Aber auch wo die Minderheit ihre Sprache zu pflegen wünscht, ist der Staat nicht ohne weiteres gehalten, sie zu fördern. Es ist ja begreiflich, daß eine frisch eingewanderte Menschengruppe sich vielfach gegen den drohenden Verlust der angestammten Sprache sträubt. Handelt es sich hier nun um ein schnell aufflackerndes unbeständiges Gefühl des Einwanderergeschlechtes oder um einen tiefsitzenden Selbsterhaltungstrieb, den auch die Kinder und Enkel teilen? Versteht diese Volksgruppe nur Forderungen zu stellen, oder hat sie

[8] Vgl. z.B. für Neu-Mexiko den auf S. 104 (*Das Nationalitätenrecht* . . .) wiedergegebenen Gesetzestext von 1889.

bewiesen, daß sie für ihre Wünsche auch materielle Opfer zu bringen bereit ist? Erst wenn sie verstanden hat, auch ihren Enkeln noch die angestammte Sprache einzupflanzen, erst wenn sie das Opfer privater Sprachenpflege mit Erfolg gebracht hat, erst wenn sie unter Beibehaltung der angestammten Sprache eingewurzelt ist, kann sie verlangen, daß der Staat ihr beisteht und sich ihrer Sprache fördernd annimmt. Ein solcher naturrechtlicher Anspruch auf Förderung steht ihr erst etwa von der dritten Generation ab zu, also erst den "natives of native parentage".

Die umfassende Duldung der Zuwanderersprachen entsprach den besten Interessen Amerikas. Wichtiger als eine möglichst rasche sprachliche Einschmelzung der Einwanderer ist ihre seelische und geistige Eingliederung. Wenn der Staat die Einwanderersprache vollständig übergeht, kann dadurch diese Eingliederung gestört werden. Bei Neueinwanderdern muß damit gerechnet werden, daß sie auf lange Jahre hinaus das Englische nicht oder nur mangelhaft beherrschen. Die Arbeit des zentralen Regierungsapparates mag davon unberührt bleiben. Aber die Arbeit der örtlichen Verwaltungsmaschinerie kann Schaden erleiden, wenn die Einwanderer die örtlichen Erlasse und Bekanntmachungen der Behörden nicht verstehen und von ihrem Inhalt keine Kenntnis nehmen. Es liegt somit im Interesse des Staates selbst, den Einwanderern der ersten Generation einer neuen sprachlichen Minderheit hinsichtlich der Sprache der amtlichen Bekanntmachungen entgegenzukommen. Bei der zweiten Generation, den Kindern der Einwanderer, kann in den Großstädten im allgemeinen damit gerechnet werden, daß die Sprache des staatsführenden Volkes gut verstanden wird; ein Interesse des Staates daran, amtliche Bekanntmachungen in ihrer angestammten Sprache zu veröffentlichen, besteht daher im allgemeinen nicht mehr. Hingegen besteht ein staatliches Interesse daran, daß diese Einwandererkinder neben der Sprache des staatsführenden Volkes auch die Sprache der Eltern noch einigermaßen beherrschen. Ist dies nämlich nicht der Fall, folgt z. B. auf eine einsprachig-italienische sofort eine einsprachig-englische Generation, so tritt ein Überlieferungsbruch ein. Die Eltern genießen bei ihren Kindern keinerlei Ansehen und üben keinen Einfluß auf sie aus. Sie können ihnen keine Normen für ihr Leben mitgeben, und die Kinder wachsen, Waisenkindern vergleichbar, ohne persönlich bildende Einflüsse auf. Dieser Zustand aber ist für den Staat äußerst gefährlich; er ist in manchen Großstädten Nordamerikas geradezu zu einer Hauptursache des Gangstertums geworden. Zum Beispiel ergab 1927 eine Untersuchung in Chicago, daß es dort neben 45 rein angloamerikanischen und 88 negerischen oder rassisch gemischten Gangs 396 gab, deren Mitglieder überwiegend oder ausnahmslos einer einzigen Einwanderernationalität angehörten, und 351, in denen sich bestimmte Einwanderernationalitäten mischten. Und zwar überwogen bei diesen 747 letztgenannten Gangs weitaus die Angehörigen der zweiten (d. h. der ersten inlandbürtigen) Generation; nur wenige Auslandbürtige gehörten ihnen an.[9]

Wie ich schon an anderer Stelle schrieb, halte ich es für eine vordringliche Aufgabe der Nationalitätenrechtler, einen Katalog der sprachlichen Grundrechte für Einwanderervolksgruppen auszuarbeiten;[10] für diese Aufgabe des internationalen Rechtes haben die Vereinigten Staaten einen überragenden Beitrag geleistet.

Es sei noch kurz auf einige Einzelleistungen hingewiesen, die Teilerscheinungen jener umfassenden Großzügigkeit in den Bereichen des Selbstbestimmungs- und Sprachenrechtes sind.

Besonders bedeutsam ist, wie oft Gebieten mit nichtenglischsprachiger Einwohner- und Wählermehrheit der Status eines Territoriums mit gewählter Volksvertretung verliehen wurde: Louisiana 1804, Neu-Mexiko 1850, Hawaii und Puertoriko 1900, Philippinen 1907. Diese Leistung wird in Amerika selber selten gewürdigt, weil man dort den Selbstregierungsgrad eines Territoriums an dem so viel höheren eines Gliedstaates mißt und feststellt, daß dieser letztere Rang Neu-Mexiko und Hawaii erst verliehen wurde, als sie eine sprachenglische Wählermehrheit erhalten hatten. Aber gemessen an den Verhältnissen in Einheitsstaaten, ob sie nun dezentralisierten Verwaltungsaufbau haben wie Großbritannien oder gar zentralistisch regiert sind wie Frankreich oder Italien, bedeutete doch auch jene Territoriumsstufe einen ungemeinen Schutz. Was würde es für Katalonien, die Bretagne, ja selbst Wales bedeuten, eine Verwaltungsform zu haben, wie sie Louisiana 1804-1812, Neu-Mexiko 1850-1912 und Puertoriko 1917-1952 besaßen!

Mit dieser Anerkennung des Rechtes bodenständiger Nationalitäten auf Selbstregierung steht in engem Zusammenhang die weitgehende sprachenrechtliche Förderung vor allem größerer bodenständiger Volksgruppen, die ihren deutlichsten Ausdruck fand in der Gleichstellung nichtenglischer Sprachen in den Parlamenten von Neu-Mexiko und Louisiana, der jahrzehntelangen Veröffentlichung deutscher Sitzungsakten des Parlaments von Pennsylvanien und vor allem natürlich der Zulassung nichtenglischer oder zweisprachiger öffentlicher Volksschulen in diesen drei Staaten und Ohio. Gerade diese Tatbestände sind in Europa weithin unbekannt geblieben.

Weitere hervorhebenswerte Besonderheiten des amerikanischen Nationalitätenrechtes sind zu verzeichnen im Bereich des Büchereiwesens und des Rundfunks. Die ausgedehnte Berücksichtigung der nichtenglischen Sprachen im Bereich des öffentlichen Büchereiwesens ist ein be-

[9] Thrasher, *The Gang* (Chicago, 1927), nach F. J. Brown und J. S. Roucek, *Our Racial and National Minorities* (N.Y., Prentice-Hall, 1937), 704.

[10] Siehe *Europa Ethnica*, 18 (Wien, 1961), H. 2, 51, 54.

sonderes Ruhmesblatt der USA; übrigens ist dies ein Gebiet, auf dem vermutlich die Zuwanderergruppen sogar eher noch besser behandelt wurden als die Altsiedler. Die umfassende Entfaltung eines Rundfunkwesens der Nationalitäten läßt auch kleinste Gruppen in den Genuß eigener Sendestunden kommen und hat überdies im American Council for Nationalities Service (früher Common Council) eine zentrale Betreuungsstelle gefunden. Der Aufschwung des nichtenglischen Rundfunkwesens ist freilich das Ergebnis der freiheitlichen privaten Struktur des amerikanischen Rundfunkwesens im allgemeinen und insofern nur mittelbar ein Teil der Nationalitätenpolitik.

Der hohe Rang des amerikanischen Nationalitätenrechtes ist dem Bewußtsein vieler Amerikaner nicht gegenwärtig. Als auf einer Expertentagung der UNESCO zu Paris im Juni 1960, die der Diskriminierung im Bildungswesen galt, der Vertreter Amerikas, J. Simsarian, sich gegen ein weitgehendes Sprachenrecht aussprach und daraufhin der Vertreter der Sowjetunion auf ihre großzügige Sprachpolitik in Gliedstaaten wie der Ukraine oder Usbekistan hinwies, antwortete Simsarian, Amerika wolle diese Sprachpolitik keineswegs beanstanden, behalte sich aber das Recht vor, seine zahllosen Einwandererminderheiten anders zu behandeln. Diese Gegenüberstellung war schief. Das Gegenstück zu den Einwandererminderheiten Nordamerikas bilden die Millionen nach Sowjetasien zugewanderten Ukrainer [11] und anderen Angehörigen sowjeteuropäischer Nationalitäten, und es ist durchaus sicher, daß diese sprachenrechtlich schlechter gestellt sind als die Einwandervolksgruppen in Nordamerika. Ein Vergleich zwischen sowjetamtlichen und exilukrainischen Sprachenkarten läßt erkennen, daß die Ukrainer z. B. nördlich von Wladiwostok und rings um Slawgorod weite Gebiete ethnisch beanspruchen, die die Sowjetregierung als fast rein russisch behandelt.[12] Man muß dabei bedenken, daß es in der Sowjetunion kaum eine staatsfreie privatrechtliche Sphäre für die Eigenbetätigung der Volksgruppen gibt und daß infolgedessen, wenn die Sprache einer Volksgruppe im Bereich der öffentlichen Hand ignoriert wird, damit automatisch auch alle die Betätigungsmöglichkeiten in Presse, Rundfunk, Vereinswesen, Buchwesen usw. entfallen, die in Amerika im Rahmen des duldenden Volksgruppenrechtes bestehen.

Einen großen Bereich echter Duldung kann es der Natur der Dinge nach nur in einem nichttotalitären Gemeinwesen geben. In allen totalitären Staaten kann von einer privaten Sphäre nur bedingt die Rede sein. In rechtstotalitären Staatswesen wie denen des einstigen italienischen

[11] Alexander Mytziuk, "Die Ukrainer in Sowjetasien", in: *Volksforschung*, 6, 1943, 79-102.

[12] Vgl. Mykola Kulyckyj, *Ethnographical Map of the Soviet Union* (Edinburgh, 1953). *Karta Narodow SSSR 1962* (sowjetamtlich).

Faschismus und des deutschen Nationalsozialismus ist sie, auch wo sie dem Rechtsbuchstaben nach vorhanden ist, faktisch völlig unter staatlicher Kontrolle und jederzeit nach Belieben einschränkbar oder aufhebbar. In linkstotalitären kommunistischen Ländern aber ist ganz offiziell fast alle "gesellschaftliche" Betätigung nur als Ausfluß staatlicher Willensbildung denkbar. Die Herausgabe einer Zeitung, die Eröffnung eines Kinos, die Gründung eines Vereins, in denen die Nationalitätensprache gepflegt werden soll, bilden Bestandteile einer einheitlichen, von Staat und Partei gelenkten Kulturpolitik. Eine wenigstens dem Namen nach staatsfreie Sphäre, in der die Nationalitätensprache auch ohne ausdrückliche Ermächtigung des Staates gepflegt werden könnte, gibt es hier allenfalls im Rahmen der Familie und der vom Staat ja nicht eben sonderlich begünstigten Kirche. In einem den Volksgruppen wahrhaftig nicht freundlich gesinnten und auch nicht eben demokratischen einstigen Rechtsstaat wie dem Königreich Preußen hingegen, das nicht daran dachte, seine Minderheiten zu fördern, konnten sich die Polen vor 1914 dank der rechtsstaatlichen Achtung vor der staatsfreien Sphäre eine Art privatrechtlicher Selbstverwaltung hohen Grades aufbauen.

Das Gegenstück zur sowjetischen Nationalitätenpolitik gegenüber der Ukraine oder Usbekistan ist die amerikanische Nationalitätenpolitik gegenüber Puertoriko. In sprachenrechtlicher Hinsicht ist sie mindestens ebenso großzügig wie die sowjetische – in staatsrechtlicher Hinsicht aber großzügiger, da sie 1952 den Puertorikanern eine echte Chance gab, in freier Abstimmung ihr Selbstbestimmungsrecht auszuüben.

Es liegt mir ferne, die Amerikaner und ihr Nationalitätenrecht romantisch zu idealisieren. Gewichtige Mängel weist es vor allem dort auf, wo es sich mit dem Rassenrecht überschneidet, wie dies der Fall ist bei der Behandlung der eingewanderten Mexikaner.[13] Die Verfolgung der deutschen Sprache im Zeitraum 1917-1923 bleibt ein schwer erklärbares und entschuldbares Phänomen (während des zweiten Weltkrieges wäre eine solche Feindseligkeit verständlicher gewesen, aber damals kam sie nicht auf). Ferner würde man im Sinne eines "perfekten" duldenden Nationalitätenrechts wünschen, daß manche Einzelstaaten nach dem Muster van Rhode Islands großzügiger in der Zulassung zweisprachigen privaten Grundschulunterrichts wären. Selbst die im Prinzip vorbildliche Regelung der Stellung Puertorikos würde doch noch wesentliche Verbesserungen vertragen.[14]

Ich möchte auch keineswegs behaupten, daß den Angehörigen der englischen Sprachengemeinschaft in den USA der gruppenegoistische

[13] Siehe S. 49 (*Das Nationalitätenrecht* . . .).
[14] Siehe S. 253 ff. (*Das Nationalitätenrecht* . . .).

Wunsch nach Ausbreitung ihrer Sprache unter den "Allophonen", den Nichtenglischen völlig fremd sei. In jeder gesunden Sprachgemeinschaft lebt der Wunsch nach Wahrung und da, wo Voraussetzungen dafür bestehen, auch nach Mehrung des sprachlichen Bestandes, entfernt vielleicht vergleichbar der Art, wie in jedem gesund empfindenden Einzelmenschen ein gewisser Drang nach Erwerb, Bewahrung und Mehrung von persönlichem Eigentum lebt. Verwerflich ist nicht, daß der einzelne den Drang zum Eigentum verspürt, sondern daß er ihm ungezügelt nachgibt. So ist es auch durchaus berechtigt, daß die Angehörigen einer Sprachgemeinschaft den Wunsch verspüren, andere Menschen ihr einzugliedern – doppelt berechtigt, wenn es sich um eine innerlich und äußerlich noch unfertige, ihrer seelischen Einheit noch nicht völlig sichere Nation handelt, wie sie im Amerika des 19. Jahrhunderts lebte; verwerflich wäre es bloß, wenn sie dabei zu das duldende Nationalitätenrecht verletzenden Mitteln griffen, statt, wie es geschah, ihre natürlichen Instinkte durch Vernunft und Rechtsgefühl zu zügeln.

Die Amerikaner haben dabei eine wichtige Erfahrung von allgemeiner Gültigkeit gemacht: daß nämlich städtische, nicht über ein geschlossenes Siedlungsgebiet verfügende Zuwanderervolksgruppen unter günstigsten nationalitätenrechtlichen Bedingungen in der Regel ihre Sprache nicht auf die Dauer aufrechterhalten können. Beweis: vorgestern und gestern der Untergang der deutschen Sprache in den Großstädten, gestern und heute der der polnischen, heute und morgen der der französischen (Neuengland!). Damit wird eine vielumstrittene Rechtsfrage als Scheinproblem entlarvt, die Frage nämlich, ob städtische Einwanderervolksgruppen in industrialisierten Landschaften das Recht haben, ihre Sprache auf die Dauer beizubehalten oder nicht. Es ist ein Scheinproblem, weil es objektiv die Möglichkeit zu einer solchen "Dauer" nur in verschwindendem Umfange gibt.[15] Die Frage muß also, wenn wir die juristische Fragestellung würzen mit dem Salz unserer soziologischen Einsicht, wie folgt umformuliert werden: Haben städtische Einwanderergruppen das Recht, den Untergang ihrer Sprache nach Kräften hinauszuzögern?

Auch andere soziologische, mit der Nationalitätenpolitik zusammenhängende Fragenbereiche sind in Amerika gefördert worden. Der Fragenbereich der Zweisprachigkeit und eines zweisprachigen Bildungswesens wurde vor allem in und für Puertoriko theoretisch geklärt und praktisch geordnet, und zwar unter dem Gesichtspunkt, wie man bei gleichzeitiger, für unumgänglich gehaltener Erlernung des Englischen die Muttersprache erhalten könne. Besonders zu nennen ist als theoretischer Beitrag der bedeutsame Bericht, den die Columbia-Universität

15 Abgesehen natürlich von Fällen, wo die Einwanderer sich durch Religion, Hautfarbe, Bildungsniveau usw. deutlich von der einheimischen Bevölkerung so sehr abheben, daß es z. B. nur ausnahmsweise zu Mischheiraten kommt.

1926 über die Zweisprachigkeit im Erziehungswesen von Puertoriko vorlegte,[16] als praktischer Beitrag die systematische Verwendung von Befunden der strukturellen Linguistik im Englischunterricht an den Volksschulen der Insel. Die Autoren des Columbia-Berichtes erklärten stolz, es sei wohl das erste Mal, daß das Problem des zweisprachigen Unterrichts irgendwo so planmäßig und gründlich erforscht worden sei; in der Tat hat ja auch in Europa erst der Zweisprachigkeitskongreß in Luxemburg 1927[17] diesem Fragenkreis eine nicht mehr auf aktuelle Regionalanliegen beschränkte Anteilnahme der Wissenschaftler gesichert. (Demgegenüber gelten die mancherlei wertvollen Untersuchungen über Zweisprachigkeit auf dem nordamerikanischen Festland im allgemeinen nicht so sehr dem Dienst an den Nationalitäten als Gruppen wie der Individualforschung.) Riesengroß ist endlich das Schrifttum über Einzelfragen des Assimilationsvorganges,[18] das hier aber nur am Rande erwähnt zu werden braucht, da es sein Thema fast ausnahmslos unter dem Gesichtspunkt behandelt, daß ein recht baldiges Verschwinden der nichtenglischen Sprachen wünschenswert sei und nur selten von der Voraussetzung ausgehe, daß zwei Sprachengemeinschaften und Sprachkulturen für längere Zeit oder gar für immer im gleichen Lande nebeneinander bestehen sollten.[19]

Nicht nur soziologische Einsichten aber verdanken wir der amerikanischen Nationalitätenpolitik, sondern auch eine ganze Reihe handfester Neuerungen und Einsichten *unmittelbar* nationalitätenrechtlichen Inhalts. Ihre entscheidenden Großleistungen bleiben: auf dem Gebiet des Sprachenrechts das Nebeneinander von sorgfältig durchgebildetem Altsiedler- und ebenso großzügig gehandhabtem Zuwandererrecht, auf dem Gebiet des Selbstbestimmungsproblems die frühe Bereitschaft zur Freisetzung kolonialen Gebietes und die Aufzeigung eines dritten Weges, der zwischen Unabhängigkeit und Integrierung vermittelt.

[16] A survey of the public educational system of Porto Rico. Made under the direction of the International Institute of Teachers College, Columbia University. Authorized by the University of Porto Rico. N. Y. 1926. Im Vorjahr hatte die gleiche Hochschule einen ähnlichen Bericht für die Philippinen veröffentlicht: *A survey of the educational system of the Philippine Islands* (Manila, 1925).

[17] Vgl. den Sammelband *Le Bilinguisme et l'Education* (Genf, 1928).

[18] Vgl. E. K. Francis, "Minderheitenforschung in Amerika", in: *Kölner Zs. f. Soziologie u. Sozialpsychologie,* 9, 1957, 517-548; 10, 1958, 233-247 und 401-417.

[19] Der europäische Leser ist vor dem Mißverständnis zu warnen, das sich daraus ergibt, daß amerikanische Wissenschaftler in den letzten Jahrzehnten nicht selten die Ansicht vertraten, es sei wünschenswert, daß die Einwanderer-*nachkommen* die "culture" ihrer Vorfahren beibehalten; was hier unter "culture" verstanden wird, ist (in der Regel) nicht sprachbedingt, und den Autoren schwebt nicht das Nebeneinander verschiedener Nationalitäten, sondern eine reizvolle Auflockerung und farbige Bereicherung der angloamerikanischen Kultur vor.

Nachdem ich ausführlich von den Vorzügen des amerikanischen Nationalitätenrechtes gesprochen habe, möchte ich nochmals auf einige Grenzen und Schwächen hinweisen:

1. Der Höhepunkt des duldenden Volksgruppenrechtes lag vor 1914, genauer um 1890, als die nichtenglische private Volksschule, an der Englisch nur Unterrichtsfach war, im größten Teil des Landes erlaubt wurde. Daß man seither – außer in einigen Außengebieten, besonders Puertoriko und Riukiu – eine so schwache Stellung des Englischen im Lehrplan nicht mehr erlaubt, ist berechtigt; bedauerlich ist aber, daß in den meisten Landesteilen (zu den Ausnahmen gehört Rhode Island) auch die zweisprachige private Schule, in der alle Fächer in beiden Sprachen gelehrt werden, nicht mehr gestattet ist.

2. Die Behandlung nichtenglischer Sprachen im Gerichtwesen war in manchen Landesteilen nicht so großzügig wie man hätte wünschen dürfen; zu Härten führte z. B. im 19. Jahrhundert die Ausschließung der deutschen Sprache von den Gerichtshöfen in Pennsylvanien.

3. Jene höchste Stufe des Nationalitätenrechtes, die in der Erhebung der Nationalität zur Körperschaft des öffentlichen Rechts (public corporations) besteht, wurde nur einmal andeutungsweise erreicht: in der Schaffung der Rechtspersönlichkeit des "People of Portorico" (1900 bis 1952). Aus drei Gründen kann dieser Ansatz nicht allzuhoch bewertet werden: Das "People of P. R." umfaßte auch die dort ansässig gewordenen Angloamerikaner und sonstigen Nichtiberer. Die Zahl dieser Nichtiberer war anderseits so gering, daß sich Gebiet und Volksgruppe, Gebiets- und Personalautonomie fast deckten. Endlich wurden diese Rechtskörperschaft und die mit ihr verbundene Institution einer eigenen puertorikanischen Staatsbürgerschaft nicht geschaffen, um den Puertorikanern etwas Besonderes zu gewähren, sondern um ihnen etwas Besonderes, die amerikanische Staatsbürgerschaft, vorzuenthalten.[20] Andere negativ zu bewertende Einzelphänomene traten entweder nur wenige Jahre hindurch auf – so die schlechte Behandlung der Deutschen im ersten, die Japaner im zweiten Weltkrieg[21] – oder entstammen dem Bereich des Rassenrechts, so besonders die weitverbreitete soziale Schlechterstellung der eingewanderten Mexikaner, die diese nicht wegen ihrer Sprache, sondern wegen ihrer Hautfarbe trifft.

[20] Vgl. S. 245 (*Das Nationalitätenrecht* . . .). Über einen Ansatz zur Zuerkennung der Rechtspersönlichkeit an eine Volksgruppe auf privatrechtlicher Basis siehe S. 31 (*Das Nationalitätenrecht* . . .).
[21] Vgl. S. 46-48 (*Das Nationalitätenrecht* . . .).

VERHÄLTNIS ZWISCHEN DER EIGENEN NATIONALITÄTENPOLITIK DER VEREINIGTEN STAATEN UND IHRER EINSTELLUNG ZUM INTERNATIONALEN MINDERHEITENSCHUTZ

Die bedeutenden Leistungen der Vereinigten Staaten auf dem Gebiete des Nationalitätenrechts legen die Vermutung nahe, daß ihre Vertreter sich auch auf internationalem Gebiet regelmäßig für einen Schutz der Volksgruppen und für einen Ausbau des Nationalitätenrechts eingesetzt haben.

Dem ist jedoch nicht so. Ich sagte weiter oben,[22] das amerikanische Nationalitätenrecht stelle einen Triumph der Rechtlichkeit über den jeder Sprachgemeinschaft in größerem oder geringerem Maße angeborenen natürlichen Egoismus und Expansionswillen dar. Aber dieser Triumph ist so wenig in das Bewußtsein der meisten Amerikaner gedrungen, daß sie sich bei internationalen Aussprachen wiederholt auf die Seite des primitiven, eher barbarischen Instinktes gestellt haben statt auf die Seite der den Instinkt bezwingenden, das Recht verehrenden Vernunft. Es kommt nicht selten vor, daß Staaten, die im Innern eine Politik der Härte und der Ungerechtigkeit verfolgen, sich vor internationalen Gremien laut zu den Idealen der Toleranz und Gerechtigkeit bekennen. Die Vereinigten Staaten bilden das seltene Beispiel der umgekehrten Haltung: bei im allgemeinen aufgeklärter, duldsamer und fortschrittlicher Behandlung der Nationalitäten in ihrem Herrschaftsbereich bekennen sie sich international sehr häufig zu den Grundsätzen einer rückschrittlichen, unduldsamen und ungerechten Nationalitätenpolitik. Eine Parallele dazu bildet die Art, wie der Vielvölkerstaat Indien im eigenen Riesenreich eine großzügige Nationalitätenpolitik praktiziert, in internationalen Gremien aber meist eher eine engherzige empfohlen hat. Und eine Art Umstülpung des von Amerika in seiner Nationalitätenpolitik angewandten Verfahrens finden wir in seiner Rassenpolitik, die auf internationalem Felde eine radikale Gleichstellungspolitik vertritt, im Inland aber die Reste der Ungleichheit bisher nur langsam abbaute.

In den Vereinten Nationen hat es von Anfang an eine starke Gruppe von Staaten gegeben, die sich für das Recht des Staates, seine anderssprachigen Bürger zu assimilieren, aussprachen, sei es, daß sie als Einwanderungsstaaten meinten, der Einwanderer habe mit dem Verlassen seines Heimatlandes freiwillig für die Sprache seines neuen Wohnlandes optiert, sei es daß sie in der Duldung oder gar Schaffung von Sondereinrichtungen für bestimmte ethnische Gruppen eine offene oder versteckte Diskriminierungspolitik witterten, sei es, daß sie von dem Ver-

22 Siehe S. 642 dieser Schrift (*Readings in the Sociology of Language*).

such der Bewahrung ererbten Sprachgutes eine Schwächung der nationalen, auf Einheit beruhenden Kraft und Solidarität befürchteten oder daß sie gar in der Pflege der sprachlichen Bande, welche Volksgruppen mit fremden Staaten verknüpften, eine Gefährdung der äußeren Sicherheit des Staates erblickten. Die Assimilationisten setzten einen Kurs in den VN durch, der zufolge Inis L. Claude "die Nationalitätenfrage unter dem weiten Problemkreis der allgemeinen Achtung der Menschenrechte subsumiert und dabei gleichzeitig stillschweigend das Recht des Staates, eine Assimilationspolitik zu betreiben, bejaht".[23]

Und Claude stellt fest, daß, wo immer im Rahmen der VN dieses Problem sich in aller Schärfe stellte, die Vereinigten Staaten an die Spitze der Assimilationisten traten.[24] Einzelbeispiele dafür lassen sich in Fülle beibringen. Die USA führten jene Staatengruppe, welche erreichte, daß in dem Entwurf einer Völkermord-Konvention die Bestimmung über "kulturelles Genocidium" d. h. gewaltsame Ausrottung einer Sprache gestrichen wurde.[25] Als 1952 von der Menschenrechte-Kommission der VN über das Selbstbestimmungsrecht gesprochen wurde, waren es die Vereinigten Staaten, vertreten durch Eleanor Roosevelt, die, gefolgt von den afro-asiatischen Ländern, verlangten, an die Bestimmung zugunsten des Selbstbestimmungsrechts keine entsprechende für den Minderheitenschutz anzuschließen, während die Ostblockstaaten und einige westeuropaische Länder, vor allem Belgien, für die Koppelung von Selbstbestimmungsrecht und Nationalitätenrecht eintraten.[26] Als Ende 1960 in der Vollversammlung der VN über Südtirol gesprochen wurde, sprach sich die amerikanische Vertreterin, Miss Willis, im ganzen nachdrücklich für den Standpunkt Italiens aus.

Es fehlt nicht an entsprechenden Zeugnissen außerhalb der VN. Schon 1938 hatten die USA auf der Interamerikanischen Konferenz in Lima einer Entschließung (XXVII) zugestimmt, daß der damals in der Alten Welt unter Völkerbund-Ägide bestehende internationale Minder-

[23] I. L. Claude, *National Minorities, an international problem* (Cambridge, Mass., 1955), 176.

[24] Claude, 166 "Whenever the issue must be squarely faced, the U. S. takes the lead ... in opposing the concept of special minority rights". Zur Behandlung der Minderheitenfragen in den VN liegt eine Studie von Professor Felix Ermacora vor, die in nächster Zeit im Rahmen dieser Schriftreihe erscheinen soll.

[25] Claude, 164.

[26] Claude, 173-175. Wegen der Erklärungen von Mrs. Eleonor Roosevelt siehe Dok. E/CN-4/SR 256 (Erklärung vom 17. April 1952) und Dok. E/CN-4/SR 73 7. Zu den Äußerungen von Mrs. Roosevelt lassen sich Parallelen in den Schriften H. v. Treitschkes nachweisen, mit denen dieser für Deutschland mit gleicher Begründung das Recht auf Assimilierung seiner Minderheiten in Anspruch nahm.

heitenschutz nicht anwendbar sei auf die westliche Halbkugel.[27] Darüber mag man in Puertoriko den Kopf geschüttelt haben. Volksgruppen wie den drei, zusammen rund 5 Millionen zählenden Gruppen der ketschuasprachigen Indianer in Peru, Ekuador und Bolivien kann man den Charakter von nationalen Minderheiten (non-dominant groups) höchstens dann absprechen, wenn man aus rassischen Gründen sie und ihre Sprache für nicht entwicklungs- und ausbaufähig hält.

Seit 1942 haben sich die Vereinigten Staaten auf jährlichen Konferenzen der Außenminister beider Amerika für den Standpunkt eingesetzt, der Minderheitenschutz erschöpfe sich in der Beachtung der Menschenrechte.[28]

Auf der Pariser Friedeskonferenz von 1946 erklärte Amerikas Vertreter Bedell Smith, sein Land verstehe nicht, wieso man die Minderheiten erhalten statt aufsaugen wolle; "wenn Sie Schutzbestimmungen für eine Minderheit in *einem* Staat treffen, müßten Sie es in allen anderen auch tun".[29] Als im Juni und im Dezember 1960 im Rahmen der Unesco in Paris eine Konvention gegen Diskriminierung im Bildungswesen vorbereitet wurde, trug der amerikanische Vertreter Simsarian dazu bei, daß die den nationalen Minderheiten geltenden Bestimmungen der Artikel 2 und 5 recht blaß ausfielen.

Mehrfach haben bei solchen Anlässen die amerikanischen Delegierten erklärt, man könne von ihnen ein Eintreten für einen internationalen Minderheitenschutz nicht erwarten, da ihr eigenes Land eine Unzahl von Einwandererminderheiten beherberge, deren Fortbestehen seine nationale Einheit gefährden würde.

Diese Haltung so vieler Sprecher Amerikas hat mancherlei Gründe. Zu den wichtigsten gehört – neben der mangelnden Kenntnis der eigenen Traditionen – die verwirrende Wirkung, die von den Komplexen der Menschenrechte und des Rassenrechts ausgeht. In diesen beiden Bereichen wird ja Gleichheit in der Regel – nicht immer! – durch die Abschaffung von Sondereinrichtungen für bestimmte Volksteile hergestellt, also z. B. dadurch, daß Angehörige aller Rassen die gleichen Schulen und Hochschulen besuchen dürfen. Diese Probleme aber haben seit dem Ende des zweiten Weltkrieges so sehr im Vordergrund der Weltpolitik gestanden, daß unvermerkt das Urteil über die Fragen des Nationalitätenrechts davon mitgefärbt und mitbestimmt worden ist. Die For-

[27] "The system of protection of ethnical, language, or religious minorities cannot have any applications whatsoever in America, where the conditions characterizing the groups known as minorities do not exist". Vgl. *Am. Jo. of Int. Law*, 34 (1940), Suppl. 198 und dazu G. Dahm, *Völkerrecht* (Stuttgart, I, 1958), 402.

[28] A. Demichel, "L'évolution de la prot. des minorités depuis 1945", in: *Rev. Gen. de Droit Int. Publ.*, 64, 1960, 27-28.

[29] J. B. Schechtmann, "Decline of the international protection of minority right", in: *West. Pol. Qu.*, 1951, 1-11 (hier 9).

derung nach Abschaffung oder Verhinderung von Sondereinrichtungen, eine im allgemeinen gerechte Forderung im Bereich des Rassenrechts, wurde übertragen auf das Nationalitätenrecht, wo sie die Billigung des Unrechts und der Ungerechtigkeit bedeutet. Man beobachtet die Wirkung dieses Mißverständnisses, wenn ein Robert F. Kennedy 1956 den Sowjets im Rahmen einer im übrigen stichhaltigen Kritik vorwirft, in Mittelasien rassische Diskriminierung zu praktizieren und das damit begründet, daß sie in Uşbekistan gestrennte Schulen für russische und einheimische Kinder unterhalten.[30]

Dieser einseitigen Begünstigung der Menschenrechte und des Rassenrechts kommen entgegen der Wunsch der Vereinigten Staaten, die – überwiegend dem Nationalitätenrecht wenig geneigten – iberoamerikanischen Staaten auf ihrer Seite zu wissen und ihre mangelnde Klarheit über den Wesensunterschied zwischen Zuwanderer- und Altsiedlerrecht.

Ein wenig mag die Sprödheid der USA gegenüber dem Prinzip internationaler Abmachungen über das Nationalitätenrecht auch dadurch verstärkt worden sein, daß laut Art. VI (2) der Bundesverfassung alle in Vollmacht des Bundes, also unter Zustimmung des Senats, geschlossenen Verträge dieselbe Kraft wie Bundesgesetze haben, wogegen sich seit etwa 1953 im Lande immer mehr Stimmen gewandt haben.[31]

Das einseitige Gesamtbild, das wir hier von dem Verhalten der USA in Fragen des internationalen Nationalitätenrechts entwerfen, wird noch etwas trüber, berücksichtigt man, daß die Vereinigten Staaten ihren wirtschaftlichen und militärischen Beistand wiederholt auch solchen Nationen leihen mußten, die, wie z. B. die Türkei gegenüber den Kurden, einen ausgesprochen minderheitenfeindlichen Kurs steuerten. Dem Prestige der USA hat diese unfreiwillige "Nationalitätenpolitik zur linken Hand" geschadet. Es ist freilich bestreitbar, ob die USA selbst bei bestem Willen an der Nationalitätenpolitik der von ihnen unterstützten Staaten viel hätte ändern können, aber kaum bestreitbar, daß ihnen das Problem kaum zum Bewußtsein gekommen ist.[32]

Das Bild, das wir hier skizzieren mußten, scheint unvereinbar mit dem Panorama inneramerikanischen Nationalitätenrechts, das wir vorher zeichnen durften. Zum Glück ist es unvollständig, denn es übergeht

[30] R. F. Kennedy: Leserbrief an N. Y. Times 25. Januar 1956: "The communists practize rigorous segregation in this area, with separate school systems for the European Russian children and for the local children."

[31] Vgl. z. B. Missouri v. Holland, 252 US 416 (1920) und dazu Heinz Guradze, *Der Stand der Menschenrechte im Völkerrecht* (Göttingen, 1956), 26 bis 29; Egon Schwelb in *Arch. des Völkerrechts,* 8, H. 1, 1959, 48-49.

[32] Der Verfasser hatte Gelegenheit, auf internationalen Kongressen kurdischer Studenten 1960 und 1961 die Auswirkungen der amerikanischen Bündnis- und Unterstützungspolitik auf die Einstellung dieses Volkes zu beobachten.

sowohl eine frühere Haupt- wie eine heutige Nebententendenz der amerikanischen Außenpolitik in Sachen Nationalitätenschutz.

Eine frühere Haupttendenz: denn vorübergehend wurden die USA unter Wilson der Hauptanwalt eines internationalen Minderheitenschutzes. Daß in die Pariser Vorortverträge entsprechende Bestimmungen hineinkamen, war in erster Linie das Verdienst Wilsons und seiner Berater, besonders des Juristen David Hunter Miller und des Historikers Archibald Coolidge.[33] Wilson hatte schon im Oktober 1917 jene "Inquiry" genannte Expertengruppe für Fragen der europäischen Nationalitätenordnung eingesetzt,[34] deren Programm sich von dem späteren Wilsons u. a. durch geringere Betonung des Unabhängigkeitsgedankens und die Einbeziehung afrikanischer Probleme unterschied. Auch Wilson selber trat ja zunächst nicht für eine Auflösung Österreich-Ungarns ein, sondern für eine als "Selbstbestimmung" aufgefaßte weitgehende Autonomie der Nationalitäten.[35] Als mit dem Zerfall der Doppelmonarchie die Unabhängigkeitsidee den Vorrang gewonnen hatte, drangen gerade die Amerikaner darauf, daß trotzdem auch für nationalitätenrechtliche Bindungen gesorgt wurde. Wilson wollte sogar in die Völkerbundsatzung einen Passus einfügen, der alle künftigen neuen Staaten, ja nach einer späteren (20. Jänner 1919) Fassung sogar alle künftigen Mitgliedstaaten auf ein Minimum von Minderheitenschutz verpflichtete.[36] Freilich war es anderseits Wilson, der (am 3. Mai 1919) endgültig die Schutzbestimmungen des Art. 93 des Vertragsentwurfes aus körperschaftlich-gruppenrechtlichen in individualrechtliche verwandelte.[37] Doch stellte er sich damit gegen seinen Hauptberater David Hunter Miller, wie auch gegen Louis Marshall, den Vertreter der amerikanischen Juden auf der Friedenskonferenz;[38] es gab damals also Amerikaner, die durchaus bereit waren, weiterzugehen als er.

[33] Zum folgenden siehe Erwin Viefhaus, *Die Minderheitenfrage und die Entstehung der Minderheitenschutzverträge auf der Pariser Friedenskonferenz 1919* (Würzburg, 1960).

[34] Vors. S. E. Mezes; unter den Mitgliedern auch D. H. Miller und Walter Lippmann; Viefhaus, 61-67.

[35] Erst in einem Brief vom 26. Juni 1918 an Lansing sprach sich Wilson endgültig gegen die Aufrechterhaltung Österreich-Ungarns aus. (V. S. Mamatey, *The U. S. and East Central Europe, 1914-1918* (Princetown, 1957), 269) – Lansing gebraucht in einem Brief an Wilson vom 21. Mai 1918 in bezug auf die Tschechen die Wendung von einer "hope of independence or at least selfdetermination" (Mamatey, 255), womit vermutlich die Selbstbestimmung im Sinne Karl Renners als Alternative zur Unabhängigkeit aufgefaßt wurde. (Denkbar wäre freilich auch, daß er zwischen bedingungslos gewährter Unabhängigkeit – independence – und Gewährung eines Plebiszits über diese Frage – selfdetermination – unterschied.)

[36] Viefhaus, 109, 113.

[37] Indem er "communities" durch "inhabitants" ersetzen ließ; Viefhaus, 158-159.

[38] Viefhaus, 82, 145, 151. Von nationalsozialistischen Wissenschaftlern, z. B.

Was damals eine Haupttendenz amerikanischer Weltpolitik war, trat im Rahmen der VN wiederholt als Nebentendenz in Erscheinung. Der amerikanische Delegierte Jonathan Daniels setzte 1949 bei der Unterkommission gegen Diskriminierung und für Minderheitenschutz eine in der Folgezeit von der ihr übergeordneten Menschenrechte-Kommission boykottierte Entschließung durch, welche die Vollversammlung aufforderte, dafür zu wirken, daß Minderheiten ihr Kulturerbe bewahren könnten.[39] Am 8. Oktober 1951 legten er und die britische Vertreterin Miss Elizabeth Monroe einen umfangreichen Entschließungsentwurf zum Minderheitenschutz vor.[40] Er forderte als Mindestrecht für volkliche Minderheiten, die ihre Sprache beizubehalten wünschen, das Recht auf Gerichtsverfahren in ihrer Muttersprache und das Recht, an den vom Staat getragenen Schulen ihre Muttersprache pflegen zu dürfen. Darüber hinaus regte der Entwurf eine vielseitige Betätigung der VN auf diesem Gebiet an: Entwerfen von einschlägigen Musterbestimmungen; ständige Berichterstattung über Minderheitenrecht im Yearbook of Human Rights; Schaffung eines Beschwerdeweges, damit die Minderheiten nicht auf den den Frieden gefährenden Umweg des Appellierens an eine ausländische Regierung angewiesen seien; schließlich Berufung eines Gremiums (panel) von Sachverständigen, die sowohl für Mitarbeit in ad hoc-Ausschüssen wie für die Beratung einzelner Regierungen zur Verfügung stehen sollten. Die Verwirklichung dieser letzteren Anregung würde z. B. dem Südtirolproblem sehr zugute gekommen sein.

Anfang 1956 wurde in der gleichen Unterkommission der Vorentwurf des Berichts von Charles Ammoun über Diskriminierung im Bildungswesen durchberaten und dabei am 11. Jänner ein in der veröffentlichten Endfassung dieses klassischen Dokumentes[41] fortgelassener Satz erörtert, der den Einwanderervolksgruppen das Recht absprach, sich "Minderheiten" zu nennen. Dazu erklärte der amerikanische Vertreter Prof. Philip Halpern, ein Jurist, laut Protokoll: "Sie (Einwanderer-

Hans J. Beyer, ist später behauptet worden, gerade die Vertreter des amerikanischen Judentums hätten sich für eine bloß individualrechtliche Regelung eingesetzt, was die Dinge auf den Kopf stellt. Beyer schrieb 1937: "Bodenständige Gruppen eines großen Volkes sollten gezwungen werden, nach den Gesetzen eines liberalen Assimilationsjudentums oder der östlichen Galuth (Diaspora) zu leben" und nennt diesen Versuch "ein raffiniertes, weil schwer in seiner Bedeutung erkennbares Werkzeug zur Vernichtung des deutschen Volkes", *Auslanddeutsche Volksforschung,* 1 (1937), 10.

[39] Claude, 162; Dok. E/CN. 4/351, 13-14.

[40] Dok. E/CN. 4/Sub. 2/ L 4.

[41] Siehe Charles Ammoun: A study on discrimination in education, New York, 1957; dieser Bericht bildete die Ausgangsbasis für die 1960 von der Unesco beschlossene Antidiskriminierungs-Konvention. Der 1956 diskutierte Vorentwurf bildete VN-Dok. E/CN. 4/Sub. 2/L 92.

gruppen) seien wie alle Minderheitengruppen berechtigt, ihre Sprache und Kultur zu bewahren, und es würde eine Verletzung fundamentaler Menschenrechte sein, wollte das Wirtsland das verhindern. Auf der anderen Seite seien sie nicht berechtigt zu besonderem Schutz und finanzieller Unterstützung seitens dieser Regierung. Sein Land habe Platz für verschiedene Kulturen und Gemeinschaften (entities); ja deren Bestehen bereichere seine Nationalkultur und stärke es als Nation. Wie er es ansehe, gründe sich wahre Demokratie auf ein Mosaik vielfältiger Kulturen." Diese Formulierung mit ihrer deutlichen Gegenüberstellung von bloß duldendem Nationalitätenrecht für die Zuwanderer und auch förderndem für die Altsiedlergruppen entsprach genau der amerikanischen Praxis.

So stehen sich in Fragen des internationalen Minderheitenschutzes in den USA zwei Richtungen gegenüber.[42] Das vorliegende Buch verdeutlicht, daß nur die von Jonathan Daniels und Philip Halpern vertretene Richtung der rühmlichen Vergangenheit Amerikas gerecht wird, – seiner Tat-Tradition mehr als seiner Wort-Tradition. Diese Tat-Tradition aber entspricht dem Geist unserer Zeit, in der alle Kräfte auf Emanzipierung, Gleichberechtigung und Entdiskriminierung drängen. Neben den Aufstiegsbewegungen der mittleren und unteren Klassen und Stände, der früher nicht tolerierten Glaubensgemeinschaften, der Frauen und der farbigen Rassen bildet der Aufstieg der Sprachgemeinschaften zu voller Gleichberechtigung die fünfte große Emanzipationsbewegung unserer Zeit – eine Bewegung, die, wie die Beispiele der Schweiz, Finnlands und vieler anderer Ländern beweisen, einer Integrierung dieser Sprachgemeinschaften zu *einer* Nation nicht im Wege zu stehen braucht und die andererseits weder die Aufgabe noch die Möglichkeit hat, alle sprachlichen Assimilationsvorgänge zu verhindern. Dieser fünften Emanzipationsbewegung in hohem Maße gerecht gewor-

[42] Aus der Tatsache, daß Miss Willis und Simsarian unmittelbar als Vertreter des US-Staates auftraten, Daniels und Halpern aber nur als Experten "à titre personnel", könnte herausgelesen werden, daß nur die ersteren die Meinung der Regierung ausgesprochen haben, die letzteren hingegen allenfalls für eine akademische Opposition. Doch ist die Grenze zwischen Regierungsvertretern und bloßen Experten durchaus fließend. Ein Großteil der Mitglieder von sogenannten Experten-Gremien von VN und UNESCO sind in Wirklichkeit Regierungsvertreter; das stellt z. B. Inis L. Claude (in: *International Organization*, Mai 1951, 300-312) ausdrücklich für die Mitglieder der VN-Unterkommission gegen Diskriminierung und für Minderheitenschutz fest; übrigens war z. B. Simsarian Sprecher der USA auf der sogenannten Experten-Konferenz über Diskriminierungsfragen, die die UNESCO im Juni 1960 in Paris abhielt. Im übrigen ist zu bedenken, daß der Meinung opponierender Fachleute international wie im eigenen Lande unter Umständen höhere moralische und logische Überzeugungskraft innewohnen kann als der offiziellen Regierungsmeinung, und daß überdies die oppositionelle Meinung von heute die morgige Regierungsmeinung werden kann.

den zu sein, bildet den nicht geringen Ruhmestitel der in dieser Schrift umrissenen Nationalitätenpolitik der Vereinigten Staaten.

From *Das Nationalitätenrecht der Vereinigten Staaten von Amerika* by Heinz Kloss (= *Ethnos*, Bd. 1, *Schriftenreihe der Forschungsstelle für Nationalitäten- und Sprachfragen, Kiel*) (Vienna, Wilhelm Braumüller, 1963), pp. 307-327. Reprinted by permission.

William J. Samarin

LINGUA FRANCAS OF THE WORLD

ORIGIN OF THE TERM

The language of the Crusaders was not the first *lingua franca* in the history of mankind, but it furnished the name for all such similar languages ever since.

The horde which descended upon the Muslims on the eastern shores of the Mediterranean had come from many parts of western Europe. The native languages (the vernaculars) of these priests and soldiers, merchants and blacksmiths, porters and page boys, were forerunners of English, French, Italian, and German. Though Latin was the language of religion and of learning, the Crusaders did not all speak Latin, nor did they speak each other's languages. While there were certainly bilinguals among them, there were with equal certainty people who did not understand even other dialects of their own language: an Englishman from the South might find it difficult if not impossible to understand an Englishman from the North on the first encounter.

Linguistic diversity (i.e., multilingualism) has always set the stage for the development of lingua francas, and the multilingual Crusaders thrown together for a common cause found a need for such a language. They found it in the language of Provençal, spoken along the southern shores of Europe between Marseilles and Genoa. Perhaps this "French language" (which is what *lingua franca* literally means, though it was most likely only a particular dialect of a Romance language) had already come to be used by native and foreign merchants and sailors whose business was in these southern ports. In any case, it became the basis of a language used among the Crusaders and with the non-French speaking peoples who had learned it.

The use of this particular form of French eventually died out, but not before having left its own name as its heritage for languages which are used in a similar fashion. Today when we find a language which is commonly used by people whose native languages are different, we describe it as a lingua franca.

A DEFINITION

If the term lingua franca is to be used with the widest possible meaning it is necessary to adopt a definition with the fewest restrictions. The following (UNESCO 1953, p. 46) is worthy of general adoption: "A language which is used habitually by people whose mother tongues are different in order to facilitate communication between them." An additional requirement included in some definitions is that a lingua franca be a *pidgin* language (a so-called "hybrid" or "mixed" language), but it is not true that all lingua francas are pidgins. A second requirement sometimes found is that a lingua franca be used for commercial purposes, but this is again not always true of lingua francas, though they frequently arise in a commercial environment.

Other terms compete with lingua franca as designations for the kind of language being discussed.

Trade language ("*langue de traité*") is usually used for some language not included among the world's majority languages and which is used by some people as a second language in commercial situations. All trade languages are therefore lingua francas, e.g., Kituba and Hausa in Africa.

Contact language (probably equivalent to French "*langue véhiculaire*") is a lingua franca whose use is not necessarily habitual. It is the most neutral of the terms.

International (or *Universal*) *language* is a lingua franca whose use is actually or virtually international. Some writers, however, make the error of using it of lingua francas indiscriminately, even of those with restricted use, e.g., English, French.

Auxiliary language is generally meant to describe an artificially devised lingua franca, e.g., Esperanto.

KINDS OF LINGUA FRANCAS

Since a lingua franca is simply a language used to communicate across linguistic barriers, it can itself be any kind of a language; *natural, pidginized*, or *planned*. By *natural language* is meant any language acquired by the normal processes of inculturation. Natural languages are thus the *mother* or *native* languages of some people. When a natural language is acquired as the *second language* of different people, it becomes their lingua franca. In the process of becoming a lingua franca, a language often loses some of its vocabulary or is simplified in its phonology or grammar. Where the structure of the language suffers serious modification, it is said to be pidginized.

A *pidginized language*, or simply *pidgin*, traces its lineage to at least one natural language. A pidgin, strictly speaking, is not a natural language (see above). However, it may become a natural language; at this point it may be called a creole (Hall, 1962).

Unlike either of the preceding kinds of lingua francas are the *planned languages*. Not all such languages are lingua francas, of course, for some are intended for very restricted use. All such languages were created ad hoc, though based on some natural languages, for express use as lingua francas.

NATURAL LANGUAGE LINGUA FRANCAS

Three natural language lingua francas have played an important role in the history of Western Civilization: Common Greek (Koiné), Latin, and French (Goad 1958).

For almost 800 years (300 B.C. to 500 A.D.) the civilized part of the Mediterranean world was unified by the Greek lingua franca. At almost every level of society, irrespective of circumstances, this language was used. Like so many lingua francas, Common Greek owes its origin to military conquest. Although the culture of the city states attracted admiration and emulation, it was not until the establishment of Alexander's empire that the language became strategic. A single empire needs one universal language.

Koiné, however, far outlived the empire. At no period after Alexander's death was there the unity and prosperity characteristic of his dynamic era. Yet for several hundred more years – even after the Romans assumed political hegemony – Greek was used by tradesmen and scholars alike. It was, however, only in the last century that we learned how widely Koiné was actually used among ordinary people. With the discovery of the papyri was revealed the unsophisticated use of the lingua franca in everyday affairs. They were written not only by Greeks but also by Egyptians, Persians, and Arabs alike. Before the discovery of the papyri, our best knowledge of the Koiné was in the Greek translation of the Hebrew Scriptures (the Septuagint version of the Old Testament), and in the Christian writings (the New Testament).

The Greek lingua franca did more than spread Greek culture. In a very real sense, it served to spread the religion with which western civilization ever since has been identified – Christianity. Had there not been such a contact language, it seems hardly possible that the propagators of the new religion would have found an audience. But in Palestine, Asia Minor, and perhaps even the Iberian peninsula, St. Paul found important groups of people whom he addressed in Greek. Like the early Christian leaders, the so-called Patristic fathers also wrote in Greek. The language of the Church for all practical purposes was Greek.

At this time, of course, Rome ruled the Mediterranean. But Latin was hardly competition for Koiné. While it is true that Latin literature reached its apogee in the works of such artists as Plautus, Virgil, Livy, or Cicero, the classic language itself seems to have been more a written than spoken one. While orations may have been delivered in the Senate in this literary language – or even Greek – it was the "vulgar" language which was used elsewhere.

Latin later became another lingua franca, identified not so much with a political institution as with a religious one. The Roman Church had continued to use it even after the fall of Rome, and out of the ruins of that civilization the Church arose, adopting a form of the spoken Latin. Its clergy learned and used this language. Political leaders like Charlemagne, by encouraging learning, encouraged its study. Western Europe was not united under one crown, but under one miter. Germans, Scandinavians, Saxons, and North Africans could carry on business and pursue scholarly activities. Until the 16th century, deeds and documents worthy of preservation were in Latin. So commonly do we think today of the English translations of the writings of the savants of the past, whether religious (like Augustine's) or not (like Bacon's and Sir Thomas More's), that we forget that these were first in Latin.

With the maturation of the Renaissance, the vernaculars began to play a greater part in the politics and art of the West. Wycliffe strove for an English translation of the Bible. Dante used the Italic dialect of Tuscany for his masterpieces. Treaties began to be written in other languages than Latin. By the 18th century, French had already become the West's new lingua franca. But it was a different kind of lingua franca, less plebeian by far than Koiné, and less regnant than Latin. A literary lingua franca, less widely known than its forerunner.

In other parts of the world too lingua francas have been or are now used by millions of people. The more important ones are here classified by language families.

Afro-Asiatic (a name proposed by Joseph H. Greenberg to include the Semitic and related languages of Africa). Between the fifth century B.C. and the fourth century A.D. Aramaic was used in Babylonia, Palestine, Syria, and Egypt. Later Arabic served as a lingua franca in some places following the Muslim conquests. Hausa, a Chadic language, serves as a trade language in Dahomey, Togo, Ghana, Upper Volta, Nigeria, and the Cameroon by several millions.

Chinese. Among the several important Chinese languages, Mandarin first became the lingua franca of education and government and then became the standard language, which by official policy is replacing local languages as on Taiwan.

Hindi. The national language of India is derived from a language of the same name spoken in the northeastern part of the Republic. Soon after the Muslim conquest of the 12th century, this language began to be used as a lingua franca of the courts, army camps, and trading centers.

Niger-Congo. In Africa several languages belonging to this family have served or are serving now as lingua francas, such as Bambara and Fulani in the West, and Ngbandi in northern Congo. Swahili and Lingala can also be included here, but because they are also commonly used in pidginized form are later classified among the pidgins.

PLANNED-LINGUA FRANCAS

Several planned-language linguage francas have been devised within the last seventy-five years. They are Esperanto, which claims 1,500,000 speakers, Ido, similar to Esperanto, Novial, Frater, and three others which compete for the name Interlingua (Ferguson, n.d.). More recently Loglan came into being. Designed by scientists, its chief claim is to simplicity and logicality.

The advocates of each planned language appear to be as loyal to their tongue as nationalists are to theirs. Dispassionate appraisals and linguistic evaluations of these languages are therefore rare.

Planned languages reveal many of the features of pidgin languages, namely, lexical syncretism and reduction of redundancy. Frater, for example, is based on Latin and Greek roots which purport to have international utility. Thus, *mutalingua* is "translation", *akusa* is "accuse", *ŭni* is "one". As for redundancy, "In Frater, there is neither article, nor flexion, nor elision, nor affix, nor concord of tense, of mood, of gender, of number." (Thai, 1957).

PIDGIN LANGUAGES

Pidgin languages as a group typify most completely the lingua francas in their development and structure. Bona fide pidgins are found all over the world and have been under observation for about one hundred years. However, it was not until recently that they have been submitted to careful analysis. The reason for this was the opinion that pidgins at their best were nothing more than poor approximations to cultural languages such as English and French.

What people failed to see was that these forms of speech were not "hodge-podge" mixtures of linguistic debris, but that in every case studied there was genuine linguistic structure. The earliest of such studies was Hall's of Melanesian Pidgin English (Hall, 1945).

The bibliography reveals that today many scholars are working on several different pidgins. The published literature has not only made available working data on the languages, but has also raised several interesting theoretical or methodological questions, such as the following: (1) Can pidgins be classified as belonging to language families like natural languages? (2) What are the psychological and social correlates of their use? (3) Can they be described with the same rigor as natural languages?

The list of pidgin languages is an imposing one. The following may possibly be a complete one for the last century.

African pidgins (Niger-Congo languages)

Bangala-Lingala: spoken in the Congo and derived from Ngala; Bangala is supposed to be the more simplified of the two.

Pidgin A70 (also known as Chauffeur Bulu, Bulu bediliva, Ewondo Populaire): spoken in the Cameroon, derived from the group of Bantu languages designated A70 (Alexandre).

Fanagalo (also known as Fanikalo, Chilapalapa, Kitchen or Mine Kafir, Isikula, Cikabanga, Cilololo, Cilungubo, "Basic Bantu"): a pidgin Zulu of Southeast Africa.

Kituba (also known as Commercial Kikongo, from which it is derived, Simple Kikongo, Kibulamatadi, Kikwango): spoken in the Congo.

Sango: derived from a language of the same name which is an intimate dialect with Ngbandi; spoken in the Central African Republic.

Swahili: derived from the language of the same name; spoken in Tanganyika and neighboring areas; the dialect of the Eastern Congo is called Kingwana.

As linguistic curios a few others might be cited: Coromanti (spoken in Jamaica around 1800, and derived from some West African language, Le Page 1960, p. 98); Nago, probably based on Yoruba and ultimately used only in certain Brazilian pseudo-African cults (Pierson 1942, p. 73).

Amerindian pidgins

Chinook Jargon: spoken in the American Northwest and neighboring part of Canada.

Island Carib (or "men's speech" Karina) can possibly be included here.

Chinese: spoken along the northwestern border of Indo-China (Whinnom 1956, p. viii).

English
Cameroon
Chinese
Hawaiian
Jamaican (and perhaps other Caribbean pidgins, excluding the last two)
Korean Bamboo English
Melanesian
Sierra Leone
Saramakan (Jew Tongo, Ningre-Tongo)
Sranan

French
Caribbean (Haiti, Louisian, Martinique)
Indian Ocean (Seychelles, Mauritius Islands)
Vietnam (?)

Portuguese
African (San Thomé, Principe, Cap Verde)
Caribbean (Papiamento)
Far East (Cochin, Malaya, etc.)

Spanish (in the Philippines)
Bamboo Spanish
Caviteño
Davaueño
Ermitaño
Ternateño
Zambangueño

If a pidgin language is used long enough in any one area, children reared in this community acquire it as their native language. When this happens the pidgin becomes the natural language of a segment of the population and is said to be *creolized*. This creolized language may outlive the competing languages or it may simply become fully naturalized. At this point it is said to be a creole (while the process here described is well known, the terminology may not represent a consensus; writers differ in the technical use of the word "creole").

The list of pidgin lingua francas scattered throughout the world hides an important fact. Though numerous and widespread, most of them are based on some Indo-European language – Dutch, English, French,

Portuguese, or Spanish. When located on a map, another significant fact appears, every one is located adjacent to a marine expanse. The history of these pidgins is therefore somehow to be connected with oceanic travel. This is, in fact, the case. What is not obvious, however, but certainly demonstrable, is the fact that a remarkable number of these lingua francas owe their origin to the heroic masters of the Age of Exploration, the Portuguese. In the fifteenth century there developed a pidgin Portuguese which may have originated in the first contacts with the Africans, but ultimately spread to the ports of the Far East (Lopes da Silva). According to Whinnom, "Even at the beginning of the eighteenth century, English trade at Canton was carried on through Eurasian Portuguese interpreters who translated the Cantonese into a Portuguese pidgin comprehensible to the English sailors (Whinnom, p. 7, fn. 13).

The influence of Portuguese pidgin on the other Atlantic pidgins was effected through the slaves for whom the language had become a lingua franca as early as the fifteenth century (the vestiges of this Portuguese sub- or ad-stratum have been documented for several languages). This language made communication possible among the slaves and with their masters until another language was learned. When this second language was pidginized, it often was pidginized along the pattern of the earlier one. For this reason Loftman speaks of a "Caribbean creole" grammar, regardless of the Indo-European language superimposed on it. To account for the differences in vocabulary Stewart has proposed the theory of "relexification" (1963).

The origin of pidgin lingua francas are for the most part hidden behind the veil of history. In only brief sketches can the origin of some be described. The past of others perhaps is buried in obscure or unknown records awaiting the scholar.

More important than knowledge of the origin of these lingua francas, however, is that of their subsequent history. What is significant about their linguistic development, about their part in the lives of human beings? What then are some of the linguistic and sociological concomitants in their use?

LINGUISTIC CHANGES

All lingua francas undergo certain linguistic changes which in their extreme form are called pidginization. As the use of a natural language is taken up by people for whom it is only a second language, either in the same or in a different area, it suffers from linguistic interference which is common in all bilingual situations. The speakers of the first (or source, S) language receive the second (or target, T) through the grid of their S language. If, for example, the S language had no gender whereas the T language did, one finds – as in the case of Hausa feminine – that one is lost. In the same way other features of the language are "re-interpreted".

This process might be called simplification, and it affects the grammatical structure as well. Many of the devices used for distinguishing various parts of sentences from one another and for showing the relationships between these constituent parts may be lost. In Ngbandi, a tone language with three levels of tone, the pronouns and verbs are intimately related in the aspectual system: different combinations of pronouns and verbs are used to mark aspect and tense. Tone is also used to derive nouns from verbs, and in other parts of the language varies considerably, but regularly, in the context of other tones. Practically all of this has been lost in Sango, the contact language derived from it. While three tones still persist in Sango, they function hardly at all to distinguish words or to mark grammatical usage (Samarin, 1963). Were it not for the fact that it is a lingua franca used almost exclusively by Africans, who already speak tone languages, the distinctive function of tone might be altogether lost.

What is lost in the morphology is to some degree compensated for in the syntax. Sango therefore uses periphrasis to mark aspect or time. One says fadé mbi goe "I shall go" (literally "now I go") and mbi goe awe "I went" (literally "I go is finished").

Lingua francas accompany – in fact, make possible – culture contact and acculturation. It is no wonder therefore that their vocabularies show dramatic changes. This happens when the natural language can no longer compete with other languages, either because it has moved into a different area or because non-native speakers predominate over the native speakers where the language is indigenous. Thus where Pidgin English is spoken one can usually describe an original situation where learners of English were not only of inferior status but also far more numerous than speakers of English (as in Jamaica, Le Page 1960). The second case might be illustrated by South African Fanagalo or even Town Bemba of Northern Rhodesia.

Lexical borrowing (using words from other languages) and innovations (by extending meanings of old words or forming new words with old stock) characterize the aforementioned changes. Notice, for example, the following French words which in Sango convey meanings somewhat different from the original ones (Taber 1964): *ça va* "to recover from an illness", *commandement* "authority", *compagne* "wife", *depuis* "for a long time", *doucement* "slowly", *jusqu'à* "for a while", *quinine* "pill, tablet".

When lingua francas are learned under controlled circumstances (e.g., in a classroom), and where there is a recognized value in attaining the normative standard, such linguistic developments occur on a much smaller scale. Yet they are nonetheless revealed in "accepted" dialects of such standard languages as English spoken in West Africa, the Caribbean, or India. Because of their close approximation to the standard there is little doubt that they will be tolerated. Difficulties will arise only when literature produced in the newer dialect is read by speakers of the standard (to some extent this already happens in reading the works of some Indians).

FATE OF LINGUA FRANCAS

What is the future of the languages now spoken by peoples whose cultures are marginal to the prestigious one? With what degree of accuracy can one predict their life expectancy? Assuming an inevitable demise, to what task can they be assigned? Can they accomplish some legitimate goal satisfactorily? These are questions to which responsible government officials and other interested people, such as religious leaders, have addressed themselves. Several fact-finding investigations have already been initiated but their reports are too often filed away with other governmental or private documents. A few conferences have been held. UNESCO convened a meeting of linguists in 1951 to discuss the use of vernacular languages in education (UNESCO 1953). In 1951 there met at Kitwe, Northern Rhodesia, a significant All Africa Conference on Christian Literature and Audio-Visual Communication. In Africa in July 1962 at Brazzaville an international congress of specialists discussed the subject of multilingualism in Africa. One of the sections, for which seven papers were presented, dealt specifically with pidgins and creoles on that continent (CCTA 1962).

The problem which faces policy makers is fraught with complexities. In every instance they are concerned with welding a heterogeneous multilingual political state into a unified and harmonious nation. To accomplish this they should like to reduce the number of languages. They also want to introduce their countries into the stream of modern civilization. For this they need either a world language in which there already is an important literature, or a local language which must be "modernized". This latter is no mean task. It is difficult enough for Arabic, which had to step from the Middle Ages into the Twentieth Century. How much more difficult it is for an undeveloped lingua franca, such as Swahili.

In many of the emergent nations, the official language is actually a marginal language, little known and little used by the population. In Haiti, for example, only about ten per cent of the population can be said to have mastered the French language (see UNESCO 1951, p. 38); the rest of the population uses Haitian Creole. Sometimes there is a blindness to the real facts. People in the more prestigious strata have been known to deny the very existence of a pidgin language (like Jamaican Creole) or to claim that "everybody knows" the official language (like French in the Central African Republic). Policy makers must therefore avail themselves of the ever-growing body of literature on all relevant subjects in addition to initiating sociological and linguistic studies; only then can they hope to have established a sound basis for operation.

Linguistic research is necessary to determine the exact nature of the lingua franca. For example, how many different forms of Swahili are there? What are the means in the language to permit it to adapt itself to growing needs? Answers to such questions are being sought for Swahili under the aegis of the East African Swahili Committee (Kampala), but such bodies are rare.

Sociological research must accompany linguistic research to assure a more probable prognosis concerning the outcome of any policy with linguistic ramifications. There are only a few ethnolinguistic monographs in circulation, although several anthropologists are currently interested in related subjects. An inescapable aspect of language use is that it is more than a communication code; it serves, among other things, to mark ethnic identification and prestige.

Some of the most interesting developments are taking place in Africa, which in many respects offers itself as an experimental laboratory to the linguists. Nida (1955), has discussed the linguistic developments on the continent. In a more recent paper by Richardson (1957) (which should be read with Epstein 1959), the competition between several languages as lingua francas is clearly presented. Briefly, there is developing in Northern Rhodesia a form of the Bemba language, a veritable lingua franca, which is gaining ascendance over Nyanja and the two other lingua francas – English and Fanagalo. Five reasons are given: (1) The mine workers in the copperbelt are linguistically heterogeneous; (2) Although Fanagalo had been used as a lingua franca until the last war, its identification with the denigrating policies of the Europeans, many of whom used only this language with the Africans, has stigmatized it; (3) The use of English by Africans is opposed by most Europeans, who see in its use an attempt to raise the Africans' status (cf. the discouragement of the learning of German and Dutch in the former colonies of the Cameroon and Indonesia); (4) Nyanja is identified with the people whose language is the lingua franca of the Army and police; (5) Bemba is spoken indigenously by over 60 per cent of the labor force.

CONCLUSION

Lingua francas have served tribal communities and vast empires from time immemorial when linguistic diversity prevented social and literary intercourse. Among them have been many drastically reconstituted languages (the pidgins) whose study is currently being undertaken in several quarters. Some dare to say that these are vanishing from the modern world (Whinnom 1956), but the ease with which Korean Bamboo English developed leads one to imagine the inevitability of pidgins in the world.

Historians might feel that all things point to "one world" where internationalism or an international federation or monolithic state would require a single lingua franca. An informed person cannot deny this possibility. But, short of a totalitarian system, the rise of such a language is beset with difficulties.

A true world lingua franca would have its advantages. But can one develop without a totalitarian state? Someone has said that Russian is grammatically too complex to serve as such a language; English, however, already meets many of the requirements. In any case, should there ever be an international lingua franca, on thing is almost certain: like all lingua francas before it, it will pass through a stage of pidginization.

REFFRENCES

Alexandre, P.
1962 "Aperçu Sommaire sur le Pidgin A70 du Cameroun", *Colloque sur le Multilinguisme* (CCTA), pp. 251-56.

Bloomfield, Leonard
1933 *Language* (New York).

CCTA (Commission de Coopération Technique en Afrique)
1962 *Colloque sur le Multilinguisme* (Brazzaville).

Epstein, A. L.
1959 "Linguistic Innovation and Culture on the Copperbelt, Northern Rhodesia". *Southwestern Journal of Anthropology*, 15, 235-53.

Ferguson, Charles A., Gode, Alexander, and Pitman, I. J.
n.d. "Interlingua and Intermedia", *The Linguistic Reporter* (The Center for Applied Linguistics), Supplement Number 3 (Washington, D.C.).

Goad, Harold
1958 *Language in History* (London).

Greenberg, Joseph H.
1963 *The Languages of Africa* (= *Indiana University Research Center in Anthropology, Folklore, and Linguistics*, Publication 25) (Bloomington).

Hall, Robert A., Jr.
1943 *Melanesian Pidgin English* (Baltimore).

Hall, Robert A. Jr.
1962 "The Life Cycle of Pidgin Languages", *Lingua*, 11, 151-56.
Le Page, Robert B. and De Camp, David
1960 *Jamaican Creole* (London).
Loftman, Beryl B.
1953 "Creole Languages of the Caribbean Area" (Columbia University M. A. thesis).
Lopes da Silva, Baltasar
1957 *O Dialecto Crioulo de Cabo Verde* (Lisbon).
Nida, Eugene A.
1955 "Tribal and Trade Languages", *African Studies*, 14, 155-58.
Pierson, Donald
1942 *Negroes in Brazil* (Chicago).
Richardson, Irvine
1961 "Some Observations on the Status of Town Bemba in Northern Rhodesia", *African Language Studies II*, pp. 25-36 (London).
Samarin, William J.
1963 *A Grammar of Sango* (Hartford).
Stewart, William A.
1963 "Relexification as a Factor in the Evolution of Creole Languages". Paper read at the Thirty-Eighth Annual Meeting of the Linguistic Society of America (Chicago).
Taber, Charles R.
1964 *French Loanwords in Sango: A Statistical Analysis of Incidence* (Hartford Studies in Linguistics) (Hartford).
Thai, Pham Xuan
1957 *Frater: The Simplest International Language Ever Constructed* (Saigon).
UNESCO
1951 *The Haiti Pilot Project: First Phase 1947-1949* (Paris).
UNESCO
1953 *The Use of Vernacular Languages in Education* (Paris).
Weinreich, Uriel
1953 *Languages in Contact* (New York).
Whinnom, Keith
1956 *Spanish Contact Vernaculars in the Philippine Islands* (Hong Kong).

From *Study of the Role of Second Languages in Asia, Africa and Latin America*, F. A. Rice, ed. (Washington, Center for Applied Linguistics of the Modern Language Association, 1962), pp. 54-64. Revised and expanded by the author. Reprinted by permission.

Section VII
THE SOCIAL CONTEXTS AND CONSEQUENCES OF LANGUAGE PLANNING

Einar Haugen

LANGUAGE PLANNING IN MODERN NORWAY

During the past century Norway has been the scene of an unusually interesting experiment in language planning. Ideas concerning linguistic engineering have here reached out from the quiet studies of linguists to the market place, where they have affected every citizen and his children. Little by little an avalanche has been set in motion which is still sliding and which no one quite knows how to stop, even though many would like to do so. When the movement began, Norway had a stable written language; today it is blessed with two competing ones, neither of which is stable. One of them claims to be the more civilized, the other the more Norwegian. Whatever truth these claims may contain, they leave the average Norwegian in the confusing position of not being quite sure whether he can manage to be both.[1]

By language planning I understand the activity of preparing a normative orthography, grammar, and dictionary for the guidance of writers and speakers in a non-homogeneous speech community.[2] In this practi-

[1] See Arne Garborg's *Vor Sprogudvikling* (1897), 10: Et selvstændigt norsk Kulturmaal er ikke opnaaet. Derimod har vi faaet to Sprog. Deraf er det ene norsk, men endnu intet udformet Kulturmaal, medens det andet vistnok er Kulturmaal, men endnu ikke "selvstændigt norsk."

[2] Linguists tend to look askance on normative linguistics, because it brings in an element which is not purely scientific. Some of them even have emotional reactions to it like that suggested by the title of Robert E. Hall Jr.'s *Leave Your Language Alone!* In Bloomfield's *Language* (e.g., 496 ff.) one will find expressed a distaste for the "authoritarianism" of the usual school norm, particularly when it is based on erroneous observation of good usage. Linguistics as such is obviously not equipped to deal with these problems, which belong in the realm of social and political values. But linguists will no doubt continue to have opinions on the subject.

cal application of linguistic knowledge we are proceeding beyond descriptive linguistics into an area where judgment must be exercised in the form of choices among available linguistic forms. Planning implies an attempt to guide the development of a language in a direction desired by the planners. It means not only predicting the future on the basis of available knowledge concerning the past, but a deliberate effort to influence it. In most countries such planning has been distributed over a long period and among many individuals, with little conscious direction. It has usually taken place at a period when the number of writers was small and standards of conformity not rigid. It has been shaped by the speech habits of a social élite which was also a governing class and automatically established its own patterns as normative for the whole nation.[3] The resulting "standard" language has had two mutually supporting aspects, on the one hand a generally accepted orthography, and on the other a prestige dialect imitated by the socially ambitious.[4]

The Norwegian experiment, however, has been conducted on a national scale and in recent times. It has been guided by men with considerable linguistic sophistication, in the full light of social criticism, and under the constant influence and supervision of a democratic public opinion. It has been done at a time of universal literacy and enforced orthographic conformity through the school system.[5] The language planners have sought deliberately to upset the status quo by rejecting the linguistic models of their social élite. Their goal has been to give the nation a language which should be the unique expression of its national individuality. The resulting bitterness and confusion have furnished striking evidence of the problems involved in such planning. By this time the Norwegians have lived through two phases of the procedure, where-

[3] For a valuable discussion of the rise of European standard languages, see Otto Jespersen's *Menneskehed, Nasjon og Individ i Sproget* (Oslo, 1925), 36-77, e.g., p. 58: "The standard language is often to a high degree a class language, an upper class language. . . ." See also Bloomfield, *Language*, 48-52, for an excellent discussion of the various types of language within a complex speech community.

[4] In the United States schools have taught the orthography and with it some kind of standard pronunciation as "correct." This teaching has unquestionably had a considerable influence on American pronunciation, though linguists are inclined to discount "schoolmarm" English (while generally following it themselves quite closely). In the absence of a true social élite, schoolteachers have felt called upon to exercise its linguistic functions in a democratic society.

[5] The Ministry of Church and Education prescribes the orthography used in the schools, following a Danish tradition that goes back to 1775 (Rolf R. Nygaard, *Fra dansk-norsk til norsk riksmål*, Oslo, 1945, p. 14). A number of changes were authorized in 1862, which led to the working out by Aars of his first book of spelling rules in 1866; its 9th edition was officially authorized in 1885, after which this came to be standard practice.

by one standard language has been created and another reborn. They are now hopefully but gingerly entering a third phase in which the claim is made that the two rivals can be fused into a new, national language embodying the best of both.[6]

In 1814 Norway was politically separated from Denmark, under whose hegemony she had fallen some four centuries earlier.[7] As citizens of a young nation, Norwegians began searching for the cultural roots that had been cut over in the Middle Ages. Among the several symbols of national individuality and independence, language was hit upon as one of the most important.[8] Many voices were raised for a restoration of the Norwegian language, reputedly lost during the union with Denmark. Norwegians had learned to write Danish, although their own speech forms were widely divergent from any of those accepted in Denmark. We may describe the linguistic situation as one in which the following speech norms could be heard in the country: [9] (1) *Danish Colloquial* from a small number of immigrated Danish officials and merchants, and from the stage which was dominated by Danish actors; (2) *Literary Standard*, a Norwegian reading pronunciation of Danish used by a small number of Norwegian-born ministers and other government officials on solemn occasions, as well as schoolmasters instructing the young in reading; (3) *Colloquial Standard*, a compromise between reading pronunciation and local Norwegian speech habits, fairly uniform throughout the official class in daily speech among themselves, with only slight local accents;

[6] See Marie Skramstad's unpublished M.A. thesis *Reform and Reaction in the Linguistic Development of Modern Norway* (University of Wisconsin, 1958). The only authoritative account in English is Alf Sommerfelt's *The Written and Spoken Word in Norway* (Oxford, 1942). A good perspective is found in Einar Lundeby and Ingvald Torvik, *Språket vårt gjennom tidene* (Oslo, 1956). The fullest source of information for the earlier phases is Achille Burgun, *Le développement linguistique en Norvège depuis 1814* (Oslo, 1919). Numerous useful brochures have been published by Didrik Arup Seip, e.g., *Fornorskingen av vårt språk* (2 ed., Oslo, 1947), *Omstridde spørsmål i norsk språkutvikling* (Oslo, 1952), *Gjennom 700 år* (Oslo, 1954).

[7] For details, see Karen Larsen's *History of Norway* (New York, 1948).

[8] The arguments of German romanticists from Herder on were repeated in Norway, but most of the arguments advanced were of a more practical nature: that school children were being seriously penalized in their education by the wide gulf between Danish writing and Norwegian speech, particularly in the countryside. This motivation has been important for the widespread support language reform has won among schoolteachers. The growth of democratic political movements was also significant, since the "folk language" was conceived as a means of diminishing the prestige and power of the official class. See Willard M. Overgaard's unpublished M.A. thesis *Political Aspects of the Language Controversy in Norway* (University of Wisconsin, 1955).

[9] The terminology here used is adapted from that of Leonard Bloomfield in *Language*, 52.

(4) *Urban Substandard*, varying from city to city and closely related to the surrounding rural dialects, spoken by artisans and working-class people; (5) *Local Dialect*, spoken by the farming class, different in every parish, with an intricate network of isoglosses crisscrossing the country and falling into broad dialectal areas determined by the lines of communication. Between the extremes of the rural dialects and the Danish heard from the stage there was a gulf which in some cases amounted to complete lack of communication. As the century wore on, a growing number of children were being sent to school and put through the discipline of learning an essentially foreign orthography.[10]

In the middle of the century two divergent responses were made to the challenge of this situation, both of them by linguist-schoolteachers, who laid down the principles for the first two stages and envisaged the third beyond. One of these reformers was Knud Knudsen (1812-95), a schoolmaster of rural origin, who agitated untiringly for a step-by-step revision of written Danish in the direction of Colloquial Standard, which he was the first to identify. He produced the first description of this language in his grammar (1856) and some years later a dictionary of proposed native substitutes for its foreign words (1881).[11] The other reformer was Ivar Aasen (1813-96), a self-taught rural linguist, who pioneered the investigation of Norwegian dialects. From these he distilled what he conceived to be their "over-all pattern" and wrote a grammar (1864) and a dictionary (1873) in which he furnished the means for writing his proposed new language. He called it *Landsmål (Lm.)* or "national language".[12] Although both of these men urged the abandonment of the entrenched Danish orthography, they outlined quite different procedures for achieving a Norwegian language: Knudsen was a gradualist reformer, Aasen a revolutionary. Yet such was the similarity of their ultimate goals that the liberal-nationalistic party of the Left (*Venstre*) could sponsor both when it came to power in 1884. In 1885 the *Landsmål* of Aasen was voted official equality with Danish. Two years later schoolteachers were instructed to abandon the reading pronunciation of

[10] Norwegian pronunciation dominated the stage after the 1860's, but the last Danish actor did not leave until 1899 (Nygaard 39). While reading pronunciation was officially abolished in 1887, it was still flourishing in many schools as late as 1904 (Nygaard 72).

[11] Knudsen first advanced his ideas publicly in 1845. In his grammar, *Haandbog i Dansk-norsk Sproglære* (Christiania, 1856), he used the term *Byfolkets Talesprog* "the spoken language of city people" (urban colloquial). In 1876 he called it *Den landsgyldige norske uttala* "the nationally used Norwegian pronunciation". See my account in *The Norwegian Language in America* (Philadelphia, 1953), 103-8.

[12] The grammar: *Norsk Grammatik* (Oslo, 1864); the dictionary: *Norsk Ordbog* (Oslo, 1873). Before his time *Landsmål* had been used chiefly to mean rural dialects, but his use of it suggested an extension to the other meaning of *Land*, viz. "entire country".

Danish in favor of the colloquial standard which Knudsen had first discovered.[13] From that time on the linguistic situation in Norway has been a race between the advocates of Aasen's all-Norwegian language and Knudsen's modified Danish which by 1900 had become a Dano-Norwegian known as *Riksmål* (*Rm.*) or "State Language".

The twentieth century has seen a rapid evolution in which the role of government has become ever more prominent. The official acceptance of literary bilingualism, which does not in any way correspond to a bilingualism in speech or otherwise resemble the situation in countries like Finland or Ireland, has inevitably led to the bureaucratic administration of the forms used in both languages. Since 1900 the language issue has been firmly intertwined with the political and social life of the country. As the government has taken over more and more functions in the welfare state, it has also assumed responsibility for establishing linguistic norms. It has rechristened both languages, has appointed numerous committees to investigate the problems involved, and has instituted a series of thoroughgoing changes in the form of each. A system of local option administered through schoolboards has ensured that the voice of the people should be heard and has made these problems part of the daily diet of even the humblest citizen. The process that was begun in the 1880's, when the *Venstre* Party made language reform a plank in its platform, has engulfed all parties, above all the Labor Party which has ruled the country since 1935. Being a socialist party, it could not at first embrace the nationalistic aspects of language reform, but brought to the discussion an emphasis on its democratic aspects. This accounts for the slogan written into the law that the development is to be guided with constant reference to the "folk language", a term that is vague enough to serve as a banner of union for proletariat and peasantry alike.

During the past half century Aasen's *Landsmål* has been considerably modified in the direction of East Norwegian dialects, accepting forms that Aasen scorned as plebeian and historically corrupt.[14] It has taken a long step in the direction of Substandard Colloquial from its first official

[13] See Nygaard 36, where it is shown that both Aasen's and Knudsen's "målstrev" were included in the thinking of the politicians. The instructions to the teachers were: "The norm for pronunciation and reading is the 'cultivated colloquial,' i.e., that pronunciation which in each part of the country is the usual one in careful, but natural everyday speech."

[14] Aasen rejected many East Norwegian dialects because their form seemed to him to be influenced by urban speech, which he regarded as un-Norwegian. In addition, he gave his language an orthographic form which should have the same dignity as neighboring Swedish and Danish, chiefly shown by silent letters and other etymological spellings. Some of this was eliminated when *Nn.* was given an official spelling ncrm in 1901. See my article "The Linguistic Development of Ivar Aasen's New Norse", *PMLA*, 48: 558-97 (1931).

norm in 1901 through reforms of 1917 and 1938 to the latest textbook norm of 1958. Known since 1929 as *Nynorsk* (*Nn.*) or New Norwegian, it is now (1958) the chief language of instruction in 2,210 school districts, all rural, comprising 23.5 per cent of all school children.[15] This is not too much to show after a century of agitation, but it could be regarded as hopeful of future growth, were it not that the years since World War II have reversed an earlier trend and led to a noticeable recession in the number of communities using it. In spite of its demonstrated serviceability in both prose and poetry, it has not achieved anything like majority status, let alone the triumph for which it once looked. Less than 15 per cent of the original books published are written in it, and it is not the editorial language of any daily newspaper.[16] It is weakened by its lack of a prestige dialect, since its speakers are limited to a spelling pronunciation if they do not simply use their native rural dialect. An important barrier to its success is its puristic resistance to universally known words of recognizably German origin. It has had an undeniable impact on the attitude towards rural speakers by raising their self-esteem and social respect, while creating also powerful antagonisms among others. Its fortunes are intimately tied to the cultural self-consciousness of the rural population and the reaction of the latter to the rapid urbanization of modern times. The growth of urban or semi-urban centers and suburbs in previously rural territory has been a serious blow to the advancement of *Landsmål*. Aasen could not foresee the rapid shift of population to the cities, nor the growth of a mass culture which by and large has been inimical to his language. Although *Lm.* is claimed to be capable of expressing any cultural phenomenon whatever, it is difficult to dissociate it from values that are widely regarded as primitive, unfashionable, and reactionary. Yet it enjoys considerable sympathy as somehow more expressive of intimate national sentiments, even among many who do not use it. And it maintains a devoted following among many schoolteachers of rural origin, who swing a big stick in the educational councils of the nation.

But the chief resistance to the forward march of *Landsmål* was the

[15] *Norsk Statistik Årbok 1960*. In 1952-53 (according to Lundeby-Torvik 96) the percentage was 28.

[16] The figure counts only book titles and includes a great many officially subsidized items, such as school textbooks and public documents; also there is no doubt that the average circulation of *Nn.* books is lower than that of *Rm.* books, so that if it were possible to get figures in terms of actual number of books sold and read, the position of *Nn.* would be still weaker. For this figure and others on recent book production, see Kaare Haukaas, *Litteraturspråket i tidsromet 1946 til 1955* (Oslo, 1957); the author is favorable to *Nn.*, but his figures appear reliable. Note that nearly all translations from foreign languages are in *Bm.*, so that if these are included the figure falls to about 11 per cent *Nn.*

surprising elasticity of *Riksmål* in the face of a serious threat to its predominance. Major reforms in 1907 and 1917 brought its spelling and morphology into substantial agreement with the Colloquial Standard, as Knudsen and his followers had been advocating for so long. In 1929 it was rechristened *Bokmål* (*Bm.*) or "book language", a term surpassed in ineptitude only by the simultaneous change of *Landsmål* to *Nynorsk* (*Nn.*). Its present government-administered form was achieved in 1938, with minor adjustments in the new textbook norm of 1958.[17] But the form of 1938 showed important innovations, following a new policy which first became apparent in 1917. It had been clear for some time that many disadvantages were attendant upon the use of two written languages, particularly in a small and not overly well-to-do nation. The cost in terms of parallel editions of schoolbooks and official documents alone was a sizeable item, not to speak of the highly divisive effects in public life. It was apparent that neither language was going to be the unqualified victor, and rather than remain in a kind of cold-war situation, many embraced a third solution, which called for one of the most delicate linguistic operations ever undertaken. This was the solution which has now been declared official policy, namely the fusion of the two languages into one all-Norwegian language at some not too distant date. A name for this dreamed-of language was coined in 1909 by the folklore scholar Moltke Moe: he called it *Samnorsk*, or "united Norwegian", and declared that what was needed was a "flowing together", a "mingling of blood" of the two languages.[18]

The committee that prepared the spelling reform of 1917 was directed by the Ministry of Church and Education to "open the way for a development towards national unity, based on the real spoken language of the people". The commission for spelling reform appointed in 1934, which prepared the reform adopted in 1938, was directed by the *Storting* (Parliament) that created it to work for "a rapprochement of the two languages in orthography, word forms, and inflections, based on Norwegian folk speech".[19] In 1951 the *Storting* authorized the Ministry

[17] For a brief list of the major changes in these spellings, see my *Spoken Norwegian* (New York, 1947), 238-39. Also Lundeby-Torvik 80-91.

[18] Moltke Moe had been writing in this vein for some years, see, e.g., his essay "Retskrivning og Folkedannelse" (1900) and "Norsk og dansk Sprogdragt" (1906), in his *Samlede Skrifter*, 1, 219-59, 2, 64-85. The term *Samnorsk* occurs in his "Nationalitet og kultur" (2, 252-64). An important book at this time was H. Eitrem's *Samarbeide mellem Landsmaal og Riksmaal?* (Oslo, 1908); the author that year became a member of an official commission which published a report in 1909 entitled *Utredning av spørsmaalet om et mulig samarbeide mellem landsmaal og riksmaal i retskrivningen.*

[19] The quotations are taken from the Bill prepared for the Storting by the Ministry of Church and Education *St. prp. nr. 1 Tillegg nr. 3. Norsk Språknemnd* (Oslo, 1950), pp. 2, 3, 21.

to appoint a permanent Language Board (*Språknemnd*) whose goal should be "to promote the rapprochement (*tilnærming*) of the two written languages on the basis of Norwegian folk speech (*folkemål*) along whatever lines may be feasible at any given time".[20] This policy directive was confirmed by the practically unanimous support of four out of five political parties in the Parliament, the fifth being the Conservative Party which fought a last-ditch fight against the setting up of the Board.[21] The method used in promoting the goal established was first of all to regulate the spelling of all words that differed in purely orthographic features in the two languages. Where some genuine linguistic difference existed, the attempt was made to find a middle ground between the two languages. Such forms were often found in the Substandard Colloquial, itself a compromise between the upper-class Colloquial Standard and the rural dialects. This is the meaning of the mysterious and frequently attacked key words of the Board directive: "on the basis of Norwegian folk speech". This has given enemies of the policy a convenient handle for attacking the new norms as vulgar: many of the forms advocated coincide with forms regarded by upper-class urban speakers as non-U. But the political parties that support the policy retort that for centuries rural children were required to learn Danish forms far more foreign to them than the colloquial forms now being encouraged among urban children. One of the serious problems facing planners is the decision on which features of the "folk language" to promote. Among the arguments advanced are those of regional spread (as imperfectly revealed by dialect monographs), of structural consistency, and of literary usage.

[20] Each one of the terms in this directive has been fought over and argued so much that it is difficult to translate it into English without a loss of connotation. In particular the term "Norwegian folk speech" (*norsk folkemål*) is a dubious one, since there is no single linguistic form which can be so designated. It is a cover term which includes all rural dialects and the urban substandard, in short, all that is not standard or "upper class". This was calculated to appeal to the voters supporting the Labor and Agrarian parties, since speakers of the standard are characteristically Conservative. But the term "folk" is ambiguous, including as it does the concept of the whole people; hence it has been argued that since Colloquial Standard is also spoken by a segment of the Norwegian people, it should be taken into account in planning. For a defense of the term see a brochure from Norsk Språknemnd entitled *Svar på kritikk av "Framlegg til læreboknormal 1957,"* pp. 4-6.

[21] The final vote on the establishment of a Language Board Dec. 14, 1951 was 95 to 24, the latter votes being those of the entire Conservative Party plus two from the Labor Party. All others voted in favor of the measure, which envisages eventual fusion of the language: the Labor Party, the Liberal Party, the Christian Peoples' Party, and the Agrarian Party. Most of these had specific planks in their platforms favoring *Samnorsk*.

The new forms are promoted through officially sanctioned spelling lists. In these lists most words have only a single permissible form, differing from older spellings in purely orthographic respects. Where the changes are more radical, alternatives are often permitted. Some alternatives are designated as equal, either one being permissible in textbooks. Others are unequal, the secondary one being permissible only in the pupils' written work.[22] In popular usage the more traditional alternatives are referred to as "moderate", the proposed innovations as "radical". Even the moderate usages are too radical for some conservatives, who have produced an unauthorized spelling list of their own which eschews most of the changes that go beyond the purely orthographic. The resulting confusion has led to a cry for limitation among the alternatives so as to simplify the task of textbook writers, teachers, and pupils. The working out of a firm textbook norm on the basis of the spelling of 1938 was one of the main tasks assigned to the Language Board after its creation in 1951. This group of 30 members, 15 for each language, was selected to represent a variety of organizations and institutions concerned with linguistic problems. Among these were the universities and teachers' colleges, teachers' and authors' organizations, radio and the press.[23] A permanent secretariat was established for the Board, consisting of two linguists, one for each language, who do the actual research and prepare the agenda for meetings.[24] After six years of intense work, this group succeeded in presenting a proposal for a textbook norm which was adopted by the *Storting* on October 7, 1958, after two days of full-scale debate, for use in the schools beginning in September, 1959. It is clear, however, that the effect of the vigorous public discussion stirred up over the past seven years, much of it a reaction to over-hasty pressure for change, has made the textbook norm a very mild step in the direction of fusion. The trend is there, but the most ardent advocates of fusion have been brought up short before the resistance of established linguistic patterns.

[22] The terminology was (1) *jamstilte former* "alternative forms" (e.g., *tru* or *tro* "believe") and (2) *hovedform* "principal form" vs. *sideform* "secondary form", the latter being placed in brackets in the spelling lists, e.g., *seter* [*sæter*] "chalet." See Lundeby-Torvik 85 ff. for details.

[23] The Ministry chooses from two sets of nominations made by each group and in addition appoints six members on its own initiative. The Board is purely advisory. Its whole membership gathers usually only once or twice a year, while its working or executive committee meets about once a month. The chairmanship rotates annually between the two languages. The bylaws are to be found in the records of the Storting for 1950 (*St. prp. nr. 1. Tillegg nr. 3*).

[24] The first secretaries were Einar Lundeby for *Bm.* and Ingvald Torvik for *Nn.* They published annual reports since 1953, a survey of Norwegian language history in 1956 (*Språket vårt gjennom tidene*), and prepared the Board's proposal for a textbook norm in 1957 (*Framlegg til læreboknormal*).

The linguist who studies this development cannot but ask himself: is it conceivable that two distinct languages can be fused, or indeed, that linguistic development can be guided by parliamentary or other governmental action? Can the welfare state extend its paternalistic concern to language, the most intimate of all social patterns? Many would be inclined to deny this *a priori*, as indeed some opponents of language planning in Norway have done, appealing even to structural linguistics for support. To clarify this problem we must make sure that we distinguish between language and orthography. The government does not pretend to be regulating pronunciation or other spoken usage; it is only concerned with writing. In general it does not prescribe vocabulary or idiom or syntax, only orthography and morphology. But a written language has to draw its models from some form of speech, which for most writers of *Bm.* has been and still is the Colloquial Standard of upper-class speakers. Insofar as *Bm.* differs from this norm, it is an artificial language imposed by government edict. This has led to a conservative counter-agitation whereby a distinction is made between *Bm.*, the government-administered form of Dano-Norwegian, and *Rm.*, the more conservative form based on the Colloquial Standard. The resistance here is based on the conception that *Rm.* is a language, a unified organism or structure, which cannot be tampered with by deliberate planning. Against this stands the conception of the planners that the Colloquial Standard itself is not firm, but is changing under the pressure of the growing democratization of society, and that this change will be accelerated as the schools adopt forms in writing that encourage the more popular speech forms, now often regarded as plebeian by many speakers of *Rm.* A form that is used in writing thereby gains prestige, and it is believed that little by little the Colloquial Standard itself will become more Norwegian and more democratic by accepting these elements. There can be no doubt that a process of liberalization in speech has been going on. Urban parents no longer exercise the control over their children's speech that they once did, particularly since the schools began counteracting their influence. But the forms of the spoken *Rm.* appear too deeply entrenched to yield to much more than a superficial infiltration of folk speech. The prestige of the Colloquial Standard is rooted in the entire social structure, which in spite of all socialism and government regulation is still basically class structured. For each folk form that is admitted, there are numbers of people who pass over from the use of dialect to Colloquial Standard when they move to the city, or get a better job, or go to an advanced school. It is thus a situation in which the government is trying to push a language in one direction by authorizing certain forms as prestigious, while the prestiges of private life are trending in the opposite direction. Though the result may be a relaxing of older standards, with a widespread adoption of some folk forms, it is hard to be sure just how much of this is due to the schools and how much of it is due to a more general social development found in other countries as well.

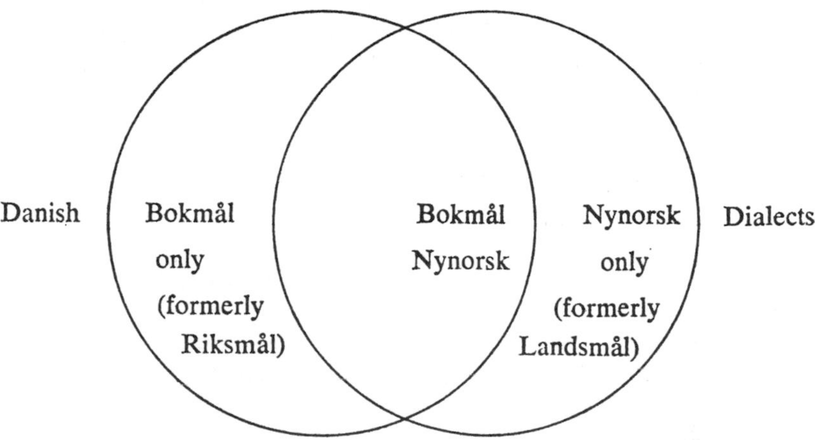

None of the planning for fusion which has here been briefly sketched would be conceivable if the two written norms with all their subvarieties were genuinely distinct languages. *Bm.* and *Nn.*, particularly in their government-administered forms, have a very large common core: (1) They have identical phonemic systems, though the phonemes are of course differently distributed in many obviously cognate words. Aasen's *Lm.* was based on the phonemic system of certain West Norwegian dialects with a different and more conservative structure, but this has been largely eliminated. (2) They have virtually identical syntax: word order is so similar that in nearly every case translation requires no change whatever; *Nn.* differs primarily in requiring gender agreement in the anaphoric pronoun (as in German), while *Rm.* has a combination of sex and gender; and in eschewing the possessive *-s* wherever possible in favor of a prepositional construction. (3) They have most of their vocabulary in common, though *Nn.* draws more freely on the rural dialects and doggedly replaces words of German origin with newly coined terms. Many of its advocates have been realizing the futility of this procedure and have suggested that this barrier between the languages might well be cleared away. (4) The chief difference today is in morphology, and it is at this point that interpenetration of the two languages is most difficult, since the forms of *Nn.* are more complex, and it seems unlikely that any of its distinctions will be introduced unless they are widespread in usage. But if they are widespread, they often occur as socially marked forms, with a stamp of rusticity or vulgarity. Only a long period of written usage will, it is hoped, gradually eliminate this association and dignify them as part of the future *Samnorsk* language.

The conflict of the two languages in Norway is thus today reduced to a conflict over the writing of forms that are either felt by many to be vulgar or rustic or that are simply unfamiliar and strange, being either coined or otherwise of limited usage. The two languages are not really distinct languages, but might rather be called stylistic norms, each one a syndrome of features that have no inner structural connection other than the fact that they are associated respectively with certain speakers and certain occasions.[25] There is no linguistic or structural reason why the use of diphthongs in *bein, stein, rein, sein* (vs. *ben, sten, ren, sen*) should be connected with the use of *-a* in the weak preterite of verbs like *kasta, hoppa, elska. hata* (vs. kastet, hoppet, elsket, hatet), or with the use of a feminine gender in *boka, døra, natta, dronninga* (vs. *boken, døren, natten, dronningen*). Both sets of forms are familiar to all, and much of the planning consists in deciding which of the forms commonly heard is to be selected as normative. In a democratic country this cannot be done by fiat, but must be carried on in a way that will win general assent. If a given "radical" form shows signs of finding favor among younger writers, it is seized upon by the planners and made obligatory in the schoolbooks. In this way the coming generation is being made the object of a stylistic re-education through forced obsolescence of older forms. This raises immense problems for the appreciation of the classic authors, who are being antiquated more rapidly than in any other country. It has reached the point where Ibsen and Bjørnson require re-writing to be read by the younger generation, and this procedure raises new problems for educators and educated alike.

In conclusion: The Norwegian experience shows that social pressure for linguistic change can be created and channeled through official organs. Although linguists generally bridle at the suggestion that language can be tampered with, it is here shown that given sufficient motivation, written and possibly spoken language like any other social phenomenon can be deliberately guided and changed. Whether the effects of government planning in this field, as in other parallel fields of social life, will be permanent and thoroughgoing, or only superficial, remains to be seen. About all the government can do is to create an

[25] The stylistic syndrome is a collocation rather than a structure, if we assume that a structure must show some statable relationship between its parts, e.g., *sg.* plus the morpheme $-Z_1$ = *pl* (in English). A collocation shows no statable relationship between its parts other than a purely spatial or co-existential selection, e.g., the co-occurrence of the phoneme /ž/ and preterites in $-D_1$ in English.

atmosphere favorable to certain kinds of linguistic change, and recognize that there are forces that escape government regulation. One of these is the cohesive force of the Colloquial Standard, which is not easily counteracted. It still seems likely that this dialect will form the backbone of the future language, as it is today of the *Bm*. But it will probably be essential to the linguistic peace of Norway that further concessions be given to the supporters of *Nn*. They have earned the satisfaction of feeling that it was they who saved the Norwegian language, even if they should have to give up the main sector of their battlefront.

FOUR PHASES OF NORWEGIAN: A SAMPLE PASSAGE

From Ivar Aasen, *Minningar fraa Maalstriden*, 1858 (pub. 1859), *Skrifter* 2.147)

1. *The Original*

(Landsmål, as written by its creator)

Det rette heimelege Maal i Landet er det, som Landsens Folk hever ervt ifraa Forfedrom, fraa den eine Ætti til den andre, og som no um Stunder, til Traass fyre all Fortrengsla og Vanvyrding, endaa hever Grunnlag og Emne til eit Bokmaal, lika so godt som nokot av Grannfolka-Maali.

Den rette Medferd med dette heimelege Maalet er, at det maa verda uppteket til skriftleg Hevding i si fullkomnaste Form, at det maa verda reinskat fyre dei verste framande Tilsetningar, aukat og rikat ved Avleiding av si eigi Rot og etter sine eigne Reglar, og soleides uppreist og adlat ved eit verdigt Bruk. Denne Hevdingi maa vera baade til Gagn og Æra fyre Landsens Folk, med di at dette er den beste Maate til at maalgreida det heimelege Laget i Hugen og

2. *Riksmål Translation*

(Danish in Norway, as written in Aasen's time)

Det rette hjemlige Sprog i Landet er det, som Landets Folk haver arvet ifra Forfædrene, fra det ene Slægtled til det andet, og som nu om Stunder, til Trods for al Fortrængelse og Ringeagt, endnu haver Grundlag og Stof til et Bogsprog, lige saa godt som noget av Nabosprogene.

Den rette Behandling af dette hjemlige Sprog er, at det maae blive optaget til skriftlig Dyrkelse i sin fuldkomneste Form, at det maae blive renset for de verste Fremmede Tilsætninger, øget og beriget ved Afledning af sin egen Rod og efter sine egne Regler, og saaledes opreist og adlet ved et værdigt Brug. Denne Dyrkelse maa være baade til Gavn og 'Ære for Landets Folk, derfor at dette er den bedste Maade til at udtrykke den hjemlige Natur i Folkets Hu

Tanken aat Folket, og til at fremja Kunnskap og Vithug (elder den einaste rette og sanne Kultur), og med det same til at visa Verdi, at ogso dette Folket hever Vit til at vyrda det gode, som det hever fenget til Arv og Heimanfylgj a fraa uminnelege Tider.

og Tanke, og til at fremme Kundskab og Videbegjær (eller den eneste rette og sande Kultur), og med det samme til at vise Verden at ogsaa dette Folk haver Forstand til at hædre det gode, som det haver faaet til Arv og Hjemmefølge fra umindelige Tider.

3. *Present-day Landsmål*
(known as Nynorsk)

Det rette heimlege mål i landet er det som landets folk har arva ifrå forfedrene, frå den eine ætta til den andre, og som no om stunder, trass i all fortrengsle og vanvørnad, enno har grunnlag og emne til eit bokmål, like så godt som noko av grannfolk-måla.
Den rette medferd med dette heimlege målet er at det må bli tatt opp til skriftleg hevding i si fullkomnaste form, at det må bli reinska for dei verste framande tilsetningane, auka og gjort rikare ved avleiing av si eiga rot og etter sine eigne reglar, og soleis oppreist og adla ved eit verdig bruk. Denne hevdinga må vera både til gagn og ære for landets folk, med di at dette er den beste måten til å målbera det heimlege laget i hugen og tanken åt folket, og til å fremje kunnskap og vithug (eller den einaste rette og sanne kultur), og med det same til å vise verda at også dette folket har vit til å vøre det gode som det har fått til arv og heimafylgje frå uminnelege tider.

4. *Present-day Riksmål*
(known as Bokmål)

Det rette heimlige mål i landet er det som landets folk har arvet ifra forfedrene, fra den ene ætt til den andre, og som nå om stunder, trass i all fortrengsle og vanvørnad, ennå har grunnlag og emne til et bokmål, like så godt som noe av nabomålene.
Den rette behandling av dette heimlige målet er at det må bli tatt opp til skriftlig dyrking i sin fullkomneste form, at det må bli renset for de verste fremmede tilsetningene, øket og gjort rikere ved avleiing av sin egen rot og etter sine egne regler, og således oppreist og adlet ved et verdig bruk. Denne dyrkinga må være til gagn og ære for landets folk, derfor at dette er den beste måte til å uttrykke det heimlige laget i folkets hug og tanke, og til å fremme kunnskap og vitelyst (eller den eneste sanne kultur), og med det samme til å vise verden at også dette folket har vett til å hedre det gode som det har fått til arv og heimefølge fra uminnelige tider.

Translation of the four versions:

The right native tongue in this country is the one that the people of the country have inherited from their ancestors, from one generation to the next, and which nowadays, in spite of all displacement and contempt, still has the basis and material for a written language just as good as any of the neighbors' languages. The right treatment of this native tongue is that it must be taken up for written cultivation in its most perfect form, that it must be purified of the worst foreign additions, increased and enriched by derivation from its own root and according to its own rules, and thus restored and ennobled by dignified usage. This cultivation must be both to the benefit and honor of the people of the country, because this is the best way of expressing the native character in the mind and thought of the people, and of promoting knowledge and zeal for the learning (the only right and true culture), and at the same time to show the world that this people, too, has the sense to honor the good which it has received as its heritage and dowry from time immemorial.

From *Scandinavian Studies*, 33 (1961), 68-81 and *Anthropological linguistics* I, 3 (1959), 8-21. Reprinted by permission.

THE USE OF VERNACULAR LANGUAGES IN EDUCATION: THE REPORT OF THE UNESCO MEETING OF SPECIALISTS, 1951

INTRODUCTION

From the foregoing survey it can be readily appreciated that the language problem in education is world-wide and therefore a proper field of investigation for the educational agency of the United Nations.

Moreover, in many of its own activities and projects Unesco has been continually confronted with one aspect or another of the problem, chiefly in relation to fundamental education. To mention but one example, the educators entrusted with carrying out the pilot project in the Marbial Valley of Haiti found that little or no progress could be made before a decision had been reached as to what language should be used as the medium of instruction.[1] Similarly the Unesco advisory missions sent to Thailand, the Philippines, Afghanistan and Burma, had to take into consideration the local version of the same problem; the reports of these missions contain useful supplementary information to the present volume and recommendations that repay careful study.[2]

Since therefore the question of the medium of instruction is a recurrent problem in fundamental education and in the development of adequate systems of schooling in so many countries, the General Conference of Unesco at its Fifth Session in 1951 recommended that it

[1] Unesco, *The Haiti Pilot Project; Phase One 1947-1949, Monographs on Fundamental Education,* IV (Paris, 1951), 83 pp.

[2] Unesco, *Report of the Mission to Thailand* (Paris, 1950), 56 pp.; *Report of the Mission to the Philippines* (Paris, 1950), 75 pp.; *Report of the Mission to Burma* (Paris, 1952), 91 pp.; *Report of the Mission to Afghanistan* (Paris, 1952), 83 pp.

should be made a subject for separate study on a world-wide scale. This decision was strengthened by a resolution previously passed by the General Assembly of the United Nations, asking Unesco to take action.

Accordingly, towards the end of 1951, specialists from all parts of the globe met at Unesco House, Paris, to discuss in particular the use of vernacular languages. The meeting considered its main task to be the provision of some answer to two important questions: under what circumstances is the use of the vernacular possible in education; and what measures might be taken to facilitate and encourage its use? The meeting recorded its findings in a draft report, which is now published in the pages that follow.[3]

To avoid ambiguity the following terms are used with the senses indicated:

Indigenous language. The language of the people considered to be the original inhabitants of an area.

Lingua franca. A language which is used habitually by people whose mother tongues are different in order to facilitate communication between them.

Mother or native tongue. The language which a person acquires in early years and which normally becomes his natural instrument of thought and communication.

National language. The language of a political, social and cultural entity.

Official language. A language used in the business of government – legislative, executive and judicial.

Pidgin. A language which has arisen as the result of contact between peoples of different language, usually formed from a mixing of the languages.

Regional language. A language which is used as a medium of communication between peoples living within a certain area who have different mother tongues.

Second language. As referred to in this report, is the language acquired by a person in addition to his mother tongue.

Vernacular language. A language which is the mother tongue of a group which is socially or politically dominated by another group speaking a different language.[4] We do not consider the language of a

[3] For preliminary matters such as terms of reference, list of members, etc., see Appendix II, p. 144, of the original (*The Use of Vernacular Languages . . .*).

[4] Unesco recognizes that, while this definition holds in the generality of cases, for it to be universally applied and comply with the conditions governing individual, particular cases, variations in emphasis and wording would be necessary. *Ed.'s Note.*

minority in one country as a vernacular if it is an official language in another country.

World language. A language used over wide areas of the world.

MOTHER TONGUE AND SECOND LANGUAGE

A General Statement

It is through his mother tongue that every human being first learns to formulate and express his ideas about himself and about the world in which he lives. This language in which he first learns to express his ideas need not be the language which his parents use; nor need it be the language he first learns to speak, since special circumstances may cause him to abandon this language more or less completely at an early age.

Every child is born into a cultural environment; the language is both a part of, and an expression of, that environment. Thus the acquiring of this language (his "mother tongue") is a part of the process by which a child absorbs the cultural environment; it can, then, be said that this language plays an important part in moulding the child's early concepts. He will, therefore, find it difficult to grasp any new concept which is so alien to his cultural environment that it cannot readily find expression in his mother tongue. If a foreign language belongs to a culture very little different from his own (as for example French is to an English child) the child's chief difficulties in learning that language will be only linguistic. But if the foreign language belongs to a culture very different from his own (as for example English to a Nigerian child), then his learning difficulties are greatly increased; he comes into contact, not only with a new language, but also with new concepts. Similar considerations apply to adults.

In learning any foreign language a child may find difficulty in mastering the alien vocabulary and syntax sufficiently to express his ideas in it. Where the foreign language belongs to a wholly alien culture he is faced with the added and much greater difficulties: to interpret to himself the new ideas in terms of his own medium of thought – his mother tongue – and to express his own ideas and thoughts through the new modes of the alien tongue. Ideas which have been formulated in one language are so difficult to express through the modes of another, that a person habitually faced with this task can readily lose his facility to express himself. A child, faced with this task at an age when his powers of self-expression even in his mother tongue are but incompletely developed, may possibly never achieve adequate self-expression.

For these reasons it is important that every effort should be made to provide education in the mother tongue. What can be done is discussed on pages 52-54 (of *The Uses of the Vernacular . . .*).

On educational grounds we recommend that the use of the mother tongue be extended to as late a stage in education as possible. In particular, pupils should begin their schooling through the medium of the mother tongue, because they understand it best and because to begin their school life in the mother tongue will make the break between home and school as small as possible.

We consider that the shock which the young child undergoes in passing from his home to his school life is so great that everything possible should be done to soften it, particularly where modern methods of infant teaching have not yet penetrated to the school. He passes from being one of a few children under his mother's eye to being one of a large group under a teacher. Instead of running about and playing and shouting he is usually expected to sit still and be quiet; to concentrate, to do what he is told instead of what he wants to do, to listen and learn and answer questions. New information and ideas are presented to him as fast as he can possibly absorb them, and he is expected to show evidence that he has absorbed them. Almost everything is different from home and it is not surprising that many children find difficulty in adjusting themselves to their new surroundings. If the language in which all these bewildering new communications are made is also different from the mother tongue, the burden on the child is correspondingly increased.

Even when the child has been at school long enough to be familiar with school life, he still has to cope with the incessant stream of lessons in many different subjects. He will find a lesson in geography or almost any other subject easier if he is taught it in his mother tongue. To expect him to deal with new information or ideas presented to him in an unfamiliar language is to impose on him a double burden, and he will make slower progress.

The use of the mother tongue will promote better understanding between the home and the school when the child is taught in the language of the home. What he learns can easily be expressed or applied in the home. Moreover, the parents will be in a better position to understand the problems of the school and in some measure to help the school in the education of the child.

There may, however, be circumstances which justify abandoning the mother tongue very early in the child's formal education. For example, the mother tongue may be closely related to a more widely used language, and the practical convenience of being able to use this language as a medium of instruction may be so great as to justify a small burden on children who find some difficulty at first in using it. In such cases as these, we urge that everything possible should be done to help the children to pass over to the new medium. They should, for example, be taught by teachers who speak their mother tongue, and their task of passing to the new medium should take priority over other tasks.

We now discuss several objections often urged against the use of the mother tongue as the medium of instruction, which we consider unsound. Later we examine others which do in fact limit the extent to which the mother tongue can be used in certain circumstances.

"*This language has no grammar and no alphabet.*" Frequently someone who has not analysed the languages of people without a modern technology or civilization is of the opinion that a language which has never been written has no grammar. This is not true. Every language, even an unwritten one, has its consistent patterns or rules by which its speakers combine words into sentences, and so on. Often such grammatical structure is as complicated or as regular as those of any world language. In fact, we hold that there is nothing in the structure of any language which precludes it from becoming a vehicle of modern civilization. Similarly, any unwritten language can be written; some of the problems involved in writing a hitherto unwritten language are discussed in pages 60-62 (of *The Uses of The Vernacular . . .*).

"*The child already knows his mother tongue.*" The second objection is that the child already knows his own language before he comes to school, and that there is no need for the school to teach it to him. There are two replies to this. In the first place, he has not completely learnt it before coming to school. He has learnt it enough for his own childish purposes, but he will still need to develop his knowledge of it as he grows older. The English or French child devotes a great part of his time throughout his school career to studying his mother tongue. In the second place, the school is not merely teaching the child his mother tongue; it is using his mother tongue as the most effective means of teaching him other things.

"*The use of the mother tongue will prevent acquisition of the second language.*" Some people claim that it is impossible for children to acquire a good use of the second language unless the school adopts the second language as a medium of instruction from the very beginning. In fact, it is on the basis of this action that some schools in the past have actually forbidden any use whatsoever of the vernacular anywhere in the school. However, recent experience in many places proves that an equal or better command of the second language can be imparted if the school begins with the mother tongue as the medium of instruction, subsequently introducing the second language as a subject of instruction.

"*Using the vernacular impedes national unity.*" It cannot be denied that the business of government is easier in a monolingual than in a multilingual nation. However, it does not follow that legislation or school policy requiring the use of the official language at all times will give the same results as actual monolingualism. On the contrary, it is fairly likely that absolute insistence on the use of the national language by people of another mother tongue may have a negative effect, leading the local groups to withdraw in some measure from the national life. In any event, it seems clear that the national interests are best served by optimum advancement of education, and this in turn can be promoted by the use of the local language as a medium of instruction, at least at the beginning of the school programme.

Practical Limitations in the Use of the Vernacular in School

We have already said that we think all children should at least begin their schooling in their mother tongue, and that they will benefit from being taught in their mother tongue as long as possible. There are, however, certain practical difficulties – some temporary, some permanent – which may compel the school authorities to abandon the use of the vernacular as the medium of instruction at some stage.

Inadequacy of the vocabulary. The first difficulty is that thc language may not yet have a vocabulary sufficient for the needs of the curriculum. In this case a second language will have to be introduced at an early stage, and as soon as the pupils have learnt enough of it the second language can become the medium of instruction. The transition to a second language should normally take place gradually and should be made as smooth and as psychologically harmless as possible. Thus, if the second language is completely different from the mother tongue it should be taught as a subject for some years, and until such time as the child has an adequate working knowledge of it, before it is brought into use as a full teaching medium. The reasons for this, and the methods to be used, are discussed on pages 55-59 (of *The Uses of the Vernacular . . .*). We would only add that the adoption of a second language as a medium need not be total, that is, one or more subjects may continue to be taught through the mother tongue, even though for others the second language has become necessary.

Shortage of educational materials. One of the most important and difficult problems connected with the use of the vernacular languages in education is that of providing reading materials. It will often happen that even a language which is quite capable of being used as a medium of instruction will be almost or entirely without school books or other materials. The difficulty is not so much in printing, since there are various machines and techniques in existence which are designed to produce books and other printed matter in small quantity. The difficulty is to find or train competent authors or translators; to obtain supplies of materials (such as paper, type and machinery) in days of general shortage; to distribute the finished product under conditions of great distances and poor communications; and above all to find the money. These are practical problems, extremely difficult and of the highest importance. We are not, however, competent to advise on those problems and we strongly urge that Unesco should investigate them by consulting those who have had to face them in different parts of the world; and that it should make available the results of the investigations.

Multiplicity of languages in a locality. If a given locality has a variety of languages it may be difficult to provide schooling in each mother tongue simply because there are too few students speaking certain of the languages. In such cases it may be necessary to select one of the languages as the medium of instruction, at the cost of using a language other than the mother tongue of some of the students. Before accepting this necessity, the school should seek ways and means to arrange instruction groups by mother tongue. If mixed groups are unavoidable, instruction should be in the language which gives the least hardship to the bulk of the pupils, and special help should be given those who do not speak the language of instruction.

Multiplicity of languages in a country. A country which faces the problem of providing schools for a number of different linguistic groups may find itself temporarily unable – for lack of resources and personnel – to provide for all of them in the mother tongue. In this case, it may have to begin with the language spoken by the largest populations or having the most developed literature of the greatest number of teachers. The ideal of education in the mother tongue for the small groups can be worked toward as conditions make it possible.

It must be recorded that there is a wide variation in the strength and validity of these reasons for not using the mother tongue. In some areas they are indeed very strong; in others they are advanced without complete justification.

We must here lay down as a general principle what must have already been made apparent by our general approach to the problem: that in order to ease the burden on the child, the mother tongue should be used as the medium of instruction as far up the educational ladder as the conditions referred to on page 50 permit (in other words that the transfer to a second language, if necessary, should be deferred to as late a stage as possible); and that authorities should do everything in their power to *create* the conditions which will make for an ever-increasing extension of schooling in the mother tongue, and make the transition from mother tongue to second language as smooth and as psychologically harmless as possible.

We now discuss the policy which should be followed with regard to the use of the mother tongue in certain specific linguistic situations.

Need for reading material. We have already referred to the practical problems that are involved in providing an adequate supply of textbooks and reading material both for children and for adults. It will be useless teaching either schoolchildren or adults to read unless they have a supply of textbooks and other reading material. Indeed to do so may easily cause disappointment and resentment, and also a reversion to illiteracy on the part of many.

This problem has three aspects:

1. Provision of textbooks and reading materials for children in school.
2. Provision of follow-up materials of all kinds for adolescents and others who have had some years of formal education.
3. Provision of suitable material for newly literate adults.

We wish to emphasize that it is not enough to provide material for the actual needs of all classes, whether for children or adults; further material must be provided for follow-up purposes. There are two main reasons why people read: one is to improve themselves, the other is for entertainment. Newspapers and periodicals are a valuable means of holding the interest and spreading the habit of reading, and government authorities can do a great deal to encourage reading by the official notices they display. If it is desired to help people who can read in their mother tongues to pass over to reading in a second language, much can be done by printing books, newspapers, and official notices in two versions. We wish to emphasize, too, that the fact that a given language may not possess an adequate supply of reading material to enable it to be used as the medium of instruction right up to the highest grades of education, does not mean that it cannot be used in the primary and possibly part of the secondary stage. It should be used in education as far as the existing resources in reading material allow, and as the efforts made to extend the supply of reading material bear fruit, the use of the language should correspondingly be extended.

The shortage of suitably trained teachers. Teachers who have themselves received their education and professional training in a second language have real difficulty in learning to teach in the mother tongue. The main reasons for this difficulty are of two kinds. First: they have to teach subjects in a language which is not the language in which they are accustomed to think about them; and some of what they have to teach involves concepts which are alien to their pupils' culture and therefore have to be interpreted in a tongue to which they are alien. Secondly, there is often a lack of suitable books to guide or help them both in teaching and in teaching through the mother tongue; they have to depend, therefore, more on their own initiative and skill than when teaching through the second language in which they themselves have been trained. In those regions where a mother tongue is spoken by a large population, it should not be difficult to give teachers much of their theoretical training and all their practice teaching in the mother tongue. In those regions where there is a multiplicity of languages, it may be very difficult to do this. Nevertheless, we urge the importance of enabling teacher trainees to do at least some of their practice teaching in the mother tongue, and that authorities should make every effort to make this possible. One very important feature of teacher training and guidance is the need, now generally recognized, for special teachers' guides and handbooks in order to prevent old-fashioned methods of teaching by rote.

Popular opposition to use of mother tongue. Some people in a locality may be unmoved by the benefits to be derived from the use of the mother tongue in education and may be convinced that education in the mother tongue is to their disadvantage. We believe that educationists must carry public opinion with them if their policy is to be effective in the long run, since, in the last resort, the people of a country must always be in a position to express their free choice in the matter of the language in which their children are to be educated; and we urge that the educational authorities should make every effort to take the people into consultation and win their confidence. The problem will lose many of its elements of conflict if the people are confident that the use of languages in the educational system does not favour any section of the population at the expense of others. If the people as a whole will not accept the policy of education in the mother tongue, efforts should be exerted to persuade a group to accept it at least for experimental purposes. We believe that when the people as a whole have had an opportunity of observing the results of education in the mother tongue, they will be convinced that it is sound policy.

Lingua franca. Sometimes, as in the case of Swahili in parts of East Africa, there is a lingua franca which is so widely used that there is a great temptation to use it instead of the mother tongue as the medium of instruction. This has the great advantages of economy and of simplicity of administration, and in particular cases in the problem of supplying textbooks and other reading matter, both for schoolchildren and adults. Our view on the use of the lingua franca will depend in each case on how familiar the lingua franca really is. If nearly all the children have some knowledge of the lingua franca as well as of their mother tongue before they come to school, it may be worth while to incur some inconvenience to the individual pupil for the sake of more efficiency in the educational system as a whole. But the lingua franca may not be as familiar as this. It may simply be the case that one or two people in each village have some knowledge of it, but that it is not used in the village as a common medium of intercourse, and the schoolchildren seldom or never hear it. If this is so, we should be opposed to its use as the medium of instruction in the lowest classes, since it is in fact a foreign language to the children. The claim of the lingua franca to become the medium of instruction at a later stage would have to be weighed against the claims of a world language.

Pidgin. In some countries pidgin languages, such as Creole and pidgin-English, are spoken. These languages are sometimes only used by a section of the population in commercial or work contacts with people with whom they have no other means of communication. But in other regions a pidgin tongue is freely used over a wide area as a lingua franca between peoples in habitual social contact, and the children become familiar with it from an early age. When this is the case, it can be used as a medium in the schools. There are, however, two main objections to this: (a) when the pidgin contains elements based upon a European language, it is feared that the use of the pidgin in schools will make it harder for pupils to learn the European language correctly; (b) the people are often opposed to it because of its association with economic and social subordination.

THE SECOND LANGUAGE IN EDUCATION

In the preceding section we have stated our view that the mother tongue should be used in the early stages of education, even when another language must be used for further training. The early training in the mother tongue should serve as a bridge for learning the second language.

Each of these languages, however, represents far more than a mere set of grammatical forms and vocabulary lists; each tends to carry with it a set of concepts and traditions which in large measure constitute a separate culture. The use of the mother tongue in learning a second language, therefore, helps to provide a foundation of culture as well as one of language.

The need of knowing a second language. If, however, a child is brought up in a community which speaks a language different from the official one of his country, or one which is not a world language with a well-developed technological and cultural vocabulary and literature, he needs to be taught a second language: in order to feel at home in the language in which the affairs of his government are carried on; and in order to have access to world history, news, arts, sciences and technology.

The teaching of the mother tongue in school is sometimes complicated by the necessity of learning the national language. Because of the intimate relations of language and sentiment, a government may desire to have its national language spoken throughout the nation as an essential common bond or as the principal earmark of its very nationality. Moreover, the national language eases the task of administration by allowing a system of communication in one language, the easier spread of information concerning its laws, policies, and economic procedures, and the more economical establishment of a school system. At times, too, identity of educational procedure has appeared to governments to be an essential part of an over-all policy of equality of treatment for all men under their domain.

Individuals, too, very often strongly desire to learn the national language – although the imposition of such a language against their will may arouse hostility instead. For specific individuals the reasons underlying their desire to learn the official language, or a world language, often differ from those given thus far, and may be locally even more influential. For them the learning of a second language may be the door to skilled jobs and leadership in commercial establishments or in the civil service; or it may be the first step toward travel and study abroad. Much more subtle, and frequently more important, may be the expressed or unexpressed conviction that the acquisition of the foreigner's tongue will guarantee a like kind of wealth, freedom, self-government, power, and social status.

The knowledge of a world language can help to promote understanding between peoples and should be encouraged as one means of increasing international sympathy and mutual appreciation of the cultural contribution of East and West, and of the important contribution from individual persons in the past. The child should be brought into the modern world as easily and as quickly as our schools can bring him, while preserving in him the traditional values of his own society.

Nevertheless, for the reasons given earlier, it is our conviction that these peoples should be counselled to be patient, and to approach the second language through the mother tongue. We believe that, in the end, their best interests will be the better served that way. Even though they must ultimately learn to think and speak and read in the second language, this goal is, we believe, psychologically and pedagogically as a rule best achieved by two short jumps (that is, from illiteracy to literacy in the mother tongue, and from literacy in the mother tongue to literacy in a second language) than by one long jump (that is, from illiteracy in the mother tongue to literacy in a second language).

We have stated our view that if the change to a second language cannot be avoided, it should at least be postponed for as long as possible, and that the transition to it should be made as smooth and as gradual as possible. We now discuss some of the practical considerations which arise.

First use of a second language in the school. Since the desire to learn the second language may be very great – enough to make the child or his parents impatient with this approach – it may be wise during the first or second year to supplement the major teaching in the mother tongue by a small amount of oral initiation into the second language. Even a small amount may be encouraging to the pupils and begin to make them familiar with the pronunciation and some phrases of the second language.

Gradual transition to the second language as a medium of instruction. From this point, the amount of the second language used may be increased gradually, with the speed controlled by local factors. At first it should be taught as a subject, that is, as a foreign language. As soon as the competence of the class allows them to understand it well enough, the second language can, if necessary, be used as the medium of instruction for some subjects, but with the vernacular used where necessary for explanations. Finally – say in the secondary school – it may have to be used almost exclusively as long as no textbooks at that level are available in the mother tongue.

Variations in the programme. Various facts may make it necessary or advisable to use a somewhat different progression. Where all or almost all the pupils speak the second language well before beginning school, it may be used from the beginning. Where many people in the community speak the second language and serve as models, or where the second language is closely related to the mother tongue, change-over to it may be much faster. Where no texts at all are available in the mother tongue or where no vernacular-speaking teachers are available or where in the same classroom several languages are represented, it may be necessary to concentrate almost exclusively for a time on the teaching of the second language as a subject, in order to use it very soon as a medium of instruction.

Goal of instruction. The degree to which the students are expected to use the second language will also modify the programme. For students who are not following a course leading to university education, more stress may be placed proportionately on learning useful things through the mother tongue; for those who are working for university entrance, the second language may become increasingly important.

As a general principle, however, we hold that the child should not begin to learn two foreign languages at the same time; where a third language is taught, its introduction should be delayed until the second is well under way.

Secondary school students who are working for certificates transferable to other countries will need to have the second language introduced soon enough and taught vigorously enough, so that by the end of their secondary training their knowledge of the second language should be not more than a year or two behind that of students whose mother tongue is that second language. We believe that with efficient teaching such a goal is possible within the general programme suggested here.

Methods and materials. In introducing a second language, the teachers should use the best available techniques for teaching foreign languages. We consider it a fallacy to assume that an adequate method for these students consists either (a) simply of using the language as a medium of instruction or (b) of teaching "grammar" to them with the same texts, goals, and pedagogical philosophy as are used for students who are studying their mother tongue. We also call attention to the fact that a large body of materials exists which deal with the teaching of English, for example; and we emphasize strongly the fact that a teacher must not be considered as trained to do an adequate job of teaching English or French or Spanish as a foreign language simply because he speaks the language as a native and has studied the conventional grammar. For this purpose special techniques and materials specially controlled in vocabulary, cultural content, and presentation of structural complexities are highly important.

Control of vocabulary is especially important. No language can be successfully used as a medium unless the student has previously acquired: an active working command of the essential nucleus of the language, consisting as a rule of about one 1,000 words, the main grammatical forms and the most necessary idioms; a semi-active, semi-passive command of an additional vocabulary; and a technique of expansion, through a dictionary using a controlled defining vocabulary. This method demands that this essential nucleus of the language be determined.

It is important that the subject matter of the course used in the teaching of the second language should be closely related to the social, economic, and other needs and interests of the pupils or students to whom it is being taught.

Interdependence of mother tongue and second language. Finally, we would emphasize that the promotion of swifter and more effective techniques of second language teaching has a very direct bearing on the use of the mother tongue as the medium of instruction. It is clear that the development and enrichment of a mother tongue can be achieved only by the interest and efforts of the people whose language it is, and their interest in and understanding of it will be stimulated by an intimate knowledge of a second language and its associated culture. Moreover, if through the use of modern techniques, pupils can acquire a good knowledge of the second language taught as a subject in one or two periods a day, then there need be no anxiety that, in order to acquire a good command of it, they should use it as the medium of instruction from the beginning of their schooling.

Languages in adult education. Wherever possible, adult education should be carried out in the mother tongue. The great majority of adults will not have the time to master a foreign language sufficiently for it to be used as an effective medium of education. Moreover the new ideas which teachers desire to convey to adults, for the purpose of stimulating and guiding community development, can best be conveyed if interpreted to the people through the medium in which they are accustomed to think. Where people of many tongues are gathered together (e.g. in towns or work centres) some form of lingua franca is usually already used between them and this can then be used also as the medium for adult education. In teaching adults to read it is always best for them to begin in the mother tongue. They will often aspire to achieve literacy directly in a second, foreign, language, particularly if this second language is the one in which their children have become literate. Such a desire should be discouraged, especially if the gap between the mother tongue and the foreign language is very wide; for if they try to begin to learn to read in a foreign language most of them will never become truly literate. The gap between the generations will be smaller if the older and the younger read in different languages than if the older cannot read at all. However, those adults who – having learnt to read in their mother tongue – want to learn a second language, should be encouraged. In townships and elsewhere where a lingua franca is freely used among the people themselves, this can usefully replace the mother tongue as a first literacy language, for it usually has the advantage of already being used for the production of news sheets, public notices, etc. Thus new literates would be assured of some reading matter on which to exercise their new skill.

Desire to study may be aroused and maintained if the efforts of the adult learners towards literacy and better citizenship are tied up with their special interests. An adult will continue to learn only as he sees that his literacy will further his economic, social or cultural improvement. It is our considered opinion that teaching for literacy alone will have ephemeral effects.

Methods and materials for teaching adults. The teaching of adults requires special techniques and materials, both of which are adapted to the needs and psychology of the mature learners. It must be borne in mind that the interests of adults are much more specific and immediate than those of children and that there must be greater variety in the contents of reading materials provided for them.

The importance in all schemes of fundamental education of providing adequate incentives and opportunities for women cannot be overestimated.

SPECIAL PROBLEMS

Certain technical issues arising from the general questions so far discussed have been reserved for fuller treatment in this section. Because we recognize the importance of a scientific basis for language policies and because the discussions have shown a divergence of opinion on fundamental matters, our procedure is to reflect these differing points of view without pronouncing judgment upon them. We feel that the importance of these problems is great enough to require further study by linguists in all parts of the world. The sections that follow deal with the choice of writing systems, problems of a multilingual area, and questions of vocabulary and structure.

Choice of Writing System

New departures with regard to language policy in education and in the social-cultural life of various countries frequently raise the question of choosing between different possible systems of writing. The language may never have been written before, or may have been recorded only by travellers or scholars for their own purposes. Again, there may be two or more distinct systems of writing used in different sections of the country, by different religious groups, or by people under the influence of different scholarly traditions. Any one system of writing may or may not have a standardized spelling for individual words.

Even where there is uniformity in the system of writing, special problems may exist. Many traditional orthographies date back to the time when the only important technique of graphic representation was handwriting. The number of separate characters was not too important, and they could be interlaced with each other in complicated ways. Modern machine writing, including the typewriter and various typesetting machines for printing, work best with simple writing systems using a limited number of characters which can be arranged in a single line.

In cases where the school uses a local mother tongue in the early years but later changes to a second language of regional and national importance as the main instrument of communication, it is advantageous to the students if both languages are written in the same way. This means that they do not have to learn to read and write a second time for the second language, but make a more or less direct transfer of their previously acquired abilities.

Where there are several major regional languages in one country or where more than one language has official status, it is of value to have relative uniformity in the way in which they are written. To the extent that they are similar, the learning of the additional language is facilitated. Even within a single country, there may be obstacles towards achieving unification of alphabets because of the attachment people may have developed towards a given form of script or because of strong feeling they may hold against another one. These same attitudes may stand in the way of achieving the simplification of a writing system along lines that may be more suitable for typewriting, machine typesetting, and telegraphy.

Where new characters are needed in an alphabetic system, they should be taken from prevailing usage in the field of phonetics. This has the effect of maintaining unity between innovations adopted for different languages.

Despite the obstacles, simplification or unification of alphabets can sometimes be achieved, notably when new opportunities for general education are opened up or when a newly independent nation is in the process of developing governmental procedures. Because it is sometimes possible to effect orthographic improvements, it is well to have a clear notion of what is desirable in this regard.

An ideal writing system should be in agreement with the actual system of sounds, recognizing that some languages make distinctions of sounds that pass, as it were, unnoticed in other languages. The speakers react to the differences which their own language forces them to make, and are largely unaware of distinctions which may exist in other languages. Language specialists speak of phonemic and non-phonemic distinctions. A writing system, to be easily learned and used, must provide a clear means of distinguishing the phonemes of a language and must ordinarily disregard any phonetic distinctions which do not show a contrast of phonemes in the given language. It may be desirable in some areas to maintain similar spellings for related but phonemically different words or elements, provided that the difference between spelling and pronunciation is not too great.

For practical needs in terms of modern machinery, the system should use a limited set of symbols written in a single line. An alphabetic system is the easiest, but a simple syllabic system is almost as good. Availability of type is a consideration, and one should prefer types which are commonly available on all the principal modern machines (typewriter, linotype, monotype, etc.). The handwritten form should be considered; it should be possible to make the letters easily in the style of handwriting which is likely to be used. For ready recognition and ease of writing, diacritics are best avoided except for the indication of accented (emphasized) syllables or for tone. Other things being equal, a single letter for each phoneme is desirable, but digraphs (sequences of two letters) may, in certain cases, be preferable to complex characters.

In so far as possible, unification between orthographies should be sought, especially among the languages within a country. If possible, the writing of a local language should agree with that of the regional, national or official language, so as to facilitate transition from one to the other. In general, care should be taken not to force distinctions in the local language because they exist in the second language. In some instances the impact of the second language on the speech or writing habits of the bilinguals may make it advisable to modify the application of this principle. If the spelling of the second language is very complicated or irregular in certain respects, this is not a reason for introducing unnecessary complexity in the writing of the local language. For example, it is not advisable to use English or French vowel spellings in other languages, even when these are local idioms within an English-speaking or a French-speaking political entity. There are cases in which a given local language is found in two adjoining countries, each with its own official language, for example, Hausa in several territories in West

Africa. In such cases it is desirable that efforts be made to achieve uniformity in the spelling used for the local language in the two places.

To summarize, where the attitudes of the population towards their orthographic traditions permit a choice in matters of orthography, one should prefer:

1. Spelling in conformity with contemporary pronunciation.
2. Agreement with phonemes of the language.
3. Simplicity in typography (available types, limited numbers of characters, etc.).
4. Letters without diacritics (if equally satisfactory).
5. Digraphs in preference to new characters unless they cause ambiguity.
6. Derivation of new characters from prevailing scientific usage.
7. Agreement between different languages of the region or country, especially with the national or official language.

Some Problems of Multilingual Areas [5]

There are places in the world where the population is divided into a great number of small language groups, some consisting of not more than a 1,000 speakers, or even less (e.g. New Guinea). In such cases the smallness of the language group goes with a simple local culture and social organization. When such a small group is brought into active relationship with a larger political unit of complex culture, special measures are needed to help the process of adaptation. Such measures should be planned and carried out according to the best practices of applied anthropology in consultation with trained social anthropologists

[5] In relation to the remainder of this report opinion was divided. The majority group approved the text of all the paragraphs as they appear here. But a group formed by Dr. C. C. Berg of the University of the Netherlands of Leyden, and Dr. Aurélian Sauvageot of the Ecole nationale des langues orientales of Paris, did not approve it. The majority groups supported the thesis that vocabulary is the main item to be treated in undeveloped languages, leaving the structure as it is found, as even the most technologically-fitted languages present inconsistencies and aberrations, although some minor features may be avoided or modified. Dr. Berg and Dr. Sauvageot maintained that languages could and must suffer structural modifications (additions or subtractions) when lacking some categories to express new concepts or when containing unnecessary features which could make learning them more difficult. It was agreed then that this divergence was itself interesting, and that the two points of view should be reflected. Dr. Berg and Dr. Sauvageot, independently, sent the Secretariat their own drafts modifying or changing the text of some paragraphs. These paragraphs are indicated, and the alternatives of Dr. Berg and Dr. Sauvageot will be found at the end of this chapter in Annexes A and B, pp. 70-75 (of *The Uses of the Vernacular . . .*).

and linguists, in order to achieve the proper understanding and co-operative effort.

If, because of the complicated linguistic situation, it is not possible immediately to provide education for children and adults in the mother tongue of each linguistic group, some other solution must be found. If one of the languages has already been used by different groups as a means of social intercourse, however superficial the previous contact may have been, this language should be encouraged in its regional function. (See Annex A, 1, p. 70.)

Such an area of small language groups may form part of a nation which wants to extend the use of the national language everywhere within its boundaries. This unquestionably has great value in that it gives the small linguistic groups a medium for talking to each other as well as to those people who speak the national language as their mother tongue. There is of course no question of insisting that the small groups stop talking their languages in their own homes and communities, but only that they acquire the use of the national language for the purpose of wider relationships, including participation in national life and the acquisition of new knowledge. In the case of the smallest linguistic groups, it is also clear that it will not be practical to conduct education beyond the first few years in the mother tongue and that the local people will have to learn the national language in order to continue their schooling. (See Annex A, 2, p. 71.)

In these areas, it is particularly valuable to devise graded materials in the national language, making it possible to impart to the learner at the outset a well-chosen limited vocabulary which can serve his purposes temporarily until he has had an opportunity to go still farther. Such materials should include much used words, so chosen as to make it possible to carry on communication in fairly satisfactory form. To some extent one can avoid grammatical complexities in the initial material while still maintaining correct and natural expression. The initial instalment of the new language meets the immediate needs of the learner and serves as the basis for subsequently perfecting and completing his knowledge.

In polyglot States, where peoples living in a simple culture have to be assimilated into a complex civilization, a simplification of text materials will be especially helpful. Precaution should be taken, however, that various degrees of complexity should not result in the development of various pidgin dialects. In addition, the long range ideal goal should be the learning of the entire standard form of the national language by all segments of the population, since the administration of the nation and the welfare of its people is likely to be best promoted thereby. (See Annex B, 1, p. 72.)

The nation may find it highly desirable, if it contains a complex linguistic situation, to establish a bureau or institute, to supervise the choice of languages for regional use and the preparation of scientifically prepared pedagogical material.

Questions of Vocabulary and Structure

Natural vocabulary development. The vocabulary of a language has a relation to the life of the people who speak it, in that there are always enough words and expressions to enable them to express, with fair accuracy, the objects and beliefs which are of importance to them. The relationship is far from rigid, since there is always a considerable flexibility in the use of words; in different languages, and even in a single language, there is usually more than one way of saying essentially the same thing, and it is possible to describe new experiences by means of the current vocabulary. Nevertheless, it is the effort to describe new experiences which gives rise to modifications in the sense of old expressions and which leads to the introduction of new terms. Much of this vocabulary growth is spontaneous, being the crystallization of many separate efforts of expression. However, in the event of new departures in education and culture, including particularly the introduction of the mother tongue into the school for the first time or the attempt to develop scientific and technical literature and training in a language which has previously been little used in this way, then the need arises for conscious planning of vocabulary development. (See Annex A, 3, p. 71 and Annex B, 2, p. 73.)

Planned vocabulary development. To be successful without requiring an overwhelming outlay of time and resources, the planned vocabulary development should make the best possible use of the natural tendencies of the language. Those who undertake such work should avoid the kind of wasted efforts which in the past has frequently resulted from an impractical approach to vocabulary building and which produced thousands of words for notions which people were not discussing or which went against the tendencies in popular usage. Consideration of these facts leads to some such guiding principles as we now offer. (See Annex B, 3, p. 73.)

1. Begin by making a study of the vocabulary already in use, including recent borrowed words and native expressions recently formed to describe new concepts. The principle methods used include giving new meanings to old terms, using native descriptive expressions or derivatives, adopting foreign terms, modelling native descriptive expressions

after convenient foreign models. The problem, then, is to determine which of these procedures are most generally used and in what way they tend to be applied to different sets of concepts. (See Annex B, 4, p. 73.)

2. Avoid coining new words where native words are already in general use or where there are words which could easily be stretched to include the new concept without special confusion. If the native word is mainly used by people in a given section of the country or by specialists in some particular craft, then the problem would be simply that of generalizing its use. Along with the employment of words of strictly native tradition, one must give full consideration to relatively new words adopted from other languages, particularly if they already have general currency. (See Annex B, 5, p. 74.)

3. Before adding a word to the vocabulary, be sure that it is really needed either at once or in the relatively near future. It is not wise to prescribe words which will not be used with some frequency, since such needs can be met by using brief descriptions. People generally will not bother to learn special words in such cases, and those few persons who go out of their way to use the prescribed terms may not be understood. A difference should be made in the case of new terms whose meaning is reasonably self-evident. (See Annex B, 6, p. 75.)

4. Where a whole set of terms applying to a given field of science has to be adopted, try to maintain general consistency among them – consistency as to type of formation and language of origin. The international terms from Latin and Greek, and other terms in widespread usage through the world, should be given special consideration.

5. Make necessary adaptations to the phonemic structure and grammar of the language.

6. Once the new terms have been chosen, try them out on a number of people to see how readily they take to them. If possible, experiment with the use of the new terms in lectures, class instruction and general conversation for a while before publishing.

Organization of vocabulary development. Where the problem is to develop a simple vocabulary for primary school purposes, it probably can be done by a small committee of experts acquainted with both the subject matter and the native culture, and advised by one or more linguistic scholars of a practical turn of mind. Where the aim is to develop the use of a language for technical purposes, a permanent commission or society would be in order. A conference to launch the new effort may have good results. Specialists in each field should be encouraged to collaborate with each other and with the commission in developing the vocabulary they need. It is further suggested that a manual or guide on the principles to be followed in adapting or coining words should be made widely available among all people who may have occasion to devise technical or literary terms. From time to time findings and recommendations should be published.

To ensure the best results of planned vocabulary enrichment, it is well to emphasize popularization rather than word coining as such. This is best done by stimulating scientific and cultural activity. The commission or society should preferably be a general literary or cultural organization devoted to the stimulation of arts and letters, considering vocabulary always in the larger context. Finally, in its programme, it should make the best possible use of modern media of diffusion, including press, radio, cinema, and theatre, in order to reach the general public as well as scholars.

Grammatical structure. In cases where a homogeneous speech community is given instruction in its mother tongue, there is no need for changing the grammatical structure of the language concerned either by adding or by abolishing categories, the main problem then being how to extend its vocabulary. In other cases, however, where a language is used for educational and cultural purposes in a multilingual society, it may be useful to reconstruct it to some extent by abolishing irregularities and by adding new useful categories in order to make it a better vehicle of modern thought. This is especially desirable if the language of education is a foreign language to the majority of the pupils concerned, and if the speech community who owns it as its mother tongue is relatively small and/or unimportant, so that it may be expected that such a community will gradually accept the reconstructed form as a result of its becoming the normal language of the greater community. (See Annex A, 4, p. 71.)

SOME FACTORS TO BE TAKEN INTO CONSIDERATION IN PLANNING A LANGUAGE PROGRAMME

Authorities who wish to extend the benefits of instruction through the mother tongue to many different language-groups under their control will naturally want to deal with those offering least difficulty first, gradually encompassing the more difficult as time and funds permit. The list of priorities need not be based on purely numerical considerations. Other factors may in fact outweigh numerical inferiority. What is needed is some sort of weighting to cover the chief factors. We suggest here some of the points to be considered in addition to that of numbers, relating to any given language-group.

Geographical

1. How intense is the community life?

2. How far is the group mixed with speakers of other languages?

3. How good are external and internal communications?

4. How far is industry developed in the region?

5. Is it likely that new developments, such as the establishment of new industries or the opening up of new lines of communication, will change the linguistic situation?

Social

1. Do many people speak another language as well – which are these second languages?

2. What is the present attitude of the people themselves on language matters, and is it likely to change?

3. Do people feel there is an economic advantage in knowing some language other than their own?

Linguistic

1. What are the linguistic relations of the language – is it a local variety of some more widely spoken language?

2. Is there a traditional system of writing, and if so, can it easily be printed and taught?

3. Has the language a traditional literary form? If so, does this differ much from the modern form, and are the people much attached to it?

4. Does the language acquire new words easily, and does it take over more easily borrowed words or native phrases?

5. Is its vocabulary already adequate for cultural and technical purposes?

Educational

1. How large is the educated population?

2. Are there any organizations concerned with developing the language?

3. Is there a present supply of trained teachers who speak the language, and can others be recruited?

4. What educational materials exist in the language, and what opportunity is there for producing more?

5. Has any work already been done in using the language in education and in publishing reading material in it?
6. Have educationists in other regions recorded their experience of similar situations?
7. How long do pupils usually stay at school?
8. If a new project for using the vernacular in education is developed, what budget, staff, and machinery for co-operation with the community are likely to be provided?

SUMMARY

1. The mother tongue is a person's natural means of self-expression, and one of his first needs is to develop his power of self-expression to the full.
2. Every pupil should begin his formal education in his mother tongue.
3. There is nothing in the structure of any language which precludes it from becoming a vehicle of modern civilization.
4. No language is inadequate to meet the needs of the child's first months in school.
5. The problems of providing an adequate supply of schoolbooks and other educational materials should be specially studied by Unesco.
6. If the mother tongue is adequate in all respects to serve as the vehicle of university and higher technical education, it should be so used.
7. In other cases, the mother tongue should be used as far as the supply of books and materials permits.
8. If each class in a school contains children from several language groups, and it is impossible to regroup the children, the teacher's first task must be to teach all pupils enough of one language to make it possible to use that language as the medium of instruction.
9. A lingua franca is not an adequate substitute for the mother tongue unless the children are familiar with it before coming to school.
10. Adult illiterates should make their first steps to literacy through their mother tongue, passing on to a second language if they desire and are able.
11. Educational authorities should aim at persuading an unwilling public to accept education through the mother tongue, and should not force it.
12. Literacy can only be maintained if there is an adequate supply of reading material, for adolescents and adults as well as for school children, and for entertainment as well as for study.
13. If a child's mother tongue is not the official language of his

country, or is not a world language, he needs to learn a second language.

14. It is possible to acquire a good knowledge of a second language without using it as the medium of instruction for general subjects.

15. During the child's first or second year at school, the second language may be introduced orally as a subject of instruction.

16. The amount of the second language should be increased gradually, and if it has to become the medium of instruction, it should not do so until the pupils are sufficiently familiar with it.

17. Efficient modern techniques should be used in teaching the mother tongue and a foreign language. A teacher is not adequately qualified to teach a language merely because it is his mother tongue.

18. Where there are several languages in a country, it is an advantage if they are written as uniformly as possible.

19. For convenience of printing, languages should as far as possible be written with a limited set of symbols which are written in a single line. For a summary of other recommendations on orthography, see p. 62.

20. For the needs of a polyglot state which is developing a national language, the materials for teaching the language should be simplified for instructional purposes, so that pupils may progress towards full mastery without having anything to unlearn.

RECOMMENDATIONS FOR UNESCO ACTION

1. Since the main obstacle to the use of the vernacular languages is shortage of educational materials, Unesco should investigate the technical questions involved – paper, type, machinery, etc. – from the point of view of the needs already known.

2. Unesco should investigate the possibility of co-ordinating scientific and technical terminology in world languages so as to help the developing languages to create their own terminology as far as possible in conformity with the terminology in world languages.

3. Unesco should investigate the possibility of promoting the exchange and extension of copyrights and the like with the particular aim of helping the developing languages to have sufficient reading and study material up to the highest level.

4. To further its work on exchange of persons, Unesco could help the younger countries which send students abroad if it pressed for having the certificates of educational achievement granted by these countries accepted in the countries to which students normally go.

5. Within Unesco's Exchange of Persons Programme some priority should be given to training in linguistic and in second language teaching.

ANNEX A

Dr. Berg's alternatives to indicated paragraphs

1. If because of the complicated linguistic situation it is not possible immediately, or even in the long run, to provide education for children and adults in the mother tongue of each linguistic group, some other solution must be found which will meet this situation. If one of the languages has already been used by different groups as a means of social intercourse, however superficial the previous contact may have been, this language should be encouraged in its regional function. If not, the simplest language of the area should be chosen, and in special cases the advantages of simplicity may over-rule the advantage of numerical superiority or wider use.

2. Such an area of small language groups may form part of a nation which wants to extend the use of the national language everywhere within its boundaries. This unquestionably has great value in that it gives the small linguistic groups a medium for talking to each other as well as to those people who speak the national language as their mother tongue. There is of course no question of insisting that the small groups stop talking their languages in their own homes and communities, but only that they acquire the use of the national language for the purpose of wider relationships, including participation in national life and the acquisition of new knowledge. On the other hand, in the case of the smallest linguistic groups, it is also clear that it will not be practical to conduct education beyond the initial stage in the mother tongue and the local people will have to learn the national language in order to continue their schooling. As the national language in such cases provides the best means to overcome isolation and backwardness, a policy of slow and gradual conversion of a polyglot (multilingual) area into a national language area should not be regarded as irreconcilable with the principle of non-insisting.

3. In the event of new departures in education and culture, including particularly the introduction of the mother tongue into the school for the first time or the attempt to develop scientific and technical literature and training in a language which has previously been little used in this way, then the need arises for conscious planning of vocabulary development.[6]

4. In general the position to take with regard to grammatical structure

[6] Dr. Berg in this paragraph dropped out all the previous sentences of the draft approved by the majority, because "According to my opinion, the theory of the introduction to this paragraph is false, as it states that language suits the needs of the people who use it. I stressed in my paper ('The Question of the Methodical Simplification and Development of Language, in Connexion with Educational Problems in Underdeveloped Areas', Unesco/EDCH/Meeting VER./9, Paris, November 1951) that people depend on the structure of the language they acquire in childhood, and that mental development is checked by the rigidness of linguistic structure. But I am aware that this point of view – which is the point of view of many biologists – is not shared by many linguists" – *Letter of the author, dated 12 January 1952.*

is the same as that which we have followed with reference to the vocabulary. One should at all times make the best possible use of the existing grammatical structure rather than undertake complex programmes of grammatical reform which would require large expenditures of time and resources and might take up the attention of the best minds for generations. It should be remembered that all the present world languages are, as it were, marred by irregularities and complexities. A good example is the presence in many world languages of arbitrary grammatical gender, which at times is related to biological sex but disregards it in many ways which are confusing not only for new learners but occasionally even for native speakers. The category of number, requiring nouns to be put in the singular or plural even when one is making a general scientific statement which is true regardless of number, is another case in point. While many world and local languages have this category, it is actually more logical to operate without it, using quantitative expressions only in these contexts where it is important to the sense. In view of these considerations, it follows that one should generally accept the native grammatical categories as they are. However, these are cases where usage is divided, where some people say things one way and some another. In such cases, it is justified to adopt and favour the simpler usage.

ANNEX B

Professor Sauvageot's alternatives to indicated paragraphs

1. To facilitate the execution of a programme of this kind, it may be necessary to undertake a judicious codification of the language selected as the national tongue of the new state or nation.

There are two possible ways of arriving at a new national tongue; (a) building on the most widely-used existing idiom; (b) combining the existing dialects to form a new codified language.

In either case, consideration should be given to the question of what can be done in the way of correction, simplification and regularization to make the new language more readily usable by those sections of the people whose mother tongues diverge in some degree from the dialect or dialects used to form it. Simplification will consist in excising forms that are too disparate; regularization, in making words and their variants more fixed and uniform; and correction, in eliminating the most glaring contradictions or anomalies. All these procedures will only be used by properly qualified experts after due consideration and with the concurrence of a majority of the best-educated speakers of the language.

These are indeed the same procedures that were applied, consciously or otherwise, in the development of the majority of the civilized languages known today. Modern linguistic knowledge makes it possible to secure results in less time.

2. It has already been pointed out that an idiom may be in such a state as to make its use difficult even in elementary teaching, either because of the inadequacy of its vocabulary or for other purely linguistic reasons.

Thanks to modern linguistics, these deficiencies can be remedied by the conscious and systematic application of procedures which have proved their effectiveness throughout history whenever a particular language has had to adapt itself to express a new type of thought for which it was not originally designed.

3. The most frequent case is one in which only vocabulary is inadequate.

Here, it is enough to provide the idiom in question with the vocables it lacks; and for this any one of the following procedures can be adopted, in the order of preference given below:

(a) The formation of new words from existing ones, in conformity with the correct word-formation rules for the language in question.
(b) The 'calquing' of foreign words by the substitution, for each of their components, of an equivalent from the native vocabulary.
(c) The borrowing of essential foreign terms, with phonetic adaptation to conform to the rules of the borrowing language.

The last of these procedures should be avoided as far as possible, as it brings with it the danger of upsetting the etymological balance of the language and causing confusion by permitting the co-existence of words similar in aspect but different in origin. In addition, borrowing on any scale has the disadvantage of introducing a large number of words which cannot be understood immediately by reference to their etymology, thus rendering the task of teaching more difficult.

4. In other circumstances the difficulty lies in the internal structure of the idiom concerned, in that it does not much lend itself to the expression of the categories which are seen to be necessary to convey a more modern and scientific type of thought.

In this case, adjustments and, if necessary, innovations must be made in the syntax or even the morphological structure of the language concerned.

For instance, should it become necessary to express the category of tense where the only existing category is that of aspect, recourse will be had to an adaptation associating tense with aspect in conformity with a prescribed system (this actually occurred in certain Polynesian languages during the nineteenth century under the impact of translations of the Bible and other European texts). Or again, in a language in which the category of number is customarily ignored, a means of expressing number will be devised by reserving a particular *construction* for the expression of that particular idea (cf. Tahitian, etc.).

Today, adjustments or innovations of this kind can be effected more quickly and surely by co-operation between qualified linguists and the users of the language, who are usually well aware of the need for such improvement and amplification of it.[7]

[7] See E. M. K. Mulira, *The Vernacular in African Education (Lantern Library Series)* (London, Longmans Green & Co., 1951), p. 13, etc.

5. It is obvious that all these endeavours must aim at providing the native with a means of linguistic expression enabling him to make contact with modern thought without thereby emasculating his own. The salvage of indigenous cultures is only conceivable given the preservation, in its essence, of the idiom in which those cultures have been expressed, and this can only be done if the idiom in question succeeds in adapting itself to the new needs. Otherwise it will gradually wither and atrophy, and finally vanish. The people speaking it will change their language, and that change will involve the death of the civilization to which they formerly belonged.

The degree to which it is considered desirable to preserve local civilizations is the measure of the need to adapt the languages which are their armature and in the absence of which they are not even conceivable. If Finnish had not adapted itself through the centuries to the successive needs with which it was confronted, the Finnish people would today speak only Swedish, and would thereby have lost all the treasures which they have inherited from their ancestors and which they have succeeded in handing down to the present generation. Many other examples of the same type could be quoted showing that, for a people desirous of preserving their heritage, no price could be too high in effort to adapt their language to the needs which circumstances impose upon them. Success in this is essential if we wish to preserve, for the future of mankind, that diversity of civilizations which enriches all, and modern linguistics vastly facilitate it.

6. To make it possible to adapt, under the best conditions, languages suffering from deficiencies in grammar and vocabulary, a sound policy would be the foundation of schools or study centres where specially qualified natives could receive the scientific training fitting them to undertake this task for their own native languages. Such institutions could be the scene of fruitful collaboration between the learned of all countries and representatives of those peoples whose languages have not yet developed sufficiently to express modern thought.

From *The Use of Vernacular Languages in Education* (Paris, Unesco, 1953). pp. 45-75. Reprinted by permission.

Elliot R. Goodman

WORLD STATE AND WORLD LANGUAGE

The Soviet grand design for transforming the present nation-state system into a Soviet world state envisages a fundamental reshaping of national languages. A national language, as the nerve center of a national memory, is probably the most important single medium through which national traditions are nurtured and transmitted. Of all of those ingredients producing a sense of national cohesion, a national language is doubtless the fundamental element, although the existence of several multilingual nation-states would indicate that national languages need not be an insuperable barrier to the growth of broader loyalties. Yet even here the continued use of national languages imparts a sense of national distinctiveness which cannot be obliterated, except through the destruction of the various national languages. If the time should ever come when all national languages are merged and transformed into a single world language, then the last glimmering of nationalism will have flickered out. The fate of national languages can therefore serve as a barometer marking the rise and fall of the very concept of a nation.

As the ultimate destiny of nations is a matter for the distant future, no Soviet theoretician has ever indicated that the extinction of all national languages or the adoption of a single world language is prerequisite to the creation of a world state. The question of a world language has therefore not been among the first problems with which the Soviet regime contended in projecting the image of a world state. But as this subject was bound to arise from any serious consideration of a world state, the Stalinist era produced a number of striking and explicit statements which both foretold the doom of national languages and predicted the formation of a single world language.

Stalin's contributions were based upon assumptions implicit in Lenin's vision of a socialist world state. Lenin foresaw the assimilation of nations and the formation of a single proletarian, non-national world culture. However Lenin's actual statements on the anticipated role of national languages were confined to his experience in the multilingual Russian Empire. He recognized "the unquestionably progressive significance of centralization, of large governmental units, and of a single language", yet he opposed the mandatory adoption of Russian as the official state language.[1] The compulsory teaching of Russian in schools in non-Russian areas, and the obligatory use of Russian in the official institutions of non-Russian regions, were part of the hated Russification policy of the Tsars. This, Lenin rightly perceived, only served to drive nations apart and retarded the process of their assimilation. Consequently, Lenin pleaded for the right of each nation to use and freely develop its own language as the first step toward the voluntary adoption of a language common to all nations. With the abolition of privileges for any one language, the objective forces of economic development would do the rest. "The demands of the economic factors will, of their own, *determine* which language of a given country the majority would *profitably* learn in the interests of trade. This determination will be the more certain and the populations of different nations will volutarily adopt it the more quickly and widely, the more democracy will be consistently introduced."[2]

THE BOLSHEVIK REVOLUTION AND THE FOSTERING OF NATIONAL LANGUAGES

This position, which Lenin assumed before the Bolshevik Revolution, underestimated the strength and tenacity of the national sentiment of the oppressed nations which were soon to be set free by the disintegration of the Russian Empire. The first few years after the revolution were consumed with the implementation of the first phase of development in which each nation rediscovered its own national traditions and language. At this point there was little talk of the second stage of

[1] Lenin, "Pis'mo S. G. Shaumianu", Dec. 6, 1913, in *Sochineniia*, XVII, 89. On the other hand, Lenin specifically favored the widespread use of Russian within the Empire, if it could be introduced without compulsion: "The progressive significance of the *Russian* language for a vast number of miserable and backward nations is indisputable."

[2] Lenin, "Liberaly i demokraty v voprose o iazykakh", Sept. 18, 1913, in *ibid.*, XVI, 596. See also, "Nuzhen-li obiazatel'nyi gosudarstvennyi iazyk?", Jan. 31, 1914, in *ibid.*, XVII, 179-81; "Razvrashchenie rabochikh utonchënnym natsionalizmom", May 23, 1914, in *ibid.*, XVII, 361.

development in which a common language would supersede the newly revitalized national languages. The suggestion of one common language for the Soviet Union was condemned as a deviation of Great Russian chauvinism, and even the very prospect of a single world language came under attack. At the height of this period, in May, 1925, Stalin said:

> Certain persons (Kautsky, for example) talk of the creation of a single universal language and of the dying away of all other languages in the period of socialism. I have very little faith in this theory of a single all-embracing language. Experience, in any case, does not speak for, but against this theory. Up until now the socialist revolution has not diminished, but increased the number of languages, since it has aroused the broad masses of humanity, pushed them onto the political stage and awakened a new life in a whole series of new nationalities, which were formerly unknown or almost unknown.[3]

This statement was made on the same occasion that Stalin introduced the idea of a "culture, national in form and socialist in content". This formula was intended to set limits upon the further development of nationalism, by standardizing the ideological content of each culture. Though it was somewhat less obvious, the formula also provided the basis for confining the development of national forms, among which language was the most important, to those modes of expression which Moscow chose to tolerate. The "national form" of a given culture, like its ideological content, was a highly manipulative concept, subject to official definition by Moscow. The handwriting on the wall now clearly warned that henceforth the integrative, not the disintegrative, phase of national development would gradually assume paramount importance. While in 1925 this formula was first directed toward integrating the content of each national culture, within a decade it was also aimed at integrating the forms of national cultures, including, first and foremost, the integration of national languages. Soon the script, vocabulary, and even the syntax of these national languages were all subjected to violent and arbitrary alterations. Thus, when Stalin returned to the language discussion in 1929 and 1930, he no longer rejected the idea of a world language.

STALIN'S CONCEPT OF A NON-NATIONAL WORLD LANGUAGE

Stalin expounded his views on a world language in an article written in March, 1929, though it was not published until 1949. It is difficult

[3] Stalin, "O politicheskikh zadachakh Universiteta Narodov Vostoka", May 18, 1925, in *Sochineniia*, VII, 138-39.

to explain the delay in its publication, since he repeated the essence of these ideas publicly in his report to the Sixteenth Party Congress in June, 1930. In these declarations Stalin claimed to revert to the Leninist tradition by acknowledging "Lenin's theses, namely, that with the victory of socialism on a *world scale*, national differences and national languages will begin to die away, that after this victory national languages will begin to be supplanted by one common language." [4] Stalin neglected to mention that this was not Lenin's original position, but only the one forced upon him by the revolution. Before the revolution Lenin had held that the process of assimilation of nations was already in progress under the bourgeoisie, and that it would be greatly accelerated by the advent of socialism. He did not then believe that national differences would only *begin* to die away *after* the formation of a socialist world state. Stalin accurately cited Lenin's statement that "national and state differences... will continue to exist for a very long time even after the dictatorship of the proletariat has been established on a world scale",[5] but failed to note that this statement, made in 1920, was at variance with Lenin's prerevolutionary views. Nor did Stalin indicate that this 1920 statement contradicted his own prerevolutionary position. In 1913 Stalin had agreed fully with the Marxian premise that " 'national differences... are now more and more vanishing', and that 'the supremacy of the proletariat will cause them to vanish still faster' ".[6] By 1929-1930 Stalin sought to extricate Lenin and himself from this contradiction, as well as to obscure his own openly heretical position of 1925, when he denounced the idea of a world language, by shifting the blame for these ideological confusions onto a scapegoat.

Stalin again dragged Kautsky onto the stage and carefully propped him up as a straw man whom he could blow over as a tour de force. Stalin now criticized Kautsky for suggesting that a revolution in the Austro-Hungarian Empire of the nineteenth century would have led to the Germanizing of the Czechs and the adoption of German as a common language. "The mere force of unshackled intercourse", Kautsky maintained, "the mere force of modern culture of which the Germans were the vehicles, without any forcible Germanization, would have converted into Germans the backward Czech petty bourgeoisie, peasants, and proletarians who had nothing to gain from their decayed nationality." [7] This statement closely paralleled Lenin's assertion that the effect of economic factors, by themselves, would determine which lan-

[4] Stalin, "Natsional'nyi vopros i Leninizm", March 18, 1929, in *ibid.*, XI, 342.
[5] *Ibid.*, XI, 346.
[6] Stalin, "Marksizm i natsional'nyi vopros", Jan., 1913, in *Sochineniia*, II, 330.
[7] Quoted in Stalin, "Politicheskii otchët Tsentral'nogo Komiteta XVI s'ezdu VKP (b)", June 27, 1930, in *ibid.*, XII, 364 (italics omitted).

guage would be adopted by the majority in any given mixture of peoples. It was also practically a verbatim quotation from Engels, who had looked upon the Germans as agents of progress and dismissed the Czechs as an ethnic by-product.[8]

Now Stalin called Kautsky "a dilettante in the national question," since he "praises the assimilating 'work' of the Germans among the Czechs, and casually asserts that the Czechs ... have no future as a nation".[9] Getting to the heart of the matter, Stalin said that Kautsky "does not understand the mechanics of the development of nations and has no inkling of the colossal power of stability possessed by nations, and believes that the fusion of nations is possible long before the victory of socialism". Here Stalin obviously shifted the onus of the prerevolutionary Bolshevik views onto Kautsky, since it is abundantly clear that, until hit by the actual impact of the revolution, neither Lenin nor Stalin had a real "inkling of the colossal power of stability possessed by nations".

This assertion of faith in the enormous staying power of nations furnished Stalin a convenient pretext for explaining away his condemnation, in 1925, of the concept of a world language. Stalin said that in excluding the possibility of a world language it must have been "evident that what I had in mind in my speech was not the period of the victory of socialism on a *world scale*, but exclusively the period of the victory of socialism in *one country*".[10] Stalin's actual statement of 1925 was that "certain persons (Kautsky, for example) talk of the creation of a single universal language and of the dying away of all other languages in the period of socialism. I have very little faith in this theory of a single all-embracing language". From this it is by no means evident that Stalin was drawing a distinction between the periods of the victory of socialism in one country and the victory of socialism on a world scale, and thereby endorsing the idea of the emergence of a world language after the creation of a Soviet world state. But it was just this distinction upon which Stalin now wished to rest his theory of a world language. He looked forward to "the flowering of national cultures (and languages) in the period of the proletarian dictatorship in one country with the object of preparing the conditions for their dying away and merging into one common socialist culture (and into one common language) in the period of the victory of socialism in the entire world".[11] Stalin indicated that the ultimate world language could

[8] Engels, "Hungary and Panslavism", 1849, in *Russian Menace*, p. 59; Engels, "Democratic Panslavism", 1849, in *ibid.*, p. 77.

[9] Stalin, "Natsional'nyi vopros", in *Sochineniia*, XI, 344.

[10] *Ibid.*, XI, 344-45.

[11] Stalin, "Politicheskii otchët", in *Sochineniia*, XII, 370.

not be identified with any one of the presently existing national languages, for "national languages must inevitably fuse into one common language, which, of course, will be neither Great Russian nor German, but something new".[12] Barmine reports that Stalin once considered Esperanto as this future non-national world language, but abandoned the idea after an unsuccessful attempt to master it.[13]

Whatever this new world language might be, Stalin warned that it could not be hurried into existence immediately after the victory of world socialism, "at one stroke, by decree from above".[14] This world language must evolve without coercion, and through a gradual series of stages. "It is a mistake to think that the first stage of the period of the world dictatorship of the proletariat will mark the beginning of the formation of a single common language." At this point the hitherto oppressed national cultures and national languages will find full freedom of expression. Only in the second stage of world socialism, when a single world socialist economy has been successfully constructed, "only in that stage will something in the nature of a common language begin to take shape, for only in that stage will nations feel the need to have a common international language in addition to their own national languages, as a convenience of intercourse and as an aid to economic, cultural, and political cooperation". In the beginning, Stalin anticipated that there might be several common international languages existing alongside national languages. "It is probable that, at first not one economic center will be formed, common to all nations and with one common language, but several zonal economic centers for separate groups of nations, with a separate common language for each group of nations, and that only later will these centers combine into one common world socialist economic center, with one language common to all nations." The final stage will arrive when the world socialist economic system has fully consolidated its gains and "when practice has convinced nations of the superiority of a common language over national languages." Only at this point will "national differences and languages begin to die away and make room for a world language, common to all nations".[15]

[12] Stalin, "Zakliuchitel'noe slovo po politicheskomu otchëtu TsK XVI s'ezdu VKP (b)", July 2, 1930, in *ibid.*, XIII, 5.

[13] Alexander Barmine, *One Who Survived* (New York, 1945), p. 260. On the fluctuation of Soviet linguistic theory toward Esperanto and the Soviet attempt to make use of the Esperanto movement, see George P. Springer, *Early Soviet Theories in Communication* (MIT Center for International Studies, Cambridge, Mass., 1956), pp. 1, 11-16, 28-37; E. Bokarev, "Esperanto – vspomogatel'nyi mezhdunarodnyi iazyk", *Literaturnaia gazeta*, July 18, 1957, p. 2.

[14] Stalin, "Natsional'nyi vopros", in *Sochineniia*, XI, 347.

[15] *Ibid.*, XI, 348-49.

These views, expressed in 1929, were fully upheld in the Soviet linguistics discussion of 1950, at which time Stalin further refined his description of the fate of national languages, both before and after the creation of a Soviet world state. "*Prior to the victory of socialism* on a world scale . . . when national and colonial oppression remains in effect, when national isolation and mutual distrust of nations are reinforced by state differences", Stalin held that the crossing of two languages "does not yield some new, third language" but rather "one of the languages usually comes out the victor, whereas the other dies away". On the other hand, "*after the victory of socialism* on a world scale . . . when national and colonial oppression has been liquidated, when national isolation and mutual distrust of nations have been replaced by mutual confidence and a drawing together of nations", then "national languages will have the opportunity freely to enrich one another on the basis of cooperation".

In this case we will not have two languages, one of which is suffering defeat while the other emerges victorious from the struggle, but hundreds of national languages from which at first the most enriched single zonal languages will emerge as a result of lengthy economic, political, and cultural cooperation of nations, and subsequently the zonal languages will fuse into one common international language, which, of course, will be neither German, nor Russian, nor English, but a new language which has absorbed the best elements of the national and zonal languages.[16]

It would seem that the limits of this inquiry had been reached, as this view offers no prospect of further identifying this future world language. Continued probing would be pointless if, in fact, the Soviet leadership considered all the existing major languages on a par, as being equally eligible to shape the form of this future common world tongue. But closer examination shows that this is clearly not the case. In the struggle for world supremacy between East and West the roles of Russian and English are cast in entirely different lights.

RUSSIAN AND ENGLISH COMPARED AS INTERNATIONAL LANGUAGES

The Soviet regime claims that "American colonizers, aspiring to world domination, are seeking to have English recognized as the world language which should replace all other languages". Accordingly, the

[16] Stalin, "Tovarishchu A. Kholopovu", July 28, 1950, in *Marksizm i voprosy*, pp. 45-47.

American motto "E Pluribus Unum" means "from the separate sovereign states to a single world government, with English as the single world language".[17] To facilitate this conquest "American linguists are hastily preparing plans for the 'simplification' of the English language in order to make it the single international tongue." These efforts are producing "the poisonous bacteria of cosmopolitanism" intended to "destroy a feeling of national dignity in the soul," and thereby to promote the capitulation of nations to the "American imperialists".[18] But such strivings will be of no avail, since an attempt "to force the English language upon all peoples" is sure to meet with "utter failure and defeat".[19]

The prospect for Russian is depicted in precisely the opposite manner. Russian is credited with a constant accretion of strength through its supposedly voluntary adoption by an ever-mounting number of non-Russian peoples. This process began in the multilingual Soviet Union and has spread to large areas outside the Soviet Union.

During the 1920s attempts to force the adoption of Russian among non-Russian peoples in the USSR were officially condemned out of consideration for the newly aroused sensitivities of the non-Russian nationalities. But even this earliest period was marked by relapses into Russification. For example, from 1920 until August, 1923, the Soviet government sanctioned the application in the Ukraine of Lebed's so-called "theory of the struggle of two cultures". In the Ukraine, Russian was widely spoken in the cities, while Ukrainian was the language of the countryside. Under the cover of proposing a natural struggle between them, Lebed's theory was really intended to produce the victory of Russian over Ukrainian, on the ground that the future belonged to the Russian-speaking urban proletariat which possessed a culture superior to the backward-looking, Ukrainian-speaking peasantry.[20]

The rediscovery of the various national languages in the Soviet Union came as a mixed blessing to the national minorities, since it often had the curious effect of elevating the importance of Russian among the non-Russian peoples. Instead of creating a common language for ethnically related peoples who were hitherto largely illiterate, Soviet policy elevated dialects into languages, even, if need be, at the cost of in-

[17] T. P. Lomtev, "I. V. Stalin o razvitii natsional'nykh iazykov v epokhu sotsializma", *Voprosy filosofii*, No. 2 (1949), pp. 136-37.

[18] A. Elistratova, "Izmenniki narodu", *Literaturnaia gazeta*, March 2, 1949, p. 2.

[19] M. Kammari, "An Outstanding Contribution to the Science of Marxism", *New Times*, No. 26 (June 27, 1951), p. 7. See also G. Serdiuchenko, "O vrednoi teorie v iazkoznanii", *Kultura i zhizn'*, June 30, 1949, p. 3.

[20] E. F. Girchak, *Na dva fronta v bor'be s natsionalizmom* (Moscow, Leningrad, 1930), pp. 18-22; Ilarion Ohienko, "Ukrainian Literary Language in the U.S.S.R.", *Ukrainian Quarterly*, VI, No. 3 (Summer, 1950), 231; Roman Smal-Stocki, *The Nationality Problem of the Soviet Union* (Milwaukee, 1952), pp. 94-96.

venting new, written alphabets. This conscious policy of fragmentation might be explained, in large part, by the fear that large, cohesive blocs of non-Russians, speaking a common tongue, would present a formidable threat to the centralized, Russian-based dictatorship. The treatment of the Moslem peoples of the Soviet Union provides the clearest illustration of this policy of parcelization. In an effort to avoid the creation of a large Moslem state in the Volga-Urals region, the Soviet regime created separate Bashkir and Tatar ASSRs, and enlarged upon the somewhat artificial distinction between the Bashkir and Tatar languages. Moreover, Moscow was happy to encourage the Turco-Tatar "Latinizers", since writing these languages in the Arabic script would have encouraged Pan-Islamic and Pan-Turkic ties, which were far more deadly sins than a tie between the Bashkirs and the Tatars. This pattern of linguistic development was later repeated among the numerous peoples of Turkic stock in Central Asia and in the Northern Caucasus.[21] While non-Russian languages were codified by the score, their development was carefully channeled and their divergencies inflated so that no new regional non-Russian language could evolve among them. The logical result of this policy was that Russian increasingly became the lingua franca of the non-Russian peoples.

THE RUSSIFICATION OF LANGUAGES IN THE SOVIET UNION

Stalin expressed opposition to Russian as an official state language for the last time in 1930. Those who urged its adoption were still condemned as Great Russian chauvinists. "Is it not evident", Stalin asked, "that those who advocate one common language within the borders of *one* state, within the borders of the USSR, are, in essence, striving to restore the *privileges* of the formerly predominating language, namely the *Great Russian* language?"[22] But the trend toward Great Russian chauvinism was, in fact, well under way. The tempo of introducing the study of Russian among non-Russian peoples was increasingly stepped up during the 1930s, and on March 13, 1938, the Soviet government

[21] Kolarz, *Russia and Her Colonies*, pp. 32-33, 41-44, 202-4, 259-62, 275, 282, 294-95; Smal-Stocki, *Nationality Problem*, pp. 152-53; Stefan Wurm, *The Turkic Languages of Central Asia: Problems of Planned Cultural Contact* (Oxford, 1953), pp. 1-53; Stefan Wurm, *Turkic Peoples of the U.S.S.R.* (Oxford, 1954), pp. 10-51; G. A. von Stackelberg, "The Second Turkmen Linguistic Congress and Its Political Significance", *Bulletin of the Institute*, II, No. 1 (Jan., 1955), 24-28; Richard Pipes, "Muslims of Soviet Central Asia", *The Middle East Journal*, IX, No. 2 (Spring, 1955), 159-62.

[22] Stalin, "Politicheskii otchët", in *Sochineniia*, XII, 365.

and the Central Committee of the Communist Party of the Soviet Union jointly decreed the obligatory teaching of Russian in all non-Russian schools.[23]

The latter half of the 1930s also marked the conversion from the use of the Latin to the Cyrillic (or Russian) alphabet for the languages of numerous non-Russian peoples. During the 1920's the Latin script had been introduced, on the theory, most sharply expressed by Trotsky, that Western Europe and not Russia would be the heart of the Soviet world state. It was assumed that the future world language would be based upon Western European, rather than Russian, roots. Furthermore, the adoption of the Latin, instead of the Cyrillic, script within the Soviet Union avoided the odious connotation of Great Russian chauvinism, an attitude that was still officially condemned during this early period.

Stalin's counterattack in the linguistic field was delayed until the mid-1930s. As late as 1933 a Soviet source reported that "72 nationalities of the USSR, formerly without alphabets, had received them, of which 64 were based on the Latin script".[24] Many more languages previously written in another script, for example, Arabic, had also been Latinized. Within a decade virtually a complete transformation occurred in all these languages. Only a few peoples who had for centuries maintained a vigorous literary language in a non-Cyrillic script (the Georgians, Armenians, Finns, Estonians, Latvians, and Lithuanians) were left untouched. Yiddish was also unaffected, but the Yiddish press in the Soviet Union was almost completely closed down by 1949.[25] All

[23] "O prepodavanii russkogo iazyka v nerusskikh shkolakh", *Pravda*, April 10, 1938, p. 6; A. M. Danev, ed., *Narodnoe obrazovanie: osnovnye postanovleniia, prikazy i instrukstii* (Moscow, 1948), p. 86; N. K. Dmitriev and V. M. Chisiakov, eds., *Rodnoi i russkii iazky v natsional'noi shkole* (Moscow, 1953), p. 3. Isolated Union Republics, such as the Ukraine and Belorussia, made the teaching of Russian compulsory before this. In the Ukraine, for example, Russian was obligatory as early as 1923: see Harold R. Weinstein, "Language and Education in the Soviet Ukraine", in *The Slavonic Year-Book, American Series*, I (1941), 144-48. Despite such scattered laws, the teaching of Russian in non-Russian schools was haphazardly executed. The Soviet press continually complained of the lack of qualified teachers and the absence of any unified methods for teaching Russian. It was not until 1938 that the teaching of Russian in all non-Russian schools began in earnest.

[24] L. Slavin and T. Khodzhaev, "Natsional'nye raiony na rubezhe dvukh piatiletok", *Planovoe khoziaistvo*, No. 3 (March, 1934), pp. 177-78.

[25] In the summer of 1956 Soviet authorities indicated that a limited revival of Yiddish literary activity could be expected, but, as a Communist source admitted, after more than a year these promises remained unfulfilled. ("Soviet Outlines Yiddish Revival", New York *Times*, Aug. 11, 1956; Chaim Suller, "Jewish Culture in USSR Today: Another Look One Year Later", *The Worker* [New York], Sept. 22, 1957.) Finally, in 1959 the Kremlin sanctioned the celebration of the centennial of Sholom Aleichem's birth by reissuing his writings in Russian and in Yid-

the remaining non-Russian languages in the Soviet Union went through a second painful metamorphosis, this time as part of an undisguised program of Russification. The Soviet leaders frankly stated the purpose of forcing these non-Russian peoples to adopt the Cyrillic script was to accelerate their learning of Russian and to broaden the influence of Russian culture.[26] The Soviet press abounded in expressions of gratitude for the "service" that this second alphabet reform had rendered. Thus a group of Kirghiz declared: "The adoption of a new alphabet based on the Russian script had played a tremendous role in elevating the culture of the Kirghiz people by bringing them into closer association with the great Russian culture."[27]

An Estonian philologist, Alo Raun, summarized the impact of this linguistic Russification. "Examining any one of the languages of the Soviet Union, e.g., Mordvinian, one is shocked by the discovery that it swarms with Russian words, and that often only the suffixes are Mordvinian. The word order, use of cases, etc., are a poor imitation of Russian."[28]

Soviet authorities, far from objecting to this characterization of their policy, only found fault with those who obstructed its implementation. A long article in *Voprosy filosofii* in 1949 complained of resistance from "local bourgeois nationalists", who were accused of "masquerading as defenders of their national language." Their treachery "consisted first of all, in attempts to eliminate international and particularly socio-political terminology, and to replace it by a provincial, nationalist terminology". That is, the non-Russian languages of the Soviet Union were required to use international terms of foreign origin in the form in which they have been adopted in the Russian language. Second, these bourgeois nationalists

> sought to use foreign languages as their models, persistently trying to minimize the importance of the Russian language. Belorussian and Ukrainian nationalists injected into their native speech elements of the Polish gentry's

dish. (Harry Schwartz, "Yiddish Writer Hailed in Soviet", New York *Times*, March 8, 1959). [Only one volume has appeared in Yiddish as of 1967. Ed.]

[26] A. E. Mordinov, "O razvitii iazykov sotsialisticheskikh natsii v SSSR", *Voprosy filosofii*, No. 3 (1950), p. 92; Kolarz, *Russia and Her Colonies*, pp. 34-38; Alo Raun, "National in Form, Socialistic in Content", *Ukrainian Quarterly*, VI, No. 2 (Spring, 1950), 115-21; E. Koutaissoff, "Literacy and the Place of Russian in the Non-Slav Republics of the U.S.S.R.", *Soviet Studies*, III, No. 2 (Oct., 1951), 124-26.

[27] "Velikomu vozhdiu sovetskogo naroda. I. V. Stalinu, ot Kirgizskogo naroda", *Pravda*, Feb. 1, 1951, p. 2.

[28] Raun, "National in Form", *Ukrainian Quarterly*, VI, No. 2 (Spring, 1950), 115-21. See also Ohienko, "Ukrainian Literary", *ibid.*, VI, No. 3 (Summer, 1950), 229-40.

speech; the Moldavian nationalists tried to drag into their language aristocratic Rumanian drawing-room words; and the Latvian nationalists, carrying out the orders of the German gentry, attempted to Germanize their tongue. The bourgeois nationalists of our Eastern Republics infused their native languages with Persian-Arabic and Turkish elements. In essence, this was a policy of betrayal of national interests, a policy of cosmopolitanism.

Only by using the Russian language as their model could these non-Russians defend their "national interests". Russian, of course, had no objectionable history, since it had never been the language of the Tsars and the Russian gentry who gathered in their drawing rooms to plot the forcible Russification of the Belorussian, Ukrainian, Polish, and other languages! And how could one resist the obvious logic of the assumption that Russian was the natural model for the languages of the peoples of Central Asia rather than Persian, Arabic, or Turkish! A third and final accusation rested on the charge that "bourgeois nationalists artifically bred local words and forms to obstruct the penetration of Russian words and forms."[29] Again, was it not obvious that the use of local words and forms in a non-Russian language was "artificial", while the use of Russian words and forms was "natural"? In contrast to the petty, narrow-minded mentality nourished by the non-Russian languages, Russian was portrayed in the following manner:

> The great Russian language has become the source of enrichment and flowering for the different national languages. . . . The Russian language is great, rich, and mighty. It is the instrument of the most advanced culture in the world. From its inexhaustible treasures, the national languages of the USSR draw a life-giving elixir.[30]

RUSSIAN AS THE FUTURE WORLD LANGUAGE

This Soviet conception of the role of Russian, both within the USSR and in the development of a world language, found its theoretical justification by means of a distorted interpretation of the works of Nicolai Ia. Marr, the father of Soviet linguistics. Marr had died in 1934, leaving a collection of linguistic theories, many of which rested upon arbitrary assumption lacking proof or consistency. In broad outline, Marr postulated the operation of a single world glottogonic, or language-forming, process. Though all languages are related, they are divided into four

29 Lomtev, "I. V. Stalin", *Voprosy filosofii*, No. 2 (1949), p. 135.
30 *Ibid.*, p. 136.

classes, representing four chronological strata, or stages of development. Those languages which somehow got stuck at a lower level are without a future, while those in the fourth stage of development represent the material for a future world language. Russian was placed in this highest stage along with all Indo-European languages. Marr considered language as an element in the Marxist superstructure dependent upon the economic base of society. Consequently, the creation of a single world socialist economy was expected to produce a single world language. Just as this base might be changed by force, so, Marr thought, the linguistic superstructure should be impelled to develop toward its ultimate goal. "Mankind, proceeding toward economic unity and a classless society, cannot help applying artificial means, scientifically worked out, in order to accelerate this broad process." [31]

By 1930 Marr had firmly grafted Marxism onto his prerevolutionary linguistic theories,[32] and depicted himself as an orthodox Marxist who put class above nation. He was interested in the evolution of a future proletarian world language, rather than in the aggrandizement of any single national language, Russian included. But the elements of Marr's theories, and the vagueness with which they were stated, lent themselves to easy perversion by his disciples, who, in the guise of following Marr's linguistic theories, joined other Soviet linguists in the systematic glorification of the Russian language.

We have already indicated the application of "artificial means" to favor the victory of Russian in the Soviet Union, where Russian was clearly considered the language of a chosen people who would assume the directing role in the future socialist world society. From this it was an easy step to assert that Russian would likewise be the future world language. As early as 1937 *Pravda* had boasted: "We love our Russian language, which is great, powerful, and rich. It is already becoming an international language. It is being studied by the leaders of humanity." [33] By 1949 Soviet theoreticians were asserting categorically that Russian was predestined to be the future world language. One Soviet writer recalled that "one world language has replaced another time and again throughout the thousands of years of the history of mankind", with the economic base of each era raising a different language to world supremacy.

[31] Quoted in A. Chikobava, "O nekotorykh voprosakh sovetskogo iazykoznaniia", *Pravda*, May 9, 1950, p. 3. See also Smal-Stocki, *Nationality Problem*, pp. 79-86; D.B.Y., "The Stalin-Marr Philological Controversy in the U.S.S.R.", *The World Today*, VI (Aug., 1950), 355-64.

[32] Lawrence L. Thomas, "Some Notes on the Marr School", *American Slavic*, XVI, No. 3 (Oct., 1957), 338-44.

[33] "Velikii russkii narod", *Pravda*, Jan. 15, 1937, p. 1.

Latin was the language of the ancient world and the early middle ages. French became the language of the ruling classes in the feudal era. It was maintained for a long time together with feudal traditions and customs, and became the language of the international diplomacy. English became the world language of capitalism. . . . Looking to the future, we see that the Russian language is the world language of socialism.[34]

THE LINGUISTICS DISCUSSION AND THE DISAVOWAL OF MARR

This simple schematic view appeared to have been upset by Stalin's abrupt intervention in the Soviet linguistics discussion in the summer of 1950. Stalin unceremoniously provided Marr with a second funeral – this time, an ideological one. Suddenly Soviet philologists "discovered" that the basis of their entire linguistic work had been unscientific. What caused this disavowal of Marr, and what effect did this have both upon the Soviet concept of a world language, and upon the role of Russian in the development of this world language?

The denunciation of Marr was explained, first of all, on the ground that his theories had introduced such chaos into Soviet linguistics that most serious linguistic work had been brought to a standstill. No doubt there was considerable justification in this complaint.[35] The newly found critics of Marr's followers charged that the literacy of the non-Russian peoples had unmistakably suffered as a result of the crude attempts to Russify the non-Russian languages.

N. Ia. Marr's followers completely ignored the specific features of national languages and, in an oversimplified and vulgarized manner, interpreted the leading role of the Russian language in the development of national languages as a mechanical hybridization of the two. The practical results of such a vulgarized approach to the development of national languages was the discarding from some alphabets of a number of letters that reflected phonetic peculiarities of the national languages. . . . This harmful approach, involving a break with the existing laws of the national languages, led to anarchy in orthography, to inumerable difficulties in mastery of the gram-

[34] D. Zaslavskii, "Velikii iazyk nashei epokhy", *Literaturnaia gazeta*, Jan. 1, 1949, p. 3.

[35] For a discussion of the charges leveled against Marr, see Jeffrey Ellis and Robert W. Davies, "The Crisis in Soviet Linguistics", *Soviet Studies*, II, No. 3 (Jan., 1951), 209-64. Aspects of this interpretation are sharply challenged by Thomas, "Some Notes", *American Slavic*, XVI, No. 3 (Oct., 1957), 323-48. For additional material on the Marr controversy, see the numerous references listed in the footnotes on page 323 of the Thomas article, and Jindrich Kucera, "Soviet Nationality Policy: The Linguistic Controversy", *Problems of Communism*, III, No. 2 (March-April, 1954), 24-29.

mar of the native language, in the work of local newspapers and magazines, etc.[36]

But the damage was not confined to non-Russian languages, since these methods had also led to an estrangement of these languages from Russian.

The "drawing together" of languages, recommended by the followers of N. Ia. Marr, actually only hampers their real harmonizing. . . . Destroying historically developed rules of pronunciation does not make it easier, but harder for the working people to master new words borrowed from Russian, i.e., yields results contrary to the aims proclaimed by the supporters of the "new teaching" on language.[37]

These critics did not object to the principle of altering these non-Russian languages so as to draw them closer to Russian, but only to the use of harsh and clumsy methods which had, in fact, obstructed the attainment of this goal. This sudden abuse of Marr was a tactical concession to the development of non-Russian languages, but it was by no means a clear-cut defeat for the Russian language. Subsequent comments make it clear that Russian was not expected to lose its dominant position, nor was the idea of its eventual victory disowned. These goals would be pursued, but with greater caution and by more skillful means. Thus, the Ministry of Education of the Uzbek SSR reported: "Thanks to the reorganization of teaching on the basis of J. V. Stalin's brilliant works on linguistics, the teaching of the Russian language and literature has been improved in Uzbek and other non-Russian schools in the Republic."[38] The subsequent denigration of Stalin left the Russifying impact of Stalin's linguistic policy intact, for the post-Stalinist period has seen a continuation, and even an intensification, of attempts to step up the teaching of Russian in non-Russian schools.[39]

Arbitrary interference with the non-Russian languages had proceeded from the assumption that language was part of the superstructure and therefore subject to artificial manipulation. Stalin attacked this

[36] Mordinov, "O razvitii", *Voprosy filosofii*, No. 3 (1950), p. 82.

[37] *Ibid.*, p. 83.

[38] "V ministerstve prosveshcheniia Uzbekskoi SSR", *Uchitel'skaia gazeta*, Nov. 15, 1952, p. 4.

[39] At the Twentieth Party Congress a Party spokesman from Dagestan, for example, simply substituted Lenin for Stalin: "An ever-increasing number of people in the Republic know Russian, the language of the great Lenin. The Russian language has become the international language of the peoples of Dagestan, and through it they gain contact with the advanced Russian Soviet and world culture." ("Rech' tovarishcha A. D. Daniialova", *Pravda*, Feb. 21, 1956, p. 7.) Typical of efforts to strengthen the position of Russian in the non-Russian Re-

practice by denying the premise that language was part of the superstructure, or, for that matter, that language was even a class phenomenon. This "revelation" had long been a commonplace assumption among those who did not pretend to understand the mysteries of dialectical materialism, but for good Marxists it came as a blow. Language, Stalin announced,

> was created not by any class, but by all society, by all classes of society, by the efforts of hundreds of generations. ... Language is the product of a whole series of epochs, in the course of which it takes shape, is enriched, develops, and is polished. A language therefore exists immeasurably longer than any base or any superstructure.

Stalin said that Pushkin's language "has been preserved in all essentials as the basis of modern Russian", and that "the Russian language has remained essentially what it was before the October Revolution".[40] Thus belatedly he did for language what he had previously done for the teaching of history, namely: assert the interests of nation above class. Far from destroying the prestige of the Russian language, he was fortifying it by drawing upon the endless stream of historical memories and traditions of Russian nationalism.

There were doubtless other unspoken reasons for the renunciation of Marr's theories. Not only did their distorted application provoke resistance among the non-Russian peoples in the Soviet Union, but they also served to insult many nations outside the USSR. In Marr's four stages of linguistic development, for example, Chinese was per-

---

publics was the announcement in the spring of 1956 of a forthcoming "inter-republican scientific conference in Tashkent on the problems of studying the Russian language in national schools". It was necessary to make "decisive improvements in this important matter. The tremendous significance of teaching the Russian language in national schools is well known, since it is the means of communication among the fraternal peoples of the Soviet Union." (M. Ismatullaev and I. Gimil'shtein, "Uchashchimsia – prochnye znaniia", *Kommunist Tadzhikistana*, May 11, 1956, p. 2.) See also H. Carrère d'Encausse, "Linguistic Russification and Nationalist Opposition in Kazakhstan", *The East-Turkic Review* (Munich), I, No. 1 (April, 1958), 96-100. A Secretary of the CC of the CP of Kazakhstan then revealed that, in addition to Russian having become "a second native language for the Kazakh people" through its study in Kazakh schools, "at the present time approximately one fourth of the Kazakh children attend schools where instruction is conducted in Russian". He berated those parents who "think it necessary to establish a system under which the children of Kazakhs could attent only Kazakh schools. This view is nothing but a manifestation of bourgeois nationalism", (N. Dzhandil'din, "Nekotorye voprosy internatsional'nogo vospitaniia", *Kommunist*, No. 13 [Sept., 1959], p. 36.)

[40] Stalin, "Otnositel'no Marksizma v iazykoznanii", June 20, 1950, in *Marksizm i voprosy*, pp. 4-7.

manently "frozen" at the lowest level. The embarrassments which this held for Soviet relations with Communist China are obvious.

Moreover, Marr repudiated the validity of comparative philology, and the classification of languages into separate linguistic families. This obviously contradicted the development of Pan-Slavic studies in the East European satellite states of Slavic origin, thus hindering their Russification.

AGAIN, RUSSIAN AS THE FUTURE WORLD LANGUAGE

What effect did the discrediting of Marr's theories have upon the Soviet concept of a world language? Chikobava, developing the newly accepted position, noted that "Marr expressed himself in favor of a single common language for future mankind. This is the only matter of principle on which, it would seem, Academician N. Ia. Marr's views are in accord with the theses of Marxism-Leninism." The prospect of a single world language was still upheld, but the "dying away of national languages and the formation of a single common world language will take place gradually, without any 'artificial means' invoked to 'accelerate' this process".[41]

One should add that the idea of "hybridization" or fusion of languages, which Stalin continued to use, was Marrist in origin. Stalin made this idea his own, in his characteristic fashion, by "reinterpreting" it to apply only to a given historical period. His distinction between the fate of national languages before and after the worldwide victory of socialism must be recalled. National languages will fuse in a gradual peaceful manner without the application of "artificial means", only *after* the creation of a Soviet world state has made possible a condition of mutual confidence and harmony among nations. Before this time, however, the crossing of national languages under conditions of national oppression will not produce peaceful fusion, but a mortal struggle in which "one of the languages usually comes out the victor, whereas the other dies away." [42] "Such was the case, for instance, with the Russian language, with which the languages of a number of other peoples mixed in the course of historical development, and which always emerged the victor." The effect which this struggle had upon the Russian language was to enlarge its vocabulary, "but this not only did not weaken, but on the contrary enriched and strengthened the Russian language".[43] Stalin gave

[41] Chikobava, "O nekotorykh", *Pravda*, May 9, 1950, p. 3.
[42] Stalin, "Tovarishchu A. Kholopovu", in *Marksizm i voprosy*, pp. 45-47.
[43] Stalin, "Otnositel'no Marksizma", in *ibid.*, p. 25.

no indication that Russian would not continue to emerge the victor in future struggles that are predicted up until the very moment of the creation of the Soviet world state.

Soviet theorists have already clearly nominated Russian as a zonal language with unlimited prospects for expansion. "In the formation of a zonal language common to many nations, Russian will undoubtedly play the decisive role in many socialist nations. With the appearance of new socialist nations the world-historic role and influence of the Russian language will steadily increase." [44] This view, expressed in 1949, does not seem to have been repudiated in the linguistics discussion of 1950. Following this discussion the importance of Russian was reaffirmed both within and beyond the borders of the Soviet Union.

> The role of the Russian language in the development of the languages and cultures of all the peoples of the USSR constantly increases. . . . Russian has therefore become an *international language* for the peoples of the USSR. But the significance of the Russian language is not limited to this. The great Russian language is becoming a second native language for the liberated peoples of the countries of the New Democracies as well as for the Chinese People's Republic. . . .
>
> In our time the Russian language is becoming the most popular and widespread language in the world. The process of steady growth of the world significance of the Russian language reflects the vanguard role of our country . . . in the struggle for the liberation of all mankind from the yoke of exploitation and oppression.[45]

The satellite states duly echoed this glorification of Russian. The Czechoslovak press supported the demand of "giving the Russian language the same rights as our own Czech and Slovak languages. It is for us the world language . . . the language of worldwide brotherhood." [46] And Chervenkov, the Premier of Bulgaria, hailed Russian as the language of "the richest and most outstanding culture in the whole world. This imbues the Russian language with a world-historic significance and makes a knowledge of it vital to every advanced fighter for the happiness of his people".[47] This bowing and scraping by provincial satraps before the mother tongue of Moscow is a meaningful part of a larger design, for Stalin was quite aware of the importance of a single language

[44] Lomtev, "I. V. Stalin", *Voprosy filosofii*, No. 2 (1949), p. 140.
[45] Mordinov, "O razvitii", *ibid.*, No. 3 (1950), p. 91.
[46] "What the Russian Language Meant and Means to Us", *Slovanský, přehled*, No. 7/8 (1949); quoted in *News from Behind the Iron Curtain*, II, No. 10 (Oct., 1953), 41.
[47] "Vsemirno-istoricheskoe znachenie russkogo iazyka", *Pravda*, Oct. 1, 1952, p. 4.

in the process of building a world empire. He specifically noted that "the empires of Cyrus or Alexander the Great or of Caesar and Charles the Great. . . were transitory and unstable military and administrative unions. These empires not only did not have, but they could not have, a single language common to the whole empire and understood by all members of the empire."[48]

It would seem that there is a fundamental contradiction in Stalin's position on a world language. On the one hand, he declared that the ultimate world language will be neither German, nor Russian, nor English, but something new. On the other hand, Russian has been accorded a favored and privileged position denied to all other major languages. The Soviet leadership has already designated Russian, but *only* Russian, as one of the world's zonal languages. Some of the offensive, chauvinistic overtones of the campaign to force the adoption of Russian by non-Russian peoples may have been eliminated by the benign assurance that the ultimate world language will not be Russian. But along with this goes the expectation that Russian will continually fight and conquer as many non-Russian languages as possible during the period before the victory of world socialism. Theoretically, Russian is only supposed to enter into open combat with other languages in the arena of national oppression and inequality, that is, in the non-Soviet world. Within the Soviet world, where, by definition, national harmony reigns supreme, the struggle for the domination of one language over others has been replaced by the mutual enrichment of one language by another. Yet it is evident that this "mutual enrichment" has been largely a one-way proposition in which Russian has been elevated, consciously and conspicuously, above all other languages.

This encouragement of the victory of Russian both within and beyond the confines of the Soviet world has definite implications for a future world language: If Russian gains a constant series of victories over non-Russian languages in the process of subduing non-Soviet nations to Soviet rule, then at the moment of the creation of the Soviet world state, Russian will have achieved an almost impregnable position of universal supremacy. Nor should this position diminish after the Soviet world state has come into operation. The "mutual confidence" and "national equality" among nations, such as is claimed for the present Soviet world, will then be of universal scope. Behind a smoke screen of verbiage about the "mutual enrichment" of languages, Russian will then be given the opportunity to triumph on a world scale. This creates the distinct possibility that Russian will, in fact, be the future world language, should the Soviet regime succeed in its ambitions.

Since the fate of national languages is intimately connected with the

[48] Stalin, "Otnositel'no Marksizma", in *Marksizm i voprosy*, p. 10.

ultimate fate of nations, this would mean that the world would become the Russian nation writ large. Lenin predicted the assimilation of nations under the world rule of socialism, but Stalin developed this into the prospect of the assimilation of all nations by the Russian nation ruling a Soviet world state.

From *The Soviet Design for a World State* by Elliot R. Goodman (New York, Columbia University Press, 1960), pp. 264-284. Reprinted by permission.

J. Berry

THE MAKING OF ALPHABETS

New alphabets are required principally for 3 purposes:
(1) to provide for the first time a means of writing languages as yet unwritten or virtually so.
(2) to provide auxiliary alphabets for languages which have already a standard script (e.g. Roman systems for Hebrew, Japanese, etc.).
(3) to provide alternatives to standardized but for some reason inadequate writing systems (e.g. Spelling Reform).

The problems of design are somewhat different in all three cases but not to the extent that generalized discussion is impossible. In this report, except if it is explicitly stated to the contrary, it should be assumed that interest is centred on alphabets of type (1).

The particular alphabet to be used for a language constitutes a problem that is always complex and more often than not unique. Generalizations about orthography are for that reason not easily established. For a start, let it be said that an alphabet is successful in so far and only in so far as it is scientifically and socially acceptable. The two interests often conflict and it would be a fallacy to assume, as it sometimes is done,[1] that the choice of an orthography can be determined solely on grounds that are linguistically or pedagogically desirable. Where systems of writing become identified (as often happens) with unreasoning and unreasonable political, national or religious passions[2] there is little

[1] Attempts at orthography making in Haiti provide classic examples of "linguistics without sociology": see D. Burns, (Social and Political Implications of the Choice of an Orthography). *Fundamental and Adult Education*, vol. 5, no. 3, pp. 80-85.

[2] Cf. the Case Histories given in UNESCO *Monographs on Fundamental Education*,

that the linguist can or should do. Nor is it profitable in all cases to make concessions to naive linguistic prejudice, traditionalism, or, a new development, its reverse;[3] there are factors in the social situation however which merit the linguist's attention and for which he should be prepared to condition his science to circumstances and seek a compromise. The extent to which such compromise can and should profitably go is a basic problem of this branch of applied linguistics.

THE SCIENTIFIC PRINCIPLES

On what grounds is it decided that an orthography is scientifically acceptable? The following are suggested:

(1) linguistic: does the alphabet represent the language system economically, consistently, unambiguously?
(2) pedagogical: how does the alphabet achieve the strictly utilitarian aim of economy of time and labour in learning to read and write?[4]
(3) psychological: how far does the alphabet respect the psychological and physiological processes involved in the reading and writing acts?
(4) typographical: how far is the alphabet suited to the needs of modern techniques of graphic representation – machine writing, etc.?

It is generally accepted that on all grounds an alphabetical system of writing is best.[5] Despite eloquent pleas, especially by Bollinger, Vachek and others,[6] that writing can and should be considered as basically a

---

VIII (Paris, 1953), or e.g., De Francis, *Nationalism and Language Reform in China* (1950).

[3] The present writer's proposed orthography for Ga, for example, was critized locally as being "unscientific" in that "it used roman not 'phonetic' letters".

[4] From the point of view of children, adults (*and foeigners?*).

[5] Though a simple syllabary is almost as good, cf. K. Pike, *Phonemics* (Michigan, 1947). Both systems use limited sets of symbols arranged in a single line. If we are to accept the assumption of the gradual evolution of writing systems it would appear that we should accept alphabets as anticipating the general linguistic development, cf. Gelb, *A Study of Writing* (Chicago, 1952).

[6] E.g. the following: D. L. Bolinger, "Visual Morphemes", *Language*, 22 (1946), p. 333; J. Vachek, "Written Language and Printed Language", *Mélanges J. M. Kořinek* (Bratislava, 1949); E. Pulgram, "Phoneme and Grapheme", *Word*, 7 (1951); I. J. Gelb, *A Study of Writing* (1952), Chapter I; W. F. Edgerton, "Ideograms in English Writing", *Language*, 17, 1941, p. 148; H. J. Uldall, "Speech and Writing", *Acta Linguistica*, vol. IV (1944); Henry Bradley, "On the Relations between Spoken and Written Language", *Proceedings of British Academy*, vol. VI; Joseph Vachek, "Some Remarks on Writing and Phonetic Transcription", *Acta Linguistica*, 5, 1945-1949; L. Hjelmslev, "Prolegomena to a Theory of Language", *Int. Journ. of American Linguistics*, vol. 19 (1953), p. 46 footnote 3; R. H. Stetson: The Phoneme and the Grapheme, Mélanges... van Ginneken 1937, p. 353; D. Abercrombie, "The Visual Symbolization of Speech", *Proceedings, International Shorthand Congress 1938*; A. McIntosh, *The Analysis of Written English* (T. P. S. 1956), pp. 27-55.

visual system independent of the vocal-auditory process, is it likely that any system of writing would be seriously proposed to-day that was not based on some attempt at a systematic correlation with the spoken language?[7] The degree of correlation held to be necessary varies between orthographers, from, for example, the absolute and transcription-like one-to-one correspondence proposed by Pike as the phonemic goal,[8] through the relatively cautious "departures from phonetic consistency" and "compromise spellings" admitted by Jones,[9] to notations as synthetic as, say, modern Pitman's shorthand, which admits abbreviations, syllable and word signs, and in which the writing of vowels is optional.

There is general agreement that phonetic ambiguity is bad and that words pronounced differently should be kept graphically apart.[10] It is also agreed that the orthography should be such that one who knows the pronunciation of a word should be able to spell it correctly. There is less agreement that the spelling should in all cases support the sound (i.e. that one who knows the spelling should be able to pronounce the word).[11]

A recurrent problem on which opinions are divided has been put by Hockett:[12] in the devising of orthographies under what conditions is it possible and advisable to omit the indication of some of the operative phonological contrasts? For example, should tones be written in a language where to omit them produces only negligible graphic ambiguity? Or, similarly, distinctions of sound peculiar to loan words and the like? e.g. the initial consonant in the Kikuyu word for "book" which in terms of a monosystemic analysis at any rate is a phoneme contrasting with other ("original") b-sounds (/β/ and /mb/) but relatively rare. Finally, in the system of native words how far is it desirable to mark only actual as opposed to potential distinctions, i.e. phonemic distinctions not used in differentiating words?[13]

It has been noted by Firth[14] and others that the removal of phonetic ambiguities in spelling reform may create other grammatical and se-

---

[7] If solely on the grounds that only a "phonetically regular alphabet" is easy to learn.

[8] *Phonemics* (Michigan, 1947), p. 208.

[9] *The Phoneme* (Cambridge, 1950), p. 229.

[10] Bradley, *Written and Spoken Language*.

[11] Ripman and Archer, *Simplified Spelling, for the Simplified Spelling Society* (London), 5th edition.

[12] The following agree: C. Hockett, Review of De Francis, "Nationalism and Language Reform in China", *Language*, 27, 1951, p. 439; K. Pike, *Phonemics*; E. Nida, *Bible Translating* (New York, 1947); D. Jones, *The Phoneme*, p. 230, holds a contrasting view.

[13] e.g. ju:/ju in English. D. Jones: *op. cit.* p. 231.

[14] *Technique of Semantics* (T. P. S., 1935).

mantic ambiguities. To what extent therefore should an orthography be grammatically as well as phonetically representative? Should it seek to distinguish for example English "find" from "fined"[15] or Polish "morze" ("sea") from "może" ("he can") by recognizing different associations and different structures? The writing of one letter to indicate two sounds is universally condemned, but of English "sex" as against "wrecks" it can be said at least that structural information is thereby signalled of a kind obscured in, say, the spellings "seks" and "reks". Finally is it desirable that the graphemic make-up of a written morpheme be retained, as in English, however different the phonic make-up of the corresponding spoken morphemes ("cats", "dogs", etc.)?

In many cases one-to-one correspondence with speech is possible only by rejecting normalization[16] as a principle. The contributory factors here are, notably –

(1) dialect: some pronunciations have to be ignored and orthographic forms adopted which are phonetic for some speakers but not all
(2) word variants due to –
  (a) synthesis (assimilation, elision, coalescence)
  (b) speed and style of utterance (strong and weak forms, etc.)
  (c) free variation between sounds
(3) personal and certain other types of proper names, in the spelling of which the orthographer has surely little say. In addition, more arbitrary departures from phonetic consistency have been advocated from time to time, in order
  (a) to avoid the cumbrous spelling of very common words[17]
  (b) to distinguish homophones[18]
  (c) to maintain the native spelling of unassimilated loans.

The need for, and advantages of, such practices are still debated; they have as yet no general acceptance.

THE SOCIAL SITUATION

Among the extralingual and external factors of which account must be taken in deciding an orthography are:

(1) *The social attitudes of the people towards their language:* Creole in

[15] Firth has suggested that these might be written "faind" and "fainnd" in a revised spelling.

[16] D. Jones, *The Phoneme*, p. 229. "Subject to rare exceptions each word should be written in one way only". M. Swadesh, "The Phonemic Principle", *Language*, vol. X, p. 126. "Normalization (would be arbitrary) and is to be avoided".

[17] Jones: *op. cit.*, p. 231.

[18] By, for example, redundant letters, cf. Firth, "Alphabets and phonology in India and Burma", *B.S.O.A.S.*, vol. VIII, pts. 2 + 3, 1935.

Haiti for example, for cultural, economic, and political reasons, is looked on by its speakers as a bridge to French; in its written form "it ought to look like French".

(2) *The status of the language:* Is it a national language? Or a vernacular? A second language? Are its speakers bilingual? The answers to these questions partly decide the symbols to be adopted.

(3) *The relations of the language with others in the region or country:* To what writing community does the language belong? Agreement with other writing systems in use for neighbouring trade or official languages is desirable where possible on pedagogical and economic grounds.

(4) *the dialectal situation:* Is there a convenient linguistic centre (i.e. an area characterized by having the greatest number of language features in common with the greatest number of speakers in the total area)?[19] Is there a dialect with the acknowledged cultural, political or commercial preponderance to merit its choice as a standard? Or must some attempt be made at a composite orthography on sociolinguistic grounds?[20]

Here too interests are likely to conflict and decisions are not easy. Is it, for example, preferable to follow the orthographic practice of the trade language[21] or that of an interlingual notational inventory such as The Africa Script,[22] The All-India Alphabet,[23] etc.? Both give areal uniformity of different kinds and both ensure availability of type, etc. Where the official language uses diagraphs for certain sounds, is it better to adopt a psychologically preferable but unrelated monographic letter form? How far should the need for uniformity override considerations of structure? Is it better, for example, that all related languages of southern Ghana write the prepalatal affricate "*tʃ*" uniformly so, or (under cultural pressure of the trade language), "*ch*", or (for structural reasons) differently in each language, k, ts, tʃ, etc.?[24]

THE SYMBOLS

In choosing symbols some balance must be kept between the conflicting claims of the "one sound – one letter" principle still held to be ideal

19 E. Nida, *Bible translating*, p. 36.

20 As was done in the case of "Union Igbo" for example.

21 C. Meinhof for example (Africa, vol. I) suggested that IPA/ ʃ/ be written "sh" in English colonies, "ch" in French colonies, "x" in Portuguese colonies.

22 *Practical Orthography of African Languages*, International Institute of African Languages and Cultures, Memo. 1, OUP 1930, revised edition.

23 *Problem of a National Script for India*, D. Jones, Hartford, 1942.

24 cf. W. E. Welmers: Review of the "Report of a Meeting of Experts on Vernacular Languages in Education", *Language*, 30, 1, 1953.

if only rarely attainable and the equally valid principle of alphabetical economy.

The majority of letters needed for a new alphabet can and should be drawn from the traditional alphabet in general use throughout the area (e.g. Roman, Cyrillic, etc.), and precise values should be assigned to each letter as far as possible in accordance with customary usage.

The graphematic deficiencies of the source-alphabet (e.g. here the "Roman alphabet") can be supplied if necessary by such additions and modifications as

(i) extra letters regarded as ordinary supplements to the original alphabet (e.g. æ, œ)
(ii) extra letters regarded as special or local supplements (e.g. Danish ø, Icelandic ð)
(iii) diagraphs and trigraphs (e.g. Welsh "ll" ..., German "sch")
(iv) diacritically modified letters (i.e. "simple" letters with e.g. supraliteral tilde or tashdid, subliteral macron or cedilla, postliteral circle or apostrophe, etc.)
(v) *ad hoc* supplements, notably of four kinds,
  (a) "restored" letters (i.e. old and rare characters reintroduced)
  (b) "borrowed" letters (i.e. borrowed from another alphabet e.g. θ, ð, from the Greek)
  (c) differentiated and adapted forms e.g.
    (1) ə/e (inversion)
    (2) ɔ/c (reversion)
    (3) g/ɡ : F/f ("swash" or small capital letters)
    (4) J/f : z/ʒ (loops, curls and tails)
    (5) (bold face, italic/normal type)
  (d) "invented" forms (e.g. ŋ, ...)

Supplementary symbols of this latter kind are perhaps best drawn from international and interlingual inventories in current use, e.g. the IPA or the Americanist symbols, the All-India Alphabet, the Africa Script.

There are no special qualities in a letter taken by itself which make it inherently superior to any other. But Sweet's comment on ŋ may be thought by some to have a point.[25]

What matters most is clearness and distinctness of the differential features in handwriting and small print as well as large, even for readers with imperfect sight: a "swash" g in handwriting, for example, is better

[25] H. Sweet, *Handbook of Phonetics* (Oxford, 1877), p. 192. "Mr. Pitman's ŋ is unquestionably superior to q as a symbol of the back nasal ng for its shape at once associates it with other nasals".

than the small-letter form if q occurs in similar contexts.[26] The differences in letters should on the whole depend on the outline of the symbol, not on other qualities: the use of bold face type as a distinguishing feature is deplored by Nida[27] and others as awkward to print and difficult to read and write. Italic (underlining on the typewriter) is less objectionable but should be used sparingly.

A. H. Smith[28] among others has considered the suitability of the existing borrowed, modified and invented supplements to the Roman alphabet from the point of view of the esthetic and practical limitations of type design. The following remarks deserve consideration. Additional letters should harmonize. Greek letters for example do not fit happily with roman; upsilon though a pleasant enough character in Greek is better replaced (as in America) by a small capital u. Runic "thorn" is for the same reason preferable to Greek "theta". Curls instead of serifs do not accord with roman face: ɲ and ŋ might have plain serifs at the foot. Archaic English ʃ for modern S (capital J inverted) is better than ʃ which is an italic form made vertical. A practical objection to curls and other excrescences is that they involve "kerning" and/or ligatures.

Characters which are outside the normal resources of the commercial printer's office and have to be specially cut are obviously uneconomical but the chief cost in the production of printed works is composition, and is not generally realized that adaptations of roman letters can be equally expensive; inversions of lower case letters and small capitals for example in machine composition must be inverted by hand, as in proof correction, or separate inverted matrices must be used in casting type.[29] Measures of typographical economy have been suggested from time to time and have included more often than not a proposal for the abolition of capital letters. Sweet was one who early suggested this[30]

[26] The Principles of the IPA, 1949, p. 19. "The IPA's treatment of a and α as different letters denoting different sounds has not met with the success originally hoped for. In practice it is found that authors and printers still generally regard the two forms as variants of the same letter". Historical examples of the confusion of insufficiently differentiated letters in English are the contractions ye, yt for "the" and "that" common in books up to the 18th Century and the spelling of the proper names Dalziel and Menzies.

[27] *Bible Translating*, p. 114.

[28] *Proceedings of the 3rd International Congress of Phonetic Sciences* (London, 1935), p. 84.

[29] Production costs are sometimes overstressed. Publishers will undoubtedly acquire the necessary founts if the market is such as to warrant the necessary expenditure. But in subliterate societies (in most of Tropical Africa for example) where book-production is at the best financially hazardous, the need for exotic type can have a deterrent effect on book production. Economic considerations in these cases do support the argument against diacritics which are apt to break off and wear out more quickly than the letter itself.

[30] *Handbook of Phonetics* (Oxford, 1877), p. 175.

on the additional grounds that they "add to the difficulty of learning an alphabet, have a disfiguring and incongruous effect among lower case letters and serve no useful purpose whatever".[31] Bradley[32] thought differently, and more recently Bollinger[33] has referred to capitals as "signs usually non-phonemic of importance". Nida[34] suggests that the pressure of usage of the trade language[35] and general convenience weight the evidence in favour of the retention of capitals. Much the same could be said of the use and kinds of punctuative and other non-phonemic marks. A compromise solution in the one case might perhaps be the use of an alternative sign for proper names such as the asterisk of the IPA.

From the point of view of handwriting the ideal is that characters should be "monographic"[36] and such as can be formed in popular hands and scripts (e.g. Chancery Cursive) by simple, and if possible, single strokes. Compare, for example, the convenience of Greek epsilon, formed by one continuous downstroke, with the difficulties of the looped 2-stroke roman *e* which is very apt to deteriorate in rapid cursive. A second advantage is when the new letter can be joined easily and naturally to others by the horizontal join or diagonal ligature. It is said of the Hausa characters ɓ, ƙ, ɗ[37] that they are unpopular with many because of the "curled" ascenders and are therefore not used in informal writing; the older forms (roman with subliteral dots) are preferred in rapid cursive. But this is probably due to other factors such as a natural linguistic conservatism.

The use of diacritically modified and conglomerate letters has been criticized[38] on many grounds but especially on those of typographical, pedagogical, and psychological inadequacy. But it must be said that Continental and Transatlantic scholars do not feel the same aversion

[31] Cf. also D. Jones, *A National Script for India*, p. 12 – "Capitals are provided for those who favour their use. It would be possible to write the languages without capitals". For the typographer's view, cf. the "scientific alphabets" originating especially in Germany in the twenties (e.g. Erbar, Futura and Kabel type faces).

[32] Report on the New English Dictionary, Letter E. T. P. S. 1891-1894, p. 262. "–We all recognize the advantage of writing proper names with initial capitals though that contrivance is purely ideographic".

[33] "Visual morphemes", *Language*, vol. 22, 1946, pp. 339.

[34] *Bible Translating* (New York), p. 108.

[35] But it should be remembered that the languages of Europe are peculiar in preserving these archaic letter forms as a second alphabet detailed to such special functions.

[36] W. K. Matthews, "Marr's Analytical Alphabet", *Archivum Linguisticum*, vol. 5, 2, 1953.

[37] F. W. Parsons in a written communication.

[38] Legros and Grant, *Typographical Printing Surfaces* (1916); E. B. Huey, *The Psychology and Pedagogy of Reading* (1913); Lloyd James, *Practical Orthography of African Languages*, Africa I. pt 1 (1928).

to these letters as do British scholars. The attitude in each case is clearly a matter of training and habit. The objections to diacritical marks may be summarized briefly: it is said (1) that a multiplicity of such marks lessens the legibility of type by blurring the bold outline, especially the top outline of a word, and by demanding an individual circumnavigation of letters by the eye impedes word recognition and slows reading, (2) that letters with diacritical marks must be separately cast and that such types are less durable. Accented capitals must be smaller in size than other capitals and do not harmonize with them. The supersigns interfere with spacing and involve "kerning". Printers in general dislike the use of diacritical marks and make mistakes in using them.[39] It is also argued that since they interfere with ease of writing they are frequently omitted with subsequent confusion. It should be noted however that certain of these alleged defects may paradoxically have advantages for the orthographer. Nida has suggested the use of sub-literal diacritics "*because* they are inconspicuous" and cites as an example Mesquital Otomi.[40] In a forthcoming dictionary of Ga-Adangme, the author has used the Americanist symbol *š* in preference to ʃ of the IPA with the hope that native users might be thus "encouraged" to abandon the graphic differentiation of a non-phonemic distinction (s/*š*) which they have hitherto insisted on retaining "in the interests of scientific (i.e. phonetic) transcription". The question of diacritically modified or monographic symbolism is perhaps best left like other typographical problems (e.g. "Fraktur oder Antiqua" in Germany) to be settled eventually on sound principles of optics by those best qualified to do so.

The need for alphabetical economy is widely recognized. Firth[41] has pointed to the danger of swamping the characteristics of an alphabet if too many new letters are employed. This may quite well result if the choice of letters is based on universal phonetic categories instead of a phonological analysis of each language *ad hoc*.[42] Inversely it must be admitted that undue regard to function in analysis may lead to symbol

[39] *Les sons du Language et leur représentation dans un Alphabet Linguistique Général* (P. W. Schmidt, Salzburg, 1907) lists 27 errata of which 21 are due to wrong diacritics.

[40] *Bible Translator*, 5 (1953). The Otomi "suffer from cultural insecurity" and are sensitive about linguistic matters. They wish their language to look like Spanish. A. N. Tucker (in conversation) reports a growing dislike of special letters in Africa since these are interpreted as an attempt at racial discrimination on the part of "White" authority. Diacritics on the other hand are welcomed as being "European".

[41] Firth, *Alphabets and Phonology in India and Burma*. Cf. also W. S. Gray, *The Teaching of Reading and Writing* (UNESCO, 1956): "Literary experts agree that other things being equal it is easier to teach children and adults to read and write when the language has a small alphabet".

[42] Cf. Nida, *Bible Translating*: "For example, a language may have the phonemes č and ǰ. There would be no point in using these comparatively rare symbols if one could use the simple forms c and j".

extravagances; for example, the desire to distinguish by letter differences, say, a nasal functioning as a term in the initial and final consonantal alternances and as a homorganic on-glide (e.g. English "bang", "bank").[43] The specializations of form for initial, medial, and final, and compound letters in the Arabic and Indian alphabets (however justifiable in abstract theory), are comparable traditional examples of alphabetical extravagance of this kind. Alphabetical economy may be achieved notably by such devices as (1) letter groups, (2) redundant letters, (3) contextual conventions. Objection to the use of letter groups is usually on the grounds that they are wasteful of effort[44] and can cause ambiguity.[45] But diagraph and even trigraph sequences are now tolerated by some who no doubt find them less than ideal, but preferable at least to, say, the use of diacritics or "special" letters: compare in this respect the two editions of "The Jamia"[46] in which the representation of vowel nasality by the tilde in the first edition is changed to a diagraphic representation in the second, and the recent decision of the Shona Language Committee to discard the six "special" characters introduced by Doke in 1932 replacing *ş*$_j$ and *z*$_b$ (the "whistling fricatives")[47] for example by the diagraphs sv and zv respectively.

Firth and others have advocated the extensive use of redundant or free letters, i.e. letters in the source-alphabet which are not required for the language either as a whole or in any particular context. "These may be used in all manner of ways even with the purely lexical function of separating homophones". It is however an advantage not to disturb the traditional phonetic associations of a letter where this is possible, however seductive the principle of flexibility may be.

Contextual conventions[48] of the type whereby the sound of IPA/ð/ in Tamil is represented in the All-India orthography by t[49] are likely

[43] Cf. Firth, "Phonological Features of Some Indian Languages", *2nd International Congress of Phonetic Sciences* (London, 1935). "Surely we are free to use the same letter without being compelled to concoct a rationalized "derivation from the letter in the shape of a phoneme theory"; and J. Entwhistle, *Aspects of Language* (London, 1952), p. 120.

[44] Arguments have been given for and against diagraphs in the teaching of reading but no comprehensive tests have been conducted.

[45] At morpheme junctions, for example, ambiguity can be avioded by the use of ligatures (undesirable on typographical grounds) or the hyphen.

[46] *The Problem of a National Script for India.*

[47] For a full description of the Shona variety of the "whistling fricatives", see Doke, *Comparative Study in Shona Phonetics.*

[48] Only –tt– occurs in comparable contexts, i.e. intervocalically.

[49] "The value of a roman letter depends on its position and context" Firth, *Alphabets and Phonology in India and Burma.* "In written English the context q(), defines the letter u as surely as the lines of the letter itself". "Expectancy and the Perception of Syllables", Brown and Hildum, *Language* 32, 3, 1956.

to meet with general approval. Somewhat similar conventions by which, for example in English, a doubled consonant shortens, or a final e (after a consonant) lengthens the preceding vowel "have been attacked on the principle that "each symbol of a notation should be self-contained" so that its significance should not depend on any other letter".[50]

Whilst stressing the need for alphabetical economy, a few linguists have cited cases where a phonetic (as opposed to a phonemic) and therefore a redundant distinction has been deliberately introduced or retained in the graphematic inventory. The conditioned variants l/r, or d/r are written in Twi, Ga-Adangme and Ewe, for example, on social grounds because both symbols are required in the trade language, English, and Nida[51] cites (without disapproval) Quechua, a language with a phonematic system of 3 vowels only, operating a graphematic alternance of 5 terms, largely because of the cultural prestige of Spanish.

CONCLUSION

The problems of alphabet-making are problems of conflicting principles, aims and needs. The solution of these problems (in so far as they are soluble) is in the nature of a calculated compromise. We have as yet to be sure in all cases of our priorities. We need to know much more than we do, for example, about the nature of the reading and writing acts, the pedagogical problems of literacy, and, perhaps, the genetic development of notational systems. Until we have this sounder knowledge, graphonomy or graphemics, call it what you will, remains a suggested not an established science. That this fact is increasingly recognized is evidenced by a marked trend towards tolerance of synthetic writing systems and away from the illusory concept of the "pure" phonetic or phonemic transcription. A consideration of Nida's more recent work (especially the *Practical Limitations of a Phonemic Orthography*) is revealing in the degrees of alphabetic latitude now permitted and (however reluctantly) approved. It is fairly safe to say in 1957 that now more than ever the words of the Simplified Spelling Society used some years ago to describe their Revised Spelling for English would meet with the general approval of linguists everywhere and might even be borrowed by some as an adequate statement of their own goals in other fields, *viz.*, "a phonetic spelling, drawing its signs from those in current use and tempered by reason and expediency".

[50] *Spelling Reform*, p. 13.

[51] "Practical Limitations to a Phonemic Orthography", *Bible Translator*, 5 (1953).

DISCUSSION

PAUL L. GARVIN: Linguistic considerations in the devising of spelling systems include not only phonemics, but also morphophonemics. The major problems in the latter area are word boundaries, and the orthographic stability of the morpheme (i.e. whether to hold its spelling constant in spite of morphophonemic variability).

These considerations must then be evaluated in terms of the speakers' cultural response to a particular orthographic solution.

In technical terms, the process is one of going from phonemes to graphemes to letters. It is in this last step that cultural considerations weigh the heaviest.

M. A. K. HALLIDAY: Language reform in China covers the reform of the Chinese script and the standardization of Pekingese as the national language. The reform of the script may bring about certain changes in the written language, but the main change has already taken place, Modern Chinese having replaced the literary language in almost all forms of written communication during the 1920s and 1930s.

The Chinese script is lexigraphic in its relation to the language, the linguistic unit represented by one symbol of the script (one character) being a lexical one. In graphic structure it is part ideographic and part phonetic. The complexity of the graphic forms, and the large number of different characters, make the script difficult to learn and unsuited to modern requirements of mass communication.

Since the seventeenth century, Chinese linguists have attempted phonetic "transcriptions" for phonological analysis, but it is only in this century that the possibility has been considered of a phonetic "script" to replace characters. Apart from the many transcriptions devised by Western scholars for research and teaching purposes, the three most important phonetic scripts of Chinese origin are (1) Chu-yin tzu-mu, (2) Gwoyeu Lomatzyh, and (3) Latinxua Sinwenz.

The first of these divides the syllable into two parts, initial (one symbol) and final (one or two symbols), its symbols being reduced forms of Chinese characters. The two latter both use the Roman alphabet, (2) being distinguished by its use of orthographic variations to indicate syllabic tone.

These three scripts were promoted by individuals and private groups, with some government support at various times, though this was mainly confined to support for their auxiliary use, for example the use of (1) in the teaching of reading. On the whole Chinese linguists throughout this period have considered that characters would eventually have to yield to some sort of phonetic script, but the issue was a live one only to a small minority of the population. Many educated Chinese were opposed to the adoption of such a script, which to them seemed to involve a loss of national identity and culture, though most linguists considered their arguments untenable.

The three main objections were (with the linguists' answers to them):

(1) The structure of Chinese, with its small number of phonetically distinct syllabic units of lexis, would render the language unintelligible in phonetic script. – But Chinese understand each other when they speak, and at the most what would be required was a closer approximation of the written to the spoken language.

(2) China is a country of divergent dialects among which the script is a unifying force. – Actually the traditional script prevents linguistic unification, since it renders the learning of the standard language by dialect speakers a vastly more difficult task.

(3) The abolition of the traditional script would cut off the Chinese from their literary heritage. – But the learning of the literary language is a special task which would be made no more difficult by the use of a phonetic script for Modern Chinese, and a phonetic script on historical principles could be devised for Classical Chinese. In any case it has long been customary to publish the classics in modern translation, and this is certainly the form in which they are most widely read.

In 1951 the Chinese (People's) Government set up a Script Reform Committee, including all leading linguists, (1) to simplify the traditional script and (2) to draft a new, phonetic script and make recommendations with regard to its use. Under (1), about 500 graphic elements, affecting 2000 characters, were simplified, and another 1000 "variant forms" abolished; these reforms were introduced into newspapers in 1956 and are now generally used in most publications in Modern Chinese. Under (2) were published in January 1956 three versions of a Draft Alphabet using Roman letters, one of which versions introduced six new symbols, four from the International Phonetic Alphabet and two from Cyrillic, with the recommendation that one version of this alphabet should gradually over a long period replace the traditional script.

After much discussion, both in the Committee and in public, the version based on Latinxua Sinwenz, and using only the letters of the Roman alphabet, was adopted by the Committee on a majority vote (about 140 out of 250, the remaining votes being spread over the other two versions and a number of other scripts submitted by individuals). But the question of the extent to which this alphabet will be used is still open. Its use in reference books, and in readers and textbooks of the standard language, is fairly certain; but there is still some opinion, expressed for example in recent issues of *Pinjin*, a journal devoted exclusively to the subject, opposed to its adoption for general use in Modern Chinese. One may however predict that the economic and social advantages of an alphabetic script will ensure its eventual adoption in place of characters. It is not to be thought that Chinese characters will disappear from the scene; but linguists everywhere may well agree with the great majority of their Chinese colleagues in thinking that this reform, for which they have been in large measure responsible, can only be of benefit to China.

DON GRAHAM STUART: It is probably useless to appeal for more objectivity and less cultural and ideological prejudice in our approaches to alphabet invention and the reform of scripts, since these are questions that are seldom taken up disinterestedly. Linguistic expressions go together with linguistic contents, and you can safely bet that any program for reforming the system of expression has designs on content as well. I should therefore only like to recommend a certain scepticism, especially wherever language reform by fiat is urged. For instance, it is obvious that the extensive changes in writing just outlined by Dr. Halliday as planned for Chinese will most certainly produce, as a most notable result, a break in the continuity of Chinese culture. Whether this is a desirable thing depends not on any linguistic consideration but upon whether one values most a certain cultural tradition or the *tabula rasa* favourable to a complete cultural reform. One may anticipate here that the end result will depend upon the extent to which nationalistic pride of culture tempers ideological extremism. This is the exclusive concern of the Chinese themselves, and we can only wish them in all good will a felicitous solution. My point is, however, that the problem of script reform in China is not produced by the inherent impracticability of the traditional Chinese characters. The extraordinary high rate of literacy in Japan proves that, at least if provided with a set of auxiliary phonetic symbols, the Chinese characters can serve very well as tools for written communication in a modern civilization.

I must also admit to feeling uncomfortable about the general assumption that an alphabetical system of writing is best. On the one hand, one would feel that much could be said for a graphic system that rested on at least a partial analysis into distinctive features; on the other, I find that Dr. Berry's admission that "a simple syllabary is almost as good" has not gone far enough. From my own experience, I am convinced that in languages which have a small number of possible syllable types a syllabary is greatly superior to an alphabetical notation, not only because of the textual economy it affords, but because it can be learned more quickly by children. My six and a half year old daughter speaks Japanese, Dutch, and English, and has played with spelling games, etc., for the past two years. Over a year ago, she began to read Japanese children's literature in *hiragana* for her own pleasure, but even though my wife and I have spent more time teaching her to read the Roman alphabet than we were able to devote to Japanese, she is only now beginning to read Dutch – which has a semiphonemic spelling. It goes without saying that she has made least progress of all in English with its completely unsystematic orthography. There can be no doubt that, in such languages as Japanese at least, syllables can be abstracted with less intellection, or at least with a simpler kind of intellection, than smaller distinctive complexes, and that this fact is reflected in the faster rate of learning which my daughter displayed in mastering the Japanese *kana* script. I should say that my daughter is a perfectly ordinary child, except for having lived in varied linguistic environments, and that in general, I believe, Japanese children begin reading earlier than European children.

Certainly, though, when it comes to an alphabetic script, the widespread use which it enjoys makes the Latin alphabet much to be preferred over all others. However, where it is to be adopted for a previously unwritten language, would it not be advisable to employ a style, say Irish uncial, in which the upper and lower case difference could be dispensed with without offending esthetic conventions? Even more important from the standpoint of typographical economy would be the elimination of the unequal widths of the letters which makes justification of the lines necessary. In the days of hand type setting, this was not an important consideration; however, in mechanical typesetting it introduces an enormous extra complication and adds greatly to printing costs. There would seem to be no reason why this difficulty should not be eliminated in planning for the adaptation of the Latin alphabet to previously unwritten languages.

KENNETH L. PIKE: The Summer Institute of Linguistics is currently working on the formation of alphabets and literacy materials for approximately 150 languages.

It, also, has found it necessary to give attention to non-linguistic factors in alphabet formation. Mr. Wonderly called such an alphabet an "ethnolinguistic" one.

One of the particular problems of a linguistic type which has faced us similar to those raised by Mr. Berry is the relation between a phonemic and a morpho-phonemic alphabet. Miss Sarah Gudschinsky found (a report which I hope will soon appear in *Word*) that in one of the Mazatec dialects (where tone is semantically very important, and where morphophonemics of tone is very complicated) that it was important to write phonemically the tone *within* a word but that changes due to mechanical tone replacement *at word boundaries* could effectively be written morphophonemically.

MARCEL COHEN: La linguistique appliquée s'est – heureusement – manifestée de diverses manières dans ces dernières années. On peut citer la publication par l'UNESCO de l'*Emploi des langues vernaculaires dans l'enseignement* (1953), l'élaboration et la discussion du *Français élémentaire* (publications de 1954 à 1957), la parution depuis 1955 de *Sprachforum, Zeitschrift für angewandte Sprachwissenschaft* (Köln-Graz).

Il ne suffit pas de considérer les applications nouvelles de l'alphabet sous la forme latine ou cyrillique. Les formes traditionnelles, différenciées par l'évolution, dont aucune n'est combinée rationnellement, pourront une fois céder à d'autres tracés.

Il faut tenir compte dès maintenant de l'abondance des sténographies, dont la création a visé à la rapidité. Une conséquence est que de nombreux usagers sont déjà habitués à l'orthographe phonétique, non traditionnelle.

Il y a d'autres écritures, phonétiques aussi, dont les formes ont été combinées à neuf pour l'apprentissage facile de la lecture et de l'écriture; certaines écritures de missionnaires, Evans, Pollard, ont connu le succès dans des régions d'Asie et d'Amérique.

On peut citer quelques autres novateurs.

Le typographe M. Passerat a donné en 1953 (sous le pseudonyme S. de Sivry) un projet de *néographie* (n'utilisant que quelques traits simples), dans une petite revue ronéotée.

Le phonéticien Martin Kloster Jensen a publié en 1956 à Bergen un système de *lalogram*(*s*) se référant pour les formes aux mouvements des articulations et qui ne se voulait destiné qu'aux étudiants en phonétique.

Un système «positionnel» non encore publié est dû à Jean Camion, architecte français. Il est combiné rigoureusement en raison des faits phonétiques, en traits simples, avec des variations d'emplacement: ainsi les occlusives sont marquées par un trait court vertical, placé différemment suivant qu'il s'agit de labiales, dentales, palatales. Le but serait de donner à toutes les langues une orthographe phonétique, avec le même tracé, facile à apprendre en relation avec les articulations.

S. Sinclair Eustace: A facile intellectualist approach is not enough in this subject, where the worker must have at his fingertips not one or two factors but twenty or thirty. An example of this intellectualism has come up this afternoon, when it was said to be a bad thing that *m* and *i* are of different width. On the contrary, this difference of width is a most useful contrastive feature, whose absence in, say, the Cyrillic alphabet probably makes that alphabet less legible than the Latin absolutely.

The most important factor not hitherto mentioned is typography. The Chinese are seriously considering using only twenty-six letters instead of a phonetically excellent alphabet with extra letters. This is amazing until you see the extra letters. They are ugly and unsatisfactory, an affront indeed to the fine traditions of Chinese calligraphy. Thus not only for Chinese but for any other new spelling it is imperative to consult the typographer, whose instinct and experience provide an essential and unexpected code of do's and don't's in letter design, which will often make the difference between the success or failure of a new alphabet.

From *Proceedings of the Eighth International Congress of Linguistics* (Oslo, University Press, 1958), pp. 752-764. Reprinted by permission.

Punya Sloka Ray

LANGUAGE STANDARDIZATION

INTRODUCTION

We ordinarily speak of standardization in relation to tools. We expect of a standardized tool that it will be cheaper to acquire and maintain, that individual specimens will be very much alike and of relatively uniform dependability. When a tool is rarely used or used by only a few people, standardization is relatively unimportant. But if it comes to be used frequently and by a large number of people, standardization is often an advantage.

When we apply the concept of standardization to languages, we stress their tool-like character. From this point of view a language is only an instrument of communication; a means, not an end. In the following discussion we consider questions of efficiency and uniformity of linguistic practices, as well as questions of policy in furthering standardization, especially insofar as it can be a deliberate and conscious operation.

In this discussion we confine our attention primarily to a single aspect of language: lexical forms, i.e. the vocabulary (as distinguished from the grammar).

QUESTIONS OF EFFICIENCY

The first thing is to dispel the notion that all linguistic practices are equal, that there are no real choices available on grounds of relative efficiency. However, a preliminary point is that we cannot simply set up an abstract scale of efficiency and grade each word or phrase of the language upon it. The expression which may be less efficient for certain purposes may be more efficient for others. We need to have therefore both an assessment of identifiable purposes and a canon for choice when an identified purpose and a small set of alternative forms are given. In brief, we do not require a method for measuring efficiency, but only for comparing it.

Let us consider what happens when the expression "vegetables" is replaced by "veg". This is often justified on the ground that the former is a mouthful compared to the latter. Yet it is also clear that "veg" requires more explanation than "vegetables". If and when the unabbreviated form is known and is not too rare, and the general technique of the abbreviation, such as "pronounce only the stressed syllable", is even better known, then the explanation required for the longer form may not counterbalance the advantages gained by the shorter form. Only in such a case may the shorter form be said to be more efficient. We shall call this type of efficiency "concision".

But there is another aspect to efficiency. Suppose that I am talking to a friend over the phone and he is being distracted by other things. In such a case, he may easily miss "veg" and ask me to repeat. "Vegetables" would not be so easy to miss. For example, if he misses "v.g...b...", but catches ".e.eta.les", there are not many alternative expressions that would fit, given the general context of the conversation. This quality has been called "redundancy" but may be also called self-confirmation of the utterance.

We shall also need to distinguish between two different concepts of frequency. "Text frequency" compares two lexical forms in their repetitions within a body of discourse. For example, in a text of 5000 words we may find that the word "set" has been used 45 times while the word "form" has been used 63 times. "List frequency" compares two lexical forms in their repetitions of pairing with other lexical forms. For example, we may find that within the same text the word "set" has been used immediately before 35 different words while the word "form" has been used before 39 different words.

A lexical form may also be identified as either relatively "familiar" or relatively "learned". It is more familiar when it has a higher list frequency and more learned when it does not. The more familiar a lexical form is, the more efficient it is to have it name a relatively fluid concept; the more learned, the more efficient it is to have it name a relatively precise concept.

Let us consider the role of associations. The higher the list frequency of a lexical form, the more diverse associations it has and if we use a more familiar word to designate a precise concept, we run the risk of being led off in irrelevant directions. But because the learned form has a lesser burden of associations, it can be used more arbitrarily and precisely than the more familiar form.

QUESTIONS OF UNIFORMITY

There are two different ways in which uniformity may be sought for a language. First, we may have a set of people who as a group identify themselves as users of the language, and yet who do not use the same forms for the same meanings. This situation is usually described as existence of dialects. All languages are fragmented into dialects, but not to an equal degree. For instance, German may be said to be more fragmented into dialects than French. That the causality of such a phenomenon might be found in another dimension, that dialects might correlate with socio-economic disparities in the population, is not relevant for the point of view adopted here. What matters here is only the ability to contrast languages. If the forms and meanings vary relatively little between smaller groups within the larger group of the speakers of the language then the language is relatively "closed".

We may have a set of people who as a group identify themselves as users of the language, and yet who do not use it for all purposes of life. For instance, up to about the Second World War, many of the chemistry textbooks in use in American universities were in German, and researchers in that subject were expected to be able to conduct discussion in that language. Indeed, not being required to use a language other than one's vernacular for some urgent purpose or other is a rather exceptional situation in history. This phenomenon leads to the question how far the forms and meanings of the first language match with those of the other languages also needed. This we shall describe as the relative "opening" of the language. We might speak, instead of "closure" and "opening", of intra-linguistic and inter-linguistic uniformity.

In summary, lack of uniformity may be shown in various ways in particular cases.[1] Firstly, there may be no common, uniform, standard linguistic practice at all within a society. Secondly, there may be one common, uniform but functionally restricted standard. Thirdly, there may be several functionally restricted standards.

Source of borrowing: "Borrowing" is a traditional term for a phenomenon we might better describe as "inheritance": no contract for repayment is involved. By a source of borrowing is meant here a source which is currently utilized, and not sources that may have been utilized in the past. English did borrow heavily from Danish at one time. But Danish is not a source of borrowing for English now, at least not a major source.

These sources may form a serial order functioning almost as one

[1] Portions of the following treatment through the end have been published as part of an article in QUEST, October 1961, the courtesy of the editor of which is hereby acknowledged.

single whole. This is the case with English, for which the major sources are French, Latin and Greek. The point to note here is that French borrows heavily from Latin and Greek, and that Latin used to borrow heavily from Greek.

Or the sources may be ordered parallel to one another. This kind of an order is exhibited for Indonesian, which borrows mostly from Dutch, French, and English. Similar is the case for German, for when it borrows it usually does it from either French or English.

Or the sources may be ordered in two unrelated and divergent groups. This is the case with Japanese, which borrows from classical Chinese as well as from modern European languages. The situation is similar for any modern Indian language, with Sanskrit (or classical Tamil or Arabic-Persian) and English as the sources. The tension which exists in the last type of relationship may be alleviated in various ways. First, one of the sources may be abandoned. This has been done in Turkey. Many words traceable to Arabic or Persian are still used, but fresh borrowing from Arabic or Persian has stopped. Second, elements from one of the sources may be used in ways which harmonize with the practice of another source rather better than they do with the original usage. Many of the new formations which German produces by recombining native elements, or Japanese by recombining elements borrowed from classical Chinese, are more or less mechanical translations of the Latin-Greek terms current in the modern European languages. Third, elements and combinations from both directions may be accommodated as stylistic variants. Japanese practices this method to the extent of matching Chinese-derived script-forms and European-derived sound forms for the same Japanese-assimilated words. One might reproduce a sample in a hypothetical English by spelling "artificial-satellite" but pronouncing "sputnik".

Dialect: There may be within a single language no one dominant dialect which can serve as the base for a common standard. This was the case in Germany before Luther, with about five major dialects. However, Luther's choice, combined with the otherwise admitted advantages of the relatively most unified dialect, did tip the scales towards a clear decision. Frequently, there is no clear awareness of the situation in this regard. This was the case in Southern Rhodesia, where Clement Duke had to research for a year before being able to recommend in favor of the very closely related Karanga and Zezuru dialects for building a written, unified Shona.

Or there may be a common, uniform but functionally restricted standard dialect, limited to formal oratory and literature. This phenomenon has been termed "diglossia" and is well illustrated by Arabic.

Formal Arabic differs little from the classical language and is used all over the Arab world. But ordinary conversation even among the highly educated is carried out in several distinct dialects in Iraq, Syria, Egypt, and the Maghreb. The long range outlook, given present political disunity, seems to favor the rise of several daughter languages on the model of the rise of French, Spanish, Italian etc. from Latin. A second possibility is the eventual dominance of one of the spoken varieties over the rest. This seems to be the drift in mainland China, where the Peking dialect is being pushed to replace all others. A third possibility is the indefinite persistence of the situation. This is the case in Switzerland's German-speaking areas, where High German and the Swiss German dialect supplement each other.

Or there may be more than one common and inadequate formal standard within the same language. One example is the situation for some decades and in some areas of Bengal. There were two formal standards, one without a spoken base in the present and the other with a spoken base in another region (besides several fairly stabilized spoken dialects structurally intermediate to the two). The situation has now been resolved by a rapid obsolescence of the first of the literary dialects.

Language: There may not be a single common language. This is rarer these days than might be supposed. Two examples are Finland and Switzerland. In Finland, Finnish is spoken by over 90 per cent and Swedish by less than 9 per cent. But Swedish was until late last century the official language, and still is the nearest equivalent to a lingua franca in the Scandinavian region. In consequence, Swedish is the official second language and the urban population is also actually more or less bilingual. In Switzerland, German is spoken by about 72 per cent, French by a little over 20 per cent, and Italian by slightly less than 6 per cent. But except for formal purposes the German speakers use a rather pronounced dialect, while French and Italian are spoken much as in France and Italy, which are powerful and often admired neighbors. Moreover, Switzerland was for a long and crucial period of her history under the influence of France. The net result is that the language most often utilized as a second language within the country is not German, but French.

Or there may be one common but not quite adequate language. In the Philippines, English is the common language and, from the third grade onwards, the only medium of instruction. The official census declares with perhaps some exaggeration that 38 per cent of the people are actually able to use it. English is clearly in the process of being transformed from an originally foreign, then upper crust second language to a mass language, although the native languages are still indispensable at the lowest levels. In Indonesia, Malay was initially used by only a small part of the population, though this small part was also the major constituent in the total urbanized and mobile section of the people.

Or there may be several common languages, each functionally inadequate in different ways. To an extent this is the case in the Philippines, where Tagalog is the dominant language of Manila and its surroundings, and Spanish too is taught in the schools, though not more than a few thousand habitually use Spanish. The best example is of course India. English is used for higher education, business and administration, though less than 7 per cent can use it. Hindi is traditionally used in the lower echelons of the armed forces, the majority of the larger market places all over the country, and a large block in the north amounting to about a third of the people, and containing the major share of the common places of religious pilgrimage. Sanskrit is used for ceremonial purposes by all Hindus, with intelligibility by a few thousand. Tamil and Bengali are to some extent used beyond their base territories, the former in the south and the latter in the east, and both have large bodies of speakers outside India, Tamil in Ceylon and Bengali in East Pakistan. If Urdu is considered to be a separate language, which it is only for formal oratory and literature, then we have to say that it is used by about a tenth of the population, almost all of which is fluent in some other Indian language. It too has an important body of users outside the country, namely in West Pakistan. Thus six languages, of which two differ only on formal occasions, qualify as common in different ways. Since eight more languages have official status in regions with considerable political autonomy, a slight change in the point of view would allow us to speak of altogether fourteen common languages (in eleven common scripts).

This kind of a situation may be resolved by several different ways. First, one of the languages may win over the rest. This seems to be the hope in the Philippines. Second, the political unit may be broken up. This happened in the case of the Hapsburg Empire, giving rise to different states, Austria, Hungary, Czechoslovakia, etc. Third, there may be a stabilized bilingualism. This is the case in Finland and Switzerland.

The question of a common language for the sciences is only slightly different. They have become a single tradition, however vaguely and incompletely defined. But even recently, relatively isolated yet highly creative schools are not uncommon. The logicians of Poland and the linguists of Czechoslovakia between the two world wars made valuable contributions in less widely accessible languages. Undoubtedly, some potential scientific talent is wasted through the dilemma of easier acquisition of science through an individual's first language versus easier acquisition of his results by other scientists through a world language.

There are just two ways of remedying such a situation. One is to step up research in both quantity and quality published in the language concerned, so that scientists elsewhere will soon simply have to learn the language in order to keep up with the field. This is the solution now being attempted in Russia. The other is early and plentiful training in any one of the leading languages of science, so that anyone who has a minimally adequate training in any science is also fluent in such a world language. This solution is slowly coming to prevail in Northern Europe. After a period in which some remarkable work was initially brought out in Dutch and Danish, it is today increasingly less likely that top quality work by Dutch or Danish scientists will be first published in those languages.

The structure of alternatives in the question of scripts, sources of borrowing, etc. is entirely analogous. The alternative that matches most closely the practice of the most accessible of the leading languages of science will always have the entire community of the scientists urging its adoption. This is only limited by the fact that cultivation of science is not the only preoccupation of any social group and that the humanistic sciences exhibit a much less uniform pattern of solidarity. There are also other considerations, such as uniformity between different classes or regions within the nation, neighbors or allies within the commonwealth, generations or traditions within the same history.

A more subtle question arises in relation to the unity of science. Is science a single enterprise at all? The answer is no, if a precisely and enduringly definite body of statements or techniques or points of view is meant. But in a vaguer, more fluid, but nevertheless real sense, the answer may be a differentiated yes. The affirmation is least ambiguous for mathematics, and most for theologies. Yet even for Hindu theology, no one language will be held sufficient today for the purposes of an authoritative scholar. One will need to operate with Sanskrit, Hindi, English and a few other languages. Hence the problems of closure and opening, of the presence or absence of common standards are all there for the languages of even this most marginally scientific of all sciences.

QUESTIONS OF POLICY

The operation of standardization consists basically of two steps, first, the creation of a model for imitation, and second, promotion of this model over rival models.

A model for imitation means a body of discourse capable of attracting the interest and the loyalty of its intended listeners or readers. If we are concerned with the spoken forms, this means the availability of people who habitually use those forms. If we are concerned with the written forms, this means the availability of literature in prose. For either, a model for imitation may be created by unorganized, multiple, obscure decisions, that is, by unplanned decisions. Or it may be done in a relatively planned way. Further, a planned model may be set up on a purely private basis, relying on nothing but persuasion. Or it may be set up on a commissioned basis, relying on more tangible rewards and punishments.

For all practical purposes, the preferred instrument of standardization is officially commissioned publications, with specific conditions as to the choice of the writing system, the source of borrowing, the dialect, etc. The administrative techniques by which literature of the desired kind can be helped into existence are variegated and complex, and need a detailed study.

A few of these administrative techniques may be barely mentioned here. Each has severe limitations in general and for some societies in particular.

1. *Approved terminologies.* This has its only use in vaguely indicating the general direction of lexical innovation, since particular recommendations can be authoritatively recommended only by those who have assumed responsibility for exhibiting them in consistent and scientifically valid use through an extended body of text.

2. *Merit awards.* Without attention to specific jobs, persistent and successful work in the desired direction may be acknowledged by public honors or cash grants.

3. *Prize contests.* A specific job may be chosen and then competition invited for its execution, with materially significant and well-publicized awards for the winners.

4. *Nominated authorship.* Specific individual writers or translators may be chosen through various means for certain specific pre-chosen jobs. Their work may be supervised and revised by appointed experts.

5. *Subsidized self-help.* The gap between those who would like to read the book and those who can afford to buy it is never either very small or very large. In the case of books which fulfill the desired conditions it may be bridged by means of a subsidy, the best proven method for which seems to be low-interest loans plus technical advice to private publishers.

6. *State enterprise.* If a published book is not read, this does not help standardization. It is rather invitingly easy to disguise such waste in State or indeed any non-profit agency enterprise, which tends to be

efficient only when publication is mainly for record, as for official or historical or cultural documents.

But the problem is not only to create a model literature in prose but also to promote its acceptance over rival models. Now there is no quick way of making the horse drink the water, if it does not want to. Only the satisfaction of genuinely felt needs can enable a literature to win the allegiance needed. If the information or exposition given is of a kind wanted and is also put in a way that does not deceive or confuse; if for all the insistence on new habits the presentation meets the intended readers more than half way, it may be successful.

Of course, needs may be created or intensified by State efforts. For example, industrialization will certainly intensify the need to have information on all kinds of technology. Or the establishment of a working democracy will create the need for a mass literature on political and subsidy for the teaching of Arabic and Persian in Turkey contributed to creation of a need for a more turkified Turkish, just as the decision to economic questions. On the other hand, the decision to withdraw the penalize any public use of the Arabic-Persian script helped the drive towards general adoption of the Roman script.

Need-creating is both relatively useless and relatively harmful without simultaneous model-creating. The stick alone without the carrot may drive the donkey into erratic ways. The argument that once the medium of administration or instruction in India is changed from English to Hindi, satisfactory literature will begin to come out in the language, is not very convincing. Productions that satisfy the best standards are expensive in terms of talent, leisure and money. Productions that satisfy the widest standards of expectation usually do not need subsidies. The essence of the problem is the disparity between the best and the widest standards.

An erratic direction of change may affect the mutual relationships of languages within a multilingual context, with the changes of linguistic habits being either convergent or divergent. Consider for example the question of technical terms in the modern Indian languages. The innovations which are pouring into these languages from English are the same for all and in this respect the change is towards greater convergence. But the technical terms which are being taken from Sanskrit into these languages are rather less convergent. It does not help much if both "sūcanā" and "ghosanā" can be met with in original Sanskrit, if one is selected by Hindi and the other by Bengali for the same English-derived concept "a notice". Even when they are mutually intelligible, and this is not always true, the Sanskrit loanwords in the different languages may be felt as mutually grotesque and barbarous. And to the extent that innovation from non-Sanskrit and non-English sources is preferred, as in Ṭheṭ for Hindi and Urdu, Arabic and Persian for Urdu, Classical Tamil for Tamil etc., the change is towards even greater divergence.

It is of course not necessary for a government to do any kind of planning. It may be just as well done by a church, as was done by Luther and others for German, or by a school of literary artists, as was done by Pramatha Chaudhury and others for Bengali, or by a communion of scientists, as was done by Linnaeus and others for botanical terminology. Even one who prefers to write "phonemic" rather than "phonematic" is doing a bit of prescriptive intervention.

Planning by the State is no guarantee that planning will succeed. One of the clearest examples is in Norway, where the long-ruling Socialists have steadily decried the actual spoken and written standard in favor of more non-Danish forms, but with less and less success. Another example is shown by Papua, where the governor thought that Neo-Melanesian, then known as Melanesian Pidgin, was a disgraceful language and ought to be abolished. The only result of his strenuous efforts has been that the language continues to flourish everywhere except Port Moresby, where it has given way, neither to English nor to any "authentic" (sic) tribal speech, but to Motu, which the governor would consider equally unpedigreed. But perhaps the most celebrated failure has been that of the Irish Republic to reinstate Gaelic.

Success in language planning depends on the already existing network of social communication, that is, on the established channels of commerce in material and intellectual goods. It matters less with whom one is free to communicate than with whom one constantly needs to communicate. Such a need may arise because the other fellow is able to supply a convenience or because association with him gives one self-respect. Prestige derives from both utility and honor. The individuals who participate in relatively more intense communication constitute what Karl Deutsch calls the "mobilized" part of the population. He has shown how changes in the status of a language no less than in its inventory of forms spread along the lines of social mobilization.

Perhaps a less misleading term for the phenomenon would be "civilization". For social mobilization in his sense does not entail anything like official control over newspapers, the radio, the publishing houses etc., or even a bringing together of people in a common task with the roles narrowly and rigidly alloted. What is of concern here are spontaneously formed habits of talking and listening to one another, increasing readiness to explain oneself to or to ask explanation from one another in unrestricted interchange of proposals and comments.

Let us consider some concrete examples. Motu prevailed over other candidates, first because it was based on the speech of the police-boys, who formed the larger part of the total "mobilized" population, and second because these police-boys were much more frequently and easily accessible to the ordinary Papuans than the English-speaking rulers. Malay prevailed over Javanese and others and was adopted as the Bahasa Indonesia because of its long-standing and wide-ranging circulation by preponderantly Malay-speaking traders, soldiers and priests. Prestige makes people want to adopt a practice, but only access enables them to do it. If different groups of linguistic forms are ordered in a scale of prestige and in one of access, the group which has the highest joint score will have the best chance for general adoption.

In other words, any formal organized action by an acknowledged authority, such as a State or a Church or a learned society or an author, can be successful in its intention to encourage or discourage linguistic habits only if it correlates maximally to informal unorganized action on the part of numerous locally more accessible lesser authorities. Artificial solutions like the IPA script or Esperanto have so little chance of success only because their teachers and texts are so few, indeed initially only one, namely the inventor and his sample composition. In contrast, any native speaker of a natural language functions as some kind of a teacher during the moments of social encounter.

BIBLIOGRAPHY

Blanc, Haim, "The Growth of Israeli Hebrew", *Middle Eastern Affairs,* Dec. 1954.

—, "Hebrew in Israel: Trends and Problems", *The Middle East Journal,* Autumn 1957.

Deutsch, Karl W., *Nationalism and Social Communication* (Cambridge, Mass., 1953).

Doke, Clement M., *Report on the Unification of the Shona Languages* (Hertford, England, 1931),

Fairbanks, Gordon W., "Frequency and Phonemics", *Indian Linguistics,* 17 (1957).

Ferguson, Charles A., "Diglossia", *Word,* 15, 2, 325-340 (1959).

Ferguson, Charles A. and J. J. Gumperz (eds.), *Linguistic Diversity in South Asia* (Bloomington, Ind., 1960).

Garvin, Paul L. and M. Mathiot, "The Urbanization of the Guarani Language", in Wallace, Anthony F. C. (ed.), *International Congress of Anthropological and Ethnological Sciences, 5th., Selected Papers* (Philadelphia, 1960).

Gerr, Stanley, *Scientific and Technical Japanese* (New York, 1944).

Grove, Victor, *The Language Bar* (New York, 1950).

Gumperz, John J., "Language Problems in the Rural Development of North India", *Journal of Asian Studies,* 16, 251-59 (1957).

Harrison, Selig S., *The Most Dangerous Decades* (New York, 1957).

Haugen, Einar, *Bilingualism in the Americas* (Alabama, 1956).

Heyd, Uriel, *Language Reform in Modern Turkey* (Jerusalem, 1954).

Hoijer, Harry A. (ed.), *Language in Culture* (Chicago, 1954).
Joos, Martin, "Semology", *Studies in Linguistics,* 13, 53-72 (1958).
Lunt, Horace G., "The Creation of Standard Macedonian", *Anthropological Linguistics,* 1, 5 (1959).
Miller, George A., *Language and Communication* (New York, 1951).
Mills, Harriet C., "Language Reform in China", *The Far Eastern Quarterly,* 15, 4, 517-540 (1956).
Morag, Shelomo, "Planned and Unplanned Development in Modern Hebrew", *Lingua,* 8, 3 (1959).
Prator, Clifford J., *Language Teaching in the Philippines* (Manila, 1950).
Ray, Punya Sloka, "A Single Script for India", *Seminar* (July 1960).
—, "The Definition of a Language", *Indian Journal of Philosophy,* August 1960.
—, "The Value of a Language", *Lingua,* 10, 220-233 (1961).
—, "The Formation of Prose." *Word,* 18, 313-325 (1962).
—, *Language Standardization* (The Hague, 1963).
Salzmann, Z., "The Analysis of Lexical Acculturation", *International Journal of American Linguistics,* 20, 137-139 (1954).
Stone, Howard, "Cushioned Loanwords", *Word,* 9, 1, 1-11 (1953).
UNESCO, *The Use of Vernacular Languages in Education* (Paris, 1953).
—, *Report on Scientific and Technical Translation* (Paris, 1957).
Weinreich, Uriel, *Languages in Contact* (New York, 1953).
Yngve, Victor H. "A Model and a Hypothesis of Language Structure", *Proceedings of the American Philosophical Society,* 104, 5, 444-466 (1960).

From *Study of the Role of Second Languages in Asia, Africa and Latin America,* F. A. Rice, ed. (Washington, Center for Applied Linguistics of the Modern Language Association, 1962), pp. 91-104, with minor revisions by the author. Reprinted by permission.

M. M. Guxman

SOME GENERAL REGULARITIES IN THE FORMATION AND DEVELOPMENT OF NATIONAL LANGUAGES [1]

I

As the collated material has shown, the main features distinguishing a national language from a folk language are not to be sought primarily in the structural characteristics of a language but in the qualitative change in the relationships of its different types, and in the change in the functional character of each of these types. This concerns the literary language first and foremost. The formation of national literary languages is, to a certain extent, in process as early as the pre-national period, inasmuch as written literary langauges are to be found even during the stage of folk existence. However, the literary language of the national formation stage gradually accumulates a series of qualitative peculiarities which distinguish it from the literary language of the preceding historical period.

In those countries (such as China, Japan,[2] or Armenia [3]), where a developed written literary language was present as early as the feudal stage, a new literary language was formed on the basis of the dialect of the territory in which the leading political and economic center of the country was located. The qualitative distinction of the new literary

[1] The conclusion was written not only on the basis of the articles included in the present collection (*Voprosy* ...), but also on the basis of other materials published earlier in various periodicals.
[2] Cf. N. I. Konrad's article "The Literary Language in China and Japan" in the present collection (*Voprosy* ...).
[3] Cf. A. S. Garibjan's article "The Armenian National Literary Language" in the present collection (*Voprosy* ...).

language, was above all expressed by its different functional character: if the medieval literary language was utilized by comparatively restricted social classes and only in its written variety, the national literary language gradually acquired a significance that was almost nation-wide and was applied in written and oral communication. In China, *pai-hua* (as only the vernacular was originally called as distinct from the classical written *wen-yen*), after it had become the state language – *kuo-yü* – became the carrier of the common national language norm. It is especially important that a new literary language exists in its written and oral varieties in China, while the very transfer of the term *pai-hua* to the new literary language seems to underscore the unity of the language sphere of the written literary and colloquial folk varieties of the national language.

Processes of the same type may be observed in Japan. The new literary language (called *hyōjungo* "normative language", or "standard language") became the common national language norm which dominated written and oral communication.

Of a somewhat different content are the processes which caused the formation of new literary language characteristics during the national formation and development stage in those countries where there existed a written literary language with a foreign base in the pre-capitalistic period: in Russia – Old Church Slavic, in Germany, France and Italy – Latin, in Norway – Danish, although the characteristics of the national literary language as distinct from the literary language of the preceding period remain essentially the same as those of China and Japan. Latin functioned as the written literary language in Germany for many years: it dominated all the prose genres of writing until the fourteenth century. The German literary language was used primarily in poetry.[4] This created a special gap between the written-literary and colloquial-folk language types of the German people. Thus, the first task in the national formation stage was the banishment of Latin from all spheres of communication. This task was not realized at once: commercial writing won out at first, then the church, and, last of all, science. The protracted dominance of a written-literary language with a "foreign" base, especially in school, not only promoted the flourishing of dialects in the colloquial-folk variety of German, but in time of extreme political and economic crisis made for the presence of several, very diverse, varieties of literary language based on German. The question was raised about effecting unity in the German literary language and overcoming regional separatism. This unity was established during the formation and development period of the German nation, first in the written, then in the oral

[4] The first significant prose works of religious content, as well as fictional prose in literary German, appeared in the thirteenth century.

varieties of the national language.[5] The difference between the German national literary language and the literary language of the German people consisted primarily in the fact that only during the formation and development period of the German nation did the German literary language dominate all spheres of communication and appear as the carrier of a united common national norm.

The formation of the French national language assumed a similar, although somewhat different, form.[6] Here, also, in the national language formation period, the French literary language gradually forced Latin out of all spheres of communication and here, also, extensive work was conducted in the formation of the lexical, grammatical, and orthoepic norms which operated in the oral and written varieties of the language. But inasmuch as a certain unity was established within the bounds of the written-literary varieties of the language as early as the pre-national period in France, the task of overcoming regional separatism was here of considerably less significance.

In Italy, however, where the developing national literary language had to fight both the protracted domination of Latin and regional separatism, the final formation of Italian literary language unity and the bridging of the gap between the written-literary and colloquial-folk varieties of the language were delayed by the restrained development of economic and political centralization, as well as foreign dominance.[7] Here too, however, as in China and Japan, as in Germany and France, the same tasks arose in the formation of the Italian national literary language.

The gradual penetration of the literary language into all spheres of communication, including the vernacular, the formation of unified grammatical, lexical, and orthoepic norms, a striving to liquidate the gap between the written-literary and colloquial-folk varieties of the language which existed earlier in many countries, and the assimilation of the styles of these two varieties – these are what characterize the formation and development period of national languages in all countries. The concrete forms in which these processes are realized, the intensity of development, and the role of the individual links do differ, but even in the formation process of the new written Bashkir national language,[8] the problem of working out a unified, supradialectal literary norm, operative in the written as well as the oral varieties of the national

[5] Cf. M. M. Guxman's article "Formation of the Literary Norm of the German National Language" in the present collection (*Voprosy* . . .).

[6] Cf. M. S. Guryčeva's article "The Initial Stage in the Formation of the French National Language" in the present collection (*Voprosy* . . .).

[7] Cf. T. B. Alisova's article "Peculiarities in the Formation of Norms of the Italian Written Literary Language in the 16th Century" in the present collection.

[8] Cf. A. A. Juldašev's article "Problems of the Formation of Unified Norms in the Bashkir National Language" in the present collection (*Voprosy* . . .).

language, was in the twentieth century just as real as it was in eighteenth- and nineteenth-century Germany or Italy.

Typical of a national literary language is its functioning in the capacity of a *unified* and *single* literary language, used both in oral as well as in written communication. The extent to which the gap between the written-literary and colloquial-folk varieties of a language is felt as an obstacle to the development of national culture and as an obstacle on a given people's road to progress, is shown not only by materials drawn from the histories of the Chinese and Japanese national languages,[9] but also by the contemporary state of affairs in countries of the Arab East,[10] and by the difficulties of language development in South America.[11]

In several cases, however, as the material indicates, two different varieties of a literary language are preserved in the period of national language formation and development. The Norwegian, Albanian, and Armenian languages may serve as examples.

In Norway, as is known, the written literary language was formed on a Danish base as early as the pre-national period. Gradually, the oral variety of this language crystallized through interaction with the urban semi-dialect of Oslo. Thus, a literary language based on a foreign (although closely related) speech form – "bokmål" – was used in oral as well as written communication. Ibsen and Björnson wrote in this language. But demands were raised in the nineteenth century in favor of creating an indigenous literary language based on the Norwegian "landsmål". Both languages perform one and the same function in Modern Norwegian, both are state languages used in artistic literature, journalism, teaching, and in oral communication; bokmål is used primarily in the east of the country, landsmål in the west. A similarity of grammatical structure, and a sufficient community of lexical items, makes the parallel use of both languages possible. The repeated writing reforms also brought together the orthographic rules characteristic of either language. The interaction of these two languages is beyond doubt. Nevertheless, even today, such a unified literary language as characterizes other nations is not to be found in Norway.

In Albania there are two varieties of literary language based on Albanian; one of them is based on the southern (Tosk) dialect, the other on the northern (Gheg) dialect. In the course of many years, both these dialects developed in a parallel fashion, but in constant interaction

[9] Cf. N. I. Konrad's article "The Literary Language in China and Japan".
[10] Cf. V. M. Belkin's article "The Problem of Literary Language and Dialect in Arab Countries", published in the present collection (*Voprosy* . . .), as well as A. F. Sultanov's article on the formation of the national language in Egypt.
[11] Cf. G. V. Stepanov's article "The National Language in Latin American Countries" in the present collection (*Voprosy* . . .).

with one another. This is explained by the specific historical circumstances of Albania. After the victory of the Albanian people in the people's war for liberation, the southern variety began to predominate considerably and, as A. V. Desnitskaja suggests, "possessed all the elements necessary to become the common Albanian literary language".[12] However even at the present time, a significant portion of artistic and political literature continues to be published in the northern variety of the literary language.

There are also two varieties in Modern Armenian which developed under entirely different historical circumstances. One of them, the eastern variety, became the main state language of socialist Armenia after the October Socialist Revolution and received every opportunity for further development. The second, the western, is the language of that portion of the Armenian people which is found abroad.

The coexistence of two literary languages was, in the first case, caused by the protracted membership of Norway in the realm of the Danish Kingdom. In the second case, the coexistence of two varieties of the literary language was the result of the protracted geographical, economic, and cultural divergence of the south and north of Albania, and of a foreign dominance which delayed the consolidation of the Albanian nation. Finally, the presence of two varieties of the Armenian language is connected with the age-old divergence of the Armenian people, divested in the past of a common territory and having therefore several cultural centers.[13]

For the Albanian language, this condition is apparently temporary, transitory. To predict the paths of development of the Norwegian and Armenian national languages would be difficult at the present time. It was noted above that during the period of national existence a literary language usually acts as the carrier of the common national norm; in fact, the literary language is called upon under such circumstances to represent the language unity of a given people and to perform the function of a common national language. This completely changes the role of the other types of the language. The introduction of mandatory elementary education in many countries still in the capitalist stage, especially the rapid tempo of the cultural revolution in those countries where socialism has been victorious, promoted the appearance of a literary language in those spheres of communication which were formerly dominated by a dialect. The press, radio, and motion pictures constitute channels for a unified literary norm. This process is most intensive

[12] Cf. A. V. Desnitskaja's article "From the History of the Formation of the Albanian National Language", page 223 (*Voprosy* ...).

[13] Cf. A. S. Garibjan's article "The Armenian National Literary Language" (*Voprosy* ...).

in socialist countries where the common national role of the literary language is fully realized.

Doubtless, the speed at which other language types are displaced by the literary language varies in different countries depending on the length of existence of both the nation and the unified literary language, on the totality of historical circumstances according to which different nations are formed, on a nation's culture in general, and its literature and language in particular. However, a general feature of national language development is the ever-growing intensity in the appearance of a literary norm in all forms of communication. For example, although the semi-dialect is still retained in oral communication in the cities off Italy and Germany, and regional dialects still retain their force in rural localities, the establishment of a unified norm and the continuous advance of the literary language on the dialect in oral communication, beginning (for example) as early as the end of the eighteenth century in Germany and in the nineteenth century in Italy, signify nevertheless an ever greater decrease in the social function of the dialect. The leading role of the literary language and the subordinate status of regional dialects is being more and more clearly defined. According to N. I. Konrad, in China and Japan it is not at all the case that everyone has a command of the common literary language – not only in rural communities but also in cities. The dialect is here, too, used in oral communication, but a progressive tendency towards its disappearance is also apparent.

In England and France the process of dialect disappearance from all spheres of communication went considerably farther. In France, in particular, the urban semi-dialect no longer plays the role it does in Germany and Italy.

In feudal times, the written variety of a literary language predominated, while, with a weak distribution of literacy, the literary language was only the property of relatively limited social circles. However, a new type of national literary language is increasingly winning over the broad masses of the people – especially in socialist countries – and is assuming a common national significance. Thus, in the stage of national existence, the character of the language unity is in fact changed. It is not to be denied that each language represents a unified system in each stage of its development, in the sense that all the types of the given language are only its modifications. In spite of dialect differentiation and the presence of a written literary language with a "foreign" base, the German and Italian languages (in the 14th and 15th centuries, for example) were perceived as a certain unity as opposed to Latin. The same is true of any language. However, not one of the language types in the feudal period functioned in the capacity of the carrier of this language unity in all spheres of communication and in various social groups.

In the colloquial variety of a folk language, there is a dominance of either a regional dialect, of modified forms of semi-dialects, or a koiné peculiar to a region. Although the local dialects in several countries were of the broadest social scope in the feudal period, not being limited by any social groups, they can in no respect lay claim to a common national character, for every local dialect is used only in one part of the territory of a given people.

II

Inasmuch as the main link in national language formation and development is the process of establishing a new type of literary language, the determination of several general features of this process is very essential.

Doubtless, a general characteristic is the completely conscious normalization of a literary language, the role of which may not be uniform in the formation and development of different national languages. It depends to a significant degree upon the interrelationship between the national literary language and the literary language of the pre-national period (whether this literary language is new, as in China and Japan, or only the modified old literary language as in France; whether the dialect base was preserved, as in France, or whether it changed, as in Holland; whether the pre-national literary language constituted a known unity, as in France, or whether it existed in the form of several varieties of the literary language, as in Germany, etc.). Nowhere, however, did the formation and development of national languages take place without the codification of a system of lexical, grammatical, orthoepic, and orthographic norms.

Literature exercizes a tremendous influence on the formation of a national language and its literary norm. In Russia, the creative work of the writers and poets of the pre-Pushkin era paved the way for the flowering of a new type of literary language, but only Pushkin, and such of his contemporaries as Lermontov and Gogol, gave final form to that new type of literary language, which became as a result expressive of the common national norm. In China and Japan, the struggle for a literary language of a new type was contemporary with the struggle for a new method and content in literature. In China, Lu-Sin, and in Japan, Shimazaki Toson, fixed these new literary language norms in their creative work. In Germany, the establishment of a unified literary language is connected with the creative work of Lessing, Goethe, Schiller, and later Heine; in France, Corneille, Racine, and Molière were to the same degree creators of a national literary language as Shakespeare in England.

In this regard, one should not separate the formation of a literary language from the activity of normative theoreticians, from the creation of normative grammars and first dictionaries, or from the activity of language societies, academies, etc. The negative sides of this normalization in the history of individual languages are widely known: the limited class character of the demands of Vaugelas in France and Gottsched in Germany was noted, the "wet feet" of Šiškov and the puristic strivings of the German normalizers of the 17th and 18th centuries were ridiculed, the striving of many normalizers both in Western as well as Eastern countries to counteract the appearance of the new vital tendencies of the colloquial variety of the language was underscored. But all these negative facts, several separate examples of which we also find in the early normative practices of our Soviet period, by no means detract from the significance of normalization itself in the process of establishing national language unity.

The direction of the normative process and the forms it assumes are different in different historical circumstances. In Socialist countries, where the establishment of orthographic, lexical, and grammatical norms is inextricably connected with the development of the general culture of the people, and with the familiarization of the broadest masses of the people with the achievements of science, literature, and art, this process assumes a national character. It is possible in this regard to refer to the establishment of the contemporary orthographic rules of the Russian language, to the discussion in China of various projects for adopting the Latin alphabet, to work on the perfection of alphabets and orthographic norms in the various Union Republics, etc. Questions, connected with the establishment of a new terminology in Armenian, Georgian, Azerbaijani, Lithuanian, and other languages, bear a direct relation to the establishment of a lexical norm in these national literary languages.

The normalization of the language in 16th- and 17th-century Italy or France was of interest, undoubtedly, to a relatively narrow social stratum. It was confined to a class also because the normalizers often proceeded from the language usage not of the broad masses of the people, but of the few layers close to the court (cf. the activity of Vaugelas in France and especially the activity of Gottsched in Germany). Sometimes connected with this was propaganda cast in a pretentious style, with words and expressions foreign to the native colloquial speech, i.e., a striving to tear the literary norm away from the use of the native colloquial language. These tendencies characterized, for example, certain historical periods in the activity of the French Academy.[14]

[14] Cf. R. A. Budagov's "The Concept of a Literary Language Norm in 16th and 17th Century France", *Voprosy jazykoznanija*, No. 5, 1956.

Consequently, the specific content of one or another of the norms which arose during the process of the development of various literary languages, depended upon the totality of historical circumstances in the development of a given literary language, and also upon the circumstances of those social relations under which the normalization was conducted. However, in order to establish general regularities in national language formation and development, it is essential to maintain the position that the formation of a new type of literary language, expressive of a common national unity, is impossible without conscious normalization, without theoretical comprehension of the norm and codification of definite rules of pronunciation, usage, and inflection. The literary language of any period has elements of choice, but in the time of national language formation and development this choice becomes especially relevant, and the striving towards language unity imparts to the developing norm a common national character. In this connection, the common national norm embodied in the literary language is never the result of a spontaneous process of language development, but to a certain degree the result of artificial selection and "interference" with this spontaneous process.

III

One of the fundamental theoretical questions concerning the study of the process of national language formation and development is the interrelationship between the literary or written literary tradition and the various manifestations of the colloquial variety of a language.

This problem has several aspects. The first of these is the question concerning the dialect base or foundation of a literary language. In the articles published in the present collection, this question was applied to the material of a series of languages. In fact, all the articles of the first section concerned this question in one degree or another.

The common national norm which crystallizes in a literary language is connected, no doubt, with one or another dialect region, but this connection may assume different forms. Thus, for example, the Eastern Middle German dialects are generally considered the foundation of the German literary language. It is also customary to claim that the norm of the Dutch national language was formed on the base provided by the dialect of the province of Holland,[15] etc. It is often mentioned that the main literary norm is the urban vernacular of the capital: of London

[15] Cf. S. A. Mironov's article "The Dialect Base Underlying the Literary Norm of the Netherlandish National Language" in the present collection (*Voprosy* ...).

– in England,[16] of Tashkent – in Uzbekistan,[17] of Peking – in China, of Tokyo – in Japan,[18] etc.

However, as material taken from the histories of various languages shows, the formation process of the literary norm of a national language is so complex, the regularities of this process so specific in comparison with the life of a regional dialect, and the forms of combination in this process of peculiarities of the colloquial speech of any one territory with the peculiarities of various intersecting traditions of the literary language so multifarious, that the literary norm is never in fact the simple codification of a system of dialect characteristics of any one region.[19]

Attention is directed to this by the various authors in their articles (S. A. Mironov, N. I. Konrad, and others). Examining the dialect base of such literary languages as Chinese and Japanese, N. I. Konrad underscores the role of regional koinés representing the result of a significant divergence from narrow dialect characteristics. The divergence from a narrow dialect base, the combination of various dialect characteristics, the influence to this or that degree of various written literary traditions are characteristic of virtually every literary language. In Germany, the literary norm of the national language is by no means a codification of the system of characteristics of the Eastern Middle German dialects, generally considered to be the basis of literary German. Practically none of the specific pronunciation peculiarities of this region were reflected in the orthoepic norm of the German literary language. This norm appeared as the result of a long process of interaction between the dialects of the Middle and Lower German regions, on the one hand, and an artificial regulation, on the other.[20]

With respect to the morphological and syntactic, and even more, to the lexical norms, the modern literary language is not only very far from the Eastern Middle German dialects, but also from the Leipzig vernacular, which represents a distinctive semi-dialect. As the analysis of the material shows, the main literary norm was the Eastern Middle German variety of the literary language of the 14th and 15th centuries (of the

[16] Cf. V. N. Jartseva's "The Change of the Dialect Base of the English National Literary Language" in the present colection (*Voprosy* . . .).

[17] Cf. V. V. Rešetov's article "The Uzbek National Language" in the present collection (*Voprosy* . . .).

[18] Cf. N. I. Konrad's article "The Literary Language in China and Japan". (*Voprosy* . . .).

[19] Urbančik (= Urbańczyk) has specially written on the complexity of the formation process of, for example, the Polish language (St. Urbańczyk "Note on the Origin of the Polish Literary Language" [in Polish], *Pochodzenie polskiego jezyka literackiego* [The Origin of the Polish Literary Language], Wrocław, 1956, pp. 82-101).

[20] Cf. M. M. Guxman's article "Formation of the Literary Norm of the German Literary Language" (*Voprosy* . . .).

pre-national stage), formed as the result of the interaction of a regional koiné and various written literary traditions.

In the Dutch language, where a change in the dialect base and re-orientation towards the colloquial speech of the province of Holland took place during the formation process of the national language, the contemporary norm of the literary language in the realm of orthoepy, grammar, and vocabulary, significantly differs from the dialect of this region. Here, especially in its written form, the literary tradition of the literary language of the pre-national period, connected with another dialect region,[21] expressed itself very strongly.

In the two varieties of the Armenian literary language, researchers [22] note not only the reflection of the interaction between different dialect currents, but also the influence of the classical written Grabar upon the formation of contemporary literary norms.

Thus, the complex interaction of regional colloquial speech (of a dialect, of a semi-dialect, of the urban vernacular) and the former tradition of the written literary language is characteristic of the formation process of the literary norm of many languages which developed under dissimilar conditions.

There are, no doubt, also those conditions under which the process reveals somewhat different tendencies. Thus, for example, in the case of an intensive repulsion from the tradition of the classical written language, as is so clearly observable in China and Japan, the infiuence of the old literary tradition upon the new literary language, formed on a colloquial base, assumes special forms. It may almost be absent in the formation of the literary norm of newly literate languages such as, for example, the Bashkir national language.[23] A definitive role in the interrelationship between the written tradition and the colloquial dialect base is played by the history of a written language in the pre-national stage, as well as by its interrelationship with various forms of colloquial speech.

However, under all circumstances, the literary norm of the national language always represents the result of a certain isolation from its dialect base. This is above all connected with peculiarities of the social functions of a literary language. Not only do marked dialect elements remain foreign to it during all the stages of literary language existence but, in the literary language itself, vocabulary layers are created, and syntactic peculiarities developed, which never existed in the dialect base. This isolation of a literary language from a dialect base assumes special

[21] Cf. S. A. Mironov's "The Dialect Base Underlying the Literary Norm of the Netherlandish National Language" (*Voprosy* . . .).

[22] Cf. A. S. Garibjan's "The Armenian National Literary Language" (*Voprosy* . . .).

[23] Cf. A. A. Juldaševʼs "Problems of the Formation of Unified Norms in the Bashkir National Language" (*Voprosy* . . .).

forms in the period of national language formation and development.

If the approximation of the functional styles of the written literary and colloquial varieties of a national language may be noted as a general tendency in the development of national languages, the interrelationship of these two varieties during the formation process and early stages in the development of national languages are very different.

Beginning with the 13th century in France, a relatively unified written literary language was formed, forcing out other written literary varieties. The edict of Francis I (in 1539) concerning the introduction of French instead of Latin into legal procedure was also directed against the use of local dialects in official practice. It is a known fact that the French normalizers of the 15th and 16th centuries oriented themselves towards the language of Paris, but towards the form in which it was spoken at court. Even then, the rather significant gap between the literary language and the colloquial language of the people – of the inhabitants of Paris – had come to light. In the other regions of France, regional dialects dominated oral communication. It is characteristic that during the French Revolution special attention was directed to the extension of a unified language over all of the French territory, on the one hand, and significant efforts were directed towards the democratization of the literary language, on the other. However, the distinct opposition of the literary language (preserving to a certain degree the traditions of French classical literature) to the colloquial language of not only the rural but the urban population is still observable in the 20th century in spite of limited dialect use. And even in the 20th century, a series of French linguists, first and foremost Dauzat, spoke out against the appearance of new vernacular vocabulary and colloquial constructions in the literary language. The controversy surrounding the conservatism of the French literary language, its simplification, the appearance of colloquial and folk speech elements in the literary language, became especially intense beginning with the period of the First World War and led to an even greater approximation of the literary variety to the colloquial folk variety of the language.

In China and Japan, where the contemporary literary norm is being created in the process of transforming the colloquial folk language into the literary language, where even the very name *pai-hua* (cf. N. I. Konrad's article) points up the connection between the literary language and the colloquial folk variety of the language, the gap between the old written and the colloquial language, which was formed here in the preceding century, is being liquidated in the process of national language formation.

In Germany, the establishment of a common national norm is above all connected with the written literary form of the language. The domination of dialects and regional koinés in the colloquial variety of the language furthered the opposition of the written form of the literary language (*Schriftsprache*) to the oral forms of the language and conditioned to a certain degree the conservatism of the syntax and phrase patterns of the literary language. However, a strong tendency towards the unification of these two spheres of German language application is observed in progressive writers of the last few decades.

The concrete historical circumstances, the period in which the foundations for a national literary language were laid, the degree of dialect persistence and, above all, the character of the language relationships of the pre-national period in this or that country, conditioned the nature of that general process of written literary and colloquial folk variety unification, which is characteristic of the period of national language formation and development. However, even here the definitive role of literary language social functions must be borne in mind. The wider the social sphere of literary language application, the more the broad social layers begin to use a literary language, the more intensive becomes the process of unifying both national language varieties. The democratization of all national culture is the basis of such a process.

IV

As was shown in the individual articles and especially noted in the conclusion, a national language differs from a folk language with respect to the fundamental character of the interrelationship between the various language types. The main feature of a system of language types is the creation of a common national norm; the carrier of this norm in any country is the literary language which first appears with such a function. The formation of such a type of literary language indicates moreover a transformation of the interrelationship between the individual elements of a general system of language types and influences the character of the unity of the language.

These processes are by no means something external in relation to the structure of a language. To a significant degree, the changes in the structural elements and the very formation of new features in the structure of the literary language are connected with its transformation as a result of normalization and conscious selection.

The concrete content of a norm is directly related to a defined language structure, outside of which it does not exist. The elements of contemporary literary languages, heterogeneous in origin, are united and related in a unified system as a result of those processes of selection and normalization which are connected with national language formation. Consequently, the changes thus brought about in the system of language types also influenced a change in the structure of the literary language. Indeed, if in the course of the struggle between competing varieties of, for example, the German literary language, the Eastern Middle German variety had not won out, the system of structural elements of the literary language would have been different; together with this, the establishment of a supradialectal type of language, the crystallization of unified norms, changed the very nature and quality of the literary language.

We are not talking about any external signs, but about the very essence of the phenomenon under study. Characteristics which are vital to the establishment of a national language may be accompanied by different changes in separate aspects of a language, for example, in the realm of syntax or vocabulary. These changes are connected with the formation of national culture. The development of a compound-subordinate complex and the formation of syntactic norms characteristic of a contemporary language take place in many languages to a significant degree in connection with the development of scientific prose and journalism; the development and complication of functional styles characteristic of that period is conditioned by the flourishing of national literatures; but the system of functional styles of a literary language changes also in connection with the change in the relationship between the written literary and colloquial folk varieties of the language. Finally, the development of the vocabulary of national literary languages is conditioned in turn by the entire development of the given society. Thus, the "external" and the "internal" factors are interwoven in a complex fashion during the process of national language formation and development.

From *Voprosy formirovanija i razvitija nacional'nyx jazykov*, M. M. Guxman, ed. (Moscow, 1960). Translated by Philip Dorf, Center for Applied Linguistics of the Modern Language Association, Washington, D.C., as part of series of "Translations of Selected Works in Sociolinguistics". Printed with permission.

Name Index[*]

Note: 10*n* indicates that the material is to be found in a footnote on page 10.

[*] Prepared by Helene K. Marer.

Subject Index[*]

Note: The following code is used in this index: 10*n* indicates that the material is to be found in a footnote on page 10; 10*f* designates material in a figure; and 10*t* shows that the material is in a table.

[*] Prepared by Helene K. Marer.

N

O